THE
MODERN
R·A·F

THE
MODERN
R·A·F

JEREMY FLACK

CROWOOD

First published in 2005 by
The Crowood Press Ltd
Ramsbury, Marlborough
Wiltshire SN8 2HR

www.crowood.com

British Library Cataloguing-in-Publication Data
A catalogue record for this book is available from the British Library.

ISBN 1 86126 616 2

All the photographs in this book were taken by the author, except where indicated otherwise.

Frontispiece: A pair of Nimrod MR.2s bank steeply in formation over their base at Kinloss. It will become the base for the rebuilt Nimrod MRA.4. Crown Copyright

Designed and typeset by Focus Publishing, 11a St Botolph's Road, Sevenoaks, Kent TN13 3AJ
Printed and bound in Great Britain by CPI Bath

Contents

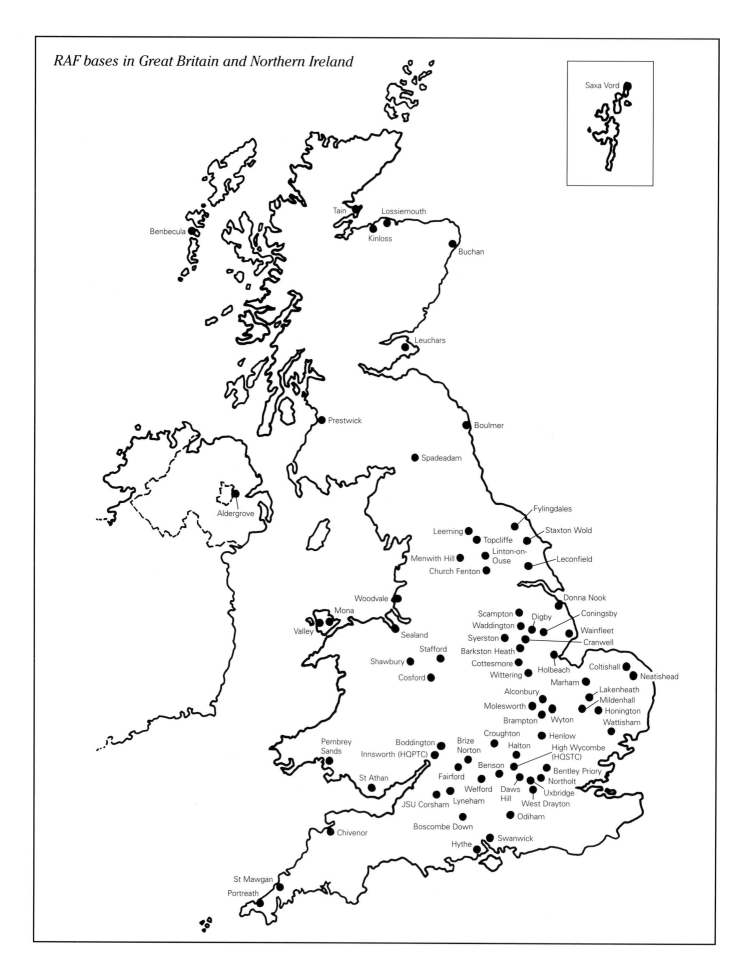

RAF bases in Great Britain and Northern Ireland

Introduction

The Royal Air Force was formed less than ninety years ago on 1 April 1918. It came into being when aviation was in its infancy and incorporated the existing flying units that had been established in the Army as the Royal Flying Corps (RFC) and the Royal Navy as the Royal Naval Air Service (RNAS). Their rapid growth during the First World War led to the decision that this new discipline, with its own unique methods of operation, had grown into a sufficiently large organization that it should be formed into a new and independent service. As a result, the Royal Air Force was born from those existing RFC and RNAS units – hence, some RAF squadrons have histories that date back further than the service itself.

In this book I have compiled a short history of the RAF's current main units and then provided information about their present role, together with a window into the future. This approach is repeated for each current aircraft type and station.

The advances in technology have seen RAF aircraft develop from fairly basic and flimsily constructed machines of wood and canvas through all-metal and now 'high tech', with increasing proportions of man-made materials such as glass or carbon-fibre. Through the use of in-flight refuelling, military aircraft are now capable of flying virtually anywhere in the world. A small RAF team is currently undergoing training with the USAF on the use of Unmanned Air Vehicles (UAV), which can play an invaluable role in reconnaissance over hostile territory without placing any aircrew at risk. While the RAF do not have any UAVs of their own yet, the acquisition is being assessed and could soon even include an Unmanned Combat Air Vehicle (UCAV) capable of launching weapons.

Today's RAF has equipment that has capabilities far in advance of that of only a few decades ago. These include GPS navigation and laser designation, which enables pinpoint navigation and weapon delivery. The more efficient use of fuel and aerodynamics allows greater ranges and/or increased payloads. Avionics within the aircraft enable the onboard computer systems to remove many of the mundane aspects of systems management, enabling the pilot and crew to concentrate on the safe, accurate and efficient completion of the mission. For the newer, larger aircraft this has resulted in reduced aircrew, with systems replacing the navigator and flight engineer. Technological advances are also widespread for most aspects of the RAF workplace, be it in computers, equipment or aircraft maintenance.

The end result is that RAF manpower levels are shrinking. Fewer personnel are now required to operate these systems. Unfortunately, many of the cuts are financially motivated rather than a reflection of efficiency. Quite often these changes have led to the cancellation of new equipment after the expenditure of large sums of money.

Following the ending of the Cold War, the general public's perception of the need for the military has reduced. Since then the Royal Air Force has undergone numerous reviews, which have included substantial cuts to equipment, units, location and manpower. Yet, for all this, the RAF has been busier than ever as the world has become less stable, with conflicts in the Gulf, the Balkans, Sierra Leone, Afghanistan and, most recently, Iraq again. Each has required the use of airpower, whether it has been combat aircraft and tanker support, or just helicopters, or frequently all three. On each occasion, substantial quantities of air transport have been required.

In addition, the trouble in Northern Ireland has taken a substantial commitment to ensure that appropriate support to the security forces has been available. Fortunately, the various parties appear to be working on peaceful solutions at last, which will eventually lead to a return to normal life for the region.

Each of the conflicts has resulted in some military remaining *in situ*. While this has not always been the RAF, those that have remained to provide a peacekeeping force have required air-transport support. Humanitarian aid also requires a substantial commitment of men and aircraft.

Following Saddam's defeat at the end of the Gulf War, the Marsh Arabs in the south of Iraq were encouraged by the Allied Forces to finish the job they started and topple Saddam. Unfortunately, the Marsh Arabs were poorly supported by the Allies and proved incapable of defeating him. Such was Saddam's remaining power that he drained their region, destroying the Marsh Arabs' economy, and then systematically tried to eliminate them. It is estimated that as many as 200,000 either lost their lives or fled the country.

In the north similar attacks were being made on the Kurds, which resulted in a massive food-aid programme, in which RAF Hercules took part. Allied forces mounted air patrols over the regions to create no-fly zones to deter some of the attacks by Saddam's forces. He still possessed a substantial number of SAMs, as these were regularly fired at the Allied aircraft and usually resulted in the launch site being targeted by LGB. Despite this, the attacks increased and, in 2002, a total of 221 missiles were fired at coalition aircraft, which included RAF Tornado GR.1s and F.3. Eventually this led to the re-invasion. Unfortunately, the invasion became too political and was conducted for the wrong stated reasons. Given their previous experience, it was hardly surprising the Iraqis were not overly joyous to see the coalition forces back again. Now substantial coalition forces continue to be needed to try to stabilize the country.

Despite the increase in operational commitments, manpower levels have steadily been eroded. Substantial numbers of military personnel have been replaced by civilians, as many jobs have been contractorized. As a result, the demands on military personnel have steadily increased. For those with families, this has resulted in greater pressure with even more

The Typhoon will become the RAF's primary multi-role combat aircraft.

time away from home, especially for aircrew and other front-line personnel.

During the Gulf War substantial numbers of reservists – ex-servicemen who can be called back to service – and Royal Auxiliary Air Force – civilians who volunteer to undergo part-time service training – have been called up to help augment the regular service men and women required for each of the conflicts. A worrying trend is that increasing numbers of these reserves are being retained in service for extended periods and even full-time, just to enable the RAF to continue to operate. These were supposed to be emergency reserves and their continued use massages the regular manpower figures.

Amongst equipment announced for withdrawal by Defence Secretary Geoff Hoon in 2004 is the whole Jaguar fleet, a squadron of Tornado F.3s, part of the Nimrod fleet and all of the RAF Rapier SAMs. During the Second World War the RAF found that the Army was unable to allocate sufficient resources to adequately protect RAF airfields, due to needs elsewhere. As a result, the RAF Regiment was expanded to provide an effective dedicated airfield-protection force. With airfield security being contractorized and SAM defences cut, one hopes that this will not be a lesson that needs to be

learned a second time. The argument for these changes is that, as part of a future coalition force, our forces' protection will come under a multinational umbrella. Unfortunately the multinational umbrella in Iraq managed to shoot down one of our ever-shrinking fleet of strike aircraft.

Also, as part of the 2004 round of cuts, we will see the manpower levels (which were 89,000 in 1991) cut yet again. This time the reduction in personnel by April 2008 will be to 41,000 from the current 48,500 – over 15 per cent.

Another worrying trend is with the current defence acquisition programmes. In the past, equipment was bought as it was required and finance was available. Over recent years, the PFI (Public Finance Initiative) syndrome has emerged, enabling new equipment to be obtained without the need for capital expenditure. This can be good for specific projects, enabling new equipment or processes to replace obsolete ones, thus raising effectiveness or reducing costs. However, the wholesale use of PFIs would appear to be a Treasury appeasement measure and approaches a buy-on-credit syndrome, which will be far more expensive by the end of the programme – as we are all aware of from personal financial experience. Unfortunately, the politicians that made

the decisions will have long departed from their posts by then and will be no longer accountable. In addition, the accumulative effect of these programmes will leave future Defence Ministers little room to manoeuvre, with most of their budgets firmly committed.

Looking on the bright side, strategic transport is getting a boost. The C-17 Globemaster has proved to be a great success. Although acquired through an expensive lease-agreement, it has been announced that they will be purchased at the end of the lease and that a fifth one will be purchased. The Typhoon is entering service, although rumours abound over the decreasing number of aircraft that will eventually enter service with the RAF. The Nimrod MRA.4, with its expanded role and much enhanced capabilities, continues to progress through rough waters. Although it has flown, the number that will eventually enter service has steadily dropped.

The munitions that are in service are progressively becoming higher tech, with laser guidance now being augmented by GPS for bombs and the missiles becoming more sophisticated. This means that fewer are needed to complete the mission. This in turn means that fewer aircraft are required for the task – hence the defence cuts. In addition, many of the weapons can be operated at a greater range, making them safer for the aircrew and because they are more accurate they will create less collateral damage and fewer civilian casualties – the usual losers in all conflicts.

It was reported during the last war against Saddam's regime that some missions were flown to hit tanks that were using heavily populated areas for cover. To reduce the collateral damage, the Paveway guidance system was fitted to inert 'concrete' bombs. Dropped from a height, the mass of the bomb was sufficient to smash through the tank's armour. This reduced the damage to the surrounding buildings due to the lack of the normally associated blast-effect.

The RAF tries to keep low-level flying-training disturbance to a minimum, but it is impossible to stop it completely. With modern technology it is possible to spot aircraft in the sky hundreds of miles away by radar. The only way to avoid getting detected by enemy forces is to fly below their radar. This means flying very low, using hills and mountains for cover, and this requires constant training. Specific areas of the country are designated 'low-flying areas' for this specialized training, with most over sparsely populated areas. However, this doesn't help those living in these areas. In an effort to reduce the load on these areas the RAF has 'exported' some of the flying. A number of pilots now undertake their advanced flying-training in Canada, while operational squadrons regularly deploy to the USA and Canada for their training.

Interestingly, a few years ago, a short piece by the BBC's *Countryfile* programme broadcast for the farming community resulted in a number of farmers around the country offering the use of their fields as practice landing grounds for the Chinooks. It being vital for aircrew to train in unfamiliar localities, these offers were highly appreciated by the RAF. Occasionally, these farmers and some of the staff and aircrew from Odiham get together for a progress briefing. During one that I attended, a comment from one of the farmers was that they loved seeing the helicopters using their fields and why didn't they use them more often. Not all farmers and country people are against low-flying – it is just that those that are tend to be the ones that are more vociferous.

The RAF is also very much aware of their integration with nature. Virtually every RAF station now has a conservation officer. A substantial amount of effort is made to nurture various animals, insects and plants and even birds in our ever-increasingly hostile environment. Surprisingly, RAF ranges can be an oasis to many species that ignore the occasional bang on the target because they have not been ploughed or sprayed to death. The same is true with archaeological sites, many of which have been saved from intensive agricultural cleansing. MoD land contains some of the most important SSSI sites in Europe. For those interested, the MoD produce an annual magazine called Sanctuary, which details some of the development and successes of various conservation projects on military land. (For a copy ring 01252 361989.)

The RAF also provides emergency manpower, termed Military Aid to the Civil Authorities (MACA). Contingency plans exist for a wide range of scenarios for military personnel to be rapidly made available in times of emergency or disaster. This can be to assist in local floods through to providing fire cover. For some five months in 2002–3 around 3,000 RAF servicemen and women provided emergency fire cover when the local fire brigades went on strike. Named Operation Fresco, it resulted in the return of the 'Green Goddesses' and a total of around 19,000 military personnel from all the services, just when they were also being tasked to prepare for war in Iraq.

Maintaining the positive note, the new-look Royal Air Force will continue to present a highly capable force with precision weapons that could only be dreamed of not long ago. It is up to the politicians to ensure that the taskings that they require of the services are matched to the capability of the personnel levels and do not exceed it. However much the technology advances, they are still reliant on the RAF's professional officers, airmen and airwomen to make it effective. In today's society with its greater freedom and personal aspirations, their needs require special attention to ensure that the right people continue to be attracted by the right incentives and then be retained in the future Royal Air Force.

I would like to take this opportunity to thank all the people who have helped me over the years with a variety of facilities – not necessarily specifically for this book. They have helped to provide information and the opportunity to take photographs, many of which have been used in this book. While this list of names of RAF personnel is too long to include here, Tim Lewis and Dale Donovan at Strike Command and Squadron Leader David Rowe and his assistant Kate Zasada at Brize Norton deserve special mention for their much appreciated help and encouragement. Thank you everybody.

CHAPTER ONE

Aircraft

The RAF operates a substantial number of aircraft types to fulfil its role as a competent military force. However, this is far fewer than those for several decades and the future will see these reduce further. The reasons for this are two-fold – modern aircraft are designed to be multi-role and, in the ever cost-conscious environment, the cost of operating two or more aircraft in the same role is an expensive luxury.

The ADV Tornado replaced the Lightning and Phantom in the fighter role while the IDS variant superseded the Canberra, Buccaneer and Vulcan within the RAF. Today the Tornado F.3 and GR.4 fleet is already being reduced and will be largely replaced by the Typhoon. Currently being delivered to the RAF, the Typhoon is also replacing the Jaguar, which, despite its highly successful operation during the Gulf War, is now to be retired earlier than originally planned. The reason why this is able to happen is that the Typhoon is the RAF's first true multi-role combat aircraft. While the Tornado was originally developed as the Multi Role Combat Aircraft (MRCA), it requires two distinctly different variants to fulfil the role of fighter and strike aircraft. The Typhoon will accomplish this with a single type, with the capabilities optimized to change from one role to another at the flick of a switch. Armed with air-to-air missiles and a range of attack weapons, the Typhoon will maintain a capability far in

excess of its predecessors and will be equipped with the latest high-tech weapons, which have an accuracy far in excess of those previously carried.

While the Tornado/Jaguar/Typhoon together with the Harrier will provide the backbone of the RAF's attack/defence capability for sometime into the future, many of the aircraft roles are also seeing significant equipment enhancements in some form. Reconnaissance will see the last Canberra variant being withdrawn, but the introduction of the Sentinel and the upgraded Nimrod R.1s, together with the JRP and RAPTOR pods, will provide a highly capable replacement as well as expanding the intelligence-gathering capability.

The Hercules fleet has been significantly improved, with half being replaced by the C-130J, and the introduction of the C-17 Globemaster has revolutionized the RAF's strategic-transport capability. The C-17 and some of the Hercules have also been fitted with enhanced defensive-aids suites, to provide improved protection for operations in potentially hostile environments. While the VC-10 and Tristars continue to provide transport/refuelling capability, a replacement is currently being negotiated in the form of the A330.

The maritime Nimrod is being upgraded, which will see it enhanced with an over-land attack capability, in view of the reduced anti-submarine threat.

On the training front, the Chipmunks and Bulldogs have been replaced by the Tutor and the development contract signed in December 2004 for the enhanced Hawk 128 will see it fulfilling the fast-jet training role from mid-2006. Meanwhile the Tucano has undergone structural improvements to continue in the basic flying-training role. The Jetstreams have been replaced by the King Air for MELIN. Eventually, when negotiations are completed, flying training will be fully contractorized.

As far as helicopters are concerned, the RAF contribution to the JHC is the Chinook, Merlin and Puma. While additional Chinook and refurbished Puma airframes are being added, there is a shortfall in capacity of support helicopters. As a result the Support Amphibious and Battlefield Rotorcraft (SABR) project is looking to replace the Pumas and Navy Sea King HC.4s with a single type.

At the end of this section are the aircraft types which the RAF intends to add to its fleet.

BAe.125 CC.3

Role: VIP transport/communications
Engine: 2 × 19kN Garrett TFE731-5R-1H turbofan
Length: 15.46m (50ft 8.5in)
Span: 14.33m (47ft)
Height: 5.36m (17ft 7in)
Speed: Mach 0.77
Weight: 11,566kg MTOW
Range: 3,336km (2,073 miles; 1,800nm)

The RAF BAe.125 is a variant of the civilian executive jet of the same name. It was originally designed and developed by de Havilland as the DH.125, which first flew

A contrast to the grey BAe.125 is the high-visibility scheme based on the old Queen's Flight livery. Both schemes are operated as part of 32 (The Royal) Sqn, to fly small numbers of VIPs or senior officers as required.

The larger BAe.146s were originally acquired for the Queen's Flight and then transferred to 32 (The Royal) Sqn, who continue to operate it for Royal flights. In addition, it is also used to fly VIPs and senior officers.

on 13 August 1962. When the company was absorbed into the Hawker Siddeley Group the aircraft became known as the HS.125 and has since been built as the Hawker 800 by Raytheon in the USA.

The RAF initially ordered twenty HS.125s in 1962, as the Dominie T.1, for navigator training. Four HS.125 Series 400s were ordered as the HS.125 CC.1 and delivered from April 1971, with an additional two delivered the following year. These were followed by two of the Series 600 and designated HS.125 CC.2, which were delivered in April 1973. All of these had their Viper turbojets subsequently replaced by the quieter and more fuel-efficient Garrett TFE731 turbofans, with a range of some 2,000 miles (3,218km). In 1982–3 six Series 700s were delivered as the BAe.125 CC.3 and had replaced the earlier models by May 1994.

All of the 125s have been operated by 32Sqn and based at Northolt, where they are operated as communications aircraft carrying up to seven passengers. The aircraft are normally used to transport high-ranking officers of all three services, Government Ministers and, since they took over the role of the Royal Flight, members of the Royal Family.

The BAe.125 CC.3 is a standard Series 700 model and externally resembles other members of the 125/Dominie family. The CC.3s are painted in two colour-schemes – medium grey with a pale blue cheat-line or a white fuselage with a black cheat-line and a red tail with red panels on the wings. The latter is the Royal scheme but may not necessarily carry Royals.

From their base at Northolt, 32 (The Royal) Sqn operate six of the BAe.125 CC.3s.

(*See also* Hawker Siddeley Dominie.)

BAe.146 CC.2

Role: VIP transport/communications
Engine: 4 × 31kN Avco Lycoming ALF502R-5 turbofan
Length: 26.18m (85ft 10in)
Span: 26.8m (86ft 5in)
Height: 8.61m (28ft 3in)
Speed: 640km/h (400mph; 350kt)
Weight: 34,473kg (76,000lb) MTOW
Range: 2,965km (1,842 miles; 1,600nm)

The BAe.146 was originally designed and launched by Hawker Siddeley as the HS.146 airliner in 1973, but was dropped the following year due to the economic turndown. In 1978 it resurfaced again as

the BAe.146. A prototype was built and this first flew on 3 September 1981.

In 1983, two BAe.146s were ordered for the RAF. These were Series 100 models and designated C.1. They were for evaluation as a possible replacement for the Andover CC.2 and were operated by an evaluation unit within 241 OCU, based at Brize Norton. After the evaluation they returned to BAe in June 1984.

In December 1983, the BAe.146 was chosen as the new aircraft type for the Queen's Flight and two aircraft ordered, designated CC.2 and operated with the rest of the Flight from their base at Benson. It was still based on the civilian 100 Series, but featured additional fuel-capacity and other modifications, including a specially designed Royal Suite. The BAe.146 is flown by a crew of six and can carry up to nineteen passengers. They first entered service in April 1986.

When the Queen's Flight at Benson was disbanded in April 1995, the role was transferred to 32Sqn at Northolt, which was appropriately renamed 32 (The Royal) Squadron. While the majority of its tasking was to transport the Royals on official engagements, these aircraft were also used to fly government ministers on official business. A third BAe. 146 was ordered in 1989, but in 2002 one was sold following a reduction in the tasking.

Two BAe.146 CC.2s are operated by 32 (The Royal) Sqn and are based at Northolt.

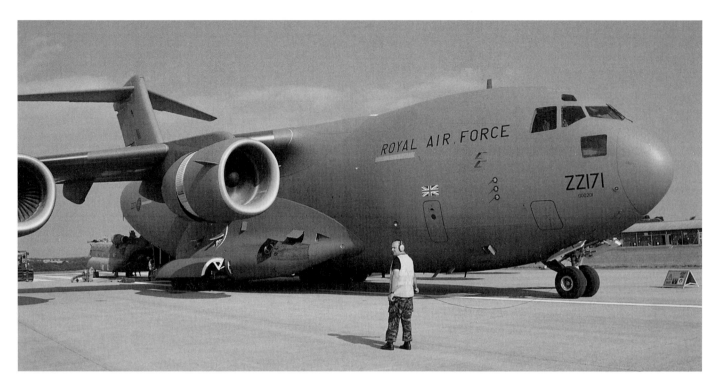

ABOVE: The C-17 is the cornerstone of the RAF's strategic-transport fleet, capable of transporting bulky loads over long distances into austere locations.

BELOW: The cavernous fuselage can accomodate a range of loads ranging from a main battle tank to troops.

Boeing C-17 Globemaster III

Role: Long-range strategic heavy-lift transport
Engine: 4 × 179.9kN Pratt & Whitney F117-PW-100
    (PW2040)
Length: 53.04m (174ft)
Span: 51.76m (169ft 10in)
Height: 16.79m (55ft 1in)
Speed: Mach 0.76
Weight: 265,352kg (585,000lb) MTOW
Range: 8,851km (5,500 miles; 4,775nm)

The C-17 Globemaster III was designed for the USAF by McDonnell Douglas. The prototype first flew on 15 September 1991 and the first was delivered to the USAF in June 1993.

Following various British assessments of potential aircraft, a ministerial announcement was made on 16 May 2000 of a seven-year £750m programme to lease four C-17s for the RAF, with the facility to extend this to nine. A further option is to buy the aircraft. The first RAF Globemaster flew in May 2001, the first example arrived at Brize Norton on 23 May and they are now operated as the RAF's primary strategic-transport aircraft.

The RAF Globemasters are what the US refers to as Block XII models. These incorporate improvements over earlier Blocks, include a Global Air Traffic Management (GATM) that enables the detection and avoidance of approaching aircraft as well as improving communications with ATC. This can be via satellite and can also include automatic reporting of the aircraft position. Another improvement is an extended-range tank, which takes 66,520lb (30,200kg) of fuel increasing the endurance by 3½ hours. The Globemaster has an impressive performance, provided by a combination of winglets and super-critical wing in addition to the powerful engines. It also features an equally impressive performance capable of short landings of less than 1,000m, even with a maximum payload. This is largely achieved by directing the engine exhaust onto large flaps extended into the exhaust stream. The aircraft has the ability to turn in a small radius, as well as reverse, thus eliminating the need for ground support at small, austere airfields.

Because of the high degree of integrated avionics and cargo systems, the Globemaster can be operated by two crew and one loadmaster. It features a comprehensive cargo-handling system that enables a wide range of roles to be conducted without any additional equipment. Down either side of the fuselage are fitted twenty-seven permanently installed seats. A further forty-eight troop seats are carried on the cargo door, which can be fitted down the centre of the fuselage, making a total of 102. Alternatively, ninety palletized passenger-seats can be fitted down the centre. A variety of freight can be carried (up to 74,797kg), which can include the Challenger II main battle tank. Such is the capacity of the Globemaster that the ramp alone can carry the equivalent of a C-130 Hercules. The cargo deck comprises a number of reversible panels with rollers to enable pallets to be loaded. The Globemaster is capable of being used for air drops but, under the conditions of the lease, the RAF aircraft will not make use of this facility.

Initial crew-training was conducted with the USAF at Altus and Charleston. Such was the pace of entry into service of the Globemaster that, following this training, the first aircraft was collected from the manufacturer with less than seven hours recorded. Ten days later the crew were flying on Exercise *Saif Sareea* to Oman with a load that would have taken three Hercules two days to complete. Ever since then the Globemasters of 99Sqn have been called upon to move a huge variety of loads to anywhere in the world.

The troubles in Afghanistan saw a major commitment by 99Sqn, who were providing an airbridge from Brize Norton to Kabul. Being a land-locked country and having poor land-communications the only means of supply was by air. Operating virtually daily, the C-17 would arrive in darkness, with no airfield aids, using its own GPS systems to guide the aircraft to the runway. Having staged through Bahrain for refuelling, the Globemaster would, without cutting the engines, be unloaded, then re-load with UK-bound passengers and freight for the return journey, taxi back out and disappear into the night. Slip crews at Bahrain enabled short stops only to refuel.

No sooner had the peak of the Afghan tasking dropped than the build up of forces for Operation *Telic* – for the Coalition operation against the Saddam Hussein regime in Iraq – saw the Globemasters being fully utilized.

The high rate of tasking for the RAF Globemasters and the ease with which this has been accomplished is of credit to the squadron as well as the aircraft. With this requirement seen to continue for the foreseeable future, with its current role plus that of supporting the Joint Rapid Reaction Force, it was announced that the four C-17s will be retained at the end of the contract. In addition, a further example is intended to be purchased.

The C-17 Globemaster is in service with 99Sqn and based at Brize Norton.

A vital part of the C-17's capability is the sophisticated cockpit, which includes advanced avionics able to monitor the aircraft's systems for the crew, advising them when there are problems. Gone is the old style yoke and it is replaced with a fighter-style control column. It even has a HUD (Head Up Display) to provide all the information needed for landing and take-off.

English Electric Canberra PR.9

A single Canberra T.4 has been retained to provide flying training for the PR.9 crews. The historical importance of this aircraft resulted in it being painted to represent the prototype Canberra — the RAF's first jet-bomber. This aircraft was placed in storage in September 2005.

Role: Photographic and electro-optical reconnaissance
Engine: 2 × 50kN Rolls-Royce Avon 206 turbojet
Length: 20.32m (66ft 8in)
Span: 20.66m (67ft 10in)
Height: 4.75m (15ft 7in)
Speed: Mach 0.82
Weight: 26,332kg (58,000lb) MTOW
Range: 1,609km (1,000 miles; 868nm)

The prototype English Electric Canberra first flew on 13 May 1949 and was Britain's first and most successful jet bomber. Over 900 Canberras were built in the UK, plus forty-eight in Australia for the RAAF and a further 403 built under licence by Martin for the USAF as the B-57. The first Canberra entered RAF service with the Handling Squadron on 8 March 1951.

Although designed as a bomber, the Canberra also served in a range of other roles – including training, research, interdiction, unmanned target, target towing, electronic warfare and reconnaissance. While most Canberras have been withdrawn and scrapped, four of the photo-reconnaissance role PR.9s and a single T.4 trainer remain operational with 39Sqn, some forty years after they were originally delivered to the RAF.

The Canberra PR.9 prototype was converted from the earlier PR.7 and the first production example was flown on 27 July 1958. Shorts built twenty-three of the Canberra PR.9 variant, which features an extended-chord wing with an enlarged span. They were also fitted with the more powerful Avon 206 engines. Such is the PR.9's performance with this power-to-weight ratio that it is capable of reaching maximum speed on just one engine. The Canberra PR.9 was never armed – relying on its speed and manoeuvrability to outfly enemy aircraft. This performance is still impressive for an aircraft of its size today. It also features an off-set fighter-style canopy and the navigator is located in the nose, which is hinged for his access.

The Canberra PR.9 can operate regularly at 48,000ft (14,630m) and, with its wide range of vertical and oblique cameras, is able to contribute significantly to the RAF reconnaissance requirements. It can fly at over 60,000ft (18,287m) if required.

The first unit to fly the PR.9 was 58Sqn, following initial delivery in January 1960. This was followed by 13 and 39Sqn and, later, 1 Photographic Reconnaissance Unit (1 PRU), which was formed in 1982 from the reduced-strength 39Sqn.

The Canberra T.4 was the standard training-variant, which originally entered service in 1954. One was retained to provide pilot proficiency and continuation training to conserve hours on the PR.9s. As it had no operational role, one was painted in an all-over blue scheme to represent the prototype.

The Canberra PR.9s have operated in a range of colour schemes during their service, ranging from bare metal to camouflage. They are currently painted in an all-over hemp colour-scheme.

Over the years the Canberra PR.9s have seen a variety of modifications and upgrades, enabling them to remain a potent tool in the RAF's inventory. In 1998 use was made of the underwing hardpoints to enable the BOZ-107 chaff/flare pods to be carried for added self-defence. Despite their age, the venerable Canberras have recently seen extensive operational service in Afghanistan, Somalia and Iraq, where their capabilities have been sought and extensively utilized in support of coalition forces. Some 150 missions were flown during Operation *Telic* in Iraq alone.

The Canberra PR.9 has also been used for non-operational tasks, which have included mapping, and in the mid-1990s one was deployed to Zaire to monitor the refugee crisis in Rwanda.

There are currently four Canberra PR.9s serviceable in the RAF. They are rapidly reaching the end of their life, especially at the rate they have been used in recent years – far in excess of their normal usage. It is anticipated that they will be withdrawn in August 2006.

39 (1 PRU) Sqn operates four of the Canberra PR.9s from their base at Marham.

ABOVE: The Canberra PR.9 has enhanced performance over previous variants, due to the more powerful Avon engines and the broader-chord inner-wing sections. Despite their age, they have been continually sought after for their reconnaissance and photo-mapping role.

RIGHT: The pilot sits in an offset cockpit in a fighter-style canopy above and behind the navigator.

BELOW: The crew positions in the Canberra PR.9 are somewhat unusual, as well as being cramped. The navigator/camera operator occupies a seat in the nose of the aircraft forward of the pilot. Access is by opening the nose.

The Chinook provides a heavy-transport capability on the battlefield — capable of carrying up to three underslung loads at a time.

These can range from fuel to guns and ammunition — here one is carrying an army Scimitar armoured reconnaissance vehicle.

Boeing Chinook HC.2, HC.2A, HC.3

Role: Heavy-lift support helicopter
Engine: 2 × 2,786kW Avco Lycoming T55-712F turboshaft
Length: 15.54m (51ft 0in) fuselage; 30.14m (98ft 10.75in) overall
Rotor diameter: 18.29m (60ft 0in)
Height: 5.78m (18ft 11.5in)
Speed: 296km/h (185mph; 160kt)
Weight: 24,267kg (54,000lb)
Range: 1,609km (1,000 miles; 868nm)

Despite the distinctive sound of the 'wokka wokka' Chinook, it has proved its worth right from when it was introduced into service with the US Army in Vietnam. It continues to provide this rugged capability and is to be seen on operations in all conditions, virtually wherever the British military are deployed.

The Boeing Vertol CH-47 Chinook is a twin-rotor heavy-lift helicopter that began development in 1956. The prototype Chinook (YCH-47A) first flew on 21 September 1961 and deliveries commenced to the US Army in spring 1963. The Chinook was built in substantial numbers for the US Army and saw extensive use in Vietnam, where its impressive lifting-power proved invaluable.

Despite a requirement for a heavy-lift helicopter since the retiring of the Belvedere in 1969, it wasn't until January 1978 that thirty Chinooks were ordered for the RAF (plus a further three in September). These were basically the CH-47C with British avionics and had a triple-hook capability. They were designated Chinook HC.1.

The first Chinook was formally received on 1 December 1980. The first recipient of the Chinook was 240 OCU and the first operational squadron was 18Sqn, which formed at Odiham in August 1981,

moving to Gütersloh in May 1983. The next unit to equip was 7Sqn.

During the Falklands campaign, four Chinooks were transported to the islands aboard the *Atlantic Conveyor*. As the ship neared the islands, the first Chinook had had its rotor blades reassembled and was undergoing an airtest, resulting in its survival when the ship was hit by an Argentinian Exocet missile. The three other Chinooks were all lost. The single Chinook was worked hard and on several occasions performed well in excess of what it said on the label. During one vital

mission over eighty fully armed troops, along with their mortars, ammunition and kit, were flown – well in excess of the peacetime maximum of forty-four. Once the war ended, 1310 Flight was formed to operate the Chinook until 78Sqn was re-established.

One Argentinian Chinook was captured and returned to the UK, but only used for ground instruction. With the war over, a batch of three replacement Chinook HC.1s were ordered and received in 1995/6, followed by an additional five.

The HC.1s underwent several modifications, including improved engines taking them to HC.1B. Of these, thirty-two were subsequently returned to the manufacturer from the early 1990s for a mid-life update that included new engines, hydraulic and

Seen here at Bagram, Afghanistan are Chinooks from 27Sqn, with the remains of ex-Soviet, Afghan AF aircraft in the foreground. With the airfield at almost 5,000ft, the mountains proved to be an obstacle but were not insurmountable.

may be two Land Rovers or twenty-four stretchers. It is also capable of carrying up to 28,000lb (12,712kg) in underslung loads, for which it is fitted with three hooks.

The Chinook HC.1 was originally painted in a grey-and-green camouflage with some having a black underside. They were later finished in an all-over drab scheme following conversion to HC.2, but some were painted pink for the Gulf War. This was an Alkaline Removable Temporary Finish (ARTF) paint that was easily stripped. However, some were further modified with ordinary black paint for night ops, which proved difficult to remove. Some were also painted white for UN duties in the former Yugoslavia.

The Chinook HC.2 and HC.2A are operated by 7, 18 and 27Sqn, which are all based at Odiham, plus 78Sqn at Mount Pleasant in the Falklands.

de Havilland Chipmunk T.10

Role: Pilot training
Engine: 1 × 108kW (145hp) de Havilland Gipsy Major 8 piston
Length: 7.75m (25ft 5in)
Span: 10.45m (34ft 4in)
Height: 2.13m (7ft 0in)
Speed: 119kt (138mph; 220km/h) MTOW
Weight: 914kg (2,014lb) MTOW
Range: 445km (277 miles; 240nm)

With enlarged sponsons, the extra range and avionics enhancement of the Chinook HC.3 will provide an added boost to an already impressive capability. Crown Copyright

electrical systems, and upgraded transmissions and flying controls, which brought them up to CH-47D standard. When they returned to RAF service they were designated Chinook HC.2.

Three more Chinook HC.2s were ordered for delivery in 1995 plus a further subsequent order for an additional fourteen for delivery from 1997. This consisted of six HC.2As and eight HC.3s, which are similar to the US Special Forces MC-47E.

The Chinook HC.3 is fitted with larger panniers on either side of the fuselage with a greater fuel capacity and it can be fitted with an in-flight refuelling probe. Although the first example flew in October 1998, the cockpit fit is a hybrid and has resulted in problems of system integration of mission equipment and software which has substantially delayed the

entry into service. A study recommended a Fix to Field as the best way forward and a proposed solution is being carefully considered. However, a sale to the USAF who have an urgent requirement and then replacement with the MH-47G has not been ruled out.

The RAF Chinooks have seen service in many parts of the world on exercises and on operations. These have ranged from the Falklands, when one lifted a total of eighty-eight troops in an emergency, to the Gulf War. More recently they have been used extensively in the former Yugoslavia, where they were operated as 1310 Flight, Sierra Leone and Afghanistan and, most recently, in Iraq.

The normal wartime capacity for the Chinook is fifty-four troops but the flexible Chinook can carry 12,712kg, which

The Chipmunk was de Havilland Canada's first design and intended as a replacement primary trainer for the Tiger Moth. Designated DHC-1, the prototype Chipmunk was first flown on 22 May 1946. There were 157 initially built in Canada and two of these were evaluated by the A&AEE for the RAF for possible use as *ab initio* trainer.

An initial order was placed for 200 Chipmunk T.10s in February 1949 to replace the RAF's Tiger Moths. This eventually led to a total of 735 Chipmunk T.10s being ordered. The first example was delivered to Boscombe Down in November 1949 and deliveries commenced to Oxford UAS in early 1950.

The Chipmunk T.10 has been used for training RAF pilots, although a number were transferred to the AAC and FAA for similar purposes. Apart from some use as a hack aircraft for a few units – communications and continuation training – the only operational use of the Chipmunk was with

114Sqn in Cyprus, where it was used on internal-security flights in 1958, and with the Berlin Station Flight. Berlin was surrounded by Soviet and East German units after the Second World War but, after the crisis and the Berlin Airlift, limited access was permitted to the city on specific routes. The Chipmunks flew these routes to maintain the right to fly over Berlin and to monitor military units bordering them.

The Chipmunk T.10 was initially replaced by the Bulldog T.1 in flying training schools and spread eventually to the University Air Squadrons (UAS) and Air Experience Flights (AEF). These have since retired and been replaced by the Tutor. The RAF retired its last Chipmunks in 1996; however, two have been retained by the Battle of Britain Memorial Flight (BBMF) to provide single-engine tail-dragger training for Spitfire and Hurricane pilots.

Two Chipmunk T.10s are operated by the BBMF at Coningsby.

Douglas Dakota III

Role: Vintage transport
Engine: 2 × 900kW (1,200hp) Pratt & Whitney R-1830 Twin Wasp radial
Length: 19.64m (64ft 5.5in)
Span: 29m (95ft 0in)
Height: 5.16m (16ft 11in)
Speed: 368km/h (230mph: 199kt)
Weight: 11,800kg (26,000lb) MTOW
Range: 2,414km (1,500 miles; 1,302nm)

The Douglas Dakota was originally designed as the Douglas Sleeper Transport (DST). It was first flown on 17 December 1935 and subsequently designated the DC-3. Developed from the DC-1 and DC-2, military interest in the DC-3 from the USN and USAAC resulted in a number of variations, which eventually led to the first C-47 being delivered to the USAAF in early 1942. When production ended, 10,692 DC-3/C-47s had been built, plus 2,485 in Russia under licence as the Li-2 and L2D in Japan.

RAF interest in the C-47 resulted in some 1,900 being obtained under the lease-lend scheme as the Dakota I, II, III and IV. Based in India, 31Sqn was the first recipient in April 1941 of DC-2s, followed by C-47s. They provided the basis of transport operations throughout the war, being used a transport, for dropping paratroops and as a glider tug. The last was retired on 4 April 1970 after twenty-seven years service.

The Dakota has returned to RAF service after a gap of twenty-three years, although this particular aircraft has no actual RAF history. It was built in 1942, delivered to

The RAF's last two airworthy Chipmunks of the BBMF enable pilots to practice flying with a 'tail dragger', so conserving the valuable flying hours on their Spitfires. Crown Copyright

the USAAF and transferred to the RCAF as KG661 shortly after. After RCAF service she was acquired by and operated by the RAE (which became DRA and is now known as QinetiQ) as KG661 for various trials until March 1992. In March 1993 she was acquired by the RAF to add to the BBMF fleet. When it was discovered that KG661 was not her previous identity, as originally thought, she was allocated the new registration ZA947.

The role of ZA947 is twofold – she is operated as a memorial to transport crews and also provides a valuable function as a crew trainer for new and current multi-engined aircrew. Thus she will reduce the number of training sorties using up valuable hours on the Lancaster.

One Dakota is operated by the BBMF and based at Coningsby. The markings are periodically changed to represent units that operated the Dakota during the Second World War.

Hawker Siddeley Dominie T.1

Role: Multi-crew advanced flying training
Engine: 2 × 14.71kN Bristol Siddeley Viper 520 turbojets
Length: 14.72m (48ft 3.5in)
Span: 14.33m (47ft)
Height: 4.88m (16ft)
Speed: 755km/h (472mph; 407kt)
Weight: 9,534kg (21,000lb)
Range: 2,156km (1,340 miles; 1,163nm)

The Dominie T.1 is a development of the HS.125 that initially flew as the DH.125 on 13 August 1962. The RAF ordered twenty Dominies in 1962 to replace the piston-engined Varsity T.1 to teach navigator training. The Dominie T.1 took to the air for the first time on 30 December 1964.

The Dominie originally entered service in September 1965 with 1 ANS at Stradishall and later served with 6 FTS at Finningley and the College of Air Warfare at Manby. When delivered, the navigators were accommodated in rearward-facing training stations, as they would be sat in the V-bombers. As these bombers were phased-out it was decided to fit forward-facing stations and conversion was undertaken during the mid-1990s. At the same time a new Thorn Super Searcher radar was fitted, which increased the length of the nose, and a new navigation system installed. At this stage consideration was given to re-designating the converted aircraft T.2 but, for one reason or another, this did not happen.

The Dominie is operated as a flying classroom and, in the navigational role, is normally flown with one pilot, a pilot's assistant, two instructors plus two students. Currently, having completed

their initial training on the Tutor and Tucano, the students progress to 3 FTS at RAF Cranwell, where they undergo fourteen hours training over twelve weeks in the art of advanced navigation and are introduced to the Dominie T.1 of 55 (Reserve) Sqn. Students are then streamed for specialist training. Fast-jet students complete a further thirty-seven hours training, maritime students forty-one hours and AT/AAR/ISTAR students thirty-two hours, each course lasting thirteen weeks. For this role the Dominie is fitted with a variety of navigation equipment that is used to teach the students to operate at high, medium and low levels. Navigators are now classified as Weapon Systems Officers (WSO).

Unique in its role, the Dominie T.1 is similar to other members of the HS.125/BAe.125/Hawker 800 family, although fitted with the older turbojets. Apart from the RAF identification markings, the Dominie T.1 is most easily recognized by its all-over black colourscheme with a white spine running from the flight deck to the tail, which first appeared in November 1997. Until they have all been re-painted, some Dominies are still operating in the old training colours of white, red and grey. With the

The BBMF's Dakota appears at airshows to commemorate the lives of airmen who flew transport aircraft and who lost their lives to maintain the freedom of this country.

reduced need for navigators, some Dominies that had not had the seating modification were retired and are used as instructional airframes at Cosford. Eleven Dominies remain in service.

The Dominie T.1 is operated by 55 (Reserve) Sqn within 3 FTS and is based at Cranwell.

(*See also* BAe.125.)

ABOVE: **The Dominie T.1 has provided navigator training for RAF aircrew since 1965.**

BELOW: **At one time the workstations on the Dominie T.1 faced rearwards, to replicate those to be encountered on the 'V' bombers. Nowadays they face forwards, as located in the Tornado.**

Slingsby Firefly 260

Role: Initial pilot training prior to multi-engine training
Engine: 1 × 194kW Textron Lycoming AEIO-540-D4A5 piston
Length: 7.57m (24ft 10in)
Span: 10.59m (34ft 9in)
Height: 2.36m (7ft 9in)
Speed: 331km/h (207mph; 179kt)
Weight: 1,157kg (2,550lb) MTOW
Range: 755km (469 miles; 408nm)

The Slingsby T67A Firefly was initially built by Slingsby under licence from Fournier of France as a two-seat touring and training aircraft based on their RF-6B. The prototype Fournier RF-6 was first flown on 1 March 1973 and the first Slingsby T67A, which was of wooden construction, first flew on 15 May 1981.

The T67M Firefly is a two-seat piston-engined trainer with a fixed undercarriage. A total of sixteen of the T67M IIs were ordered, to be operated by Huntings with

The Firefly is now only used to provide an initial training for pilots who will subsequently join the multi-engine lead-in course.

civilian registrations to equip the Joint Elementary Flying Training School (JEFTS) at Topcliffe in July 1993. They were to replace the previously operated Chipmunks. An additional two ex-Royal Hong Kong Aux AF examples were subsequently acquired to replace one that crashed. These were powered by 119kW (160hp) Textron Lycomings AEIO-320-D1B and used mainly for staff training. In 1996 a further twenty-five T67M-260s were ordered.

The lower-powered Fireflies are used for the initial grading of navy and army students, while the more powerful T67M-260 was used for elementary flying training of students of all three services. This role for the RAF has now been taken over by the UAS with the Tutor T.1 and RAF students will now only fly the Firefly as part of the multi-engine lead-in course, flying thirty hours prior to joining 45 (R) Sqn. This is operated by a DEFTS Flight based at Cranwell. When this change happened in July 2003 the JEFTS was renamed Defence Elementary Flying Training School (DEFTS). Around the same time the Firefly 160s were transferred to Middle Wallop for flying grading and the 200s sold.

The Firefly 260 is operated by DEFTS at Barkston Heath.

Westland Gazelle AH.1

Role: Scout
Engine: 1 × 440kW Turbomeca/RR Astazou IIIN turboshaft
Length: 9.52m (31ft 2.75in) fuselage; 12.09m (39ft 8in) overall
Rotor span: 10.5m (34ft 5in)
Height: 3.02m (9ft 11in)
Speed: 265km/h (166mph; 143kt)
Weight: 1,800kg (3,968lb)
Range: 650km (404 miles; 351nm)

The Gazelle was originally designed by Sud as the SA.341 Gazelle and the prototype was first flown on 7 April 1967. It became one of three Anglo-French development projects in 1967, which resulted in the acquisition of one French prototype by Westland and the building of 215 AH.1s for the Army Air Corps and Royal Marines, thirty-five HT.2s based on the SA.341C for the Fleet Air Arm and thirty HT.3s based on the SA.341D for the RAF.

The Gazelle HT.3 entered service in July 1973 and was mainly used for pilot training and as a communications helicopter. It has now been replaced by the Squirrel. The RAF use Army Gazelles, as required, with 7Sqn, who use them to check low-level night-flying routes for their Chinooks. When JHC took control of all helicopters the remaining Gazelle HT.3s

were retired and 7Sqn's Gazelles were replaced with AH.1s to reduce the cost of operating the different variants.

The FAA HT.2s were retired and replaced by the Squirrel. One continued to fly with ETPS, together with one ex-RAF HT.3. QinetiQ continues to operate three HT.3s for trials and has one more in storage – all located at Boscombe Down.

Two Army Gazelle AH.1s operate with 7Sqn at Odiham as required.

Bell Griffin HT.1

Role: Advanced multi-engine flying training
Engine: 2 × 671kW P&W Canada PT6T-3D turboshaft
Length: 17.11m (56ft 1.57in) overall
Rotor span: 14.02m (46ft)
Height: 4.59m (15ft 0.85in) overall
Speed: 260km/h (163mph; 140kt)
Weight: 5,397kg (11,900lb) MTOW
Range: 744km (462 miles; 401nm)

The Griffin HT.1 is the RAF's training variant of the Bell 412EP. It is derived from the outstanding single-engined UH-1 Iroquois, which first flew on 16 August 1961 and proved so effective during the Vietnam War. The first of nine HT.1s entered RAF service in April 1997 and a further two were ordered in 2002.

ABOVE: The RAF Gazelles to the right and left have now been withdrawn from the training and communications roles. The sole operator now being 7Sqn, which operates the AH.1 on loan from the army as required.

BELOW: A Griffin HT.1 of 60(R)Sqn, DHFS during a low-level training sortie, part of which includes flying under electricity wires.

The Bell 412EP is the enhanced-performance variant of this twin-turboshaft, utility helicopter, which is in wide service throughout the world. Although operated with a military registration, the Griffin HT.1 is a civilian-owned helicopter operated by the Defence Helicopter Flying School. It is used for advanced multiengined training of RAF aircrew and training in the specialized SAR role prior to progressing to Puma, Chinook and Sea King squadrons, as well as 84Sqn with the Griffin HAR.2.

The Griffin HT.1 is operated by 60 (R) Sqn at Shawbury and the SARTU at Valley – both of which are training units within the DHFS.

Bell Griffin HAR.2

Role: Search and rescue
Engine: 2 × 671kW P&W Canada PT6T-3D turboshaft
Length: 17.11m (56ft 1.57in) overall
Rotor span: 14.02m (46ft)
Height: 4.59m (15ft 0.85in) overall
Speed: 260km/h (163mph; 140kt)
Weight: 5,397kg (11,900lb) MTOW
Range: 744km (462 miles; 401nm)

The Griffin HAR.2 is the RAF's latest variant of the Bell 412 to enter service. Four of these have been supplied by FB Heliservices under a contract to provide the helicopters and servicing for the next five years. Like the Griffin HT.1s, the HAR.2s are commercially owned but military registered and flown by RAF crews.

The Griffin HAR.2 differs from the HT.1 variant in having a permanently fitted hoist and FLIR, as well as some instrument differences.

The Griffin HAR.2 has replaced the Wessex HC.2 in 2003 with 84Sqn at Akrotiri in Cyprus, where it provides SAR cover for the RAF aircraft at the base, including the regular Armament Practice Camps (APC). They also provide support for British Army units in the UN and Sovereign Base Areas, replacing the Army Gazelles.

The Griffin HAR.2 is operated by 84Sqn and based at Akrotiri in Cyprus.

BAe Harrier GR.7A, GR.9, GR.9A

Role: STOVL multi-role combat
Engine: 1 × 95.6kN RR Pegasus Mk.105 vectored-thrust turbofan
Length: 14.12m (46ft 4in)
Span: 9.25m (30ft 4in)
Height: 3.56m (11ft 8in)
Speed: Mach 0.89
Weight: 14,061kg (31,000lb) MTOW
Range: 1,046km (650 miles; 564nm)

The origins of the Harrier date back to the P.1127, which made its first tethered-hover flight on 21 October 1960. This led to the world's first operational VSTOL aircraft – the Harrier GR.1, which entered RAF service on 1 April 1969. The first recipient for the training programme was 233 OCU and 1Sqn became the first operational unit in July 1969.

These served with four RAF operational squadrons and two flights (1, 3, 4 and 20Sqn, 1417 and 1453 Flights) plus 233 OCU until finally retired in May 1994, by which time, following upgrades, the survivors had been designated GR.3s. A two-seat model had also been built as the T.2 and eventually modified to T.4. The RAF Harrier GR.3s and RN Sea Harrier FRS.1s were deployed in 1982 to the South Atlantic on Operation *Corporate*. With their V/STOL capability, they were the only British strike aircraft that could be deployed to the South Atlantic and provided the total air strike/defence capability. After all these years it remains the world's only operational strike aircraft capable of V/STOL apart from helicopters. The nearest is the Yak-36, which has limited performance and is no longer thought to be in service, and the Yak-141.

The current Harrier is a totally revised design. McDonnell Douglas developed the AV-8B and the RAF ordered a variant, which was partially built and assembled by BAe and designated Harrier GR.5. Two pre-production models were ordered and the first flew on 30 April 1985. An order for sixty production models followed in 1982 and on 29 May 1987 the first Harrier

The Harrier GR.7 comes from a sizeable family of variants, of which an early P1127 (RAF) leads the line. Behind are a GR.3, T.4, Sea Harrier FRS.1, Harrier T.4N, T.4, GR.5, GR.7 and Sea Harrier FA.2.

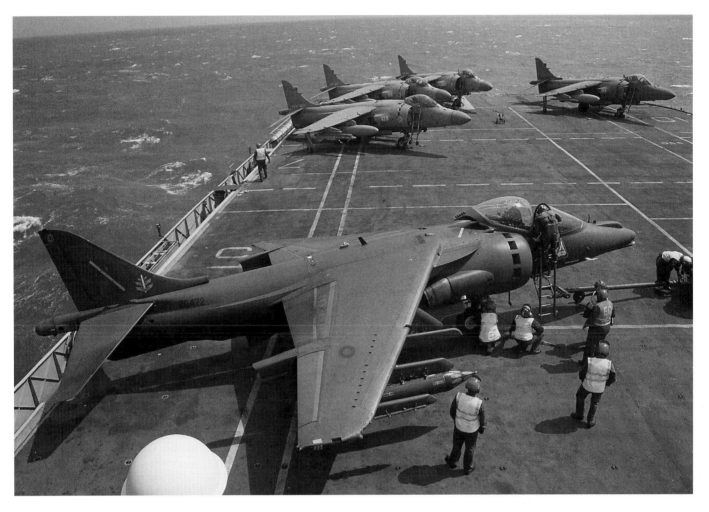

A Harrier GR.7 of the SAOEU (now Fast Jet OEU) undergoes trials on HMS *Invincible* alongside Sea Harrier FA.2s. Current planning sees the Sea Harriers being replaced by Harrier GR.7s from 3Sqn to form 801 NAS.

GR.5 was delivered to the RAF. Although this retains the name Harrier, it is a completely new aircraft. It resembles the earlier aircraft but has a stretched fuselage and larger wings plus a raised cockpit.

However, the GR.5 was little more than an interim model without the FLIR and a few other minor differences. Of the ninety-six new Harriers that were eventually ordered, sixty-two were built as the GR.5 or GR.5A by the time that the definitive GR.7 variant came off the production line. The first GR.7 entered service with 4Sqn in September 1990. Once sufficient GR.7s had been delivered, the earlier GR.5s were returned to BAe to be modified to GR.7 standard.

The GR.7 is fitted with a Forward-Looking Infra-Red (FLIR), from which an image is displayed onto a wide-angle Head-Up Display (HUD), and a terrain-following radar, giving it true night-capability. The HUD gives the pilot a view out of the aircraft with the FLIR image superimposed. The HUD also provides the normal flight data, reducing the pilot's need to look down into the cockpit. The pilot can also wear Night Vision Goggles (NVG), which can transform a star-lit environment into virtual day, thus providing all-round vision for the pilot twenty-four hours a day.

The Harrier has nine hardpoints onto which a range of weapons and equipment may be attached according to the mission. These can include up to sixteen 500lb or six 1,000lb bombs but rockets and missiles can also be fitted, to which the Maverick and CRV-7 have more recently been added. For long-range ferrying the Harrier can be fitted with 250 gallon (1,135ltr) drop tanks.

Forty of the GR.7s are being upgraded to GR.7A standard by fitting the improved Pegasus Mk.107. These are being remanufactured by Rolls-Royce from the Mk.105 under a £150m contract. This will give the Harrier GR.7A a valuable additional 3,000lb of thrust.

In January 2003, BAe Systems was awarded a £150m contract as the first stage of the GR.9 and T.12 upgrade programme, which is expected to cost around £500m. This initial contract was for non-recurring elements of the programme with a further contract to follow for the actual upgrade. This will include new digital systems that include the capability to operate Brimstone and the new precision-guided bombs. Various other enhancements will include a new INS/GPS system, plus improved cockpit displays and a ground-proximity warning-system, plus secure communications. A new rear-fuselage is also to be fitted. The first Harrier GR.9 was flown on 30 May 2003 and it is anticipated that the first will be delivered in November 2004. The upgrade programme on seventy Harriers is planned to be completed by December 2006.

A range of weapons displayed around a 4Sqn Harrier, with mission markings indicating missions flown over Iraq on Operation *Telic*.

LEFT: With shark's teeth and mission markings applied, these Harriers had just returned from Operation *Telic*.

BELOW: The two-seat trainer variant of the Harrier — the T.10 — has a fully operational attack-capability. Although it is not equipped with the nose-mounted laser-designator, it can be fitted with a TIALD instead. Kevin Wills

The previously modified GR.7As will subsequently become GR.9As following their completion of the full upgrade programme. These upgrades are planned to extend the service life of the Harrier through 2012 and the arrival of the JSF.

In February 1999 it was announced that the RAF Harrier GR.7s and FAA Sea Harrier FA.2 would be combined to form Joint Force 2000 (JF2000) and that they would be based at Cottesmore and Wittering. In February 2002 a further announcement declared that the FAA's Sea Harrier FA.2 would be withdrawn from 2004. As a result, FAA pilots are being trained to fly the Harrier GR.7. Once sufficient crews have been trained, one of the RAF Harrier GR.7 squadrons will be disbanded and re-formed as an FAA squadron. It is probable that 3Sqn will be the one that disbands due to its shorter length of total service. During the transition period, the RAF air and ground-crew will be reduced as those from the FAA increase in numbers.

Deliveries of the Harrier GR.7 commenced with 4 (AC) Sqn in 1990; they did not participate in the Gulf War as the crew were still converting and were not fully operational. Harriers have since been deployed on operations in former Yugoslavia, where they first dropped bombs in anger – some 80 tons in total. They also formed part of the *Northern Watch* force that patrolled over Iraq, as well as taking part in the disposing of Saddam's forces in Iraq during Operation *Telic* in 2003.

According to an announcement by the Secretary of State for Defence on 22 April 2004, based on current assumptions, the Harrier GR.9 will remain in operational service until the middle of the next decade.

Twelve Harrier GR.7/7As equip each of 1, 3 and 4Sqn, which are based at Cottesmore, and a further nine equip 20 (R) Sqn, which is based at Wittering. The Fast Jet OEU also operates three GR.7s for trials and is based at Coningsby.

BAe Harrier T.10

Role: STOVL multi-role combat training
Engine: 1 × 95.6kN RR Pegasus Mk.105 vectored-thrust turbofan
Length: 15.79m (51ft 9.5in)
Span: 9.25m (30ft 4in)
Height: 4.09m (13ft 5in)
Speed: Mach 0.86
Weight: 8,527kg (18,800lb) MTOW
Range: 740km (460 miles; 400nm)

The Harrier T.10 is the two-seat trainer-variant of the Harrier GR.7, of which thirteen were ordered in February 1990. Unlike the USMC TAV-8B, the RAF two-seat Harrier trainer is fitted with the same number of hardpoints and weapon system as the GR.7. If required, the T.10 could fly the same operational missions as its single-seat counterpart with one or two crew – the only difference being the weight penalty of the larger fuselage, which reduces the weight of fuel/weapons that can be carried and also reduces the G-limit for the T.10.

The Harrier T.10 entered service with the RAF in 1995 and will undergo a BAe

Systems upgrade programme similar to that for the GR.9, which will result in their being designated T.12.

A Harrier T.10 is operated by each of the operational squadrons at Cottesmore – 1, 3 and 4Sqn – plus a further five with 20 (R) Sqn at Wittering.

Hawk T.1, T.1A, T.1W

Role: Fast-jet advanced flying training
Engine: 1 × 25.4kN RR/Turbomeca Adour Mk 861 turbofan
Length: 11.8m (38ft 10in)
Span: 9.39m (30ft 10in)
Height: 4.0m (13ft 2in)
Speed: 1038km/h (649mph; 560kt)
Weight: 7,530kg (16,600lb) MTOW
Range: 1040km (646 miles; 561nm)

Design of the Hawk commenced in the late-1960s as the HS.1182, a private venture by Hawker Siddeley to replace the Gnat and some Hunter variants. In 1971 an order was announced for 175 of these new trainers, still only on paper. Unusually, a prototype was not built, the first aircraft being constructed on the

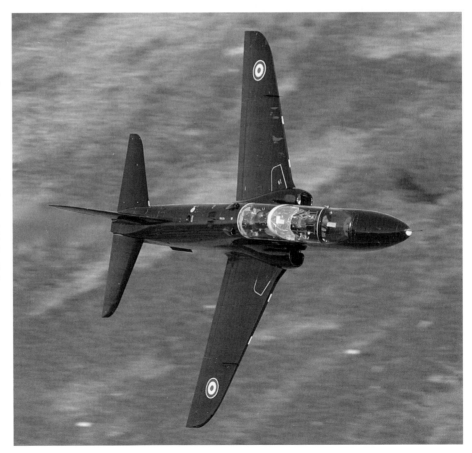

production line. The first Hawk was initially flown on 21 August 1974.

The first six Hawk T.1s were initially used for flight development and then refurbished prior to entry into service, with the exception of the first aircraft, which was retained for continued manufacturer's trials. The first Hawk T.1 was delivered to the RAF in November 1976 and entered service with 4 FTS at Valley. Later deliveries equipped 1 TWU at Brawdy in 1978, followed by 2 TWU at Lossiemouth, which subsequently moved to Chivenor in 1980.

The Hawk quickly proved to be a popular aircraft, with excellent handling qualities, good field of vision from front and back seat, and comfortable cockpit. Its safety record also proved to be much better than provisioned for.

Initially, Hawk students would have undergone basic training on the Chipmunk T.10/Bulldog T.1 before progressing to the Jet Provost T.5. The advanced course then included seventy-five hours on the Hawk before being posted to the TWU and then OCU, where they would fly the Buccaneer, Harrier, Jaguar, Phantom or Tornado. Today this would be Tutor, Tucano, Hawk then Harrier, Jaguar and Tornado and soon the Typhoon – the Hawk being the first jet that these students will fly.

The Red Arrows converted onto the Hawk T.1 in 1979 and were based at Kemble – now at Scampton. The CFS operated their Hawks at Valley to train instructors. Chivenor-based 1 TWU consisted of shadow squadrons 79 and 234Sqn while Brawdy- and later Lossiemouth-based 2 TWU consisted of 63 and 151Sqn, indicating their potential war role. All the TWU units have since disbanded and their tasks transferred to 4 FTS. In addition ETPS plus QinetiQ operated several Hawks at Boscombe Down.

As a weapons-training platform, sixty-five of the TWU Hawks were modified to carry weapons, with a 30mm Aden cannon on the centre line plus a 68mm SNEB rocket pod under the starboard wing and a CBLS (Carrier Bomb Light Stores) for practice bomb. These modified Hawks were designated T.1W. Another designation was the T.1N, which was used at Valley for Hawks fitted with a stopwatch used in navigator training. However, this designation appears to have fallen into disuse with 100Sqn, who now undertake this training.

A further war role was given to the Hawk – that of second-line air defence. A contract was awarded to BAe in January 1983 to modify the TWU and Red Arrows Hawks. As a result, eighty-eight Hawks were modified during the mid-1980s to T.1A standard with the capability of operating Sidewinder missiles for an air-defence role.

Initially, 4 FTS aircraft were flown clean in standard red, white and grey training colours and the TWU aircraft were camouflaged. Subsequently, the T.1As were painted an overall light-grey and all are now painted an overall high-gloss black. The Red Arrows maintain their own scheme.

On 30 July 2003, the MoD announced the selection of the Hawk 128 as its new Advanced Jet Trainer, powered by the Adour Mk.951. Twenty aircraft are being ordered with options on a further twenty-four. These will enter service from 2008 and will form part of the proposed Military Flying Training System (MFTS), which should be in place by then. They will also enable some of the T.1s to be retired.

The Hawk 128 will enable the easy transition of qualified fast-jet pilot students to the Typhoon and later the JSF with a state of the art digital-cockpit. This is not available in the currently operated Hawk T.1.

In the meantime, eighty existing Hawk T.1/T.1As have been put through a fuselage-replacement program, which is intended to extend their service life to 2010. The Hawks were flown to DARA at St Athan, where the aircraft was dismantled. The fuselage is despatched to BAe Systems at Brough, where new centre-aft and aft fuselage-sections were fitted. When completed, the fuselage was completed to a Hawk Mk.65 standard before being returned to St Athan. This modification was undertaken depending on where the aircraft was in its maintenance schedule. The completed aircraft remained designated T.1A.

The Red Arrows currently fly the Hawk T.1 and T.1A, which have a few additional modifications for their aerobatic role – the main one being the carrying of diesel fuel in a ventral fuel-tank, plus plumbing enabling it to be squirted into the exhaust to provide the smoke.

From 1995, the Royal Navy received a total of fourteen ex-RAF Hawks, for use with their Fleet Requirements and Aircraft Direction Unit (FRADU) at Yeovilton, to replace their Hunters. Subsequently, they moved to Culdrose where they are currently based. They operate in the same black markings as those with the RAF – their main visible difference being the 'Royal Navy' wording forward of the serial.

A groundcrew from the TAF Det at St Athan loads a 3kg No. 2, Mk.3 practice bomb into the CBLS 100 pod. Once released they replicate the trajectory of a 1,000lb bomb and give off a small flash and puff of smoke to enable ground observers to calibrate the accuracy of the attack.

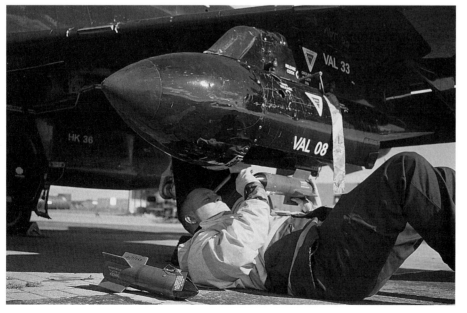

The Hawk is operated by 4 FTS, which comprises 19 (R) Sqn and 208 (R) Sqn with T.1/T.1As and T.1Ws, based at Valley. 100Sqn is based at Leeming with T.1/T.1As, which are also used by the JFACTSU (Joint Forward Air Control Training and Standards Unit). The RAF Centre of Aviation Medicine based at Henlow operates T.1As but these are housed at Boscombe Down. The Red Arrows operate Hawk T.1/T.1As from their base at Scampton. QinetiQ and ETPS also use Hawks.

Lockheed Hercules C.1

Role: Tactical support and transport
Engine: 4 × 4,910eshp Allison T56-A-15 turboprop
Length: 30.63m (100ft 6in) including probe
Span: 40.41m (132ft 7in)
Height: 11.71m (38ft 5in)
Speed: 621km/h (388mph; 335kt)
Weight: 70,370kg (155,000lb) MTOW
Range: 5,468km (3,398 miles; 2,950nm)

RAF humour is seldom in short supply! A Hercules at Lyneham is suitably painted for Comic Relief Red Nose Day, while another happy Herc looks on.

The Hercules design was originally selected as a USAF transport aircraft in July 1951. On 23 August 1954 the prototype YC-130 took to the air and has since become the world's most successful postwar transport aircraft. The first USAF squadron deliveries commenced in December 1956.

By 1965 some 800 C-130 Hercules had been delivered to the USAF and nine other countries when MoD interest was manifesting itself for RAF use. The Labour Government had cancelled the British-designed HS.681 transport, along with a number of other RAF aircraft projects, the previous year, leaving a serious gap in RAF capabilities.

An announcement of an intended order was made in February to replace the Hastings and Beverley with a new variant of the Hercules based on the C-130E. The first of sixty-six C-130Ks flew on 19 October 1966 and was delivered to Marshalls at Cambridge on 19 December. They had been appointed as the UK design authority and took delivery of each aircraft, making final modifications before they entered service with the RAF.

Following trials at Boscombe Down, deliveries commenced to 242 OCU at Thorney Island in April 1967 and 36Sqn became the first squadron to form, in July at Lyneham. Next was 48Sqn. It was to be based at Changi, so equipped at Colerne prior to taking its aircraft out to Singapore. In February 1968, 24Sqn commenced their deliveries at Lyneham, while 47Sqn formed at Fairford in May 1968, plus 30Sqn in June. In November 1970, 70Sqn took delivery of some Hercules at Akrotiri.

In 1972, one Hercules was modified for the Meteorological Research Flight as a W.2, with a long nose-probe and the radar mounted above the fuselage. This aircraft is currently in open storage at Boscombe Down, where its future is uncertain.

Gradually all the Hercules squadrons migrated to Lyneham. In February 1971, 30 and 47Sqn were the first. These were followed by 70Sqn in January 1975, 48Sqn in September and 242 OCU in October. Thinning out then became the order, with 36Sqn disbanding in November and 48Sqn the following January. During March 1975, RAF Hercules assisted in the withdrawal of civilians from Phnom Penh, Cambodia.

In July 1992, 242 OCU was re-named 57 (R) Sqn and was subsequently disbanded in November 2001. In September 1995, the Hercules Operational Evaluation Unit (HOEU) was formed to assess and develop the various roles and equipment for the Hercules models that are perceived to be of value to the squadrons. The HOEU is actually part of the Air Warfare Centre based at Waddington.

While the squadron situation remained static for a few years, changes were to be made to the aircraft. Modifications of the fuselage introduced in 1979 resulted in the lengthened C.3 variant.

When the Falklands were invaded by the Argentinians the RAF discovered that they had no transport aircraft capable of operating the distances required. An urgent programme by Marshalls delivered the first Hercules C.1P, with a nose probe for air-to-air refuelling, in three weeks. This enabled Victor K.2s to refuel the Hercules to provide vital re-supply missions. The C.1P and C.3P designation reverted to C.1 and C.3 once the whole fleet had been modified.

While this was under way, Marshalls were also tasked to convert four Hercules as tankers (this was later increased to six). The first aircraft was operational just seventy-six days from the order as a C.1K – all have since been converted back or withdrawn.

The Hercules rapidly became the workhorse of the RAF: whether it was exercise or operation, the Hercules usually arrived first with advanced and reception parties, including movers – then undertook the resupply. It was then the last to depart, recovering the final elements, which included the movers again.

While exercises have always been the run of the mill, the number of operations has continued to increase. These have

ABOVE: **For many years the Hercules has provided the RAF with its only means of transporting large loads. One here is disgorging an army Lynx at Split, for use with the UN force in the Balkans.**

LEFT: **The flexibility of the Hercules is its greatest attribute and a formation is seen here air-dropping MSPs (Medium Stressed Platforms), which contain vehicles and artillery for the Paras.**

fallen into a number of categories including conflict, policing and humanitarian. Each has required heavy utilization of the Hercules fleet. For a medium-range transport the regular shuttles to the Falklands and major airlift for the Gulf War – which was greater than the Berlin Airlift – together with subsequent operations, have taken their toll on the airframe.

As a result a replacement was sought. A European solution was the FLA (now designated A400M), however, political wrangling and indecision has made the possibility of this aircraft entering service seem less likely. However, in 2003 the Germans eventually made their mind up and confirmed their order, enabling the project to proceed.

When Lockheed proposed their solution a number of existing operators, including the RAF, became interested. This solution was a re-designed Hercules, which was designated C-130J. With a number of their airframes getting close to a decision on scrapping or major refurbishment the RAF opted for twenty-five C-130Js.

As deliveries of the C-130J were made, existing C-130Ks were handed over to Lockheed Martin, as agreed in the contract. Some of these have been refurbished

and re-sold (for example, Austrian AF), offered for sale (for example, Polish AF), stored or have been scrapped.

Over the years the colour-scheme of the Hercules has changed. Initial deliveries from Lockheed were made in natural finish and then were painted in a light- and dark-stone with black undersides. Light-grey and green followed, as Middle East commitments were reduced, and they are now finished in an overall light-grey. Variations on these schemes included various underside permutations of black, including an underseal black, light-grey and all-over camouflage. Several special schemes have also been applied to the Hercules using an Alkali-Removable Temporary Finish (ARTF) paint, including pink (of which a couple were later used during the Gulf War) and white.

RAF Lyneham is due to close in 2012 and, while the new Hercules C.4 and C.5 will transfer to Brize Norton, six of the older C.1s will remain at Lyneham along with the C.3s until they are retired.

Hercules C.1s are flown by 47 and 70Sqn and operate from Lyneham. One is also operated by 1310 Flight, which is based at Mount Pleasant on the Falkland Islands.

Lockheed Hercules C.3

Role: Tactical support and transport
Engine: 4 × 3,645kW Allison T56-A-15 turboprop
Length: 35.20m (115ft 6in) including probe
Span: 40.41m (132ft 7in)
Height: 11.71m (38ft 5in)
Speed: 507km/h (317mph; 273kt)
Weight: 72,640kg (160,000lb)
Range: 1,850km (1,150 miles; 998nm)

The Hercules C.3 is a modified version of the existing C.1, with a similar fuselage stretch to the L-100-30 Hercules used by many civilian operators.

It had frequently been the situation that the Hercules 'bulked out' (that is, the maximum size of the load was reached before the Hercules maximum weight). As a result a programme was instigated in 1978 to convert thirty Hercules to C.3s by increasing their length by 15ft (4.57m). This was achieved by inserting a section fore and another aft of the wing box. Not only did this increase the volume by 37 per cent but the capacity for fully equipped troops increased from 92 to 128.

After the conversion by Lockheed of an initial aircraft in 1979 used for trials, a further twenty-nine were converted by Marshalls. The first Marshalls-converted C.3 was delivered to Lyneham on 28 August 1980 and the programme completed in 1985. By 2004, twenty C.3s remained in service; they will remain at

A few Hercules have been fitted with the DIRCOM defensive-aids system. This is to provide enhanced protection from surface-to-air missiles (SAM) when operating in potentially hostile environments such as Iraq or, as shown here, in Afghanistan. Unofficially they have been designated C.3a.

Lyneham with the C.1s until their withdrawal.

It is anticipated that the A400 will replace the Hercules C.3, with delivery expected from 2009.

Hercules C.3s are flown by 47 and 70Sqn and operate from Lyneham.

Lockheed Hercules C.4

Role: Tactical support and transport
Engine: 4 × 3,424kW Rolls-Royce AE.2100D3 turboprop
Length: 34.37m (112ft 9in)
Span: 40.41m (132ft 7in)
Height: 11.81m (38ft 9in)
Speed: 656km/h (410mph; 354kt)
Weight: 79,380kg (175,000lb) MTOW
Range: 5,500km (3,418 miles; 2,967nm)

The Hercules C.4 is the RAF's designation for the stretched C-130J-30. This stretch was incorporated in the initial build on the production line by Lockheed Martin rather than later as a conversion.

The C-130J was designed and built as a private venture by Lockheed Martin to replace the original family of C-130 Hercules, which was nearing the end of its production after some 2,100 examples had been built. The prototype was first flown on 5 April 1996.

Although it looks very similar to the Hercules C.3 it is, in fact, a very different aircraft, readily identifiable by the distinctive six-blade composite Dowty Aerospace R391 propellers. It also has a black panel on the lower front of the fin. While all of the C.1/C.3 Hercules feature a permanently fitted refuelling probe, the C.4/C.5 will normally only have one fitted when the mission requires it. It is also unusual in that, when fitted, it is located halfway down the left-hand side of the cockpit.

The propellers are the highly visible portion of a redesigned propulsion system based on four Rolls-Royce AE 2100D3 engines. They develop 29 per cent more thrust than the old Hercules engines and at the same time are 15 per cent more fuel efficient. This can enable greater ranges to be flown at higher speeds. The cockpit is designed around a two-crew operation with a loadmaster to look after the hold. There are provisions for an additional crew member if required. Much of the workload is undertaken by computer systems and displayed in the fully digital glass-cockpit. A HUD reduces the pilots' need to look down in the cockpit. A new radar enables ground-returns to be viewed as a picture. The cockpit is also NVG compatible.

The Hercules C.4 is capable of carrying up to 128 troops or ninety-two paratroops. It also has a medevac role, in which ninety-seven stretcher patients can be carried plus four attendants.

The RAF became the lead customer for the C-130J with an order for twenty-five aircraft in December 1994. This order was split into fifteen of the longer C.4s (C-130J-30) and ten standard C.5s (C-130J).

The first C.4 was due to be delivered to Boscombe Down in November 1996. Although the first aircraft was rolled out in 1996 and first flew on 5 April, technical delays meant that it did not arrive until August 1998. The first aircraft to arrive at Lyneham was on 21 November 1999 for 57 (R) Sqn, who were the OCU. As part of the contract, C-130Ks were returned to Lockheed on a one-for-one basis as the new Hercules were delivered.

The C-130J has received some adverse publicity regarding the delays in its achieving operational clearance due to various problems with software and airflow patterns. It also caused the RAF a number of problems. The old aircraft still required a navigator, the new did not. As a result, a plan to retain existing crew and train up new navigators was required. Plus, because the new C-130Js were without the necessary clearances, the reduced fleet of the old, fully cleared Hercules was being worked increasingly harder. However, in June 2002, a defence-aids suite had been installed and the new Hercules was cleared sufficiently to enable it to deploy operationally. The new Hercules first deployment was to Afghanistan to support British forces.

About the same time 30Sqn was stood up to operate as the second C-130J squadron at Lyneham.

In 2003 the Hercules C.4s were operated in support of coalition forces in Iraq and a pair remained in theatre after the Iraq War to continue this role, as well as the humanitarian role.

The Hercules C.4s are operated by 24 and 30Sqn from their base at Lyneham.

Lockheed Hercules C.5

Role: Tactical support and transport
Engine: 4 × 3,424kW Rolls-Royce AE.2100D3 turboprop
Length: 29.79m (97ft 9in)
Span: 40.41m (132ft 7in)
Height: 11.84m (38ft 10in)
Speed: 640km/h (400mph; 345kt)
Weight: 70,305kg (155,000lb) MTOW
Range: 5,250km (3,262 miles; 2,832nm)

The Hercules C.5 is the C-130J equivalent of the C-130K C.1 with the standard length fuselage.

The RAF ordered ten of the Hercules

The C-130J version of the Hercules features a bolt-on probe that is normally only fitted when the mission requires air-to-air refuelling.

C.5, which can carry ninety-two troops or sixty-four paratroops. They can also carry seventy-four stretcher patients with four attendants for the medevac role.

It is proposed that the RAF C-130J will have a tanker capability and it is anticipated that Mk.32 refuelling pods will be acquired from Flight Refuelling. These can be fitted to the C.5s when required. They will then be able to refuel the Merlin HC.3 and the Chinook HC.3 or its replacement. In addition, they will also have the capability to refuel some fixed-wing aircraft.

While the C-130J initially offered substantial savings in operating costs, the new technologies incorporated in the design initially caused difficulties in achieving the RAF's necessary operation clearances, resulting in increased operating costs. However, these problems have now been resolved.

The Hercules C.5s are operated by 24 and 30Sqn from their base at Lyneham.

Hawker Hurricane IIc

Role: Vintage fighter
Engine: 1 × 98kW (1,300hp) Rolls-Royce Merlin XX
Length: 9.83m (32ft 3in)
Span: 12.19m (40ft 0in)
Height: 4.04m (13ft 3in)
Speed: 526km/h (327mph; 284kt)
Weight: 3,425kg (7,544lb) MTOW
Range: 740km (460 miles; 399nm)

The Hurricane was designed by Hawker as a private venture around the same time as the Spitfire. It was not as advanced as the Spitfire and never had its reputation. It had metal wings but the fuselage consisted mainly of a canvas-covered metal tubular frame with wood stringers and formers. The prototype was first flown on 6 November 1935.

With its simpler design, the Hurricane was easier to put into production. When war broke there were eighteen squadrons of Hurricanes but only nine of Spitfires. During the Battle of Britain the Hurricanes still maintained their two-to-one lead and, when production ended in

ABOVE: The Hercules is remarkably agile and the enhanced capabilities of the 'J' model provide a quieter but more capable performance at low, as well as higher altitudes.

BELOW: The two Hurricanes of the BBMF are regularly displayed at airshows. It provided the majority of the fighter defences during the Battle of Britain and shot down more enemy aircraft, although the Spitfire (in the background) is often given greater credit.

The Jaguars that were operated over Iraq during Operation Granby were painted pink to provide camouflage over the desert. This one also features a dummy cockpit painted on the underside to further confuse the enemy.

1944, 14,533 had been built in two basic fighter-models – the Mk.I and Mk.II. A fighter-bomber Mk.IV and Canadian-built Mk.X were also produced.

Two Hurricanes are operated by the BBMF and can be seen flying at airshows and official functions. Both are the Mk.IIc and both are historical. LF363 has remained in RAF service since she was delivered to the RAF in January 1944. On 11 September 1991 disaster struck when the engine failed during a routine flight. Due to his skill, the pilot managed an emergency landing at Wittering but LF363 was extensively damaged in the ensuing fire, to the extent that normally it would have been declared a write-off. However, the historical significance of this individual aircraft was such that one of the BBMF Spitfire PR.19s was sold to provide funds for the rebuild. LF363 returned to the air in 1998.

The other Hurricane IIc is PZ865 – the last Hurricane built by Hawker. Both aircraft are regularly repainted in authentic markings to represent squadrons that operated the Hurricane in the Second World War.

The two Hurricane IIcs are operated by the BBMF and are based at Coningsby.

Britten Norman Islander CC.2, CC.2A

Role: Communications and survey
Engine: 2 × 238.5kW Allison 250-B17C turboprop
Length: 10.86m (35ft 7.75in)
Span: 14.94m (49ft 0in)
Height: 4.18m (13ft 8.75in)
Speed: 314km/h (196mph; 169kt)
Weight: 3,175kg (7,000lb) MTOW
Range: 1,595km (991 miles; 861nm)

The BN-2 Islander was originally designed and built with piston engines. The prototype was first flown on 13 June 1965. The British military variant is fitted with 298kW (400shp) turboprops, which have been flat-rated at 238.5kW (320shp) and have the Britten Norman designation BN-2T.

Seven Islander AL.1s were ordered for the Army Air Corps (AAC) to replace their Beavers and deliveries commenced in 1989.

The Northolt Station Flight was formed in August 1991 and took delivery of the first of two BN-2T Islanders in December. Their exact role is unclear but they are officially used for light communications and photographic mapping. A subsequent CC.2A model was delivered to the Flight.

An Islander CC.2 and a CC.2A are operated by Northolt Station Flight and are based at Northolt.

SEPECAT Jaguar GR.3, GR.3A

Role: Offensive counter-air, close air-support and tactical reconnaissance
Engine: 2 × 38.6kN RR Adour Mk 106 turbofan
Length: 16.83m (55ft 2.6in) including probe
Span: 8.7m (28ft 6in)
Height: 4.92m (16ft 1.75in)
Speed: Mach 1.2
Weight: 15,436kg (34,000lb) MTOW
Range: 1,315km (817 miles; 709nm)

The Jaguar was the subject of a joint Anglo-French programme that was originally announced in 1965. The first prototype made its initial flight on 8 September 1968.

Initial plans were for a high proportion of two-seat advanced trainers, but this was later changed to 165 single-seat strike GR.1s with just thirty-five Jaguar T.2 two-seat operational trainers, due to a high operating-cost. This was in addition to the three prototypes.

The first British prototype single-seat Jaguar was first flown on 12 October 1969 and the first production GR.1 on 11

October 1972. The first Jaguar GR.1s entered service on 30 May 1973 with 226 OCU at Lossiemouth. The first operational squadron to receive the Jaguar in March 1974 was 54Sqn and eventually eight front-line squadrons were operating the aircraft – 2, 6, 14, 17, 20, 31, 41 and 54Sqn.

The Jaguar was originally fitted with a sophisticated navigational system and a laser rangefinder. Improvements commenced in 1978: these included fitting the more powerful Adour 104, in place of the 102, and an inertial navigation system. As a result of these upgrades the aircraft were designated GR.1A. In 1995, several GR.1Bs were delivered; these had been modified to operate the TIALD target-designation pods.

The Jaguar is well used to operating in different environments. Jaguars regularly deploy to the often hostile environment of Norway for various joint exercises with other NATO members. Occasionally the aircraft are painted in winter camouflage schemes.

Not all the areas of operation for the Jaguar are cold. The Jaguar was extensively used during the Gulf War, with over 600 missions flown by twelve aircraft on strike and reconnaissance. A wide range of weapons was carried by the Jaguars during these missions, with AIM-9 Sidewinders being standard on overwing rails. Four 1,000lb iron and LGB bombs were usually

A Jaguar armed with 1,000lb bombs under the wings, AIM-9 Sidewinder air-to-air missiles on rails above the wings and fitted with Phimat chaff dispenser-pods flies over the Adriatic during missions over the Balkans.

carried, but they also used BL755, CBU-87 and CRV-7 rockets.

Besides these weapons, the Jaguar is fitted with a single 30mm Aden cannon and can carry a range of the Paveway LGBs. In addition, while all three operational squadrons are able to conduct attack and reconnaissance missions, 6Sqn and 54 (F) Sqn are primarily attack squadrons, while 41 (F) Sqn is primarily a reconnaissance squadron. While the TIALD pod is carried for the attack role, various reconnaissance pods have been carried over recent years, including the BAe recce pod with conventional wet film sensors and an Infrared Line Scan or the Vinten Vicon recce pod that combines wet film and Electro-Optical (EO) sensors. Most recently, the Jaguar Reconnaissance Pod (JRP) GP1 Electro-Optical (EO) pod has been used. The only squadron to operate the JRP pod in the low-level tactical reconnaissance role is 41Sqn.

Although the Gulf War was quickly over, the Jaguars continued to operate over Iraq as part of the *Northern Watch* to protect the Kurds in the north of the country – a job that that the Jaguar squadrons shared on rotation with the Harriers until 2003 with Operation *Telic*.

Subsequently, operations in the former Yugoslavia have seen Jaguars based in Italy for close air-support and reconnaissance over Bosnia and Kosovo.

Despite its age the Jaguar proved highly capable during Operation *Granby* and has since undergone some significant upgrades.

Jaguar 96 saw the integration of a GPS system, together with a MIL-DTD-1553 databus, a ground-proximity warning-sensor, a wide-angle Head-Up Display (HUD) and the addition of the TIALD pod. Once the aircraft had undergone these modifications, it was designated the Jaguar GR.3. The two-seat trainers were designated T.4.

The next upgrade programme was Jaguar 97. This took forty-four of the GR.3s and added a Helmet Mounted Sighting (HMS), which also enabled the AIM-9 Sidewinders to be aimed off-boresight for the first time. It also had a large-format Active Matrix Liquid Crystal Display to replace the small CRT unit. An improved Paveway II and III aiming capability and terrain-referenced navigation system, as well as provision for the ASRAAM were also included. Once complete these were designated the GR.3A.

Another further upgrade is underway, resulting in the aircraft being modified to take the Adour Mk.106 engine. This engine has had a sizeable portion replaced by that fitted to the Hawk's Adour Mk.871. While this has not produced the anticipated added power-boost, it does substantially increase its reliability and ease of maintenance. The £105m contract was signed in 1998 and provided for sixty aircraft to be modified, with fifty-eight being modified at St Athan remaining as the GR.3A. The first was delivered to Coltishall in February 2002.

Following an announcement, 16 (R) Sqn and 54Sqn were disbanded on 11 March 2005. In 2006 41Sqn will disband, followed by 6Sqn in 2008. It is intended that the Jaguar will be replaced by the Typhoon around 2008/9.

The Jaguar GR.3/GR.3A and T.4 are flown by both 6 and 41Sqn based at Coltishall. The Fast Jet OEU at Coningsby operates the GR.3.

SEPECAT Jaguar T.2A, T.4

Role: Offensive counter-air, close air-support and tactical-reconnaissance training
Engine: 2 × 7,900lb RR Adour Mk 104 turbofan
Length: 16.43m (53ft 11in)
Span: 8.69m (28ft 6in)
Height: 4.92m (16ft 1.75in)
Speed: Mach 1.2
Weight: 15,700kg (34,612lb)
Range: 1,315km (817 miles; 709nm)

Initial plans were for the two-seat Jaguar trainer to fulfil the role of advanced trainer to replace the Gnat T.1. However, this was subsequently dropped as being too expensive in favour of the Hawk and a total of thirty-eight Jaguar T.2 two-seat operational trainers were ordered. This included three aircraft for the ETPS and RAE (later to become DERA then QinetiQ).

The British prototype two-seat Jaguar was first flown on 30 August 1971 and the first production T.2 on 28 March 1973.

Like the single-seat model, the two-seat Jaguar has four underwing and one centre-line pylon but has just a single 30mm cannon. It also lacks the laser system that is fitted in the nose of the strike model. It does feature a weapon-carrying capability and so could be used operationally if required.

The T.2s followed the GR.1 upgrade programme with the replacement Navigation and Weapons Aiming Sub-System (NAVWASS), which led to the designation T.1A. The subsequent GR.3 modifications brought the two-seat model up to T.4.

While most of the Jaguar T.2s were used to equip 226 OCU at Lossiemouth, each of the operational squadrons (2, 6, 14, 17, 20, 31, 41 and 54Sqn) would have had at least one for refresher and check training purposes. 226 OCU was re-numbered 16 (R) Sqn and joined the operational squadrons at Coltishall in July 2000.

The Jaguar T.4 is operated by both 6 and 41Sqn, which are based at Coltishall. The ETPS at Boscombe Down also operate two Jaguar T.2s.

Loading a live 1,000lb GP bomb under a 41Sqn Jaguar G.3 ready for a training sortie on a range in Alaska. The RAF regularly use training areas overseas to try to reduce the amount of low-level flying in the UK.

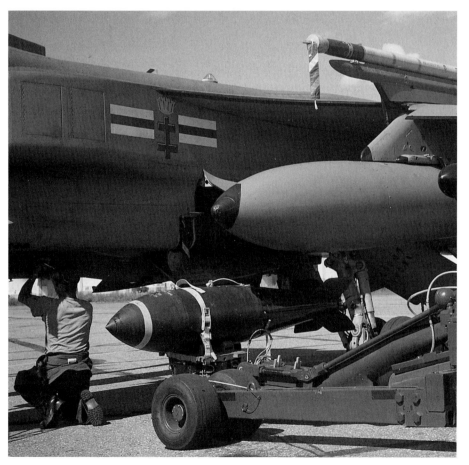

Raytheon King Air B200

Role: Multi-engined advanced pilot-training
Engine: 2 × 634kW P&W Canada PT6A-42 turboprop
Length: 13.36m (43ft 10in)
Span: 16.61m (54ft 6in)
Height: 4.52m 14ft 10in)
Speed: 422km/h (255mph; 222kt)
Weight: 5,670kg (12,500lb) MTOW
Range: 3,283km (2,040 miles; 1,771nm)

The design of the Raytheon King Air B200 commenced in 1970 as the Beech Super King Air. The twin-turboprop aircraft was geared toward the civil market as a pressurized light-transport for passenger, business or cargo. The prototype was first flown on 27 October 1972 and, since then, over 5,500 aircraft have been built, of which well over 2,000 are the B200 model.

In 1996, the 'Super' prefix was dropped, which established the King Air as a comprehensive range of light twin-engined aircraft, capable of carrying 7–8 seats on the C90B through to the 350 model with 8–11 seats.

In June 2003 SerCo was awarded the £60m RAF Cranwell Multi-Activity Contract (MAC) and Multi-Engine Pilot Training Interim Solution. The MAC is primarily admin and services, however,

The King Air B200 has replaced the Jetstream for training pilots to fly multi-engined aircraft.

the Multi-Engine Pilot Training has resulted in seven King Air B200s being leased from Raytheon, replacing the existing Jetstreams.

The flight training aspect includes some 5,500 flying hours per year on the King Air B200 and 3,000 simulator hours per year. The first two aircraft arrived on 16 December 2003 and all were delivered by February 2004. The contract came into full effect on 1 April 2004.

The King Air B200 is flown by 45 (R) Sqn and operated by SerCo from Cranwell.

Avro Lancaster B.I

Role: Vintage bomber
Engine: 4 × 954kW (1,280hp) RR Merlin XX piston
Length: 21.13m (69ft 4in)
Span: 31.09m (102ft)
Height: 6.25m (20ft 6in)
Speed: 462km/h (287mph; 249kt)
Weight: 32,688kg (72,000lb) MTOW
Range: 4,023km (2,500 miles; 2,170nm)

One of only two remaining airworthy Lancasters is flown by the BBMF from Coningsby to commemorate the thousands of aircrew of Bomber Command who lost their lives defending this country.

The Avro Lancaster was developed from the underpowered twin-engined Manchester bomber. The prototype was first flown on 9 January 1941 and entered service in with 44Sqn in December 1941. When production ended a total of 7,377 had been built, of which 3,349 had been lost on operations during the Second World War. The Lancaster was the corner post of Bomber Command and

took part in many famous operations – the most famous probably being the dambusting attacks by 617Sqn. Their bomb-carrying capability developed from 4,000lb to the massive 22,000lb Grand Slam bomb.

PA474 is not a significant airframe; she was built at Chester in 1945 and was earmarked for Tiger Force for operations against the Japanese in the Far East, but the war ended before she was deployed. The turrets were removed and PA474 served with 82Sqn for photo reconnaissance duties in Africa. On her return home she was transferred to the College of Aeronautics for trials. However, PA474 is now one of only two remaining airworthy Lancasters in the world. The other is located in Canada.

In 1973, PA474 joined the BBMF, with whom she has been displayed before millions. Through dedicated restoration and servicing over the years, she has been returned to her original configuration and the fitting of new spars in 1995–6 will help to ensure that she will continue to be displayed for many years to come, as a memorial to bomber crews lost in the Second World War. PA474 is regularly repainted with squadron markings representative of those that operated the Lancaster in the Second World War and can be seen at numerous airshows.

The Lancaster is operated by the BBMF and is based at Coningsby.

The Merlin is the RAF's latest helicopter transport. Although it suffered some initial problems during its entry into service, a twelve-month deployment to Bosnia soon put these in the past. With high levels of serviceability and a substantial payload, it was quickly sought after to undertake a wide range of roles, due to its reliability and capability.

GKN Westland Merlin HC.3

Role: Ground-force tactical and strategic support
Engine: 3 × 1,394kW (1,870shp) RR Turbomeca RTM 322-02/8 turboshaft
Length: 22.81m (74ft 10in) overall
Rotor Span: 18.59m (61ft 0in)
Height: 6.65m (21ft 10in)
Speed: 309km/h (192mph; 167kt) MTOW
Weight: 14,600kg (32,188lb)
Range: 648km (403 miles; 350nm)

The Merlin HC.3 is the RAF's variant of the EH101 and is operated as a medium support-helicopter. The EH101 became a joint project between Agusta and Westland in 1980, as a result of a broadly similar specification by the Royal Navy and Italian Navy for a Sea King replacement. The prototype EH101 first flew on 9 October 1987. The RAF ordered twenty-two in March 1995 and the first entered service with 28Sqn in January 2001.

The Merlin HC.3 is a next-generation multi-role helicopter that has an all-weather, day- and night-capability. It is fitted with an effective defensive-aids suite that incorporates the Nemesis DIRCM turret with missile approach and laser warning-sensors. The cockpit has been

modified for low-level operations with a sophisticated navigation system and is fully NVG compatible. Although not currently utilized, the Merlin HC.3 is unique in being the RAF's first operational helicopter capable of in-flight refuelling, enabling greater ranges to be flown. Another feature of the Merlin is an active vibration-damping control. As a result, the internal noise and vibration levels are reduced, providing a more comfortable flight for passengers, reduced crew fatigue and increased airframe life.

As a multi-purpose helicopter, the Merlin HC.3 can carry Land Rovers and Light Strike vehicles internally or thirty-five fully armed troops, in addition to underslung loads up to 5,443kg (12,000lb). It can easily be converted to the Casevac role, with sixteen stretchers plus the medical team. Future proposals include the fitting of a nose turret with a 0.5in gun, in addition to pintle-mounted machine guns in the doors. Another proposal is to fit stub wings with pylons, enabling the carrying of anti-tank and air-to-air missiles, as well as rocket pods.

The latest flight simulators at the Medium Support Helicopter Aircrew Training Facility (MSHATF), also located

Soldiers rapidly deplane from a Merlin HC.3, which is capable of carrying thirty-five of them fully armed. Agusta Westland

at Benson, include three for the Merlin HC.3. These are capable of being linked together and can provide valuable prior training for a particular sortie, enabling tactics to be developed and rehearsed.

Early production Merlin HC.3s were delivered to Boscombe Down, where QinetiQ carried out the Military Aircraft Release trials. Further deliveries were then made to 28Sqn from January 2001.

The Merlin HC.2 is operated by 28Sqn, which was officially re-formed in July 2001 at Benson. Initial work by the squadron was to undertake instructor training and course validation. Once this was completed, the job of building up the squadron proper with a full complement of air and groundcrew could commence, to achieve operational status.

In April 2003 two Merlins were deployed on the squadron's first operation deployment to Banja Luka in Bosnia, where they were operated in support of the multi-national SFOR peacekeeping force. During this deployment the Merlins were in constant use and were found to operate well in excess of expectations. This significantly increased the SFOR capability and effectiveness.

The last Merlin HC.3 was handed over to the RAF on 19 November 2002 and each is undergoing various upgrades, which means that not all of the fleet are operational at any one time. The original intention was that some of these aircraft would be used to equip a Flight of 72Sqn when the Wessex was withdrawn. Instead, that squadron was disbanded

and it would appear that plan has been abandoned.

The Merlin HC.3 is operated by 28Sqn and is based at Benson.

BAe Nimrod R.1, MR.2

Role: Reconnaissance and electronic intelligence-gathering, anti-submarine and anti-surface warfare, and search and rescue
Engine: 4 × 54kN RR RB.168-20 Spey 250 turbofan
Length: 40.16m (131ft 9in)
Span: 35.08m (115ft 1in)
Height: 9.08m (29ft 8.5in)
Speed: 926km/h (579mph; 500kt)
Weight: 80,510kg (177,500lb) MTOW
Range: 12 hours endurance

Design of the Nimrod commenced in 1964 as a new maritime-reconnaissance aircraft to replace the piston-engined Shackletons. An order for two prototypes was placed in January 1966 and the first flew on 23 May 1967. The first of forty-six Nimrod MR.1s entered RAF service on 2 October 1969.

The Nimrod is based on the de Havilland Comet 4C airliner. However, the unique shape is due to it being fitted with a weapons and operational-

The development of the Comet airliner to Nimrod can be seen in this line up. In the middle is the ill-fated Nimrod AEW.3 variant, which didn't enter service and was replaced by the Sentry AEW.1.

equipment bay 15.85m (52ft) long, in an extension under the fuselage.

Commencing in 1975, thirty-two Nimrod MR.1s underwent a major upgrade to their systems. These incorporated the advanced Searchwater system – completed, the total computer power was about sixty times that of the MR.1. This resulted in the designation being changed to MR.2. The first Nimrod MR.2 was handed over to the RAF on 23 August 1973. During Operation Corporate, when Nimrods needed to fly extended ranges, a hurried programme was introduced to enable air-to-air refuelling. The resulting modification resulted in the MR.2P; although the 'P' was later dropped once all of the fleet had been modified.

AIM-9 Sidewinders can be carried on underwing pylons for air defence against other aircraft and chaff/flares can be fitted to distract incoming missiles. This was an additional Operation Corporate modification.

The primary role of the Nimrod is Anti-Surface Vessel (ASV) and Anti-Submarine Warfare (ASW). For ASV missions the Searchwater radar provides an impressive surveillance medium for detection of surface vessels. Not only can

it provide information as to the length but also present an identification image of the ship. Yellowgate ESM sensors are also able to detect and classify radar transmissions. Once detected, enemy vessels can be dealt with by an arsenal of weapons, which can be carried in the massive bomb-bay as well as under the wings – these can include Harpoon missiles. Alternatively, secure communications can advise other friendly forces to enable them to attack.

For the ASW role, the Searchwater radar can be optimized to search for a periscope or any other part of a submarine that breaks the surface. The Magnetic Anomaly Detector (MAD), which is fitted in the tail extension, traces any discrepancies in the Earth's magnetic field that indicate the location of a submarine. The Nimrod carries around 150 active and passive sonobuoys that can be dropped to more accurately detect and identify the submarine. The active sonobuoy emits a ping, which is reflected and enables a distance to be calculated – three sonars enable an accurate position to be plotted. The passive sonobuoy listens for any noises that can be used to identify an individual submarine. The information from the sonar buoys is transmitted to the

Nimrod's Tactical Computer and can appear on a number of displays. Once identified, an attack can be launched with a range of torpedoes or depth charges.

Apart from training and exercises, the main peacetime role for the Nimrod is Search and Rescue (SAR). One aircraft and crew are maintained on 24-hour standby for 365 days per year. For this role it carries multi-seat life rafts, which can be airdropped and will self-inflate. The Nimrod then remains on station to co-ordinate the recovery of the survivors by ship or helicopter.

The Nimrod is fitted with four powerful Rolls-Royce Spey turbofans, which enable it to combine the advantages of a high-speed and high-altitude transit with good low-level manoeuvrability. Once it reaches the patrol area it is normal for the Nimrod to be flown on just two of the engines, which conserves fuel and extends the time on patrol.

The Nimrod fleet consisted of 42Sqn and 236 OCU at St Mawgan and 120, 201 and 206Sqn at Kinloss plus 203Sqn at Luqa, Malta. In 1992, those at St Mawgan moved north to Lossiemouth.

In addition to the numerous SAR operations in which the Nimrod had been successfully employed, the Nimrod was deployed into the South Atlantic from Ascension Island during Operation Corporate in 1982. They participated in

The Nimrod R.1 is instantly recognisable due to the lack of the MAD boom at the rear of the aircraft. It also features more aerials and has fewer windows.

ABOVE: The Nimrod MR.2 was conceived for the anti-submarine (ASW) and anti-surface vessel (ASV) warfare role. The search radar also has proved valuable for SAR. More recently, the Nimrod has taken on additional 'over land' tasking, for which additional equipment includes the BOZ pod for self protection and extra sensors.

RIGHT: Working at their stations in a Nimrod MR.2 are the routine and tactical WSOs (seated left). Over-looking them is the sensor and communications co-ordinator WSO. Behind the bulkhead are three 'wet' systems WSOps, who work the acoustics equipment monitoring the sonobuoys. In addition, on the right side with only one visible are a further four 'dry' WSOps, who manage various avionics and weapons systems. Crown Copyright

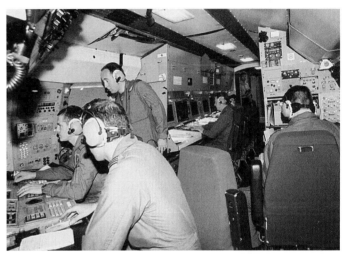

BELOW: The Nimrod MR.2 can carry a variety of equipment and weapons depending on its task. These can include the Harpoon missile, life rafts, sonobuoys, torpedoes and depth charges. It can even be fitted with AIM-9 Sidewinder missiles for self defence.

A rack of Sting Ray torpedoes ready to be loaded into a Nimrod's bomb bay. **BAE Systems**

operational airframes, as well as new examples still on the production line. When the programme was cancelled in December 1986, due to massive cost-over-runs, all of the Nimrod AEW.3s were scrapped.

Until early 2005, twenty-one Nimrod MR.2s were being operated, but recent re-appraisal of capability requirements have resulted in this being reduced to sixteen. As a result, 206Sqn was disbanded on 1 April 2005. The MR.2s will be replaced with the Nimrod MRA.4 when it enters service from 2009 and, with its superior performance, will result in this fleet being further reduced to twelve. Earmarked to be the first recipient is 42Sqn.

The Nimrod R.1 is operated by 51Sqn and based at Waddington. The Nimrod MR.2 is in service with 42 (R), 120 and 201Sqn, all of which are based at Kinloss.

surveillance operations in the Gulf War, the former Yugoslavia, Afghanistan and Iraq.

In addition to the original MR.1, three Nimrod R.1s were built to replace the Comet C.2Rs. They have a highly specialized reconnaissance and ELINT role examining routine radar and radio transmissions and are fitted with a substantial number of additional small aerials. They are also readily identified by the lack of the MAD boom on their tails. As a result, they are 4.3m (14ft 1in) shorter, at 35.86m (117ft 8in). One was lost during a test flight in 1995 and an MR.2 was modified as a replacement. In 2000, Raytheon were awarded a £100m contract to upgrade all three aircraft with new mission systems, as well as providing ground support and simulators. In May 2004, a further upgrade-contract was announced as Project *Helix* and is intended to maintain the mission capability out to 2025. Due to their role, which is highly secret, the Nimrod R.1s of 51Sqn, believed to have a mission crew of twenty-three, have been highly utilized before, during and after the conflicts in Afghanistan and Iraq.

In a programme to replace the AEW Shackleton, eleven airframes were selected to be modified in 1977 as the Nimrod AEW.3. These were a mixture of

Westland Puma HC.1

Role: Battlefield tactical support
Engine: 2 × 970kW RR/Turbomeca IIIC4 turboshaft
Length: 14.10m (46ft 2in) fuselage
Rotor span: 15.1m (49ft 7in)
Height: 4.50m (14ft 9in)
Speed: 265km/h (166mph; 143kt)
Weight: 7,400kg (16,280lb) MTOW
Range: 572km (355 miles; 309nm)

The Westland Puma HC.1 is an anglicized model of the Sud (later Aérospatiale then Eurocopter) SA.330 Puma, which was designed for a French Army requirement and first flew on 15 April 1965.

The RAF had a similar requirement for a light support-helicopter and, in 1967, an Anglo/French agreement was signed for joint production of the Gazelle, Lynx and Puma. The prototype Sud SA.330E was delivered to Westland in 1968 and was subjected to trials after modification to meet the British requirement.

Initially, forty Puma HC.1s were ordered and the first was flown on 25 November 1970. The Puma entered service with 33Sqn on 29 September 1971 at Odiham. Subsequent operators have been 18Sqn, 27Sqn, 230Sqn, 240 OCU and 1563 Flt.

A production line was reinstated for an additional seven (subsequently increased

When required, the Puma can be fitted with a pintle-mounted GPMG machine-gun for self protection.

The battlefield tactical-support helicopter, the Puma HC.1 is capable of fulfilling a range of roles: here it is about to land on an aircraft carrier while flying in support of UN operations.

to eight) attrition replacements in 1979, of which the first was delivered in May 1980. Built to a revised standard, they incorporated composite main rotor-blades and multi-purpose air intakes, which were gradually fitted to the rest of the fleet.

The Puma HC.1 is a light support-helicopter and can carry sixteen troops or 5,500lb (2,497kg) of freight internally or as an underslung load. It also has a medevac role capable of carrying six stretchers and four attendants

During Operation *Corporate* to relieve the Falkland Islands, several helicopters were captured and returned to the UK. One was a Prefectura Naval Argentina (Coast Guard) SA.330L Puma, built in France and serial PA.12. To ensure that the Argentinians were unable to make further use of it, British soldiers had detonated a hand grenade in the gearbox. Once the war was over, the Puma was brought back to the UK and allocated the maintenance serial 9017M. After a period

at RAF Odiham, it was allocated the active RAF serial ZE449 in 1984 and, the following January, transferred to Westland for a rebuild. Due to a combination of damage and mod state, as well as it being a French-built example, the rebuild was not straightforward. It wasn't until March 2001 that the completed Puma eventually reached 33Sqn.

A further increase in the Puma fleet will occur in 2006, with the delivery of four ex-South African AF Oryx, which are currently being modified at Westlands.

The sole Puma operator in Northern Ireland is now 230Sqn, having absorbed 72Sqn's aircraft when it disbanded in March 2002. These additional aircraft now make 230Sqn one of the RAF's larger units, with fifteen on strength. For operations in Northern Ireland the Pumas are fitted with various sensors and defences for protection from missile attack. They are fitted with infra-red spotlight and armed with the GMPG. The crews are fully

NVG-trained and operate their Pumas frequently at night. They are normally armed with a 7.62mm machine gun in the cabin when on operational missions.

33Sqn normally operate in support of exercises in the UK, but recently they have been on operations in Afghanistan and Iraq.

The Puma HC.1 is operated by 33Sqn at Benson and 230Sqn at Aldergrove.

Sea King HAR.3/HAR.3A

Role: Search and rescue
Engine: 2 × 1,238kW RR Bristol Gnome H.1400 turboshaft
Length: 17.1m (56ft 2in) fuselage
Rotor span: 18.9m (62ft)
Height: 5.13m (17ft)
Speed: 208km/h (130mph; 112kt)
Weight: 9,752kg (21,500lb) MTOW
Range: 1,482km (921 miles; 800nm)

The Westland Sea King is an anglicized variant of the US-designed Sikorsky SH-3 Sea King, which was first flown on 11 March 1959. The Westland-built aircraft are a development of the SH-3D,

ABOVE: The RAF's HAR.3 is one of a family of Sea King helicopters. Behind is one of the Fleet Air Arm's 'Junglie' Sea King HC.4s.

BELOW: The flood disaster at Boscastle saw RAF and Fleet Air Arm Sea Kings scrambled to rescue many villagers who climbed onto roofs to escape from the torrent of water that almost destroyed their village in 2004. Crown Copyright

RIGHT: The Sea King HAS.3a is being fitted with the Forward Looking Infra-Red (FLIR) system, which greatly enhances their search capability.

incorporate British engines and the early models were fitted with specialized-role equipment to meet a Royal Navy need for an anti-submarine helicopter.

One SH-3D was imported, along with three sets of components that were assembled as pre-production models, with the first flying on 8 September 1967. Production then commenced with an initial batch of fifty-six HAS.1s for the Royal Navy, the first of which flew on 7 May 1969.

RAF interest in the Sea King did not manifest itself until much later, when fifteen aircraft were ordered as HAR.3s on 24 September 1975, as replacements for the Whirlwind HAR.10 and to augment the Wessex HAR.2 in the Search and Rescue (SAR) role. The first example flew on 6 September 1977. Initial deliveries were made to the Sea King Training Unit (SKTU), which was formed on 17 February 1978 at RNAS Culdrose – the home of the RN Sea Kings. Further deliveries continued and were used to re-equip some of the Flights of 22 and 202Sqn. An additional four HAR.3 were ordered and delivered in 1985.

In 1982, 1564 Flight was established to provide SAR facilities for British Forces operating in the often hostile environment of the Falklands. They were also painted grey for tactical reasons. The Flight was re-named 78Sqn in May 1986. The SKTU was re-named SK OCU briefly in 1996, before becoming 203 (R) Sqn.

A further order was announced on 19 February 1992 for an additional six Sea Kings, which were designated HAR.3A. The first of these flew in 1995 and, although basically similar to the earlier model, these benefited from Thorn EMI colour-radar and a new Racal navigating-computer plus improved communications. Initial introduction was undertaken by the HAR.3A OEU at St Mawgan, prior to entry into service with 22Sqn. It has been further enhanced by the fitting of a Forward Looking Infra-Red (FLIR) thermal imaging and daylight TV-camera system. This is capable of detecting a 1°C difference in temperature at over 1km range. The first was delivered to 'A' Flight of 22Sqn in March 2004 and will eventually be fitted across the fleet.

The role of the Sea King in RAF service is SAR, primarily to rescue servicemen and women. However, in peacetime the bulk of their tasking is to assist the civil authorities. This comes mainly in the form of rescuing holidaymakers stranded on rocks or in difficulty in the water through to winching injured seamen from ships.

The Sea King HAR.3 is operated by 202Sqn and the HAR.3A by 22Sqn at their various Flights. 78Sqn based at Mount Pleasant and 203 (R) Sqn at St Mawgan operate the HAR.3.

Boeing Sentry AEW.1

Role: Surveillance and airborne command-and-control
Engine: 4 × 107kN CFMI CFM56-2 turbofan
Length: 46.62m (152ft 11in)
Span: 44.42m (145ft 9in)
Height: 12.72m (41ft 9in)
Speed: 800km/h+ (500mph+; 435kt+)
Weight: 152,090kg (335,000lb) MTOW
Range: 9,268+km (5,759+ miles; 5,000+nm)

The Sentry AEW.1 is the RAF's version of the E-3 AWACS, which is based on the 707-320 with the addition of an external radome. The prototype was converted from an existing 707 and first flew on 9 February 1972 as the EC-137D. The first production E-3A was delivered for USAF service on 24 March 1977.

In February 1987, six AWACS were ordered to replace the cancelled Nimrod

The Sentry AEW.1 is the RAF's equivalent of the USAF E-3, which is based on the 707-330 airliner.

AEW.3s at a total cost, including spares, system trainers and support equipment, of approximately $1.3bn. An offset agreement was made to give British industry 130 per cent of the value, which included the installation of the mission equipment. An additional AWACS was ordered the following October. These Sentries are the equivalent of the E-3D, but powered by the CFM56 turbofan in place of the P&W TF33s. The first aircraft was handed over on 24 March 1991; 8Sqn retired its remaining six Avro Shackletons in July, when it had converted to and been declared operational on the Sentry AEW.1.

The Sentry AEW.1 brought a tremendous leap forward over the venerable Shackleton, which had been struggling to maintain an effective service with an antiquated system.

The Sentry can operate effectively at a various altitudes up to 10,668m (35,000ft). At 8,839m (29,000ft) a total of 312,000sq km can be covered by the radar and processing system. Ships and low-level aircraft can be detected at ranges of 200 miles (320km) and medium-altitude aircraft at 270 miles (434km). The information is then presented on the nine mission-consoles. The system can auto-matically indicate friendly forces and help the operator prioritize other returns so as to direct appropriate action. Information can be distributed to various agencies through secure data-links to ground command and other forces, as well as aircraft.

In addition to the AEW role the Sentry can also provide a maritime surface-surveillance service to naval forces, providing a much increased area of survey due to the altitude at which it operates. A further role is as a co-ordination platform for search and rescue operations. Tasking is provided by the NATO Airborne Early Warning Force Command (NAEWFC) located at Mons in Belgium. NAEWFC co-ordinates the NATO and RAF E-3s to fly national and NATO missions throughout the world.

The Sentry is normally manned by a crew of seventeen, which includes the flight crew of four (pilot, co-pilot, navigator and flight engineer). The thirteen-strong mission crew is led by a tactical director with weapons and surveillance teams. A communications operator manages external links and three technicians provide support to ensure the maximum effectiveness of the systems.

The Sentry can operate a ten-hour sortie, which can be further extended by in-flight refuelling if required. It has retained the USAF boom refuelling-system but has the standard RAF probe-and-drogue system added as well. Substantial quantities of hot and cold food and drink are available in a galley at the rear of the aircraft.

The Sentry AEW.1s are operated by 8 and 23Sqn with aircraft pooled. Both squadron markings are carried by the aircraft. Since entering service, the Sentries have seen extensive and extended operations around and over the former Yugoslavia during NATO operations in Bosnia and Kosovo, and subsequently in Afghanistan – where it was flown for fifteen months – and Iraq.

The RAF Sentry AEW.1 is recognisable from other E-3s by the refuelling probe (which is also fitted to French AF E-3Fs) and the Loral Yellow Gate ESM pods on the wing tips (which are also fitted to NATO E-3As).

The Sentry AEW.1s are operated by 8 and 23Sqn on a pool basis and based at Waddington. Squadron markings for both units are applied to each aircraft.

Two of the controllers occupy their stations aboard a Sentry, from where they are able to detect enemy aircraft. They are then able to monitor, advise and control other air assets to safely conduct operations at ranges of up to 200 miles.

Information from the large radome is processed then presented on a monitor for the controllers. This sanitized image shows the Bosnian 'No Fly' zone with a UN route from Sarajevo to Zagreb.

Supermarine Spitfire

data for Vb
Role: Vintage fighter
Engine: 1 × 1,102kW (1,470hp) RR Merlin 45
Length: 9.12m (29ft 11in)
Span: 11.23m (36ft 10in)
Height: 3.47m (11ft 4.75in)
Speed: 594km/h (371mph; 320kt)
Weight: 2,911kg (6,417lb)
Range: 1,827km (1,135 miles; 986nm)

The Spitfire was designed by Reginald J Mitchell, built by Supermarine (later Vickers Supermarine) and the prototype first flown on 5 March 1936. The first examples were delivered to the RAF in 1938. It remained in production throughout the Second World War, with maximum speed increasing from the 349mph (562km/h) of the Mk.1 to the 460mph (740km/h) of the PR.XIX. When production ended a total of 20,351 Spitfires had been built.

The RAF retains five airworthy Spitfires and these are all operated by the Battle of Britain Memorial Flight (BBMF). They are flown by the BBMF at various airshows and official functions as a reminder of those who died to keep Britain free.

A variety of Spitfires are operated by the BBMF: the oldest being the Spitfire II, P7350, which actually served in the Battle of Britain and was credited with three kills. The Mk.Vb was fitted with the more powerful Merlin 45 and the BBMF example – AB910 – was made famous by taking off with groundcrew LACW Margaret Horton still holding on to the tail. Fortunately, the pilot realized that something was wrong and quickly landed. The Mk.IX was one of the standard Spitfires with over 5,600 built and MK356 – an LF.IXc – was the last Spitfire to join the BBMF. Previously it had been a gate guard, then a static museum example, until it underwent a five-year restoration to airworthiness prior to joining the BBMF in 1997.

The BBMF has two photo-reconnaissance PR.19s on its strength. They feature a longer nose, which houses the more powerful Griffon that replaced the original Merlin engine. This model was the fastest of all production models and a total of 225 were built.

Along with the other aircraft for the Flight, they can regularly be seen at airshows. They are re-painted every few years in new marking to represent

One of the BBMF's Spitfires painted with D-Day recognition stripes on the wings. These living memorials to those fighter pilots who were killed during the Second World War are regularly repainted to represent the various units that operated the type.

squadrons that operated them during the Second World War.

The Spitfires are flown by the BBMF from their base at Coningsby.

Eurocopter Squirrel HT.1

Role: Single-engine rotary-wing training
Engine: 1 × 732shp Arriel 1D1 turboshaft
Length: 12.94m (42ft 5.5in) overall
Span: 10.69m (35ft 0.75in)
Height: 3.14m (10ft 3.5in)
Speed: 248km/h (155mph; 134kt)
Weight: 2,250kg (4,960lb) MTOW
Range: 670km (416 miles; 361nm)

The AS.350 Ecureuil (Squirrel) was originally designed by Aérospatiale as a five/six-seat general-purpose helicopter. The prototype made its maiden flight on 27 June 1974.

The AS.350BB variant was ordered as the Squirrel HT.1 for the Defence Helicopter Flying School (DHFS) for basic flying training of pilots of the three services. The Squirrel is civilian-contractor owned but operated with a military registration.

The Squirrel entered service at RAF Shawbury in April 1997 to fulfil the role previously undertaken by the Gazelle HT.3s of 2 FTS. They are operated as a basic trainer by DHFS and operated by 660Sqn, AAC, for basic rotary-training and then 705Sqn, FAA, for advanced rotary-wing training. Students for all three services progress through these squadrons with courses tailored to suit the need of their service. RAF students fly 36 hours with 660Sqn and 37 hours with 705Sqn, before progressing to the Griffin for the advanced multi-engine course.

The Squirrel HT.1 is also used by the CFS at Shawbury to train instructors. They borrow DHFS Squirrels as required.

The Ecureuil has been built in a number of variants, for different purposes and

The external differences of the Squirrel HT.1 and Twin Squirrel HCC.1 are mainly centred around the upper fuselage behind the cabin, which is enlarged to accommodate the second engine.

customers, both for the military and civil markets. The Squirrel HT.1 is fitted with a more powerful engine than the earlier AS.350A and AS.350B models, together with wider-chord main- and tail-rotors.

A Squirrel HT.2 variant is operated by the Army Air Corps for further training of student pilots at Middle Wallop. They are basically similar, with minor differences in instrumentation and radio fit, and the cockpit lighting is NVG compatible. The HT.2 is fitted with a hook to enable training in the carrying of underslung loads.

The Squirrel HT.1 is operated by 660 and 705Sqn of the DHFS at Shawbury.

Eurocopter Twin Squirrel

Role: VIP transport and communication
Engine: 2 × 343kW Allison 250-C20R turboshaft
Length: 12.94m (42ft 5.5in) (overall)
Span: 10.69m (35ft 0.75in)
Height: 3.14m (10ft 3.5in)
Speed: 222km/h (139mph; 120kt)
Weight: 2,600kg (5,732lb) – MTOW
Range: 722km (449 miles; 390nm)

The French-built Ecureuil 2 is a twin-engined development of the earlier single-engined Ecureuil/Squirrel. The prototype was first flown on 28 September 1979. Designated AS.355F1 by the manufacturers, but unlike most other RAF aircraft, does not have a designation after the name.

Two AS.355F1 Squirrels were initially acquired by McAlpine Helicopters on the second-hand market and prepared for RAF use with a five/six-seat corporate configuration. They were then handed over to their subsidiary – Operational Support Services Ltd – prior to being delivered to 32 (The Royal) Sqn on 30 March 1996, with whom they are operated as a replacement for the Gazelle HCC.4. Although they remain contractor-owned, these Twin Squirrels are operated as military aircraft and have military registration. A third Twin Squirrel was subsequently added to the squadron.

Of similar size and shape, the Twin Squirrel differs visually from the HT.1 in the size of the engine cowling. However, the VIP overall white colour-scheme, with red spine and tail plus dark-blue cheat line, is the easiest identification feature.

The twin-engined capabilities of the Twin Squirrel means that this helicopter is not subjected to the same CAA restrictions as a single-engined helicopter, especially when flown over built-up areas.

In April 2005 it was announced that the Twin Squirrels at Northolt would be replaced by two of the AgustaWestland A109 Power helicopters on 1 April 2006.

Three Twin Squirrels are operated by 32 (The Royal) Sqn and based at Northolt. A further Twin Squirrel is also operated in military marking by the ETPS at Boscombe Down.

Panavia Tornado GR.1, GR.1 (T), GR.1A, GR.1B

Role: All-weather strike or reconnaissance
Engine: 2 × 38.5kN Turbo-Union RB.199 Mk.103 turbofan
Length: 16.72m (54ft 10.25in)
Span: 8.60m (28ft 2.5in) swept; 13.91m (45ft 7.5in) spread
Height: 5.95m (19ft 6.25in)
Speed: Mach 1.3 max
Weight: 27,215kg (60,000lb) MTOW
Range: 2,780km (1,727 miles; 1,500nm)

The basic Tornado design commenced as the tri-national (Germany, Italy and UK) MRCA (Multi Role Combat Aircraft), which eventually came into being in 1969. Two variants were to be built – the ADV which was specifically for the RAF and the IDS (InterDiction/Strike). The latter was the first to be constructed and the prototype took to the air for the first time on 14 August 1974. The first production Tornado GR.1 was flown on 14 March 1980.

The IDS was to become the Tornado GR.1 in RAF service and was to initially replace the Vulcan, then Phantoms and Buccaneers. Designed for high survivability and to be effective against heavily defended enemy positions, it is capable of carrying an impressive warload over long ranges and in all weather. It is fitted with an automatic terrain-following system for low-level operation together with accurate navigation.

The Tornado was the RAF's first operational swing-wing aircraft and capable of varying the sweep from 25 to 67 degrees. The purpose of this was to combine the better low-speed handling of a straight wing for landing with the high-speed performance of a swept wing. The angle can be set manually by the pilot or automatically by the flight-control system to match the angle of attack.

The Tornado GR.1 has a Mauser 27mm cannon and is designed to carry a comprehensive range of other weaponry and defensive aids on the four underwing pylons, with a further three under the fuselage. These can range from bombs and rockets to weapon dispensers and missiles

and include nuclear weapons, although these are no longer in the RAF inventory. A BOZ-107 pod is fitted on the right wing to dispense chaff and flares and a Sky Shadow-2 Electronic Counter Measures (ECM) pod is on the left wing.

A sub-variant of the GR.1 was the GR.1(T), which was fitted with dual controls, enabling an instructor to fly in the back seat. Fifty-one of the GR.1(T)s were built but fully retained their operational capabilities.

A further variant of the GR.1 was the reconnaissance GR.1A. This model did not have the Mauser cannon but was fitted with BAe Sideways Looking Infra-Red (SLIR) reconnaissance system designed for low-level reconnaissance. Fourteen Tornado GR.1s initially were modified, plus two built from scratch. These were subsequently followed by a further fourteen new GR.1As. Deliveries commenced in 1987.

Yet another variant was the GR.1B, optimized for the maritime role and armed with the Sea Eagle anti-shipping missile.

Twenty-six Tornado GR.1s were modified and the first delivered to 617Sqn in February 1994.

Initial deliveries of the GR.1 were to the multinational TTTE (Tri-national Tornado Training Establishment), which formed in January 1981 at Cottesmore. This was followed by the TWCU (Tactical Weapons Conversion Unit) at Honington, which was also designated as a 'shadow' unit and sported 45 (R) Sqn markings.

The Tornado GR.1 commenced equipping 9Sqn from January 1982 and was officially re-formed with the type in June 1982. Subsequent squadrons to form were 2, 12, 13, 15, 16, 17, 20, 27, 31, 39, 45 and 617 plus the SOEU, TTTE and TWCU. The TTTE operated most of the GR.1 (T)s; 2 and 13Sqn flew the GR.1A; 12 and 617Sqn flew the GR.1B.

The TTTE at Cottesmore disbanded on 31 March 1999, together with 17Sqn at Bruggen.

A number of Tornado GR.1 and GR.1As were deployed to the Middle East during the build up for the Gulf War. They were some of the first aircraft to enter combat, using the JP233 airfield-denial weapon, 1,000lb bombs and the ALARM

Bread and butter tasking for the Tornado F3 during the Cold War was escorting Soviet 'Bears' away from UK airspace. Nowadays, it is more likely to be an unidentified airliner.

missiles to attack Iraqi airfields, mainly at very low-levels at night, during which six aircraft were lost. Buccaneers were later deployed to provide laser designation with the Pavespike pods, enabling Paveway LGBs to be dropped. Later still, in February, a few Tornados were fitted with the Thermal Imaging Airborne Laser Designator (TIALD) and flown out to Tabuk, from where they flew thirty-six missions dropping LGBs at the safer medium-level. By the end of the 100-day war some 1,500 operational missions had been flown.

In 1999, the GR.1s saw further operational missions during Operation *Allied Force* to try to halt the Serbian attacks in Kosovo, with 14Sqn operating from Bruggen, and 9 and 31Sqn deployed to Corsica.

A programme to upgrade 142 GR.1/GR.1As to GR.4/GR.4A commenced in 1999 and was completed in 2003. Of the twenty-four surviving GR.1Bs only eight were modified, with the rest being retired as instructional airframes, spares, gate guardians or to museums.

There are no GR.1s operational within the RAF, although a few are flown by BAe Systems at Warton and QinetiQ for trials with the ETPS at Boscombe Down.

Panavia Tornado F.2

Role: Air-defence interceptor
Engine: 2 × 42.95kN Turbo-Union RB.199 Mk.103 turbofan
Length: 18.06m (29ft 3in)
Span: 8.60m (28ft 2.5in) swept; 13.90m (45ft 7in) spread
Height: 5.70m (18ft 8in)
Speed: Mach 2.27 max
Weight: 27,986kg (61,700lb)
Range: 1,852km (1,151 miles; 1,000nm)

The F.2 was the interim Air Defence Variant (ADV) of the Tornado that was built for an RAF specification to replace the Lightning and Phantom. Three ADV prototypes were built; the first was flown on 27 October 1979 and the first production model was flown on 5 March 1984 as the Tornado F.2.

The ADV was specifically designed for the RAF requirement of a long-range interceptor and no production models were built for the other members of the original consortium – Germany and Italy. Only Saudi Arabia subsequently ordered the ADV. Despite the difference

in role, the fighter retains approximately 80 per cent commonality with the strike variant.

Eighteen Tornado F.2s were built and, after development trials, the initial deliveries went to 229 OCU during 1984. Due to problems with the new radar for the fighter they were initially fitted with the Blue Circle radar – a block of concrete ballast named after a certain cement manufacturer.

The two-seat, variable geometry, fly-by-wire Tornado F.2 was designed to climb to 30,000ft in less than two minutes, loiter for a lengthy time, which could be extended by in-flight refuelling, and have a high-speed-dash capability. The Foxhunter radar enabled the crew to detect and engage targets at ranges of up to 100 miles, for which it carried four Sky Flash medium-range missiles. For closer ranges it was equipped with four AIM-9 Sidewinder short-range missiles (currently replaced by the ASRAAM on the F.3). It was also fitted with a 27mm cannon.

As the F.3 squadrons built up, the OCU F.2s were withdrawn and placed in storage or used for ground training. When a number of F.3 wings were irreparably damaged during contractorized major servicing, a number of the F.2s had their wings removed and used as replacements.

Although the RAF no longer flies the Tornado F.2, one is still operated by QinetiQ for trials.

Panavia Tornado F.3, EF.3

Role: Air-defence interceptor or suppression of enemy air-defences
Engine: 2 × 40kn Turbo Union RB.199-34R Mk.104 turbofan
Length: 18.7m (61ft 1in)
Span: 8.6m (28ft 2in) swept; 13.9m (45ft 7in) spread
Height: 5.94m (19ft 6in)
Speed: Mach 2.2
Weight: 27,986kg (61,700lb) MTOW
Range: 3,704km (2,302 miles; 1,998nm)

The Tornado F.3 is the Air Defence Variant (ADV) model that was specifically designed to meet an RAF requirement for a long-range interceptor to replace the Lightning and Phantom. Despite the difference in role, the fighter retains approximately 80 per cent commonality with the strike variant. The prototype ADV was first flown on 27 October 1979, followed by the first

production Tornado F.2 on 5 March 1984 and F.3 on 20 November 1985.

This two-seat, variable geometry, fly-by-wire aircraft can climb to 30,000ft in less than two minutes, loiter for a lengthy time which can be extended by in-flight refuelling and has a high-speed-dash capability. With a longer fuselage than the GR.1/GR.4 attack variant, this space in the F.3 forward fuselage is used to accommodate the Foxhunter radar in the extended radome. This piece of kit enables the crew to detect and engage targets at ranges of up to 100 miles. For this role it was armed with four Sky Flash medium-range missiles, which have been replaced more recently by the AIM-120 AMRAAM. For closer ranges it was fitted with the AIM-9 Sidewinder and these have been replaced by four ASRAAM short-range missiles. Additional space in the fuselage is used to accommodate avionics plus a further 900 litres of fuel. It is also fitted with a 27mm Mauser cannon.

Avionics in the Tornado F.3 includes a Joint Tactical Information Distribution System (JTIDS), which increases the situational awareness of the crew with live information from other aircraft. It can allow the crew to effectively switch their radar off, thereby not transmitting identifying radiation that can be detected by an enemy aircraft's EW sensors. The target information for the missiles can be transmitted by JTIDS from a Sentry/AWACS and missiles fired with next to no warning to the target aircraft. The Radar Homing and Warning Receiver (RHWR) provides information about enemy radar and missile transmissions, enabling effective countermeasures with chaff and decoy flares. This is in addition to the standard and secure radios.

The F.2 was an interim model of the Tornado fighter, of which eighteen were built; they were basically used as trainers until sufficient F.3s were delivered. In 1988 they were withdrawn and placed in storage, apart from one each retained by BAe Systems and QinetiQ for trials.

The Tornado F.3 entered service with the RAF in 1986 and deliveries were initially made to 229 OCU at Coningsby.

Following a series of trials in the USA, Tornado F.3 ZE155 made the first non-stop un-refuelled crossing of the Atlantic by a British jet fighter in September 1987 – a distance of 2,540 miles (4,087km)

Deliveries of the Tornado F.3 steadily

The Cold War scenario of RAF fighters intercepting Soviet bombers may have ended and some of the Tornado F.3 squadrons have disbanded (such as 5Sqn). However, with the terrorist threat, Tornados are still scrambled to intercept and identify aircraft that cannot be identified from the ground. Fortunately, this is usually due to an avionics fault but, after 11 September 2001, this remains a serious business.

progressed and it eventually saw service with 5, 11, 23, 25, 29, 43 and 111Sqn and 1453 Flight operationally, plus 229 OCU/65Sqn and 56 (R) Sqn in the training role.

Coningsby, Leeming and Leuchars were the operational Tornado F.3 stations – the first two making up the Southern Quick Reaction Alert (Interceptor) Force and Leuchars the Northern Quick Reaction Alert (Interceptor) Force. The Tornados would be launched to intercept Soviet bombers over the North Sea and were supported by Victor, Tristar and VC.10 tankers. While this was once a regular occurrence, the ending of the Cold War

saw this drop to virtually nil. Coningsby gradually reduced its complement of F.3s, with 5 and 29Sqn disbanding and, finally, 56 (R) Sqn moving to Leuchars in March 2003.

In 1995, the first of twenty-four RAF Tornado F.3s were leased to the Italian AF to enable them to replace the Starfighters of 360 and 530 Stormos and fill the gap until the entry of the Eurofighter. Under the terms of the lease they were all returned by December 2004.

In 1996, a £125m Capability Sustainment Programme (CSP) contract was awarded to enable 100 F.3s to carry the new AMRAAM and ASRAAM

missiles. A further CSP in 2002 further increased their capabilities, including new navigation systems, IFF and secure communications packages.

111Sqn became the first squadron to be AMRAAM/ASRAAM compatiable in mid-2002.

An interesting and new role for some Tornado F.3s is that of SEAD (Suppression of Enemy Air Defences). Having undergone trials, some Tornado F.3s been re-designated EF.3. They have initially entered service with 11Sqn based at Leeming and flown with a pair of ALARM missiles under the fuselage. Previously carried by Tornado GR.1/GR.4s, these aircraft now have an extensive range of weaponry and their payload capability is required for ordnance. With recent past conflicts posing only limited requirement for fighters but a continual need for SEAD, the EF.3 option could maximize

ABOVE: **A Tornado GR.4 of 617Sqn, readily identifiable with the addition of a second bulge under the nose to incorporate a new thermal-imaging and laser-designator system. This complements the laser ranger and marked-target seeker in the original pod. Crown Copyright**

LEFT: **Recognisable by the rectangular panel just aft of and below the pitot head, the Tornado GR.4A is used in the reconnaissance role. They are still fully capable of being used as bombers, as can be seen with this example from 2Sqn, which is armed with Paveway II LGBs.**

use of the Tornado fleet with the new fighter/SEAD swing-role capability.

Eighteen Tornado F.3s were deployed during Operation *Granby* and flew some 2,500 sorties, of which around 700 were during the conflict. They continued to fly during Operations *Bolton* and *Resolute* to maintain the no-fly zone over southern Iraq and the peacekeeping operations over the former republic of Yugoslavia. In 2003 the F.3 saw active service again during Operation *Telic*, with crews from all four operational squadrons participating.

It is anticipated that the Tornado F.3 will remain in service until 2010.

The Tornado F.3 is operated by 11, 25, 43, 56 (R) and 111Sqn, 1435 Flt, and F3 OEU. The Tornado EF.3 is operated by 11Sqn.

Panavia Tornado GR.4, GR.4A

Role: All weather strike or reconnaissance
Engine: 2 × 38.5kN Turbo-Union RB.199 Mk.103 turbofan
Length: 16.72m (54ft 10.25in)
Span: 8.60m (28ft 2.5in) swept; 13.91m (45ft 7.5in) spread
Height: 5.95m (19ft 6.25in)
Speed: Mach 1.3
Weight: 27,950kg (61,619lb) MTOW
Range: 2,780km (1,727 miles; 1,500nm)

The upgrade to the GR.4/GR.4A standard, which includes new systems and avionics, has now been completed by 142 Tornado GR.1/GR.1As. Part of this includes optimizing some of the systems away from the very low-level missions of the Cold War era to the medium-level, as experienced in more recent conflicts.

The programme commenced in 1994 to integrate new weapons systems, including the Storm Shadow stand-off weapon, Brimstone anti-armour missile and the Enhanced Paveway LGB. New equipment for the GR.4 includes TIALD and the VICON reconnaissance pod. The latter has already been replaced by the Goodrich Reconnaissance Airborne Pod for TORnado (RAPTOR) recce pod on the GR.4A. The modification programme saw the first development GR.4 fly on 29 May 1993, but RAF first examples were not handed over until October 1997 and deliveries were completed in 2003.

The GR.4A has substantially increased computing-power and a full avionics data-bus and incorporates updates to the displays, controls and onboard defence-systems, armament control and radar. A FLIR has been fitted under the nose and can be displayed on cockpit monitors or on the HUD. The port cannon has been removed and replaced with a video-recording system. In December 2003, the DLO announced that a £82m contract had been awarded to BAe Systems to provide a cockpit upgrade known as TARDIS (Tornado Advanced Radar DISplay). This will replace the 1970s wet-film and display-processing technology with a multi-function display for the pilot and a new radar and map processor for the navi-gator. Deliveries to stations are enabling the TARDIS to be fitted during routine maintenance; the upgrade should be completed by August 2006.

Plans are in hand for a next-generation electronic warfare self-protection system that will replace the existing Sky Shadow. This will help to maintain the effectiveness of Tornado, which, it is anticipated, will remain in service until 2018/2020.

In 1996 the MoD began a £35m feasibility study into a replacement for the Tornado. The project, known as the Future Offensive Air System (FOAS), is looking at manned and unmanned solutions, with low-observable designs being preferred. Although the Tornado will continue to be operated for some time, a decision on a replacement will be required soon.

The Tornado GR.4 are operated by 9 and 31Sqn at Marham, plus 12, 14, 15 (R) and 617Sqn at Lossiemouth, plus the Fast Jet OEU at Coningsby. Tornado GR.4As are operated by II (AC) and 13Sqn at Marham.

Lockheed Tristar K.1, KC.1

Role: Long-range passenger/freight transport or air refuelling
Engine: 3 × 222kN (50,000lb) RR RB.211-524B4 turbofan
Length: 50.85m (166ft 10in)
Span: 50.15m (164ft 6in)
Height: 16.87m (55ft 4in)
Speed: Mach 0.885
Weight: 245,000kg (540,127lb)
Range: 12,050km (7,488 miles; 6,500nm)

The design of the Lockheed L.1011 Tristar commenced as an airliner; the prototype was first flown on 16 November 1970, and deliveries commenced in April 1972. At the time it was an advanced design, with fully powered controls and all-moving horizontal-stabilizer, as well as a sophisti-cated autopilot and autoland systems. When production ended in 1983, a total of 250 Tristars had been built.

A post-Falklands MoD review high-lighted the importance of air-to-air refuelling, which had been reliant on the converted Victor bombers – well through their fatigue life. ASR411 was issued for a large strategic tanker that would augment

The Tristar crew on finals to land, at their home base of Brize Norton.

the Victors and also be able to carry freight and passengers.

The Tristar and DC-10 were both put forward, but both required substantial modification for the new role. Marshalls had established their Lockheed reputation with the Hercules and so their proposal for a modified Tristar was selected. A total of six Tristar 500s, surplus to British Airways requirements, were acquired by the RAF.

Two Tristars were modified to K.1, with a pair of the Mk.17 Hose Drum Units (HDU) fitted in the rear fuselage. Additional fuel tanks were fitted in the cargo compartment, resulting in the MTOW increasing from 504,000lb to 540,000lb. A refuelling probe was also fitted, enabling it to receive fuel if necessary. A remote TV-camera was also fitted under the fuselage, to enable the refuelling operating to be visually monitored from the cockpit. The cabin is split into cargo and seating areas, with accommodation for 187 passengers, but has no cargo door.

In the cockpit, which had been increased in size by moving the bulkhead back by some 16in, the flight engineer had an enlarged position. This was to accommodate the extra equipment, including the monitor, required for the management of the refuelling operation in addition to normal duties. Certain avionic and communications equipment also needed upgrading for RAF compatibility. The K.1 is also capable of carrying up to 204 passengers.

Four of the Tristars were modified to KC.1 standard. In addition to the modifications of the K.1s, the KC.1 has a freighter capability. For this additional role, a hole was cut into the left-hand side of the fuselage, forward of the wings. Into this was installed a 140in × 102in hydraulically operated cargo-door and the area reinforced. The floor was also reinforced to enable palletized freight to be carried. No refuelling probe was fitted. The first KC.1 was handed over to the RAF on 24 March 1986.

The Tristar tankers have seen various periods of deployment during operations in the Middle East and the former Yugoslavia. Apart from their early days, when they were flown in a modified BA scheme, they have been operated in an overall white colour-scheme with a blue cheat line. Two were painted in a tempo-rary pink desert-camouflage for Operation *Granby*.

Tristar K.1s and KC.1s are operated by 216Sqn from their base at Brize Norton.

Lockheed Tristar C.2, C.2A

Role: Long-range passenger/freight transport
Engine: 3 × 222kN (50,000lb) RR RB.211-524B4 turbofan
Length: 50.85m (166ft 10in)
Span: 50.15m (164ft 6in)
Height: 16.87m (55ft 4in)
Speed: Mach 0.885
Weight: 233,000kg (513,671lb)
Range: 9,270km (5,760 miles; 5,000nm)

In addition to the Tristar K.1 and KC.1, two C.2s and one C2A are operated purely as transport aircraft with no provision for refuelling. They are ex-Pan American that were acquired in the 1980s and can carry up to 242 passengers.

Although it has been given a sub-variant designation, the C.2A is externally identical to the C.2, with a slightly different radio-configuration and a few other small avionics-differences. This was to instigate a programme to modify the

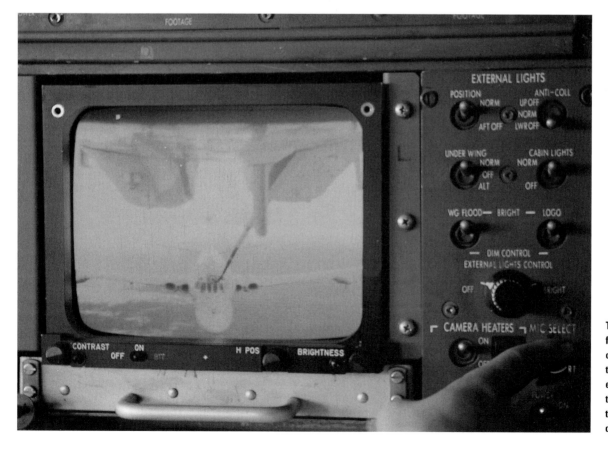

The Tristar tankers are fitted with a remotely controlled TV camera to enable the flight engineer to monitor the correct aspect of the receiver — in this case a Nimrod R.1.

Not fitted with refuelling equipment, this Tristar C.2 is used solely for carrying passengers and cargo.

C.2s to align them with the avionics of the ex-BA K.1s. In the end only the one was modified.

The Tristar C.2 and C.2A are operated by 216Sqn and are based at Brize Norton.

Short Tucano T.1

Role: Pilot and weapons systems officer (WSO) basic
    flying training
Engine: 1 × 820kW (1,100shp) AlliedSignal TPE331-12B
    turboprop
Length: 9.86m (32ft 4in)
Span: 11.28m (37ft)
Height: 3.4m (11ft 1in)
Speed: 504km/h (315mph; 272kt)
Weight: 3,178kg (7,000lb) MTOW
Range: 1,665km (1,035 miles; 898nm)

The RAF Tucano T.1 is a licence-built modified-variant of the Brazilian EMB-312 Tucano, which was originally designed and built by Embraer and first flown on 16 August 1980.

The two-seat tandem Tucano was the winning submission to the RAF's AST412

and was selected to become the RAF's basic flying trainer. It took over the role from the Jet Provost, which had been in service since the early 1960s. The design was altered to suit British requirements, which included replacing the PT6 engine with the more powerful AlliedSignal (previously Garret) TPE331. The cockpit instrumentation was also altered to make the transition to the Hawk easier.

A total of 130 of the Tucano T.1s were ordered from Short's and the first aircraft flew on 30 December 1986. The first example was delivered to the RAF on 16 June 1988. They have been operated by the CFS, 1, 3, 6 and 7 FTS and the last aircraft was delivered in January 1993.

The Tucano is used to train student pilots in general and all-weather aircraft-handling, take-off and landings, as well as formation flying, low-level navigation and night flying. Although still noisy, the turboprop-powered Tucano T.1 is much quieter than the Jet Provost and is also more economical.

Following a reduction in the amount of flying training, the Tucanos of 3 and 6 FTS

were put in storage with Aircraft Maintenance & Storage Unit (AM&SU) at Shawbury. Here the Tucano fleet is rotated to ensure that the airframe hours even out. A modification programme has been carried out to strengthen the central fuselage and wing-attachment fittings, which were showing some fatigue.

The Tucano T.1 is currently operated by 72 (R) and 207 (R) Sqn of 1 FTS at Linton-on-Ouse, which also operate the CFS Tucano Squadron. It is also flown by the Tucano Air Navigation Squadron (TANS), which is also part of 1 FTS.

Grob Tutor

Role: Elementary flying training and air experience
Engine: 1 × 134kW Lycoming AEIO-360-A1B6 piston
Length: 7.59m (24ft 9in)
Span: 10.0m (32ft 9.75in)
Height: 2.8m (9ft 2.25in)
Speed: 250km/h (156mph; 135kt)
Weight: 990kg (2,183lb) MTOW
Range: 1,150km (715 miles; 620nm)

The Grob 115 is a two-seat training aircraft, which first flew in November 1985.

The Grob 115E was selected in

ABOVE: **A mass formation of Tucano T.1s from 1 FTS during a rehearsal for a flypast.**

LEFT: **The Tutor gives air cadets the opportunity to experience and fly the same aircraft that future RAF pilots are being taught on.**

June 1998 for use in the, then new, RAF training PFI. The first of ninety-nine entered service in September 1999 as the Tutor, replacing the Bulldog T.1, under a ten-year contract with Bombardier Contract Services, which became VT Aerospace in 2000. As a result the Bulldogs, which were RAF-owned and civilian-contractor maintained, were retired and disposed of, mainly by sale to the civil market, with the type being finally retired on 30 May 2001. The Tutor is civilian owned and maintained and operated with RAF roundels, but with civil registrations.

The Grob 115 is of an all-composite construction, with a two-seat cockpit providing a good environment for student and instructor, who sit side by side. Current RAF planning anticipates an annual usage of 500 hours per aircraft. It is claimed to have a structural life of 24,000 hours and is stressed at +6/–3g. Unlike the Bulldog, the cockpit is arranged so that the student can fly from the right-hand seat with a right-handed control-column and a left-handed throttle, as in fast jets. This facilitates the conversion to the Tucano.

The last of the ninety-nine Tutors was delivered in December 2001 and they are used by the UAS (23,500 hours flown per annum) to train student pilots, both from the universities and the Direct Entrants,

plus the Air Experience Flights (17,500 hours), which provide air experience flying for ATC and CCF (RAF) cadets. They are also used by the CFS Tutor Squadron (5,000 hours) for QFI Instructor and Navigator training and 1 EFTS UAS Standards Flight (1,000 hours) for UAS QFI continuation training.

The Tutor is operated by the fourteen University Air Squadrons at their various locations and pooled with the twelve AEFs. They are also operated by the CFS and the CFS Tutor Squadron as well as the UAS Standards Flight, which are also pooled with the UAS and AEF Flight at Cranwell.

Eurofighter Typhoon T.1, T.1A, F.2

Role: High-performance multi-role fighter
Engine: 2 × 90kN Eurojet EJ200 turbofan
Length: 15.96m (52ft 4.25in)
Span: 10.95m (35ft 11in)
Height: 5.28m (17ft 4in)
Speed: Mach 2.0
Weight: 23,000kg (50,706lb) MTOW
Range: 1,389km (863 miles; 749nm)

The Typhoon is the RAF's latest fighter. Initially conceived as the Eurofighter in 1986, the prototype was first flown on 27 March 1994. It represented a milestone in the achievements of the multinational Eurofighter GmbH, which comprises aircraft manufacturers from Germany, Italy, Spain and the UK.

Seven development aircraft were built to confirm, test and develop the systems and characteristics that are being incorporated into the production Typhoon. The first British single-seat prototype was ZH588 (DA2), which was first flown on 6 April 1994, and the first British two-seat prototype was ZH590 (DA4), which was flown on 14 March 1997. The first British IPA (Instrumented Production Aircraft) was first flown on 15 April 2002. DA4 undertook the first fully guided test of AMRAAM

by a Typhoon on the ranges at Benbecula, also in April. The first production T.1 made its initial flight on 14 February 2003 and the F.2 on 21 December 2004.

The first order was placed in September 1998 for a total of 148 for all partner nations, of which fifty-five were for the RAF. Initial production aircraft have been delivered to a Typhoon Operational Evaluation Unit established at Warton, to enable any technical problems to be quickly resolved. First RAF deliveries were slated for July 2002 but Type Acceptance was not formally given until July 2003. BAe Systems was contracted to deliver thirteen two-seat trainers to the OEU, which it will directly support for eighteen months. During that time it will fly 1,300 hours, to train sixteen instructors and 190 ground personnel.

The initial OEU course has been completed and the instructors and ground-crew moved to the OCU, which is now established at Coningsby. The role of the OEU will be to continue to develop the standard operating procedures, as well as tactics, for the Typhoon.

The OEU has already been renamed 17 (R) Sqn and the OCU 29 (R) Sqn. Concurrently, the Eurofighter Ground Maintenance School will have been established at Coningsby to provide training for all levels of ground personnel.

After two years of training the instructors and developing the procedures, the first batch of pilots will be posted to squadrons. They will consist of existing fighter or ground-attack pilots, together with a number of new pilots who have just completed their flying training on the Hawk. These pilots will become the first operational Typhoon squadron when it is declared operational around 2006.

The whole Typhoon 'package' is a complex system, with paperless records maintained on computer along with aircrew and servicing documentation. Even the pilot's role will be computer assisted to a much greater degree than at present. Not only will his Flight Reference Cards be digitally stored in the cockpit, but he will also wear a Helmet Mounted Sight that will provide a wealth of information for day and night operations. A Direct Voice Input will reduce the need to look down into the cockpit by interpreting his instructions, increasing his external visual-awareness and contributing to increased safety, especially at low level.

While the Typhoon is being established as the primary fighter for the RAF and will replace the Tornado F.3, it has also been designed as a multi-role aircraft. From around 2007 the first ground-attack squadron should be forming at Leeming and replacing the Jaguar. With added capabilities, this variant of the Typhoon will also be able to carry a range of air-to-ground weapons for the attack role, in

Although more logical, it is unusual for the two-seat trainer to be the first initial variant of a combat aircraft, as with the Typhoon T.1.

addition to fully maintaining the air-to-air capability.

The fighter variant will be fitted with AIM-120 AMRAAM as the primary weapon, plus ASRAAM air-to-air missiles, in addition to the 27mm Mauser BK27 cannon. The Meteor missile will be added when deliveries commence around 2008.

Depending on the attack role for the Typhoon, it will be armed with:

- Air interdiction – 2 × Storm Shadow, 2 × Alarm, 4 × AMRAAM, 2 × ASRAAM, with 2 × 1,500ltr and 1 × 11,000ltr fuel tanks
- Close air-support – 18 × Brimstone, 4 × AMRAAM, 2 × ASRAAM, with 1 × 11,000ltr fuel tank
- SEAD – 6 × ALARM, 4 × AMRAAM, 2 × ASRAAM, with 1 × 11,000ltr fuel tank
- Maritime Attack – 4 × Penguin, 4 × AMRAAM, 2 × ASRAAM, with 2 × 1,500ltr and 1 × 11,000ltr fuel tanks

In order to increase the Typhoon's endurance, conformal fuel tanks are being developed for introduction later. These will increase fuel capacity by 1,500ltr and could increase the range by 25 per cent.

On 21 February 2003, the first production two-seat trainer, c/n BT001, was delivered to QinetiQ at Boscombe Down as ZJ800. From 2005 it is anticipated that deliveries for all customers will reach a total of fifty-two per year from all four final-assembly sites. The order for the second tranche will be for 236 aircraft, of which eighty-nine will be for the RAF.

On 30 June the first Typhoon was accepted by the RAF and it was announced the the two-seat trainer variant would be designated T.1 and T.1A and the single-seat fighter F.2. The first Typhoon T.1 was delivered to 17 (R) Sqn on 18 December 2003.

The difference between the T.1 and the T.1A is the result of a problem between fuel systems and flight control systems. The F.2 required major rework, whilst the initial T.1s were accepted but the redesign was incorporated into the T.1As. While the initial tranche comprises a substantial number of Typhoons for training and evaluation, the second will be enhanced to give it the true multi-role capability.

The Typhoon initially equipped the Typhoon OEU – 17 (R) Sqn – followed by 29 (R) Sqn, which moved to Coningsby in July 2005. The first operational squadron will be 3Sqn, which will form in 2006,

followed by 12Sqn in 2007. Both will be based at Coningsby and should be ready to take over the southern QRA from the Tornado F.3s shortly after. Later, operational Typhoon squadrons will be formed/converted at Leuchars, commencing with 6Sqn.

BAC VC.10 C.1K

Role: Passenger/freight transport or air refuelling
Engine: 4 × 9,890kg Rolls-Royce Conway 301-550 turbojet
Length: 50.63m (166ft 1.4in)
Span: 44.55m (146ft 2in)
Height: 12.04m (39ft 6in)
Speed: 920km/hr (575mph; 496kt)
Weight: 146,500kg (323,000lb) MTOW
Range: 6,436km (4,000 miles; 3,472nm)

The design of the Vickers VC.10 commenced as a civil airliner in 1958. The prototype first flew at Brooklands on 29 June 1962.

The RAF became interested in the VC.10 as a transport and five aircraft were initially ordered in September 1961; this was subsequently increased to fourteen. The RAF examples differed from the civilian models in taking the Standard VC.10 fuselage (which was shorter) and fitting

One of the single-seat prototype Typhoons, which is designated F.2 in service with the RAF.

The longer VC.10 K.3 (nearest) leads a VC.10 C.1K, showing the difference between the Super and Standard models.

this with the larger Super VC.10 wing, tail and engines. These improvements significantly improved its performance and range. As a result, the RAF VC.10 became one of the fastest multi-purpose transports anywhere in the world. They also incorporated a cargo door, strengthened floor and were capable of receiving fuel in-flight. Up to 137 passengers could be carried in rearward facing seats, which were considered safer than the airliner arrangement, which relied on the seat-belt to retain the passenger in their seat in the event of an accident. However, a substantial amount of 10Sqn's tasking later involved mixed-role, with passengers and cargo. In a purely cargo role, the VC.10 can carry 54,000lb (24,495kg) of freight. The VC.10 C.1 can also be operated in the casevac role and is capable of carrying up to seventy-eight stretchers.

The VC.10s were initially delivered to the VC.10 Air Training Squadron (ATS) at Brize Norton. However, the first squadron VC.10 C.1 entered service with 10Sqn on 7 April 1966 and the last was handed over in 1968 at Fairford. In May

1967 the squadron moved to nearby Brize Norton.

In June 1970 the Britannia ATS arrived from Lyneham and was combined with the Belfast and the VC.10 ATS to form 241 OCU in July.

Initially, much of the VC.10 C.1 tasking consisted of route flying to various bases overseas that required regular support. These stretched from the Far and Middle East across to the USA. The 1968 Defence White Paper announced dramatic reductions of British forces outside Europe. This resulted in greatly reduced 10Sqn scheduled services, which were operated almost like an airline.

The VC.10 C.1s continued to provide vital strategic-airlift capability with exercise commitments. One aircraft was lost in 1970 when it was provided to Rolls-Royce as a testbed, with one of their new RB.211s replacing two Conways on the port side. When the trials were completed it was discovered that the airframe had been twisted, making its conversion back for RAF use uneconomic.

An additional VC.10, in the form of an

ex-BUA Type 1103, flew in military markings, although it didn't arrive at Brize until its flying days were over and was never operated by the RAF. This aircraft was purchased by the Ministry of Technology in 1973 and operated on various trials with the RAE at Bedford. It was subsequently broken up and the fuselage ended up at Brize as an instructional airframe.

The VC.10 C.1s were used many times in the humanitarian role. In 1974 the aircraft assisted in the evacuation of some 13,000 civilians from war-torn Cyprus and 5,700 from Angola the following year. In 1977, Guatemalan forces threatened the British protectorate of Belize: as a result, British troops and a force of Harriers were rapidly deployed.

A further role for the VC.10 C.1 was VIP transport, flying members of the Royal family, government or officers, although this ceased in 2002.

The withdrawal of the Comets in 1975 and Britannias in 1976 saw the VC.10 gain extra tasking.

The Gulf War demonstrated how vital in-flight refuelling was to modern operations. With the Victors rapidly reaching the end of their lives it was decided that the VC.10 C.1 should have a refuelling capability. A modification program

commenced that resulted in the fitting of a pair of refuelling pods onto strengthened wings, modification to the fuel system and the fitting of monitoring equipment for the flight engineer in the cockpit. The first aircraft was completed in June 1992. The pods are removable and so are normally only fitted for refuelling sorties.

The VC.10 is operated with two pilots, a navigator and a flight engineer, who also manages the refuelling operation.

In 1997, XR806 was severely damaged when it sat on its tail due to a refuelling error. Such was the damage and the limited life left on the airframe, it was decided that repair of the damage was uneconomic and so it was scrapped.

Plans are in hand for the VC.10 fleet to be replaced by 2013 by the winner of the Future Strategic Tanker Aircraft (FSTA) with A330-200 being the preferred option. Commencing in June 2005, three VC.10s were withdrawn and used for spares recovery which will include the engines that are in short supply. It is anticipated that one C.1K will be withdrawn. On October 14th, 2005 10 and 101 Sqns were merged, resulting in the disbanding of 10 Sqn.

VC.10 C.1Ks are currently operated by 101Sqn from their base at Brize Norton.

The K.3s are ex-East African Airways Super VC.10s that have been refurbished and modified for the aerial-refuelling role.

BAC VC.10 K.3

Role: Passenger/freight transport or air refuelling
Engine: 4 × 9,890kg Rolls-Royce Conway 301-550 turbojet
Length: 54.59m (179ft 1.4in)
Span: 44.55m (146ft 2in)
Height: 12.04m (39ft 6in)
Speed: 896km/hr (550mph; 483kt)
Weight: 152,090kg (335,000lb) MTOW
Range: 6,436km (4,000 miles; 3,472nm)

In addition to the VC.10 C.1s that were built specifically for the RAF, an announcement was made in 1978 that a number of ex-airline aircraft were purchased. These were to be modified for RAF use as tankers to augment the converted Victor bombers.

Five ex-Gulf Air Standard VC.10s were initially converted as VC.10 K.2s and the first took to the air again in June 1982. Being the oldest airframes of all, the K.2s were retired in mid-2001 and scrapped.

The balance of four aircraft were ex-East African Airlines Super VC.10s and these were converted to K.3 standard.

The conversion process of the VC.10

airliners to tankers was considerable. The RAF requirement was that all aircraft should be as common as possible to the C.1. In addition, each would have three refuelling points, have additional fuel capacity and be capable of operating independent of ground support.

The aircraft were completely stripped down by BAe at Filton. Additional cylindrical fuel-tanks were fitted onto the cabin floor, enabling a total of 78 tonnes of fuel to be carried. All of the cabin was stripped down to a bare minimum, apart from small section towards the front that is fitted with seventeen seats behind a bulkhead, to enable technicians or support crew to be carried.

A centre-line Hose Drum Unit (HDU) was fitted with a 24.38m (80ft) hose in the former rear-fuselage cargo bay. This is used to refuel larger aircraft, such as the Nimrod or Sentry. Wing-mounted pods with 16.76m (55ft) smaller-diameter hoses were fitted under each wing, enabling a pair of fighters or strike aircraft to be refuelled at the same time.

Various other modifications included

the fitting of an Auxiliary Power Unit (APU), refuelling probe and fuel system modification. The first VC.10 K.2 was delivered to the RAF in July 1983 and by May 1987 all nine K.2s and K.3s aircraft had been delivered to 101Sqn.

Like all tanker aircraft, they are a force extender, enabling combat aircraft to increase their endurance. As a result the VC.10s, which were initially augmenting the Victor tankers, eventually took over their role as the Victors were retired when they reached the end of their life in 1993.

In 1991, during the Gulf War, all nine of the VC.10 K.2 and K.3s of 101Sqn were deployed to Saudi Arabia to provide air-to-air refuelling for RAF and US Navy aircraft. They have seen virtually continuous operations since, with deployments for the northern and southern watches of Iraq, operations in Bosnia and Kosovo, and the latest operations in Afghanistan and Iraq. An interesting comment from a US Navy pilot was that they preferred to operate with RAF tankers as they were always on station and on time and had a flexible attitude. These operations were in addition to the normal exercises and trials, such as *Red Flag* and *China Lake* in the USA as well as around the UK.

The VC.10 fleet is now beginning to struggle as it, too, is approaching the end of its fatigue life. A consultation document has been released for a Future Strategic Tanker Aircraft (FSTA). This Private Finance Initiative (PFI) is intended to result in a 27-year contract for a tanker replacement to enter service in 2008, with AirTanker's A330-200 bid being the MoD's preferred option. However, in 2004 the VC.10 was given a two-year stay of execution, which will see them continue to operate until 2013.

The VC.10 K.3s are operated by 101Sqn from Brize Norton.

BAC VC.10 K.4

Role: Passenger/freight transport or air refuelling
Engine: 4 × 9,890kg Rolls-Royce Conway 301-550 turbojet
Length: 54.59m (179ft 1.4in)
Span: 44.55m (146ft 2in)
Height: 12.04m (39ft 6in)
Speed: 880km/h (550mph: 475kt)
Weight: 146,500kg (323,000lb) MTOW
Range: 6,436km (4,000 miles; 3,472nm)

By 1981 British Airways had retired their Super VC.10s and fourteen were bought by the RAF, together with spares. They were stored at Abingdon and Brize Norton awaiting their fate until 1989, when it was decided to convert five into tankers and dispose of the rest – mainly for spares recovery with the remains scrapped. As these had been built for BA, they were to yet another standard and these conversions were designated K.4.

The program followed a similar one to the previous conversions, only these ones didn't feature the additional fuel-tanks in the fuselage. The process for the K.2 required a hole cut in the fuselage to get the tanks in, but it was considered that this would weaken these airframes. The K.3s had cargo doors so didn't require that drastic action. Instead, they retained more seats. As a consequence, the K.4 can only carry 74 tonnes of fuel. The fact that they had been stored for so long meant that additional rectification work was also required. However, once completed they featured a more modern cockpit-fit than the earlier models. The first K.4 was flown on 30 July 1993 and deliveries to 101Sqn were made the following April.

Recent modifications to the VC.10 fleet have seen the use of a low-infra-red paint, which resulted in their colours changing

Most of the fuselage of the K.3s has been stripped and additional fuel tanks fitted to provide additional off-loadable fuel. These are not fitted in either the C.1K or the K.4. Crown Copyright

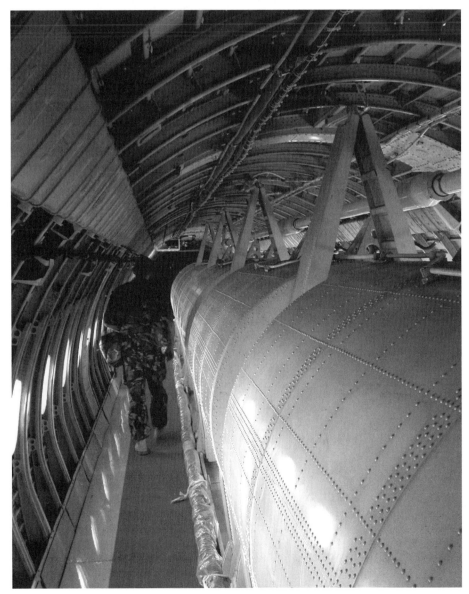

from hemp to grey. They have also been fitted with Radar Warning Receivers (RWR) and the Matador IRCM missile-protection system, which will assist in their remaining operational until 2013.

The VC.10 K.4s are operated by 101Sqn from Brize Norton. However, in June 2005 it was announced that the VC.10 fleet would be reduced by three aircraft and these would be used as a source for some spares to maintain the others fully operational. It is believed that two of these three aircraft will be K.4s.

Grob Vigilant T.1

Role: Single-engined motor glider
Engine: 1 × 67.1kW Grob 2500 flat-four piston
Length: 7.92m (26ft 0in)
Span: 17.37m (57ft 0in)
Height: 1.68m (5ft 6in)
Speed: 240km/h (150mph; 130kt)
Weight: 850kg (1,874lb)
Range: 1,798km (1,117 miles; 970nm)

The Grob G.109 is a two-seat motor-powered glider that was developed in the late-1970s. It became the first glass fibre motor-glider and the prototype was initially flown on 14 March 1980.

The G.109B is a complete redesign of the original G.109 and was first flown in March 1983. Fifty-three G.109Bs were ordered as the Vigilant T.1s to replace the Venture T.1 motor-gliders of the Air Training Corps (ATC). They are used to provide air experience and airmanship training for ATC cadets.

Three more Vigilants were delivered in 2002, including one that had been sold back to Grob after a Cat 4 accident in 1991. This aircraft had been rebuilt prior to being bought back.

Due to its glider style of design, the Venture has a low drag that, combined with a high-aspect-ratio wing with a laminar-flow profile, results in good operating economy. The wings can also be folded if needed, reducing the required hangar space and enabling recovery by trailer if necessary.

The Vigilant T.1 is operated by the sixteen Volunteer Gliding Schools (VGS) located around the country.

Grob Viking T.1

Role: Two-seat high-performance glider
Engine: n/a
Length: 8.18m (26ft 10in)
Span: 17.5m (57ft 5in)
Height: 1.55m (5ft 1in)
Speed: 250km/h (155mph; 135kt)
Weight: 580kg (1,279lb)
Range: n/a

The Grob G.103 Twin II Acro first flew in 1979.

A total of 100 G.103s were ordered for the Air Training Corps to replace the Cadet Mk.3 and Sedberg gliders, which had been in operation since the early 1950s. The G.103 formally entered service with the Air Cadets on 5 October 1984 and was named Viking T.1. With tandem seating and a glass-fibre construction resulting in a lighter weight, combined with vastly superior aerodynamics over its predecessors, the Viking gives a greatly improved performance, as well as making maintenance easier.

The ATC operate the Viking T.1 to provide Air Cadets with air-experience flying and airmanship training.

The Viking T.1 is operated by eleven of the VGS located throughout the country.

Forthcoming Types

Airbus A330

Role: Passenger/freight transport or air refuelling
Engine: 2 × 252kN RR Trent 700 turbofan
Length: 59m (193ft 6.75in)
Span: 60.30m (197ft 10in)
Height: 17.89m (58ft 8.25in)
Speed: Mach 0.86
Weight: 217,000kg (478,400lb) MTOW
Range: 11,852km (7,365 miles; 6,394nm)

The Future Strategic Tanker Aircraft

The Vigilant T.1 provides air cadets with a valuable training. It is able to combine some of the basics of glider training but able to self launch and extend flight-time with its own motor.

The Viking glider is constructed of glass fibre, combining strength with reduced weight. It therefore has a much higher performance capability over the previous wood-and-canvas Cadet Mk.3 and Sedberg gliders.

(FSTA) will replace the existing fleet of Tristar and VC.10 tankers with a private Finance Initiative (PFI) fleet. Two consortia bid for the 27-year contract, which is potentially worth £14bn; each had their own solution for the task, which specified an entry into service of 2008.

The two consortiums were AirTanker, consisting of KBR, Cobham's FR Aviation, EADS, Rolls-Royce and Thales, who based their solution on new Airbus A330 airframes, and the Tanker Transport Support Company (TTSC), which comprises BAe Systems, Boeing, SerCo and Spectrum Capital, who offered ex-British Airways 767-300ERs. The latter incorporated the Smiths refuelling system that Boeing is offering to the USAF and which has been chosen by Italy and Japan.

Apart from the aircraft acquisition and operating costs, a factor in the package is that the aircraft will be offered onto the civilian market when not required for RAF use. The revenue from this would enable reduced costs. Initially this may appear a strange idea but, in times of peace, public confidence in flying results in high passenger-levels and the airlines

need additional capacity, while the military are only using aircraft for routine training on exercises. During times of tension or war, public confidence drops and airlines need fewer aircraft while the military need is greater. Therefore, the theory would appear to provide a good solution, achieving increased aircraft utilization and, therefore, lower operating-costs.

It is thought probable that a total of twenty aircraft will be needed to fulfil the requirement, which will consist of a mix of two and three refuelling points.

With an in-service date of between January 2008 and January 2020, it was originally planned that contract signing would be in early 2003. However, continual delays have resulted and it was January 2004 before the MoD announced that AirTanker had been selected as providing the best solution. Final negotiations continue before the contract is finally signed.

While the PFI system is promulgated as a good solution for government financing, under PFI arrangements competing organizations have to be self financing and incur considerable costs and these increase

with the delays. Unfortunately, the PFI does not allow for the loser to recoup any costs, leaving them in a weaker position to bid for future business.

Subject to final approvals, the A330 will be based at Brize Norton and is due to enter service in January 2008.

Airbus A400M

Role: Tactical and strategic airlift
Engine: 4 × 7,450kW EPI TP400-D6 turbo-prop
Length: 42.2m (138ft 5in)
Span: 42.4m (139ft 1in)
Height: 14.7m (48ft 2.75in)
Speed: Mach 0.72
Weight: 130,000kg (286,600lb) MTOW
Range: 4,540km (2,821 miles; 2,449nm)

The A400M originally commenced life as the Future Large Aircraft (FLA). This was managed by Euroflag as a transport contender for a number of European Air Forces, including the RAF. In September 1994, the project was transferred to the new military division of Airbus.

The A400M proposal was adopted in 1999 and, in May 2000, the MoD was the first to order an initial batch of twenty-five aircraft. Others followed, leading to a Declaration of Intent for 225 aircraft being signed by eight European ministers at Farnborough 2000. However, the project has suffered from a lack of financial commitment, especially by the German partner. As a result, Portugal pulled out from her stated requirement for three, Turkey reduced her requirement from twenty-six to ten and Italy decided to go for the C-130J instead of sixteen A400Ms. By 2003 this figure had been reduced to 180 aircraft (eight for Belgium/Luxembourg, fifty for France, sixty for Germany, twenty-seven for Spain, ten for Turkey and twenty-five for the UK).

After many continued delays, German confirmation came and, on 27 May 2003, the signature was finally signed for the contract to purchase the above total of 180 A400Ms for the seven NATO customers. The Airbus timetable anticipates a first flight in January 2008, first delivery to commence in late 2009 and series production deliveries in 2010. The A400Ms will replace the remaining Hercules C.1s and C.3s.

The A400M will be capable of carrying approximately half the mean-payload of a C-17, but it is planned to operate at a substantially cheaper cost. In comparison with the C-130J, it will carry twice the load. In addition, Airbus have also proposed an additional role for the A400M as a tanker, with an in-flight refuelling pod fitted under each wing.

Capable of operating at altitudes of 12,191m (40,000ft) down to 45m (150ft), the A400M will carry up to 116 paratroops or up to 37 tonnes of freight. It will also be capable of operating from semi-prepared strips.

Brize Norton has been selected to be the A400M base when it enters service in 2010.

Lockheed Martin Joint Combat Aircraft (F-35B JSF)

Role: STOVL multi-role fighter/attack
Engine: 1 × 177kN P&W F135 turbofan
Length: 15.39m (50ft 6in)
Span: 10.70m (35ft 1.25in)
Height: 4.57m (15ft 0in)
Speed: Mach 1.6 max
Weight: 27.215kg (60,000lb) approx. MTOW
Range: 835km (519 miles; 450nm)

The Joint Strike Fighter (JSF) is the next-generation fighter aircraft, which is being developed in the USA as the F-35. The project commenced in November 1974 and the US DoD instigated a competition between Boeing and Lockheed Martin, with prototypes being built and subjected to intense evaluation. The UK joined the programme in December 1995 as a collaborative partner. The British name for the project is the Joint Combat Aircraft (JCA). In October 2001, Lockheed Martin were awarded the first stage of what could eventually be a US$19bn contract for some 3,000 of their F-35s.

The F-35 has been designed with three variants: the F-35A conventional take-off and landing aircraft (CTOL) for the USAF; the F-35B Short Take-Off and Vertical Landing (STOVL) variant for RAF, RN and USMC; the third a carrier-operable F-35C for the USN.

The British F-35B features a lifting fan located behind the cockpit (replacing some fuel). It will have a broader and higher spine with a shorter cockpit-canopy than the other F-35Bs.

The prototype F-35A made its maiden flight on 24 October 2000 and, after twenty-five sorties totalling twenty-five flight hours, was returned from Edwards AFB to Palmdale for conversion to the F-35B configuration. Having completed a number of hover-pit trials, the F-35B made its first vertical take-off and landing on 23 June 2001. The prototype F-35C made its first flight on 16 December 2000.

One of the features of the JSF will be a reduction in the amount of pilot work-load during the VSTOL portion of the flight. This requires a substantial amount of additional training for the Harrier pilots but, following trials by the DERA (now QinetiQ) VAAC Harrier at Boscombe Down, this can be reduced to an acceptable level and could lead to a fully automated vertical-landing system.

Production agreements will entail Lockheed Martin being responsible for the forward fuselage, cockpit and leading edges, as well as the final assembly. Northrop Grumman will build the mid-fuselage and wing box, while BAe Systems will produce the rear fuselage.

Initially, a total of nineteen pre-production flying examples will be built. Five will be the F-35A, four F-35Bs and five F-34Cs. In addition, a further eight will be built for non-flying trials. The first F-35A is scheduled to fly in October 2005, F-35B in early 2006 and F-35C in late 2006. However, by 2004, the complexities of a multi-purpose aircraft surfaced when it was revealed that the aircraft was 3,300lb overweight.

On 30 September 2002 it was confirmed by the Defence Procurement Minister – Lord Bath – that the F-35B would be ordered for the RAF and RN to replace the currently operated Harrier and Sea Harriers. It is anticipated that ninety will be ordered for the RAF and sixty for the RN, with deliveries commencing from around 2010.

The F-35B/Joint Combat Aircraft will replace the Harrier GR.7/GR.9.

BAe Nimrod MRA.4

Role: Anti-submarine and anti-surface warfare, and search and rescue
Engine: 4 × 68.9kN BMW/Rolls-Royce BR710 turbofan
Length: 38.71m (126ft 9in) excluding probe
Span: 38.71m (17ft)
Height: 9.14m (30ft)
Speed: Mach 0.77 (MTOW)
Weight: 105,378kg (232,316lb) MTOW
Range: 15 hours endurance

With the Nimrod MR.2 starting to become considered obsolete, the Government announced in July 1996 that BAe had won the £2.5bn RMPA (Replacement Maritime Patrol Aircraft) contract. Their proposal was the Nimrod 2000 upgrade of twenty-one of the Nimrod MR.2s, but this was subsequently reduced to eighteen.

The upgrade is more than just replacement of some of the components – it actually represents a total of over 80 per cent new aircraft. Initially, four fuselages were moved to FRA at Hurn for work to commence on re-lifeing, but they were moved to Woodford shortly after.

The MR.4 variant airframe, as it later was designated, comprises a merger of the existing pressurized fuselage and tail of the MR.2, with a new wing incorporating the Rolls-Royce BR710 engines. BAe Systems has used its experience in the design and building of Airbus wings to apply the technology to the Nimrod, whose new wings are 25 per cent greater in surface area. Equipment wise, the MR.4 will feature a new mission system with well over five million lines of software code plus new general systems comprising hydraulics, fuel and electrics. It also features a new state-of-the-art cockpit designed for a two-man crew and incorporating a seven-screen electronic flight-instrument system.

The resulting aircraft will have greater thrust but lower fuel consumption, which, combined with increased fuel capacity, increases sorties to over fifteen hours. This can be further increased with air-to-air refuelling. Lower noise and vibration will reduce fatigue for the tactical crew of seven on long sorties. New fourth-generation sensors will give improved capability and reliability, while the Advanced Armament Control System has been designed to accept all current and future weapons for its role. These systems will place Nimrod as a world leader.

Once in service, the Nimrod MRA.4 will have been re-lifed for a further twenty-five years of service. Its new improved systems will increase its reliability and capabilities not only for its military role but also when assisting civilian authorities. The first aircraft was rolled out in August 2002 and was first flown on 26 August 2004.

The original programme called for deliveries to the RAF to commence in 2001, but the various problems resulted in delays, with official estimates now stating the first aircraft is expected to fly in 2004. Early difficulties resulted in the contract with FRA being cancelled in 1999. One major problem that has been encountered was that the original MR.1 production was virtually hand-built, resulting in each aircraft being slightly different to each other. This has not been a major problem until now but, with modern computerized production-techniques capable of producing components to fractions of millimetres, these variations have caused a major headache when trying to mate the new wing to the old fuselage.

BAe initially paid a £45m penalty for delays back in 2000 but, such are the problems, that work is only being carried out on the first three aircraft, with the others being held until a significant risk reduction of the programme has been achieved. Although totally unrelated, it is estimated that the BAe Systems Astute submarine and the Nimrod MRA programmes are running at around £1bn over estimates.

Once complete, the Nimrod MRA.4 will have a capability far in excess of the MR.2. It will have four underwing hard points in addition to the cavernous bomb-bay. As blue-water operations have reduced, the role of the Nimrod is being expanded elsewhere. As the designation

indicates, it will be capable of an attack role in addition to its original role. This can include SEAD (Suppression of Enemy Air Defences) with the Alarm anti-radiation missiles and deep strike with Storm Shadow. Maverick and ASRAAM are also to be considered as future weapons. Overland surveillance capabilites will be expanded, in addition to the traditional ASW role with torpedoes and sonobuoys.

The contract was re-negotiated in February 2003 and, as a result, MoD will increase the budget from £2.7bn to £2.97bn. This requires for the Nimrod MRA.4 to be in service (namely the sixth production aircraft) by 2009. The contract also required production on the subsequent fifteen to halt until significant risk-reduction work has been completed. In 2004 it was announced that the total order was being reduced to twelve MRA.4s following a detailed examination of future capability requirements.

Bombardier Sentinel R.1

Role: Airborne stand-off radar
Engine: 2 × 6.65kN BMW RR BR710
Length: 30.3m (99ft 5in)
Span: 28.6m (93ft 10in)
Height: 7.95m (26ft 1in)
Speed: Mach 0.80
Weight: 43,584kg (96,000lb) MTOW
Range: 7 hours endurance (approx.)

Sentinel is what was previously referred as the ASTOR (Airborne Stand-Off Radar) project. It is the RAF's new surveillance and target-acquisition aircraft based on the Global Express and ordered from Raytheon with a £800m contract in 1999. The decisions that led to the ordering of Sentinel were as a result of experience gained during the Gulf War with the USAF J-STARS and U-2R aircraft.

A total of five Sentinels are being modified from the Bombardier Global Express aircraft for the RAF order. These are being equipped with a radar-surveillance system capable of observing deep into enemy territory using various radar modes. These will provide photograph-like images using Synthetic Aperture Radar (SAR), as well as Moving Target Indicators (MTI) showing vehicle movements at ranges of hundreds of miles with the ASARS-2 derivative radar. The SAR can be used in a swath setting to cover an area to get a general picture. The spot setting is a much

higher setting, which can be used to determine the type of vehicle or weapon. These systems can be used individually or together to enable battlefield commanders to have accurate up-to-the-minute information on the enemy. Images can even be transmitted to other aircraft via Link 16, to provide target information for strike aircraft using a Narrowband Datalink Subsystem (NDLS) or a wideband based on the Common Data Link (CDL).

Sentinel is manned by a crew of five, of which two are the pilot and co-pilot. The three mission crew are able to process the information received from the radar before it is transmitted via the secure data-links to various locations, such as headquarters and intelligence analysis units. The information obtained by Sentinel will greatly improve potential-target information during a fast-moving conflict, enabling attack aircraft and artillery to have up-to-the-moment target co-ordinates.

A Bombardier Global Express ASTOR development aircraft with representative aerodynamic modifications made its first flight on 3 August 2001, the first production airframe was then delivered for modification to Raytheon's facility at Greenville, Texas on 31 January 2002 and is due to arrive in the UK in mid-2005.

As part of the programme, a new Raytheon facility has been established at the old British Aerospace airfield at Broughton, where the modification and system integration of the RAF's second Global Express, ZJ691, and subsequent three aircraft plus ground stations will be completed. The first Global Express was delivered to Broughton on 29 January 2003, having already completed handling trials with the two mission-antenna radomes. Raytheon is currently finishing designing and manufacturing the systems and equipment prior to the fitting out of the aircraft.

Plans for the introduction of Sentinel are already well underway, with initial personnel being posted in from September 2003 and 5Sqn officially reforming on 1 April 2004. The first Sentinel R.1 was flown on 26 May 2004 at Major's Field, Greenville, Texas and thus began a series of flight trials. The first Sentinel will be delivered in 2006 and the complete system, which includes six Tactical Ground Stations and two Operational Ground Stations, is scheduled for final delivery in 2007.

Sentinel R.1 will equip 5Sqn at Waddington from 2006.

CHAPTER TWO

RAF Locations

In this section I detail briefly the history of each RAF station and provide information on its current role and occupants. This list of stations is constantly shrinking as the RAF reduces in size and recent reviews continue the trend. With old aircraft being retired and new ones delivered the individual roles of each station may change from time to time.

During the 1930s, 1940s and 1950s the RAF had bases spread virtually throughout the world, but today it is almost entirely based in the UK. Only stations located in Ascension, Cyprus, Falklands, Gibraltar and Goose Bay in Canada provide a permanent overseas presence. Long gone are the strategic bases of RAF Far East and

RAF Near East. The post-Second World War requirement to station RAF aircraft in West Germany finally ended with the withdrawal of the last squadrons in 2001.

This withdrawal of stations has not brought an end to deployments for RAF aircraft. Training exercises regularly see squadrons deploy to USA for *Red Flag* at Nellis and *Distant Frontier* in Alaska or *Maple Flag* in Canada. In fact, so frequent are these deployments that aircraft – mainly Tornados – are usually kept as a pool in North America for a season to save the cost of flying them back and forwards.

Not all RAF stations are airfields, these others provide a variety of other functions ranging from radar and communications

through to ranges and storage. A number of other locations are occupied by the US military and designated USVF (United States Visiting Forces). These comprise airfields and communications bases, plus a US Army boat maintenance depot.

Each RAF station has a similar structure, although the actual balance at each individual location will vary according to its role. Admin Wing provides various services, including accounts, catering, dental, medical, supplies and transport, which enable the station to function. The Ops Wing is normally the core of the station, responsible for the management of the airfield (if there is one), security, intelligence and planning. If appropriate, it would include flying support and air traffic control. Eng Wing provides the servicing and some repair faculties for aircraft and most other mechanical equipment, including vehicles. It may also

Every RAF airfield has an established structure of manning, from the CO and his executives through to operational and admin staff and security. This small team was running Kabul airport. Each location will vary the proportions of the make-up depending on its role.

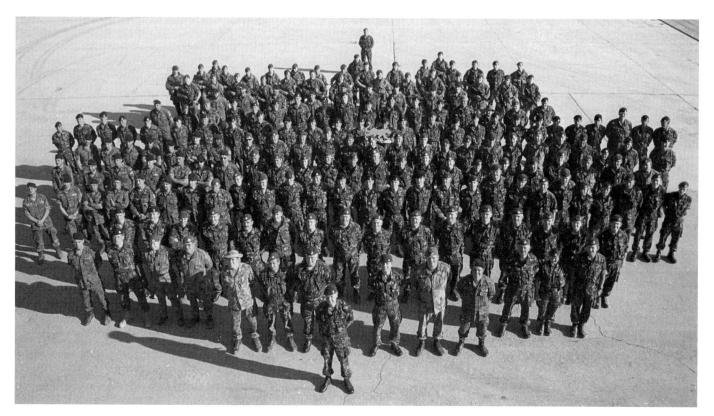

include armaments, electrical and safety-equipment sections.

Although each station's role is just a part of the overall RAF capability, they function as an individual self-contained community. Accommodation is provided for single personnel, while housing is available for those who are married and their families. Like all businesses, supplies come from various sources – in the case of the RAF both military and civilian. As far as the local civilian community is concerned, this can mean additional business worth many millions of pounds a year.

Unfortunately, this comes at a cost. Most military combat aircraft are noisy and pilots need constant training to keep them fully capable. This means that active flying stations, especially those designated front line, can be noisy. Major effort is incorporated into planning to try to reduce the impact of this noise on local communities. Where possible, some flying is conducted on simulators, while night flying and weekend flying is strictly controlled. Low-level flying is part of most pilots' training, to reduce their vulnerability to enemy radar. This is undertaken in designated low-populated parts of the countryside. This is fine as long as you don't live in these areas. To try to reduce the amount of their use, the RAF has been making increased use of overseas training areas, especially in North America. Participation in *Red Flag*, *Maple Flag* and *Distant Frontier* exercises enables RAF to fly almost totally unrestricted over large unpopulated areas and usually in conjunction with other air forces for mutual beneficial training. However, although worthwhile from most aspects, this form of training is more expensive.

A few of the RAF stations described are extremely small in terms of manpower, although they can still cover a large expanse of land – these are the ranges. Most ranges date back to the early days of the RAF – some even further! One aspect of these that is not often appreciated is how, because of their very nature, the landscape has been so little changed during their use. Despite the fact that they have been subjected to explosions and are thus cratered, this is very local and the majority of the range is to provide a safety margin. Archeologists and nature conservationists have discovered that most ranges and even some RAF stations have provided a haven from the ravages of

intensive farming. As a result, most MoD sites have a conservation officer, whose job it is to monitor the local species, often encouraging their development and providing warning on any potential threat. This also includes archeological finds. As a result some RAF stations include designated SSSIs (Site of Special Scientific Interest).

RAF Akrotiri

Overseas
Motto: *Acra Semper Acria* – Always remain alert

Akrotiri opened on 1 October 1955, but it was January before an aircraft arrived. In November 103 MU arrived; 13Sqn with Meteors were the first residents of the Near East Strike and Reconnaissance base, joined by 208Sqn Meteors and 6Sqn Venoms shortly after. Soon, 3 Wing RAF Regiment arrived to provide base protection and Hunters of 1 and 34Sqn deployed in August. Most were active during the Suez Crisis

In 1956, 13Sqn re-equipped with the Canberra and, by 1958, four Canberra squadrons were at Akrotiri. In July 1960 Cyprus became a Republic, however, the Sovereign Base Areas (SBA) of Akrotiri and Dhekelia remained separate under British jurisdiction. Princess Mary's Hospital (TPMH) was opened in 1963. Javelins and Lightnings arrived in 1964 followed by 1563 Flight Whirlwinds for the SAR role.

The role transfer from El Aden in 1964 resulted in Akrotiri becoming the RAF's main staging post to the Middle and Far East. LXXSqn Hastings arrived to become the resident transport squadron. In 1967, 56Sqn Lightnings arrived and the Argosy began to replace the Hastings. At its peak Akrotiri housed seven squadrons and had 14,500 personnel.

In 1969 the Canberra squadrons were disbanded and replaced by Vulcans of 9 and 35Sqn. In November 1970, Hercules began to arrive to partially replace the Argosy. In 1971 1563 Flight was re-named 84Sqn.

When Turkish forces invaded Cyprus and fighting erupted in July 1974, the RAF were required to rescue and evacuate visiting tourists, as well as British Service families. People were moved by 70Sqn to Akrotiri, from where some 9,000 souls were flown out under RAF control, for

which Akrotiri was subsequently awarded the Wilkinson Sword of Peace.

During the mid-1970s Akrotiri's role was slashed – 103 MU was closed and only 84Sqn remaining flying. Personnel had dropped from 4,000 to 350. In 1986, 34Sqn RAF Regiment returned and, from 1988, joint units were established with the army to provide logistic and engineering support.

Akrotiri is the RAF's largest overseas airfield. Its current role is to support British Forces in Cyprus and to operate as a strategic Forward Mounting Base for British operations. It also accommodates armament-practice camps for fighter squadrons. This includes receiving detachments from 100Sqn, who provide the target towing facilities with their Hawks. The Red Arrows are also normally an annual visitor, taking advantage of the good weather to complete intensive training before the airshow season commences.

SAR duties are maintained by 84Sqn, which disposed of their Wessex in early 2003, which were replaced for a while by a detachment of 203 (R) Sea Kings as a temporary measure until the arrival of their Griffin HAR.2s.

The station commander also is responsible for nearby Episcopi, for which Akrotiri provides administrative support as the collectively known Western Sovereign Base Area (WSBA). Episcopi has been predominately army but various changes have resulted in it being occupied by some RAF personnel and army personnel at Akrotiri. As a result, much of the normal station functions of Ops and Admin Wings are also partially manned by army personnel.

Akrotiri hosts a number of lodger units, most of which are joint service with the army. These include what was a detachment of 12 Signals Unit but is now named the Cyprus Communications Unit. Medical support is provided by the Princess Mary's Hospital (TPMH). During Operation *Telic*, the hospital was augmented to act as an aeromedical evacuation staging-post for British and US casualties. Many of the support and security tasks are run as joint operations with the army. The majority of the station Engineering Wing function is performed by the Cyprus Service Support Unit – also a lodger unit with RAF and army (75 per cent/25 per cent) personnel. Likewise, security is jointly manned, with the Cyprus Joint Security Unit protecting

Akrotiri and the Cyprus Police Unit protecting Episcopi.

In 1990, Akrotiri became an important staging post once more for Operation *Granby* following the Iraqi invasion of Kuwait. During October 1990, 3,162 aircraft movements were recorded – far different from the normal eighty-four of the previous April. This was followed by Operation *Haven* in support of the Kurds and later Afghanistan and further Iraq operations and humanitarian supplies.

Akrotiri was even busier in 2003. Following a major and rapid construction programme, not only did it handle some 80 per cent of the air cargo that was delivered for Operation *Telic* but it also housed air-to-air refuelling tankers that provided 20 per cent of the fuel transferred to receivers. In addition, two USN carrier groups had all their air-delivered cargo routed via Akrotiri. During the three and a half month operation, some 12,000 movements were recorded.

Akrotiri is the home of 84Sqn with Griffin HAR.2s, but a variety of other units are frequently deployed for short periods.

RAF Alconbury

USVF
Personnel and Training Command

Alconbury opened on 15 May 1938 as a satellite airfield initially to Upwood and then Wyton. It was first occupied by 63Sqn from Upwood and, temporarily, 52Sqn – both operating Battles and Ansons. In April 1940, 15Sqn temporarily deployed from Wyton with Blenheims but left the following month. In February 1941 40Sqn arrived with Wellingtons. A detachment flew out to Malta in October and the rest moved out to the Middle East the following February. They were replaced by 156Sqn, which re-formed with Wellingtons and departed by 1942.

Alconbury was then transferred to the USAAF's 8th AF as Station 102. The 93rd Bomb Group (328th, 329th, 330th and 409th BS) arrived with B-24 Liberators in July 1942. They were replaced by 92nd Bomb Group (325th, 326th, 327th and 407th BS) in December with B-17 Flying Fortresses, as a Combat Crew Replacement Unit (CCRU). In September 1943 they were replaced by 95th Bomb Group with B-17s. They

departed in June and 482nd Bomb Group arrived in September, operating as a Pathfinder unit with B-17s and B-24s until June 1945. In the meantime, from March 1944, Alconbury also housed an operational radar-development unit.

Alconbury returned to RAF control and housed a sub-site of Abbots Ripon 264 MU from November 1945 until September 1948. Alconbury then closed and went into a period of care and maintenance.

The USAF then returned and, from June 1953, Alconbury underwent a modernization programme, which included a new extended runway and new hangars, prior to the arrival of the first units in September 1955. First to arrive were the 86 BS with B-45 Tornados, which converted to B-66 Destroyers before departing in August 1959. It was replaced by 10th TRW (1st and 10 TRS) with RB-66 then RF-4C Phantoms in 1965. Then 42nd Transport Carrier Squadron (42 TCS) operated various transports for 3rd AF from May 1956 until it disbanded in December. In April 1976, the arrival of 527 TFTAS with F-5E Tiger IIs brought with them a new role of an aggressor squadron. They sported various colour schemes and flew enemy tactics for realistic training of RAF as well as USAF units. In October 1982, 17th RW with the TR-1/U-2, took residence and an extensive Avionics and Photograph Interpretation Centre was established. In August 1987, the 10th TRW became the 10th TFW and converted to the A-10 Thunderbolt II, which was heavily utilized during *Desert Storm*. In July 1991 when the role reduced, 17th RW was inactivated but 95th RS remained. In spring 1992 the A-10s returned to the USA and the 95th RS was inactivated. However, U-2 operation continued with a detachment from 9th RW until March 1995. Also in 1992, the 39th SOW, with MH-53J Pave Low and MC-130H and HC-130N/P Hercules variants, took advantage of the quieter base. Later that year it became the 352nd SOG and departed in February 1995. By mid-1995 all flying at Alconbury had ceased.

The airfield at Alconbury was returned to the RAF and is currently operated by Alconbury Developments Ltd. The domestic site remains a USVF base and is operated jointly in conjunction with facilities at Molesworth and Upwood. It is operated by the 423rd ABS.

RAF Aldergrove

Joint Helicopter Command
Motto: Ours to hold

Aldergrove initially opened for just one year in 1918. Although 2Sqn temporarily operated a detachment of F.2b fighters in 1922 on an exercise, it was 1925 before it was reopened as an RAF station.

The first unit to occupy Aldergrove was 502 (Ulster) Sqn, when it was formed with Vimys in May 1925, replacing these later with Hyderabads and then Virginias. In 1933 some civilian flights were operated, but their operation was moved to Newtonards the following year. 502Sqn re-equipped with the Wallace followed by Hinds in April 1937. It became part of the Auxiliary Airforce in July but was transferred to Coastal Command in January 1939 with Ansons. In December 1939, 23 MU was formed.

In August 1940, 233Sqn arrived with Hudsons, followed by a 236Sqn Flight in September with Blenheims. This was used to re-form 272Sqn in November, staying until the following April and being replaced by 254Sqn. In October 1940, 502Sqn had converted to the Whitley and continued to operate these until it departed at the end of 1941. In April 1941 252Sqn replaced 233Sqn with Blenheims, was re-numbered 143Sqn in June and departed the following month.

During the Second World War, Aldergrove was an important Coastal Command station with various units, including 220Sqn with their Fortress Is from April 1942 until the following March. Aldergrove's location enabled patrols to be operated further out into the Atlantic.

In October 1946, 202Sqn reformed at Aldergrove with the Halifax to fly weather-reconnaissance sorties out into the Atlantic, providing valuable meteorological data for military and civil weather-forecasting. The Halifax gave way to the Hastings MET.1 in October 1950 and the squadron disbanded in 1964. Meanwhile, 502Sqn returned in 1951 with Vampires but disbanded in March 1957. In September 1959, 'A' Flight Sycamores from 228Sqn arrived, transferred to 118Sqn in May 1960 and continued to be operated until August 1962, when it too was disbanded.

A new civil air-terminal was built and

Belfast Airport opened for civil operations in 1963.

During 1968–1970 23 MU was responsible for delivery acceptance and issue of the RAF's 116 F-4M Phantoms. It remained active until April 1978, when it was closed.

In 1981 72Sqn arrived at Aldergrove with their Wessex HC.2s to provide support for the security forces. These were joined by 230Sqn in April 1992. February 1997 saw the first Pumas delivered to 72Sqn.

The Wessex- and Puma-equipped 72Sqn was retired in March 2002, leaving the Puma HC.1s of 230Sqn to provide the tactical support for the security forces. No Chinooks are based in Northern Ireland – although they do operate there, they tend to deploy for specific tasks. The JHC influence has resulted in the deployment of FAA Sea King HC.4s to operate alongside the Pumas. Ground protection is provided by 3Sqn, RAF Regt.

Lodgers at Aldergrove include the AAC Gazelle AH.1s of 665Sqn, Lynx AH.7s of 655Sqn and Islander AL.1s of 1 Flight. A detachment of Sea King HC.4s is deployed from Yeovilton and regularly rotate.

Aldergrove houses Puma HC.1s of 230Sqn and 3Sqn, RAF Regt, The airfield is shared with Belfast International Airport.

RAF Ascension Island

Overseas
Motto: *Auxilium Trans Mare* – Help across the sea

Ascension Island is a British airfield but was initially built by some 4,000 US Army Engineers, who commenced in April 1942 and completed in June. The first aircraft to land was a RNAS Swordfish, a month before the airfield named Wideawake was officially opened on 10 July 1942. It provided an important communications link and included a small RAF and RN presence. By the end of the war it is estimated that some 20,000 aircraft transited through Wideawake to and from the USA, en-route to Europe or Africa. The US Forces left and the airfield was decommissioned in May 1947, however, nearly a year later it was used as part of the US Eastern Test Range.

In 1982, the airfield at Ascension provided a vital link for British forces in the South Atlantic, when it was used as a FOB (Forward Operating Base), being the nearest British airfield to the Falklands – though still 3,375 miles away. Its limited facilities were vastly overstretched by Hercules, Nimrods and Victor tankers, with VC.10 C.1s and Belfasts used to fly in urgently needed vital supplies.

In addition to the role of tanker, the Victors flew recce and on the first one flew 7,000 miles – the world's longest reconnaissance mission and, at 14 hours 45 mins, the longest a Victor K.2 had ever flown up until then. The first of six *Black Buck* attacks on Stanley by Vulcans of 195 (A) Composite Squadron were mounted from Ascension on 30 April, although one was aborted. They required eleven Victors to provide the air-to-air refuelling capacity for the single Vulcan plus one spare. A further two Victors were require to support the return on what was then the world's longest bombing mission – 7,900 miles (12,711km). Three Harriers from 1Sqn were also used to provide CAP for the island, while 18Sqn Chinooks helped RN Sea Kings and Wessex in airlifting stores and 202Sqn Sea Kings provided SAR cover.

After the war ended, Ascension was used to provide the launch point for the Hercules Air Bridge, with two Hercules and a Victor required to get each Hercules to Stanley with reserves to return to Ascension if necessary. On completion of the longer runway and improved aids at Mount Pleasant, the Hercules Air Bridge ceased and the flights are mainly carried out by a 216Sqn Tristar or a chartered aircraft.

Ascension Island has no permament aircraft based there, but is a vital staging post for aircraft en-route to Mount Pleasant on the Falkland Islands. Flights from Brize Norton regularly stage through Ascencion. Cargo and resupply vessels also provide stores and fuel supplies for the island.

RAF Barkston Heath

Personnel and Training Command

Barkston Heath originally opened as a RLG for Cranwell in 1941. In April 1943 the flying units from Cranwell moved over, while hard runways were built at the college. Once they returned, preparations

Barkston Heath operates as a satellite from Cranwell and is able to operate with minimal staff actually based on the airfield. It houses the Defence Elementary Flying Training School (DEFTS) with the Firefly 260 two-seat basic trainer.

were made to convert the airfield to a Heavy Conversion Unit and runways were constructed.

When the airfield re-opened in January 1944 the plans had changed and it became known as Station 483 by the USAAF. It became the home to the 9th AF's 61st Troop Carrier Group (TCG) (14, 15, 53 and 59th TCS) equipped with C-47s plus Horsa and CG-4 Hadrian gliders. During the run-up to D-Day it was joined by 349th TCG (23, 312, 313, 314th TCS) with C-46 Commandos. It was also a launch point for 81st and 101 Airborne and elements of the British 1st Airborne Division for Operation *Market Garden*.

Returning to RAF control in June 1945, Barkston Heath 256 MU was established for disposal and operated until December 1948 when it closed. It then reverted to being a RLG for Cranwell and a Sub Depot for 2Sqn, RAF Regt.

In October 1963, 25Sqn was re-formed at North Coates as a SAM unit with Bloodhound missiles and operated 'A' Flight at Barkston Heath from March 1983 until October 1989, when the site then came under 85Sqn as 'D' Flight, which disbanded in December 1990.

Joint Elementary Flying Training School (JEFTS) was established in April 1997 to provide elementary flying training to student pilots of all three services. A fleet of civilian registered T67M II Firefly and Firefly 260s were used and flying carried out at Barkston Heath and Church Fenton. In June 2003 the contract was not renewed by the RAF – all their elementary training is now conducted through the UAS. However, some the services of DEFTS are still used by the RAF for the Multi-Engine Lead-In (MELIN) course at Cranwell, which is run through 45 (R) Sqn. DEFTS continue to occupy Barkston Heath, where they provide elementary pilot training to Army and Navy pilots.

Barkston Heath is home to the Defence Elementary Flying Training School (DEFTS) with the Firefly 260 two-seat basic trainer and is also used a Relief Landing Ground for Cranwell.

RRH Benbecula

2 Group
Strike Command
Motto: *Faireachail* – Watching

Benbecula was originally established as an airfield near to Balivanich, which opened as a grass airfield in 1936. The RAF took it over in 1941 and it was soon operating anti-U-Boat and convoy-escort patrols into the North Atlantic.

In July 1942, 206Sqn arrived with the Fortress and departed in September. In 1943 220Sqn flew the Fortress from March and had departed by September. In September 1944, 304 (Polish) Sqn brought its Wellingtons to Benbecula then departed in March 1945. Also in September, 842 Naval Air Squadron was attached to Coastal Command and operated from Benbecula, departing again the following month. They were immediately replaced by 36Sqn, also with Wellingtons, which it operated until disbanding in June 1945.

In 1947 the airfield returned to civil control and only sees occasional military traffic in conjunction with the South Uist missile range.

Since then then there have been various sites operated by the RAF. The first radar site was at Borve Castle on the southern coast of Uist. The second site was established on the airfield and operated from 1972 until 1982. This was replaced by the third site at Benbecula, located just off the airfield. This housed the CRC but has no radar and was sold in 2003. These have all closed, leaving just the fourth site, which was established at South Clettraval, was initially a Control and Reporting Centre (CRC) and regularly tracked Soviet 'Bears' and transport aircraft. Technology advances provided the ability to transmit the radar picture directly to the mainland and into the UK air defence system. As a result, in 1992 it was downgraded to a Remote Radar Head (RRH) and remains a vital element of the UKADGE. Parented by Buchan, it provides controllers and surveillance officers there with long-range coverage of the North Atlantic. This data is then fed into the Integrated Command and Control System and is used to provide part of the UK's air defence. A further sub-station is also maintained at Aird Uig on the Isle of Lewis and forms part of the NATO Atlantic monitoring network. The installation of a NATO-funded Type 92 long-range radar enabled operations personnel to be finally withdrawn from South Clettraval in May 1999. From September 2004 the reporting chain will change to Boulmer, as Buchan becomes a remote radar-head, although this is planned to change again following the April 2004 announcement that Scampton would be the new location for communications-based units.

Benbecula is a remote radar head.

RAF Benson

Joint Helicopter Command
Motto: *Spectemur Agendo* – Let us be known by our actions

Benson opened in 1939 during the build up of military forces prior to the Second World War. The Battles of 103 and 150Sqn were the first occupants, but were quickly deployed to France as part of the Advanced Air Striking Force. The King's Flight arrived at Benson later that year but was disbanded in 1942. In April 1940, 12 OTU was also formed with Battles and Ansons – replaced with Wellingtons the following year – and departed in August.

In 1941 the Photographic Reconnaissance Unit (PRU) was established at Benson to develop urgently needed quality reconnaissance-photography. They were equipped with Spitfires, specially modified with additional fuel tanks that enabled them to fly long missions over enemy positions. In 1942, 1 PRU was expanded, split into 540, 541, 542, 543 and 544Sqn and deployed detachments to various locations. These squadrons flew huge number of missions all over Europe, gaining vital information about targets before and after attacks by the Allies. On just one mission the pilot was able to fly for three quarters of an hour over Berlin, during which he obtained an almost complete mosaic-coverage of the city.

At the end of the war 540Sqn returned to Benson and was joined by 58Sqn in October with Mosquitos and Ansons. In 1946 the King's Flight was re-formed. October saw 82Sqn re-form from a 541Sqn Flight with Lancasters and Spitfires, which were used for various surveys in Africa, before moving to Kenya in May 1947. In July 1947, 237 OCU was formed to train reconnaissance pilots on the Mosquito and Spitfire, then left the following April. October 1951 saw the formation of the Radar Reconnaissance Flight with Lincolns, departing in March 1952. In 1953 58Sqn departed and the Transport Command Ferry Wing arrived, with the responsibility of delivering aircraft to various units throughout the world. The Wing

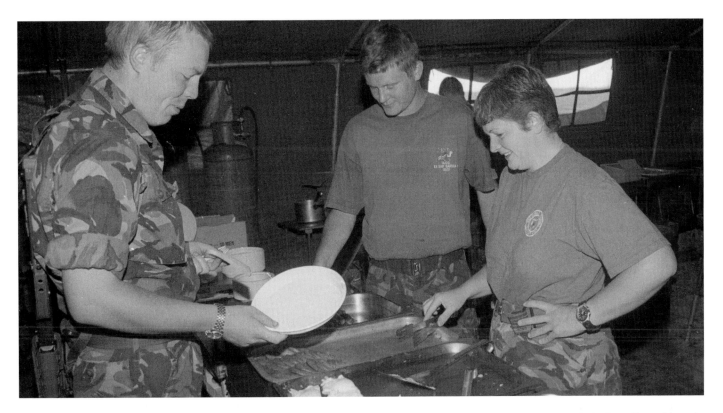

Benson is a larger, more conventional station. Within the station are several tactical units, which permanently maintain a small core-structure but which can rapidly be established to an appropriate size by taking appropriate staff and then be rapidly deployed. The Mobile Catering Support Unit (seen here at Kabul) will relocate to Wittering in 2005 and the Mobile Met Unit to Scampton by 2006.

disbanded in 1960 and November 1961 saw the arrival of the first Argosy C.1 and the establishment of the Argosy OCU – which departed in April 1963. This was followed by 105, 215, 114 and 267Sqn. A Wessex training flight was formed in November 1980 but disbanded again in April 1982.

In January 1983, 115Sqn moved its radar calibration Andovers to Benson from Brize Norton, together with the Andover Training Flight.

In 1992, 60Sqn re-formed with the Wessex HC.2, while London and Oxford UAS, together with 6 AEF, moved across from Abingdon when it closed as an RAF station. In addition, the Mobile Catering Support Unit moved in. In 1993, the Support Helicopter Force HQ arrived from Gütersloh and 115Sqn disbanded in October. In April 1995 the Queen's Flight was disbanded and its aircraft transferred to 32Sqn at Northolt. 60Sqn disbanded in March 1997.

In June 1997, 33Sqn moved across from Odiham with their Puma HC.1s. This was followed by the Operational Conversion

Flight in December. In October 1997, the RWOETU & SH STANEVAL (R&S) Wing was formed to provide the Rotary OEU function as well as training instructors for the SH and SAR units and the SH standards and examining functions. In October 1999, the London UAS moved to Wyton.

New policies saw the opening of the Medium Support Helicopter Aircrew Training Facility (MSHATF) in July 2000. The contract for this was awarded to CAE Aircrew Training Services in October 1997. It represented the first transfer of a complete military function to a commercial contractor, as a Private Finance Initiative (PFI) with a contract to last forty years.

The MSHATF facility includes six simulators – one Puma HC.1, three Chinook HC.2 (two reconfigurable to HC.3) and two Merlin HC.3. These simulators can be operated as stand-alones for single-crew training or can be linked together to provide force training. Various complexities of mission can be rehearsed, which can incorporate 500 computer-generated play-

ers. These can include friendly and hostile forces, radar and SAM sites and even oil rigs.

The contract for the MSHATF eliminates the need for the RAF to incur the high capital-cost of the simulators. Payment is based on an hourly rate with a guaranteed minimum usage. A penalty scale can be applied should the training fail to reach agreed standards. Surplus capacity can be marketed to other approved operators of these helicopter types.

In October 1999, the London UAS moved to Wyton. The first of the new Merlin HC.3 support helicopters arrived in November 2000 for 28Sqn.

Besides the Oxford UAS and 6 AEF, lodger units at Benson include the RAF Infrastructure Organization – formed in January 1997 to manage RAF estate and property and to ensure effective planning and implementation of RAF top-level budgets, DARA, JHC and HQ Northern Ireland Capital Works Programmes. Another is the Support Helicopter Engineering Development and Investigation Team (SHEDIT), which studies and develops engineering solutions to improve safety as well as capability for the Merlin and Puma.

Two Royal Auxiliary AF Units are located at Benson. They are 606Sqn, providing heli-

Despite its old appearance, Bentley Priory retains its high technological capability, being a major unit within the UK's Air Surveillance and Control System (ASACS). It monitors airspace for hundreds of miles to detect and provide early warning of any hostile attack. Crown Copyright

copter support, and the Mobile Meteorological Unit. The latter unit comprises specialists who are able to deploy to provide weather forecasting facilities for RAF units operating from remote airfields.

Benson provides the home for 28Sqn with the Merlin HC.3, 33Sqn with the Puma HC.1, Oxford UAS with the Tutor and 6 AEF, which borrows UAS aircraft on demand.

RAF Bentley Priory

3 Group
Strike Command
Motto: *Traditio Inspirat* – Tradition inspires

Bentley Priory was opened in 1926. It was established on the site of an Augustinian Friars' Priory dating back to the twelfth century, given to private owners by Henry VIII. Having been demolished, a new Priory was built in the 1770s, away from the original site. After various occupants, the Priory became a girls' school in 1908, until it closed in 1922. Having remained empty, the Air Ministry bought the Priory and some forty acres of surrounding land.

HQ Inland Area (part of UK's Air Defences) moved in during May 1926

from Uxbridge and stayed until it returned as Training Command in May 1926. In July, HQ Fighter Command moved in from Uxbridge and was the base for Air Marshal Sir Hugh Dowding during the Second World War.

When Fighter and Bomber Commands were amalgamated into Strike Command, in April 1968, Bentley Priory became the HQ for 11 Group – responsible for the air defence of the UK in time of war. In peacetime it was responsible for the integrity of the UK Air Defence Region (UKADR). It also provided an air-defence capability, as required, overseas. As a result, elements were deployed to the Falklands and Gulf War, as well as the former republic of Yugoslavia (FRY).

In April 1996, 11 Group was amalgamated with 18 Group from Northwood following the end of the Cold War. The Group was then responsible for the air-defence and air-maritime operations within Strike Command. In March 2002 the RAF Inspectorate of Flight Safety became part of the tri-service Defence Aviation Safety Centre.

Bentley Priory has since taken onboard several units, including the Defence Aviation Safety Centre, Air Historical Branch and the RAF Support Unit, in

addition to the supporting Air Battle Management role.

The old house remains and the Dowding Room has been restored as it was in the Second World War. Pre-arranged visits can be made (Tel: 0208 838 7378). Plans are underway for a move of all units to Northolt under project MODEL followed by closure of the site.

Bentley Priory has no flying units.

DCSA Boddington

Personnel and Training Command
Motto: *Aetherem Vincere* – Command of the ether

Boddington became an RAF establishment on 1 July 1969. It first became a military installation in 1940, as a military telephone and telegraph facility manned by the Auxiliary Territorial Service. Prior to that it had been a GPO facility.

In 1949, the operation of the unit passed to the Royal Corps of Signals. The increasing volume of telegraph traffic led to a new telegraph switching-centre, known as 1 Tape Relay Centre, in 1954. In May 1965 the first computerized automatic-routing equipment – the ATS 102 – entered service, enabling work to be undertaken at rate a thousand times faster than the old manual systems.

When the RAF took control of Boddington it was parented by Stanbridge. In 1974, a second-generation computer system – the ADX 6400 – was introduced, followed in 1976 by the Ferranti Argus 600 project, which is a dual-suite system that can automatically reject corrupt messages.

On 1 October it ceased to be parented by Stanbridge. Now being independent, it was designated 9 Signals Unit (9 SU).

January 1992 saw the introduction of the SCICON computer system to replace ADX 6400.

In April 1996, Boddington ceased to be independent and became parented by Innsworth. In 1998, the site and personnel became part of the Defence Communication Services Agency (DCSA) based at Corsham and is now referred to as DCSA 9 Signals Unit Boddington. However, parenting support is still provided by Innsworth.

In 2004, 9 SU became the Primary Management Centre for AMSCERP (Automated Message Switching and ComCen Equipment Replacement Programme), which is used by all Army and RAF units. It currently provides formal 24-hour 365-days per year messaging services to MoD units on fixed and mobile sites worldwide.

Boddington houses 9 Signals Unit.

RAF Boulmer

2 Group
Strike Command
Motto: *Semper in Excubitu Vigilans* – Always the vigilant sentry

Boulmer was originally established as a decoy airfield in 1940, to distract Norwegian-based Luftwaffe aircraft attacking Acklington. In 1943, it began to be used as a relief landing-ground for Spitfires of 57 OTU from Eshott. Concrete runways were built and defence units arrived, but when the war ended Boulmer was closed.

In 1953, the site was re-opened to house 500 Signals Unit and operated as an air-defence control-centre. Steadily, the role of Boulmer developed and by 1957 it had become a Group Control Centre, with radars at Buchan and Killard Point. It then became part of the centralized air-defence system with the construction of one of the new high-powered radars. These included the Type 84 and 85 radars; the latter being part of the Linesman air-defence system, which included a passive detection system

By 1974, Boulmer had been developed into a Sector Operations Centre, as well as

a Control and Reporting Centre (CRC) tasked to detect and monitor Soviet aircraft that probed the UK's air defences and to scramble fighters to intercept them.

When Acklington closed, the Whirlwind HAR.10s of 202Sqn 'A' Flight moved to Boulmer to provide Search and Rescue (SAR) cover. In September 1978 they were re-equipped with the Sea King HAR.3 and, when Finningley closed in 1989, their HQ also moved to Boulmer.

Currently lodged at Boulmer is 1 Air Control Centre (ACC). It provides a mobile command-and-control capability that can be deployed at short notice to anywhere in the world. It was deployed to Iraq in 2003 for Operation *Telic*, where it co-ordinated air defence in southern Iraq.

Another lodger unit that arrived in 1985 is the School of Fighter Control, which provides ground training for Fighter Control and Aerospace System Operators. It is also maintains part of the RAF Air Surveillance and Control System (ASACS) with a standby Control and Reporting Centre (CRC) as part of the UKADGE system, providing air defence for the UK. During 2003, the systems were refurbished with a Modular Airspace Synthetic Environment Trainer. This is to provide improved basic skills-training plus intercept control, as well as identification-officer training.

Within Boulmer's engineering squadron is the Air Defence Ground Environment Maintenance Training School. This is a lodger unit, which is tasked directly from Strike Command to provide pre-employment training of engineering personnel who are posted to air surveillance and control units. A further lodger is the Air Surveillance and Control Safety and Standards Unit (ASSU) Detachment, which independently assesses the ASACS and maintains standards of personnel and procedures, as well as ensuring that the correct rules, regulations and functional safety are applied.

Having undergone a major refurbishment, the air-defence bunker was re-opened in 1993. During the down-time Buchan and Neatishead took operational control and Boulmer operated as a reserve. Following a further upgrade, it is was announced that Buchan is to be downgraded to a Radar Head, resulting in the CRCs operating just from Boulmer and Neatishead with Buchan retaining a back-up capability. Boulmer is responsible for the radar facilities at Brizlee Wood and High Buston.

In April 2004, following an MoD Review, this all changed, with the announcement that all communications-based units would be moved to Scampton. Consequently, 1 ACC will move to Kirton-in-Lindsey as a temporary measure and the School of Fighter Control will move to Scampton by April 2010. Boulmer will lose its CRC to Scampton by 2012 and become a RRH, although the HQ and 'A' Flight of 202Sqn will remain, while Brizlee Wood and High Buston will continue to be operated as RRHs.

Boulmer houses the HQ and 'A' Flight of 202Sqn with the Sea King HAR.3.

RAF Brampton

Personnel and Training Command
Motto: Pride in Service

Work to construct a camp at Brampton commenced in May 1942. Two months later, USAAF personnel began to arrive and a provisional HQ was established in June in the Grange Hotel. This was followed by the activation of USAAF 1st Bomb Wing Headquarters in August. As soon as the war ended most US personnel were returned home, while the 1st BW HQ moved up the road to Alconbury in September 1945.

During the spring of 1946, RAF Technical Training Command HQ moved from Shinfield Park. By 1955, a decision was made to make the establishment permanent and a two-year building programme was initiated, resulting in the old Nissan huts and some of the buildings being replaced.

Once complete in 1957, the Central Reconnaissance Establishment (CRE) and Joint Air Reconnaissance Intelligence (JARIC) became lodgers. In 1968, the Flying Training Command and Technical Training Command merged to become HQ Training Command and occupied a new building. That October, the HQ Air Cadets moved in from White Waltham and occupied the Grange building.

The HQ Air Commander of the Home Defence Forces moved to Brampton from Shinfield Park in July 1968. The CRE disbanded in October 1970 and in 1975 HQ Air Cadets moved to Newton.

In June 1977, Support Command and Training Command merged, resulting in a new Support Command. In October 1985, the HQ building was destroyed by fire and a new building was constructed and completed in February 1988.

Support Command changed its name and role in April 1994 and became HQ Logistics Command, until that too changed. It was subsequently replaced with the tri-service Defence Logistics Organization, which has its HQ in Bath. Also in 1994, nearby Wyton was downgraded and administratively merged with Brampton. In April 2001, Henlow was similarly merged with Brampton.

JARIC produces intelligence from all forms of imagery and supplies trained and experienced service-personnel to provide intelligence in support of operations. It is now part of the Defence Geographic and Imagery Intelligence Agency (DGIA), which was formed on 1 April 2000.

Brampton currently provides an admin function for the three sites. It also provides support for the DLO and JARIC, Defence Security Standards Organization and RAF Infrastructure Organization East Region, plus the flying UAS/AEF/VGS units at Henlow and Wyton.

Brampton is an administration site and has no flying units.

RAF Brize Norton

2 Group
Strike Command
Motto: *Transire Confidenter* – Pass through confidently

Brize Norton officially opened on 13 August 1937, 2 FTS arriving the following month equipped with Audax, Furies and Harts. In October 1938, 6 MU was established and quickly built-up its stock of aircraft, having over 200 by the following February. The FTS began replacing its biplanes with Harvards and Oxfords and was renamed 2 Service Flying Training School (2 SFTS).

In 1940, thirty-five Oxfords and eleven Hurricanes were lost following an attack by two Ju88s. The Heavy Glider Operational Unit (HGOU) arrived in July 1942, with Whitley bombers for use as tugs and Horsa gliders to train army pilots. Albemarles of 296 and 297Sqn replaced the Whitleys in 1943 as tugs, as well as for dropping paras. On D-Day, these squadrons dropped the main body of 5 Para Brigade on Normandy. The HGOU moved out at the end of 1945 and was replaced by the Transport Command Development Unit, with various aircraft.

In September 1947, a USAF C-54 Skymaster made the first fully automatic transatlantic flight and landed at Brize Norton after a 2,400-mile flight without the joint RAF/USAF crew having touched the controls.

Due to the tension that rose from the perceived threat from the Soviet Union, in 1950, USAF personnel began to arrive in preparation for their taking control of the station in April 1951. Their arrival heralded the deployment of B-29/B-50s, B-36s, B-47s, KC-97s and, later, B-52s and KC-135s.

Brize Norton returned to RAF control in 1965 and construction commenced to create the RAF's new principal strategic-transport terminal. This included the base hangar which, at the time, was the largest cantilever structure in Europe. The VC.10 C.1s of 10Sqn arrived in 1967 and were joined by 53Sqn with the Belfast C.1 plus 99 and 511Sqn with their Britannia C.1s and C.2s in 1970. Each of these main types had their own Air Training Squadron (ATS) and, in July 1970, they were merged to form 241 OCU, which borrowed aircraft as required.

Following the 1974 Defence White Paper, the Belfasts and Britannias of 53, 99 and 511Sqn were withdrawn, leaving just the VC.10s. In February 1976, 115Sqn moved in with the Argosy, used for calibration. These were replaced with the Andover in January 1978, prior to their moving to Benson in 1982. Brize Norton's 241 OCU absorbed the Andover ATS and even trained RNZAF crews when some of these aircraft were sold.

In 1976, the Joint Air Transport Establishment (JATE) moved in, along with the Tactical Communications Wing (TCW), RAF Movements School and the No. 1 Parachute Training School (1 PTS). The PTS also added the Falcons parachute display team, which had formed in 1961 and consisted of parachute-jump instructors who volunteered to perform at airshows in their spare time.

Brize became highly active following the Argentinian invasion of the Falklands, with 10Sqn operating a continuous shuttle of their VC.10s to Ascension carrying troops and freight.

Another influx of units came in 1983, with the forming of 2624 Regiment and 4624 Movement Auxiliary AF Squadron. Later in the year 101Sqn was reformed with the VC.10 K.2 and 216Sqn with the Tristar. In addition, 241 OCU received a

pair of BAe.146s to evaluate for potential use by the Queen's Flight. In 1986, 19 RAF Regiment Squadron was established at Brize with the Rapier SAM and tasked with providing air-defence protection for USVFs at Fairford and Upper Heyford.

During this period Brize Norton had grown from a relatively quite station to an extremely busy one. But life was to become even harder following the Iraqi invasion of Kuwait and the subsequent Operation *Granby* – or *Desert Shield/Desert Storm*, as the US called it. Brize's aircraft were heavily utilized and all 101Sqn's tankers were deployed. Despite USAF assistance with their C-5As, a number of charter aircraft were hired-in, including the giant Russia An-124.

In October 1995, 240 OCU was re-named 55 (R) Sqn, but disbanded again in March 1996.

In 1999, Brize Norton became the temporary base for twelve KC-135R Stratotankers of the USAF ANG, which were used to refuel NATO aircraft participating in Operation *Determined Force* to halt the Serbian aggression against other regions in the former Yugoslavia. At the same time 216Sqn Tristars were deployed to Ancona in Italy.

In May 2000, the first of four C-17 Globemasters arrived for the recently reformed 99Sqn. Initial crews were trained in the USA but, almost as soon as they arrived, these aircraft were being tasked, as their capabilities were quickly appreciated.

In 2003, the VC.10 and Tristar tankers were in action over Afghanistan against the Taliban and Al Queda, and over Iraq against the Saddam Hussein regime shortly after. The C-17s were tasked with maintaining an airbridge that was flown virtually on a daily basis. This was especially vital in land-locked Afghanistan, where everything had to be flown in.

During the period after the Gulf War, tankers were also deployed to provide support for combat aircraft patrolling *Northern Watch* and *Southern Watch* over Iraq. This was all in addition to providing a tanker for the Falklands, plus exercises and trails, not only around the UK but abroad as well.

Brize Norton has been home for 1 Parachute Training School since it arrived in 1976, providing para-training primarily for the Army. The instructors also form the RAF Falcons parachute display team, which appears at many airshows and other venues around the country. In addition to using a training hangar at Brize Norton, the nearby airfield at Weston on the Green is used for live jumping. Initially, Skyvans operated by Huntings are used for live jumps, then students progress to the Hercules tasked from Lyneham. Typically, some 10,000 descents are made by 1 PTS staff and students per year.

The RAF Movements School trains personnel from all three services, MoD and other countries in all aspects of air-movement staff. To assist in this the school has a number of transport-aircraft fuse-lages – real and mock-up – for practical loading-training. A variety of loads include time-expired helicopters.

These are two lodger units at Brize Norton. The Joint Air Transport Establishment (JATE) has been a long-time resident at Brize Norton. It is a tri-service unit that designs, trials and documents the techniques of carrying loads in aircraft and helicopters, which are loaned as required.

The other lodger unit is the Tactical Communications Wing (TCW). It is joint Army- and RAF-operated and looks after ground-based communications equipment and radar. It also has a Mobile Communications Flight, which can provide teams to move immediately and establish VHF and HF communications wherever needed in Northern Europe. A further Strategic Communications Flight provides a similar HF communications facility worldwide.

In October 2003, the Integrated Tasking and Operation Centre (ITOC) was established to task and co-ordinate the tanker and transport fleet.

In April 2004, following an MoD Review, it was announced that TCW would move to Scampton in 2006 and linked with the transfer of Hercules from Lyneham, UKMAMS would also move in along with the Tactical Medical Wing (TMW). Also in the announcement was that the VC.10s will remain in service for a further two years pending the arrival of the FSTA programme extending their life until 2013. In June 2005 this changed to

the withdrawal of three VC.10s for critical spares recovery and the amalgamation of 10 Sqn into 101 Sqn. Some of the crew and ground crew will be converted to the Tristar before joining 216 Sqn.

Brize Norton houses 99Sqn with the C-17 Globemaster III, 101Sqn with VC.10 C.1K K.3 and K.4s and 216Sqn with Tristar K.1, KC.1, C.2 and C.2As. It also houses 1 PTS and JATE, which use aircraft from other units as required, plus TCW, 501Sqn and 4624Sqn, R Aux AF.

RAF Buchan

3 Group
Strike Command
Motto: *Au courant* – Well informed

Construction of Buchan commenced in 1952 as an Air Defence Radar Unit and to provide a Ground Control Intercept (GCI) capability as part of the ROTOR Programme. In April 1953, 409 Signals Unit arrived but, due to various delays, it was August 1953 before the site actually became operational.

A Control and Reporting Centre (CRC) was commissioned in Sept 1954, to co-ordinate all aspects of air defence

Brize Norton is the home of the RAF strategic-airlift force, operating C-17s, Tristars and VC.10.s. All require maintenance and the huge base-hangar visible in the top left is able to accommodate a number of these large aircraft.

within the Caledonian Sector roughly north of Newcastle. It uses this information to provide an accurate Recognized Air Picture (RAP) and Weapons Control Capability (WCC) for the United Kingdom's Air Surveillance and Control System (ASACS). This is further co-ordinated with a number of radar units, not only in this country but also Scandinavia, as well as NATO ships and AWACS aircraft, to provide defence of the NATO region.

To assist in this role, Buchan parented the remote radar-heads Saxa Vord in the Shetlands and Benbecula in the Hebrides, which provided further radar coverage. From April 2004 it ceased to parent Saxa Vord and will also lose Benbecula soon. Buchan was one of three operational CRCs, along with Neatishead and Boulmer. However, each could also provide cover should one cease to be operational.

In addition to maintaining an up-to-date RAP, the CRC also have fighter controllers who will provide the tactical control for the fighter jets in any required interceptions, to maintain an effective air-defence.

In 2003, it was announced that a drawdown of personnel would result in a reduced manning level from 400 to just 14 engineering staff by April 2005, due to the change in role of the station. The control and reporting centre will be reduced to a remote radar-head. The CRC service that Buchan was providing was to be transferred to Boulmer, but that changed following an April 2004 announcement that Scampton would be the new centre for communications-based units. From April 2005, Buchan became a remote radar-head.

Buchan is a remote radar-head.

RMB Chivenor

3 Group
Strike Command

Chivenor commenced its existence as a civil airfield, opening in 1934, initially as Barnstaple airfield and then North Devon Airport. It was taken over and expanded by the RAF in May 1940 for use by Coastal Command. Work commenced building the runways and it opened as Chivenor on 1 October. The first arrivals were Blenheims of 3 OTU, along with Ansons and Beauforts.

The Blenheims of 252Sqn arrived in December 1940 and remained for five months, being replaced briefly by 272Sqn with Beaufighters. In July, 3 OTU departed, to be replaced by 5 OTU with Ansons, Beauforts and Oxfords. During November there was excitement when a Luftwaffe Ju88 landed following a night-mission over the Irish Sea. The pilot mistook the North Devon coast for France and provided the RAF with an airworthy bomber that went to Farnborough. In April 1942, 172Sqn was formed with Wellingtons from 1417 Flight, which had only formed there a few weeks previously. The Wellingtons were modified with the Leigh Light in an attempt to locate and attack U-Boats at night. They were first used operationally in June and immediately spotted and began attacking the German submarines. This proved highly successful and detachments were operated from the Azores, Gibraltar and Malta. In May 1942, 5 OTU departed to make space for 51 and 77Sqn, which were temporarily attached to Coastal Command to augment 172Sqn while it was still training with the Leigh Light. They returned to Bomber Command in October. The Beaufighters of 235Sqn arrived in July 1942, to help combat the growing threat from the Ju88s.

Along with several of the Cornish airfields, Chivenor was heavily utilized in providing a refuelling stage for aircraft transiting to Gibraltar and beyond, especially during the lead up to Operation *Torch*, which commenced in November 1942. At the beginning of 1943, 235Sqn departed and was briefly replaced by 404 (RCAF) Sqn with Beaufighters, departing in March. By this time, 172Sqn was receiving Wellingtons fitted with ASV Mk.III radar, which enabled the U-Boats to be detected and approached before the light was turned on to aid the attack – thus maintaining the element of surprise. Fortresses of 59Sqn operated for a few weeks in February, being replaced by 407 (RCAF) Sqn and 547Sqn with Wellingtons, who were joined by 612Sqn in May. June saw 547Sqn departing, while 407Sqn's Wellingtons were fitted with Leigh Lights for U-Boat hunting. In September 1943, 407Sqn departed, followed by 612Sqn in November – both returning several times during 1944. The Wellingtons of 304 (Polish) Sqn arrived in February 1944. As the Allies advanced into Europe, the use of French ports by the U-Boats was curtailed, so their threat diminished in the south west approaches and Bay of Biscay. In September 172Sqn departed and, although it was replaced by 179Sqn in October with Wellingtons, it too departed the following month and was replaced, in turn, by 407Sqn. However, as a result of no enemy sightings it was disbanded the following June. In June 254Sqn arrived with Beaufighters and was joined by 248Sqn the following month with Mosquitos. 248Sqn departed first and was re-numbered 36Sqn in September 1946, while 254Sqn had left by November.

On 1 October 1946, Chivenor was transferred to Fighter Command and soon 691Sqn arrived with Martinets, Oxfords and Spitfires for anti-aircraft co-operation duties. In February 1949 691Sqn was re-numbered 17Sqn, continuing in the role until March 1951, when it was disbanded. Meanwhile, 203 Advanced Flying School (203 AFS) arrived in September 1947 then departed in July 1949.

Chivenor was transferred to Transport Command in 1950 and was occupied by 1 Overseas Ferry Unit but, with most deliveries needed to the East, it soon disappeared. Chivenor returned to Fighter Command and, in March 1951, 229 OCU arrived with Meteors and Vampires. These were augmented by Sabres until the arrival of the Hunter. Various reserve units were formed within the OCU, including 63, 79, 127, 145 and 234Sqn. In September 1974, 229 OCU departed Chivenor to become 1 TWU at Brawdy. With just 'A' Flight of 22Sqn operating the Whirlwind and 624 VGS operating the Cadet and Sedbergh gliders, the airfield entered a period of care and maintenance. This didn't last long, as the airfield underwent a period of re-build from 1979 in preparation for the arrival of Hawks of 2 TWU from Lossiemouth, to teach the advanced-jet pilots the art of delivering ground-attack weapons. The first Hawks arrived in August 1980 with 63 and 151Sqn operating as shadow squadrons within the TWU. In April 1992, 2 TWU was re-numbered 7 FTS and, in September, the shadow squadrons were renumbered 19 and 92 (Reserve) Sqn and moved to Valley in October. Following the departure of the Hawks, Chivenor was transferred to the Royal Marines.

Chivenor currently houses the Sea King HAS.3As of 'A' Flight, 22Sqn and the Vigilant T.1s of 624 VGS.

RAF Church Fenton

Personnel and Training Command

Church Fenton was one of the airfields built in the mid 1930s, in response to the re-armament in Europe. Although incomplete, it was opened on 1 April 1937 and occupied by 72Sqn with Gladiators and 213Sqn with Gauntlets. Their role was to provide fighter cover to protect the industrial region of West Yorkshire as part of 13 Group. In May 1938, 213Sqn left, to be replaced by 64Sqn, who arrived with Demons then converted to Blenheims. In August 1939, 72Sqn converted to Spitfires and departed to be replaced by 242Sqn, which was re-formed in October 1939 with Blenheims, plus 245Sqn. Battles were added and, in early 1940, Hurricanes were being delivered, prior to them both departing by June. In January 72Sqn returned, then departed again in March, while 64, 242 and 245Sqn also left in May. They were replaced by 87Sqn with Hurricanes and 234Sqn with Spitfires.

In August 1940, Church Fenton was transferred to 12 Group for the training of specialist night-fighters using the new radar. Also that August, the first all-Polish unit – 306 (Polish) Sqn – formed with Hurricanes, followed by the first US Eagle unit, in the form of 71Sqn, in September with the Buffalo, although they were soon replaced with the Hurricane prior to departing in November. In December 1940, 4 OTU was formed, but was re-numbered 54 OTU shortly after. It was equipped with a variety of aircraft, including Blenheims, Defiants, Masters and Oxfords.

May 1942 saw the arrival of 25Sqn's Mosquitos, which remained until December 1943. The Spitfires of 308 (Polish) Sqn arrived in April 1943, departing in July, while 307 (Polish) Sqn brought its Mosquitos in May 1944 and departed the following January. In November 1944, 288Sqn arrived with the Vengeance for target towing, continuing to fly it until disbanded in June 1946

In March 1945 63Sqn arrived, but was disbanded the following month.

In April 1946 Church Fenton began operating the jet-powered Meteors of 263 and later 257Sqn, although it wasn't all jets. In April 1947, 19Sqn arrived with Hornets and 3Sqn with Mosquitos. In 1950, 609 Aux AF Squadron arrived with Spitfires before converting to Vampires

briefly. However, by 1951, all were flying the Meteor.

In 1951, 19Sqn replaced their Hornets with the Meteor F.4 and later the Hunter. In January 1957 609Sqn disbanded, 72Sqn continuing with various Meteors until April 1959, when it converted to the Javelin. From July, 60 MU had a presence here but had left again in early 1962. In June 1959, 19Sqn moved to Leconfield and the primary role of Church Fenton changed from fighter to training.

In March 1962, Church Fenton became the home for 7 FTS with Jet Provost T.3s. These were operated until November 1966, when it was disbanded. The CFS's Primary Flying School (PFS) arrived in January 1967 with Chipmunks and was re-numbered 2 FTS in January 1970. In 1968, Yorkshire UAS was formed from the UAS of Hull and Leeds in March 1969 then moved out in August 1975. In April 1973, Royal Navy Elementary Flying Training School (RNEFTS) moved in with Bulldogs, then departed in 1975. In December 1974, 2 FTS were disbanded and the airfield was placed in care and maintenance.

In 1979 Church Fenton was brought back to life when 7 FTS was re-formed with the Jet Provost, to boost the number of pilots needed for the soon to be introduced Tornado. Once this had been achieved the airfield became a victim of the Governments 'Option for Change' – 7 FTS was disbanded once more and the airfield was designated an RLG for Linton-on-Ouse.

Yorkshire UAS returned from Finningley in October 1995, along with 9 AEF, when that airfield was closed. In February 1999 they were joined by a detachment of the JEFTS with the Firefly, which was used to provide elementary training to RAF student pilots. In 2000 the UAS converted to the Tutor T.1 but, in 2003, the RAF contract for the contractorized JEFTS was ended, with the training to be carried out by the UAS organization. As a result the detachment at Church Fenton was closed.

Although the airfield and the immediate buildings are still very active, much of the domestic site has been largely abandoned to nature and it has been offered for sale. The old family quarters were sold to private developers, who refurbished them and sold them on to private owners.

Church Fenton is the home of Yorkshire UAS and 9 AEF, who jointly operate the

Tutor T.1. It is also used as a relief landing ground (RLG) for the Tucano T.1s from 1 FTS at Linton-on-Ouse.

RAF Coltishall

1 Group
Strike Command
Motto: Aggressive in defence

Construction of Coltishall commenced in February 1939 and was planned to be completed as a bomber base. However, events resulted in it being opened in May 1940 for fighters. The Spitfires of 66Sqn were first to arrive, followed by Hurricanes of 242Sqn. The latter consisted of mainly Canadian pilots and was led by Squadron Leader Douglas Bader.

Coltishall was declared fully operational on 23 June 1940 and the same day recorded its first Luftwaffe aircraft destroyed, by a Spitfire of 66Sqn – the first of eighty aircraft destroyed by Coltishall squadrons. During the Battle of Britain, in addition to 66Sqn, Coltishall was briefly home for 72, 74, 242 and 616Sqn. In December, 257Sqn arrived with Hurricanes and stayed almost a year. August 1941 saw the formation of 133 (Eagle), before they took their Hurricanes to Duxford later that month. In March 1942, 68Sqn arrived with Beaufighters and flew with mainly Czech pilots through to February 1945, with just a few short periods elsewhere. It converted to the Mosquito in July 1944.

The arrival of 133 Polish Wing HQ together with 303, 306, 307, 309, 315 and 316Sqn during 1944–5 was a prelude to the station being handed over to the Polish AF in August 1945 and it became known as Coltishall (Polish). In February 1946 the station was returned to Fighter Command and 315 was disbanded in January 1947.

In June 1946, 141Sqn arrived with Mosquitos, later joined by 23Sqn. In September 1951 they were withdrawn and replaced with the Meteor NF.11. During 1957 the runway was lengthened, during which the aircraft operated from Horsham St Faith. At the same time, the squadrons were re-equipped with the Javelin.

The Air Fighter Development Squadron (AFDS) of the Central Fighter Establishment (CFE) arrived, along with the first Lightnings to enter service. These were pre-production models and the first

RAF Coltishall opened in 1940 and in 2000 a Jaguar was painted up in celebration of their sixtieth anniversary. Sadly, Coltishall's days are numbered, as it is due to close around 2008. Kevin Wills

of these arrived on 23 December 1959. On 29 June 1960, 74Sqn became the first operational Lightning squadron. In April 1964, 226 OCU was formed to train pilots to fly the Lightning and, by the time it disbanded in 1974, over 800 pilots had successfully completed the course.

The Historic Aircraft Flight arrived in April 1963 with Hurricanes and Spitfires. 'C' Flight of 202Sqn arrived in 1973 with Whirlwinds to provide SAR. The Lightnings left in 1974 – they were replaced by the Jaguar. On 8 August 1974, 54Sqn was the first Jaguar unit to arrive, followed by 6Sqn in November and, later, 41Sqn in April 1977. However, space was tight, resulting in the HAF, which had by now been re-named Battle of Britain Memorial Flight (BBMF), being moved on to Coningsby in March 1976. In the summer of 2001, 16 (R) Sqn moved down from Lossiemouth, making Coltishall the home of the Jaguar – 6 and 54Sqn concentrating on the strike role and 41Sqn photo reconnaissance.

In 1990, the Jaguars were deployed to the Middle East, as part of the coalition forces to halt the Iraqi invasion forces. A composite squadron was formed and ten Jaguars were painted in a desert-pink camouflage in just five hours, before being flown out.

Having re-equipped with Sea Kings in 1978, the 202Sqn Flight departed in July 1994, as part of the reorganization of the Royal Air Force's search and rescue assets.

Following the transfer of 41Sqn's RIC to Marham in July 2003, 41 Tactical Imagery Intelligence Flight was formed as an independent unit.

Sadly, it was announced that the Jaguar fleet was to be withdrawn, resulting in 16 (R) and 54Sqn being disbanded on 11 March 2005. These will be followed by 41 (F) Sqn in 2006 and 6Sqn towards the end of 2007. Finally, Coltishall will close shortly after the departure of the last Jaguars. While it survived a previously announced closure in the early 1990s, it has been announced that Coltishall will close on 31 December 2006.

Coltishall is home for 6 and 41Sqn, both of which operate the Jaguar GR.3A and the T.4A.

RAF Coningsby

1 Group
Strike Command
Motto: Loyalty binds me

Although construction of Coningsby commenced in 1937, it didn't open as a bomber station with 5 Group until 4 November 1940. 106Sqn with Hampdens.

Manchesters arrived in February 1941 and began converting to Lancasters in May. In March 97Sqn arrived with Manchesters, converting to Hampdens later that year, before taking delivery of Lancasters in January 1942 and departing two months later. Coningsby aircraft took part in the 'Thousand Bomber' raid on Cologne in May 1942, however, from September until the following August flying was all but halted while hard runways were constructed.

The Lancasters of CO Wing Commander Guy Gibson's 617Sqn arrived in August 1943, but moved to Woodhall Spa the following January. A special Marker Force was established at Coningsby; this resulted in a substantial increase in night-bombing success for the rest of the war. This force included 83 and 97Sqn, which arrived in April 1944. They were joined briefly by 61 and 619Sqn in early 1944.

As the war came to a close, Lincolns began to arrive. These were replaced with Mosquitos in 1946, which continued to be operated until March 1950. For six months all was quiet, until the arrival of the B-29 Stratofortress – named Washington in RAF service. These were operated until the arrival of the Canberra in 1953. The following year Coningsby was closed once more while the runways were extended. This and other work resulted in the airfield not opening again until 1956.

Coningsby quickly returned to full activity but, in 1961, the Canberras left, to be replaced the following year by the Vulcans of 9, 12 and 35Sqn. In 1964 these moved out, as the station was being prepared for the arrival of the TSR2 but was placed under Care and Maintenance when the aircraft was cancelled.

Coningsby's future brightened with the decision in 1966 that it would be the first recipient of the Phantom. Following a transfer from Bomber to Fighter Command and more construction, a further change ensued before even the first Phantom arrived. In December 1967, the station was transferred to Air Support Command. Re-formed in February 1968, the first Phantom was delivered to 228 OCU in August 1968. As training progressed and deliveries of aircraft built up, 6Sqn became the first operational unit to convert, in January 1969, followed by 54Sqn in September. The Phantoms of 54Sqn were taken over by 111Sqn from July 1974, when it converted to Jaguars. October 1974 saw Coningsby transfer from 38 Group and the close air-support role, to 11 Group for air defence. In January 23Sqn arrived and 29Sqn replaced 111Sqn when it departed in October 1975.

In March 1976 the BBMF arrived from Coltishall with its historic fleet of Spitfires, Hurricanes and Lancaster.

The year of 1981 saw another building programme, with the construction of Hardened Aircraft Shelters (HAS) and other protective buildings and the resurfacing of the runway. This work was completed in October 1984 and left the station ready for yet another new era.

In November 1984, 229 OCU re-formed, received its first Tornado F.2 and was allocated the shadow squadron identity of 65Sqn. In 1987, 29 (F) Sqn became the first operational squadron to convert from the Phantom to Tornado F.3. Also in April 1987, the shrinking Phantom OCU moved out from Coningsby to Leuchars. The Tornado F.3 Operational Evaluation Unit was formed in April 1987 and, in December, 5 (AC) Sqn arrived and re-equipped with the Tornado F.3.

During *Desert Storm*, 5 (AC) and 29 (F) Sqn were both active, flying CAP for the troops and aircraft. They have also been deployed to Gioia del Colle to police the no-fly zones over Bosnia and Iraq. They also provide support for 1435 Flight in the Falklands. The ex-satellite airfield at Woodhall Spa is no longer active, but a facility for maintaining and repair of the RB.199 engines has been established there.

On 1 July 1992, 229 OCU, which had 65Sqn identity, was re-numbered 56 (Reserve) Sqn.

In October 1998 29 (F) was disbanded, followed by 5Sqn on 28 September 2002. On 27 March 2003, 56 (R) Sqn moved to Leuchars, the BBMF to Barkston Heath and the Tornado OEU to Waddington, while work on the runway was carried out for the Typhoon. This marked the end of operational Tornado flying at the station. With the runway completed in March 2004, the Tornado F.3 OEU returned on 1 April, to become the Fast Jet and Weapons OEU whon amalgamation with the SAOEU from Boscombe Down and the Air Guided Weapons OEU from Valley. Coningsby is currently undergoing further preparations for the arrival of the Typhoon, prior to the arrival of 17 and 29 Reserve Squadron.

It has been announced that 6 Sqn Jaguars will arrive from Coltishall by 31 March 2006, then disband towards the end of 2007.

Coningsby is home to the Fast Jet and Weapons OEU, with the Tornado F.3 and GR.4 and the Harrier GR.7, plus the BBMF, which operates five Spitfires, two Hurricanes, a Lancaster, a Dakota and two Chipmunk T.10s. The BBMF also has a small museum. It will also be to home for 17 and 29 (R) Sqn with the Typhoon.

JSU Corsham

Personnel and Training Command

Corsham was originally a quarry site, providing the much sought-after Bath stone. During the First and Second World Wars this quarry and a number of adjacent ones were used to store munitions and were referred to as the Central Ammunition Depot. As it was next to Box Tunnel on the London to Bristol railway line it had its own railway spur. On the surface, the main building was designed to resemble a monastery.

Brown Quarry had links underground and housed an RAF Sector Command, while Spring Quarry was a Ministry of Aircraft Production factory with Bristol Aircraft Co building engines. Later, Spring Quarry became a store for the Royal Navy. Subsequently, part of this site was developed as one of the Hawthorn Central Government (War) Headquarters (GCHQ) sites and this still exists, although it is now kept on a care and maintenance basis.

The Tunnel Quarry site was retained by MoD, with part referred to as the Corsham Computer Centre, while the other is operated as Rudloe Manor, previously an RAF station until 1998.

Corsham currently houses the Defence Communication Services Agency (DCSA), which was formed in 1997 to provide an integrated communications service to all three services. It is a Direct Administered Unit of P&TC Command.

Corsham is now a Joint Support Unit and provides support to a variety of units, especially those in the communications business, who occupy the majority of the site. It remains a Direct Administered Unit of P&TC Command with an Admin Department to support the RAF elements of the JSU.

RAF Cosford

Personnel and Training Command
Motto: *Seul le premier pas coute* – Only the beginning is difficult

Cosford was opened in 1938 to provide technical training, as well as storage and maintenance. No. 2 School of Technical Training (2 SoTT) was established in February with a planned strength of 4,000 personnel. This has remained the bread and butter of Cosford ever since. Storage and maintenance was provided by 9 MU.

During the war Spitfires were assembled, followed later by Horsa gliders in preparation for carrying troops on D-Day. A major military hospital was built in 1940 and provided a valuable facility for the military and the local community until 1977. At the end of the war Cosford played a major part in the repatriation of prisoners-of-war.

Despite the major cuts in RAF personnel at the end of the war, Cosford has been maintained as a centre of training, which in more recent years has been expanded. In 1965, it commenced Avionics Apprentice training and, in 1994, the aircraft engineering training of 1 SoTT at Halton completed its movement to Cosford. This resulted in the re-naming of the 2 SoTT to 1 School of Technical Training (1 SoTT). This was followed by ground electronic and communications training transferring from Locking into a new state-of-the-art facility.

Cosford became the RAF's largest ground-training station and consisted of three schools. These were the No. 1

School of Technical Training, 1 Radio School, the Joint School of Photography and the RAF School of Physical Training.

The 1 SoTT, whose roots date back to Halton in March 1920, has provided basic, further, and advanced-further training courses for a range of disciplines for new recruits and for further training. For this the school ran a number of units, comprising the Principles and Advanced Training Squadron, Engineering Skills Training Squadron, Airframe Training Squadron, Avionics Systems & Electrical Training Squadron, Propulsion & Weapon Training Squadron, Line Training Flight and Airfield Flight. Besides having gained the appropriate skills, at the end of the courses the students are awarded a range of certificates ranging from City and Guilds, through BTEC and HNC to NVQ. The students are trained using a number of grounded instructional airframes, which include the Andover, Dominie, Gnat, Harrier, Jaguar, Jet Provost and Tornado. On 1 April 2004, 1 SoTT became an establishment within the tri-service Defence College of Aeronautical Engineering (DCAE).

The newly formed DCAE has its HQ at Cosford and, in addition the former 1 SoTT, it is now responsible for aeronautical training at St Athan (formerly 4 SoTT), plus the Army AE training at Arborfield Garrison and RN AE training at HMS Sultan. It continues to provide the breadth of training of 1 SoTT and time will see some rationalization of training courses run at the various locations.

In addition to the regular RAF units, Cosford houses lodgers in the form of the Air Cadets Regional Headquarters (Wales and West) and Headquarters West Mercian Wing Air Training Corps.

A further substantial occupier of space and hangars on a sectioned-off part of the airfield is the RAF Museum Cosford, which opened in 1979. This impressive museum contains a substantial collection of aircraft, including many rare research and captured enemy Second World War aircraft. It is a reserve for the RAF's main museum at Hendon, although it is highly unlikely that many will be moved. When the restoration facility at Cardington closed in 2000, the Michael Beetham Conservation Centre was established at

Cosford to continue the valuable work. While this not normally open to visitors, pre-arranged tours can be made (Tel: 01 902 376 200 for details).

Cosford is the HQ of DCAE and the school has a number of time-expired airframes – some of which are taxied. It is also home to the Birmingham UAS with the Tutor and 8 AEF, who borrow UAS aircraft on demand, plus 633 VGS with Vigilant T.1s. The RAF Museum maintains a large museum on the airfield.

RAF Cottesmore

1 Group
Strike Command
Motto: We rise to our obstacles

Cottesmore was opened 11 March 1938 as a bomber station within 2 Group. In April 1938, 35 and 207Sqn arrived with Wellesleys. These were quickly replaced with Battles but, by September 1939, both had departed. They were replaced by 185Sqn with Ansons, Hampdens and Herefords. By the end of the year this had become 14 OTU. Also in September 106Sqn arrived with Hampdens, but departed the following month.

In May 1942, 14 OTU provided Hampdens to take part in the 'Thousand Bomber' raids on Bremen, Cologne, Dusseldorf and Essen. Altogether, 14 OTU flew 151 sorties, losing nine aircraft and twenty-three aircrew. Later that year it re-equipped with Wellingtons, then departed at the beginning of August as preparations were being made for the airborne assault into Europe. Cottesmore had been selected as a storage centre for the Horsa glider.

A year later, in September 1943, with the invasion of Europe still looking some way off, the USAAF HQ Troop Carrier Command took over the airfield as Station 489. The 316th Troop Carrier Wing arrived (36, 37, 44 and 45 TCS), operating the C-47 Skytrain and C-53 Skytrooper. Large numbers of American paratroops were accommodated just prior to the D-Day landings in Normandy. CG-5 Hadrian gliders were launched for Operation *Market Garden* and over 1,300 paratroops were dropped. Within days after the end of the war the Americans were returning home.

Cottesmore returned to the RAF and 1668 HCU moved in with Lancasters. It

Technical training at Cosford is now carried out by the Defence College of Aeronautical Engineering (DCAE). A number of time-expired airframes are utilized to enable trainees to undertake some of their practical training on real aircraft, such as the Harrier GR.3. Crown Copyright

was replaced by 16 OTU with the Mosquito and Oxford briefly, before 7 FTS arrived in 1948 with Tiger Moths and then the Prentice, Harvard and Balliol. In March 1954, 7 FTS moved out, to be replaced by Canberras from 15, 44, 57 and 149Sqn, but their stay was brief, as they had all departed by February 1955.

Cottesmore had been selected to be a V-bomber base and the runway was extended before 10 and 15Sqn were re-formed in 1958 with Victors. By October 1964 they had both disbanded and were replaced by the Vulcans of 9, 12 and 35Sqn. These Vulcans were deployed to the Far East during the Indonesian confrontation in 1965 and, by 1969, all three squadrons had moved to Akrotiri.

May 1969 saw the arrival of 231 OCU with Canberras to Cottesmore, which was transferring to 90 (Signals) Group. This was followed by the arrival from Watton of 115Sqn with the Argosy and Varsity and then 98 and 360Sqn with Canberras. However, another round of changes saw 360Sqn leave in September 1975, 98Sqn disband in February 1976 and 231 OCU depart along with 115Sqn's Argosies, leaving the airfield empty.

An agreement was reached whereby Tornado flight crews from the RAF, German AF and Navy, plus the Italian AF would complete their operational training at a single unit. Cottesmore had been selected and preparations commenced from 1976 for the introduction of the Tornado GR.1. The unit was to be the international Tri-National Tornado Training Establishment (TTTE). The first course commenced in October 1980; it

Cranwell is where Trenchard established his cadet college to provide basic officer and flying training. Cranwell continues in this role and strives to be a centre of excellence.

could take students who had never flown a Tornado and, by the end of thirteen weeks, teach them everything they needed to know, from flying low-level to avoid detection by hostile radar to formation flying.

The TTTE disbanded on 31 March 1999 after training almost 3,500 aircrew, following the decision to relocate the training to home nations. The Tornados were rapidly replaced by the Harrier GR.7s from 3 and 4Sqn returning from Laarbruch, which was closing as part of the withdrawal of forces from Germany. Several months later, 1 (F) Sqn moved in from nearby Wittering.

It was also proposed that the Royal Navy Sea Harrier FA.2s of 800 and 801Sqn from Yeovilton were to move to Cottesmore from 2003, to form the Joint Force 2000 as outlined in the Strategic Defence Review. However, a subsequent announcement of the early withdrawal of the Sea Harriers by 2006 resulted in the move being cancelled as uneconomic and the combined squadrons were then referred to as Joint Force Harrier (JFH). From November 2004 the major servicing of Harriers transferred from St Athan to Cottesmore.

At the end of 2003, 3Sqn joined a mixed force with Jaguars and Tornados on an annual exercise in Jordan and returned in January. Within a short time they were being deployed back to the same region as part of the Harrier force on Operation *Telic*.

The Harriers are undergoing a mid-life

upgrade that will see then being converted to GR.9/GR.9A. 3 (F) Sqn is due to become a Royal Navy squadron in 2006.

Cottesmore is the home of 1 (F), 3 (F) and 4 (AC) Sqn, each of which operate thirteen Harrier GR.7/GR.7As and a single T.10. It is also home to 504 (County of Nottingham) Sqn, R Aux AF.

RAF Cranwell

Training Group Defence Agency
Personnel and Training Command
Station motto – *Alitum Altrix* – Nuturer of the winged
College motto – *Superna Petimus* – We seek higher things

Cranwell was originally built as an RNAS training station, following its acquisition by the Admiralty in November 1915. It opened on 1 April 1916, as the RNAS Central Training Establishment Cranwell, to train naval officers to fly all types of aircraft, as well as balloons. Unnamed naval establishments were borne on the books of HMS *Daedalus*, a depot-ship hulk in the Medway, and, as a result, the site became incorrectly known as HMS *Daedalus*. A Boys' Training Wing was also formed, to train ratings as air mechanics and riggers. When the RAF was formed on 1 April 1918, it was transferred from the Navy, re-named Cranwell and continued with the training role.

When the First Wold War ended, Trenchard selected Cranwell as a cadet college to provide basic officer and flying training. Cranwell became the first Military Air Academy in the world when the first course commenced on 5 February 1920 – now referred to as 'Founders Day'. In 1922 it was decided to commence developing Cranwell as a permanent college, a decision that led to the laying of the foundation stone for the College Hall in 1929 and its official opening on 11 October 1934 by HRH The Prince of Wales.

While it was an RNAS establishment a volunteer orchestra was established; this continued when it was transferred to the RAF. On 5 February 1920 the RAF College Band was officially formed. During the Second World War they provided many moral-boosting concerts and marches, and, during Operation Granby, they became medical assistants and stretcher bearers.

The Electrical and Wireless School was based at Cranwell from November 1938. It operated a range of semi-obsolete aircraft, such as the Wapiti, Hendon, Valencia and Wallace. It subsequently became 1 Signals School in September 1940, adding types such as the Harvard, Wellington and Whitley, and then became 1 Radio School in March 1941, with Bothas, Halifaxes and Ansons included. In December 1938, the HQ for 21 Group Training Command was re-formed at Cranwell and remained until July 1944.

The College itself closed in September 1939; however, training continued at Cranwell with the establishment of the RAFC SFTS, flying Ansons, Blenheims, Magisters and Spitfires and operating through to May 1945. Cranwell also housed a number of other units. These included 2 Flying Instructors School in September 1940 with the Monospar, Oxford and Tutors, which two months later became 2 CFS and continued until June 1941.

During this period the Gloster E28/39 arrived at Cranwell, where the W1 flight engine was fitted; it was first flown on 15 May 1941 – the first flight of a British jet aircraft.

In August, 3 Coastal Officers Training Unit was established, along with 3 Operational Air Training Unit, with the Anson, Lysander, Martinet, Wellington and Whitley. Both departed in June 1943. In January 1943, 1 Radio School became 6 Radio School, operating Halifaxes, Hurricanes, Masters and Oxfords. The

Beam Approach Technical Training School was established in January 1944 with Oxfords. In March 1944 the Officers Advanced Training School was established with Magisters, Masters, Mustangs, Proctors and Spitfires. At the same time 17 SFTS arrived with a variety of aircraft, including the Blenheim, Beaufort, Hector and Tiger Moth. It was joined by 19 FTS in May 1945 with Ansons, Harvards and Tiger Moths. By June 1947 both had departed.

The College officially reopened in April 1947 and, in July 1948, King George V1 presented the College with his Sovereign's Colour – the first such award to any RAF unit.

As with most wars, technology advanced apace. As a result it was desirable that all officers of the main branches should be trained together. During the 1960s, the number of initial officer training units reduced and the more specialist training was undertaken at Cranwell. Rising standards of civilian education and aspirations resulted in the recruitment of a higher proportion of university graduates. In September 1970, No. 101 Entry became the final intake of flight cadets and, in the 1970s, Cranwell became the gateway to the RAF for most graduates. From December 1979, further rationalization of officer training resulted in all initial officer training being undertaken at Cranwell. This remains the case today, with entrants coming direct from school, university or civilian employment, together with serving airmen and airwomen.

The airfield at Barkston Heath became parented by Cranwell in 1949 and is operated as a satellite of Cranwell.

Currently Cranwell houses a number of units, including the Directorate of Recruiting and Selection, which incorporates the Officers and Aircrew Selection Centre (OASC), the Officers and Air Crew Training Unit (OACTU), No. 1 Elementary Flying Training School (1 EFTS), Headquarters Central Flying School (CFS), Headquarters Air Cadets, and the Department of Specialist Ground Training (DGST). Lodger units include the Air Warfare Centre and the Band of the RAF Regiment.

For those wishing to join the RAF as a Direct Entry officer the OASC is the first stage. They make the initial selection for both Ground Branch and Aircrew. Having successfully passed the initial stage, cadets will spend twenty-four weeks with

OACTU. Here cadets will be trained to become officers by developing their management and leadership skills, as well as their commitment. On successful completion they graduate and progress on to towards their chosen career.

For Ground Branch Officers, they will proceed to the DSGT for their specialist training. For aircrew, they will proceed to the UAS for their elementary flying training.

During January 2003, Cranwell began receiving the King Air T.1 to replace the Jetstreams of 45 (R) Sqn.

Cranwell is the home for 3 FTS, which comprises 45 (R) Sqn with the King Air T.1, 55 (R) Sqn with the Dominie T.1, a CFS Tutor Flight that, together with the Navigator and Aircrew School, uses the Tutors loaned from RAFC AS and RAF College Air Squadron with the Tutor. East Midlands UAS is also based there with the Tutor, along with 7 AEF, who borrow aircraft on demand.

RAF Croughton

USVF

Personnel and Training Command

Construction of Croughton airfield was undertaken in 1938 on land previously occupied by three farms. It was initially referred to as Brackley landing ground and was used by Harts and Hinds once it had opened.

In 1940, it was used by 16 OTU as a satellite for Upper Heyford, to train Commonwealth pilots to fly using Blenheims, Hampdens and Wellingtons. In 1941 it became known as Croughton. From 1942, the airfield was used for glider training by 23 Group, using Hotspur and Horsas of 1 Glider Training School. Dakotas, Hectors, Harvards and Masters were used for the aero tows.

With the war ended, flying ceased and the airfield was used to store ammunition. In January 1951, the airfield was transferred to the USAF, who used it to establish a communications base for the USAF in Europe.

'Radio' Croughton has provided information on flight patterns, weather conditions, clearances and flight levels covering more than two million square miles of Atlantic Ocean. Croughton also provides links with the USA and nearly 30 per cent of all US military communications between Europe and the USA. It has also provided support for three of the Apollo missions.

The end of forty-nine years of manned HF communications came on 14 December 2000 with the beginning of the System Capable of Planned Expansion, or SCOPE, Command era. This new automated-system provides a similar service to aircrew, but no longer needs manning at Croughton. Instead, communications specialists at Central Net Control Station, Andrews Air Force Base, Md run the system, with only maintenance support needed on site. Besides the service to aircrew, emergency aid has also been provided to drifting yachtsmen and downed balloonists.

Croughton parents outstations at Barford St John, Chelveston, Daventry, and Uxbridge.

Croughton is assigned to the 100th ARW at Mildenhall and is manned by the 422nd Air Base Squadron (ABS).

RAF Daws Hill

USVF
Personnel and Training Command

The site of Daws Hill was opened in May 1942, purchased from a local school. Designated Station 101, it was occupied by the HQ of the USAAF's 8th Bomber Command, which became the 8th AF. Daylight missions all over Europe were co-ordinated from an underground bunker.

In 1945, the USAAF left the site and it was returned to the school. In 1952, the Americans returned to use Daws Hill for Strategic Air Command's (SAC) 7th Air Division supported by 3939th ABS. In June 1965, it was deactivated and Daws Hill was transferred to 3rd AF supported by 7563rd ABS. In August 1966, they were joined by 322nd Airlift Division of MATS. Following the 322nd's deactivation in December 1968, the site remained dormant until 1975, apart from the arrival

of the DoD's London Central High School. In July 1975, 7500th ABS arrived and Daws Hill became a Detachment of the 20th TFW until April 1984, when it was re-designated 7520th ABS. In June 1987, it reverted to 3rd AF control until June 1993, when the 7520th ABS was deactivated.

In July 1993, Daws Hill was taken over by the US Navy, who currently occupy it as a storage and supply unit.

Daws Hill is a USVF ground station occupied by the US Navy.

RAF Digby

Personnel and Training Command
Motto: *Icarus Menatus* – Icarus reborn

Digby was originally opened on 28 March 1918 as Scopwick and was referred to as 59 Training Depot with the Avro 504, FE.2b and Handley Page 0/400. However, in 1917, it was being used as a RLG for the RNAS at Cranwell. A number of squadrons returned home from France and Germany in 1919 and were disbanded by

Flying at Croughton ended soon after the Second World War. It was transferred to the USAF in the early 1950s and has remained a communications base ever since.

January 1920. These included 11, 25, 203, 209, 210 and 213Sqn.

In April 1920, Scopwick was renamed Digby. It resumed training with 3 FTS, operating Avro 504s, Snipes and F.2b Fighters, until 1922 and, following a period of care and maintenance, 2 FTS from 1924 until 1937. In August 1937, it became a 12 Group Sector Fighter Base and saw the arrival of 46 and 73Sqn with Gauntlets and Gladiators, joined by 504Sqn in September 1939 with Hurricanes and 611 (West Lancashire) Sqn in October with Spitfires. In November 229Sqn re-formed with Blenheims. Having converted to Hurricanes, 46 and 73Sqn departed in June 1940, along with 229Sqn, and were replaced by 29Sqn with Blenheims, followed by 151Sqn with Spitfires converting to Defiants. During this period of the Battle of Britain, 56, 79, 111, 222Sqn also made short visits. In December, 46Sqn returned for a few months.

Digby became heavily utilized by RCAF units from 1940. First to arrive was 2Sqn RCAF, which was re-numbered 401 the following March to avoid confusion with RAF squadrons. This was followed by 1Sqn RCAF which became 401 – both flew the Hurricane. In June, 409Sqn formed with Defiants, along with 411 and 412Sqn with Spitfires. All had departed by November and were replaced by 92 and 609Sqn with Spitfires and 288Sqn, which formed with Blenheims, Hurricanes and Lysanders. Hudsons replaced the Blenheims and were joined by Defiants and Oxfords before 288Sqn departed in March 1942. Some of the RCAF squadrons returned for short periods, along with short stays by RAF squadrons, including 19, 167, 242, 310, 349, 350 and 416 with Spitfires, 198 with Typhoons. In January 1943, 288Sqn returned with various aircraft for Army co-operation and was replaced by 116Sqn in 1944.

A further influx of Canadians to Digby saw more units form, including 438Sqn in November 1943 with Hurricanes. It was followed by 441, 442 and 443Sqn with Spitfires in February 1944. In April 1944, 527Sqn arrived with various aircraft for radar-calibration duties in south and south-east England, along with 528Sqn. The two were merged to form an enlarged 527Sqn in September, which now included types ranging from Wellingtons to Hornet Moths.

With the war approaching an end, Digby reverted to the training role with the arrival of 1 Officers Advanced Training School (1 OATS) in July 1945. It was joined by 19 Flying Training School the following January with Tiger Moths. In 1947, 1 OATS closed and was replaced by 1 Initial Training School in October 1947, which was, in turn, replaced by 2 Initial Training School in September 1950, then 2 Air Grading School with Tiger Moths in February 1951. All flying came to an end at Digby at the end of 1953.

The station was transferred to 90 (Signals) Group and, in 1955, 399 Signals Unit (399 SU) arrived. This was later joined by 591 SU, providing the RAF with various communications functions. Both are now part of the Joint Services Defence Communication Services Agency with its HQ at Corsham.

In September 1959, the Aerial Erectors School arrived. It currently provides a range of courses ranging from the fourteen-week Basic Erector Course and twenty-three-week Aerial Erector Further Training Course, to the two-week Advanced Fibre Optics Course. In addition, it provides a range of aptitude and safety courses. The aptitude test takes place using a 100m (365ft) tower that was built in the 1930s as part of the Chain Home Defence System at Stenigot and is now a Grade 2 listed building.

In 1995 a project commenced to restore the former Operations Room and the Fighter Direction Post back to their Second World War condition. In May 1997, it was opened as a Museum, although some restoration work still continues. (Tel: 01526 327262 for details.)

In September 1998, 399 SU was renamed to the Joint Service Signals Unit (JSSU) to reflect its tri-service operation. Also based at Digby are members of the US armed forces, who work alongside members of the JSSU and 591 SU.

Digby is home to 591 SU, the Aerial Erector School and JSSU.

RAF Donna Nook

1 Group
Strike Command
Motto: Defend and Strike

The use of Donna Nook commenced in 1926, when it was used as an air-to-ground target facility for 1 Air Gunnery Training School based at North Coates. In 1936, a relief landing ground (RLG) was established for use by North Coates and, in 1938, plans were made for the airfield to be developed into a bomber station with concrete runways, but this did not proceed.

Donna Nook was established as a decoy airfield in 1940 before being taken over by Coastal Command, with whom various aircraft were operated, including a detachment of Hudsons from 206Sqn, from August 1941 for almost a year. When concrete runways were being built at North Coates, the three Beaufighter squadrons of the 16 Group Strike Wing (143, 236 and 254Sqn) operated out of Donna Nook. From 1944 the airfield housed some 3,000 prisoners of war, until it closed in 1945.

The bombing range at Donna Nook continued to be used and was administered by Theddlethorpe but, following the closure of that station, Donna Nook became established in its own right in 1974. The range currently comprises some 10km of coastline and, despite its role, a large proportion of its area has remained undisturbed. EOD personnel from Coningsby regularly work at the range to dispose of any live weapons that come to light.

In July 2002, the range became the first National Nature Reserve on MoD land, in recognition of the undeveloped landscape that was providing homes to many species of birds, animals and plants. Donna Nook is jointly managed with the Lincolnshire Wildlife Trust.

Donna Nook is an air weapons range.

RAF Fairford

USVF
Personnel and Training Command

Fairford was originally the site for the US 32nd Field Hospital, opened on 16 September 1943 and operated until May 1944. Construction of the runways also commenced in 1943 and, on 18 January 1944, the airfield opened as one of fourteen sites in the Berkshire, Wiltshire and Gloucestershire area to house British and American troop carriers and gliders in readiness for D-Day. For some reason the main runway was not aligned into the prevailing wind, which still results in problems for pilots of some aircraft today.

The first of fifty Stirlings from 620Sqn arrived on 18 March, joined by 190Sqn with 100 Horsa gliders a week later, to enable RAF and Army Glider Pilot Regiment crews to undergo a period of intense training. On 2 June the airfield was sealed off. However, bad weather resulted in a delay until 5 June, when 887 paratroops of the 6th Airborne Division were flown out to Normandy by forty-five Stirlings towing Horsas. The next day saw SAS raiding-party drops in France, Belgium and Luxembourg.

In mid-September 1944, preparations were underway for the second major airborne-force operation at Arnhem, code-named Operation *Market Garden*. Fairford was sealed again on 16 September and, the following day, commenced with the dispatch of pathfinders, airborne troops and their equipment.

With the war in Europe over, flying all but came to a halt, until September 1946 when 47Sqn arrived with Halifaxes, followed by another three units, including 295Sqn, to make Fairford the RAF's airborne-forces base in the UK. But all departed in September 1948, leaving just a care and maintenance party.

In June 1950 Fairford opened once more. Work was undertaken to extend the runway in readiness to receive USAF aircraft from SAC. In February 1953, B-36s deployed on exercise – one crashing nearby in bad weather. In June, forty-five B-47 Stratojets arrived with KC-97 Stratofreighter tankers in support. The deployment lasted ninety days, but the increased tension of the Cold War saw further deployments. In 1954, the USAF deployed nuclear weapons to UK airfields. By 1964, the threat had diminished, the USAF deployments ended and the 3919th Combat Support Group, which looked after the airfield, disbanded.

In June 1964, the airfield reverted back to RAF occupation with the arrival of the CFS Gnats. The following year saw the arrival of the Red Arrows and, between 1969 and 1976, the airfield was used for Concorde test-flying. From September 1978 it provided a base for USAF KC-135s.

Fairford has continued to be maintained as a NATO Forward Operating Base (FOB) by the 424th Air Base Squadron and has seen a variety of USAF aircraft deploy for various exercises. These have included B-1s, B-2s, B-52s, C-130s, F-111s, KC-10s, KC-135s and U-2s. In 1986,

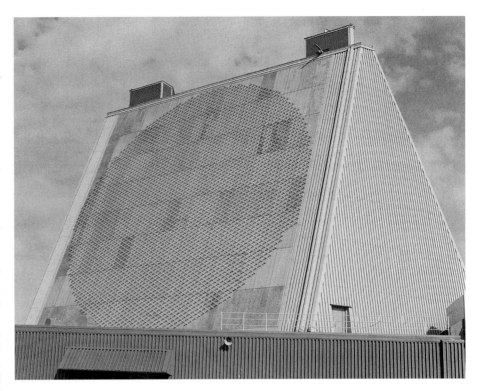

Fylingdales used to have large 'golf ball'-like structures. In the mid-1980s they were replaced by large Solid State Phased Array Radar for use by the Ballistic Missile Early Warning Squadron (BMEWS). Crown Copyright

tanker elements of the *Eldorado Canyon* raid on Libya flew from Fairford and, in addition, *Desert Storm* saw B-52s operating over Iraq and *Determined Force* saw operations over Kosovo in 1998. Commencing in June 2000, the airfield underwent a major upgrade of its runways and taxiways. It has since seen further deployment of B-1s and B-52s during Operation *Enduring Freedom* in Afghanistan and, most recently, Operation *Iraqi Freedom*.

Fairford is currently a NATO standby base that is occupied by the USAF. No aircraft are based there, but deployments arrive for exercises or operational reasons. Fairford is also an emergency diversion base for NASA's Shuttle.

RAF Fylingdales

3 Group
Strike Command
Motto: *Vigilamus* – We are watching

Fylingdales was opened within the North York Moors National Park in 1962 and declared fully operational in September 1963 with the Ballistic Missile Early

Warning Squadron (BMEWS). Prior to this, the site was an MoD artillery range dating back at least as far as the First World War. For this new role it was equipped with large phased-array radars that were mounted inside large radomes which, due to their appearance, were nicknamed 'golf balls'.

In 1986 a major upgrade to the facility saw the end of the 'golf balls', which housed 112-ton scanners, and their replacement by a single pyramid-like structure with a Solid State Phased Array Radar (SSPAR) mounted on its three surfaces.

Fylingdales is a non-flying station operating the BMEWS.

RAF Gibraltar

Overseas
Motto: Guard the gateway

The history of flying at Gibraltar dates back to 1903, when two officers and sixteen NCOs arrived to operate a captive balloon from the southern end of the Rock for reconnaissance. A seaplane base was

Gibraltar is the gateway to the Mediterranean and has been considered a vital strategic position. Despite a public road across the runway, the airfield frequently has RAF aircraft deployed on training exercises.

established by the RNAS in 1915 at North Front, with Short Seaplanes and Curtis H4 flying boats that were used for submarine spotting. A few Caudrons and BE.2cs were also operated from the racecourse.

In August 1918, 265Sqn became Gibraltar's first RAF unit when it was formed with Short 184s and Felixstowe F3s from the various RNAS Flights. It didn't last long – disbanding in January 1919.

During the 1920s, the Governor of Gibraltar and his counterpart in Algeciras planned to construct a landing strip, but this was rejected by both governments. However, in 1931, permission was granted for an air passenger-service to Tangier. This was operated from the racecourse, but suspended after just three months due to maintenance problems.

In September 1934, a grass strip was constructed, completed in March 1936 and followed by the arrival of 210Sqn with Rangoons and Singapores. But it wasn't until 1939 that construction of the first of two RAF camps commenced at North Front Camp – on land that was previously a racecourse and included a solid runway. Shortly after, construction of a second camp commenced on reclaimed land, next

to Montague Bastion and named New Camp.

In September 1939, 202Sqn arrived equipped with Londons and was joined by 3 Anti Aircraft Co-operation Unit flying the Swordfish. Additional Swordfish arrived for 202Sqn, plus another unit in the form of the Navy's 810Sqn, followed by a detachment from 228Sqn with Sunderlands. In July 1940, 202Sqn over-flew the French port of Oran to photograph the Vichy warships, which were subsequently attacked by the RN to prevent them falling into German hands. In April 1941, 202Sqn started to convert to Catalinas.

In 1940, most of the civilian population of Gibraltar was evacuated to Jamaica and Madeira, as well as the UK, and replaced by British servicemen. Gibraltar became an important transit-base for aircraft flying on to the Middle and Far East. The runway was extended into the sea with a large quantity of the rock obtained from the expanded network of tunnels constructed in the Rock. By 1942, over 30,000 service-men were based at Gibraltar – most of whom were accommodated within the rock.

Spitfires arrived in crates and were

hastily assembled, prior to being loaded onto Ark Royal for delivery to Malta. However, when HMS Ark Royal was torpedoed in November 1941, 812 and 814Sqn, with Swordfish, diverted to North Front, from where they operated as lodgers for a while, providing anti-submarine cover for ships in the locality, together with 813Sqn.

In late 1941, work requiring major recla-mation commenced, to lengthen the runway and provide a dispersal capable of accommodating some 600 aircraft. Rock was blasted from the north face of the Rock and taken from further tunnel construction, resulting in some 7,500 tons per day being utilized. By the time it was finally completed in 1943, operations from Gibraltar were reducing, although numbers of aircraft in transit remained high.

Having operated a Flight at Gibraltar from August 1941 with Hudsons, the rest of 233Sqn arrived in June 1942. During May, U-573 was attacked and sunk, followed by a number of others, with depth charges and later with rockets. They also destroyed two Condors before departing in February 1944.

Various squadrons spent short periods at Gibraltar, flying operations before moving on. These included 89, 95, 200 and 204Sqn while, in November 1942, 43, 72, 81, 93, 111, 152, 600 and 608Sqn arrived for Operation *Torch* in North Africa. In addition, a number of other squadrons or detachments operated for the period to provide support, including 179, 500, 540, 544 and 608. These were to support the US troops invading North Africa and were joined by others from the USAAF, also operating out of North Front.

With major activity reducing, 87Sqn arrived with Hurricanes in November and 179Sqn with Wellingtons, followed in December 1942 by 48Sqn with Hudsons for maritime patrol. April saw the formation of 1676 Gibraltar Defence Flight with Spitfires. Various detachments continued, including 541Sqn with Spitfires in October 1942 and 59Sqn with Liberators, which arrived in May 1943.

Sadly, an accident in July 1943 resulted in the death of General Sikorski – the Polish Prime Minister in exile – when the 511Sqn Liberator in which he was flying crashed into the sea on take-off. After being buried in Newark, he was finally taken home in 1993. In September 1943, 520Sqn was formed for the meteorological role, initially with Gladiators and later Halifaxes. Due to increased U-Boat activity, a Wellington detachment from 172Sqn arrived in October, plus 272Sqn with Beaufighters for anti-shipping attacks.

Repatriation of the civilian population commenced in 1944 and, while most had returned by 1946, it took some six years to complete the task. During the early part of the year a number of aircraft departed, including 48 and 233Sqn in February, but were replaced by 52Sqn with Baltimores. However, this squadron disbanded at the end of March. The following month 179Sqn also left, plus 202Sqn in September. This left some US Navy Liberators, on detachment from VPB-112 and VB-114, providing the anti-submarine capability. They were joined by 22Sqn SAAF, with Venturas. August 1944 saw aircraft return, when a large number of Dakotas arrived at North Front for Operation *Dragon* – the successful Allied invasion of southern France. In January 1945, 458 (RAAF) Sqn arrived with Wellingtons for anti-submarine patrols and disbanded in June.

Once the war ended, the aircraft numbers reduced to 520Sqn with Halifaxes and detachments of Lancasters. It disbanded in April 1946 and the meteorological duties were undertaken by a 518Sqn Detachment with Halifaxes. It

was re-numbered 202Sqn in October 1946 and augmented by a 224Sqn Detachment from mid-1948, before the whole squadron moved to North Front in August. In July 1951, it began to convert to Shackletons and, in January, a Flight was used to re-form 269Sqn, which departed in March.

In 1955, the runway was lengthened again from 5,400ft to its current 6,000ft. This enables all RAF aircraft to use the airfield, apart from the Tristar and VC.10. In October 1966, 224Sqn was disbanded and so ended the permanent basing of a squadron at Gibraltar. The AHQ Gibraltar was disestablished and the station re-named RAF Gibraltar.

The tension with Spain over the ownership of Gibraltar has remained a problem and has led to the border being closed for various periods of time. During the mid-1960s a detachment of Hunters from 229 OCU were deployed, remaining for over a decade.

In 1982, Gibraltar became a strategic point for shipping bound for the South Atlantic during Operation *Corporate*. Several helicopters were based on the airfield, assisting in the movement of passengers and cargo. More recently it was used during operations in Bosnia and Sierra Leone.

In 1985, the RAF Marine Craft Unit was disbanded and the SAR role taken over by the Royal Navy with Patrol Craft and RIBs. The station currently forms part of HQ British Forces Gibraltar and is also used as a civil airport.

Although the number of RAF personnel at Gibraltar is fewer than forty-five, it remains a strategic base that also acts as an international airport. It has no based aircraft but aircraft are frequently deployed on exercises and training – it sees types as diverse as Dominies and Nimrods.

RAFU Goose Bay, Canada

Overseas
Motto: *Tingijub Akkarvinga* – Where the big bird lands

The RAF have maintained an interest at Goose Bay, Canada since the airfield was completed in November 1941 for the Canadian Armed Forces. It provided a valuable refuelling point and refuge for aircraft transiting between North America and Europe using the Great Circle route.

The RAF Unit was established in its current form in 1982. In addition to

providing facilities for transit aircraft, it provides support for aircraft detachments visiting to use the low-level training ranges in Labrador and eastern Quebec. These exercises are normally conducted between April and October and consists of up to eighteen combat aircraft supported by transport and tanker aircraft. The largely uninhabited areas enable the crew to train with various other air forces at all altitudes down to 100ft (30m) with minimal disturbance. In 2002 the number of permanent personnel was reduced from 120 to around fifty, but the number of training flights is planned to continue by temporarily deploying crew and hiring local personnel.

RAFU Goose Bay has no permanent aircraft, it only operates them on detachment or in transit.

RAF Halton

Personnel and Training Command
Motto: Teach Learn Apply

In 1914, Alfred Rothschild offered the use of his estate at Halton Park to the army for training purposes. His only stipulation was that it should be restored and returned within six months of the end of the war.

It wasn't until 1917 that the RFC arrived and established its School of Technical Training (SoTT) and Boys Training Depot. When Alfred Rothschild died in 1918, the War Office bought the estate. In March 1920, the SoTT was renamed No 1 SoTT. In 1922, the Apprentice Scheme was created by Lord Trenchard to ensure that the RAF had sufficient skilled technicians to maintain their aircraft. Such was this standard of training that a light aircraft – named Mayfly – was designed and built by the school and was successful in air races during the late 1920s.

The apprentices, who became initially known as 'Trenchard's Brats' (later 'Halton Brats') were soon to raise the quality of aircraft maintenance within the RAF. In 1927, Princess Mary's RAF Hospital opened, providing further student training facilities as well as medical care. The hospital also included the Institute of Pathology and Tropical Medicine.

In addition to the school buildings, which included a number of large hangars and workshops full of time-grounded aircraft, the airfield was used to accommodate a number of instructional airframes. It also accommodated some flying aircraft. In March 1943, 1448 Flight arrived and was re-numbered 529Sqn in June. It was equipped with Hornet Moths and the Avro Rota autogyro, which were used for highly secret radar-calibration duties. It departed in August 1944. In addition, Bomber Command operated a communications flight from Halton.

The training role of Halton remained broadly similar until 1993, when the 1 SoTT moved to Cosford, so ending the RAF Apprenticeship Scheme that had seen some 40,000 boys trained.

Halton's current role continues with initial recruit training and it is the 'Gateway to the RAF' for all non-commissioned personnel. Each year 2,000 new recruits join the RAF: civilians arrive and undergo a nine-week course for basic training prior to progressing to their specialist training. Approximately one-third of these recruits remain at Halton, where additional training is provided for a number of trades, including chefs, police and suppliers. Also based at Halton is the Airmen's Command Squadron, which provides management and leadership courses for newly promoted NCOs. Such are the standard of these courses that spare capacity and resources are frequently offered, not only within MoD but also to the business market. Besides the recruit and specialist training courses, with some 20,000 personnel passing through per year, Halton offers a wide opportunity for sport.

Lodger units include the Defence Dental Agency (DDA) Headquarters, which was formed in March 1996, and the Provost & Security Services (Southern Region). In June 2004, the RAF Gliding and Soaring Association (RAFGSA) arrived from Bicester.

Besides being the 'Gateway to the RAF', Halton is the home of No 613 VGS, which provides Air Cadets with air experience and training on its Vigilant T.1 powered gliders.

RAF Henlow

Personnel and Training Command
Motto: *Labor Arma Ministrat* – Hard work provides armour

The initial land purchase for Henlow was made in the summer of 1917 and it opened on 10 May 1918 to establish 5 Eastern Area Aircraft Repair Depot. Following the end of the war, surplus aircraft were disposed of here, with fighters sold for 10 shillings (50p) and bombers for £1. In April 1919, airmen awaiting demob mutinied over increased working hours, resulting in fifty-six courts martial. In 1920, the airfield was further expanded and, in March, became the Inland Area Aircraft Depot, working on an extensive range of aircraft from Avro 504s to Vimys. The Officers Engineering School was established in 1924 for specialist engineering training.

In July 1925, 23 and 43Sqn were re-formed with Snipes, as part of the home defence. These were replaced shortly after with Gamecocks. In September, the Parachute Test Section was formed. In April 1926, Henlow became the Home Aircraft Depot within 21 Group. In October the Parachute Training Section moved in from Northolt. It was merged with the Test Section to become the Parachute Test Unit and used Vimy bombers.

In December 1926, 43Sqn departed, followed by 23Sqn the following February. It was while in charge of the engine test-bays that Flight Lieutenant Frank Whittle began developing his jet-engine ideas.

During October 1935, the Pilotless Aircraft Section from Farnborough arrived with the radio-controlled Queen Bee target aircraft. The depot had been expanding from 1935 and, in December 1936, the Officers Engineering School was re-named the School of Aeronautical Engineering.

In 1936, 64Sqn formed with Demons, followed by 80Sqn, who arrived in March 1937 with Gauntlets, re-equipping with Gladiators in May but departing again in June. Meanwhile, the ground-training role of Henlow was rapidly expanding, however, the majority of the Wing moved to St Athan and the remaining third – 1 Wing – moved to Halton in April 1939. Meanwhile, the depot was renamed 13 MU in October 1938 and was to become one of the RAF's largest MUs.

In February 1940, the Queen Bees moved out and, in June, some 3,000 men of 21 Aircraft Depot arrived to assemble, test and repair Hurricanes. Henlow assembled and modified over 1,000 of the 1,077 Canadian-built Hurricanes that were shipped. The ATC Control Tower is reputed to be built from old Hurricane packing-cases. Over fifty men from Henlow were deployed to prepare Hurricanes aboard the aircraft carriers that were ferrying them to Malta.

Later, 14 School of Technical Training was formed from the old Training Wing and the School of Aeronautical Engineering became the RAF Technical College in August 1947. The Signals Development Unit transferred from West Drayton from 1947 and the Radio Calibration Unit was formed in 1948. It became the Radio Engineering Unit (REU) in 1950, servicing, modifying and manufacturing radio equipment. The Radio Warfare Engineering Flight was added in 1955 to develop radio counter-measures. The technical college continued to expand as various units moved in. By 1953, it consisted of an HQ and five Wings. In 1960, it amalgamated with the RAF College at Cranwell but, by 1980, all that remained was the Radio Engineering Unit. The calibration elements of the REU were separated in 1972, to form the Test Equipment Wing, which moved to Sealand in June 1993.

Meanwhile, in 1958, 616 Gliding School was formed with Cadet Mk.3 and Sedbergh gliders. Henlow was also selected to provide a store for a number of the RAF Museum's aircraft during the 1960s. In 1964 it became one of the locations for filming *Those Magnificent Men In Their Flying Machines* and has been chosen for a number of other films since.

The RAF Officer Cadet Training Unit (OCTU) arrived from Feltwell in 1966. It provided initial basic training for over 60 per cent of newly commissioned officers for General Duties Branch. Once completed, the officers would undergo their specialist training. Although this increased to 80 per cent by the mid-1970s, it was decided that the OCTU would move to Cranwell.

The year 1973 saw the establishment of the RAF Support Signals Command HQ (RAFSCSHQ), which has spawned several smaller units. These proved of great value during Operation *Granby*, when their capabilities were in great demand. They have now been absorbed into the tri-service Defence Communications Services Agency.

In 1978, the 616 VGS gliders were replaced with Venture motor gliders and, subsequently, the Vigilant in 1991.

Joint Arms Control Implementation Group (JACIG) moved into Henlow in May 1996 and, in September 1998, the

Centre of Aviation Medicine (CAM) was formed. In November 1978, the HQ RAF Provost and Security Services (HQ RAF P&SS) arrived from Rudloe Manor. In June 2000, the Aviation Medicine Flight became a detached unit at Boscombe Down.

Henlow is also home to the RAF Signals Staff, which is responsible for the RAF element of the Defence Communications Network (DCN), including radio and telegraphic communications

A private RAF Signals Museum has been established on the station, with wireless and other signalling equipment dating back to the First World War.

Henlow is home for the Centre for Aviation Medicine, HQ Provost and Security Services, 3Sqn, R Aux AF, JACIG, DCSA, plus 616 VGS, which operated the Vigilant T.1.

RAF High Wycombe

Strike Command
Motto: *Non sibi* – Not for ourselves

Construction of High Wycombe commenced in November 1938 to provide a permanent, concealed location for Bomber Command HQ. As a result, this new command, which formed in July 1936, was temporarily located at Uxbridge.

Bomber Command moved to High Wycombe in March 1940 in great secrecy. The Air Ministry instructions were for the station to be known as Southdown and its postal address was c/o GPO, High Wycombe. Some of the buildings were constructed to resemble houses.

An Air Staff recommendation in 1963 for the forming of a single front-line command started to be implemented in 1967. Bomber and Fighter Commands were initially merged in April 1968 to form Strike Command. A year later Signals and Coastal Commands were absorbed.

During the early 1980s a new command bunker was constructed on the site.

In April 1986, 7006Sqn RAF VR AF was formed and became an Auxiliary AF unit in 1997, before moving out in October 2000.

On 1 January 1969 the station was formally re-named High Wycombe.

In April 1996, High Wycombe became the location for a new 1 Group – formed by the merging of 1 and 2 Groups, and also became the HQ for 38 Group.

On 27 June 1995, the Franco-British European Air Group was formed at High Wycombe to improve inter-air-force co-operation. It was enlarged to include other countries and, in January 1998, it was re-named the European Air Group. The Combined Air Operations Centre Nine (CAOC9) was established on September 1st, 1999 as part of NATO's Allied Air Forces North (AIRNORTH).

In April 2000, HQ Strike Command was reorganized, which resulted in the formation of a number of multi-service organizations, including the Joint Rapid Reaction Force, Joint Helicopter Command and the Joint Force Harrier. However, a number of historical units were lost, including 11, 18 and 38 Groups. These were incorporated into the new 1, 2 and 3 Groups, which have since undergone a number of smaller changes.

In June 2005 it was announced by the Armed Forces Minister Adam Ingram that after due consideration High Wycombe was to be the single site location for Strike Command and the Personnel & Training Command HQs. This co-location will result in the saving of some 1,000 military and civil posts plus £420m over 25 years producing a more efficient and effective HQ structure.

High Wycombe is the HQ of Strike Command plus 1, 2 and 3 Groups, Combined Air Operations Centre 9 and the European Air Group.

RAF Holbeach

1 Group
Strike Command
Motto: Defend and Strike

Holbeach has been used as an air weapons range since the 1920s. The range is currently used by various combat aircraft, including the Tornado GR.4, Harrier GR.7 and USAF F-15E Strike Eagle. They fire 20mm and 30mm cannon and drop 4kg and 15kg practice bombs, as well as 500lb and 1,000lb inert bombs. On this range – which includes ship and land targets – no live bombs larger than 15kg are now dropped.

Because of the use of this area as a range and the appropriate safety area that is required, despite the disturbance of the aircraft and the weapons, the wildlife is flourishing from over eighty years of virtual protection.

Holbeach is an air weapons range.

RAF Honington

2 Group
Strike Command
Motto: *Pro Anglia Valens* – Valiant for England

Honington opened on 3 May 1937 as a bomber station within 3 Group. In July, 77Sqn arrived with the Audax and Wellesley, together with 102Sqn with Heyfords. In July 1938, they were replaced by 215Sqn with Harrows and were re-equipped with Wellingtons a year later.

In September 1939, the empty airfield returned to activity with the arrival of 9Sqn with Wellingtons who, in December, flew one of the first bombing raids of the Second World War. From June 1940, 103 and 105Sqn flew Battles briefly. In July 1940, 311Sqn was formed as the only Czech bomber squadron, was equipped with Wellingtons and departed in September. Three Beam Approach Training Flights operated until later in 1942. In June 1942, Honington was allocated to the USAAF and, so, 9Sqn departed in August 1942, by which time it had lost seventy-nine Wellingtons on operations. It was replaced by 8th Air Service Command, which arrived at Station 375 to set up a depot for the maintenance of 3rd Air Division B-17s. The 364th Fighter Group (383, 384 and 385th FS) arrived in February with P-38 Lightnings and P-51 Mustangs . The 364 FG departed in November 1945, having destroyed 449 enemy aircraft over 342 missions, at a loss of 143 of their own. The depot closed in February 1946 and Honington returned to the RAF once more.

Due to light soil, a hard runway had never been built, despite the airfield being used by B-17s. The USAAF simply constructed a steel-plank runway. Immediately post-war, Honington was used by 58 MU, who were responsible for recovering crashed aircraft, and 94 MU, who disposed of wartime bombs and ammunition. They operated until the early 1950s, when a concrete runway was eventually built. This was completed in 1955, allowing the arrival of 10, XV, 44 and 57Sqn with Canberras. They were deployed shortly after for operations during the Suez Crisis. The arrival of the Valiant came in 1956 with 7Sqn, followed by 90 and 199Sqn, and then Victors of 55 and 57Sqn from 1960. The V-bombers departed in 1966 and the station was closed to await the F-111, which was subsequently cancelled.

Honington re-opened when 12Sqn became the first RAF Buccaneer unit in October 1970. It was joined briefly by XVSqn, which departed for Laarbruch in January 1971. In March 1971, 237 OCU was re-formed, along with 208Sqn in July 1974. Meanwhile, 204Sqn arrived in April 1971 with the Shackleton, operating in the maritime surveillance and SAR role until April 1972. Until 1978, 809 NAS were here, when not aboard HMS *Ark Royal*. In 1979, 2623Sqn, Aux AF Regt was formed to provide airfield defence. In July 1979, 216Sqn briefly formed with Buccaneers, before it moved to Lossiemouth in 1980.

The exodus of the Buccaneer to Lossiemouth was led by 12Sqn, which departed in 1982, followed by 208 in July 1983 and 237 OCU in 1984, leaving Honington empty to prepare for the Tornado.

The Tactical Weapons Conversion Unit (TWCU) was established in August 1981 with the Tornado GR.1. It was allocated the shadow squadron status of 45Sqn in January 1984. At the same time, IXSqn commenced working up on the Tornado

prior to re-forming in June. In 1985, 20Sqn RAF Regt was formed to provide Low-Level Air Defence (LLAD) with Rapiers for USAF units. In 1986, IXSqn moved to Bruggen. In January 1990, 13Sqn re-formed with the Tornado GR.1A, in the reconnaissance role. Both 13 and 20Sqn were deployed to the Middle East for Operation *Granby*. In April 1992, 45Sqn was re-numbered XV (R) Sqn, prior to it departing in November 1993. By the end of 1993, 13, XV (R) and 218Sqn had all departed and flying operations ceased.

In March 1993, 16Sqn, RAF Regt and the Rapier FSC Conversion unit arrived, marking a change in role for Honington. In 1994 the RAF Regiment Depot from Catterick arrived. This provides the support and training for the Regiment, including all of the basic and advanced field and air-defence training. They were followed by 2Sqn, plus 15Sqn – which was re-formed from 20Sqn at Honington in 1996. In 1999 the title of RAF Regiment Depot was dropped.

G Squadron of the Army's 1st Royal Tank Regiment arrived in Honington to become part of the Joint Nuclear, Biological and Chemical Reconnaissance unit (Jt NBC Regt) with 27Sqn RAF Regt and formed on 1 April 1999. On the same day, the Joint Rapier Training Unit (JRTU) was formed. The Survive to Operate Centre was re-named Force Protection Centre in April 2004 and, in

the same month, 2623Sqn re-roled from a GBAD unit with Rapier to a Biological Detection unit augmenting the Jt NBC Regt.

An RAF Regiment Museum can be viewed by prior arrangement (Tel: 01359 269561 ext 7824).

Honington is home to 2, 15 and 16Sqn of the RAF Regt, Jt NBC Regt (comprising 27Sqn, RAF Regt and the Army's G Squadron, 1RTR), Training Wing, JRTU, the Force Protection Centre and 2623 (East Anglian) Sqn, R Aux AF.

RAF Hythe

USVF
Personnel and Training Command

Hythe was originally opened by the Admiralty during the First World War with the construction of some sheds for flying-boat production. Amongst those built were some fifty Felixstowes, designed by Squadron Commander Porte and based on a design by Curtiss. The production was conducted by May, Harden and May, although some of the final assembly may have been undertaken elsewhere.

In 1925, Supermarine took over the site and it was used for assembly of some of its seaplanes, including Southamptons. From the late 1930s, Imperial Airways occupied part of the site as a maintenance base for its Empire flying-boats.

In 1940, Imperial Airways became part of the newly established BOAC and Hythe continued to be used as a maintenance base. It was also used to provide maintenance for the Sunderlands of Coastal Command.

With the war over, Hythe reverted to BOAC for commercial flying-boat operations with Hythes, Seafords and Sunderland/Sandringhams, until they ended in 1950. In 1952, the site was taken over by the Royal Navy as HMS *Diligence*, a maintenance base for inshore and coastal minesweepers.

When France pulled out of NATO in 1967 and US Forces based there were required to withdraw, part of the site at Hythe was made available, enabling about half of the watercraft to be relocated. In 1974, the RN withdrew from the site and it was transferred to RAF control.

In addition to the slipways, two of the original aircraft-hangars remain in use. One for stores and maintenance and

With the old seaplane hangars still in use – albeit for stores – the old base at Hythe continued to be a hive of activity. Strangely, it is the US Army who are in situ and, even stranger, they maintain maritime craft!

the other as the main workshop for the various watercraft, which includes tugs and landing craft. Hythe is unique within the US Army, being the only such unit outside the USA maintaining vessels for the Prepositioned Afloat Programme. It operates as a sub-element of the US Army Material Command and is operated as a US Army Combat Equipment Battalion.

Hythe is a USVF base with no aircraft.

RAF Innsworth

Personnel and Training Command
Motto: *Multos sustentare* – To support the many

Innsworth opened in 1940 with 7 School of Technical Training, tasked with instructing engine- and airframe-fitters. The first course was delayed when 1,500 airmen arrived, following the evacuation of Dunkirk. It eventually commenced training in July 1941. With some 2,000 personnel based at Innsworth, a hospital was also established.

In December 1941, 2 WAAF Depot was opened and provided instruction as mechanics, carpenters and drivers for the WAAF NCOs. With numbers rapidly passing the 4,000 mark, it was decided that Innsworth would become exclusively a WAAF training establishment. It remained thus until May 1944, when it was handed over to the RCAF as a reception base for its personnel.

In January 1945, Innsworth returned to RAF control; Records Office arrived, followed by RAF Base Accounts later that year, and it later became the Central Pay Office. In 1946, the Airman's Recruit Centre arrived, but departed a year later. A school of cookery arrived later, plus an RAF Regiment Wing, the RAF Education Book Depot, 7 and13 School of Recruit Training and the HQ 4 Police District.

A major reorganization resulted in the forming of Personnel and Training Command (P&TC) in 1974. Subsequently, a number of new organizations have been established under the P&TC umbrella. The more important of these include the Personnel Management Agency (PMA), the Training Group Defence Agency (TGDA) and the Armed Forces Personnel Administration Agency (AFPAA).

Innsworth is the home of Personnel and Training Command.

Innsworth is the HQ of P&TC, housing a large administrative complex. During the announced restructuring of the RAF in 2004, it was revealed that P&TC and Strike Command HQs would be co-located by 2008, with High Wycombe subsequently selected as the location. Crown Copyright

RAF Kinloss

3 Group
Strike Command
Motto: Power to the hunter

Construction of the airfield at Kinloss commenced in 1938 and it opened on 1 April 1939. First occupant was 14 FTS with the Hart, Hind, Anson and Harvard. Joined shortly after by 45 MU, the FTS was replaced by 19 OTU in 1940. Remaining until 1945, the OTU operated the Anson, Whitley and Wellington.

Once the war was over, Kinloss transferred to Coastal Command and 6 (Coastal) OTU arrived. Between then and 1951, it operated Mosquitos, Beaufighters, Warwicks and Lancasters. It then split into the School of Maritime Reconnaissance and 236 OCU.

In 1950, Kinloss's first operational squadron arrived in the form of 120Sqn with the Lancaster 3 and, later, the Shackleton. In 1952, it was replaced by 217Sqn with Neptunes, until it was disbanded in 1957. In October 1956, 236 OCU, which had been operating the Shackleton I and Neptune, became the Maritime OTU (MOTU) with the arrival of the Shackleton T.4 and moved to St Mawgan in 1965. In 1959, 120Sqn returned with Shackleton MR.3s and later

was joined by the similarly equipped 201 and 206Sqn.

In 1970, 201Sqn converted to the Nimrod MR.1, followed by 120Sqn and 206Sqn. The last ASW Shackleton departed in December 1970. The Shackleton returned briefly in 1972, when 8Sqn brought their Shackleton AEW.2s, prior to being based at Lossiemouth from the following year.

In 1979, a Nimrod Conversion Flight was formed as the modified MR.1s were returned from the manufacturer as the upgraded MR.2. The Flight facilitated the return to service of the aircraft with its new avionics, sensors and systems.

Lodger units at Kinloss includes the Aeronautical Rescue Centre (ARCC), which controls and co-ordinates RAF rescue resources (Sea King HAR.3s, Nimrod MR.2s and the Mountain Rescue Teams, plus RN and Coast Guard helicopters) and works closely with the civilian emergency services. It is responsible for an area that extends to the Faroes in the north, English Channel to the south, halfway across the Atlantic to the west and halfway across the North Sea to the east. On average, some 2,000 scrambles are launched by RAF aircraft each year and around 1,500 people assisted – by far the majority being civilians.

Other lodger units at Kinloss include Kinloss Mountain Rescue Team, Nimrod AEDIT (Aircraft Engineering and Design Implementation Team), Nimrod Major Servicing Unit and the 633 VGS.

While the first four Nimrod MRA.4s have been undergoing their re-build, the airfield has been subjected to preparations, including a new simulator, and other buildings built or modified. Even taxiways and aprons have required attention for the increased-span aircraft.

In December 2004, it was announced that 206Sqn would be disbanded on 1 April 2005. This was a result of the defence cuts announced earlier that year and would result in the reduction of the Nimrod MR.2 fleet from twenty-one to sixteen aircraft.

Kinloss provides the home to the Nimrod fleet and houses 42 (R), 120 and 201Sqn. In addition, 663 Volunteer Gliding School operates Vigilant T.1s. Kinloss also houses the Fulmar Gliding Club of the RAFGSA.

Kirton in Lindsey

2 Group
Strike Command

Kirton in Lindsey opened in December 1916 and housed B Flight of 33Sqn, RFC, which operated the F.2B Fighter and Avro 504. In June 1919 the squadron disbanded, the site was vacated and the airfield returned to agricultural use.

In May 1940, Kirton in Lindsey re-opened as a fighter station once more with 253Sqn, initially operating Hurricanes. In May, 65 and 222Sqn also stayed briefly, while 264, 74, 307 and 85Sqn followed, in short succession, with Defiants, Hurricanes and Spitfires, to recover from the intense operations of the Battle of Britain.

In November 1940, 255Sqn was formed with Defiants, then converted to Hurricanes in March, before departing in May. In November, 71Sqn with its American crew also arrived to convert to the Hurricane and departed in April 1941. A couple of days later, 452Sqn, RAAF was formed with Spitfires, departing in July. Meanwhile, in May, the second Eagle Squadron – 121 – was formed with Hurricanes, converting to Spitfires in October, before departing in December. Its place was taken by the

third Eagle Sqn – 133 – which converted to the Spitfire V, before departing in May 1942. At the same time, 136Sqn had been formed with Hurricanes in August 1941, departing for India less than three months later. In May 1942, 457Sqn, RAAF arrived with Spitfires and departed for Australia the following month.

June 1942 saw the arrival of the USAAF, in the form of the 94th FS with the P-38 Lightning. It stayed for two months and was followed by the 91st with P-39 Airacobras in October, staying until December.

In May 1943, Kirton in Lindsey became a training station, housing the Masters and Spitfires of 53 OTU until May 1945. During this time Hibaldstowe and Caistor were used as satellite airfields.

In April 1946, 7 SFTS began to arrive with Harvards and Oxfords. The title reverted to 7 FTS at the beginning of 1948 and it received some Tiger Moths and Prentices, before it moved on to Cottesmore in April 1948. The station continued its training role with non-flying units until August 1951, when 2 ITS arrived. A couple of Tiger Moths were borrowed, as required, for part of the training. In May 1951, 4 ITS was formed from a 2 ITS Flight for a few months then re-absorbed. In July 1957, 2 ITS was re-designated 1 ITS and fulfilled its role until it was moved in July 1957. The airfield then closed and the station was placed on care and maintenance.

In August 1959, Kirton in Lindsey re-opened as a training station once more, housing 7 SoTT, plus 22 Gliding School in August 1960. The latter was re-designated 643 VGS in September 1955. These remained active until 1965 and, shortly after, the station was transferred to the army as Rapier Barracks for 22nd Air Defence Regt. It closed again in March 2004.

As part of the co-location of RAF Air Combat Support and Air Combat Service Support units, Kirton in Lindsey reverted back to RAF control on October 6th, 2004 and is currently the home for 1 ACC which moved in from Boulmer at the end of January 2005. This was announced as a temporary move with Scampton being the designated location no later than 2009.

Kirton in Lindsey is currently the home of 1 ACC.

RAF Lakenheath

USVF
Personnel and Training Command
Motto: Ut aquilae volent – Where eagles dare

Military use of the land on and around the current site of Lakenheath dates back to the First World War. A number of training grounds were established for the RFC during the war, but reverted to their original farm use after its end.

During 1939, a decoy airfield was built at Lakenheath Warren, intended to draw attacking aircraft away from nearby Mildenhall. However, construction of a permanent airfield commenced in 1940 and the first recorded aircraft to land was a Proctor in September 1941. November 1941 saw the arrival of Wellingtons of 20 OTU and, between January and April 1942, the Stirlings from 149Sqn at Mildenhall transferred over. During May, they took part in the first 'Thousand Bomber' raid on Cologne.

While at Lakenheath, Australian pilot Pilot Officer R H Middleton was posthumously awarded the VC. In November 1942, he was captain of a Stirling from 149Sqn that was damaged during an attack on Turin and he was badly injured. Despite the loss of an eye he completed the attack and managed to fly back to the English Channel, where, running out of fuel, he ordered the rest of the crew to bale out when near the coast. He lost his life when the plane crashed as he turned back out to sea to avoid civilian casualties.

In July 1943, 199Sqn arrived with more Wellingtons. They flew numerous similar operations, initially attacking the V-weapon development site at Peenemunde and later mine-laying. Both squadrons departed in May 1944, as this station was one of three selected for upgrade for heavy bomber ops with the new B-29s. However, this work was not completed until April 1947.

In 1948, it became a USAF transit and TDY base. In June 1950, Lakenheath was officially handed over to the Americans. Increased tension came to a head later in the month when the Korean War commenced and, by August, there were twenty-nine B-29s, plus twenty-four B-24s.

Various bomber, tanker and reconnaissance squadrons came and went, until January 1960 and the arrival of F-100 Super Sabres of the 48th Tactical Fighter Wing (TFW), following France's ejection

ABOVE: The HS.125 CC.3s are operated in two colour-schemes by 32 (The Royal) Sqn to provide transport for VIPs. This the low-visibility light-grey scheme.

RIGHT: The BAe.146, which is painted in the high-visibility scheme, is used to transport groups of VIPs and members of the Royal Family.

BELOW: The C-17 Globemasters have been at the centre of the RAF's strategic-transport capability since their initial delivery.

LEFT: Although the Canberra design dates from shortly after the Second World War, the upgrades to the PR.9 variant have meant that it is still capable of fulfilling a vital reconnaissance role.

ABOVE: The Chinook HC.2 provides the heavy-lift capability for the JHC, be it from land or ship.

LEFT: Although superseded for mainstream RAF pilot-training, a couple of Chipmunk T.10s remain with the BBMF for tail-dragger experience for those pilots fortunate enough to fly the Hurricane and Spitfire. Crown Copyright

ABOVE: The oldest airworthy transport aircraft in the RAF is the BBMF's Dakota, which is displayed at airshows in memory of the aircrew of Transport Command who lost their lives during the Second World War.

RIGHT: The Dominie T.1 continues to serve as a navigation trainer with No 55(R)Sqn for the RAF's Weapon Systems Officers.

BELOW: The role of the Firefly has recently been significantly reduced and it is now only used for the lead-in course for multi-engine pilots.

ABOVE: Following the withdrawal of the HT.3, the only Gazelles still flown by the RAF are the Army's AH.1s, operated by 7Sqn in the recce role.

BELOW: The Griffin HT.1 is used by the DHFS to provide advanced multi-engine training to RAF aircrew prior to their being posted to operational squadrons.

LEFT: The Griffin HAR.2 provides the SAR cover for the British forces in Cyprus with 84Sqn, based at Akrotiri. Crown Copyright

ABOVE: Aircraft of the three operational Harrier GR.7 squadrons based at Cottesmore – 3, 1 and 4 – caught in formation during a training exercise. Kevin Wills

RIGHT: The two-seat T.10 trainer-variant of the Harrier features an extended nose and tail, but retains the operational capability of the single seat GR.7 (note TIALD pod under the fuselage).

BELOW: The Hawk is the RAF's advanced trainer. It is also used by the Red Arrows, as well as by 100Sqn (illustrated) for Dissimilar Air Combat Training (DACT) and other specialist duties such as target-towing.

ABOVE: The Hercules C.3 was stretched to give an increased capacity. It is seen here in the Red Arrows support role at an airshow in Slovakia.

LEFT: The Hercules C.1 was the original variant to see service with the RAF as a tactical transport. All are based at Lyneham, as part of the Lyneham Tactical Wing.

Demonstrating its impressive take-off capability, the Hercules C.4 is the stretched variant of the new C-130J, which has increased performance whilst being quieter and more economical.

The Hercules C.5 is the standard length C-130J.

ABOVE: **The two Hurricanes of the BBMF continue to provide a living memorial to the fighter pilots of the Second World War.**

RIGHT: **A pair of Islanders of Northolt's Station Flight are officially used for communications and photographic mapping.**

RIGHT: **A formation comprising each of the current Jaguar squadrons plus 16(R) and 54(F)Sqn, who disbanded in early 2005. By 2008, the Jaguar will have been finally withdrawn.** Crown Copyright

BELOW: **The T.4 provides the two-seat operational-training capability for the Jaguar force at squadron level.** Crown Copyright

LEFT: **The King Air B200 replaced the Jetstream for multi-engine training in 2004.**

ABOVE: **The RAF's last Lancaster provides a fine tribute to the members of Bomber Command who lost their lives during the Second World War.**

LEFT: **The Merlin HC.3 is the RAF's next-generation transport helicopter. Its self-diagnostic fault-detection system significantly reduces maintenance, enabling more time in the air and less on the ground.**

of NATO forces. These were replaced by the F-4 Phantom in January 1972 and then the F-111F in March 1977, which resulted in the construction of sixty Hardened Aircraft Shelters (HAS). These aircraft participated in Operations *Eldorado Canyon* on Libya in 1986 and *Desert Storm* against Iraq in 1991.

From February 1992, the F-111s returned to the USA and were replaced by the F-15 Eagle fighter and F-15E Strike Eagle attack aircraft. These aircraft have flown in operations in the former republic of Yugoslavia, Northern Iraq, Afghanistan and, most recently, Iraq again during Operation *Iraqi Freedom*.

Lakenheath is a USVF base, housing 48th Fighter Wing (48 FW). This comprises 492 and 494 Fighter Squadron with F-15E Strike Eagles and 493 Fighter Squadron with F-15C Eagles.

Leconfield

3 Group
Strike Command

Leconfield opened as a Bomber Command airfield in December 1936 and Heyford bombers of 166Sqn arrived the following month, swiftly joined by 97Sqn. In June 1938, they undertook air-observer training. Aircraft were pooled and, from June 1939, they began converting to Whitleys before departing in September.

In October 1939, Leconfield was transferred to Fighter Command and 72Sqn Spitfires arrived for the first of a number of short stays, followed by 616Sqn. This was a feature of station life, with various squadrons being moved north for a short break from the continuous attacks from the Luftwaffe on airfields in the south. In addition, a few new squadrons were formed. In August 1940, 302 (Polish) Sqn was formed with Hurricanes and departed in October. April 1941 saw 60 OTU form with Blenheims, Defiants and Oxfords for night-fighter pilot training, but it departed in June. Its space was taken by 129Sqn, which re-formed with Spitfires paid for by the people of Mysore in India. Very quickly 129Sqn clocked up a Ju88 and a Bf110 – shot down before it was declared operational. It was joined by 81Sqn, which arrived in July, with Hurricanes and 313 (Czech) Sqn with Spitfires, then 129 departed in August. It was replaced by 610Sqn, which stayed until mid-January.

Meanwhile, as the Luftwaffe attacks were dwindling, Leconfield began to change role to training, with the establishment of 28 Conversion Flight (28 CF) in October and 107 CF in December. By the end of the year both had departed, by which time the station was closed for a period while it was converted for use by heavy bombers.

Leconfield re-opened in December 1942. First to arrive was 196Sqn with Wellingtons, followed by the similarly equipped 466 (RAAF) Sqn, which continued to operate until June 1944, although it converted to the Halifax in September 1943. The departure of 196Sqn had come in July 1943. In January 1944, 640Sqn was formed with the Halifax and remained at Leconfield until May 1945, when it was disbanded. In June 466Sqn departed and 96Sqn re-formed in December 1944 as a transport unit with the Halifax, departing for the Middle East in March. In April 1945, 51Sqn arrived with more Halifaxes, converting to Stirlings in June, before departing in August.

Central Gunnery School (CGS) arrived in November 1945 and operated a wide range of aircraft. The courses were split into fixed guns, with aircraft such as the Meteor, Mosquito, Sabres, Spitfire and Vampire, and free guns, as in the turrets of Wellingtons and Lincolns. In March 1953, one of a pair of their Lincolns on a fighter affiliation training flight inadvertently flew into East Germany and was shot down by a Soviet AF MiG-15. Within the school were a number of smaller organizations, such as the Central Fighter Establishment (CFE) and a Trials Flight. The CGS was re-named Fighter Weapons School in January 1955, departing in October 1957.

Sycamores of 275Sqn arrived in October 1957 to provide search and rescue cover. Whirlwinds were later added and, in September 1959, it was re-numbered 228Sqn. The last Sycamores were retired in January 1961 and, in September 1964, 228Sqn was re-numbered 202Sqn.

In April 1959, 72Sqn arrived with Javelins but, in June 1961, it was disbanded. June 1959 saw 19Sqn arrive with Hunters, followed by 92Sqn in May 1961, also with Hunters. In October 1962, 19Sqn converted to Lightnings, followed by 92Sqn in December. During the 1964 season, 92Sqn formed a display team. In September 1965, 19Sqn transferred to Gütersloh and became the first Lightning squadron based overseas. In December, 92Sqn also departed to Germany.

In February 1966, 60 MU moved into Leconfield, taking some tasking from 33 MU at Lyneham when it was closed in December 1966. Part of its tasking included major servicing of Lightnings and Phantoms. It also stored and disposed of the Bassets, when they were withdrawn in 1974. In November 1976, 60 MU closed down and the tasking passed to Abingdon.

The HQ and 'B' Flight of 202Sqn departed just prior to the station being handed over to the army in 1976. It was then used by the Army's School of Mechanical Transport from 1977 and was renamed Normandy Barracks.

In October 1979, 22Sqn's 'D' Flight arrived, operating the Wessex until November 1988, when it was replaced by 202Sqn's 'E' Flight with the Sea King.

In April 1988 the driving school was renamed the Defence School of Transport (DST) and it now trains some 15,500 drivers from all three services. It uses a specially built cross-country training area that was constructed with hills, lakes, obstacles and tracks on part of the old airfield.

Leconfield is base for 'E' Flight of 202Sqn, which are equipped with the Sea King HAR.3.

RAF Leeming

1 Group
Strike Command
Motto: Straight and True

The origins of Leeming date back to early 1938, when an airfield was established for Yorkshire Air Services. Towards the end of the year, the airfield was acquired by the Crown and construction of the military airfield of Leeming commenced. It opened on 3 June 1940.

Blenheims of 219Sqn were the first aircraft to arrive, on detachment from Catterick. The first true residents were Whitleys of 10Sqn, which arrived in July 1940 – their first operation was flown just nineteen days later. A string of new squadrons formed at Leeming over the following months before moving on. In August 1940, 7Sqn became the first Stirling unit and was joined briefly by 35Sqn in November with the Halifax. In September 1941, 77Sqn joined with Whitleys and remained until May. Operations were ceased while concrete runways were laid in 1941. Wellingtons of

A line-up of 100 Sqn Hawks at Leeming.

419 and 420Sqn, Royal Canadian AF (RCAF) arrived in August 1942. After just a week, 419Sqn moved out and 10Sqn departed the following month. During September, 420Sqn converted to the Halifax and 408Sqn arrived with Hamdens to also convert to Halifaxes. By January 1943, Leeming had become an RCAF base with a Canadian station commander.

While most of the other RCAF units moved out after a short while, 427 and 429Sqn arrived and remained at Leeming, operating Halifaxes and, later, Lancasters. Their last operation was flown on 25 April 1945. After VE day they brought prisoners and Allied troops home. In June 1946, both squadrons disbanded and Leeming returned to RAF control.

In July 1946, 228 OCU arrived with Brigands and Mosquitos for training. The runway was lengthened and, in July 1952, the Meteor arrived. The runway was further lengthened and strengthened in 1956 and other improvements made in readiness for the Javelin. Some Meteors continued to be operated for training, along with the Valettas, which were replaced by Canberras in 1959.

Defence policy decreed that air defence would change from manned aircraft to surface-to-air missiles in 1957. As a consequence, the need for the OCU declined, until it was disbanded in 1961. However,

Leeming survived by becoming the home for the re-formed 3 FTS the following month, equipped with the Jet Provost T.3.

Training continued and, in 1975, it expanded with the arrival of the Royal Naval RNEFTS Bulldogs and School of Refresher Training Jet Provost T.4s. Northumbrian UAS arrived in 1974 with their Bulldogs and the Swords aerobatic team was formed with 3 FTS Jet Provosts. CFS transferred their Bulldogs in 1976 and their Jet Provosts in 1977. Around the same time the METS Jetstream T.1 was added to 3 FTS. Despite the use of the relief landing-grounds of Topcliffe and Dishforth, the circuits were considered too busy and the METS moved to Finningley in 1979.

Following a change of Government in 1979, the Conservatives increased the number of fighter squadrons, to balance the perceived threat from the Soviet Union. In 1982, it was announced that Leeming would house three Tornado F.3 squadrons. In 1984, 3 FTS and the CFS moved out and preparations commenced on hardening the airfield for its new role. A huge building programme costing some £148m was completed by January 1988, in time for the arrival of the first Tornados.

In July 1988, XI (Fighter) Sqn began their work-up on the Tornado and were declared operational by November. They

were followed by 23Sqn. The Lockerbie disaster saw a sombre end to the year, with the station's mountain-rescue team deploying in less than an hour to search for bodies and wreckage, following the blowing up of the Pan Am 747 in-flight.

The third Tornado unit to be established at Leeming was 25Sqn. It commenced flying from July 1989 and officially re-formed in September 1989. With three operational fighter-squadrons, Leeming was a potential target and so, on 1 October 1989, 34Sqn RAF Regiment was formed to provide defence with Rapier SAMs. On 31 October, 23Sqn Tornado F.3s were scrambled and intercepted a pair of Soviet Navy 'Bears' that had entered the UK Air Defence Region (UKADR) – the first of many live intercepts from Leeming.

August 1990 saw major activity at Leeming following the Iraqi invasion of Kuwait, with some crews deployed to Dharhan and, subsequently, the rest of XI (F) Sqn deployed to Akrotiri, but their stay was short-lived and they returned home. Meanwhile, a programme was being put in place to upgrade the F.3s at Leeming. While this was going on, crews from each squadron were deployed to form a XI 'Composite' Squadron in Dhahran. Eighteen modified aircraft were flown out to replace the initially deployed F.3s. By the end of December, most of the personnel had returned home, to be replaced by others from Leuchars.

In April 1993, new operations saw six F.3s initially deployed to Gioia del Colle in Italy to enforce the no-fly zone over Bosnia – a task which was to keep all three squadrons busy. In February 1994, 23Sqn disbanded as part of the 'Options for Change'. This was followed by 15Sqn RAF Regiment, which had been re-numbered from 54Sqn in August 1990.

In September 1995, 100Sqn arrived with its Hawks, primarily operating as a target-facilities squadron. As a result of the ending of the Cold War, in January 1997, Leeming F.3s units were given a new primary task – that of providing the air-defence element of an Immediate Reaction (Air) Force (IRF (A)), requiring to be able to deploy anywhere in the world at short notice. This has resulted in various exercises, involving the deployment of the squadrons to operate from other bases.

Lodger units include the Northumbrian University Air Squadron, which converted from the Bulldog to the Tutor T.1 in February 2001, and 11 AEF, which provides air experience flying for ATC cadets, using the UAS Tutors as required. Other units are the 2 Force Protection Wing HQ (2 FP Wing HQ), 34Sqn, RAF Regt and 609 (West Riding) R Aux AF Sqn, which provide operations support, plus Leeming Mountain Rescue Team.

In June 2004, it was announced that the Tornado F.3s at Leeming were to be withdrawn. On 31 October 2005, 11 (F) Sqn would be disbanded, and will be followed by 25Sqn during 2008.

Leeming currently is home for 11 (F) and 25Sqn equipped with Tornado F.3s, 100Sqn with Hawk T.1As, Joint Forward Air Control Training and Standards Unit, which pools Hawks with 100Sqn, Northumbrian University Air Squadron and 11 AEF with the Tutor T.1. Non-flying units include the 609 (West Riding) R Aux AF Sqn, 34Sqn RAF Regt and 2 FP Wing HQ.

RAF Leuchars

1 Group
Strike Command
Motto: Attack and Protect

Leuchars began its military career in 1911, as the home of a Royal Engineers balloon squadron. In 1917, it was designated as a Naval Fleet Training Unit teaching personnel to be gunnery spotters for Royal Navy ships.

Leuchars came under RAF control in March 1920, although the RN continued to visit for training. In April, 205Sqn was re-formed as a fleet reconnaissance unit with Panthers and disbanded in April 1923 when it was split to form 440, 441 and 442 Flights. In 1935, 1 FTS arrived and the station was used for range-work and practice bombing. In 1938, 1 FTS moved out to Netheravon and Leuchars became part of Coastal Command, housing 224 and 233Sqn.

On the second day of the war, a Hudson of 224Sqn became the first British aircraft to come in contact with the enemy, when it attacked a Dornier Do18 over the North Sea. In 1940, another 224Sqn Hudson spotted a German prison ship, enabling it to be intercepted and 200 British prisoners to be released. However, most of Leuchars operations were spent on long, lonely, uneventful maritime patrols. In October 1940, 320 (Dutch) Sqn arrived with Hudsons. In August 1941, 489Sqn, RNZAF was formed with Beauforts and then Blenheims. This and 320Sqn were replaced, in April 1942, by 455Sqn, RAAF with Hampdens, later converting to Beauforts and Beaufighters. In August 1942, 415Sqn, RCAF operated briefly with Hampdens. In April 1943, the Mosquito element of 1477 Flight formed and, in April, it was re-numbered 333 (Norwegian) Sqn as did the original flight at Woodhaven with Catalinas.

Post-war, Leuchars housed a reconnaissance school and St Andrews UAS with Tiger Moths, prior to its transfer to Fighter Command in May 1950 and the arrival of 222Sqn with their Meteors. In June 1965, 228 OCU was re-formed to train additional Javelin crews, required due to the troubles in Indonesia and Malaysia. It was disbanded in November 1966. In addition to operational Javelins, Leuchars later operated Hunters and Lightnings.

In 1955, 'C' Flight of 275Sqn, equipped with Sycamores, was established for the SAR role. The squadron was re-numbered 275Sqn in 1964. These were replaced by the Whirlwind, and later the Wessex, and departed in 1973.

In September 1969, 43Sqn re-formed with Phantoms, followed by the joint RAF/RN Phantom Training Flight in September 1972. They were joined by 111Sqn when it re-formed in July 1975. It also provided the shore base for 892 NAS when not on HMS *Ark Royal*. In 1989, the Tornado F.3 began to replace the Phantom. In April 1987, 228 OCU/64Sqn arrived with Phantoms and was disbanded in March 1991. In the meantime, Aberdeen UAS arrived in December 1980 and was followed by what was the St Andrew UAS element of East Lowlands UAS, to form the Aberdeen, Dundee & St Andrew UAS in 1993.

In March 2003, 56 (Reserve) Sqn arrived from Coningsby as part of the preparations for the Typhoon.

Tornado F.3s from Leuchars have been involved in most recent operations, such as the Gulf War, as well as *Deny Flight* in Bosnia and *Bolton* and *Resinate* over Iraq and, most recently, four Tornado F.3s of 111Sqn provided fighter cover for coalition forces during operations to free the Iraqi people from the regime of Saddam Hussein during Operation *Telic* in 2003.

In September 2003, the Aberdeen, Dundee and St Andrews, plus the East Lowlands UAS were merged to form the East of Scotland University Air Squadrons

Lodgers at Leuchars include the Leuchars Mountain Rescue Team. Another being 612 (County of Aberdeen) Sqn R Aux AF – the air-transportable surgical squadron.

The army also has three lodgers at Leuchars, which are all TA units: 3 Flight (Volunteers) of the AAC, which is equipped with Gazelle AH.1s, 71 (Eng) Regt (Volunteers), which provides a wartime airfield support and 277 Field Squadron (ADR) (Volunteers), who provide airfield damage-repair capability.

As deliveries progress, Leuchars squadrons will re-equip with the Typhoon.

Leuchars is the home of 43 (F), 56 (Reserve) and 111Sqn, who operate Tornado F.3s. In addition, it also houses 603 and 612Sqn of the R Auxiliary AF, the East of Scotland UAS and 12 AEF, operating the Tutor.

RAF Linton-on-Ouse

Personnel and Training Command
Motto: *A flumine impugnamus* – Strike over the river

Linton-on-Ouse opened on 13 May 1937 as a bomber airfield and was the home for the 4 Group HQ until April 1940. The first aircraft to arrive were Whitleys of 51 and 58Sqn in April 1938. They were used to drop propaganda leaflets over Germany from the first day of the war, but this soon changed to live bombs. However, both had departed by December 1939.

The Whitleys of 78Sqn arrived in December 1939 and 58Sqn returned in February, after a short spell with Coastal Command. In July, 78Sqn moved on and was replaced by 77Sqn Whitleys the following month. In October they had also departed. Briefly, 102Sqn operated here, before 35Sqn arrived as the first Halifax squadron in November. Initial problems delayed the first operational sortie until the following March. In May 1941, 76Sqn re-formed, also with the Halifax, but left in June. In April 1942, 58Sqn departed, having flown some 200 sorties during which forty-nine Whitleys were lost. In August 35Sqn left, having been selected as a pathfinder unit. Both 76 and 78Sqn returned in September 1942 and remained until the following June.

In 1943, Linton-on-Ouse transferred to 6 Group, operated by the RCAF. In June 1943, 426Sqn arrived with Lancasters, converting to the Halifax the following May. In August 1943, 408Sqn arrived with Lancasters, converting to the Halifax for a while from September 1944. In May 1945, 426Sqn transferred to Transport Command and departed, having flown 269 sorties on the Halifax with eight aircraft lost.

In May 1945, 405Sqn, RCAF moved in briefly with Lancasters, prior to their return home to Canada with 408Sqn in June. By the end of the war, a total of 339 bombers from Linton-on-Ouse had failed to return home, either lost on operations or training.

In November 1945, 1665 Conversion Unit arrived flying Stirlings and Halifaxes, which were operated as transports until July 1946.

In July 1946, Linton-on-Ouse was transferred to Fighter Command. From July to August 1946, 264Sqn were based with Mosquitos. These were replaced by 64 and 65Sqn with Hornets from August 1946; they converted to Meteors from March 1951 and December 1950 respectively. Both departed in August 1951. In the meantime, 66Sqn had arrived with its Meteors in October 1949, together with 92Sqn. In December 1951, 264Sqn returned with its Mosquitos, re-equipping with the Meteor in 1955. 'A' Flt of 275Sqn was formed in March 1953 with Sycamores for the SAR role and left in November 1954. In December 1953, 66Sqn had converted to the Sabre, to be replaced by the Hunter in March 1956, departing in January 1957, followed by 264Sqn in February. In April 1956, 92Sqn converted to the Hunter and departed in July 1957.

On 9 September 1957, 1 FTS arrived with the Provost and Vampire to train RAF and FAA pilots. It also trained students from a number of Commonwealth and other foreign countries. During July 1966, 23 Group HQ moved in, disbanding in 1975.

The Jet Provost replaced the Provost and Vampires from June 1960 and these were replaced by the Tucano in 1993. In 1997, the CFS Tucanos were incorporated into 1 FTS. In July 2002, 1 and 2Sqn of 1 FTS became 72 (R) and 207 (R) Sqn.

In addition to 1 FTS, Linton-on-Ouse parents Church Fenton and Topcliffe, which are used as Relief Landing Grounds (RLG).

Linton-on-Ouse is the home of 1 FTS, which comprises 72 (R), 207 (R) Sqn CFS (Tucano) plus TANS and operates a total of seventy-eight Tucano T.1s. It is also the home of 642 VGS, which operate the Vigilant T.1.

RAF Lossiemouth

1 Group
Strike Command
Motto: *Thoir An Aire* – Be alert

Construction of Lossiemouth commenced in 1938 and it was opened on 1 May 1939, with 15 FTS Oxfords and Harvards, joined by 46 MU in August.

Lossiemouth was transferred to Bomber Command the following spring and 20 OTU Wellingtons replaced the FTS. In May 1940, 21Sqn arrived, followed by 57Sqn – both with Blenheims – as a result of the German invasion of Norway. A satellite airfield was opened at Bogs O'Mayne (later renamed Elgin) and saw 57Sqn move across. During a 20 OTU training flight an air gunner – Sergeant Geoff Pryor – spotted a Luftwaffe Ju88 and opened fire, causing the Ju88 to crash into the sea. By November 1940, 21 and 57Sqn had departed – although 21 returned several times as a detachment during the war. They were replaced by 232Sqn flying Hurricanes and operating from Bogs O'Mayne, as the grass airfield at Lossiemouth was becoming more difficult to operate from. In the meantime, 46 MU's operation was expanding and a couple of satellite landing grounds were established for it to maintain and store aircraft.

The approaching winter conditions saw 20 OTU Wellingtons temporarily operate from Lakenheath, but Bomber Command operations saw Lossiemouth involvement. The first RAF attacks on the Tirpitz were launched from here, while 20 OTU involvement in the 'Thousand Bomber' raids resulted in casualties. Construction of a concrete runway was completed before the winter of 1942 by USAAF engineers and resulted in uninterrupted training. After another unsuccessful attack on the Tirpitz, staged through Lossiemouth, 617Sqn launched their successful attack in November 1944. Events in Europe were seeing the Germans being constantly pushed back and, in May 1945, 20 OCU stopped taking new trainees and was disbanded in July 1945. Meanwhile, 46 MU operations continued, with some aircraft being prepared for Far East operations as well as for storage. The following month saw the arrival of 111 OUT, with Liberators and Halifaxes from Bermuda, and 1674 Heavy Conversion Unit. A detachment of 280Sqn added Warwicks for air-sea rescue.

After the war, Lossiemouth initially became a satellite for Milltown, before it became HMS *Fulmar* with the RN from 1946 until 29 September 1972, when it returned to RAF control. The SAR Wessexes of 202Sqn were the first to return, then Shackleton AEW.2s of 8Sqn, followed by Jaguars of 226 OCU. In 1978, 2 TWU arrived with their Hunters, plus 48Sqn, RAF Regt with their Rapier SAMs. They were joined by 2622 (Highland) RAF Aux Regt, when they formed in 1979.

Buccaneers of 12Sqn arrived in 1980 and the Hunters departed. By 1984, the remaining Buccaneer fleet (12, 208 and 237 OCU) had moved to Lossiemouth, as this was considered to be nearer to their designated area of operations. In 1991, the Shackletons were retired and, in October, 237 OCU disbanded – its reduced role being conducted by the Buccaneer Training Flight with 208Sqn.

In 1993, the Buccaneers began to be replaced with the Tornado GR.1. October 1993 saw 12Sqn disbanded and Marham's 27Sqn re-numbered 12Sqn, prior to moving to Lossiemouth with the Tornado. In April 1994, 208Sqn was disbanded and was replaced by 617Sqn. Both were to be operated in the maritime attack-role with the Tornado GR.1B and 48Sqn, RAF Regt left in 1996.

Providing aircrew training in aircraft weapon systems is15 (R) Sqn, the Tornado Weapons Conversion Unit (TWCU). When the TTTE at Cottesmore disbanded in March 1999, most of the GR.1s were transferred to 15 (R) Sqn to form a national Tornado OCU. To make room for this influx of aircraft, the Jaguar OCU – 16 (R) Sqn – moved to Coltishall.

Lossiemouth provides such an ideal training base – with its topography, the nearby weapons ranges of Tain and Rosehearty and its good weather – that it is frequently used by other squadrons on exercise.

As with most airfields, a number of non-flying units operate to assist in its protection. At Lossiemouth these include 48Sqn RAF Regiment, which provides air defence with the Rapier SAM and 2622Sqn, R Aux AF Regt for ground defence. In addition, the Army's 237 Airfield Damage Repair (ADR) Squadron provides a quick repair capability for runways and taxiways damaged by air attack.

In 2002, the first of two new Tornado GR.4 simulators built by Thales Training and Simulation (ACE) Ltd was opened, as one of the latest training systems installed in a PFI contract. This will enable Tornado crews to undertake a substantial amount of their training, including realistic emergency drills and operations in hostile environments, without endangering themselves or their aircraft. A third simulator is located at Marham.

Lossiemouth is the home for 12 (B), 14, 15 (R) and 617Sqn, which are equipped with the Tornado GR.4, plus 'D' Flt of 202Sqn, which operates the Sea King HAR.3 in the search and rescue role. Airfield protection is provided by 51Sqn, RAF Regt, 2622Sqn, R Aux AF and the Army's 237 Airfield Damage Repair (ADR) Squadron.

RAF Lyneham

2 Group
Strike Command
Motto: Support, Save, Supply

RAF Lyneham was established on 18 May 1940 as the home for 33 Maintenance Unit (33 MU). It assumed a training role in August 1941 with the arrival of 14 SFTS with Oxfords. Six months later, it was replaced by the Ferry Training Unit. The MU also expanded its recovery-from-storage role. Various types were being held in storage and modified prior to delivery overseas – these included Blenheims, Lysanders, Spitfires and Wellingtons. As numbers built up, 45 Satellite Landing Ground at Townsend near Calne was allocated to 33 MU.

The number of units at Lyneham expanded in 1942, with 1 Flight Ferry Training Unit being formed in March. This was followed in April 1942 with the arrival of 1425 Communications Flight, operating Liberators and later Albemarles – it was re-numbered 511Sqn in October 1942. It was joined by 1444 and 1445 Flights for ferrying aircraft by June and merged together with 1 FFT, to form 301 Ferry Training Unit in November and 1 Ferry Crew Pool the following July. BOAC moved in from Whitchuch with its Liberators. This was the beginning of Lyneham's transport role, with the operation of BOAC flights from 1943 until 1945.

In the meantime, 33 MU was assembling the wooden tank-carrying Hamilcar gliders with components built by a number of furniture manufacturers. In February 1944, 301 FTU moved out, following the arrival of 525Sqn with Warwicks. 242Sqn arrived to take over some of 511's Liberators –it was gradually re-equipping with Dakotas and Yorks – while 525Sqn departed in July.

In December 1945, 1359 Flight was formed as a VIP transport unit with Lancasters and Yorks, departing in February. Once the war ended, 33 MU became busy with the storage of surplus aircraft. By late-1946, there were approaching 750 aircraft in store, of which the majority were Spitfires.

In November 1947, 99 and 206Sqn were re-formed with Yorks. Lyneham crews served with distinction during the Berlin Airlift of 1948–9. From 1950, 99, 242 and 511Sqn converted to the Hastings, while 206Sqn disbanded with its Yorks. In November 1950, 24Sqn arrived to also convert to the Hastings, although it still operated the York for a couple more years.

Many of 33 MU's Spitfires were disposed of, a number of which were supplied to foreign air forces. By now, jet fighters in the form of the Vampire were arriving and being issued to squadrons.

In May 1950, 242Sqn disbanded and was replaced by 53Sqn, also with Hastings. Almost immediately Lyneham was plunged into flying troops and supplies for the Korean War. Its transport role was a cornerstone to numerous operations over the following few years in the Middle East and Africa.

November 1955 saw 216Sqn move in with Valettas. The following year it introduced the jet age to Lyneham's transport fleet when it re-equipped with the Comet 2. Operations continued – now with the Suez Crisis. In 1957, 53 departed and 511Sqn was re-numbered 36Sqn in September 1958. In 1959, the last of the Hastings departed, to make room for the 'Whistling Giant' – the Britannia which served with 99 and 511Sqn. The larger Comet C.4 augmented 216Sqn's fleet from 1962 for extensive VIP use. Thus, Lyneham became the centre of the RAF's long-range transport operations.

The year of 1966 saw the run down of 216Sqn's Comet C.2s and, in 1967, 33 MU closed, but Lyneham's future was looking good. The RAF's first squadron Hercules was delivered to Lyneham for 36Sqn on 1 August 1967. 48Sqn established their strength at Lyneham before deploying to Changi, Singapore, in October 1967. They were replaced by 24Sqn, which arrived in January 1968.

A rationalization of RAF air transport resulted in the move of the Britannia fleet to Brize Norton in 1970. This was followed the next year by the movement of the two Fairford-based Hercules squadrons – 30 and 47 – to Lyneham. With the run down of commitments in the Far East, 48Sqn returned later that year. The 1974 Defence Review brought further consolidation, with the arrival of 242 OCU from Thorney Island and the deep-servicing organization transferring from Colerne. LXX also returned from Cyprus, bringing all the Hercules operations together. However, 36 and 48Sqn were disbanded in November 1975 and January 1976 – 216Sqn having disbanded in June 1975.

The Hercules fleet quickly became a cornerstone of military operations, both on exercises and for real. Wherever army or RAF units needed to deploy, the Hercules were tasked with helping to both move them out and return. Depending on the nature of the deployment, they would also be tasked with the re-supply. Another task that the RAF Hercules has become well-respected for is the air supply of

Lyneham has been the home of the Hercules since the early 1970s. Despite it being known as the 'Home of the RAF Hercules' and the Lyneham Tactical Wing (LTW), it was decided that the airfield will close by 2012. The operations will, by then, have moved to Brize Norton.

humanitarian aid. These tasks have kept Lyneham air and ground crews busier than most other stations.

The Falklands became a major logistical headache for Lyneham with the huge distances involved – 8,000 miles (13,000km). Using the Forward Operating Base (FOB) of Ascension – still some 3,800 miles (6,100km) from the Falklands – the Hercules provided a lifeline for the Task Force. Using in-flight refuelling they were able to deliver urgently required support by air-drop into the sea throughout the campaign. Once the war was over, Lyneham maintained an air-bridge into Stanley – flights which sometimes lasted twenty-eight hours.

The Hercules has provided the backbone to RAF operations – by March 1990 the fleet had flown one million hours. Then came the Gulf War, which resulted in a greater airlift of tonnage than the Berlin Airlift. Since then there have been major conflicts in the Balkans, Afghanistan and Iraq, all of which have required major involvement for the Hercules, both for transport from the UK and back, and in-theatre.

The first C-130J was delivered to Lyneham on 23 November 1999 and this has led to the introduction of a number

training devices, including two dynamic-mission simulators. For aircrew converting to the C-130J, this means a total of thirty-two simulator-based training missions, plus four or five live flights.

In June 2002, 30Sqn became operational on the C-130J and were soon joining 24Sqn in providing aircraft and crews to be based in Oman – for operations flying into Afghanistan to support British and coalition forces there. This has resulted in a split, with 47 and LXXSqn flying the remaining twenty-nine C.1/C.3s, plus 24 and 30Sqn flying the twenty-five new C.4/C.5s.

Lyneham hosts a number of lodger units. Just across the road from the airfield, on the site originally occupied by 33 MU, is 47 Air Despatch (47AD). This army unit is responsible for preparing army equipment prior to loading onto the Hercules. This can range from packing small quantities of vital supplies to constructing Medium Stressed Platforms (MSP) that enable vehicles and field guns to be air dropped. A 47AD air despatcher would also normally fly with the load, to assist with the drop.

The UK Mobile Air Movement Squadron (UKMAMS) provide a vital ground-handling service for RAF trans-

port aircraft. UKMAMS supplies teams to airfields where no suitable RAF organization exists, to organize, load and unload freight and passengers. It is usual for the UKMAMS team to be on the first aircraft to an exercise or operation and the last one out.

The Hercules OEU was established in 1995 to flight-trial and evaluate new equipment, as well as assess tactics and operating procedures. It is part of the Air Warfare Establishment and borrows Hercules as and when required.

Another unit located at Lyneham is the Tactical Medical Wing (TMW), which was formed in April 1996 to provide and support medical service to all deployed RAF personnel worldwide. This ranges from a Deployable Aeromedical Response Squadron to Aeromed. It is supported by 1 Air Evacuation Squadron and 4626 (County of Wiltshire) Aeromedical Evacuation Squadron, R Aux AF.

During 2003, the RAF Tactical Survive to Operate HQ moved in from Honington. At the same time, part of their force had been deployed to Ali Al Salem to provide command and control of the protection elements during the build up of Operation *Telic*.

On 5 July 2003, it was announced that Lyneham would be closed by 2012. The new Hercules C.4 and C.5 would be relocated to Brize Norton, while the older C.1 and C.3 would continue to operate from Lyneham until withdrawn. As a part of this relocation, UKMAMS and TMW will also move to Brize Norton.

In March 2004, Lyneham celebrated 50,000 hours flown by the C-130J Hercules in just two years of operations.

Lyneham currently houses 24 and 36Sqn, which pool the Hercules C.4 and C.5, plus 47 and 70Sqn, which pool the Hercules C.1 and C.3.

RAF Marham

1 Group
Strike Command
Motto: Deter

The origins of Marham can be traced back to August 1915, when RNAS Narborough was opened near Marham village. It was initially used to provide a satellite landing-ground for RNAS Great Yarmouth, which was tasked to combat the German Zeppelin threat to the Midlands.

By the summer of 1916, it had become an RFC airfield and was initially occupied by 35Sqn with the BE.2 FB.5 and FK.3. By the time they were deployed to France in January 1917, they had converted to the FK.8. Formed in August 1916 with RE.8s, 59Sqn deployed in February 1917. In November, 191Sqn was formed to provide night-flying training for pilots on the BE.2d, BE.2c, FE.2b and the DH.7 but, in July 1918, it departed. A number of reserve units were also formed at Marham, including 48Sqn in November 1916, with the DH.6 Shorthorn and RE.8. In 1919 the airfield was closed.

Marham re-opened on 1 April 1937 and first to arrive were Hendons of 38Sqn – 115Sqn was formed from 'B' Flight and re-equipped with the Harrow. By 1939, both had equipped with the Wellington. In December 1939, they flew their first operation. On 22 June, Marham had their first experience of being under attack, when Luftwaffe aircraft dropped bombs on the station. In November, 38Sqn was deployed to the Middle East and was replaced by 218Sqn. In 1942, the squadron re-equipped with Stirlings and moved out to the satellite airfield of Downham Market.

In September 1942, Marham transferred from 3 to 2 Group. The Wellingtons of 115Sqn moved to Mildenhall and were immediately replaced with Mosquitos of 105 and 139Sqn. The first squadron to equip with the Mosquito bomber had been 105Sqn and they developed the low-level (50–100ft) bombing technique that they used to attack Gestapo HQ in Oslo in September 1942. In July 1943, 139Sqn departed, followed by 105Sqn in March 1944. Marham then underwent a major upgrade, including construction of a new, hard runway.

In February 1946, the Central Bomber Establishment was the first to move in, undertaking various trials on a variety of aircraft, including Lancasters, Lincoln and Mosquitos. It departed in 1948, to be replaced in July by USAF B-29s of 340th BS. The Berlin Crisis resulted in further units deploying and the HQ of the 3rd Air Division was established.

Further B-29s arrived in March 1950, but these were actually the first of seventy Washingtons for the RAF to operate as a stopgap whilst awaiting the Canberra. The Washington Conversion Unit was formed in March (later becoming 35Sqn), followed by 115Sqn then equipped 90 and 207Sqn plus 15, 44 and 149Sqn which

moved on to Coningsby and 192Sqn to Watton. During December 1953, two-thirds of the fleet were returned to the USA as Canberra deliveries progressed. First to equip was 90Sqn, followed by 115, 207 and 35Sqn. Although it soldiered on with other units, Marham's Canberras began to be replaced by 'V' bombers.

In January 1956, 214Sqn re-formed at Marham with the Valiant B.1, followed by 207 and 148Sqn. Shortly after, the Suez Crisis resulted in six Valiants being deployed to Malta and used to bomb Egyptian airfields at the beginning of November. All operations ceased following UN pressure and the aircraft returned home.

AT Marham, 214Sqn worked closely with Flight Refuelling in developing air-to-air refuelling. This included a number of long-distance route-proving trials, which resulted in their breaking many records, including non-stop to Changi – 4,350 miles (6,999km) in 15 hours 35 minutes. Their work led to 90 and 214Sqn becoming exclusively tanker units.

In October 1959, 242Sqn had been re-formed with Bloodhound SAMs to provide air defence, but was disbanded

again in September 1964 and the Marham Station Flight consisted of three Chipmunks and two Ansons. In December 1964, the Valiant fleet was grounded as a result of major fatigue problems, which resulted in their being withdrawn and scrapped virtually overnight. In May 1965, the first hastily converted Victor B (K).1A tanker arrived with 55Sqn. and the Tanker Training Flight (TTF) formed the following month. Deliveries to 57Sqn commenced in December. In July 1966, 214Sqn re-formed with the Victor K.1. In February 1970, 232 OCU was reformed, taking over and expanding the role of the TTF and continuing to train crews until disbanding in April 1986.

In January 1976, 100Sqn arrived with Canberras for the target-facility role. It was augmented with further examples when 98Sqn disbanded. It was joined shortly after by 231 OCU – the Canberra training unit.

In 1977, work commenced on preparing Marham for the Tornado, including the construction of twenty-four Hardened Aircraft Shelters (HAS). In January 1982, 100Sqn moved to Wyton. The first

Marham houses the remaining Canberras plus Tornado GR.4/GR.4As. In 1993 it hosted a Royal Review of the RAF, which included a number of Tornado squadrons that no longer operate.

Tornado GR.1 for 617Sqn arrived in March 1983 and July saw the Canberras of 231 OCU depart. In May 1983, 27Sqn re-formed, while 57Sqn disbanded in June 1986. TWCU Tornados from Wyton and 42Sqn Nimrods temporarily deployed during 1987–8, while runways were rebuilt at Wyton and St Mawgan.

The year 1990 saw 27 and 617Sqn deployed to the Middle East in response to the Iraqi invasion of Kuwait – 55Sqn deployed at the end of the year. Following intense action, the squadrons all returned home in June. In December 1991, II (AC) Sqn arrived from Laarbruch to introduce a new role of reconnaissance to the station. In September, 27Sqn disbanded, reformed as 12Sqn and moved to Lossiemouth in January 1994.

Following the defeat of Iraq, a system of monitoring Saddam's military activity on the Marsh Arabs resulted in the establishment of Operation *Southern Watch* to enforce the southern no-fly zone – 617Sqn commenced the patrols that were to see most GR.1 squadrons deployed for a tour.

Marham hosted the RAF's seventy-fifth anniversary celebration in April 1993. Attended by most of the Royal Family, the event was marred by bad weather, causing the flying display to be cancelled. In October, the last of the V-bombers retired, with the disbanding of the Victors of 55Sqn. Their place was filled with 39 (1 PRU) Sqn, which moved in from Wyton. In February 1994, 13Sqn also officially arrived with their reconnaissance Tornado GR.1As from Honington, to co-locate the Tornado reconnaissance assets. This was followed by the departure of 617Sqn for Lossiemouth in April.

In July 2001, IX (B) Sqn arrived, followed by 31Sqn from Bruggen, which was closing. These four Tornado and one Canberra squadrons were then known collectively as the Marham Wing.

The Tactical Imagery Intelligence Wing (TIW) was formed on 1 April 2002 from the RICs (Reconnaissance Intelligence Centre) of each of the three reconnaissance squadrons. These RICs were then designated Tactical Imagery Intelligence Flights (TIF) and came under the control of the TIW, which provided the HQ function – responsible for such areas as

operations, admin and training. In April 2003, the 41 (F) RIC also became part of the TIW, following which it was classified as an Air Combat Support Unit.

From June to October 2003, three Tornado F.3s were deployed on Quick Reaction Alert (QRA) to provide 24-hour cover for the south while the Coningsby runway was resurfaced.

Non-flying units at Marham include the Armament Support Unit, Tornado Maintenance School and 3 Force Protection Wing HQ, who are assisted by 2620 (County of Norfolk) Squadron, R Aux AF in providing security for the station in a hostile environment. More recently the Storm Shadow Central Training Facility was established and Marham was re-elected to provide the Forward and Depth Support sections for the Tornado GR.4 fleet.

Marham have established a history room, which may be visited subject to prior arrangement (Tel: CRO on 01760 337261 ext 7332).

Marham is the home for IX (B) and 31Sqn, which operate the Tornado GR.4, II (AC) and 13Sqn, which are both equipped with the Tornado GR.4A, plus 39 (1 PRU) Squadron with the Canberra PR.9.

RAF Menwith Hill

USVF
Personnel and Training Command

The site was opened in 1960 and occupied by the US Army Security Agency as Menwith Hill Station, operating as a high-technology communications site.

In 1966, the administration of the site transferred to the DoD and the number of military personnel dropped, although overall numbers increased. In February 1996, the site became an RAF station.

Menwith Hill is now operated as an out-station of the National Security Agency (NSA), but includes UK staff from MoD and GCHQ who are integrated to provide intelligence support for the UK, USA and NATO. In addition, the site is the European Relay Ground Station (RGS-E) for the US Space-Based Infra-Red System (SBIRS), which is designed to detect and warn of hostile infra-red targets, such as a missile launch. Still under construction, this is planned to become operational in 2006 and will replace the current Defence Support Programme (DSP). This system was used during the Gulf War to provide warning of Scud missile launches to UK and US troops.

Menwith Hill is a USVF ground station.

RAF Mildenhall

USVF
Personnel and Training Command

The land for an airfield was originally purchased in 1929. The airfield eventually opened on 16 October 1934, to be one of the largest bomber-stations at that time. However, the first arrivals were the competitors for the Royal Aero Club's England to Australia air-race that

Just some of the 'Golfballs' at Menwith Hill, which provide weather protection for the enclosed satellite-tracking dishes. Crown Copyright

commenced on 20 October 1934. At the time it was the longest race and attracted some 70,000 spectators. It was won by pilots C.W.A. Scott and T. Campbell Black, flying the de Havilland Comet 'Grosvenor House', in less than seventy-two hours.

Heyfords of 99Sqn were the first aircraft to arrive in 1934, however, Mildenhall was the subject of another major event on 6 July 1935 when 356 aircraft from thirty-eight squadrons were assembled for the first Royal Review of the RAF by King George V. The following year more Heyfords arrived with 38 and 147Sqn, to be joined by 73Sqn Furies and Gladiators and 211Sqn Audax. In October 1938, 99Sqn became the first squadron to receive the Wellington and, in April 1937, 149Sqn was formed from 99Sqn's 'B' Flight

The storm clouds were building over Europe and on 3 September 1939 – three days after Germany invaded Poland – three Wellingtons from 149Sqn were launched from Mildenhall to attack the German Naval fleet at Wilhelmshaven. In December 1941, 419Sqn, RCAF was formed with Wellingtons and 115Sqn arrived in September 1942, but left two months later. Operations were halted briefly while concrete runways were laid. In April 1943, 15Sqn arrived with Lancasters and 622Sqn formed in August 1943 with Stirlings, converting to Lancasters towards the end of the year. While the Wellingtons had given way to Stirlings and later to Lancasters, they also operated from the satellite airfields of Newmarket, Tuddenham and Lakenheath.

By the end of the war some 8,000 sorties had been flown, during which over 23,000 tons of bombs had been dropped and 2,000 mines laid. Over 200 Mildenhall aircraft were lost during these operations, together with 2,000 aircrew.

With the war in Europe over, Mildenhall's role changed to humanitarian – flying PoWs home and dropping food to Holland. By the late-1940s the station had been reduced to care and maintenance. Only the HQ of 3 Group remained, staying on until 1967.

On 12 July 1950, the USAF's 93rd Bomb Group arrived and from October 1951 until 1958 Mildenhall came under control of Strategic Air Command (SAC). From then on Mildenhall has been the home of various USAF units, as well as others on TDY. In 1959, Mildenhall became the Air Passenger Terminal for the UK for Military Air Transports Service (later Military

Airlift Command). In 1965, 7120th Airborne Command and Control Squadron (7120 ACCS) arrived from France with the Silk Purse Control Group, equipped with C-118s then EC-135s. On 8 June 1966, the base received yet another unit, the 513th Troop Carrier Wing (513 TCW) arrived from France with two C-130 squadrons. It was later re-designated 513th Tactical Airlift Wing (513 TAW). In 1972, the 3rd AF HQ moved in from Ruislip. In 1979 Detachment 4, 9th Strategic Reconnaissance Wing (9 SRW) arrived, operating the SR-71 and U-2. During these thirty years the base has seen aircraft ranging from B-29s to SR-71s.

On 1 February 1992 the 100 ARW was re-activated at Mildenhall and, as part of the 3rd Air Force, has remained the USAF's sole air-refuelling wing for Europe. In 1995, the 352nd Special Operations Group (352nd SOG) moved in from Alconbury with 7th Special Operations Squadron (7th SOS) flying the MC-130H, 21st Special Operations Squadron (21st SOS) the MH-53 and 67th Special Operations Squadron (67th SOS) the MC-130.

Mildenhall continues to be a USVF (United States Visiting Forces) location with only USAFE aircraft based there.

RAF Molesworth

USVF
Personnel and Training Command

Molesworth opened in November 1941 as a bomber base and was initially occupied by 460Sqn, RCAF, which was formed that month with Wellingtons. It departed at the end of the year to be replaced by 159Sqn, which formed in January 1942 with Liberators. It departed the following month, prior to the airfield being handed over to the USAAF, becoming Station 107.

The runways were extended and Americans began to occupy the airfield from May 1942 and saw 5th Photo Reconnaissance Squadron arrive the following month with F-4 Lightnings. They were joined by 15th Bomb Group flying RAF A-20 Havocs, converting to B-17s in August. The following month both units departed, to be replaced by 303rd BG (358th, 359th, 360th and 427th BS) with B-17s, who remained until April 1945.

In May 1945, 441Sqn, RCAF arrived, followed by 442 in August – both flying

Mustangs. However, they were disbanded later that month.

In July 1945, Molesworth returned to RAF control and 1335 Conversion Unit arrived with Meteors, along with 124Sqn. They were followed by 19Sqn in September with Mustangs, converting to Spitfires in March and then 234Sqn. However, all soon departed, with 19Sqn being the last during June 1946, and the airfield then entered a period of care and maintenance.

In July 1951, the USAF returned to Molesworth – runways were lengthened and facilities on the airfield modernized, prior to the arrival of the 582nd Air Resupply Group with B-29s, C-119s and SA-16s in February 1954. In October 1956, it became the 42nd Troop Carrier Squadron with C-54s and SA-16s. In May 1957 the 42nd TCS returned to the USA and Molesworth reverted back to care and maintenance, with just a few small ground units remaining.

September 1985 saw major construction commence, following the selection of Molesworth as a cruise missile facility. Large protective bunkers were built to house the missiles and the 303rd Tactical Missile Wing was activated in December 1986. Following the signing of the US/Soviet Intermediate-Range Nuclear Forces Treaty in 1988, the missiles began to be withdrawn and, in January 1989, the 303rd TMW was inactivated.

In 1991, the Joint Analysis Center (JAC) arrived. Its role is to process, analyse and consolidate data to produce comprehensive intelligence on various countries across Europe, Africa and the Middle East.

Molesworth is a USVF site maintained by the 423rd ABS.

RAF Mona

Personnel and Training Command

Mona was originally opened in 1915, when it was known as Llangefni Airship Station and, at one time, had twenty-two hangars. When the war ended, dirigibles were flown under the Menai Bridge as part of the celebrations, before the station was closed.

When Mona was re-opened in 1942, the first unit to arrive was 3 Air Gunnery School (3 AGS) in December, operating forty-eight Bothas plus Battles and Martinets. Ansons subsequently replaced the Bothas and 3 AGS departed in October 1943. It was replaced by 8 (O) AFU in November 1943 with Ansons and they remained until June 1945, with up to forty-five Ansons training 200 air gunners, bomb aimers and navigators at a time. In June 1945, 8 (O) AFU disbanded and the airfield was placed in care and maintenance.

Mona was re-opened again in 1951 as a relief landing-ground for Valley.

Mona has no based aircraft, but operates as a RLG for Valley.

RAF Mount Pleasant, Falkland Islands

Overseas

Mount Pleasant was officially opened on 12 May 1985, to provide a military replacement for the airfield at Stanley on the Falkland Islands, which was handed back to civilian operations on 1 May 1986. Mount Pleasant had already been declared fully operational on that date.

Following Operation *Corporate*, to regain the Islands from the Argentinians, initial operations were flown in and out of Stanley Airport. However, this small airfield was impracticable for sustained operations. The 2,000ft (610m) runway and apron were covered in AM2 reinforced-runway matting and the air-defence Phantoms required an arrester wire for landing. The Hercules airbridge was also expensive and limited in capacity.

Vital to the protection of the Falklands and even more urgent than the new airfield was the construction of radar sites to establish the Falkland Island Air Defence Ground Environment system (FIADGE). Mount Kent was initially selected to house the first permanent land-based radar, plus a Control and Reporting Centre. Because of the difficult terrain, much of the transport had to be carried out by Chinook. By early 1983, a Control and Reporting Centre was fully operational. A requirement for two further forward radar-sites was deemed necessary, to replace the temporary system and to replace that being provided by Royal Navy warships to give long-range early warning. The location of these sites was complicated. Maximum coverage was not the only factor. Because of the remoteness of the landscape, especially in the Western Falklands, ease of construction and future supportability were also major

The Tristar provides a regular airbridge to the Falklands from the UK using the airfield at Mount Pleasant.

considerations. Such was the urgency that a temporary southern site was established at Cape Orford while the main site at Mt Alice was built, enabling the system to be re-located.

Although the Mt Kent installation was complex, the logistics were simplified by the closeness of the airfield at Stanley and the available support. The West Falklands was completely different. The solution was for two ships to be anchored as close as possible to the sites, with materials and equipment stored to enable sequential access. These Ships Taken Up From Trade (STUFT) also required heli-decks, not only for the loading but to provide overnight accommodation. In concert with Army Royal Engineers, major planning and training was required for what was to become a major task, with over 1,000 Chinook flying hours. Detailed recce of the site and weather conditions provided valuable further components of the planning.

By November 1983, the construction teams were on site. Byron Heights to the north had plenty of locally available sand and stone, but suffered badly from weather, especially hilltop cloud-cover. Meanwhile, Mt Alice had better weather but no hard-core, resulting in the need to transport materials from Port Stanley. As a result

both projects suffered from intermittent continuity. Despite this and to the credit of those involved, the sites were ready for the AR3D radars in April as planned. This stage was conducted flawlessly, although the 29-mile (46km) transfer from Cape Orford to Mt Alice required a fuel stop due to the weight of the system, which complicated life. By late-April, both sites were handed over and were declared operational by mid-summer. Sadly, the crew of an army Lynx were lost during the operation.

Each site is self-contained, with an integral processing and power-generation facility, and run by its own ops and engineering sections. Each is designated a separate unit – Byron Heights was 7 SU, Mt Alice 751 SU and 303 SU at Mt Kent. Their projected life was five years, however, they continue to provide an effective component of the defence of the Falkland Islands. All three sites are now designated Reporting Posts and the CRC is operated by 303 SU.

While this work was being undertaken, various sites were surveyed for a new airfield. Eventually, the site of Mount Pleasant was selected and the new airfield built, complete with a hangar capable of accommodating a Tristar. While the problems of building were different to the radar sites, they were also impressive, due to the huge scale of the operation and the remoteness. Substantial quantities of materials had to be supplied from the UK and so a port was built at Mare Harbour, to enable ships to unload relatively close to the site.

Since opening the airfield, a regular airlink to Brize Norton has been operated, either by 216Sqn Tristar or a contractor airline routing via Ascension.

The Phantoms of 23 (F) Sqn moved over from Stanley, where it was re-numbered 1435 Flight in November 1988 and, in July 1992, was re-equipped with the Tornado F.3.

The 1312 Flt Hercules also moved over from Stanley in 1985. Initially the tanker K.1Ps were used, but were replaced with the C.1 when the Hercules tankers were withdrawn and replaced by VC.10s in 1986. The Hercules have provided a maritime reconnaissance capability and resupply to South Georgia.

In 1986, the pair of Chinooks of 1310 Flight at San Carlos and Sea King HAR.3s of 1564 Flight at Naval Point were amalgamated to re-form 78Sqn and established at Mount Pleasant.

The Falkland Island Government Air Service (FIGAS) also operate their Islanders from Mount Pleasant, providing air communications around the Islands for the civilian community. Sikorsky S-61s are also operated by British International.

Mount Pleasant is home to 1312 Flight with a VC.10 tanker on detachment from 101Sqn and a Hercules from Lyneham, 1435 Flight with Tornado F.3s, 78Sqn with Chinook HC.2 and Sea King HAR.3 and a Rapier Detachment from the RAF Regiment.

RAF Neatishead

3 Group
Strike Command
Motto: *Caelum Tuemur* – We watch over the sky

Neatishead was opened in June 1941, to provide a Ground Control Intercept (GCI) service using a Type 8C mobile radar. Following training, it conducted its first intercept in March 1942 with a 255Sqn Beaufighter from Hibaldstow. This resulted in damage to a He 111 but, the following month, the first successful kill was achieved with a 604Sqn Beaufighter from Coltishall.

In January 1942, the constantly rotating Type 7 radar was installed in the happidrome, but took a full year before it was fully operational.

In March 1947, Neatishead became a Sector Operations Centre and, in July 1953, was re-named 271 Signals Unit. The radars were upgraded but, in 1961, it ceased operations and was placed on care and maintenance. It re-opened in 1963 as a Master Radar Station and was equipped with a Type 84 radar.

Disaster struck in February 1966, when fire completely destroyed the underground operations-complex, closing the station once more until 1974. It re-opened in April, equipped with a new data-handling system in the old, 1942 building. As a result, it became responsible for controlling fighters at Binbrook, Coltishall, Coningsby, and Wattisham, plus Marham's Victor tankers and the AEW Shackletons at Lossiemouth. It also provided control for the UK-based fighters of the USAF.

The Integrated Command and Control System (ICCS) was introduced in the 1980s, to provide a highly advanced air-defence system. This involved the refurbishment of the underground bunker with a new data-handling system, together with new digital, phased-array, transportable 90-series radars. The idea being that these new radars could be rapidly deployed to pre-positioned sites and transmit their data back via secure communications, making them less vulnerable. It was April 1993 before the new system became full operational.

The nearby site at Trimingham also dates back to the Second World War, when it was a Chain Home (Low) station. From 1954, it fed radar data into Neatishead. During the mid-1980s it was re-equipped with the mobile T90 series radar. Due to its mobility, it was designated 432 SU but, following the end of the Cold War, it was decided to erect a weatherproof dome and the now-static site became a subordinate of Neatishead.

Neatishead houses one of the two operational Control and Reporting Centres and is responsible for the Southern UK Air Defence Region, which comprises the area roughly to the south of Newcastle. It provides a vital part of the UK Air Surveillance and Control System (ASACS) and the Combined Air Operations Centre (CAOC) located within Strike Command at High Wycombe. Here the overall picture is compiled, enabling the appropriate decision to be taken regarding necessary action. A third site at Boulmer houses a standby CRC. Following the downgrading of Buchan from CRC to RP, the role of Neatishead expanded to include that of Buchan's CRC.

In addition to its operational role, Neatishead also is the location for the award-winning RAF Air Defence Radar Museum. It was opened in October 1994 in the 1942 building and traces the history and development of Air Defence Radar during the period 1935 to 1993.

In April 2004, the results of a Strike Command study concluded that the Air Surveillance and Control System units would benefit by being located at Scampton. As a consequence, the CRC function at Neatishead moved to Scampton and operational staff moved to Boulmer. On 1 April 2005, Neatishead was downgraded to a remote radar-head.

Neatishead is currently a remote radar-head.

RAF Northolt

2 Group
Strike Command
Motto: *Aut Portare Aut Pugnare Prompti* – Ready to carry or to fight

Despite several failed attempts to establish a civilian airfield at Northolt from 1910, it was in 1914 that the land was requisitioned for the RFC. On 3 March 1915, BE.2cs of 4 Reserve Aeroplane Squadron (4 RAS) arrived from Farnborough and became the first occupants, with Longhorn pusher-biplanes. Later that year, Northolt was designated a Home Defence night landing-ground, with a BE.2c maintained at readiness to be scrambled. The first recorded instance of their being launched was on 4/5 June, during a Zeppelin raid over Kent.

On 1 May 1915, 18Sqn was formed with a mixed fleet of Gunbus, DH.2 and Scouts, followed by 11 RAS in November, when 18Sqn was deployed to France. In March 1916, 43Sqn arrived for a temporary stay, while it re-equipped and trained on the Sopwith 1½ Strutter before deploying to France in January 1917.

On 13 June 1917, a 35 RAS F.2b Fighter intercepted a formation of enemy bombers over Ilford – believed to be the only contact Northolt-based aircraft had during the First World War.

In July 1917, 74Sqn was formed at Northolt, but moved out shortly after. Northolt had been involved in training for some while and, when the RAF was formed from the RFC and RNAS, the station became RAF Northolt and operated as a training base, although this role declined rapidly once the war ended.

In May 1919, Northolt Flight was established to provide refresher training and, following several name changes, became 12 (Bomber) Sqn in 1923. Around the same time, 41 (Fighter) Sqn was re-formed and remained until it moved to Aden in September 1935.

When the Government decided to establish the Royal Auxiliary Air Force in 1925, Northolt became home to the first two units – 600 (City of London) and 601 (County of London) Bombing Squadron with DH.9As and Avro 504s, although both moved to Hendon in 1927.

In 1925, the Cairo–Cape–England Flight was formed with Fairey IIIDs, to pioneer scheduled flights to South Africa. In January 1927, 24 (Communication) Sqn was established at Northolt to fly VIPs on urgent business, with various two-seat

aircraft including the Avro 504, DH.9A, and the F.2b Fighter, although these were later mainly replaced by the Fairey IIIF.

In 1933, 24Sqn departed, replaced by 111 (Fighter) Sqn with Bulldogs in 1934, re-equipping with Gauntlets in 1936. London UAS was formed in October 1935 with Tutors and Harts. Northolt aircraft frequently participated in the nearby Hendon displays and 41Sqn was one of the favourites. From 1935, Northolt held their own annual Empire Air Days, with a crowd of 22,000 attending in 1938 – the war made 1939 the last.

During the late 1930's Rearmament Programme, there was much toing and froing of units based at Northolt. With war looming, 111Sqn re-equipped again in January 1938, to become the RAF's first Hurricane squadron. When war broke out, Northolt was home to 111Sqn plus 600 (City of London) Sqn with Blenheims. In January 1940, 604 (County of Middlesex) Sqn arrived and was later joined by 257 and 609 (West Riding of Yorkshire) Sqn with Hurricanes and Spitfires. Northolt housed a Sector Operations room as part the defences within 11 Group

As the Battle of Britain broke, 257Sqn departed, to be replaced by 1Sqn,

followed by 43Sqn and 1 (RCAF) Sqn – both with Hurricanes – in August. Also in August, the leading elements of 303 (Polish) Sqn arrived to form the unit. By the end of the Battle, it was calculated that some 4,000 bombs had been dropped within a two-mile radius of the well-camouflaged airfield, of which fewer than twenty actually fell on the airfield. Northolt squadrons had put up a fine fight, with 148 enemy aircraft destroyed with a further twenty-five probables, plus fifty-two damaged.

As the war continued, Northolt squadrons conducted fighter sweeps over France. 306 and 308Sqn arrived to form 1 Polish Fighter Wing. On 19 August 1942, the wing took part in the raid on Dieppe.

When RAF Transport Command was formed in March 1943, Northolt was designated the command's main London Terminal. By August 1943, Northolt's Spitfire Wing, which included 124Sqn, were operating over Germany. Although most had already previously operated from Northolt earlier in the war, 1943 saw an influx of Polish fighter squadrons – hence the Polish War Memorial just outside the airfield. These units included 302, 303, 308 and 317 (Polish) Sqn. In April 1944, Northolt become a forward aerodrome in the Tangmere Sector and saw various reconnaissance units use its facilities, including 16Sqn with Spitfires, 69Sqn with Wellingtons and 140Sqn with Mosquitos. In June 1944, a C-54 Skymaster was delivered for use by the Prime Minister – Winston Churchill

Immediately after the war, 271Sqn commenced a scheduled service to Brussels with Dakotas. In February 1946, Northolt was loaned to the Ministry of Civil Aviation and operated as a civil airport. At its peak in 1950, it handled 47,697 movements, while 773,000 passengers were handled in 1952. For seven years it was the busiest airport in Europe.

RAF control returned in 1954, but it was 1957 before aircraft were based there again, when the Metropolitan Communications Squadron arrived from Hendon. Their continuation-flying role ended in 1960, resulting in the loss of the Anson and Chipmunks, although they continued to operate Devons, Pembrokes, Sycamores and Valettas. The Southern Communications Squadron arrived in 1969 and the two were subsequently renamed 32 and 207Sqn. Later, 32Sqn re-

RAF Police provide security for a BAe 146 while awaiting a VIP at Northolt.

equipped with the Andover, Basset, HS.125 and Whirlwind, however, the Basset was retired overnight on 29 April 1974.

During the 1960s there were several incidents with civil airliners, including a Pan-American 707 landing – just! – at Northolt in error for Heathrow. In 1970 an Indian AF Constellation caused mayhem when it overshot a bad approach and turned south to cross Heathrow's approach. Not quite as dramatic, the No 1 Aeronautical Information Documents Unit (1 AIDU) arrived at Northolt during that period and 207Sqn disbanded with the RAF's last operational Devons.

When the Queen's Flight disbanded at Benson, the closeness to London of Northolt and its squadron role resulted in 32 (The Royal) Sqn taking over the task (and gaining the new title). The BAe.146 CC.2 and Wessex HCC.4 were added to the squadron, but the latter were withdrawn in April 1998.

April 1991 saw the formation of No. 1 (County of Middlesex) Maritime Headquarters Unit – a R Aux AF unit formed to provide support for the Coastal Command HQ at nearby Northwood. It was re-named 600 (City of London) Sqn in November 1999. This was followed by the formation of the Station Flight in August 1991 and the arrival of the first of two Islanders. A new operations-building opened on the south side of the airfield in January 1995 and marked an increase in the use of the airfield by civilian business-aircraft.

Future plans for Northolt have been included in the MoD Estate London (MoDEL) project, which was launched in October 2002. The plan is to reduce the number of MoD sites in London, which will make funds available to improve accommodation at the core sites and reduce operating costs in the long term, as well as improving security. As a core site, Northolt would take some units from Uxbridge and all from Inglis Barracks, Mill Hill and Bentley Priory.

Remaining a Lodger Unit is 1 AIDU, producing Flight Information Publications and maintaining a worldwide digital database of aeronautical information, aimed primarily at the Armed Forces.

Northolt is the home for 32 (The Royal) Sqn, which is equipped with BAe.125 CC.3, BAe.146 CC.3 and the Twin Squirrel, plus Northolt Station Flight with the Islander CC.2 and CC.2A.

RAF Odiham

Joint Helicopter Command
Motto: Promise and Fulfil

During the middle of 1925, Odiham was used as the site for a summer camp for army co-operation aircraft, but reverted to pasture afterwards. Later, an airfield was constructed and opened on 18 October 1937 by General Erhard Milch – the Chief of Staff of the Luftwaffe – an interesting guest considering the time. A story exists that he was so impressed with the airfield that he told Hitler he would use it as his headquarters once England was conquered. As a result, he ordered his pilots not to bomb the airfield.

Following the outbreak of war, 614Sqn moved to France and was replaced by Lysanders of 225Sqn. Odiham subsequently housed various training units for Canadians and included 400Sqn with Lysanders, as well as escaped French and Belgian airmen. Fighter Command took over Odiham in June 1943, with Mustangs followed by Typhoons.

Odiham became a transit base for the D-Day follow-up units and then housed a PoW Reception Centre. Some of the tin hut remains can still be seen in an old nearby quarry.

In mid-1945, a Canadian AF Transport Wing was briefly established at Odiham, followed by 271Sqn Dakotas, prior to the arrival of aircraft from Fighter Command. These included the Spitfire, Hunter and Javelin. In July 1948, six 54Sqn Venoms took off from Odiham and flew to the USA via Iceland, Greenland and Labrador, to make the first jet-crossing of the Atlantic. In 1953, Odiham was the site for the Coronation Review of the RAF. Statically 318 aircraft were displayed, while a further 641 took part in the flypast.

The first Hunter display team – the Black Knights – was formed by 54Sqn in 1955 and, the following year, 46Sqn became the first to fly the Javelin. By July 1959 flying had ceased and Odiham reverted to care and maintenance.

In February 1960, Odiham re-opened under Transport Command with the Sycamore. This was followed by the Whirlwind in May and Belvedere in November. A small fixed-wing unit – the Pioneer Conversion Flight – also existed, to train pilots on the Pioneer and Twin Pioneer. The Wessex arrived in 1961, to gradually become the mainstay of Odiham

operations until the arrival of the 33Sqn Pumas in September 1971. In December 1971, 240 OCU was formed, to provide training for Wessex and Puma aircrew.

In November 1980, 230Sqn Pumas were moved to Gütersloh in Germany, while 18Sqn converted from Wessex to Chinook. In 1981, 72Sqn Wessex moved out to Benson and was replaced by the Chinooks of 7Sqn in September 1982. The Joint Helicopter Support Unit (JHSU) was hastily formed from a mixture of army and RAF personnel, to provide specialist support for the Chinook. In May 1983, 18Sqn also moved to Gütersloh.

For the next ten years the unit situation remained static, with 33Sqn operating the Puma HC.1 and 7Sqn with the Chinook HC.1, plus 240 OCU providing aircrew training for both types. During 1993, the Chinooks underwent an upgrade programme, from which they emerged as HC.2s. In October, the OCU was re-numbered 27 (R) Sqn.

In 1997, the Support Helicopter Force underwent a reorganization. As a result, 33Sqn took its Pumas to Benson, 27 (R) Sqn lost its Pumas and was designated a fully operational squadron and 18Sqn returned from Germany. In 2000, 657Sqn AAC arrived from Dishforth.

The squadrons and personnel of Odiham have been heavily committed on many operations over recent years, first with the Falklands and then the Gulf War, when seventeen Chinooks and nineteen Pumas were deployed. More recently, they have been to Bosnia, Sierra Leone, Afghanistan and Iraq. This is in addition to the standing commitments to Northern Ireland and the Falklands and emergency aid to the civil community.

Odiham is the home of 7, 18 and 27Sqn, which all operate the Chinook HC.2. Also, 7Sqn makes use of Army Gazelle AH.1s and are due to receive the Chinook HC.3. It is also the home of 657Sqn AAC, with the Lynx AH.7.

RAF Pembrey Sands

1 Group
Strike Command

The airfield at Pembrey opened 3 September 1939 and 2 Air Armament School were the first occupants. In June 1940, 92Sqn Hurricanes arrived, followed by 79Sqn in September, forming part of the 10 Group defences during the Battle of Britain. In 1941, 1 Air Gunnery School (AGS) arrived and remained until 1945, providing periods of gunnery training for the Group's squadrons. These included 32, 238, 248 and 256Sqn, each visiting for a month or so. In February 1941, 316Sqn formed with Hurricanes, as one of the Polish units.

On 23 June 1942, one of the latest Luftwaffe fighters – a Fw.190A – landed as a result of a navigation error, was captured and was subjected to evaluation by the RAE.

From October 1946, 595Sqn was based at Pembrey to provide anti-aircraft co-operation duties, flying various aircraft, including Spitfires and Vampires. It was re-named 5Sqn in February 1949.

In October 1949, Pembrey was placed into care and maintenance and, the same year, RAF Regt 21 Depot Wing arrived, remaining until October 1952.

In September 1952, 233 OCU was formed with Vampires, to train fighter pilots. It was later equipped with Hunters, before disbanding in September 1957. The station then went into care and maintenance until April 1964, when it became a range. In August 1997, part of the airfield was opened as a civil airport.

Pembrey is an air-weapons range, primarily used by 19Sqn Hawks from Valley.

RRH Portreath

3 Group
Strike Command
Motto: Ever alert

Portreath opened on 14 March 1941 as a Fighter Sector Station. Its role, and that of the satellite stations opened at Perranporth and Predannack in April and May, was to provide fighter defence for much of the south-west coast, including convoys in the approaches. In the distant past, parts of Nancekuke common had been used as a Victorian rifle range.

The first inhabitants were 263Sqn with Whirlwinds, who were replaced by Spitfires of 152Sqn during April. In June, 130Sqn was formed with Spitfires and flew in support of Blenheims attacking German targets. In August, 152Sqn departed and was replaced by 313 (Czech) Sqn. An Overseas Air Despatch Unit was established in October as a final UK stopping

point prior to flying mainly to Gibraltar and the Mediterranean. In addition, substantial numbers of aircraft stopped to refuel either prior to or after crossing the Atlantic. With most transit aircraft operating at maximum weight, four runways were built, one of which was about a mile long.

The German battleships *Gneisenau* and *Scharnhorst* operating from Brest were the subject of numerous attacks – with only limited results. A number of these attacks were launched from airfields in the south west and included 22Sqn's Beauforts, which had arrived at Portreath for a couple of months from March 1942 before deploying on to Ceylon. In April, 234Sqn arrived with Spitfires and remained until the end of the year, although it operated from the RLGs when Portreath became overloaded with transit aircraft. Meanwhile, 152Sqn departed in August.

Plans to attack Italy from North Africa led to Operation *Torch* and saw large numbers of aircraft in transit. At one point, the airfield was manned by 2,250 personnel and recorded as having 107 aircraft on it. Transit aircraft included the Blenheim, Halifax, Mosquito and Spitfire and even Horsa gliders. In addition, USAAF units also passed through, flying C-47s and B-24 Liberators and even P-47 Thunderbolts and P-38 Lightnings. From March 1943, 295Sqn operated Halifaxes, also frequently towing Horsas to Gibraltar then on to North Africa for Operations *Beggar Husky* and *Elaborate*. In August 1943, 235Sqn arrived, followed by 143Sqn – both equipped with Beaufighters. In February 143Sqn departed and was replaced by 248Sqn with Mosquitos – 235 converted to Mosquitos and both flew operations in support of the D-Day landings before departing by September.

During 1945, the Transport Command Briefing School moved in and was joined in 1946 by the Polish Resettlement Air Corps, but they moved out in 1948, when the station was placed under care and maintenance. The Polish airmen farmed a portion of the airfield for their needs – this is still referred to as the 'Polish Farm'.

In May 1950, the site was transferred to the Ministry of Supply and housed the Nancekuke Chemical Defence Establishment (CDE). During its early years, it was involved in the small-scale production of various chemical agents. In 1956, when the UK declared that it would cease its chemical-weapons programme, the plans for full-scale production were halted. From then

on it operated in support of Porton Down, providing research into defence against CW and the production of anti-riot agents, such as CS Gas, until it was closed in 1976. It became increasingly involved in the development of medical countermeasures, training stimulants and the development of the charcoal cloth that is in NBC suits used today by all of the British Forces.

Following a 1976 defence review, the CDE role transferred to Porton Down, Nancekuke began to decommission and, by 1979, the site had been decontaminated and dismantled. A team of international inspectors from the Committee of Disarmament visited in March, to witness the decommissioning. Verification being an important part of disarmament, the site remains open to inspection by members of the Organization for the Prohibition of Chemical Weapons (OPCW).

In July 1979, 1 Air Control Centre (1 ACC) deployed to Portreath to provide a GCI capability for the south-west approaches.

With the CDE closed, the airfield returned to the RAF control in September 1979, when 1 Air Control Centre (1 ACC) deployed to Portreath to provide a GCI capability for the south-west approaches. By September 1980, the various facilities were upgraded, Portreath was given full station status and 1 ACC was disbanded. In 1995, the manning level was reduced and Portreath was classified as a Control and Reporting Post and parented by St Mawgan.

Using surplus capacity leased out by Defence Estates to Cornwall County Council, the Cornwall Fire Brigade have established a training and development department at Portreath, which they use for a variety of small and major incident training.

Between 2002 and 2004, various surveys and investigations were conducted as a result of concerns that the decontamination processes of forty years ago did not meet the stricter standards of today. A major land-quality survey is underway and the RAF have undertaken to take remedial action on five sites in which debris was buried. This could take seven years to complete, commencing from summer 2005. Despite all of this, parts of the site have been designated as a Site of Special Scientific Interest (SSSI).

Following several rounds of restructuring within Strike Command, between 2000

Although the runway at Portreath is only occasionally used, the airfield continues to play an important role, with its powerful long-range radar monitoring the South West Approaches.

and 2003, Portreath was re-titled a remote radar-head (RRH) in October 2003. Command of Portreath transferred to Neatishead, although St Mawgan continues to provide extensive parenting support.

Currently, one runway is maintained in good repair to act as a relief landing-ground (RLG), purely for helicopters from St Mawgan and Culdrose

Portreath is currently a Radar Reporting Post parented by St Mawgan and has no resident flying units.

Prestwick

3 Group
Strike Command

Prestwick originally opened as a civil airfield in 1934; although it never became an RAF station, a variety of military aircraft have used the airfield.

Developed by David McIntre, Prestwick became home to Scottish Aviation, providing training on Tiger Moths from 1935. When war broke out, the airfield was used by a number of aircraft – 141Sqn with Blenheims was one: briefly staying in October 1938 and returning the following year with Defiants. Prestwick was also used for military aircraft being delivered on the lease-lend programme from the USA for the RAF. The USAAF also began to operate at Prestwick from 1942 and, similarly,

used it an arrival point for aircraft being delivered to the 8th AF. At its peak, deliveries of anything up to 300 aircraft were arriving in a day.

In 1944, the RAF opened a flying control centre at Prestwick, which formed part of the beginning of an air traffic control system for the UK.

With the war over, the military use subsided, but the production facilities established by Scottish Aviation continued, with aircraft such Pioneer and Twin Pioneer being built for the RAF and later the Bulldog and Jetstream. In 1977, it was absorbed into British Aerospace and currently houses their Aerostructures and Regional Aircraft Divisions.

The civil airport also grew as a major terminal for transatlantic air traffic, having excellent weather and being one of the closet airfields to the USA. A new Oceanic and Scottish Airways Centre was established in 1959 – Oceanic controlling transatlantic air traffic. In 1978, a new Scottish Air Traffic Control Centre was opened and was the first in the UK to operate a fully processed radar-system. In 1999, approval was given for a new Centre at Prestwick. A complete upgrade of the SATCC was approved in 1999, but stalled after the 9/11 terrorism. In 2003, approval was given again, which, together with Swanwick, is being seen as enabling the UK to be at the forefront of the Single European Sky, once completed in 2009.

The RAF presence at Prestwick is maintained through the Scottish Air Traffic Control Centre (Mil) (ScATCC (Mil)), which is controlled by the HQ Military Air Traffic Operations (MATO). It provides a radar service to military and civil aircraft, and monitors a distress and diversion cell for emergencies.

The Royal Navy also formed a presence in 1971 when HMS *Gannet* was established. It has housed various helicopter squadrons, providing anti-submarine duties to defend the submarine base at Faslane and also providing an SAR capability. Wessex and, later, Sea King squadrons that have been based there are 814, 824 and 819Sqn. In November 2001, 819Sqn decommissioned and was replaced by HMS *Gannet* SAR Flight, a detachment of 771 NAS. HMS *Gannet* also provides parenting for RAF personnel at ScATCC (Mil).

Prestwick houses the Scottish Air Traffic Control Centre (Mil).

RAF St Athan

Personnel and Training Command
Motto: *Y Siafft I Flaen Y Bicell* – The shaft for the spearhead

Land to build the airfield at St Athan was purchased in June 1936 and, from September 1938, RAF personnel began to arrive at the new station. The 4 School of Technical Training (4 SoTT) was formed, with various training airframes, including Harts, Furies and Avro 504Ks. A training flight was also established with Magisters.

A total of thirty-six hangars had been built during the construction of the station, which was the largest RAF airfield at that time. While some were occupied by 4 SoTT, most of these were occupied by 19 and 32 MUs. Established in February 1939, 19 MU was mainly civilian manned and looked after stored aircraft, including Ansons, Blenheims, Hampden and Hurricanes – by the end of 1939 they had some 300 aircraft on charge. Established in July of the same year, 32 MU was mainly made up of reservists, who consisted of a range of trades. They worked on aircraft preparing them for issuing to the flying units. This included converting Blenheim bombers to fighters and preparing Ansons for the Empire Training Programme. They were also responsible for the scrapping of a number of obsolete aircraft.

As Project *Red Dragon* is completed, the DARA aircraft maintenance is being consolidated into large purpose-built hangars at St Athan.

A few flying units were also based at St Athan in the early days, for a short time. These included 11 (Fighter) Group Pool with Hurricanes in June 1939, which departed the following March. The School of Air Navigation with Ansons arrived in September 1939 and left the following August. In September 1943, 12 Radio School with Ansons and Oxfords arrived, to be joined by 14 Radio School in June 1944 and the Signals Instructors School.

A number of nationalities who had escaped from the advancing Germans were located at St Athan, including Belgians, Czechs and French. Some French even arrived in French AF aircraft, which were used to re-establish their École de Pilotage No 23 before being absorbed into the RAF as 1 French Training School.

To disperse stored aircraft following some Luftwaffe raids, 6 Satellite Landing Ground (SLG) was established near St Brides and another – 7 SLG – temporarily at Chepstow race course. By the end of 1945, 661 aircraft were with 19 MU.

Post-war the MUs were tasked with disposing of large numbers of surplus aircraft, as well as accepting the new jets for preparation for delivery to the squadrons. Sadly, a number of historical aircraft were scrapped during this period, resulting in many of the Second World War types no longer being in existence. Fortunately, the establishment of the Historic Aircraft Collection in the 1960s saw the preservation of a number of the survivors, which became established as the RAF Museum's reserve collection.

The University of Wales Air Squadron was formed at St Athan in September 1963 with the Chipmunk T.10, which were replaced with Bulldogs in the early 1970s and now with the Tutor T.1.

By 1968, the work of the MUs had significantly decreased and they were reduced to sub units in November within the St Athan Aircraft Engineering Wing.

In 1992, the Repair and Salvage Squadron (RSS) facilities at Abingdon were transferred to St Athan and, in 1995, the Non-Destructive Testing Squadron (NDT Sqn) was formed. Prior to their merging, it had previously been the Structures Squadron and the Aircraft Integrity Monitoring Squadron at Swanton Morley within the Maintenance Group Defence Agency. It provides the NDT capability, support and training for the RAF, using various NDT techniques. It has since become a tri-service unit, under the Assistant Director Aircraft Integrity Monitoring based at Gosport, and remains a lodger at St Athan.

On 7 April 1999, 19 and 32 MUs finally closed and became the fixed-wing division of the Defence Aviation Repair Agency (DARA). It currently provides the scheduled major maintenance, repair and overhaul of the RAF's fixed-wing aircraft, including Dominies, Hawks, Jaguars, Tornado F.3s and VC.10s, as well as Royal Navy Sea Harriers. Harrier and Tornado GR.4 servicing moved to Wittering and Marham respectively following the End-to-End Logistics Review, in which it was concluded that greater use of service personnel should be made in peacetime to maintain a sufficient deployable manpower level. Although no flying examples are based at St Athan, small numbers of these types may be retained in storage.

February 2003 saw Project *Red Dragon* commence, with the cutting of turf for a new £77m super-hangar for DARA. Once complete it will enable consolidation of the thirteen separate sites at St Athan. It will be capable of housing forty-eight fast-jets and was officially opened on 14 April 2005. In May 2003, St Athan saw a new, additional role with the army and the arrival of the 1st Battalion Welsh Guards.

On 1 April 2004, 4 SoTT became part of the tri-service Defence Training College of Electro-Mechanical Engineering, which is centred at HMS *Sultan*, Gosport.

St Athan houses a mountain rescue team and the Tactical Armament Flight Detachment (TAF Det) from Valley operates to refuel and re-arm 19 (R) Sqn Hawks. They use St Athan as a forward-operating base (FOB) due to its closeness to the ranges at Pembrey, thus saving around forty minutes of flying time.

St Athan is home for the University of Wales Air Squadron, which is equipped with the Tutor T.1. It also houses the 634 VGS, which operates the Viking glider to give ATC cadets air experience. The Engineering Wing, operated by DARA, provides maintenance for the Hawk, Jaguar, Tornado F.3 and VC10.

RAF St Mawgan

3 Group
Strike Command
Motto: *Vigila* – Ever watchful

The airfield at St Mawgan was originally known as Treblezue Big Field and operated several civilian services from May 1939. This was suspended in September 1939 and, by 1941, it had become a satellite landing ground for St Eval, which had been build a few miles further up the coast.

Treblezue Big Field transferred from Coastal Command to 44 Group Ferry Command at the end of 1941 and saw a large number of flights passing through, transiting to and from many overseas locations. The RCAF became the first units to be actually based at St Mawgan. They operated Mustangs and Mosquitos from the end of 1942 until February 1943.

On 23 February 1943, Treblezue Big Field was re-named St Mawgan. Hard runways were built and then many USAAF aircraft joined the list of transiting aircraft. During one week in November 1944, 120 new aircraft arrived from the USA. St Mawgan also provided a link on the route operated from Prestwick to Naples. In 1947 St Mawgan was closed, although some limited civilian pleasure and charter flights and a weekly scheduled service commenced in 1950.

In 1951, St Mawgan reopened for military use, in the hands of Coastal Command once more, and the civil flying stopped. The Air Sea Warfare Development Unit (ASWDU) arrived in May, followed by the School of Maritime Reconnaissance in June. 'A' Flight of 22Sqn arrived in April 1956 June with Whirlwinds, to be joined by their HQ in June. The school continued to operate Lancasters until it departed in October 1956. Its place was taken by 220 and 228Sqn with Shackletons. These were re-numbered 201 in October 1958 and 206Sqn in April 1959 respectively. In August 1957, 220Sqn became the first squadron to take delivery of the Shackleton MR.3. The ASWDU departed in September 1958 and was replaced by 42Sqn the following month. In June 1959, Starways began a summer tourist-service with DC-3s and DC-4s. The MOTU arrived in June 1965 from Kinloss, while 201 and 206 moved the other way.

The civil operations were expanding and so a small terminal was built on the north side of the airfield. Westpoint added a Heathrow service in 1963 and British Eagle replaced Starways for the 1964 summer season, operating Viscounts. During the winter, the terminal was further expanded. From early 1966, the Shackletons lost their squadron identities and the aircraft were pooled. In addition, the servicing was centralized. While this was more efficient, it chipped away at the squadron spirit. Meanwhile, the civil operations continued to grow, with British Midland Airways commencing holiday flights in 1996 and British Eagle introducing BAC 1-11s. The grounding of British Eagle in November 1968 was a set-back, from which the airport did not seem to recover until the arrival of Brymon in 1972.

In July 1970, 7Sqn re-formed with Canberras for target towing. In August 1970, the Maritime Operational Training Unit (MOTU) was re-named 236 OCU and re-equipped with the Nimrod. April 1974 saw the 22Sqn HQ move out. Gradually, all of the Shackletons were phased out and replaced by Nimrods. In January 1982, 7Sqn was disbanded.

From 1977, Brymon was able to operate its Heralds with little competition, enabling a viable and successful service to be expanded; it became a subsidiary of British Airways in 1993. In September 1994, a civil airport-terminal was opened by Prince Charles on the airfield and this has continued to flourish, with flights operated by Air Southwest, Ryanair and Sky Bus.

In July 1992, 42Sqn moved to Kinloss and, in August, the School of Combat Survival and Rescue (SCSR) arrived from Mount Batten – its role being to teach personnel all aspects of survival on land or in the sea. Although primarily for the RAF, the school also trains personnel from the FAA and AAC, as well as Commonwealth and some civilian organizations. Whilst the majority are aircrew, they can include physical education and safety equipment personnel and medical officers. Whilst the SCSR makes good use of the bleakness of Dartmoor, it also trains personnel at other locations around the world, preparing for that emergency everybody hopes will not happen to them.

In September 1992, 3 (County of Devon) Maritime HQ Unit, R Aux AF, also from Mount Batten, arrived to provide trained staff to augment the Nimrod units on exercises and operations. In October 1999, it was merged with 1 Maritime HQ to form 600Sqn, R Aux AF at Northolt.

In October 1992, 42Sqn disbanded and 236 OCU moved to Kinloss, resulting in the end of regular Nimrod operations from St Mawgan. However, Nimrods continue to operate detachments for exercises that also included Tornados.

The School of Combat Survival and Rescue plus 3 Maritime HQ moved in from Mount Batten by the end of 1992. The Sea King maintenance facility arrived in December 1992 and now all RAF Sea King maintenance is carried out at St Mawgan. Also resident on the airfield are 1 Squadron RAF Regiment and 2625 (County of Cornwall) Squadron, RAuxAF.

St Mawgan is the parent unit to the Joint Maritime Facility (JMF). Formed on 18 August 1995, JMF consists mainly of US Navy plus Royal Navy and RAF personnel, making up an Integrated Undersea Surveillance System command. Its primary role is to providing a link between US and UK maritime forces and their respective HQs. It supports anti-submarine warfare forces and their commands by detecting, classifying and tracking submarines and issuing reports.

St Mawgan also parents CRP Portreath, located nearby along the North Cornish coast, and provides limited parenting for 22Sqn HQ and Flight at Chivenor.

In 2004, it was announced that 203 (R) Sqn would relocate to Valley by June 2006, thus bringing to an end St Mawgan's lengthy association with the RAF's maritime operations. It was also announced that the RAF Sea King first-line servicing would be contractorized and deep servicing undertaken by DARA at Fleetlands..

St Mawgan is currently the home for 203 (R) Sqn, which is equipped with the Sea King HAR.3.

RRH Saxa Vord

3 Group
Strike Command
Motto: *Praemoneo de Periculis* – Forewarned of danger

The Saxa Vord site in the Shetland Islands has had radar since it became operational on 15 October 1957. It was established within 90 (Signals) Group and the Rotor III programme to provide coverage for Fighter Command.

The radar was operated by 91 Signals Unit (91 SU) and parented by Bishopbriggs. Initially, it was equipped with a T80 as the primary radar and a T14 surveillance radar as the secondary – a third T13 was a height finder. Serviceability was beginning to be a problem and in March 1973 – nine years after the demise of the T14 – 1 ACC deployed with a S259. The following February it was formally handed over to 91 SU.

In 1975, Saxa Vord was subject of a £10m upgrade funded by NATO. The radars were replaced with T96 and HF200 and an ATC service added, due to the increasing traffic from the North Sea oil business. This became known as Shetland Radar. Link 11 was later added, together with UKAEGIS, although the Link 11 suffered in December 1991, when 230mph winds blew it down and all four radomes were destroyed. Shetland radar continued by deploying personnel to Sumburgh and a new T93 radar was installed at Saxa Vord.

In 1993, 91 SU Saxa Vord was disbanded and it officially became RAF Saxa Vord. However, the role has not changed – providing early warning of any aircraft approaching from the north. This data is fed into the Integrated Command and Control System within the UK. It had been parented by Buchan but, from 1 April 2003, it became independent.

Due to the changing threat, it was announced in July 2005 that Saxa Vord would cease operating and be placed in Care and Maintenance from April 2006.

Saxa Vord is a remote radar-head.

RAF Sealand

2 Group

Strike Command

Motto: *Manus nostrae alas sustinent* – Our hands sustain the wings

The site at Sealand was originally opened as the civilian Murrey Dutton Flying School in 1916. The following year it was taken over by the RFC. At the same time, additional land was taken over for use as an aircraft acceptance park and operated as North and South Shotwick. In May 1919, 4 Training Squadron was re-formed and then re-named 5 FTS in April 1920, with various aircraft including Harts, Audax and Magisters. In 1924, the two sites were amalgamated and became known as Sealand. In October 1936, 36 MU was established, taking over the RAF Packing Depot.

In 1938, East Camp was formed as the technical and admin site, which remains active today. In September 1939, 5 FTS was renamed 5 SFTS, departing for Ternhill in November 1940. In July 1939, 30 MU was established as a Service Repair Depot. May 1940 saw 36 MU re-named 47 MU in as a Packing and Storage Unit. In January 1940, 19 EFTS was formed with Tiger Moths and continued to operate until the end of 1941, when it was disbanded. It was replaced by 34 EFTS in February 1942, also operating Tiger Moths, continuing to operate until March 1945, when it departed for Rochester.

The Sealand site remained active throughout the war, with the repair of engines, instruments, armament and wireless equipment. Some of the manpower was provided by a large contingent of Polish airmen. Sealand suffered substantial damage during enemy bombing raids, as it was on the route to the nearby Mersey Docks.

The role of Sealand changed to heavy vehicle repair and maintenance after the war, until March 1951, when 30 MU moved to Stoke Heath, 47 MU moving to Hawarden in May. It then became a storage depot with the USAF's 3rd AF. Initially, it was occupied by the 30th Air Depot Wing, then the 7558th Air Depot Group. In September 1957, it was returned to RAF control.

Meanwhile, 2 MU had been formed in March 1955, initially as a packing unit then later as an equipment supply depot. In February 1959, 30 MU was re-formed from Stoke Heath's 24 MU and from Handforth's 290 MU, to provide a radio and radar repair service, which operated on a direct-exchange basis – much as it does today. In 1965, electrical and instrument repairs were added to their services and the Ground Radio Servicing Centre moved in from North Luffenham during the mid-1990s.

In June 1963, 631 VGS arrived with Sedberghs and Cadet Mk.3s to provide gliding for air cadets.

Although the role of Sealand expanded in 1965, with 30 MU now also maintaining electrical instruments, a large portion of the site was sold. In June 1969, 2 MU closed, Sealand becoming a sub site for 7 MU then 16 MU at Stafford. As a result of the government's 'Competing for Quality' review, in 1995, Sealand's organization had to compete with industry for future work. This it won and, following further reviews, it was established as the electronics division of the MoD's Defence Aviation Repair Agency (DARA), when it formed in April 1999.

Sealand currently operates two sites, split by a main road. South Camp is the RAF site, with most of the admin and accommodation plus various lodger units. East Camp is occupied by DARA.

The lodger units on South Camp include the Expeditionary Radar and Airfield Squadron, which arrived in 1996 as the Ground Radio Servicing Centre. It was transferred to DCSA in 1999, but taken over by Strike Command in August 2002 and operated as an Air Combat Service Support Unit. It is capable of providing immediate worldwide support for a range of vital airfields, and also most radars, navigational aids, aerials and radomes. They are also able to assist civilian organizations, such as NATS, in an emergency. Another lodger – and the only one flying – is 631 VGS with the Viking T.1. Also operated from South Camp is Fishers Sealand. This is a civilian contractor, which provides spares support for aircraft fourth-line maintenance.

The workforce of Sealand is in the region of 1,700, consisting of service and civilian personnel and providing its service for all three branches of the British armed forces. In addition, it also undertakes work for German, Italian and Saudi Air Forces, amongst others. In April 2004, it was announced that, following a review, the RAF units at Sealand would be moved to Scampton and the station would be closed in April 2006. An option to retain some civilian staff, to maintain some equipment until it goes out of service in 2009, was also being considered. This decision would not affect the DARA operation.

The only flying activity at Sealand is undertaken by 631 VGS, which arrived in 1963. It operates the Viking TX.1 for cadets of the Air Training Corps.

RAF Shawbury

Personnel and Training Command

Motto: *Doceo Duco Volo* – I teach, I guide, I fly

Shawbury originally opened in June 1917 as 9 Training Depot Station with 29 (Flying Training) Wing. It consisted of 10, 29 and 67 Squadrons, operating an assortment including the Avro 504, Camel, DH.5, Bristol and Nieuport Scouts and Shorthorn. Around the same time, an RFC Aeroplane Repair Section was also established. When the war ended, it became a repatriation unit for Canadian, South African and US pilots and, by 1920, the airfield had closed.

Many previous airfield sites were reactivated in the build up to the Second World War – Shawbury being one in 1938. In February, 27 MU became the first occupant, followed by 11 FTS. The airfield, which also eventually operated some twenty RLGs, operated a variety of aircraft, including the Audax, Battle, Blenheim, Fury and Gladiator. In 1942, the FTS was re-named 11 (Pilot) Advanced Flying Unit (11 (P)AFU), further training pilots taught overseas for operations with Oxfords. It departed in January 1944 and was replaced by the Central Navigation School (CNS)

Shawbury has become the Joint Service Centre for helicopter training. Operated by the Defence Helicopter Flying School (DHFS), it comprises of three squadrons. They fly the Squirrel HT.1 with the Army's 660Sqn and RN's 705Sqn for basic helicopter training and the Griffin HT.1 with the RAF's 60(R)Sqn, which is used for advanced training.

with Stirlings and Wellingtons and renamed Empire Air Navigation School in 1944. The first of the Aries was born, to ensure research and develop long-range navigation. 'Aires 1' was a modified Lancaster and, in October 1944, departed on the first round-the-world flight by a British aircraft. Its purpose was to establish a physical link between the unit and RAAF and RNZAF units.

The School of Air Traffic Control arrived in February 1950 and the CNS, which had reverted to its old title in 1949, became the Central Navigation and Control School and re-equipped with Lincolns and Ansons. These were later replaced with Vampires in 1954 and Provosts in 1958. The navigation school departed in 1963 and the ATC school was re-named Central Air Traffic Control School (CATCS) and re-equipped with the Jet Provost in 1970.

By 1972, 27 MU had closed, however, a similar reduced-level function has been conducted by the Aircraft Maintenance & Storage Unit (AMASU) from 1981. Operated by civilian contractors, it maintains and stores well over 100 training aircraft.

The Whirlwinds and Gazelles of 2 FTS moved in from nearby Ternhill in 1976. The Wessex replaced the Whirlwinds in December 1980 and continued in the training role through to 1997, when the task was contractorized as a Joint Service operation.

In April 1997, the Defence Helicopter Flying School (DHFS) was formed, to take over the role of 2 FTS under a PFI initiative. This tri-service training school operates the Squirrel HT.1 with 660 and 705Sqn and the Griffin HT.1 with 60 (R) Sqn.

The Army's 6 Flt (V) is a lodger unit operating Gazelle AH.1s.

Shawbury is the home of DHFS, which comprises 660 and 705Sqn with the Squirrel HT.1 and 60 (R) Sqn with the Griffin HT.1. It is the location for the Aircraft Maintenance & Storage Unit (AMASU), which services and stores a variety of aircraft and helicopter types.

RAF Spadeadam

1 Group

Strike Command

Motto: *Si vis pacem para bellum* – If you wish peace prepare for war

Spadeadam opened as the Electronics Warfare Tactics Range (EWTR) on 12 May 1976. Prior to that, it had originally been used from the late 1950s as a test site for the British Intermediate Range Ballistic Missile (IRBM) – known as Blue Streak. The RZ 2 engines were designed by Rolls Royce and the first engine was fired in August 1959. However, the project for these missiles was cancelled in 1958, once the American Thor missiles had been deployed.

Development of Blue Streak continued for launching satellites, but was eventually cancelled following unsuccessful firing in Australia. Although some of the buildings were demolished, a number remain, including the rocket and test plinths, and these may be scheduled as historic monuments to Britain's initial attempt to get into the space business.

In 1976, work began on the 9,000-acre site known as Spadeadam Wastes to build a full-scale Electronics Warfare Tactics Range (EWTR), which opened in 1976. It is the only such establishment in the UK. Only one other exists in Europe and so it is in great demand, not only by the RAF but also by other NATO Air Forces.

The EWTR has a variety of equipment, emitting various electronic signals. Aircraft flying within the range have to detect, identify, categorize and, if necessary, take appropriate action to avoid or destroy the source of the emission, while carrying out their original briefed task. The signals can include a range of radars – some of which may be for SAMs or AAA requiring immediate action, while others may be search radar needing less drastic action.

A number of simulated targets have been laid out on the range. However, the recent ending of the Cold War has enabled actual ex-Warsaw Pact equipment and vehicles to be added. While a dummy airfield complete with aircraft and vehicle convoys provides realistic targets, there are also a number of missile sites, AAA batteries and other simulated threats scattered over the range.

It is the job of the pilot to prepare for all eventualities whilst preparing his flight plan, as if on a live operation. This will enable him or her to be able to quickly take the correct appropriate action. If required, specific threats can be requested for individual training or a realistic environment as would be expected over the battlefield. As a result, the pilot of a single-seat Harrier or two-seat Tornado or even a Hercules can be better prepared for real operations when required.

Spadeadam houses the EWTR to provide realistic electronic-warfare tactics training.

RAF Stafford

2 Group
Strike Command
Motto: *Instrumenta Fundamenta* – Supplies are the foundations

The site of Stafford was purchased in September 1949 and 16 MU was formed on 1 December. The first storage units were handed over in March 1940 and the first receipts were delivered. Work constructing more storage and engineering units continued throughout the war, with accommodation taking second place using tents and huts. It wasn't until the mid-1950s that the airmen's facilities were modernized.

During the 1960s, the site covered some 362 acres and had its own railway. The workload steadily increased, with the civilian workforce rising by 50 per cent to around 1,200. By October 1969, it had become operational and was later being linked to a central computer, which enabled stocks to be viewed worldwide. Movement of Tornado spares to and from Italy and Germany within the Tri-National Movements Organization became the responsibility of 16 MU.

When the Density Activity Complex was opened in May 1977, it was the largest warehouse in north-west Europe and provided 80 per cent of the depot's workload. It contained all of the small and more frequently used items.

The 1980s saw refurbishment of the storage units, which was completed in 1994. Plans were then implemented to make Stafford the sole RAF Equipment

Supply Depotn which was achieved in 1996n resulting in the depots at Quedgeley and Carlisle closing.

The Defence Storage and Distribution Agency took over 16 MU, continues to fulfil its role as an air-equipment supply depot and is a lodger unit. It operates nearly 350,000sq m of secure storage-space and runs a twice-daily distribution service to all military aviation operational- and repair-bases in the UK.

The Stafford-based Tactical Supply Wing provides mobile fuel-handling facilities for helicopters on exercises or operations away from normal airfield facilities. This has included a continual presence in Northern Ireland since the 1970s and twice in Iraq – 140 members of the TSW were deployed to the war under Operation *Telic*, as part of the coalition forces refuelling aircraft of various nationalities.

In 1958, 2 Mechanical Transport Squadron, whose origins date back to July 1940 at Cambridge, arrived at Stafford. It provides the transport required for moving units, as well as large or abnormal loads. Consequently, 2 MT is regularly involved in exercises and were deployed during the operations in Yugoslavia and Afghanistan, as well as both *Granby* and *Telic* in Iraq.

The 85th Expeditionary Logistics Wing is collectively formed by 2 MT Squadron together with 5001 (EAF) Sqn (Expeditionary Airfield Facilities), which provides engineering support, also involving building temporary structures including hangars, and the Mobile Catering Support Unit (MCSU). In April 2004, it was announced that 87 EL Wing would be relocated to Wittering as part of the MoD Review.

Stafford is also the HQ for the RAF's mountain-rescue teams. It co-ordinates the activities of the five teams, which are based at Kinloss, Leeming, Leuchars, St Athan and Stafford. Each of the MRTs consist of seven full-time staff and up to thirty volunteers. Their role is, primarily, to search for and rescue crashed aircrew, a role which dates back to the Second World War. In practice they are often called out to assist in the rescue of civilians lost or injured in difficult terrain.

A lodger within Stafford is the Research Centre and Reserve Collection of the RAF Museum. It moved from Cardington from September 1999 and provides a store facility for the museum collection that is

Spadeadam is a large tract of land in Northumberland that houses the RAF's Electronics Warfare Tactics Range (EWTR). Operational aircraft can often be seen flying around the range, where a variety of electronic warfare equipment will be pitted against the aircraft above to confuse and threaten the crew, as they would expect when overflying enemy territory. In recent years a quantity of ex-Soviet kit has found its way onto the range, such as this SA-8 'Gecko' SAM launcher. Crown Copyright

not on public view. While most of these are small items, there are a number of dismantled aircraft, including a Swordfish and pieces of Stirling. It also has in store the last four remaining gate-guard Spitfires plus another.

Stafford is now designated a Defence Storage and Distribution Centre.

Stafford is a non-flying ground station and is the home of 16 MU, 2 Mechanical Transport Squadron, the TSW and the HQ of the Mountain Rescue Team.

RRH Staxton Wold

3 Group
Strike Command
Motto: *Vigilamus et Defendimus* – We stay awake to defend

The site at Staxton Wold was originally used for early warning as long ago as the fourth century by the Romans, who had a beacon located here, according to archaeological discoveries in 1999.

In 1937, the site was selected for the early warning role once more, when it became one of the sixteen locations that made up the Chain Home System. This became operational in 1939 and played an important part in the defence of the UK during the Second World War, including giving early warning of raids by the German Luftflotte V from bases in occupied Denmark and Norway.

It continued to provide radar coverage within the post-war Rotor system, and then became a Master Radar Station. It operated the Linesman/Mediator system from the mid 1960s, with Type 84 and 85 radars.

Staxton Wold is currently a radar reporting-post, manned by Tactical Radar Operators (TACROs) who process the data, reducing clutter and unwanted 'noise' from the radar picture, which provides information regarding all aircraft movements within its sector. This is passed on to the Air Surveillance and Control System (ASACS), together with similar information from our NATO allies, warships and AWACS aircraft. Fighter Control Officers of the Operations Support Branch who, supported by airmen Aerospace Systems Operators, compile information to produce the Recognized Air Picture (RAP). This information is then used by the Air Defence Commander to identify potential threats from uniden-

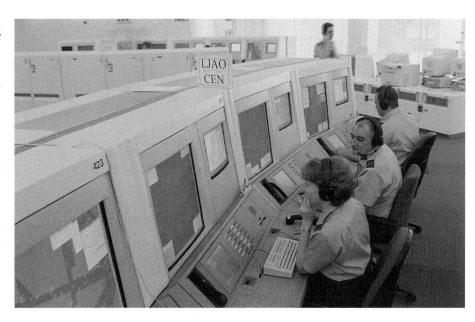

Swanwick is the new London Area Control Centre for NATS and includes an RAF element to co-ordinate military traffic. Crown Copyright

tified aircraft. The United Kingdom Combined Air Operations Centre – CAOC9, who co-ordinate the air defence, ground attack and maritime-air elements, are advised and a decision made to scramble a fighter for interception and identification, or even its destruction by SAM.

Staxton Wold continues in the early warning role, as a radar reporting-post within the Air Surveillance and Control System (ASACS) and parented by Fylingdales. It is believed to be the world's longest-lasting operational radar-site.

Staxton Wold is a Radar Reporting Post.

Swanwick

3 Group
Strike Command

The Swanwick Centre houses the National Air Traffic Service's newest and largest air traffic control centre in the UK – the London Area Control Centre.

Opened on 27 January 2002, although NATS is a civilian organization, an RAF element of some forty personnel of the London Joint Area Organization (LJAO) work as part of the team of controllers to co-ordinate military flying within the UK.

Swanwick is a NATS-owned and operated site, incorporating the RAF's London Joint Area Organization.

RAF Syerston

Personnel and Training Command
Motto: *Praesta in Officiis* – Excel in service

Syerston opened on 1 December 1940. Its first occupants were the Wellingtons of 304 and 305 (Polish) Sqn. They were replaced by 408Sqn of the RCAF in July 1941, which operated Hampdens until it departed in December 1941 to the satellite airfield of Balderton, when construction of hard runways commenced.

In May 1942, 61Sqn arrived to convert to Lancasters and were joined by 106Sqn in October. In November 1943, Flight Lieutenant Bill Reid pressed home an attack despite being attacked by enemy fighters, which damaged his aircraft, injured him and killed his navigator. For this he was awarded a VC. Shortly after, both squadrons departed and the role of Syerston changed to training, with 1668 Heavy Conversion Unit. This was renamed 5 Lancaster Finishing School when a shortage of Lancasters resulted in crews being trained on other bombers, prior to finishing their training at Syerston.

In November 1944, 1690 (Bombing) Defence Training Flight arrived with the Hurricane, Spitfire and Wellington to provide training for the Lancaster gunners.

By April 1945, the need for bomber crews was waning and 5 LFS disbanded, being replaced by Lancasters of 49Sqn.

They only flew a single operation from Syerston before the war ended.

Syerston was transferred to Transport Command, prior to the arrival of 22 FTS in 1948 to train Royal Navy pilots, until 1957, when 2 FTS arrived to train RAF pilots with the Provost T.1. These were soon being replaced by the Jet Provost from 1959. In 1963, the first course to have only flown jets received its wings.

During the 1958 Battle of Britain display disaster struck, when the prototype Vulcan broke up during a flypast with the loss of the whole crew.

Flying training ended in 1970 at Syerston and the airfield was placed on care and maintenance. In 1975 it had a reprieve, when the Air Cadets Central Gliding School (ACCGS) moved in from Spitalgate, together with 644 VGS, followed by 643 VGS from Binbrook in June 1992.

Syerston is currently the home of ACCGS, which operates the Vigilant T.1 and the Viking T.1, 643 VGS with Vigilant T.1 and 644 VGS with Viking T.1. The Four Counties Gliding Club, which is a part of the RAF Gliding and Soaring Association (RAFGSA), is also located at Syerston and operates a variety of gliders.

RAF Tain

1 Group
Strike Command

The Morrich Moor in Ross-shire had been used for various manoeuvres dating back to at least the 1920s and at some point use commenced as a bombing range.

Following the opening of Evanton in 1937, a relief landing-ground was built alongside the range. A variety of aircraft used the range, including Battles, Blenheims, Hampdens and Heyfords, as well as Swordfish operating from carriers. As a result of the Luftwaffe attacks against Scottish targets, the grass strip was blocked with old cars and wooden poles.

As the need for airfields increased, the RLG at Tain was enlarged and opened on 16 September 1941, initially as a fighter station with three runways. First to arrive was 17Sqn, soon after, with Hurricanes. It only stayed briefly, departing the following month and was replaced by 123Sqn with Spitfires.

In February 1942, 417Sqn, RCAF with Spitfires deployed for a month, as did 801

NAS in March 1942 with Sea Hurricanes. Around the same time, 76Sqn used the airfield as a launch point for attacks on the *Tirpitz*. A 254Sqn Det with Blenheims arrived in November and remained for most of the war.

Wellingtons of 547Sqn arrived for two months in January 1953 and were replaced by 404Sqn Blenheims, which deployed briefly in April 1943. It was joined by 144Sqn with Beaufighters, which stayed for a couple of months before departing overseas in June. It returned in August, but then left in October.

In January 1944, 186Sqn Spitfires arrived and left in March. A 547Sqn detachment arrived at the same time and remained until September 1944. In June 1944, 86Sqn arrived with the Liberator and was joined by 311Sqn. As the end of the war came closer, the Liberators were used as transports to repatriate freed PoWs, before departing in August 1945.

Although the airfield at Tain was placed into care and maintenance in 1946 before being closed, the range next to the airfield has remained in virtually continuous use, not only by the RAF but also the Royal Navy and various NATO aircraft. When Lossiemouth was transferred to the RN they also manned the range. It reverted to RAF operation in 1972, when Lossiemouth was returned to RAF control. Being a short flying time away, a substantial portion of its trade emanates from that station. Personnel from Tain are also deployed to the Cape Wrath/Garvie Island range, when live bombing exercises are being conducted.

Tain is the most complex of all the weapons ranges in the UK, with multiple and opposing patterns. The range is considered to be one of the busiest in the UK.

RAF Topcliffe

Personnel and Training Command

Topcliffe opened in September 1940 and was first occupied by 77Sqn with the Whitley the following month. They were joined by the similarly equipped 102Sqn in November. A year later, both squadrons had departed, while concrete runways were constructed. In June 1942, 102Sqn returned with the Halifax. It was joined by the Squadron Conversion Flight, but both departed in August and were replaced by 405Sqn, RCAF with Halifaxes.

A few days later, 405Sqn was joined by 419Sqn, RCAF but departed a few weeks after that. In October, 405Sqn temporarily moved to Beaulieu to fly anti-submarine patrols with Coastal Command and was replaced by 424Sqn, RCAF, which was formed in October with Wellingtons. In January 1943, Topcliffe was designated an RCAF station. In March, 405Sqn returned, only to move out again later that month. The same month, 1659 Heavy Conversion Unit (1659 HCU) arrived, representing a change in role for the station to training from bombers, but still flying the Halifax. The following month 424Sqn departed. In November 1944, the HCU converted to the Canadian-built Lancaster, then disbanded in September 1945.

Topcliffe returned to RAF control and was initially home for 5 Air Navigation School (5 ANS) from September 1946 – later redesignated 1 ANS operating Ansons and Wellingtons. In April 1954, 1 ANS departed. In the meantime, 53Sqn had been re-formed in August 1949 with the Hastings and was joined by 47Sqn. During October 53Sqn left, to be replaced by 297Sqn in December. Temporarily, 242 OCU located to convert to the Hastings before returning to Dishforth. In November 1950, 297Sqn disbanded, then 24Sqn arrived with Hastings in February 1951, staying until May 1953, when it departed along with 47Sqn, leaving the airfield empty.

The station changed role again when it was selected to be a Coastal Command Neptune base. First to arrive was 210Sqn with Lancasters, in October 1952. Neptune conversion courses were taken at Kinloss and aircraft received at Topcliffe in February 1953. During March 1953, 203Sqn had arrived and converted, while 36Sqn formed on them in July. From June 1953 until June 1956, 1453 Flight operated with the Neptune in the AEW role. The rest of the squadron continued to operate in the maritime reconnaissance role until September 1956, when 203Sqn disbanded, followed by 210 in January and 36 in February 1957.

Topcliffe returned to the training role, with the re-forming of 1 ANS in March 1957 equipped with the Marathon, Valetta and Vampire. The Varsity replaced the Marathon from February 1958. In January 1962, 1 ANS moved to Stradishall.

The Northern Command Communications Squadron operated the Basset from June 1965. In February 1969, it was re-numbered 26Sqn, then departed the same month.

Topcliffe entered a period of care and maintenance before it was transferred to the army in 1972, with whom it became Alanbrooke Barracks. However, the runways continued to be maintained and it was used as a relief landing-ground (RLG).

The Joint Elementary Flying Training School (JEFTS) was formed at Topcliffe with Fireflies in April 1993, but then moved to Barkston Heath in April 1995. It was replaced by the Tucano Air Navigation School (TANS), which also departed in 2003. Topcliffe then returned to being used as an RLG for Linton-on-Ouse.

Topcliffe is an RLG for Linton-on-Ouse.

RAF Uxbridge

Personnel and Training Command
Motto: *Juventutem Formamus – We form youth*

Uxbridge was first utilized by the RFC in December 1917 as an Armament School. Prior to that it had been a private house, which had been sold to the Government in 1915 and used as a convalescent hospital for Canadian soldiers.

Hillingdon House and the grounds were transferred to the RAF in April 1918 and, in October 1919, the RAF depot was opened in the grounds, while the house was used to accommodate HQ Southern Area. This became HQ Inland Area in April 1920 and moved to nearby Bentley Priory in May 1926. In June 1925, the Air Defence of Great Britain (ADGB) arrived, followed by HQ Fighting Area a year later. In 1936, the ADGB ceased to exist as a separate unit and the Home Air Force was re-organized into four functional commands – Bomber, Fighter, Coastal and Training. Training Command was formed in May 1936, before moving to Buntingsdale Hall at Market Drayton in July.

Fighter Command's 11 Group was established in Hillingdon House, while a bunker was constructed to house its control centre. Also located there briefly was Bomber Command HQ, while its new HQ at High Wycombe was being constructed. During the early days of the Second World War the squadrons controlled by 11 Group took on the brunt of Luftwaffe might in the legendary Battle of Britain. The control centre of operations in the south-east of England

continued to be 11 Group's HQ, which also covered the French and Belgian coasts as the German forces were being pushed back. In 1958, the HQ of 11 Group moved to Martlesham Heath.

The RAF's Central Band was formed at Uxbridge in 1920 from the School of Music, which was formed in 1918, plus the establishment of RAF Music Services. During the Second World War this organization expanded to provide a medical support role, as it continues to provide today. With the war over it reduced in size but, in 1960, Music Services still operated ten established bands. Today the HQ Music Services is responsible for three bands of which the Central Band of the RAF remains based at Uxbridge. The other two – the Band of the RAF College and the Band of the RAF Regiment – are based at Cranwell. During Operation *Granby* the Central Band was deployed to provide medical support for the Allied forces.

A ceremonial drill unit was also formed in the 1920s. This was designated the RAF Drill Unit and, in November 1960, became the Queens Colour Squadron (QCS). The QCS represents the RAF on Royal and State occasions and mounts guards of honour for visiting Royalty and Heads of State, as well as our Royal Family.

The underground bunker, which was vital during the Battle of Britain, was closed down in 1958. However, during the 1970s, restoration commenced to return it to the state it was in on 15 September 1940. It eventually opened in 2000 as a museum. Visits to the bunker can be made, subject to prior arrangement (Tel: 01895 816400).

The main role of Uxbridge is to provide administrative, logistic and training support to RAF personnel who have no separate administrative backing. This means most of the London sites, including MoD, Joint Service Units and those personnel on loan with other services or civilian businesses, as well as nearby West Drayton. It also provides temporary accommodation through the London Transit Centre.

Uxbridge is the home of the RAF Learning Forces, which assists members of the RAF, their families and other members of MoD to plan their personal development through further education. It parents nearby West Drayton.

Under MoDEL project (described under Northolt), it is proposed that some RAF

units will move to Northolt. Once the move is complete, the site may be closed o developed to accommodate other units.

Uxbridge is the home of the Queen's Colour Squadron, 63Sqn RAF Regt, HQ Music Services and the Central Band of the RAF.

RAF Valley

Personnel and Training Command
Motto: *In Adversis Perfugium* – A refuge in adversity

Valley was originally opened on 13 February 1941 as Rhosneigr, but was re-named Valley two months later. It came under the command of 9 Group to become a base for fighter detachments protecting the north-west. Because of its location, Valley became the Sector Operations Centre to control the fighters protecting the approaches to Belfast and Merseyside. They were also responsible for the protection of ships in the Irish Sea.

When it arrived on 3 March 1941, 312 (Czech) Sqn, with Hurricanes, became its first unit. They departed again on 25 May, but not before shooting down a Ju.88. They were replaced by 615Sqn's Hurricanes from April to September 1941. A number of one-month detachments saw various units at Valley, including 'A' Flight of 219Sqn with Beaufighters, 302 (Polish) Sqn with Hurricanes and 68Sqn with Beaufighters.

In June 1941, 456 (RAAF) Sqn became the first unit to form at Valley. Equipped with Defiants, they were declared operational in September and then re-equipped with Beaufighters. In January 1943 they were re-equipped with Mosquitos, before moving on to Middle Wallop in March.

In October 1941, 275Sqn was formed with the Walrus and Lysander for the SAR role. This followed the failed rescue of the crew of four from a Botha, who were lost along with eleven rescuers in heavy seas near the airfield. Next to form, in November 1941, was 350Sqn. Equipped with Spitfires, this was an all-Belgian unit, which moved out the following April. A number of other squadrons were temporarily deployed to Valley, including 131, 125, 157, 315, 406 and 452Sqn.

With enemy raids in their sector on the wane, the Sector Operations Centre closed in October 1943, leaving just 125Sqn Beaufighters for air defence and

The rear seat of a Hawk provides an excellent view as the pilot returns to Valley after another training sortie.

275Sqn, which departed the following April, for SAR. Valley was prepared for use as a ferry terminal for USAAF transatlantic aircraft. USAAF personnel moved in and, before long, up to seventy aircraft a day were arriving at Station 568, eventually totalling over 5,000. Even when the war in Europe ended the role continued, with some 2,500 aircraft despatched for operations in the Far East, before halting in September and the departing of the USAAF Transit Unit. After the end of the war, most 8th AF aircraft returned to the USA through Valley.

The only unit to remain was 1528 Beam Approach Training Flight, which had been at Valley with Oxfords since November 1944, but they left in December 1945. In July 1946, the station was transferred to Flying Training Command and was placed on care and maintenance; remaining so, although designated a Master Diversion Airfield in 1947.

In April 1948, it was passed on to 12 Group, Fighter Command, but it was fifteen months before it became active with 20Sqn. They brought a diverse collection of aircraft, including Beaufighters, Martinets, Spitfires and Vampires. Until disbanding in October 1951, 20Sqn remained and then Valley came under Flying Training Command once more.

No. 202 Advanced Flying School arrived in February 1951 with Meteor T.7s and various Vampires. On 1 June 1954, 202 AFS was re-numbered 7 FTS, becoming an all-Vampire T.11 unit by October

1959 and training RN pilots for the Fleet Air Arm (FAA).

In 1955, 6 Joint Services Trials Unit was formed as a lodger unit to trial the Fireflash AAM, which failed to become operational. This was re-named 1 Guided Weapons Development Squadron in 1957 and equipped with Swifts for further trials, then re-named again to 1 Guided Weapons Training Squadron, with Javelins for the Firestreak AAM trials.

In January 1955, 1113 Marine Craft Unit formed at Holyhead Harbour and was assisted by 22Sqn's 'C' Flight with Whirlwinds from September. These were later replaced by the Wessex in October 1976.

In 1958, the training of pilots for the RN was transferred to Linton-on-Ouse and Valley took over the advanced pilot-training of Worksop's 4 FTS, replacing 7 FTS. The actual move took until August 1960 to complete. Around the same time, 4 FTS took delivery of some Varsity T.1s, to operate alongside the Vampire T.11s for the multi-engined training of pilots for Coastal and Training Commands.

From November 1962, the Gnat T.1 began to replace the Vampire and these were used in 1964 as the mount for the 4 FTS aerobatic team – the Yellow Jacks. The Hunter F.6 and T.7 augmented the Gnat from 1967 and continued to be operated until the arrival of the Hawk in October 1976. CFS established a Hawk squadron in 1977 and, by 1979, both Gnat and Hunter had been replaced, enabling all training to be centred around the Hawk. In

October 1992, 74 (R) Sqn was formed within 4 FTS and was joined by 234 (R) Sqn in April 1994. These were subsequently re-numbered 19 and 208 (R) Sqn.

Another change in 1962 was when 1 Guided Weapons Development Squadron disbanded to be replaced by Fighter Command Missile Practice Camp. This was renamed Strike Command Missile Practice Camp (STCAAME) in April 1968. Their role was to provide a facility for squadrons to fire live air-to-air missiles at targets over Cardigan Bay. These targets have usually been the radio-controlled Jindivik drones launched from the Qinetiq facility at Llanbedr or the supersonic Stiletto missile launched from a Canberra. In 1996, this became the Air Guided Weapons Operational Evaluation Unit (AGWOEU) and it currently provides the planning, briefing and facilities for the missile practice camps. On 1 April 2004, the AGWOEU amalgamated with the SAOEU and the Tornado F.3 OEU, to form the Fast Jet and Weapons OEU at Coningsby.

A further arrival in 1962 was the Central Flying School Helicopter Detachment (CFS (H)), which moved in with Whirlwind HAR.10s from Ternhill in May, to train SAR crews. This role was later taken over by a detachment of 2 FTS, which had its HQ based at Ternhill and then Shawbury from September 1976.

The Search and Rescue Training Squadron from Finningley arrived in December 1979 and later became the Search and Rescue Training Unit (SARTU). It was equipped with the Whirlwind HAR.10 and converted to the Wessex HAR.2. Their role was to train navigators, winchmen and instructors, as well as pilots. In April 1997, these were replaced by the Griffins of the DHFS.

A further lodger at Valley is the Hawk Aircraft Engineering Development and Investigation Team (AEDIT), which tests and analyses new or problem items for the Hawk.

By June 1997, 22Sqn's 'C' Flight had converted to the Sea King HAR.3 and the last UK-based Wessex retired. Despite all the moves that the SAR unit have undergone over the years, 'C' Flight is the only one still operating from its original base.

Valley is the home for 4 FTS, which comprises 19 and 208 (R) Sqn equipped with the Hawk T.1 and T.1A, plus the Central Flying School Advanced Training Unit, which is parented by 19 (R) Sqn. Lodger units are 'C' Flight of 22Sqn with the Sea King HAR.3 and the Search and Rescue Training Unit, which is part of the DHFS and operates the Griffin HT.1.

RAF Waddington

3 Group
Strike Command
Motto: For faith and freedom

RAF Waddington was opened in November 1916 as an RFC flying training unit and closed in 1920.

It re-opened in 1926 as a bomber base with various types of aircraft. In March 1937, 44Sqn arrived and converted from the Hind to the Blenheim, later re-equipping with the Hampden. It was joined in May by 50Sqn, which moved on to Lindholme in July 1940, and briefly by 142Sqn. During the Battle of Britain, 44Sqn attacked German invasion barges. In November, 207Sqn was re-formed with the Manchester and moved out later that month. During the daylight operations 44Sqn suffered heavy losses and changed to night bombing. In February 1941, 97Sqn was re-formed with Manchesters and departed the following month. The Hampden was replaced with the Lancaster by the end of 1941 and, in April 1942, the CO – Squadron Leader Nettleton – was awarded a VC. He led six Lancasters on an attack against the diesel-engine factory at Augsberg. They were bounced by German fighters, which shot four down. The two remaining aircraft continued their attack, from which only Nettleton's aircraft survived, managing to return to the UK despite severe damage. In December 1941, 420Sqn, RCAF was formed with Hampdens and 9Sqn arrived in August 1942. It converted from the Wellington to the Lancaster and stayed until April 1943. The operations of 44Sqn continued from Waddington until it, too, moved out the following month, to enable concrete runways to be laid.

On completion of the runways, in November 1943, 467Sqn arrived, providing a nucleus of personnel to form 463Sqn later in the month. These Australian squadrons consisted of a substantial proportion of British crews and continued to operate until mid-1945. During this period they flew nearly 6,400 sorties, with some 29,000 tons of bombs dropped at a cost of over 1,300 aircrew lost. in July 1945, 9Sqn returned briefly, before departing for the Far East.

Post-war, Waddington was reduced to care

and maintenance. The station re-opened on 1 June 1s 1955, ready for the arrival of 21 and 27Sqn Canberras. In May 1957, 83Sqn became the RAF's first operational Vulcan squadron, moving to Scampton in October 1960. By August 1961, the Waddington Wing consisted of 44, 50 and 101Sqn.

The arrival of the Tornado saw the Vulcan being phased out. Waddington was the last base to still have Vulcans when the Argentinians invaded the Falklands in 1982. As a result, an urgent plan was put together to prepare the remaining Vulcans and crews for conventional bombing – a role that had long been discontinued. Due to the lack of space available at Ascension, only two Vulcans were deployed and conducted several missile and bombing attacks on Stanley at distances that were the longest operational bombing missions ever flown.

Operation *Corporate* had shown that the RAF needed additional tankers and so six Vulcans were quickly modified and then flown by 50Sqn, until they disbanded in March 1984. Around this time, a new unit was established to prepare for the arrival of the Nimrod AEW.3. This was later cancelled and the Sentry ordered, but it was June 1991 before 8Sqn was re-equipped and the Sentry entered service.

On 1 April 1995, 51Sqn with its Nimrod MR.1s took up residence. These were joined by 23Sqn, which was re-formed in July 1996 to become the second Sentry squadron. With only a total of five aircraft in service, the aircraft are pooled and both squadrons' markings have been applied to each aircraft.

A cadre unit of 5Sqn was formed but not formally established on 1 April 2004, although the Sentinel R.1 will not arrive until 2006. 5 September 2005 saw the re-forming of 54(R) Sqn to provide aircrew training for the four operation squadrons borrowing aircraft as required.

Lodgers at Waddington include the Air Combat Manoeuvring Instrumentation (ACMI) facility, which became operational on 22 September 1990. This facility sees a substantial number of aircraft from various countries using the base for support and briefings during detachments. Operated by BAe Systems, the aircraft fly simulated operational tasks over the North Sea Air Combat Range, where a number of towers accurately track and record their progress in 3D enabling a comprehensive debrief to access their performance.

Another lodger is the College of Air

Warfare, which arrived in July 1984 and became the Air Warfare Centre (AWC) in October 1993.

No. 2503 (County of Lincoln) R Aux AF Field Squadron are based at Waddington to support 26Sqn RAF Regt and 7006 (VR) Sqn provide intelligence.

Waddington houses 8 and 23Sqn with pooled Sentry AEW.1s and 51Sqn with Nimrod R.1s; 26Sqn RAF Regt with Rapier SAMs provides air and ground defence of the airfield. Also located at Waddington are 2503 (County of Lincoln) R Aux AF Field Squadron and 7006 (VR) Sqn. 5Sqn will operate the Sentinel R.1. and 54 (R) Sqn with no aircraft.

RAF Wainfleet

1 Group
Strike Command
Motto: Defend and strike

The recorded use of Wainfleet as a range dates back to 1890, when it was used by army artillery. However, it is believed that musketry practice was carried out back in Napoleonic times. Use of the range by aircraft commenced in 1914, with RNAS aircraft from HMS *Daedalus* – now RAF Cranwell – and 4 School of Aerial Fighting at Freiston. It continued to be used by the RAF, as well as the army artillery, through to March 1920, when the school closed.

Wainfleet was opened as an RAF bombing and gunnery range in 1928. It continued to be used by the artillery, as well as aircraft throughout the war. Some of the trials for the 617Sqn and Barnes Wallis bouncing bomb were carried out at Wainfleet, while the Central Gunnery School was based at nearby Sutton Bridge. During Operation *Corporate*, Vulcan crews practised their high-level bombing before putting into effect on Stanley airfield in the Falklands. It is thought that virtually every type of RAF bomber has used the range at some point or another, as well as numerous other USAAF and USAF types.

As with the other ranges around the Wash, Wainfleet has substantial numbers of wildlife on its large area of undeveloped coast, ranging from plants and birds to insects and animals. This has led to the range being designated a Site of Special Scientific Interest (SSSI). The assortment of wildlife includes many rare or unusual species and Wainfleet proves to be a popular site for visitors when the range is not in use.

Apart from the bread and butter use of the range at Wainfleet by RAF and USAF aircraft, trials were undertaken in 2001 with Raptor pod and Storm Shadow and, later, with Brimstone missiles to confirm that they would separate from the aircraft cleanly. An inert Enhanced Paveway III was also dropped from 20,000ft, creating a large crater despite the lack of explosive.

Wainfleet is an air-weapons range.

Wattisham

3 Group
Strike Command

Construction of Wattisham airfield commenced in 1937 and it opened on 1 April 1939. The following month, the first aircraft began to arrive in the form of Blenheim bombers of 107 and 110Sqn.

The day after war was declared, aircraft from 107 and 110Sqn attacked warships at Wilhelmshaven, during which five of the ten Blenheims were shot down. In May 1941, 107Sqn departed and was replaced by 226Sqn. It departed in December 1941, as did 110Sqn in August 1942. In February 1942, 236Sqn arrived with Beaufighters, but also left in July. Preparations commenced to build Wattisham into a heavy-bomber base, but this soon halted. Instead, the USAAF 8 Air Force moved into the base and established a central supply depot. October 1942 saw the 68th Observation Group (16 and 122 OS) arrive with Havocs and depart by the end of the month. In May 1944, it was joined by the 479th Fighter Group (434, 435 and 436 FS) with P-38 Lightnings. These were replaced by P-51 Mustangs in September 1944, before they returned home in November 1945.

Following the return of Wattisham to the RAF, 56 and 266Sqn arrived in late 1946, but departed again the following April. In 1949, the airfield was upgraded with new runways, in readiness for the arrival of Meteors from 257 and 263Sqn. These were later replaced by Hunters, but they departed to allow further airfield construction including runway rebuilding, in 1957.

Wattisham re-opened with the arrival of 111Sqn with Hunters in June 1958. They were better known as the Black Arrows aerobatic team. In 1958, they performed the twenty-two-Hunter loop at the Farnborough airshow, assisted by 56Sqn, which had arrived in July 1959 and oper-

ated their Hunters until 1961, when they both converted to the Lightning. In 1960, 41Sqn arrived with the Javelin. In 1963, 56Sqn formed the Firebirds aerobatic team, departing for Cyprus in 1967. Meanwhile, 41Sqn were disbanded in December 1963. They were replaced by 29Sqn with Lightnings in May. In September 1974, 111Sqn disbanded; 29Sqn disbanded in December and were replaced by the return of 56Sqn in January 1975.

January 1976 saw 56Sqn start converting to the Phantom, followed by 23Sqn the following month. 'C' Flight of 25Sqn arrived in 1981 (although it was initially temporarily numbered 'E' Flight of 85Sqn). In August 1984, 74Sqn were re-formed with ex-USN Phantoms. March 1983 saw 23Sqn deployed to the Falklands. In March 1989, the Bloodhounds were transferred to 85Sqn becoming 'E' Flight again. July 1991 saw 85Sqn disband. With the demise of the Phantom, numerous examples from various squadrons arrived for spare reclamation before scrapping. In 1992, 56Sqn disbanded, followed by 74Sqn. On 31 October 1992, RAF Wattisham was closed and was handed over to the army in March 1993, later becoming home for the 16 Air Brigade.

Despite Wattisham being army owned and operating Gazelles and Lynx, 'B' Flight of 22Sqn arrived in July 1994 from Manston with Sea King HAR.3 to provide SAR cover for the East Coast.

Wattisham provides home to 'B' Flight of 22Sqn with the Sea King HAR.3A.

RAF Welford

USVF
Personnel and Training Command

Construction of RAF Welford commenced in 1942 for use as an OTU but, instead, it was handed over to the USAAC in September 1943 as Station 474. It became home for the 315th, 434th Troop Carrier Group (TCG) (comprising 71st, 72nd and 74th TCS) of the 8th AF and later 435th TCG (75th, 76th and 77th TCS) of the 9th AF. It became one of many bases flying paras into Europe for D-Day, Operations *Dragon*, *Market Garden* and others, using transport aircraft and gliders.

It was returned to the RAF in June 1945 and occupied by 1336 Conversion Unit

with Dakotas and Horsas, but closed in March 1946. It was subsequently used for signals from October 1946 until 1952, when it was reduced to care and maintenance. Some flying activity took place during 1946–7, when Elliotts of Newbury were given permission to conduct flight testing of their new Eon light aircraft. In September 1955, it re-opened as a logistics site for the USAF 3rd AF, storing and preparing munitions, parented by Upper Heyford.

Welford played a significant part in *Desert Storm*, in preparing and dispatching large quantities of munitions. In April 1995, Welford became a joint RAF/USAF base. During operations in Kosovo and Serbia some 48 per cent (11,590 bombs) of all munitions expended came from Welford. In April 1990, the RAF withdrew from Welford and the Defence Munitions Agency (DMA) took over its role. However, DMA closed their facility at the end of 2000 and, on 1 October 2002, DM Welford became RAF Welford once again, with the USAF taking full control of the storage facility parented by Fairford.

Welford is a USAFE storage site and has no aircraft based there.

West Drayton

3 Group
Strike Command
LATCC motto – *Viatores caeli tutare* – Protect the traveller through the heavens.

In 1919, the Admiralty established a RNAS shore station at West Drayton, which was transferred to the RAF in 1924.

West Drayton was used for training and evaluating recruits and SNCOs until 1945, when it became an education and vocational training centre for personnel being demobilized. It also housed the Signals Development Unit but, in 1947, it began a move to Henlow, following a decision to use West Drayton to house contestants for the 1948 Olympic Games. In 1951, it was transferred to the USAF and operated by the 3911th Air Base Group.

In 1962, West Drayton was designated as the site for a joint civil/military air-traffic control centre (ATCC) to cover the south of England and, in 1967, Southern ATCC moved across from Heathrow, becoming London ATCC in 1971. In 1989, a new military airspace operations room was declared operational.

The original WW2 layout of hangars at Welford remains visible, although the hangars are now used for other purposes.

In April 1994, West Drayton ceased to be an RAF station, but the London Air Traffic Control Centre (Military) (LATCC (Mil)) continues to operate in the London Terminal Control Centre (LTCC) within the National Air Traffic Service's (NATS) building. The London Joint Area Organization (LJAO) moved to Swanwick, with the opening of the new civil ATC facilities in January 2002.

The Military Area Service Operations Room (MASOR) provides an area-ATC service to military and civil aircraft over eastern England and the North Sea out to the national boundary, and western England, Wales, the Irish Sea and Atlantic to the national boundary. In addition, a distress and diversion service provides help to military and civil aircraft in an emergency. The emergency-fixer service enables an immediate position to be given to lost aircraft.

An Aeronautical Information Service (Military) is able to facilitate searches for obscure aeronautical information when required. It also monitors the progress of Royal and VVIP flights within the UK. In addition, it provides an initial trace of air misses and other potentially hazardous incidents, as well as receiving low-flying complaints and even UFO reports from the public.

LATCC (Mil) also provides admin support for the Military Flying and Airspace Co-ordination Squadron. In April 2004, it was announced that the low-flying element of the Squadron would move to Wittering as part of the MoD Review.

West Drayton continues to house the London Air Traffic Control Centre (Mil) (LATCC (Mil)).

RAF Wittering

1 Group
Strike Command
Motto: Strength is freedom

Wittering was originally opened as RFC Stamford, as a training airfield on Wittering Heath in 1916. In July 1917, 1 Training Depot was established with a number of aircraft types, including the Avro 504, Camel, DH.4, F.2B Fighter and Pup. Just west of Stamford, a further airfield was opened at Easton on the Hill, shortly after. This housed 5 Training Depot, which was formed in September 1917, and was subsequently re-named Collyweston. It was operated as a satellite of Stamford, although they both operated independently. In 1919, Stamford closed.

In 1924, the airfield re-opened as Wittering and became the home of the CFS. In 1935, it was replaced by 11 FTS, who continued the training role until April 1938, when it was transferred to Fighter Command. In December 23 and 213Sqn arrived, with Demons and Hurricanes respectively. In December, 23Sqn re-equipped with the Blenheim and left in August 1940, while 213Sqn left in June. In October 1939, 610Sqn arrived

with Spitfires and departed the following April. During the Battle of Britain, Wittering was a Sector Operations Centre within 12 Group, seeing 74, 229 and 266Sqn spending short breaks from action in the south. In December 1940, 151Sqn arrived with Defiants, adding some Hurricanes. In July 1941, 1453 Flt was formed with Turbinlite-equipped Havocs, becoming 532Sqn in September 1943 and departing in November. In April 1942, 486 (NZ) Sqn arrived with Hurricanes and converted to Typhoons in July, before departing in September.

Collyweston was amalgamated with Wittering in 1943 and, as a result, their combined runways were used to provide an emergency diversion for damaged aircraft throughout the rest of the war. In April 1943, 141Sqn arrived with Beaufighters, re-equipping with Mosquitos before departing in December. In June 1943, 349 (Belgian) Sqn re-formed with Spitfires and stayed briefly. Arriving in August 1943, the USAAF's 55th Fighter Squadron with the P-38 Lightning was provided with temporary accommodation for nearly a year. While, in December, 438 (Canadian) Sqn arrived with its Hurricanes, before departing the following January. Also in 1943, 1426 Enemy Aircraft Flight located to Collyweston with a number of airworthy captured aircraft, used mainly for evaluation and recognition training. In February 1945, 68Sqn came over from Coltishall briefly before returning again later that month. By the time the war ended, Wittering-based aircraft had accounted for 151 aircraft and 89 flying bombs confirmed destroyed and a further 112 damaged or possibly destroyed.

With the war over, Wittering was transferred to Flying Training Command and became the home for 1 Initial Training School. Also, 23Sqn returned, re-forming with Mosquitos in September 1946, but all had departed before Wittering was handed over to Maintenance Command in 1947. A new runway was laid and the airfield prepared for its new role as a bomber station. During 1953, 49, 61 and 100Sqn arrived with Lincolns and all took part in operations against the Mau Mau terrorists in Kenya. November 1953 saw 49Sqn convert to the Canberra, followed by 61 and 100Sqn in August and April the following year.

August 1953 saw the arrival of the Bomber Command Armament School to train armourers on the new generation of nuclear weapons. It was subsequently renamed the Armament Support Unit (RAFASUPU or ASU). Initially the ASU was tasked with escorting weapon moves throughout the UK. More recently, this role has developed into providing weapon preparation for exercises and operations and EOD. While the ASU and the Tactical Armament Squadron moved to Marham in 2002, the EoD function remains at Wittering with 5131 (Bomb Disposal) Sqn.

The Valiant was the first of the V-bombers to operate from Wittering, with 138Sqn from July 1955. It was joined by 49Sqn, which was to drop the UK's first atom bombs, during trials in October 1956 in Australia, and hydrogen bombs, in 1957–8 in the Christmas Islands. Meanwhile, 138Sqn was one of the units deployed to Malta to drop conventional bombs during the Suez crisis at the end of 1956. March 1958 saw 61Sqn disband, followed by 100Sqn in September 1959. The discovery of metal fatigue in the Valiant was disastrous and saw them grounded in December 1964.

In February 1962, 139Sqn was re-formed with Victors from the Victor ITU, followed by the re-forming of 100Sqn in May – both were later armed with the Blue Steel stand-off missile. In September 1968, 100Sqn disbanded, prior to the nuclear deterrent passing to the Royal Navy in June 1969, and 139Sqn disbanded in December.

Following the transfer of Wittering to Air Support Command in February 1969, 230Sqn arrived with Whirlwinds in March, the Harrier OCU (HOCU) formed in April and 51Sqn, RAF Regt arrived. In July, 1Sqn received its first Harrier GR.1 and was officially formed as the world's first VTOL-fighter squadron on 1 October. Wittering's last addition for 1969 was 15Sqn RAF Regt, which arrived in December.

In a blaze of publicity, the HOCU took part in the *Daily Mail* Transatlantic Air Race in May 1969. Flying from the Post-Office Tower, London to New York's Empire State Building, the Harrier used its unique capability to take off from St Pancras Station in a cloud of coal dust. It won, beating the supersonic RN Phantom, which flew for a shorter time but, by landing on the Manhattan waterfront, the VSTOL Harrier achieved a total time of 7 hours 6 minutes. In October, the HOCU was re-named 233 OCU.

No. 5 Wing of the RAF Regt was tasked with protecting the Harriers when

deployed. It arrived in 1970 with 15 and 51 Field Squadron. In September 1972, 45Sqn arrived, followed by 58Sqn in August 1973 with Hunters. Their role was to train pilots in ground attack prior to converting to the Buccaneer, Harrier or Jaguar. This was only an interim measure to resolve a training bottleneck and both squadrons were disbanded in 1976. In September 1992, 233 OCU was re-named once again, becoming 20 (Reserve) Sqn.

In February 1999, it was announced that Wittering, along with Cottesmore, would operate the Joint Force Harrier, which was to see the RN Sea Harriers moving up from Yeovilton. However, when it was subsequently announced that the Sea Harriers were to be withdrawn by 2006, this was cancelled. As a result, RN pilots are currently being trained to fly the Harrier GR.7 and one of the Cottesmore squadrons will become a RN unit.

Following the departure of 1Sqn, Wittering became solely a training base for the Harriers. It also accommodates various lodger units, including 5131 (Bomb Disposal) Sqn, whose war tasking is to ensure an airfield or airstrip is sufficiently clear from munitions to ensure aircraft can operate safely. In peacetime they are busy clearing munitions that have been left from the past. They also provide a Military Aid to the Civil Power by maintaining a team on ten-minute notice to deal with criminal and terrorist bombs.

Another lodger is 1 Force Protection Wing HQ (1 FP Wing HQ), which provides a command-and-control expertise in ground defence matters. Also a lodger is 37Sqn, RAF Regt, which now comes under the command of 1 FP Wing HQ.

Although not based at Wittering, the tri-service MoD Hospital Unit (MDHU) at Peterborough is parented by Wittering. As a result, the station provides not only admin support but also accommodation and social facilities.

In April 2004, it was announced that the Air Combat Service Support Units of 85 Expeditionary Logistics Wing would be transferred from Stafford, along with the Low-Flying Booking Cell from West Drayton, over the following two years.

Wittering is the home of 20 (R) Sqn, which is equipped with the Harrier GR.7/GR.9 and T.10. It also houses 1 FP HQ, 37Sqn, RAF Regt and 5131 (Bomb Disposal) Sqn.

RAF Woodvale

Personnel and Training Command
Motto: *Ut aquiale volent* – In supply of eagles

Woodvale airfield officially opened on 1 December 1941, although parts of it were still being built. It was originally planned as a fighter station to provide protection for Merseyside, however, these attacks had abated and it was initially used to provide units with a rest and/or re-equip location. The first unit to arrive was 308, followed by 315 (Polish) Sqn, both with Spitfires and 285Sqn with Defiants. A detachment of 776 NAS arrived in May 1942 to operate target tugs for use over the nearby gunnery range at HMS *Charlotte*. This squadron was equipped with Chesapeakes, Blenheims, Rocs and Skuas. While more squadrons came for a rest, a number visited to re-equip with the Typhoon and, in June 1943, 322 (Dutch) Sqn was formed by the re-numbering of 167Sqn.

Towards the end of 1943, 12 (Pilot) Advanced Flying Unit arrived with Blenheims, followed by 650Sqn for target towing duties.

When the war ended, the station came under Royal Navy control and became HMS *Ringtail II*, until January 1946, when it was transferred back to the RAF. 611 (West Lancs) In the summer of 1946, Aux AF Sqn arrived with Spitfires and converted to Meteors in 1951. Following their departure, the Temperature and Humidity (THUM) Flight arrived in July 1951, operating Spitfires and then Mosquitos prior to disbanding in May 1959. Also in 1951, the Liverpool UAS was re-established, followed by Manchester UAS in 1953, both equipped with Chipmunks. In December 1957, the 5 Civilian Anti-Aircraft Co-operation Unit (5 CAACU) arrived and continued operating the Meteor until disbanded in 1971. In August 1958, 10 AEF was formed with Chipmunks to provide Air Cadets with air experience flying.

Uniquely, the squadron commander for the UAS also has the responsibility of the station commander.

Woodvale is the home for the Liverpool University Air Squadron and the Manchester & Salford Universities Air Squadron, who operate the Tutor T.1, and 10 AEF, who loan UAS aircraft as required.

RAF Wyton

Personnel and Training Command
Motto: *Verum Exquiro* – to seek the truth

Military activity at Wyton dates back to 1916, when wooden buildings were occupied by the RFC and used for training. One unit was 96Sqn, which formed in September 1918 with the Salamander to teach ground-attack techniques, but was disbanded in December. However, it wasn't until 1935 that a permanent airfield was constructed, during the RAF's expansion programme, opening in July 1936.

In September 1936, 139Sqn re-formed, followed by 114Sqn in December – both with Hinds, but they converted to Blenheims before war broke. It was a 139Sqn Blenheim that was the first RAF aircraft to make an operational sortie in the Second World War, when it flew a reconnaissance mission to photograph the German Fleet in preparation for an RAF attack. They both moved to France in December and were replaced by 15 and 40Sqn with Battles and immediately began converting to Blenheims. In April, 15Sqn then moved to the satellite airfield of Alconbury. In June 1940, 57Sqn arrived briefly and, together with 15 and 40Sqn, re-equipped with Wellingtons. In November, 57Sqn departed, when 15Sqn converted to the Stirling. In February 1941, 40Sqn moved to Alconbury. No. 4 Beam Approach Flight (BAT) arrived, was re-numbered 1504 BAT and departed in August.

In August 1942, 83 and 109Sqn arrived with Lancasters as part of the original Pathfinder Force, while the Stirlings of 15Sqn moved out to Bourne. Immediately, 109Sqn converted to Mosquitos, which were the first to be fitted with the OBOE blind bombing-system, using a pair of transmitters to determine the target. Following some development and after calibration flights over Holland, they were used operationally for the first time in December 1942 as part of the 8 Group Pathfinder Force. In July 1943, 109Sqn departed and was replaced by 139Sqn. In January 1944, 1409 Meteorological Research Flight arrived with Mosquitos. In February, 139Sqn left, while 83Sqn departed in April 1944.

In September 1944, 128Sqn was reformed with Mosquitos and departed in June 1945. In January 1945, 163Sqn reformed with Mosquitos, but disbanded again in August. Meanwhile, 1409 Flight had departed in July. They were replaced by 156Sqn, which arrived with Lancasters in June and was occupied repatriating PoWs from Germany and troops from Italy, until disbanding in June 1946.

In February 1947, 15, 44, 90 and 138Sqn began arriving with Lancasters and converting to Lincolns. In September 1950, 90 and 138Sqn both disbanded, while 15Sqn left in November, followed by 44Sqn in January. Following the lengthening of the runway in 1952, Wyton became home to the Strategic Reconnaissance Force. This included 82Sqn with Lancasters, plus 58, 540 and 541Sqn with Mosquitos. First to convert to Canberras was 540Sqn in December 1952. It was followed by 58Sqn in December 1953, then 82Sqn in November 1954, but it disbanded September 1956. May 1954 saw 542Sqn reform with Canberras, but it disbanded in October 1955. It was re-formed again the following month from 1323 Flight. In November 1955, 543Sqn arrived with the Valiant and were joined by 237 OCU, which was formed from 231 OCU's 'C' (PR) Sqn, in October 1956, but reverted to being part of 231 OCU in January 1958.

In March 1963, 51Sqn arrived with the Comet and Canberras. When the Valiants were grounded by metal fatigue in December 1964, their role was taken over by the Victor SR.2. Provision was made for nuclear weapons to be held at Wyton for use by Victor bombers when deployed but were not stored, as Wyton was never classified as a main nuclear-base.

In February 1969, the Northern Communications Squadron was re-numbered 26Sqn but disbanded in April 1976. In April 1969, 360Sqn arrived and continued to provide EW training with its specialized Canberra T.17s until October 1994, when it was disbanded. In March 1970, 58Sqn departed. In October 1970, 39Sqn arrived from Malta. In May 1974, 543Sqn disbanded, while 51Sqn Canberras and Comets were replaced by Nimrods later in the year. In January 1982, 100Sqn arrived with its Canberras for the target facilities role, while 39Sqn was disbanded in May 1982 and re-formed as 1 PRU. March 1983 saw 25Sqn HQ arrive, along with 'B' Flight – equipped with Bloodhound SAMs. In March 1989, the squadron was absorbed into 85Sqn and the Flight became 'F'. In December 1990, 231 OCU was re-named the Canberra Standard-ization Training Flight, reverted to 231 OCU in May 1991, then disbanded in April 1993. Meanwhile, the Bloodhounds were withdrawn during 1990. In 1991, 100Sqn began converting to the Hawk before moving to Finningley in September 1993. In July 1992, 1 PRU expanded and was re-named 39 (1 PRU) Sqn then moved to Marham in December 1993. In January 1995, 51Sqn moved out to Waddington, along with the Electronic Warfare Operational Support Establishment (EWOSE).

By April 1995, the last aircraft had departed and the south-east aircraft dispersals became a site for new buildings for use by the Logistics Command from Harrogate, which subsequently became part of the joint service Defence Logistics Organization (DLO). The domestic site and airfield were separated by a fence and plans were made to sell the airfield. However, the 1996 Strategic Defence Review halted that and resulted in the airfield becoming active once more. In September 1999, Wyton returned to a flying station with the arrival of Cambridge UAS and 5 AEF from Cambridge Teversham Airport. They were followed by London University.

The 2000 MoD re-organization resulted in the DLO providing logistics support for all three services. The DLO comprises a number of business units, of which Equipment Support (Air) (ES Air) is the largest, primarily located at Wyton. It also houses the Corporate Technical Services.

On 1 April 2001, Brampton, Henlow and Wyton were merged. Whilst maintaining their own identity, they have a single station-commander based at Wyton and many of the support functions are centralized. The role of the stations is to support the various lodger units.

Having come under Logistics Command, Wyton houses the central supplies procurement centre. The 500 Range Managers are responsible for the provisioning of the supplies and services that enables the RAF to function on a day-to-day basis with a spend of some £1.2bn per year.

A Pathfinder Museum has been established at Wyton and this can be visited subject to appointment (Tel: 01480 52451 ext 4553).

Wyton provides a home to the Cambridge UAS and London UAS, plus 5 AEF, which all operate the Tutor T.1.

CHAPTER THREE

Units

The RAF consists of a substantial number of units, of which the majority are squadrons or flights, each with a specific role and collectively providing its capability. The following section provides details of most of the major and smaller units together with a brief history.

The front-line flying squadrons are usually considered to be the vital portion of the RAF, but they only form part of the overall force. There is the RAF Regiment, which provides the operational security and ground defence for deployed flying squadrons and home bases in times of tension. In addition to these Strike Command units, the Personnel and Training Command (P&TC) comprises a range of training units needed to maintain the personnel requirements of the operational units. It also operates a range of service units that

provide support capability. In addition, the Auxiliary AF squadrons provide additional manpower, in the form of civilian volunteers who are being increasingly required to maintain manpower levels during the mounting number of operations to which the RAF is being tasked.

The number of units that are based overseas has now reduced to just a handful – mainly in Cyprus and the Falklands. However, the increasing number of operations has seen whole units or flights being deployed for short periods of time. Where possible, these deployments have been rotated through other similarly tasked units, enabling personnel to be away from home for as short a period as possible. Inevitably, with reduced numbers of units, some of these deployments will require units to return more than once.

The RAF operates a system whereby the front-line squadrons with the longest history are retained, hence the reason why some have changed number and why the old OCUs were allocated squadron numbers to preserve some of their histories. As always there are exceptions, the most obvious being 617Sqn, which was only formed in the Second World War – specifically for its famous Dam-busting role – but remains in service.

In RAF life, the unit organization – especially the squadron – provides a valuable point of focus, with units striving for levels of excellence over their colleagues in other units. However, when operations dictate composite units the rivalry is forgotten and the levels of excellence benefit all.

Strike Command

RAF High Wycombe
Motto: Defend and Strike

On 30 April 1968, Strike Command was formed by the merging of Bomber and Fighter Commands at High Wycombe. On 28 November 1968, Coastal Command also merged into Strike command and formed 18 (Maritime) Group. In May 1972, 90 (Signals) Group was transferred to Maintenance Command. In July 1972, 38 Group was absorbed, followed by 46 Group in September. This resulted in the disbanding of Air Support Command and brought most RAF aircraft, except training aircraft, under a single command for the first time, thus reducing the size of the chain of command.

In April 2000, 11 Group – previously formed from the merged 11/18 Groups – 18 Group and 38 Group were all disbanded and re-established as 1, 2 and 3 Groups. No. 1 Group was responsible for all strike aircraft, plus Tornado F.3s, but excluding

the Harriers. No. 2 Group was responsible for support aircraft, including transport and tankers, plus the Nimrod R.1 and Sentry, as well as the RAF Regiments. The newly re-formed 3 Group became responsible for the Joint Force Harrier (which included RAF and Royal Navy aircraft), plus the maritime patrol Nimrods, Search and Rescue helicopters and the RAF's mountain-rescue teams. Uniquely, the first AOC of 3 Group was a Royal Navy officer – Rear Admiral Scott Lidbetter.

During 2003–4, Strike Command underwent a refinement to its operation It retains the three-Group structure, with each formed according to the operational capability of its component units, and a further four divisions provide the appropriate support to the Groups, to achieve the overall objectives of the Command.

The effect of this refinement is that 1 Group is responsible for Air Combat, and now includes the Harriers and Sea Harriers, plus the Typhoons as they are

delivered. No. 2 Group is responsible for Air Combat Support and remains fairly similar, but without the Nimrod R.1s and Sentries. No. 3 Group is now responsible for Air Battle Management and has lost all of the Harriers, but gained the Nimrod R.1s and Sentries, plus Joint Helicopter Command, and will receive the Nimrod MRA.4s and Sentinel.

The divisions consist of Chief of Staff Operations (CoS Ops), Chief of Staff Support (CoS Spt), Command Secretary and Plans. In addition to supporting the CinC to deliver, sustain and develop air power, the CoS Ops also is the senior Air Operations adviser. He is supported by the Commandant of the Air Warfare Centre and Director of the Defence Electronic Warfare Centre. The CoS Spt is the logistics, CIS and personnel-support adviser, while the Command Secretary provides the administration and Plans Division provides management for future exercises and operations.

As part of the re-structuring of the armed forces, in 2004, it was announced that Strike Command and the Personnel and Training Command would be co-located in 2008. This would result in a new structure, together with a reduced staff level – thought to be around 2,000. Once completed, this will then determine the new needs, followed by the selection of a suitable location. It is anticipated that the co-location will be completed in 2008.

Strike Command is based at High Wycombe and comprises 1, 2 and 3 Groups.

No. 1 Group

RAF High Wycombe
Strike Command
Role: Air Combat
Motto: Swift to Attack

A Harrier GR.7 of 1(F)Sqn fires a salvo of SNEB rockets at the target. These rockets have now been replaced by the CRV-7. BAE Systems

On 1 April 1918, 1 Group was formed in London as part of 1 Area, which became South Eastern Area. It became 1 (Training) Group in August 1918, but reverted in April 1920. Following a move to Kenley, in May 1924 it was re-numbered 6 Group and a new 1 Group was formed the same day at Kidbrooke. In April 1926, it was re-numbered 21 Group.

In August 1927, 1 Air Defence Group was formed in London, but re-named 6 Group in May 1936.

The Air Defence of Great Britain – Central Area was re-named 1 (Bomber) Group at Abingdon in May 1936, which was absorbed into Bomber Command when it was formed in July. It was re-titled Advanced Air Strike Force (AASF) in August 1939, when it was deployed to France.

In September 1939, 1 (Bomber) Group was re-formed at Benson, only to be disbanded in December. However, it was reformed in June 1940 at Hucknall from the returning AASF, retaining its identity through until April 1968. It initially controlled squadrons at Binbrook, Newton, Swinderby and Syerston. Following a move to Bawtry Hall in July 1941, six more were added by the end of the year. By the time the war ended, 1 Group aircraft had flown a total of 57,900 operational sorties, during which 238,500 tons of bombs had been dropped and 8,147 mines laid.

In November 1967, 1 Group absorbed 3 Group and, the following April, it was re-titled Bomber Command, within the newly formed Strike Command. It reverted to 1 Group in September 1972 and it continues through to today.

In addition to the lineage changes, 1 Group has also undergone numerous structural changes. In November 1983, 38 Group were absorbed and, in April 1996, while at Benson, 1 and 2 Group at Rheindahlen were merged, then moved to High Wycombe, where they were formed as a new 1 Group.

In January 2000, it controlled offensive and defensive operations.

In 2003–4, 1 Group underwent a further re-organization under Project Future Strike, which resulted in the Joint Force Harriers coming under its control.

The role of 1 Group is Air Combat and, as such, it now operates all attack, offensive support, tactical reconnaissance and air-defence aircraft.

The attack and offensive support comprise the Tornado GR.4, Harrier GR.7 and Jaguar GR.3. Tactical reconnaissance is made up from the Tornado GR.4A, Jaguar GR.3 and Harrier GR.7. Air Defence consists of the Tornado F.3. In addition, 100Sqn is incorporated, as it provides a training facility for fighter pilots and fighter controllers, as well as providing targets for air-defence exercises.

1 Group is based at High Wycombe.

No. 1 (Fighter) Squadron

RAF Cottesmore
BAe Harrier GR.7, GR.7A & T.10
1 Group
Strike Command
Role: Offensive Support
Motto: *In omnibus princeps* – Foremost in everything

On 13 May 1912, 1 Squadron was formed, as one of the first four squadrons of the Royal Flying Corps (RFC). It was initially equipped with observation balloons and kites from No 1 Airship Company, Royal Engineers and was based at Farnborough.

A cadre was formed at Brooklands in May 1914 with a few training aircraft, but these were seconded by active squadrons at the outbreak of war. It moved to Netheravon in November, prior to the squadron deploying to St Omer in March 1915 as part of the British Expeditionary Force (BEF). It was equipped mainly with Avro 504s, which were flown in the reconnaissance role. By early 1917, it had re-equipped with the Nieuport 17, was designated a fighter squadron and undertook numerous combat sorties against the German forces. During January 1918, it converted to the SE.5a but, after the war ended, it was reduced to a cadre the following year, returned to London Colney in March 1919 and disbanded in January 1920.

The following day, 1Sqn was re-formed

at Risalpur on the Indian North West Frontier with the Snipe. It took these to Iraq in 1921, as part of the policing force, where it remained until 1 November 1926, when it disbanded. During this time it had also operated some of the Mars VIs, which had been converted from Nighthawks.

The squadron re-formed again at Tangmere in February 1927 with Siskins, which were replaced with Furies by May 1932 and then Hurricanes in 1938.

When war broke, 1Sqn was deployed to France from Tangmere as part of 67 Wing of the Advanced Air Striking Force, but returned to Tangmere following the German offensive in June 1940. Within a month, the squadron was operational again and immediately pitched into the Battle of Britain, shooting down two Bf.110s. In September, the squadron was temporarily moved to Wittering for a rest, before returning south to Northolt at the end of the year. From here, Kenley, Croydon and Redhill, it undertook fighter sweeps and bomber-escort duties. Substantial numbers of Czechs and Poles who had escaped the German invasion had joined the RAF as volunteers – some helped to boost 1Sqn numbers. Gradually the role changed to night fighter. Having returned to Tangmere, in November 1941, the role changed once more, to intruder patrols over France.

In July 1942, the squadron moved to Acklington to replace their Hurricanes for the Typhoon. Once operational, in September 1942, it moved to Lympne, where it commenced daylight bombing-attacks on airfields and shipping and countering the new threat – the V1s – shooting thirty-nine down over the UK. In April 1944, it converted to the Spitfire IX at Ayr, followed by brief stays at Predannack and Harrowbeer. In June, it was allocated to anti-V1 patrols from Detling, with short moves to Lympne and Manston before arriving at Coltishall. It received the Spitfire F.21 the following year while at Ludham.

The war over, 1Sqn returned to Tangmere, where it re-equipped with the Meteor F.3 in 1946. With the wind-down of RAF strength, August 1947 saw 1Sqn reduced to an instrument-training squadron flying Harvards and Oxfords. June 1948 saw it return to the front line with Meteors, until they were superseded by the Hunter F.5 in September 1955. The squadron was deployed to Cyprus in 1956 during the Suez crisis, but returned home

soon after. It was disbanded once more on 23 June 1958, but reformed on 1 July with Hunters, following the re-numbering of 263Sqn at Stradishall. It moved to Waterbeach and, in March 1960, began to receive the Hunter FGA.9, prior to it becoming part of the newly formed 38 Group and its ground-attack role. It subsequently moved to West Raynham.

In July 1969, 1Sqn received its first Harrier GR.1 and, following conversion, officially formed as the world's first VTOL-fighter squadron on 1 October. It quickly built up to full strength and was soon taking part in exercises, making its first overseas deployment to Akrotiri in March 1970.

The squadron was given three major roles: the first being as a part of the AMF (Allied Mobile Force); the second as a contribution to SACEUR's strategic reserve; and finally it has a commitment to our National Contingency Operations. As such, the squadron frequently deployed to such places as Norway, Denmark, Germany and Italy to exercise these various options and is still a regular visitor to Norway.

In November 1975, 1Sqn deployed six aircraft to Belize at very short notice, as a National Contingency Operation in response to a threatening posture from Guatemala. The speed of the deployment, assisted by air-to-air refuelling, resulted in the situation being defused. The aircraft returned home the following April, but the situation flared up again in July 1977 and six of the new GR.3s were deployed. As a result, it was decided that 1417 Flight would be formed as a semi-permanent detachment with four Harriers.

On 8 April 1982, Wittering were given warning that they were likely to be deploying Harriers to the South Atlantic, following the Argentinian invasion of the Falklands. A fleet of a dozen Harriers was assembled, with half coming from 1Sqn, who also provided six of the sixteen pilots that were deployed. They underwent a rushed preparation: not only the pilots, who had to use the ski jump at Yeovilton for the first time, but also the aircraft, which had to be cleared to use the Sidewinder AAMs, 2in rockets and Paveway bombs. They also were given an improved sealing and drainage for the salt environment, as well as other items that enabled them to be operated from a carrier. Due to the time required, they missed the sailing from Liverpool of the *Atlantic*

Conveyor, which was to transport them, and so had to be ferried to Ascension. During the deployment the Harrier force flew 125 operational sorties, during which the laser-guided Paveway bombs were used for the first time.

Once the war was over, 1Sqn established a shore-based detachment on 26 June, which was handed over to 4Sqn in November. It subsequently became known as HarDet, was then established as 1453 Flight and was manned by the squadrons and OCU on rotation.

In November 1988, 1Sqn became the first squadron to receive the Harrier GR.5, followed by the first GR.7s in 1992, as well as being first to be cleared for night operations. The squadron became part of the newly formed Joint Force Harrier (JFH) in 2000 and moved to Cottesmore in July.

Apart from numerous exercises, since 1992, 1Sqn Harriers have been deployed on Operation *Warden* over Northern Iraq, Operation *Deny Flight* over Bosnia, Operation *Allied Force*, during which over 800 missions were flown over Kosovo, and, more recently, Operation *Bolton* in Iraq. In early 2003, they were deployed to the Middle East once again for Operation *Telic* over Iraq. In October 2003, eight Harriers flew to Romania to take part in an MoD outreach exercise.

1Sqn operate the Harrier GR.7A plus a T.10 from their base at Cottesmore.

No. II (Army Co-operation) Squadron

RAF Marham
Panavia Tornado GR.4 & GR.4A
1 Group
Strike Command
Role: Reconnaissance
Motto: Hereward

On 13 May 1912, 2 Squadron (normally referred to as II (AC) Squadron) was formed at Farnborough – the day that the Royal Flying Corps (RFC) became effective. It moved to Montrose, Scotland soon after and returned south after a short stay.

II (AC) Sqn became the first fixed-wing RFC unit, along with 3Sqn, flying a mixture of aircraft built by Maurice Farman, Breguet and Cody, as well as the BE.2c. The squadron trained in the reconnaissance role and was deployed to France at the beginning of the First World War.

The squadron soon achieved a number of firsts, starting when it flew the first RFC aircraft into France. It achieved the first aerial victory by forcing down a German aircraft and it was the first unit to use a camera to photograph enemy trenches. It wasn't long before bombing was added to its tasking. During one such mission in 1915, Lieutenant Rhodes-Moorhouse was badly wounded while dropping a 100lb bomb. He was injured a second time from ground fire, but managed to return to base and insisted on giving his report before being taken to hospital – sadly, he died the following day. For his gallantry and courage he was awarded a posthumous VC – the first for the RFC.

In 1918, Second Lieutenant A A Macleod was also awarded a VC. Having destroyed one aircraft, the FK.8 that he was flying was attacked by eight enemy aircraft. He managed to manoeuvre his aircraft, enabling his observer to shoot down two of the enemy. Unfortunately, the fuel tank was hit and the petrol set alight. Having to stand on the wing and side-slip to avoid the flames, the observer – Lieutenant Hammond – was able to shoot down another aircraft. The aircraft crashed into no man's land, during which Hammond was badly injured. Macleod managed to drag him back to friendly

lines. Macleod was further wounded by a bomb and was awarded the VC for his heroic actions on his recovery. At the end of the war, II (AC) Sqn returned home to Andover and disbanded in January 1920.

Just a few days later, II (AC) Sqn was re-formed in Ireland with the F.2b Fighter. It moved to the UK, then to Ulster by May 1922, and left a detachment while the HQ moved to Farnborough by the end of the year. In April 1927, the squadron was despatched to Shanghai, China, although it was back at Manston in September. It flew the Atlas, Audax and Hector until it re-equipped with the Lysander at Hawkinge for the outbreak of the Second World War.

In October 1939, the squadron deployed to France, where they were used as bait to draw out enemy aircraft for waiting Hurricanes. After reconnaissance and SOE roles, II (AC) Sqn converted to the Tomahawk in 1941 and then to the Mustang in 1942.

After D-Day, II (AC) Sqn deployed again to France, providing reconnaissance for the Canadians. November 1944 saw it re-equipped with the Spitfire XIV. While in Germany, in 1946, PR.XIXs were added, resulting in two flights being formed – one for high-level and the other for low-level tactical reconnaissance. In 1951, it returned to low-level only and re-equipped with the Meteor FR.9. It

operated from various locations in Germany and re-equipped with the Swift in 1956. These were replaced with the Hunter F.6 in 1961 at Gütersloh. In December 1970, a new II (AC) Sqn re-equipped again – this time with the Phantom – and moved to Laarbruch in May 1971.

The Reconnaissance Interpretation Centre (RIC), which is responsible for processing and interpreting reconnaissance images, merged with II (AC) Sqn in 1974.

From March 1976, the Phantoms were replaced by the Jaguar, which proved to be a highly effective aircraft, with II (AC) Sqn crews excelling in tactical evaluations and exercises. On 1 January 1989, II (AC) converted to the GR.1A, becoming the RAF's first Tornado reconnaissance, using a new infra-red Linescan video system. During the Gulf War, six crews from II (AC) Sqn were deployed to form 2 (Composite) Squadron together with 13Sqn, as the tactical reconnaissance unit for the coalition forces operating at night – a role that no other Allied squadron could fill. When the war ended, II (AC) Sqn returned to Laarbruch

Six Tornado GR.1As were deployed to Dhahran during the build up to the Gulf War, as 2 (Composite) Sqn, with crew from both II (AC) and 13Sqn. While there, they flew only night-time low-level tactical reconnaissance missions, being the only Allied unit which could perform the role.

On 3 December 1991, II (AC) Sqn

II (AC) Sqn is one of the two RAF squadrons to operate the Tornado GR.4a fitted with CBLS (Carrier, Bomb, Light Stores) pods, just visible behind the drop tanks. Kevin Wills

moved to Marham as part of the RAF's Tactical Reconnaissance Wing.

No. II (AC) Sqn have been regularly deployed to patrol the northern and southern no-fly zones over Iraq. They were required to bomb Iraqi targets during Operation Bolton in early 1999 and were deployed again during Operation *Telic* in 2003.

II (AC) Sqn operate the Tornado GR.4A from their base at Marham.

No. 3 (Fighter) Squadron

RAF Cottesmore
BAe Harrier GR.7, GR.7A & T.10
1 Group
Strike Command
Role: Offensive Support
Motto: *Tertius primus erit* – The third shall be first

On 13 May 1912, 3 Squadron was formed at Larkhill and was the first RFC squadron to operate a heavier than air aircraft – the Blériot XI. It was deployed to France on 13 August 1914, initially for reconnaissance patrols and artillery spotting, later operating the Morane Parasol. In 1917, its role

changed to fighter with Camels and, by the end of the First World War, the squadron had destroyed fifty-nine enemy aircraft. It returned to the UK in February 1919 and disbanded in October.

The squadron was re-formed in India on 1 April 1920 and operated Snipes until the end of September 1921, when it took over the identity of 205Sqn at Leuchars, which operated the DH.9a prior to re-equipping the the Walrus then moving to Gosport. In April 1923, 205Sqn was disbanded when it was split into 421 and 422 Flights.

Twelve months later, 3Sqn was re-formed at Manston and operated a variety of aircraft during the 1920s and 30s, including Snipes again, followed by the Bison, in 1922, while based at Gosport and later the Woodcock, Gamecock and the Bristol Bulldog while at Upavon. However, basically it remained a fighter unit.

In the mid-1930s, 3Sqn briefly deployed to the Sudan. On return, it equipped with Hurricanes at Kenley in 1938, although these were temporarily replaced by Gladiators for a while, before the squadron moved to Biggin Hill and then Croydon with Hurricanes, then brief stays at

Hawkinge and Kenley. It deployed to France in May 1940 for an even briefer period, but suffered heavy losses and was brought home to defend Scapa Flow. From 1941, it specialized in the night-fighter role, operating from Martlesham Heath and Stapleford Tawney. Typhoons replaced the Hurricanes in February 1943 and were changed again, a year later, to Tempest Vs. During their *Diver* Operations, 3Sqn managed to destroy 288 flying-bombs while on anti-V1 patrols during the last year of the war.

At the end of the war, 3Sqn was deployed to Germany as part of 2 TAF. The first jet to operate with 3Sqn was the Vampire from April 1948. This was followed, in mid-1953, by it being one of the first RAF squadrons to re-equip with the F-86 Sabre. This was ordered as a stop gap while waiting for Swift and Hunter deliveries. The Hunter arrived in 1956, but the squadron was disbanded in June 1957. In June 1959, it took over the identity of 96Sqn at Geilenkirchen to operate the Javelin. This lasted until the end of 1960, when it then took the identity of 59Sqn, at the same base but operating the Canberra B (I).8. It was with these aircraft that the squadron won the Salmond Trophy bomb-aiming competitions in 1965 and 1967. In January 1968, it moved to Laarbruch and disbanded in December 1971.

3Sqn Harrier GR.7s were deployed to Kandahar in Afghanistan in 2004 to support the ISAF Coalition forces, who continue to rid the country of the remnants of the terrorist factions. They have been rotating the task with 1 and 4 Sqns.

IV (AC) Sqn Harrier GR.7 with an AIM-9 Sidewinder acquisition training-round leads a pairs formation.

In 1972, 3Sqn was reformed with the Harrier GR.1A at Wildenrath in the fighter/ground-attack role. It took part in the development of the off-base role for the Harrier force and often exercised in field or road sites. Many of these sites were no bigger than those originally used when the squadron was first formed. On 1 April 1977, the squadron moved to nearby Gütersloh and took delivery of the improved Harrier GR.3.

When the Argentine Forces invaded the Falkland Islands, two of 3Sqn's pilots were detached to the Royal Navy and three to 1 (F) Sqn to fly Harriers from aircraft carriers, as part of Operation *Corporate*. At the end of the conflict, 3 (F) Sqn deployed a detachment to Stanley for over two months.

In March 1989, the squadron received its first Harrier GR.5 and commenced conversion onto the new aircraft, becoming the first operator of the type in Germany. However, the GR.5 was only an interim model and was superseded by the GR.7 in 1991. Before it had completed its pre-service bomb-release trials, 3Sqn was required to deploy four of its aircraft to Incirlik in Turkey. They were required to provide protective cover for the Kurds in northern Iraq from Saddam Hussein's forces as part of Operation Warden. In November 1992, it moved to Laarbruch and was deployed for active service on

Operations including *Provide Comfort*, *Deny Flight/Decisive Edge* in Bosnia and *Deliberate Force* in Kosovo. In November 1999, it returned to the UK at Cottesmore and joined the RAF/RN Joint Force Harrier (JFH) as part of 3 Group. Most recently, 3Sqn flew missions in Operation *Telic* in Iraq.

No. 3Sqn is due to disband in April 2006, when 801 NAS will have become fully trained on the Harrier GR.7. In the meantime, trained naval crews are being integrated into 3Sqn, enabling the trained crews to built up to full strength and Sea Harriers to be withdrawn. It will then be re-formed as the first operational Typhoon squadron and be based at Coningsby.

No. 3Sqn operate the Harrier GR.7A plus a T.10 from its base at Cottesmore.

No. IV (Army Co-operation) Squadron

RAF Cottesmore
BAe Harrier GR.7, GR.7A & T.10
1 Group
Strike Command
Role: Offensive Support
Motto: *In Futurum Videre* – To see into the future

On 16 September 1912, 4 Squadron was formed at Farnborough from a IISqn

Flight. In August 1914, it was deployed to France with BE.2C. It was while in France that the squadron's title – IV (Army Co-operation) Sqn – was earned due to the close work that it undertook with the British Army. It re-equipped with F.2b Fighters and one Flight was detached to Northern Ireland in November 1920, before the whole squadron was deployed to San Stefano, Turkey during the Chanak Crisis.

During the inter-war years, IV (AC) Sqn was equipped with the Atlas, Audax, and Hector. Just prior to the commencement of hostilities, it re-equipped with the Westland Lysander.

The squadron deployed to France, but were soon pushed back with other members of the BEF by the German offensive. By May 1940, the Lysanders of IV (AC) Sqn were the only BEF Air Component aircraft still operating in France. The squadron re-equipped with the Mustang in 1942 and conducted offensive fighter-sweeps over France and the Low Countries, until they were re-equipped once more. This time it was with the Spitfire and Mosquito, from August 1943, from Odiham for high-altitude photo reconnaissance. On 31 August1945, IV (AC) Sqn disbanded in Germany.

The following day, IV (AC) Sqn took over the identity of 605Sqn at Celle, oper-

A 6Sqn Jaguar GR.3 prepares for flight back to Coltishall after a major refurbishment by DARA at St Athan. 6Sqn will be the last to fly the aircraft as the Jaguar fleet is withdrawn.

ating the Mosquito. These were replaced by the Vampire in 1950, the Sabre in October 1953 and Hunter in 1955. Initially, it operated as a light-bomber unit followed by day-fighter. At the end of 1960, it took over the identity of 79Sqn with the Hunter FR.10 and was based at Gütersloh. On 1 September 1969, it also absorbed 54Sqn, when that unit converted to the Phantom.

The UK Flight Hunters were replaced with the Harrier in April 1970 and, in May, the German-based Flight disbanded. The following month, IV (AC) Sqn took its Harriers to Wildenrath. The original GR.1s were replaced by upgraded GR.3s in 1976 and, in January 1977, it moved back to Güsloh, from where it operated in the ground-attack and reconnaissance role, losing the reconnaissance role in May 1989. It was the last operator of the Harrier GR.3. In September 1990, it became the first to re-equip with the Harrier GR.7 and, in November 1992, moved to Laarbruch. It returned to the UK in November 1999 when Laarbruch closed and became part of the Joint Force Harrier (JFH) at Cottesmore.

No. IV (AC) Sqn has frequently been required to share tasks with 3Sqn, which has had them deploy to Incirlik in Turkey, providing protective cover for the Kurds in Northern Iraq as part of Operation *Warden*

and including reconnaissance missions. They were also deployed for Operation *Deny Flight* in Bosnia, *Allied Force* in Kosovo operating out of Gioia del Colle in Italy and, most recently, Operation *Telic* in Iraq.

No. IV (AC) Sqn operates the Harrier GR.7A and a single T.10 from its base at Cottesmore.

No. 6 Squadron

RAF Coltishall
SEPECAT Jaguar GR.3A & T.4
1 Group
Strike Command
Role: Offensive Support
Motto: *Oculi Excercitus* – The eyes of the army

No. 6 Squadron was formed at Farnborough on 31 January 1914 with two BE biplanes. Having transferred most of its aircraft to other squadrons in August, it did not reach full strength until October. Then an advanced party, led by Captain Dowding (later to become Air Chief Marshall) departed for France followed by the whole squadron for the army co-operation role. This included tactical reconnaissance, artillery observation, photography, and trench mapping with BE.2s, BE.8s and Henry Farmans.

In July 1915, one of the squadron pilots – Captain L G Hawker – located and attacked three German aircraft in quick succession whilst flying his Bristol Scout, onto which he had unofficially mounted a Lewis machine-gun. The last of these aircraft was shot down in flames. For his endeavour, Captain Hawker was awarded the Victoria Cross – the first to be awarded for air-to-air fighting. He was, sadly, killed in action the following year.

Later, the squadron's role changed to low-level bombing, flown in close support of the cavalry and other units on the Western Front. In September 1915, 6Sqn attempted to land an intelligence agent behind enemy lines with a BE.2c. Unfortunately, the aircraft was damaged on landing and the secret papers had to be destroyed before they were captured.

In 1919, 6Sqn was deployed to the Middle East and initially operated F.2b Fighters and RE.8s in co-operation with the army in Iraq, Kurdistan and Palestine. These were replaced with the Gordon in April 1931. The squadron role changed in 1935, when it was re-equipped with the Hawker Hart and Demon. These were frequently used for Arab-Jewish peace-keeping operations.

In Palestine, 6Sqn was located at Ramleh and Haifa with Hardy and Gauntlet biplanes and later the Lysander, by the time war broke out. By 1940, it had resumed its army co-operation role. One flight was equipped with Hurricanes and operated with the 2nd Armoured Division and two further flights were equipped with the Lysander and based at Tobruk. Over the following two years this make-up fluctuated. At one point the squadron only operated Hurricanes, while at another it was just Lysanders, and then Gladiators and Blenheims IVs. This changed again in April 1942, when Hurricane IIDs were delivered. These were fitted with the 40mm cannon, which proved effective in the tank-busting role. The squadron became so extremely proficient in this role that they were nicknamed the 'flying can-openers', which has resulted in an appropriate logo being applied to their aircraft. In February 1944, the squadron moved to Taranto with rocket-firing Hurricanes and was mainly tasked with anti-shipping patrols until the end of the war.

With hostilities over, 6Sqn returned back to the Middle East and then Cyprus, where it re-equipped with the Tempest. The squadron was deployed to Somaliland to quell local unrest in early 1948 and was assisted by 8Sqn. It moved to various locations in the Middle East, during which time it re-equipped with the Vampire and then Venom.

King Abdullah of Jordan presented his personal standard to the squadron in 1950. When Queen Elizabeth presented her standard in 1954, 6Sqn became the only RAF unit with two standards.

In 1956, 6Sqn deployed to Akrotiri and flew attack missions against Egyptian airfields during the Suez Crisis. The squadron remained in Cyprus and re-equipped with the Canberra in 1957, becoming part of the Middle East Air Force Strike Wing. In 1969, 6Sqn returned to the UK for the first time since 1914 and became the RAF's first Phantom squadron at Coningsby on 16 January 1969.

On 30 September 1974, 6Sqn re-equipped with the Jaguar at Lossiemouth and then moved to Coltishall on 6 November. In 1990, it led the first deployment of the Coltishall squadrons to Oman, as the JagDet, as part of the force to counter the invasion of Kuwait by Iraq. Once over, 6Sqn then deployed to Turkey, where they took part in Operation *Warden*, protecting the Kurds from attack from Iraqi forces until 1993. In July, it deployed to Gioia del Colle to fly operational close air-support and reconnaissance missions from southern Italy over the former Yugoslavia. It returned in 1999 for more operations over Kosovo. In August 2002, eight Jaguars took part in

joint exercises in Bulgaria, operating with MiG and Sukhoi aircraft.

No. 6Sqn is the RAF's longest-operated unit. Of the original seven RFC squadrons formed in January 1914, 6Sqn is the only one that has been in continuous service since day one. With the run down of the Jaguar force, it is expected that the last examples to be operated by the RAF will by by 6Sqn and will be withdrawn around the end of 2007. No. 6Sqn will then convert to be the first Typhoon squadron to be formed at Leuchars.

No. 6Sqn operate the Jaguar GR.3A and T.4 from Coltishall. Moving to Coningsby by 31 March 2006.

No. IX (Bomber) Squadron

RAF Marham
Panavia Tornado GR.4
1 Group
Strike Command
Role: Strike Attack
Motto: *Per Noctem Volamus* – We fly by night

No. IX (B) Sqn was initially formed on 8 December 1914 at St Omer in France from the HQ Wireless Unit, but disbanded the following March, its personnel distributed to boost other units. It was re-formed the following month with the BE.2c at Brooklands as an Army co-operation unit and then deployed to France in November.

It flew reconnaissance missions in the Somme and Ypres until re-equipped with the RE.8 for the bomber role in May 1917. By February 1919, F.2b Fighters were beginning to arrive, when it was recalled home and disbanded at the end of the year.

On 1 April 1924, the squadron re-formed with the Vimy bomber at Upavon and later moved to Manston. Virginia heavy-bombers were received the following January and these were replaced with Heyfords in 1936. During this period they developed long-range day- and night-flying, which would become invaluable just a short time later.

In February 1939, IX (B) Sqn moved to Honington, where they were re-equipped with the Wellington, which they flew on the first offensive operation of the Second World War on Brunsbuttel. The Wellingtons were briefly replaced by Manchesters but, in September 1942, these were replaced with the Lancaster. They moved to Bardney, where they specialized in dropping large munitions, including the 12,000lb 'Tallboy' bomb. They took part in the successful attack on the *Tirpitz* in 1944. Following one mission to Germany in 1945, Flight Sergeant George Thompson – an RAFVR wireless operator on a Lancaster – was awarded a VC for saving two of his crew in their burning Lancaster. Sadly, he died shortly after from his injuries.

Once the war in Europe ended, IX (B)

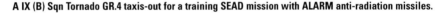

A IX (B) Sqn Tornado GR.4 taxis-out for a training SEAD mission with ALARM anti-radiation missiles.

Sqn received the Lancaster VII and deployed to the Far East as part of Tiger Force to fight the Japanese. With the war ended in the Far East, IV (B) Sqn undertook aerial survey for a while in India. The Lancasters were replaced by Lincolns and, in 1952, these gave way to the Canberra, which was later deployed for operations in Malaya and then Suez. In April 1962, the Canberra was replaced by the Vulcan. From February 1969, IXSqn was deployed to Akrotiri for six years, operating as part of the Near East Air Force until 1975, when the squadron returned to the UK at Waddington. During the late 1970s. the squadron's high quality of operation was reflected by their regularly winning trophies in various bombing and navigation competitions. The squadron disbanded in April 1982.

On 6 January 1982, IX (B) Sqn received its first Tornado GR.1. However, it didn't officially reform until 1 June at Honington, when it became the first operational squadron on the type. In 1986, it became part of RAF Germany and moved to Bruggen. In 1990, the squadron was deployed to Dhahran during the Gulf War.

From here it was tasked with a number of missions with JP233 and 1,000lb bombs against Iraqi targets.

Shortly after returning to Bruggen, IX (B) Sqn moved to Marham as part of the RAF's programme of vacating German bases. Since then it has participated in operations against Serb targets during the protection of Kosovo and in Operation *Telic* in Iraq in 2003.

No. IX (B) Sqn is based at Marham and is equipped with the Tornado GR.4.

No. 11 (Fighter) Squadron

RAF Leeming
Panavia Tornado F.3
1 Group
Strike Command
Role: Air Defence
Motto: *Ociores acrioresque aquilis* – Swifter and keener than eagles

On 28 November 1914, 11Sqn was formed at Netheravon from a nucleus of 7Sqn. However, it wasn't until 14 February that it became an independent unit. In July, it

deployed to France with the FB.5 Gunbus, to become the first all-fighter squadron to be deployed to the Expeditionary Force. In November 1915, Second Lieutenant Insall was awarded a VC for his actions in shooting down a German aircraft, dive bombing the aircraft whose crew were about to fire. While returning to base, he and his gunner had to stop and repair the aircraft overnight before completing the mission. By mid-1916, 11Sqn began converting from the Nieuport Scout to the FE.2b, and the F.2b Fighter the following year. In September 1919, it returned to Scopwick and was disbanded at the end of the year.

In January 1923, 11Sqn was re-formed at Andover, with personnel from the Air Pilotage School but with the role of communications. Following re-equipment with the DH.9As, it moved to Bircham Newton. These were replaced by Fawns and Horsleys in 1926. In 1928, these were passed on to 100Sqn when the squadron was deployed to Risalpur, India and re-equipped with Wapitis to patrol the North West Frontier. Following the arrival of Harts during the early 1930s, a series of reinforcement exercises were flown to Singapore and Egypt.

Blenheims arrived in July 1939 and 11Sqn moved to Singapore the following month. Next May, it moved to Egypt and

A dual-role Tornado EF.3 armed with ALARM missiles for a SEAD role, as well as its usual one of a fighter. MBDA/GH Lee

12Sqn have ceased their maritime attack-role specialization and have exchanged their Tornado GR.1Bs for the standard GR.4 attack variant.

then to Aden the following month, to participate in the Abyssinian Campaign, before withdrawing to Egypt. In January 1941, it moved to Greece, then Palestine and Iraq, and returned to Egypt by September.

In March 1942, 11Sqn was deployed to Ceylon and then to Burma the following January. In September, the Blenheims were replaced with Hurricanes, until June 1945, when it moved to India. Here it re-equipped with the Spitfire, prior to the invasion of Malaya. This was cancelled following the Japanese surrender in August 1945 and, instead, it deployed to Kallang, Malaya aboard HMS *Trumpeter*. In May 1946, it deployed to Japan to be part of the British Commonwealth Air Forces of Occupation, prior to disbanding in February 1948.

In October 1948, 11Sqn re-formed with the Mosquito at Wahn, having taken over the identity of 107Sqn, and later moved to Celle and then Wunsdorf. It then re-equipped with Vampire in August 1950 and the Venom in August 1952 and continued to operate these until being disbanded in November 1957.

In January 1959, 256Sqn surrendered its identity to enable 11Sqn to re-form at Geilenkirchen with Meteors, which were exchanged for Javelins the following year. Various marks were flown prior to disbanding in December 1962.

In April 1967, 11Sqn was reformed with the Lightning F.6 at Leuchars, moving south to Binbrook in March 1972. It became the last RAF squadron to operate the Lightning and, in April 1988, 11Sqn was re-equipped with the Tornado F.3.

In August 1990, 11Sqn deployed to Dhahran, to relieve aircraft and crews that had hastily been previously deployed for operations during the Gulf War.

In November 2002, 11Sqn became the first RAF squadron to be deployed operationally with the ASRAAM missile. The occasion was when the Squadron was deployed to the Middle East as part of Operation *Resinate (South)*.

In January 2003, 11Sqn became the first RAF squadron to operate the Tornado EF.3 and was assisted in the work-up period with crews from 25Sqn, being declared operational in the SEAD role by the end of the month.

In 2003, an 11Sqn Tornado EF.3 participated in Exercise *Elite* – a German-hosted NATO electronic warfare and SEAD exercise.

In July 2004, it was announced that 11Sqn would be disbanded in October 2005, due to the reduced need for RAF fighter aircraft. However, 11Sqn will not disappear for long, as it has also been announced that it will be re-formed in 2007 as the second Typhoon squadron.

No. 11Sqn operates the Tornado F.3 and EF.3 from their base at Leeming.

No. 12 (Bomber) Squadron

RAF Lossiemouth
Panavia Tornado GR.4
1 Group
Strike Command
Role: Strike Attack
Motto: Leads the Field

On 14 February 1915, 12Sqn was formed at Netheravon from a nucleus provided by 1Sqn and equipped with the BE.2c. It was deployed to France and operated the RE.8 during operations over Cambrai, the Somme and Loos. It became part of the Army of Occupation and, by the time it was disbanded in July 1922, it was the sole operational RAF squadron in Germany.

The squadron was re-formed at Northolt in April 1923, from Inland Communications Flight with the DH.9A at Northolt. In March 1924, it moved to Andover and re-equipped with the Fawn and then the Fox in 1926. This resulted in the use of the Fox in the emblem painted on their aircraft – the Fairey Fox was the first all-metal aircraft. The increased performance of the Fox led to it winning many bombing trophies. In 1931 it re-equipped with the Hart and was deployed for a short period in Abyssinia, during the crisis there in 1935. It returned to Andover, where it re-equipped with Hinds in December 1936 and then Battles in 1938.

For the outbreak of war, 12Sqn was deployed to France as part of the Advanced Air Striking Force (AASF). In May 1940, Flying Officer Garner and his

XIII Sqn is the RAF's second dual-role Tornado GR.4A reconnaissance/attack-unit based at Marham. Crown Copyright

observer Sergeant Gray, led a flight of five Battles to attack a vital bridge over the Albert Canal. They met strong opposition, which resulted in all bar one aircraft being shot down. However, the bridge was destroyed and Flying Officer Garner and Sergeant Gray were posthumously awarded the Victoria Cross – the first RAF VCs of the war.

Following the withdrawal from France in June 1940, the Battles were replaced by the Wellington at Binbrook and then Lancasters in 1942 at Wickenby. These continued to be operated until August 1946, then they were replaced by the Lincoln in August 1946. During 1952, 12Sqn re-equipped with the Canberra and these were flown during Operation *Firedog* in Malaysia and Operation *Musketeer* in Suez. The squadron was disbanded in July 1961.

In November 1962, 12Sqn was reformed with the Vulcan at Coningsby, but disbanded at the end of 1967.

In October 1969, 12Sqn was re-formed at Honington, to become the first RAF squadron to equip with the Buccaneer. The squadron moved to Lossiemouth in 1980, from where it could cover the Faroes Gap in the maritime strike-role in addition to its normal strike-role. When it was

called to fly its Buccaneers operationally there was no water – just the Iraqi sand. The Buccaneers were deployed during the Gulf War to provide laser designation for the Tornados, as well as for their own bombing missions. It is an interesting fact that their first Gulf War mission was against a bridge over the Euphrates. Their first Second World War mission had been on the Dutch Maastricht bridges, for which the RAF's first two VCs were awarded to a squadron crew.

On 1 October 1993, 12Sqn finally disbanded with its Buccaneers and was re-formed at Marham by taking over the role and identity of 27Sqn, which was equipped with the Tornado GR.1B. The squadron took its Tornados to Lossiemouth in January 1994, continuing to operate them in the maritime role. During December 1998, the squadron took part in the four-day campaign against Iraq in Operation *Desert Fox*, using TIALD pods for laser-designating LGBs. Following the withdrawal of Sea Eagle, the dedicated Tornado GR.1Bs were retired from April 2001 and have now been replaced by the upgraded GR.4, which flew operationally against Iraqi targets in 2001.

No. 12Sqn operate the Tornado GR.4 from their base at Lossiemouth.

No. XIII Squadron

RAF Marham
Panavia Tornado GR.4 & GR.4A
1 Group
Strike Command
Role: Reconnaissance
Motto: *Adjuvamus Tuendo* – We assist by watching

On 10 January 1915, XIII Squadron was formed at Gosport. It was deployed to France with the BE.2c, where it performed army co-operation duties and later undertook bombing raids.

In those early days, XIIISqn helped to evolve tactics and technology in respect to reconnaissance and bombing, as well as pioneering formation flying. Bristol Scouts were added and, by 1918, it was operating the RE.8, with which it took over 14,000 photos, until reduced to a cadre in March 1919 then disbanded at the end of the year.

Re-formed on 1 April 1924, XIIISqn initially operated F.2b Fighters from Kenley and, in June, moved to Andover. It converted to the Atlas in September 1927, moved to Netheravon in September 1929 and was re-equipped with the Audax by February 1932. April 1935 saw it move to Odiham and take delivery of Hectors.

In January 1939, XIIISqn received the Lysander, with which it deployed to France in October. By mid-1940 it had been withdrawn to the UK at Hawarden and, later, at Hooton Park. However, a year later, XIIISqn was equipped with Blenheim bombers at Odiham, which it operated in army-support training as well as operationally. This was followed by a move to the Mediterranean theatre in November 1942, initially for tactical bombing and then anti-submarine patrols. The following November saw the Ventura arrive for the patrol and escort tasks. In December 1943, it replaced these with Baltimores, following a move to Egypt. In February, it moved to Italy, where its role changed to interdiction in May, and was then involved in the invasion of southern France. In October, it re-equipped with Bostons and moved to Hassani, Greece in September 1945, where it disbanded in the following April.

In September 1946, XIIISqn re-formed at Ein Shemer, Palestine with Mosquitos, by taking over the identity of 680Sqn, and returned to the reconnaissance role, followed by a move to Egypt in December. During a recce sortie a Mosquito was shot down by an Israeli Mustang. By February 1952, the Mosquitos were replaced by the Meteor, a detachment of which was deployed to Kenya for operations against the Mau Mau terrorists. The Meteors were replaced by the Canberra in May 1956, following a move to Akrotiri, Cyprus. While there, Canberras were flown on reconnaissance missions over Egypt, Lebanon and Syria, prior to the Suez War,

during which one was shot down over Syria. It moved on to Malta in September 1965 and became the last RAF squadron to operate from Malta, undertaking many survey detachments before returning to the UK, in October 1978, to Wyton. It subsequently disbanded in January 1982.

On 1 January, 1990 XIIISqn re-formed at Honington with the Tornado GR.1A. Once again the squadron was at the forefront of technology. Instead of cameras, the Tornado was fitted with the Linescan system, which used infra-red sensors and video recorders capable of operating with a night and all-weather capability. However, they had little time to train with the equipment before they had to use it for real.

Just prior to the commencement of the Gulf War hostilities in January 1991, six Tornado GR.1As of XIIISqn were deployed to Saudi Arabia. They successfully located several Scud sites and then were tasked with locating Iraqi ground forces. Although the coalition forces flew most of their missions at medium level to avoid ground fire, XIIISqn flew most of their missions at night and at low level. By the end of the war, XIIISqn had flown a total of 128 reconnaissance sorties.

In addition to the reconnaissance role, four XIIISqn crews were rapidly trained to use the TIALD (Thermal Imaging and Laser Designation) pod, which was still in development. With their work up

completed, these crews were deployed to Tabuk, where they flew seventy-two successful missions.

The squadron have played their part in Operation *Jural*, in which their aircraft patrolled over southern Iraq to enforce the United Nations No-Fly Zone directive to protect the population from Saddam's oppressive regime. This was followed by Operations *Bolton* and *Warden*.

On 1 February 1994, XIIISqn moved to Marham, where it became part of the Tactical Reconnaissance Wing, which has since been re-named the Tactical Imagery Intelligence Wing, providing photos and data to the appropriate forces.

In 2003, it returned to the Middle East, where it flew on Operation *Telic* over Iraq, flying low-level reconnaissance missions, initially trying to locate Scud missile sites.

No. XIIISqn operates the Tornado GR.4/4A from their base at Marham.

No. 14 Squadron

RAF Lossiemouth

Panavia Tornado GR.4

1 Group

Strike Command

Role: Strike Attack

Motto: I spread my wings and keep my promise (an extract in Arabic from the Koran)

On 3 February 1915, 14Sqn was formed at Shoreham from a nucleus provided by 3 Reserve Squadron and flew a number of types before they deployed to the Middle East in November. They flew in the army co-operation role in Egypt, Palestine and

As with all attack aircraft, it is necessary to train at low level in order that they can approach targets undetected below radar. This 14Sqn Tornado GR.4 is using one of the specially selected low-flying routes that tries to avoid areas sensitive to noise. Philip Stevens – TargetA

Arabia until November 1917, when they received RE.8s for a reconnaissance role. They were located in Greece for a short while, before returning to the UK in February 1919 and disbanding.

The squadron was re-formed the following year at Ramlah, Palestine with the F.2b Fighter from the re-numbered 111Sqn, for various air-policing and flag-waving tasks. The DH.9A, Fairey IIIF and Gordon were operated successively from the early 1930s, followed by the Wellesley from March 1938, which was flown from Amman, Trans-Jordan and, later, Sudan. In June 1940, they were re-equipped with Blenheims and moved to Egypt. A Flight of Gladiators was added a few months later. Following operations in Iraq, the squadron moved to the Western Desert and re-equipped with Marauders in August 1942, continuing various maritime roles from Algeria from March 1943. In September 1943, it disbanded.

In September 1943, 14Sqn was re-formed at Chivenor with Wellingtons, to operate in the anti-submarine role, but disbanded again on 1 June 1945.

The same day, it was re-formed at Banff,

taking the identity, role and Mosquitos from 143Sqn, until it disbanded once more on 31 March 1946.

The following day, 14Sqn re-formed with Mosquitos again. This time it was at Wahn, Germany from the re-numbered 128Sqn. These were operated until February 1951 when, at Fassberg, they were replaced by Vampires, followed by Venoms in 1953. Hunters arrived in 1955 and were operated as a day-fighter squadron until disbanded on 17 December 1962.

Once again, 14Sqn was re-formed on the same day, when 88Sqn was re-numbered at Wildenrath with Canberras in the strike role.

Keeping their period of service intact, yet again 14Sqn disbanded on 30 June 1970 and re-formed the same day – this time with Phantoms at Bruggen. These were operated until April 1975, when the squadron converted to the Jaguar. These were operated for the next ten years, until replaced by the Tornado GR.1, which were operated in the strike role with conventional and nuclear weapons.

In August 1990, 14Sqn was deployed to

the Middle East and flew operations during *Desert Storm* and again in April 1999, when operations were flown against Serb targets direct from Bruggen, using the TIALD pod to designate dropped laser-guided bombs. However, when Bruggen closed – the last RAF station in Germany – as part of the draw-down of British Forces in Germany, 14Sqn returned to the UK, to be based at Lossiemouth in January 2001.

Since then, 14Sqn have been deployed operationally to Ali Al Salem, along with other RAF Tornado units, to fly the *Southern Watch* missions monitoring Saddam's forces in southern Iraq. It also flew operations against Iraqi targets in 2003.

No. 14Sqn operate the Tornado GR.4 from their base at Lossiemouth.

No. XV (Reserve) Squadron

RAF Lossiemouth
Tornado GR.4
1 Group
Strike Command
Role: Tornado GR.4 OCU
Motto: Aim Sure

On 1 March 1915, 15Sqn was formed at South Farnborough from a nucleus provided by 1 Reserve Squadron. It was

A pair of 15(R)Sqn Tornado GR.4s line up at the end of the runway for the beginning of another training sortie. The student pilot will either have successfully completed the advanced jet-training course and be progressing to his or her first posting or alternatively he/she may already be a qualified pilot and be undergoing refresher training after a non-flying tour, or converting from another type. Kevin Wills

17(R)Sqn became the first RAF unit to receive the Typhoon T.1, followed by 29(R)Sqn (at the rear).
Eurofighter GmbH

deployed to France in December and operated the BE.2c to provide artillery spotting and reconnaissance. In June 1917, it re-equipped with the RE.8, but returned to the UK in February 1919 and disbanded at Fowlemere at the end of the year.

The squadron was reformed in March 1924 at Martlesham Heath, where it performed numerous trials with various aircraft with the Aeroplane and Armament Experimental Establishment (A&AEE). In June 1934, it moved to Abingdon, where it was equipped with the Hart for a bomber role. While there, the squadron adopted the title XVSqn, which it continues to use today.

In early 1936, part of XVSqn was used to re-form 52Sqn and, later, 106Sqn, passing on its old aircraft, while the rest of the squadron re-equipped with the Battle in June 1938. These it took to France in September 1939 as part of the Advanced Air Strike Force (AASF). It withdrew in December and re-equipped with the Blenheim at Alconbury, before moving to Wyton. In November 1940, these were replaced by the Wellington, which gave way, in turn, to the Stirling the following April. It then moved to Bourn in August 1942 and Mildenhall the following April.

In December, it re-equipped with the Lancaster and operated these through the end of the war, until they were replaced by the Lincoln in February 1947. In 1953, XV took delivery of the Washington (ex-USAF B-29 on loan) prior to entering the jet age with the Canberra in May of the same year. These it operated until April 1957, when it was disbanded.

In September 1958, XVSqn was re-formed at Cottesmore with the Victor, but disbanded again in October 1964.

In October 1970, XVSqn was re-formed at Honington with Buccaneers. It moved to Laarbruch, Germany in January 1971 and the Buccaneers were flown until July 1983, when it disbanded and the aircraft and crews were transferred to 16Sqn. During this period a few Hunters were also used for training

The same day, an embryo XVSqn commenced training on the Tornado GR.1, although it didn't officially re-form until 1 September 1983. Having participated in the Gulf War, during which it flew over 200 sorties and lost two aircraft, the squadron was disbanded once more in December 1991.

On 1 April 1992, XVSqn took over the identity of 45 (R) Sqn – this squadron had

previously provided the squadron identity of the Tornado Weapons Conversion Unit (TWCU). As a result, the unit became XV (R) Sqn and was based at Honington. In November 1993, it moved to Lossiemouth and, when the TTTE at Cottesmore closed in March 1999, it became the sole training-unit for the RAF's Tornado aircrew. Their courses range from several weeks to around six months, depending on whether the pilot is undergoing refresher training or is on his or her first posting.

No. XV (R) Sqn operate the Tornado GR.4 from their base at Lossiemouth.

No. 17 (Reserve) Squadron

Warton
Eurofighter Typhoon T.1 & F.2
1 Group
Strike Command
Role: Typhoon OEU
Motto: *Excellere Contende* – Strive to excel

On 1 February 1915, 17Sqn was formed at Gosport with the BE.2. It deployed to Egypt, flying its first mission on Christmas Eve. Its reconnaissance role saw it move to Greece in July 1916 and, later, to Macedonia. It also operated the DH.2 and Bristol Scout in the fighter role, but these were transferred to form 150Sqn in 1918. It converted to the FK.8 and, by the end of

20(R)Sqn provide the training for Harrier pilots using the GR.7 and two-seat T.10. Since the announcement that the Fleet Air Arm will get a squadron of Harriers to replace the Sea Harriers, training is also given by 20(R)Sqn to navy pilots.

Unit was formed at Waddington in April 2002 and was moved to Warton in September and designated 17 (R) Sqn. It received the first Typhoon T.1 on 18 December 2003 and, having completed training with BAE under the Case White programme, moved to Coningsby on 1 April, together with its first single seat F.2. On 15 May it was officially re-formed.

No. 17 (R) Sqn operates the Typhoon T.1/1A and F.2 from its base at Coningsby.

No. 20 (Reserve) Squadron

RAF Wittering
Harrier GR.7A & T.10
1 Group
Strike Command
Role: Harrier OCU
Motto: *Facta non verba* – Deeds not words

On 1 September 1915, 20Sqn was formed at Netheravon and deployed to France in January 1916, with FE.2bs in the fighter-reconnaissance role. These were replaced by the F.2b Fighter in August 1917. During one patrol over Belgium, Sergeant Mottershead was attacked by enemy aircraft at 9,000ft, during which the petrol tank caught fire. He and his observer were unable to escape. Despite the fire, Mottershead managed to fly back to base, where the aircraft collapsed on landing. The observer was thrown clear, but Mottershead remained trapped. He was rescued but died of his injuries four days later and was posthumously awarded a VC. The F.2b Fighters continued to be operated in France until June 1919, when the squadron deployed to Bombay, India. It patrolled the North West Frontier and re-equipped with the Wapiti in 1932, Audax in 1935 and the Lysander in 1941.

From mid-1942 it flew in support of the Chinese Army against the Japanese, converting to the Hurricane the following February. By May, it was flying the heavier-armed Hurricane IID, with 40mm cannons and rockets, through to September 1945. It had already begun to convert to Spitfires in May and later moved to Thailand and then India, where it received Tempests in May 1946. In August 1947, the squadron disbanded.

In February 1949, 20Sqn was re-formed at Llanbedr by taking the identity of 631Sqn and its role of anti-aircraft co-operation, for which Martinets and Vampires were operated. In October 1951, it was disbanded again.

the war, these were being replaced by Camels, to augment the DH.9s already being flown. In January 1919, the squadron was split with 'A' Flight assisting the White Russians and 'B' and 'C' Flights located in Constantinople. In November 1919, the Squadron was disbanded.

On 1 April 1924, 17Sqn was re-formed with Snipes at Hawkinge. These were later replaced by Woodcocks in 1926, followed by Gamecocks, Siskin IIIAs and Bulldog IIs. Equipped with Gauntlets from August 1938, 17Sqn moved from Kenley to North Weald in May 1939 and then re-equipped with the Hurricane, which it operated variously from Croydon, Debden and Martlesham Heath, prior to brief deployment to France in June 1940, returning home to Debden and, subsequently, operating also from Tangmere and Martlesham Heath during the Battle of Britain. In April 1941, it moved to various airfields in Scotland, before deploying to the Far East in November 1941.

Too late to help defend Singapore, 17Sqn was diverted to Burma to help stem the Japanese advance. Having to withdraw, the squadron then assisted in the defence of India from Calcutta. A move was made to Ceylon in August 1943, where it converted to Spitfires in March and then moved to Burma in November.

To prepare for the invasion of Malaya, 17Sqn was pulled back, but the atom bombs and the subsequent Japanese surrender brought this to a halt. Instead, the squadron was transported by carrier. In April 1946, it formed part of the Commonwealth Air Forces of Occupation in Japan, where it remained until disbanded in February 1948.

In February 1949, 691Sqn at Chivenor was re-numbered 17Sqn and took on the role of an anti-aircraft co-operation unit. This it did with the Martinet, Oxford, Spitfire and Vengeance, until disbanded in March 1951.

It was re-formed in June 1956 with Canberras at Wahn, Germany in the photo-reconnaissance role. In April, it moved to Wildenrath, but was disbanded in December 1969.

From July 1970, 17 (Designate) Sqn began to operate Phantoms at Wildenrath and officially re-formed in October at Bruggen. Phantoms were operated until 30 January 1976, when they were replaced by the Jaguar the following day. On 1 March 1985, the sequence of events was repeated with the conversion to the Tornado GR.1. 'Options for Change' and the withdrawal of RAFG resulted in the disbanding of 17Sqn on 31 March 1999

The Typhoon Operational Evaluation

On 1 July 1952, 20Sqn was re-formed at Jever with the Vampire, moving to Oldenburg later that month. It converted to the Sabre in 1953 as a day-fighter squadron and then the Hunter in November 1955. It moved to Tengah, Singapore, where it operated in the ground-attack role. In 1962, it was deployed to Thailand, where missions were flown against communist guerrillas. It inherited a few Pioneers from 209Sqn, in 1969, for use in the FAC role, prior to disbanding in February 1970.

In December 1970, 20Sqn re-equipped at Wildenrath with the Harrier. These aircraft were transferred to 3 and 4Sqn in March 1977 and 20 (Designate) Sqn became officially formed the same day with Jaguars at Bruggen. In June 1984, there was a similar occurrence for the transition to the Tornado GR.1 at Laarbruch. During the Gulf War, 20Sqn was operationally deployed to Saudi Arabia, where it operated as part of the Tabuk Wing. Options for Change saw the run-down of RAFG, which resulted in 20Sqn disbanding on 1 September 1992.

To keep the spirit of the squadron alive, the 233 OCU at Wittering (formed September 1952) was re-designated 20 (Reserve) Squadron the same day. In time of conflict, and should the need arise, 20 (R) Sqn, as with other 'Reserve' units, would cease to be a training unit and become operational, with the instructors flying the missions.

The normal peacetime role of 20 (R) Sqn is the training of student pilots new to the Harrier and refresher training for pilots who have previously flown the Harrier, as well as training of Qualified Weapons Instructors (QFIs) and Electronic Warfare Instructors (EWIs). From September 2002, it commenced training RN pilots in readiness to form the first RN GR.7 squadron.

Ab initio pilots arriving straight from advanced flying training at Valley will undergo the long course, which incorporates 87 hours flying (34 hours on the T.10) plus 32 hours on the simulator. A conversion course for RN pilots crossing over from the Sea Harrier to the Harrier incorporates 23 hours flying (18 hours in the T.10) plus 23 hours in the simulator.

In September 1992, 20 (R) Sqn was formed by the renumbering of 233 OCU and maintains the role of the Harrier OCU at Wittering.

No. 20 (R) Sqn flies the Harrier GR.7A and T.10 from its base at Wittering.

No. 25 (Fighter) Squadron

RAF Leeming
Panavia Tornado F.3
1 Group
Strike Command
Role: Air Defence
Motto: *Feriens Tego* – Striking I Defend

On 25 September 1915, 25 (F) Sqn was formed at Montrose from 6 Reserve Squadron (formed at Montrose in July 1915), which was a elementary training unit. With the weather so bad, it was decided to use the airfield for advanced training only. As a result, 6 (R) Sqn was re-numbered 25Sqn and operated a mixture of types, including the G.102 Elephant and S.7 Longhorn. Initially, 25Sqn was used to provide replacement pilots for the Expeditionary Force in France. By the end of the year, it had moved to Thetford and equipped with trainers, before the arrival of FE.2b and Bristol Scouts – most of which were presentation aircraft.

In February 1916, 25Sqn was deployed

An unarmed Tornado F.3 from 25Sqn flies a training mission from Leeming out over the North Sea.

to St Omer in France, initially to intercept German bombers heading for England, prior to moving to the Western Front. Initially, they flew patrols to protect the GHQ and then as escorts for reconnaissance aircraft, which were increasingly under attack from German fighters, especially with the appearance of the Fokker E.III Eindekker. On 18 June 1916, Lieutenant McCubbin and Corporal Waller shot down the German Ace Max Immelmann.

During this period, 25Sqn were tasked with bombing, photo reconnaissance and even balloon bursting, in addition to their fighter role. They also practiced night flying, prior to undertaking night-bombing and conducted offensive/close air-support missions. FE.2ds replaced the FE.2b, followed by the DH.4 with its increased range. The squadron frequently moved and, at the time of the armistice, DH.9s started to be delivered. The squadron then moved into Germany as part of the Army of Occupation before returning home, in September 1919, to South Carlton and finally disbanding at Scopwick in January 1920.

In February 1920, 25Sqn re-formed at Hawkinge with Snipe fighters. In fact, it was the RAF's only fighter squadron and so was named 25 (Fighter) Squadron the following month. It was deployed to Turkey in September 1922, returning to Hawkinge a year later. During this period, it took part in the Hendon Air Pageants, re-equipped with the Grebe, then Siskin IIIs, Furies, Demons and Gladiators, before progressing onto the Blenheim in early 1939. These it took to Northolt for London's defence and it was declared a night-fighter squadron the following month. A few days later it moved to Filton to provide cover for ships transporting troops to France. It then returned to Northolt, before moving to North Weald in January 1940. A detachment was maintained at Martlesham for AI-radar trials. When war broke out they were tasked to detect enemy raiders but, in the early days of the 'phoney war', nothing happened. The squadron's first operation took place in November against shipping. In July 1940, a squadron Blenheim became the first aircraft to shoot down another using AI radar.

A pair of Whirlwinds were received in May 1940, but 25 (F) Sqn continued with the Blenheims in September, until radar-equipped Beaufighters arrived in early

1941. Later, it moved to Debden and then Wittering in March 1941, before going to Ballyhalbert (Northern Ireland) in January 1942 for convoy protection. In May, it moved to Church Fenton and took delivery of a few Havocs, prior to becoming re-equipped with the Mosquito from October. These were flown as night-fighters and progressively on 'Rangers' attacks on targets of opportunity. In mid-1943 a detachment was located in Cornwall to fly patrols over the Bay of Biscay, to protect Coastal Command aircraft from Ju.88s.

The Mosquitos had Mk.X radar fitted from September 1943 and joined the bomber streams on 'Mahmoud' and 'Flower' trials. The 'Mahmoud' trials aircraft were fitted with rearwards-facing radar. As a Luftwaffe fighter approached 3,000 yard behind the Mosquito, the pilot would snap around to attack the enemy. This successful technique was then introduced to other night-fighter squadrons of 100 Group. These were only undertaken on bright, moonlit nights to enable the pilot to visually spot the enemy aircraft. In March 1944, five Luftwaffe bombers were shot down on a single night. During this period, 25 (F) Sqn was based at Acklington from December 1943 and Coltishall from February 1944, before moving into Castle Camps in October 1944.

The squadron reverted to the 'Ranger' attacks and were given the latest Mosquito NF.XVIIIs. Such was the radar definition that it even experimented with night air-sea-rescue searches. It was tasked with intercepting the V-1 flying bombs from May until November 1944. It provided cover for the D-Day forces and for the advance on Germany, plus intruder attacks as well as home defence, and eventually contributed to the Occupation Forces when the war ended at Lübeck.

In September 1946, 25 (F) Sqn moved to West Malling and received Mosquito NF.36s and, in November 1951, became the first night-fighter squadron to equip with a jet – the Venom. These were replaced with the Meteor in January 1954. It moved to Tangmere in 1957, before being disbanded in June 1958.

On 1 July 1958, West Malling-based 153Sqn was re-numbered 25 (F) Sqn and continued to operate the Meteors until they were replaced with Javelins in March 1959. Two years later, the squadron moved to Leuchars. It remained there, apart from

a detachment to Nicosia, until November 1962, when the squadron was re-numbered 11Sqn and 25Sqn was disbanded.

In October 1963, 25 (F) Sqn was re-formed at North Coates, as the RAF's first Bloodhound unit protecting the V-bomber bases. During April 1970, the squadron moved, establishing its HQ and 'A' Flight at Bruggen, 'B' Flight at Wildenrath and 'C' Flight at Laarbruch. In 1983, it returned to the UK, locating its HQ, along with 'B' and 'D' Flights, at Wyton. 'A' Flight was based at Barkston Heath and 'C' Flight at Wattisham. On 2 July 1989, the squadron disbanded, when all the Flights were merged into 85Sqn.

The following day, 25 (F) Sqn was reformed with the Tornado F.3 at Leeming, to form part of the UK Air Defence region. In August 1990, they were deployed to the Middle East in response to Saddam's invasion of Kuwait.

Since then, 25 (F) Sqn has taken part in Operation *Deny Flight* in Bosnia and Operations *Bolton* and *Resinate* to enforce the no-fly zone over southern Iraq.

In July 2004, it was announced that 25 (F) Sqn would be disbanded by 2008 and bring to an end to Tornado F.3 flying at Leeming.

No. 25 (F) Sqn operate the Tornado F.3 and are based at Leeming.

No. 29 (Reserve) Squadron

RAF Coningsby
Eurofighter Typhoon T.1/T.1A and F.2
1 Group
Strike Command
Role: Typhoon OCU
Motto: *Impinger et Acer* – Energetic and keen

On 7 November 1915, 29Sqn was formed at Gosport and was deployed to France early the next year with the DH.2. From March 1917, it was re-equipped with the Nieuport 17, 24 and 27. These were replaced with the SE.5a in April 1918, which it continued to operate on the Western Front until the end of the war. The squadron disbanded at Spittlegate in December 1919.

In April 1923, 29Sqn re-formed at Duxford with the Snipe, followed by the Grebe and, in April 1928, the Siskin, with a move to North Weald. These were to be replaced with the Bulldog and then Demon, the latter of which it took to

29(R)Sqn Typhoon T.1 proudly on display at the Royal International Air Tattoo.

Egypt in 1935. It returned to the UK in 1937 to Debden, where it re-equipped with the Blenheim the following year. They moved to Digby then Wellingore, before converting to the Beaufighter in September 1940.

The Blenheims were used as light bombers when the war broke out but, by the Battle of Britain, following heavy losses, 29Sqn were operating the Blenheim as a night-fighter at West Malling from April 1940 until February 1941. The squadron started to take delivery of Mosquitos in May while at Bradwell Bay. Following a move to Ford in September, they moved to Drem, followed by West Malling, Hunsdon, Colerne and Manston, staying just a few months at each.

With the war over, 29Sqn continued to develop their night-fighting role with the Mosquito at West Malling, followed by Meteors from August 1951. These were replaced by the Javelin at Acklington in November 1957, with which it moved to Leuchars in July 1958. The squadron moved to Nicosia, Cyprus in March 1963,

from where it deployed a nine-month detachment to Zambia in December 1965 during the Rhodesia Crisis, returning in August. In May 1967, 29Sqn moved to Wattisham and were re-equipped with the Lightning, which they flew until December 1974 when they were disbanded.

On 1 January 1975, 29Sqn was officially re-formed with the Phantom at Coningsby, using aircraft from 6Sqn. In August 1979, it became the first squadron to fire a Sky Flash missile, destroying a radio-controlled Meteor. It was deployed to the Falklands in October 1982, to provide air defence for the islands after the Argentinian invasion, and was subsequently replaced by 23Sqn in March 1983.

In April 1987, 29Sqn re-formed with the Tornado F.3, to become the first operational squadron with the new variant.

The squadron was in Akrotiri, changing over with 5Sqn for their APC in August 1990, when instructions cancelled the training. They were deployed to Dhahran, where they flew their first CAP within a couple of hours of arriving, during the

build up that led to the Gulf War. By the time the war ended, 29Sqn had flown some 500 missions during the three-month deployment. The squadron also took part in Operation *Deny Flight*, maintaining the no-fly zone over Bosnia.

Following the Strategic Defence Review, 29Sqn was disbanded on 31 October 1998.

No. 29 (R) Sqn is currently training instructors on the Typhoon T.1, T.1A and F.2 as the OCU at Coningsby, when formal OCU training courses commenced.

No. 31 Squadron

RAF Marham
Panavia Tornado GR.4
1 Group
Strike Command
Role: Strike Attack
Motto: *In Caelum Indicum Primus* – First in the Indian skies

'A' Flight of 31 Squadron was formed on 11 October 1915 at Farnborough with the BE.2c and Farman and deployed to India

A 31Sqn Tornado GR.4 in formation with a Typhoon T.1. Eventually the Typhoon will replace the Tornado in the strike role. Crown Copyright

at the end of November. This flight located at Risalpur and was joined by a further two flights by the following May, these having been formed in early 1916. They flew in the army co-operation role with the Indian Army along the North West Frontier. In September 1919, they re-equipped with the F.2B Fighter. In 1929 they took part in the evacuation of Kabul, escorting Victoria transports. They continued their co-operation role with Wapitis from February 1931, until they converted to Valentias for bomber/transport duties in April 1939.

In April 1941, 31Sqn commenced delivery of seconded DC-2s and these were used, together with the Valentias, to get supplies to the isolated forces at Habbaniya, which had been surrounded by the Iraqi military. By September, they were all DC-2s, but these were gradually replaced by the Dakota from April 1942. Their main task became flying between Calcutta and Rangoon to drop supplies to the XIVth Army following the Japanese invasion of Burma and recover casualties.

When the war ended, 31Sqn moved to Java. While there, one of their Dakotas crashed. Before a rescue party arrived, Indonesian rebels reached the site and

hacked the survivors to death. In September 1946, the squadron disbanded.

At Mauiput, India, 31 Squadron re-formed briefly with Dakotas from the renumbered 77Sqn, continuing as a transport unit until the end of 1947, when it disbanded once more.

In July 1948, 31Sqn was re-formed from the Metropolitan Communications Squadron at Hendon. It was equipped with various transport aircraft, including the Anson and Proctor, and even included Spitfires and Tiger Moths. In 1955, the squadron reverted to its original title, while on the same day in November a new 31Sqn was formed at Laarbruch with the Canberra PR.7. These were replaced with Phantom FGR.2 in October 1971 and Jaguar in January 1976 at Bruggen.

From September 1984, 31 (Designate) Sqn began training on the Tornado GR.1 and was officially formed on 1 November 1984. In 1991, the squadron was deployed to the Middle East to form part of the Tornado Force that operated in the Gulf War. Once the war ended, 31Sqn continued to operate over southern Iraq as part of Operations *Bolton* and *Resinate*. In January 1995, 31Sqn was re-rolled into Suppression of Enemy Air Defences

(SEAD) and carried the ALARM anti-radiation missile. In 1996, the squadron received the Tornado GR.4, as well as being deployed on Operation *Engadine* for NATO tasking over the former republic of Yugoslavia. On 21 August 2001, 31Sqn became the last permanently based RAF combat unit to leave Germany.

In August 2001, 31Sqn moved to Marham where it now operates as a part of the Marham Tornado Wing with II (AC) IX (B), XIII and 39 (PRU) Sqn.

In 2003, 31Sqn was deployed to the Middle East, where it took part in Operation *Telic*.

No. 31Sqn operate the Tornado GR.4A from their base at Marham.

No. 41 (Fighter) Squadron

RAF Coltishall
SEPECAT Jaguar GR.3A & T.4
1 Group
Strike Command
Role: Reconnaissance
Motto: Seek and destroy

On 14 July 1916, 41Sqn was formed at Gosport and deployed to St Omer in France with FE.8s that October – hence the Arms of St Omer in the badge. It later operated the DH.5 and SE.5a, flying offensive patrols, escort, reconnaissance and ground-strafing missions. It returned to the UK and was disbanded at Croydon in October 1919

Re-formed in April 1923 at Northolt, 41Sqn was initially equipped with the Snipe, followed by the Siskin. In 1931, these were replaced with the Bulldog and then the Demon in 1934. During this period, 41Sqn performed many a star role in the Hendon Air Pageants. In September 1935, it moved to Khormaksar, Aden, then Sheikh Othman during the Italian/Abyssinian War. In October 1937, it was re-equipped with the Fury.

In January 1939, 41Sqn re-equipped to the Spitfire at Catterick, before moving to Hornchurch, from where it took part in aerial cover for the evacuation of Dunkirk, and then to London during the Battle of Britain. Although predominately based in the south east, it made numerous moves over the following couple of years and was involved in fighter sweeps, interception of Luftwaffe raiders and, later, the V-1 flying bombs, of which forty-three were claimed destroyed. During June 1944, it assisted with fighter cover for the D-Day landing and the following push into Europe. Six months later it was deployed into France

with the 2 TAF, where it continued to fly offensive patrols until the war ended. In September 1945, it converted from the Spitfire, which it had operated throughout the war, to the Tempest.

The squadron returned to the UK at Wittering, where it returned to operating Spitfires. However, in 1947, it became an instrument-flying training unit at Church Fenton and re-equipped with Harvards and Oxfords. In June 1948, it reverted to an operational unit and re-equipped with Hornets, before entering the jet age with the Meteor in 1951 at Biggin Hill and, in 1955, the Hunter. In February 1958, the Hunters disbanded, but a reconstituted 41Sqn was formed the same day by the re-numbering of 141Sqn at Coltishall with the Javelin. Having moved to Wattisham in 1960, these continued to be operated until December 1963, when it disbanded.

In September 1965, 41Sqn re-formed with Bloodhound SAMs at West Raynham. It undertook a number of deployments in the UK and Near East, before being disbanded in September 1970.

April 1972 saw 41Sqn re-formed as a

tactical reconnaissance squadron at Coningsby, with the EMI Reconnaissance Pod-equipped Phantom. Around the same time, 41 Reconnaissance Intelligence Centre (RIC) was formed to process and interpret their images.

On 1 October 1976, 41Sqn was re-equipped with the Jaguar GR.1 at Coltishall. Following a work up, the squadron took on the role of day reconnaissance and officially re-formed on 1 April 1977. The squadron is also the air force's declared Arctic specialist and regularly deploys to Norway for exercises in the often hostile environment.

Along with other RAF Jaguar, and Harrier units, 41Sqn has undertaken its role on *Northern Watch*, with regular deployments to Incirlik in Turkey.

Jaguars of 41Sqn received the Joint Reconnaissance Pod in 2000 and, on 4 July 2003, the squadron's Reconnaissance Intelligence Centre (RIC) was amalgamated into the new Tactical Imagery Intelligence Wing (TIW) at Marham.

The Jaguar is gradually reaching the end of its operational life and, in 2004, it was announced that this had been brought forward, which will result in 41Sqn being disbanded on 31 March 2006.

No. 41Sqn operates the Jaguar GR.3A and T.4A from its base at Coltishall.

A Jaguar GR.3 of 41Sqn flies a training mission out of Coltishall equipped with CBLS practice bomb pods. Although designated a tactical reconnaissance squadron, 41Sqn maintains its proficiency in the attack role.

No. 43 (Fighter) Squadron

RAF Leuchars
Panavia Tornado F.3
1 Group
Strike Command
Role: Air Defence
Motto: *Gloria finis* – Glory is the end

On 15 April 1916, 43 (F) Squadron was formed at Stirling from a nucleus provided by 19 (Reserve) Squadron. After a period on Home Defence, it deployed to France in January 1917 with Sopwith 1½ Strutters and, in September, converted to Camels, becoming the first squadron with the Snipe in September 1918. In August 1919, it returned from Germany and was disbanded at Spittlegate at the end of the year.

The squadron re-formed at Henlow in July 1925, flying with Snipes and converting to Gamecocks in March 1926 – the latter led to it becoming known as the 'Fighting Cocks'. It moved to Tangmere in December 1926, converting to the Siskins in June 1928 and then the Fury in May 1931, before the arrival of the Hurricane in November 1938.

Having been based at Acklington and Wick since late 1939, 43Sqn returned to Tangmere in May 1940, prior to a move to Northolt in July. From there it covered the withdrawal from Dunkirk and then the

Battle of Britain and was credited with sixty kills. It moved back to Tangmere, prior to moving north to Usworth in September, then Drem in December, which enabled a break while the squadron was brought back to strength. During this time the squadron took on a training role, as well as conducting defensive patrols.

Following a further period at Acklington, 43Sqn returned to Tangmere again in June 1942 and flew offensive operations over France until September, when it began preparations at Kirton in Lindsy to deploy to the Mediterranean. Having arrived in Gibraltar in November, it moved on to Algeria, where it converted to Spitfires in February 1943. It then moved to Malta, from where it provided cover for the Sicily landings in June, prior to moving to Sicily. It assisted in the landing in southern France from Sicily, before moving into Italy. Having taken a part with the Occupation Forces in Austria and Italy, 43Sqn was disbanded in May 1947 at Treviso, Italy.

In February 1949, 43 (F) Sqn was re-formed with Meteors at Tangmere by the re-numbering of 266Sqn and moved to Leuchars in November the following year. In August 1954, it became the RAF's first Hunter squadron. In June 1961, it moved to Cyprus, then Aden in March 1963, where it was disbanded in October 1967.

In September 1969, 43Sqn re-formed at

Leuchars with the Phantom for the Maritime Air Defence role. On 1 July 1989, 43Sqn flew the last RAF Phantom mission.

In July 1989, 43 (F) Sqn re-equipped with the Tornado F.3, to provide air defence for the UK. It was deployed to Saudi Arabia in November 1990, where it was the lead F.3 squadron at Dharhan during the Gulf War, providing CAP until it returned in March 1991. Since then, it has taken part in the patrols in southern Iraq, as well as providing air and ground crews for the Falklands.

No. 43 (F) Sqn is equipped with the Tornado F.3 and operates from its base at Leuchars.

No 54 (Reserve) Squadron

RAF Waddington
3 Group
Strike Command
Role; C2ISTAR OCU
Motto; Audax Omnia Perpeti - Boldness prevails

54 Sqn was formed at Castle Bromwich on 15 May 1916, with the BE.2c and Avro 504 and deployed to France later that year with the Pup – the first RFC unit to operate the type. In December 1917, 54 Sqn re-equipped with the Camel which it operated in the ground attack role. After the end of the war, 54 Sqn returned to the UK and was disbanded at Yatesbury in October 1919.

43Sqn operate the Tornado F.3 out of Leuchars. This example is armed with the ASRAAM missile.

In January 1930, 54 Sqn re-formed at Hornchurch with the Siskin, converting to the Bulldog, then Gauntlet and Gladiator biplanes prior to taking delivery of the Spitfire from March 1938, which it operated from Hornchurch and Rochford with periods at Catterick. The Squadron was the RAF's top scoring squadron during the Battle of Britain with 92 kills – 37 occurring on one day! They re-equipped with the Spitfire IV during a rest period at Catterick before returning to Hornchurch in February 1941 to operate fighter sweeps over Northern France. During March 1941 54 Sqn achieved its 100th kill. In November 1941 it moved to Caithness.

In August 1942, 54 Sqn moved to Richmond, Australia and then locations around Darwin. Here it undertook occasional attacks against the withdrawing Japanese. On 20 July 1944, three Spitfires intercepted a Japanese AF 'Dinah' on a reconnaissance mission near Truscott airfield. This was the last Japanese aircraft shot down over Australia. In October 1945 it was disbanded at Melbourne.

54 Sqn was re-formed at Chilbolton with Tempest IIs in November 1945 from 183 Sqn. The following June it moved to Odiham, where it began to re-equip with the Vampire in October and became the first squadron to operate them as night-fighters. In July 1948 six 54 Sqn Vampire F.3s made the first jet-powered trans-atlantic flight.

The Vampires were replaced by the Meteor in 1953 followed by the Hunter in February 1955. In July 1959 it moved to Stradishall and the following year returned to the ground attack role with the FGA.9. In November 1961 it moved to Waterbeach where it joined 38 Group's Offensive Support Wing. It then deployed to Aden to assist in policing the protectorate's border prior to moving to West Raynham in 1963. In September 1969 the Hunters were absorbed into 4 Sqn.

A fresh 54 Sqn emerged from 229 OCU in September 1969 equipped with the Phantom at Coningsby. The following May the Squadron notched up another first by flying their deployment to Singapore non-stop in 14 hours, 8 minutes.

On 29 March 1974, 54 Sqn became the first Jaguar squadron when it re-equipped with the GR.1 at Lossiemouth for the ground attack and tactical reconnaissance role - the Phantoms being used to re-equip

111 Sqn. On 9 August 1974 it moved to Coltishall where, together with 6 and 41 Sqns, it formed the Air Element of the United Kingdom Mobile Force

54 Sqn frequently deployed overseas on exercises and in August 1990 it provided aircraft and crew for the JagDet at Thumrait during the build up of Coalition forces prior to the Gulf War. They took part in some of the 600 sorties that were flown by Jaguars.

Once the war ended, 54 Sqn provided detachments to Incirlik in Turkey to fly over Northern Iraq on Operation Warden and provide protection of the Kurds from Saddam's forces. Deployments were rotated with the other Jaguar and Harrier GR.7 squadrons.

Due to the run-down of the Jaguar fleet, 54 Sqn was disbanded on 11 March 2005. Its demise was only for a short while, as it was re-formed on 5 September 2005 at Waddington, where it became the Command and Control, Intelligence, Surveillance, Target Acquisition and Reconnaissance (C2ISTAR) Operational Conversion Unit (OCU). Its task is to train aircrew initially for the Nimrod R.1 and Sentry AEW.1 as well as the Sentinel R.1 when it enters service. While it has no aircraft of its own, 54 (R) Sqn borrows aircraft from the front line squadrons at Waddington as required.

54 (R) Sqn fly the Nimrod R.1 and Sentry AEW.1 from their base at Waddington to which the Sentinel R.1 will be added in 2006. As they are borrowed from other squadrons none will appear in 54 (R) Sqn colours.

No. 56 (Reserve) Sqn

Tornado F.3
RAF Leuchars
1 Group
Strike Command
Role: Tornado F.3 OCU
Motto: *Quid si coelum ruat* – What if heaven falls?

On 8 June 1916, 56Sqn was formed at Fort Rowner, Gosport and operated the BE.2c and Bristol Scout prior to moving to London Colney in July. It became the first RFC unit to receive the SE.5a and deployed to France in April 1917, where the first German aircraft was destroyed the following day – the first of 427 and all on the SE.5a! During this period Captain James McCudden was awarded a VC for

his continued bravery, exceptional perseverance and a high devotion to duty in attacking the enemy and protecting new crews. By March 1918, he had been credited with fifty-one enemy aircraft destroyed; was killed in action in July. Captain Albert Ball flew with 13 and 60Sqn before joining 56Sqn and was awarded a VC for his continuous actions – sadly, posthumously. After the end of the war, 56Sqn returned to the UK and operated from Narborough, until it moved to Birch Newton, where it disbanded in January 1920.

It was re-formed at Aboukir, Egypt in February 1920 with Snipes by the re-numbering of 80Sqn, but was disbanded again in September 1922. Although officially disbanded, the deepening Chanak crisis in Turkey resulted in the hasty assembly of a Flight in September 1922, which remained in theatre until August 1923.

While this was happening, 56Sqn was officially re-formed at Hawkinge in November 1922 with various aircraft, prior to standardizing with the Grebe from 1924. In October 1927, it moved from Biggin Hill to North Weald with the Siskin IIIA. In 1936, it re-equipped with the Gauntlet. 'B' Flight was used as a cadre to form 151Sqn. In 1937, Gladiators arrived and were replaced with the Hurricane in April 1938. At the outbreak of war, it moved temporarily from North Weald to Martlesham Heath. In May 1940, 56Sqn was deployed to Belgium and then France, but was soon providing cover for the Dunkirk evacuation, before taking part in the Battle of Britain from North Weald. In September, it moved to Boscombe Down for a rest, having lost a substantial number of pilots. During November and December, it was at Middle Wallop, before returning to North Weald, at the end of 1940, with new Hurricanes.

Following a move to Duxford in June 1941, 56Sqn converted to the Typhoon in September 1941, with which it attacked German targets from various east-coast airfields. By the summer of 1944, it had re-equipped with the Tempest at Newchurch and was concentrating on the V1 flying bombs. It moved to France as part of the advancing Allied forces and, by the end of the war, had claimed 130 enemy aircraft shot down. It was disbanded on April 1946 at Fassberg, Germany by being re-numbered 16Sqn.

The Typhoon F.3s of 56(R)Sqn provide conversion training for pilots and navigators prior to their posting onto an operational F.3 fighter squadron. Kevin Wills

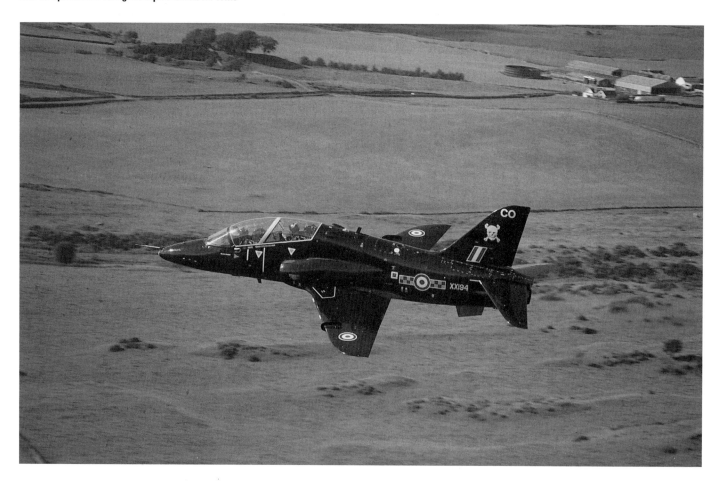

A Hawk T.1 of 100Sqn flies low-level to provide a difficult target for opposing forces – be that Tornado F.3s from above or Rapier SAMs from below. These vital training exercises are conducted in special areas and routes to minimize disturbance to people on the ground.

On the following day, 56Sqn was re-formed at Bentwaters, with Meteors from the re-numbered 124Sqn. From February 1954, it undertook trials with the Swift but, in 1956, converted to the Hunter. It moved to Wattisham in 1959 and re-equipped with the Lightning in December 1960. It was with the Lightning that 56Sqn formed the Firebirds aerobatic team and provided numerous displays. In April 1967, they moved to Cyprus and, in 1974, they provided protection to the Sovereign Base Areas (SBA) during the Turkish invasion. While at Akrotiri, they were also equipped with two Canberras for target-towing duties.

From March 1975, 56Sqn began to convert to the Phantom at Coningsby. It moved to Wattisham in November 1976 and continued to operate until 31 July 1992, when it was disbanded.

From December 1986, 65Sqn had been the shadow squadron for 229 OCU, but was re-named 56 (R) Sqn in July 1992. Various courses are taught: typically, it provides training for newly qualified pilots who have just completed the advanced training on the Hawk, followed by a six-week ground school at Coningsby. This long course lasts for twenty-one weeks, which includes fifty-eight hours flying. For experienced pilots converting back to one of the operational Tornado squadrons, their short course lasts eight weeks and includes thirty-seven hours flying. In addition, it operates the Qualified Weapons Instructor Course for suitably experienced pilots. These last for twenty-one weeks during, which they will fly fifty-eight hours.

On 27 March 2003, 56 (R) Sqn moved to Leuchars as part of the preparations of Coningsby for the Typhoon.

No. 56 (R) Sqn is equipped with the Tornado F.3 and operates from Leuchars.

No. 100 Squadron

RAF Leeming
BAe Hawk T.1A
1 Group
Strike Command
Role: Target Facilities
Motto: *Sarang Tebuan Jangan Dijolok* – Never stir up a hornet's nest

On 23 February 1917, 100Sqn was formed at Hingham and mobilized at South Farnborough, before being deployed to France the following month with FE.2bs as the RFC's first specialized night-bomber unit. It also added the BE.2e in April and, later that month, destroyed von Richthofen's flying circus aircraft during raids on Douai. In August 1917, it converted to the Handley Page O/400, with which it was able to reach targets in western Germany. During the war it flew 213 raids, dropped 185 tons of bombs, fired 450,000 rounds of ammunition and lost only five aircraft. It returned to the UK in September and then disbanded.

In January 1920, it was re-formed at Baldonnell, from cadres of 117 and 141Sqn, with F.2B Fighters, to operate in the army co-operation role against Sinn Fein. It moved to Spittlegate in 1922, where it took delivery of the DH.9a and Vimy bombers. In 1924, it converted to the Fawn, followed subsequently by the Horsley torpedo-bombers with which it moved to Donibristle in 1930. In November 1932, the Vildebeest arrived and it deployed with these to Seletar, Singapore in January 1934, where it stayed until January 1942. In 1941, it was expecting to take delivery of Australian-built Beauforts, but was attacked by the Japanese while still awaiting their arrival, consequently suffering heavy losses with the obsolete Vildebeest. Many were killed or taken prisoner, while the remains of the squadron were absorbed into 36Sqn and, shortly after, withdrew.

In December 1942, 100Sqn was re-formed with Lancasters at Waltham Grimsby and continued to operate from there until it moved to Elsham Woods in April 1945. During this period in Bomber Command, 100Sqn flew over 100 missions and dropped 17,500 tons of bombs.

In 1946, 100Sqn converted to Lincolns at Scampton. In 1950, it was deployed to Tengah, Singapore on Operation *Firedog* to combat communist terrorists and, in 1954, another deployment saw it sent to Kenya to help combat Mau Mau terrorists. The squadron returned to Wittering, where it converted to the Canberra from April 1954. It took part in the British nuclear tests in the Pacific and disbanded in September 1959 at Wittering.

In May 1962, 100Sqn re-formed at Wittering with the Victor, armed with Blue Steel missiles, and remained part of the V-Force until disbanded in September 1968.

In February 1972, it was re-formed at West Raynham in the target-facilities role. For this, it was equipped with various marks of Canberra, a number of which were absorbed from 7Sqn. It moved to Marham in January 1976 and then to Wyton in January 1982. It finally retired its mixed fleet of sixteen Canberras and replaced them with the Hawk T.1 from 1991. In September 1993, it transferred to Finningley and then moved into Leeming on 20 September 1995.

In RAF operation 100Sqn is unique, in that it provides a Dissimilar Air Combat Training (DACT) or aggressor capability for front-line units to train. The Hawks can be flown to simulate enemy aircraft or missiles, to provide realistic enemy attacks against aircraft, and even helicopters, at medium and low-level. The squadron can provide multi-ship formations of 'enemy' aircraft to provide defence training. In addition, it provide a target facility for various purposes, including banner towing for APCs at Cyprus, as well as fighter-controller training. It also assists in training forward air-controllers through the JFACTSU. In October 1999, the Navigator Training Unit from Valley was absorbed into 100Sqn, to expand their role even further.

No. 100Sqn operates the Hawk T.1A from their base at Leeming.

No. 111 (Fighter) Squadron

RAF Leuchars
Panavia Tornado F.3
1 Group
Strike Command
Role: Air Defence
Motto: *Adstantes* – Standing by (them)

On 1 August 1917, 111 Squadron was formed at Dier-el-Belah, Palestine from a 14Sqn Flight. It was the region's first dedicated fighter squadron. It was equipped with various aircraft, including Bristol Scouts and Nieuport 17s. Its role was to counter German aircraft flying over Suez. Later, it converted to the F.2b Fighter and SE.5a, in support of army units that were in combat with Turkish units in Palestine and Syria. It moved to Egypt in 1918, but was disbanded in February 1920, when it was re-numbered 14Sqn.

In October 1923, 111Sqn was re-formed at Duxford, where it was involved in high-altitude flight trials, flying a mixture of aircraft, including the Grebe, Snipe and Siskin. It moved to Hornchurch in April

1928. In 1931, it converted to the Bulldog, which it took to Northolt in 1934, re-equipping with the Gauntlet in 1936. In March 1937, 213Sqn was formed from one of 111Sqn's Flights. In January 1938, 111Sqn became the first Hurricane squadron and soon established a speed record between London and Edinburgh of 408mph, taking just forty-eight minutes. Following a brief period at North Weald, 111Sqn moved on to Croydon. From here the squadron flew cover for the Dunkirk evacuation and then through the Battle of Britain, during which it was credited with destroying sixty-five enemy aircraft.

It converted to the Spitfire in April 1942 and, in November, deployed to Gibraltar in preparation for Operation *Torch*. It took part in the move through Algeria and Tunisia and then provided cover, from June 1943, for the invasion of Sicily from Malta, before moving into Italy. After the end of the war it spent some time in Austria, before disbanding in May 1947.

In December 1953, 111Sqn was re-formed at North Weald with the Meteor. It converted to the Hunter F.4 in 1955 and repeated the London to Edinburgh speed-record run, this time at 717mph. During the 1958 Farnborough Airshow, 111 achieved their unique feat of looping twenty-two Hunters in formation. It moved to Wattisham

A 111Sqn Tornado F.3, assisted by 43Sqn, escorts a Russian AF Ilyushin Il-78 Midas tanker. Interception of Soviet aircraft used to be a frequent occurrence. Following the end of the Cold War this has almost ended. This Russian aircraft is being met and guided through British airspace to Fairford for the Royal International Air Tattoo. Crown Copyright

in 1957, where it re-equipped with the Lightning in 1961.

At Coningsby, 111Sqn formed a cadre unit, which commenced flying the Phantom in July 1974, while the Lightning element of the Squadron remained at Wattisham until September. The Phantoms were provided by 54Sqn, which had disbanded in April to convert to Jaguars. The squadron moved to Leuchars in October 1975. It received the ex-RN Phantom FG.1s, following the disbanding of 892Sqn, in December 1978. The last Phantom sortie was flown on 20 January 1990 and the squadron was re-equipped with the Tornado F.3 on 30 January 1990.

The squadron have been providing a combat-ready aircraft as part of the Quick Reaction Alert (QRA), ready to launch immediately to investigate unidentified aircraft detected approaching UK airspace. If necessary, they may be required to shoot down a hostile intruder. In addition to this primary role, the squadron has also been involved in Operation *Deny Flight* over Bosnia, as well as Operations *Bolton* and *Resinate* over Iraq, and, in 2003,

provided four Tornados to assist in providing CAP for coalition forces during the invasion of Iraq.

No. 111Sqn is equipped with the Tornado F.3 and based at Leuchars.

No. 617 Squadron

RAF Lossiemouth
Panavia Tornado GR.4
1 Group
Strike Command
Role: Strike Attack
Motto: *Après moi le déluge* – After me, the flood

On 21 March 1943, 617Sqn was formed as 'X Squadron' at Scampton, commanded by Wing Commander Guy Gibson. Although he was aware that the task he was to undertake involved flying Lancasters at low-level over water, he was not told about the mission until nearer the time. He was cleared to select the best Lancaster crews for this special mission and, once assembled, the crews undertook their training over the dams and reservoirs of Derbyshire.

617Sqn are equipped with the Tornado GR.4 for the strike role. On their sixtieth anniversary they became the first RAF unit to operationally use Storm Shadow when it was launched at a target in Baghdad.

On the night of 16–17 May 1943, nineteen specially modified Lancasters departed Scampton with their bouncing bombs on Operation *Chastise*, to attack the Mohne, Eder, Sorpe and Schwelm dams in the German Ruhr, flying at exactly 60ft and 220mph (354km/h). Wing Commander Guy Gibson radioed back the code word 'Nigger' to signify that they had breached the Mohne dam and was subsequently awarded the VC for his gallantry in repeatedly flying over the dams to draw the enemy fire. He was later killed in action in September 1944. The Eder dam was also breached, but eight of the Lancasters failed to return from their missions and fifty-three crew members (40 per cent) lost their lives. Thirty-two crew members were decorated.

Despite having only been formed for the single mission, 617Sqn continued to serve on other specialized operations. During the D-Day landings it dropped 'window' – metallic strips to cause radar to indicate large formations. This was to cause a distraction by indicating an invasion force approaching Pas de Calais. In November 1944, it also flew the attack with 9Sqn that sank the Tirpitz with 12,000lb 'Tallboy' bombs. It also carried the 22,000lb 'Grand Slam' bombs, which destroyed targets such as the Bielefeld viaduct. In January 1946, 617Sqn were allocated to the Tiger Force, but they didn't deploy because of the Japanese surrender.

In September 1946, 617Sqn re-equipped with the Lincoln at Binbrook, before receiving the Canberra jet-bomber in 1952. They spent four months in Malaya on Operation *Firedog* in 1955, prior to disbanding in December 1955.

In May 1956, 617Sqn was re-formed at Scampton with the Vulcan. In June 1963, it conducted the first non-stop flight to Australia, covering the 11,500 miles in just over twenty hours. It continued to operate until it was disbanded again on December 1981.

On 16 May 1982, 617Sqn was re-formed at Marham with the Tornado GR.1, which it operated in the strike role. In October 1993, it moved to Lossiemouth, where its role changed to that of maritime-strike, armed with the Sea Eagle anti-ship missile, replacing the Buccaneers of 208Sqn.

By the end of 2002, the dedicated maritime-strike role ceased and the squadron traded their Tornado GR.1s for the upgraded GR.4.

In 2003, 617Sqn was deployed to the Middle East as part of the Operation *Telic* force. On 21 March – the squadron's sixtieth anniversary – it became the first RAF squadron to operationally launch the new Storm Shadow stand-off weapon (SOW). It had been chosen as the first squadron to equip with this new weapon and was still completing training when the squadron was deployed. During the first attack with the Storm Shadow, a pair of Tornados were fired at by Iraqi AAA and targeted by SA-2 SAM, but successfully launched the missiles, which were reported as having hit their intended targets.

No. 617Sqn are equipped with the Tornado GR.4 and are based at Lossiemouth.

No. 1435 Flight

RAF Mount Pleasant, Falkland Islands
Panavia Tornado F.3
1 Group
Strike Command
Role: Air Defence

On 4 December 1941, 1435 Flight was formed as a night-fighter squadron at Luqa, equipped with Spitfires to provide air defence for the island, but disbanded in June 1942.

In July 1942, it was re-formed as a day-fighter squadron with men and Spitfire Vs of 603Sqn. Gradually, the Flight increased in strength and, in August 1942, it was re-classified as a squadron. By January 1943, it had converted to the fighter-bomber role and was used on operations against Sicily and Italy. Subsequently, 1435Sqn conducted operations against targets in Albania and Yugoslavia. On 9 May 1945, 1435Sqn was disbanded.

On 1 November 1988, 1435 Flight was re-formed at Mount Pleasant by the re-naming of 23Sqn. It was equipped with four Phantom FGR.2s, which were named 'Faith', 'Hope', 'Charity' and 'Desperation' in recognition of its Second World War connection with Malta. With these it undertook the role of air defence of the Falkland Islands.

1435 Flight has been providing the Falkland Islands with fighter cover since 1988. Initially it operated Phantoms from Stanley but now flies the Tornado F.3 from Mount Pleasant Airport.

In July 1992, 1435 Flight was re-equipped with the Tornado F.3 with which it continues to provide air defence for the islands with air-to-air refuelling support from the VC.10 tanker from 1312 Flight. Because of their remoteness, the Falklands provide an excellent training area for the Tornados, which can operate with all three services and undertake low-level training with next to no restrictions.

No. 1435 Flight operate the Tornado F.3 from their base at Mount Pleasant.

Battle of Britain Memorial Flight

RAF Coningsby
de Havilland Chipmunk T.10, Douglas Dakota III, Hawker
    Hurricane IIc, Avro Lancaster B.I, Supermarine Spitfire
    IIa, Vb, IXe & PR.19
1 Group
Strike Command
Role: Memorial Flight
Motto: Lest we forget

The Battle of Britain Memorial Flight (BBMF) was originally formed on 11 July 1957, as the Historic Aircraft Flight at Biggin Hill. It was initially equipped with three Spitfire PR.19s (PM631, PS853 and PS915) and a Hurricane IIc (LF363). PS915 was swapped for the gate guardian Spitfire XVI (TE330), which had been the gate guard at West Malling. A further two Spitfire XVIs (TE476 and SL674) were acquired later in 1957, after their use in the Royal Tournament.

In 1958, the BBMF moved temporarily to North Weald, before settling in at Martlesham Heath. Meanwhile, PS853 departed to become gate guardian at West Raynham and TE330 was presented to the USAF. Sadly, the BBMF suffered two casualties with the Mk.XVIs in 1959. The first was a landing accident and the second an engine failure during the annual London flypast, resulting in a forced landing. In both cases the aircraft were grounded but, more significantly, the forced landing resulted in single-engined aircraft no-longer being allowed to overfly London. BBMF then moved to Horsham St Faith in November 1961, with a single Hurricane and Spitfire.

The move to Coltishall in April 1963 represented a change for the better in BBMF fortunes. PS853 returned to the BBMF in 1964 and Vickers Armstrong presented their airworthy Spitfire Vb, AB910, in 1965. The making of the Battle of Britain film in 1968 did a great deal to help the restoration of Second World War aircraft, especially Spitfires and Hurricanes. All of the BBMF aircraft took part in the film, however, during the search for more suitable aircraft a Mk.II was located in the Colerne museum. Such was its state that it was easily restored to an airworthy condition. When the filming finished, P7350 was added to the BBMF fleet, to become the only member of the flight that actually took part in the Battle of Britain.

In 1972, Hawker had completed trials which incorporated their Hurricane G-AMAU, but instead of retiring it, they refurbished it and then presented it to

the BBMF. In 1973, 44Sqn handed the airworthy Lancaster PA474 over to the BBMF to extend the memorial to bomber crews. A Chipmunk was added to the flight during the early 1970s for single-engine tail-dragger training. In 1976, space at Coltishall was becoming a premium, so the BBMF moved to Coningsby in March.

In 1984, PS915 was recovered from West Malling and restored to flying condition by British Aerospace before rejoining the BBMF. A Devon was added to the Flight in 1985 as a communications and multi-engined trainer. When a Dakota was acquired in 1993, it took over the role of the Devon, which was retired. It also enabled the BBMF to provide a visible memorial to transport crews. Two more Chipmunks replaced their original example.

When one of the Hurricanes was all but destroyed when it suffered an engine failure and caught fire in 1991, Spitfire PS853 was sold to provide funds for a restoration and LF363 returned to the air once again in 1998. Spitfire LF.IXe MK356 was restored and added to the fleet in 1997 to replace PS853.

From June 2003 until October, the BBMF temporarily operated from Barkston Heath during runway maintenance.

The BBMF aircraft can be regularly seen at airshows. Visits can be made to the BBMF base and their Heritage Centre at Coningsby (Tel: 01526 344041 for details).

The BBMF currently operates five Spitfires, two Hurricanes, one Lancaster and one Dakota, plus two Chipmunks.

The BBMF operates a mixed fleet of vintage aircraft to provide a living memorial to those servicemen and women who lost their lives to protect our freedom. These aircraft regularly appear at airshows and other events.

Joint Forward Air Control Training & Standards Unit

RAF Leeming
BAe Hawk T.1A
1 Group
Strike Command
Role: Forward Air Control training

The Joint Forward Air Control Training & Standards Unit (JFACTSU) was formed at Chivenor in 1964, where it operated some of the last Meteors under the auspices of 79Sqn. It then moved to Brawdy in 1977, where it flew camouflaged Jet Provosts until 1993. It then moved to Leeming, from where it now operates Hawks.

The role of the JFACTSU is to teach and standardize Forward Air Control, to enable strike aircraft to launch weapons accurately and safely onto the target. Having established its reputation for excellence,

the unit provides student training for a number of countries, including Sweden, Norway and the USA, in addition to the Army, RAF and Royal Marines.

The JFACTSU operate the Hawk T.1 from their base at Leeming. These aircraft are pooled with 100Sqn, but retain their own markings.

No. 2 Group

RAF High Wycombe
Strike Command
Role: Air Combat Support
Motto: *Vincemus* – We will conquer

On 1 April 1918, 2 Group was formed at Norham Gardens in 1 Area and transferred to South-Eastern Area in May. It became 1 (Training) Group in August 1918, but this role was dropped in July 1919. In September 1919, it was absorbed into Southern Area and disbanded in March 1920.

It was reformed at Abingdon in March 1936 as 2 (Bomber) Group within Central Command. It was initially responsible for

Hucknall, Turnhouse, Abbotsinch and Worthy Down. It moved to Bomber Command in July. Following a move to Wyton, eight Blenheim squadrons were added from Wattisham, Watton, West Drayton and Wyton. It was transferred to be part of 2 Tactical Air Force (2 TAF) in June 1943. After bearing the brunt of day bombing during the early days of the war and moving numerous times, 1 Group was disbanded in May 1947, having played its part in the British Air Forces of Occupation (BAFO).

In December 1948, it was re-formed as part of BAFO again. This time it was located at Sundern, Germany and it transferred to 2 TAF in September 1951, but then disbanded in November 1958.

Following the end of the Cold War, RAF Germany ceased to be a Command and became 2 Group within Strike Command in April 1993, based at Rheindahlen. In April 1996, it was absorbed into 1 Group.

In January, 2 Group was re-formed as one of the three Groups in the restructured Strike Command, where it formed the support component. As such, it controlled the air transport and tankers, plus the

The Joint Forward Air Control Training & Standards Unit (JFACTSU) operates two Hawk T.1as to train Forward Air Controllers the art of effectively directing aircraft onto a target.

Nimrod R.1 and Sentry.

A further reorganization in 2003–4 saw it responsible for Combat Support, which included the air transport and tankers and now includes the RAF Regiments plus Combat Support Units.

No. 2 Group is based at High Wycombe.

No. 24 Squadron

RAF Lyneham
Lockheed Hercules C.4 & C.5
2 Group
Strike Command
Role: Air Transport
Motto: In Omnia Parati – In All Things Prepared

On 1 September 1915, 24Sqn was formed at Hounslow Heath with elements from 7Sqn. They initially flew Blériot, Curtiss and Farman aircraft and later the BE.2c and the Gunbus. By the end of 1915, they had become the first DH.2 squadron and were ready to deploy to France, where they operated in the fighter role from February 1916. They were the first single-seat fighter squadron to deploy to France and, later, operated various aircraft, including the DH.5 and SE.5a. By the time the war ended, 24Sqn had been credited with 297 enemy aircraft destroyed, including that of Lieutenant Wüsthoff, a German Ace with

twenty-seven victories, and Hauptmann Boelcke, with forty. Having handed its SE.5s to 1Sqn, 24Sqn returned to the UK to London Colney in February 1919 and was disbanded in November 1920.

Re-formed in April 1920 at Kenley as a communications and training squadron with F.2b Fighters, it participated in the early Hendon Pageants, winning a number of the events. In January 1927, the squadron moved to Northolt. While there, aircraft operated included the Avro 504, DH.9A, F.2b Fighter and Moth. As the only air-transport squadron at that time, it was tasked with flying VIPs on urgent business. In April 1928, it became the first RAF squadron to fly a member of the Royal Family, when the then Prince of Wales was flown in a F.2b Fighter. Later the following year, he was being given flying instruction by the squadron. From 1930, it was equipped mainly with Fairey IIIFs, with a few Wapitis.

In January 1933, the first Hart was received by 24Sqn and, in July, it moved to Hendon, although 'C' Flight remained at Northolt. By the following year, the inventory included the Tiger Moth, Gipsy Moth, Audax, Tomtit and a Bulldog, to which a Dragon Rapide was added the year after. In 1937, 24Sqn received the first Don and DH.86 Express, venturing as far as Khartoum. When war broke out the

communications role was greatly expanded, including operating many clandestine flights. The aircraft operated continuously changed, with many being requisitioned civil aircraft. These included the DH.86 Express, Electra, Ensign, Flamingo, Heston Pheonix, Magister, Percival Q6 and Vega Gull, as well as Savoia and Douglas types from Sabena. Military aircraft arrived in the form of the Anson, Dominie, Hornet Moth, Mentor, Oxford and Roc. However, in October 1940, 'A' Flight hangar was hit, destroying a number of the aircraft.

During the early war, 24Sqn flew many flights into France, where their unarmed aircraft were often attacked and, occasionally, forced down. Some managed to take off again and get their passengers home. VIP passengers included His Majesty King George VI and the squadron also operated Sir Winston Churchill's personal Avro York. A total of 323 flights of vital supplies were flown by unarmed Hudsons into besieged Malta and when the Island was awarded the George Cross, in May 1942, 24Sqn had the honour of delivering the medal.

'A' Flight was used to form 510Sqn in October 1942, with various aircraft for local duties. When Transport Command was formed in March 1943, 24Sqn immediately came under its control, although its

An LTW Hercules C.5 being flown into Baghdad Airport, Iraq fires off a number of flares due to the potentially high threat from SAMs. Many of these missions were being flown by 24Sqn crew. MSgt Hargreaves Jr – USN

role didn't change. The following month, twelve Dakotas were added to the fleet and, shortly after, a York. The York was one of the prototypes and had been modified internally for use by Churchill. Operating almost everywhere in the UK, Europe and the Mediterranean, 24Sqn's short-range routes were transferred to another off-shoot – 512Sqn, in August 1943. In January 1944, the squadron commenced operations to Bombay. By September 1944, the squadron fleet was consolidated on Dakotas and Ansons and a three-aircraft flight was established in the Far East to maintain communications.

In February 1946, 24Sqn moved to Bassingbourn and were involved in the testing of flying aids to assist in development of blind flying. In June, 1359 Flight was absorbed, along with its fleet of VIP Dakotas, Lancastrians and Yorks. In 1947, it became known as 24 (Commonwealth) Squadron, when it absorbed RAAF, RNZAF and SAAF crews from the Dominion Air Force.

24Sqn participated in the Berlin Airlift prior to moving to Waterbeach in June 1949. By 1950 the Lancastrians had been retired and replaced later in the year by Valetta in February following a move to Oakington. It re-equipped with the Hastings in November when it moved to Lyneham. In February 1951 the Squadron

moved on to Topcliffe, then Abingdon in 1953 and Colerne in 1957.

On 6 January 1968, 24Sqn arrived at Lyneham, to become the second RAF Hercules squadron. Since then the squadron has served on all operations with deployments, including Belize, Cyprus, Rhodesia, the Falklands, the Gulf and the Balkans. In addition, it has participated in numerous humanitarian missions, including Nepal, Turkey, Cambodia and Ethiopia. The famine relief in Nepal resulted in the Khana Cascade technique being developed, to drop food to remote Himalayan villages using steep approaches.

Shortly after the end of the Falklands Campaign, the squadron operated some Hercules K.1s that had been converted for the air-to-air tanking role. It also operated the Air Bridge from Ascension to the Falklands. Since then, 24Sqn has been kept busy with virtually continuous humanitarian and operational taskings, in addition to its normal role.

By May 2000, 24Sqn had completed re-equipping with new C-130J Hercules and, in November, the first operational route was flown to Gibraltar. Having initially acted as the conversion unit, in early 2003, the squadron provided a number of crews to 30Sqn to enable it to become the second RAF C-130J unit. The squadron

specializes in route flying and it is planned that it will move to Brize Norton.

C-130J crew training is also undertaken by 24Sqn. Being a new aircraft, the latest simulators are a major factor in reducing airframe hours on the course, with students undertaking thirty simulator 'flights' and just three in the aircraft.

No. 24Sqn operates the Hercules C.4 and C.5 from their base at Lyneham. The aircraft are pooled with 30Sqn and carry no squadron markings.

No. 30 Squadron

RAF Lyneham
Lockheed Hercules C.4 and C.5
2 Group
Strike Command
Role: Air Transport
Motto: Ventre à terre – Belly to the floor (Flat out)

In November 1914, 30Sqn was originally established at Farnborough as an untitled unit that later sailed to Egypt. On 24 March 1915, this unit was designated 30Sqn at Ismailia, Egypt with five Farmans. Its role was to provide reconnaissance, bombing and fighter duties, along with army co-operation, throughout the Mesopotamia campaign. It performed its

30Sqn is the second unit to operate the new C-130J. This is the longer Hercules C.4 model.

first bombing mission just three days after having been formed. In April 1915, a flight was formed at Basra to support operations in that theatre and, in October, the rest of the squadron joined it, to become the only RFC unit in Mesopotamia.

Intense operations continued in the harsh conditions. In March 1916, 30Sqn were tasked in the resupply of the besieged garrison at Kut-el-Amara, where 13,850 troops and 3,700 Arabs were surrounded by the Turks. A desperate operation was mounted, with four BE.2cs, a Farman, Voisin and three Short Seaplanes on the first transport support operations. Over 140 missions were flown, dropping 19,000lb (8,600kg) of food despite some aircraft losses. Unfortunately, this was insufficient and the garrison had to surrender. A number of squadron personnel were lost but, after the arrival of a number of new members, it was able to regain air superiority over the Germans and support the army in driving the Turks back up north.

SPADs and Bristol Scouts arrived in 1917, to be joined by RE.8s; DH.4s followed. Although operations against the Turks had ended, in October 1918 further

activity continued in Persia. In 1929, it re-equipped with the Wapiti at Mosul and, in 1935, these were replaced by the Hardy, with a move to Habbaniya the following year. The Hardys were passed on to 6Sqn and were replaced by the Blenheim, which it took to Ismailia in August 1939.

At the beginning of the Second World War, 30Sqn moved to the Western Desert, where they flew fighter operations with Browning gun-packs fitted in the Blenheim's bomb-bay. In October 1940, they were ordered to move to Greece to oppose invading Italian forces. When Hitler declared war on Greece in April 1941, the RAF's eighty combat aircraft were quickly overwhelmed by 900 from the Luftwaffe. Within two weeks the British forces underwent a major evacuation.

Along with the surviving Hurricanes from 33Sqn, 30Sqn were moved to Crete to defend the convoys operating Greece–Crete–Egypt. However, Hitler pushed hard against Crete, which was also overwhelmed. During intense fighting, twenty-nine members of 30Sqn were killed and some sixty taken prisoner.

The squadron was re-formed with

Hurricanes to fight in the desert and then, in 1942, it was moved to Ceylon on HMS Indomitable. On 5 April they destroyed fourteen Japanese aircraft, with another eleven probables or damaged, but at a cost of five of their own pilots plus sixteen aircraft lost or damaged. In February 1944, they moved forward to Burma and the Arakan front. In June, they pulled back to India to re-equip with the Thunderbolt, returning to Arakan that October. They were tasked with various fighter-escort and ground-attack missions and, in 1945, took part in the invasion of Rangoon. Once the Japanese had been pushed out of Burma, they returned to India to prepare for the invasion of Malaysia. However, the Japanese surrendered before that commenced.

Following a re-equipping with Tempests and a move to Bhopal in the summer of 1946, 30Sqn was disbanded that December, concluding what had been, then, the longest period serving abroad for any RAF squadron.

In November 1947, 30Sqn was re-formed at Oakington with Dakotas and was fully operational when the Soviets attempted to blockade Berlin in June 1948. During the airlift, 30Sqn carried 8,729 tons of freight, 25,136 passengers and 123.5 tons of mail. In 1950, the squadron was re-equipped with the Valetta and moved to Abingdon, followed by Benson in 1952 and Dishforth in April 1953. From here, VIP and courier flights were flown and one aircraft was detached to Northolt from April 1957. At the same time, the Beverley arrived and, in November 1959, it moved to Eastleigh, Kenya. Amongst its taskings were a number of emergency-aid and refugee-evacuation operations. On just one, a total of 1,783,000lb (809,500kg) were dropped in only seventy flights.

In September 1964, 30Sqn moved to Muharraq, Bahrain, but was disbanded once more in September 1967.

On 10 June 1968, 30Sqn was re-formed at Fairford with the Hercules C.1 and moved to Lyneham in 1971. In addition to training, exercises and scheduled flying, the squadron continued to be involved in many humanitarian operations, including ones in Nepal and Ethiopia. The Falklands campaign saw a heavy commitment, which continued with the air-bridge from Ascension to Stanley until 1989 and included provision of air-to-air tanking crews for 1312 Flight.

More humanitarian taskings continued to Ethiopia, Jamaica, Nepal and Monserrat and, in 1990, events in the Middle East saw 30Sqn involved in the massive build-up of forces for Operations *Granby* and *Desert Storm* against, Iraq during which it flew over 8,500 hours. Since then, further humanitarian relief for the Kurds and operations in the former Yugoslavia, Afghanistan and Iraq again have seen 30Sqn as busy as ever, specializing in route flying. It also conducts some tactical flying. In June 2002, 30Sqn completed the conversion to the Hercules C.4 and C.5.

No. 30 Squadron operates the Hercules C.4 and C.5 from its base at Lyneham. The Hercules are pooled with 24Sqn and carry no squadron markings.

No. 32 (The Royal) Squadron

RAF Northolt

BAe.125 CC.3, BAe.146 CC.2, Aérospatiale Twin Squirrel HCC.1

2 Group

Strike Command

Role: VIP communications

Motto: *Adeste Comites* – Rally round, comrades

On 12 January 1916, 32Sqn formed at Netheravon from a nucleus that had been provided by 21Sqn. After a period of training on the FB.5 and Henry Farman, they were deployed in May, initially to Auchel, France, as a fighter squadron with DH.2s. During July, their CO – Major LWB Rees – spotted a formation of eight enemy aircraft and, despite being out-numbered, decided to attack. In the ensuing battle, he forced two down out of control, despite being injured in the leg, before he ran out of ammunition. For this action he was awarded the Victoria Cross. During the later stages of the war, 32Sqn used their DH.5s and SE.5as to strafe-attack enemy troops on the Western Front. With the war over, the squadron returned home to Tangmere and were disbanded at Croydon at the end of the year.

On 1 April 1923, 32Sqn was re-formed at Kenley with Snipes, converting to Grebes, followed by Gamecocks, Bulldogs, Gauntlets and, eventually, the Hurricane in October 1939, by which time it had moved to Biggin Hill. Abbeville in France was used as a forward-operating base for a while in May 1940. However, heavy losses were suffered during the Battle of Britain and 32Sqn was moved to Acklington in August 1940. In December, it moved to Middle Wallop and then commenced convoy patrols from Pembrey and Angle. It returned to the south east in November 1941 and was deployed to North Africa in December 1942, still with Hurricanes. In August 1943, it converted to Spitfires, before moving through Italy and Greece and finishing in Palestine when the war ended.

In 1948, 32Sqn moved to Cyprus, where

The HS.125 CC.3 and BAe.146 CC.2 are both operated by 32(The Royal)Sqn to fly high-ranking officers, VIPs and the Royals. The Twin Squirrel is used for shorter distances.

it converted to the Vampire, continuing to operate these until 1955, when they were replaced with the Venom. In 1957, the squadron's role was changed to bomber, for which it received the Canberra. In February 1957, it was transferred to Akrotiri and became part of the Middle East Air Force Strike Wing. In February 1969, the squadron was disbanded.

It was re-formed the following day at Northolt by the re-numbering of the Metropolitan Communications Squadron whose role it continued, transporting military and government officials around the country. It was equipped with the Andover, Basset, Pembroke and Sycamore. The Sycamore was replaced by the Whirlwind and withdrawn in 1972. Bassets were withdrawn overnight on 29 April 1974 and, when 60Sqn disbanded in March 1992, the Andover C.1s transferred to 32Sqn.

In 1997, the Queen's Flight at Benson (which had originally formed in 1936 as the King's Flight) was finally disbanded

and the role of flying members of the Royal Family was transferred, together with the three HS.146 CC.2s and two Wessex HCC.4s, to 32Sqn. In recognition of this, the squadron was re-titled 32 (The Royal) Squadron.

The pair of venerable Wessex HCC.4s were retired in March 1995. It was decided that they would not be replaced, but the tasking would be contractorized, resulting in the establishment of the civilian-operated Queen's Helicopter Flight, which is equipped with a leased Sikorsky S-76. One of the HS.146s was also sold.

On 1 April 1996, the four Gazelle HT.3s were replaced by three Twin Squirrels, which are on long-term lease from McAlpine Aviation. As a result the Gazelles were retired. In April 2005 it was announced that AgustaWestland will provide two A109 Power helicopters to replace the Twin Squirrels from April 2006. The contract will continue the practice of Civil Owned Military Registered operation.

No. 32Sqn currently operate six HS.125 CC.3s, two BAe.146 CC.2s and three Twin Squirrel HCC.1s from their base at Northolt.

No. 47 Squadron

RAF Lyneham
Lockheed Hercules C.1 & C.3
2 Group
Strike Command
Role: Air Transport
Motto: *Nili Nomen Roboris Omen* – The name of the Nile shall be an omen of our power

In March 1916, 47Sqn was formed at Beverley, prior to being deployed to Salonika that September for operations against the Bulgarians on the northern frontier of Greece and Macedonia. Aircraft were operated in the fighter and reconnaissance roles and included the BE.2c, BE.12, DH.2, FK.3 and FK.8. The fighter elements were transferred to become the basis of 150Sqn in April 1918.

In April 1919, the squadron deployed to Russia to help support General Denikin's

Seen at Skopje, Macedonia, a line of RAF Hercules transporting troops, vehicles and equipment on peacekeeping duties. 47Sqn continue to operate the Hercules C.1 (front) and C.3.

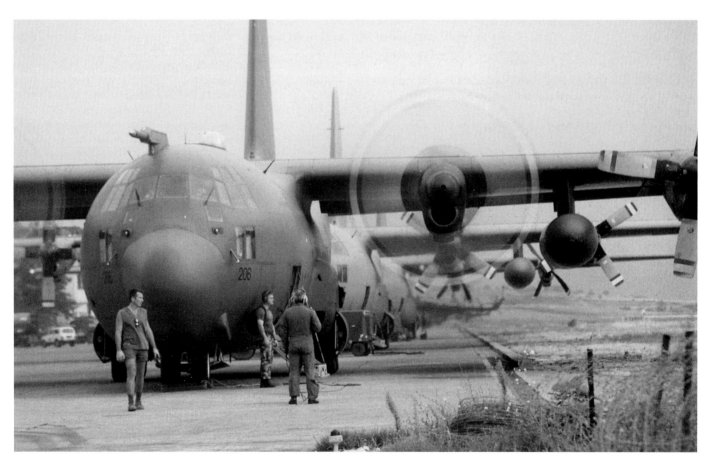

White Russian Forces in their ill-fated attempt to repel the Bolshevik armies. However, the government was criticized in the House of Commons for participating in a foreign civil war. As a result, 47Sqn was disbanded in October and formed as 'A' Sqn, RAF Mission, operating without the RAF Ensign and flying their own flag instead. This flag is still worn by squadron aircrew as their shoulder flag.

On 1 February 1920, 47Sqn was reformed at Helwan in Egypt from the re-numbered 206Sqn and spent most of the inter-war years in East Africa, especially in Sudan at Khartoum. Here they flew the DH.9, DH.9a, Fairey IIIF, Gordon, Vincent and Wellesley. The Vincents remained until August 1940, although they were largely replaced by the Wellesley from June 1939. The squadron's motto and badge were derived from this period, when petrol was poured onto the Nile and set alight by bombing to impress the locals and gain their confidence. One chieftain stated that 'the name of the Nile shall be an omen of your power' and so it was adopted. The badge contains the Crest, which is a native bird of the Nile, and the blue and white background represents the two Niles.

The squadron was tasked with attacking Italian units in Eritrea and Ethiopia through to May 1941 and then, later, undertook anti-submarine patrols. Beauforts were added from July 1942, enabling strikes against enemy ships, plus Beaufighters the following June. In March 1944, 47Sqn moved to India, where it started to receive Mosquitos. However, the high humidity softened the glue of the wooden wings. As a result, it took until February 1945 for improved fighter-bombers to be delivered. After the end of the war, 47Sqn was deployed in November to Java, to help combat the communist terrorists. In March 1946, the squadron was disbanded at Butterworth, Australia.

In early September 1948, 47Sqn re-formed with the Halifax at Qastina, Palestine from the re-numbered 644Sqn. However, it was called home almost immediately, to operate from Fairford using the Halifax as a transport aircraft. In September 1946, it moved to Dishforth, where it became the first squadron to operate the Hastings and participated in the Berlin Airlift, before moving to Topcliffe in August 1949. In March 1956, while at Abingdon, 47Sqn became the first to receive the Beverley C.1, which it contin-

ued to operate until October 1967, when it was disbanded again.

On 25 February 1968, 47Sqn was re-formed at Fairford with the Hercules C.1 and moved to Lyneham in February 1971. Almost immediately, the squadron was making well-publicized humanitarian flights, evacuating civilians caught up in the East/West Pakistan war. The squadron has also participated in most of the many humanitarian and operational activities in which the Lyneham squadrons have been involved, in addition to its normal peacetime duties and exercises.

Operation-wise, 47Sqn has been frequently seen at the forefront, with first in and last out being very much part of their role, flying troops and supplies, providing resupply, then recovery. During Operation *Corporate*, 47Sqn were tasked with conducting the bulk of the resupply by air of Ascension Island. They were also heavily tasked during Operation *Granby* and flew the first Hercules into Kuwait International Airport while Iraqi forces were still being pushed out. Subsequent operations have seen 47Sqn's Hercules highly active in the former republic of Yugoslavia, Sierra Leone, Kosovo, Afghanistan and, most recently Iraq.

No. 47Sqn specializes in the tactical Air Transport Support Role, which involves air-dropping troops and equipment onto the battlefield. It also trains crews for this specialist role.

No. 47Sqn operates the Hercules C.1 and C.3 from their base at Lyneham.

No. 70 Squadron

RAF Lyneham
Lockheed Hercules C.1 & C.3
2 Group
Strike Command
Role: Air Transport
Motto: *Usquam* – Anywhere

On 22 April 1916, 70Sqn was formed at Farnborough with the Sopwith 1½ Strutter, prior to deploying one Flight to France in May, followed by the other two shortly after. It operated over the Western Front, flying bombing, fighter and long-range reconnaissance, as well as escort missions. One of the commanding officers at that time was Major A W Tedder – later to become Marshal of the Royal Air Force Lord Tedder. The squadron re-equipped with Camels in July 1917 and continued to

operate these until disbanded in January 1920.

In February 1921, 58Sqn, with the Handley Page O/400 and Vimy, was re-numbered 70Sqn at Heliopolis, Egypt. During this period, it was involved in the development of air dropping – a role it carries out today. The following year, it moved to Iraq, where it assisted in the developing of a mail route from Cairo to India via Baghdad, using Vernons then Victorias. Commencing in December 1928, it flew 586 people of various nationalities out of Kabul during a revolution – the first major airlift in aviation history. In 1934, it began to convert to the Valentia and, in August 1939, it returned to Egypt where it re-equipped with Valentines, exchanging these for Wellington the following year.

The early war years were spent at various locations in the Western Desert, especially Libya, until December 1943, when 70Sqn moved to Italy. It converted to Liberators in January 1945 and, in October, moved back to Shallufa, Egypt, where it was disbanded in March 1946.

Two weeks later it was re-formed with Lancasters when 178Sqn was re-numbered, but was disbanded again a year later.

In May 1948, 70Sqn was re-formed from the re-numbered 215Sqn at Kabrit, Egypt with Dakotas. During 1950, 70Sqn re-equipped with Valettas, which were heavily tasked while operating in the Canal Zone. Following a move to Cyprus in December 1955, these were gradually replaced by the Hastings from January, which took part in the dropping of paras on El Gamil airfield during the Suez Crisis. The Hastings was replaced by the Argosy in December 1967.

In 1970, 70Sqn began to receive the Hercules C.1, which were operated alongside the Argosy at Akrotiri as part of RAF Near East and flew many missions in support of British forces throughout the Middle East. They were also tasked with evacuations in West Pakistan in 1971 and Egypt and Cyprus in 1974.

Following the reduction of commitments in the Middle East, 70Sqn returned to the UK to be based at Lyneham. Overseas tasking continued, including deployments to Rhodesia in 1980 to assist in Operation *Agila* during their transition to independence and Nepal for Operation *Khana Cascade* in 1981 for famine relief.

Following the Argentinian invasion of

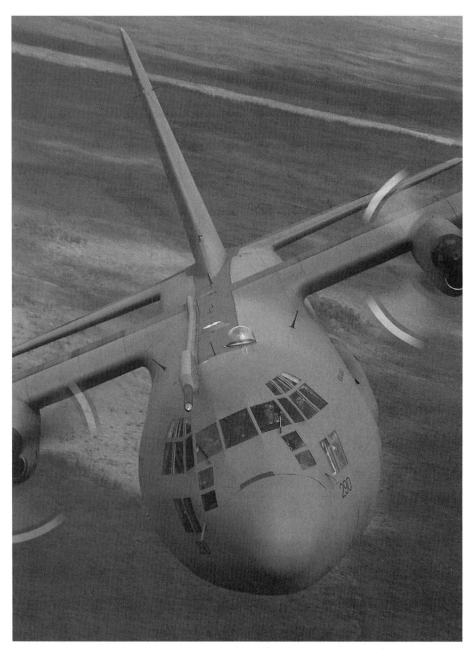

70Sqn operate the Hercules C.1 and C.3 variants within the Lyneham Tactical Wing (LTW).

the airfield shortly before their arrival. Due to the tight safety margins, they had little alternative other than to return to Ascension. The weather change resulted in headwinds once again and, as a consequence, they were airborne for just over twenty-eight hours.

Stanley was closed for two weeks during that August, while the runway was lengthened and covered in AM-2 matting (aluminium panels). In that time 47 and 70Sqn were tasked with covering the airbridge and used a grappling-hook system to collect mail for the return to Ascension. Despite these long remote flights, the 650 airbridge flights were operated safely and without any major incident, although one flight came close.

On 3 March 1984, a Hercules took off from Stanley for Ascension. It was a standard flight with a reasonable met forecast. Ten hours into the flight all was well, but some 75nm out from Ascension they were advised of a rapidly developing storm. Having completed three missed approaches and been advised that a tanker could not be launched because of the conditions, with sixty passengers and insufficient fuel to get anywhere else the crew were planning a ditching. As the co-pilot prepared to overshoot for the final time the engineer spotted the approach lights and the captain managed a successful landing, much to everybody's relief. The co-pilot – Flying Officer Paul Oborn – is now station commander at Lyneham.

The primary role of 70Sqn is route flying, which means that a summary of their tasking sheets looks like a world atlas. Humanitarian operations, including such as Operation *Bushell* in Ethiopia, exercises, such as *Red Flag* in the USA, and major full-scale conflicts, such as Operations *Granby* and *Desert Storm* in the Middle East, are just the tip of the iceberg. More recent operations have seen the squadron in Oman, Afghanistan and Iraq.

The C-130K training is also provided by 70Sqn. During the fourteen-week course, seventy-nine hours will be flown plus forty-seven hours in the simulator – forty-three and a half of the flying hours will be role-training, flying tasked sorties. The difference in the number of flying hours training on the C-130K compared with the C-130J (see 24Sqn) is due to the different generation of simulators – the C-130J being brand-new state of the art.

No. 70Sqn operates the Hercules C.1 and C.3 from their base at Lyneham.

the Falkland Islands, 1982 saw active operations. The squadron was heavily tasked with missions to the South Atlantic, dropping vital, urgent freight to ships of the Task Force. As the ships progressed south, the transit distance became longer – approaching the Hercules range. Initially, a pair of Andover ferry tanks were fitted, but this would still not be enough. The solution was fitting refuelling probes, to enable refuelling from Victor tankers, and subsequently Hose Drum Units (HDU), to enable operation as tankers. By 3 June,

70Sqn, together with 24Sqn, had flown 10,000 hours on Operation *Corporate* missions.

Once the Argentinians surrendered on 14 June, flights to Stanley were made to drop supplies – landings didn't commence until 24 June, as the runway was being repaired. These flights lasted around twenty-six hours. From 26 June, the airbridge was maintained by all four Hercules squadron plus the OCU. On one of these flights the crew had a headwind en route to Stanley, where bad weather closed

No. 99 Squadron

RAF Brize Norton
Boeing C-17 Globemaster
2 Group
Strike Command
Role: Air Transport
Motto: *Quisque Tenax* – Each Tenacious

On 15 August 1917, 99Sqn was formed at Yatesbury from a cadre provided from 13 Training Unit. It was deployed to France the following April with DH.9 bombers and flew seventy-six raids against enemy positions by the time the war ended, with a total of some sixty-one tons of bombs dropped.

With the war over, 99Sqn was deployed to India with the DH.10a, where it operated in the policing role along the North West Frontier. In April 1920, the squadron was renumbered 27Sqn and not re-formed again until April 1924. It then operated as a heavy-bomber squadron with various aircraft, including the Hyderabad and, later, the Heyford. In April 1937, 'B' Flight

was brought up to full squadron strength and re-numbered 149Sqn. September 1939 saw it re-equipped with the Wellington at Newmarket. In March 1941, it became the first occupant of the new airfield at Waterbeach.

Wellingtons were flown on missions in Europe until February 1942, when the squadron was deployed to Ambala, India to attack Japanese units in Burma. After various moves, the Wellingtons were replaced by Liberators in September 1944. In November 1945, 99Sqn was disbanded while based on the Cocos Islands. This was only for a short while as, later, in November 1945, 99Sqn was re-formed at Lyneham as a transport unit with the York. During 1948–9 the squadron was heavily committed to flying essential supplies during the Berlin Airlift.

The Yorks were replaced by the Hastings, which were flown around the world in support of British forces, as well as in the humanitarian role. In March 1959, the Hastings were replaced by the 'Whispering Giant' – the Britannia –

which the squadron continued to fly until it was disbanded in January 1976. During this period, it had moved to Brize Norton.

On 23 May 2001, 99Sqn was officially re-formed at Brize Norton, although it had already received the first of four C-17 Globemasters and undergone crew training at Charleston AFB. Almost immediately after the squadron was declared operational, it was being tasked. Within a year, the operations in Afghanistan and, subsequently, Iraq resulted in substantially higher tasking than had been planned for the squadron. With Afghanistan being a landlocked country without any reliable communications, all of the personnel and equipment had to be flown in and supported by air. The squadron were heavily committed to this operation and operated virtually a daily service to Kabul.

Before operations in Afghanistan were ended, 99Sqn were in the thick of it again, with operations in Iraq. Despite the ending of the war, 99Sqn continues to fly support missions into both countries.

No. 99Sqn operate the C-17 Globemaster from their base at Brize Norton.

Almost immediately it re-equipped with the C-17 Globemaster, 99Sqn was in great demand to haul freight and outsize loads around the world. This demand continues and so it has been decided to add an additional one to the fleet.

No. 101 Squadron

RAF Brize Norton
BAC VC.10 C.1K.3 & K.4
2 Group
Strike Command
Role: Air Transport/Tankers
Motto: *Mens Agitat Molem* – Mind over matter

On 12 July 1917, 101Sqn was formed at Farnborough as the first night-bomber unit and equipped with the FE.2b. It was deployed to France in August and saw much action on the Western Front. In March 1919, the squadron returned home and disbanded in December at Filton.

The squadron re-formed at Bircham Newton in March 1928, initially with the DH.9A, then the Sidestrand at Andover from October 1935 and, subsequently, the Overstrand. The latter bombers were armed with the first enclosed, powered turrets, which led to a castle turret being included in their badge

Based at West Raynham with Blenheims at the beginning of the war, 101Sqn flew their first daylight sortie to Germany in July 1940. By mid-August it was operating at night and attacking enemy invasion barges. Following a move to Manston in April 1941, 101 established a successful operation to close the Straits of Dover to enemy ships during daylight.

Later in 1941, 101Sqn re-equipped with the Wellington, with which it attacked Turin and took part in the 'Thousand Bomber' raids. It moved to Bourne in February 1942. In October 1942, it moved to Holme-on-Spalding Moor, where it re-equipped with the Lancaster. Whilst operating these on bombing raids, an extra crew member was carried to operate special broadcasting equipment. From October 1943, 101Sqn took part in *Airborne Cigar* (ABC) – jamming German radio transmissions and making false broadcasts to Luftwaffe pilots. The fluent German-speaking crew member, who was sometimes actually a German who had been expelled by the Nazis, would frequently imitate the Luftwaffe controllers, to send the fighters in the wrong direction. During January 1944, the squadron flew 900 hours on operations, during which it dropped 600 tons of bombs, in addition to its ABC role and dropping 'window'. By April 1945, it had flown 2,477 ABC sorties.

While at Binbrook, in September 1945, 101Sqn's Lancasters were replaced with Lincolns. In May 1951, it re-equipped once again, this time it was to become the RAF's first jet-powered Canberra squadron. In 1956, it became the first Canberra unit to drop bombs in anger, during attacks on terrorists in Malaya on

Operation *Firedog*. The following year, it returned to Binbrook and disbanded in February 1957.

In October 1957, 101Sqn re-formed with the Vulcan at Finningley and moved to Waddington in June 1961. In-flight refuelling had become a well-established practice with RAF bomber and fighter crews and, in 1963, three of the Vulcans were flown non-stop to Australia in less than eighteen hours. In February 1982, 101Sqn was disbanded.

On 1 May 1984, 101Sqn re-formed with five VC.10 K.2s, specially modified for the refuelling role from civilian airliners. The following year, the first of a further four Super VC.10s arrived, designated K.3.

The squadron quickly fitted into its new role and made a major contribution to RAF capabilities as a force extender. It regularly takes part in exercises and deployments, as well as establishing new achievements, such as the first refuelling of a fully laden passenger-jet. It even manages to break records: it flew to Australia non-stop in sixteen hours on its seventieth anniversary in 1987, breaking the earlier record by two hours (also made by 101Sqn, when equipped with the Vulcan).

During Operation *Granby*, the whole of 101 Squadron was deployed to the Middle East . In 1992, two VC.10s were deployed for Operation *Warden*, refuelling aircraft patrolling Iraq's northern no-fly zone. In 1993, two VC.10s were deployed to Italy for Operation *Deny Flight*, policing the

Bread and butter for 101Sqn – a VC.10 K.3 refuelling combat aircraft. In this case the receivers are a Tornado F.3 from 111Sqn and another unmarked.

former Yugoslavia, plus a further two to Bahrain to support the *Southern Watch* aircraft.

From mid-1994, a further five VC.10 K.4s were added to 101Sqn's fleet, enabling the dual role of carrying passengers as well as refuelling. This allows the squadron not only to refuel aircraft on deployment but also to carry their ground crews.

In March 1996, 101Sqn took over the refuelling task in the Falklands from the Hercules and has maintained a single aircraft on alert to support the Tornado F.3s. During Operation *Desert Fox* in December 1998, 101Sqn tankers provided tanker support for RAF and US Navy aircraft over Iraq. In March 1999, they supported Tornados from Bruggen bombing Serb targets and, later, deployed to Ancona, Italy.

These continuous operations have been taking their toll on the squadron's VC.10s, which had all previously been used by airlines. As a result, all of the K.2s were retired by late-1999.

The operational tasking continued, with further deployment to the Middle East for Operation *Oracle* over Afghanistan, where an intensive three months of flying were conducted out of Seeb, Oman, refuelling RAF and US Navy aircraft. This was followed by Operation *Telic*, during which some 4.2 million kg were dispensed. The squadron also assisted in the aeromed role, during which over 1,000 personnel were evacuated.

No. 101Sqn continues to be the RAF's main refuelling unit and regularly flies sorties to designated refuelling areas around the UK. It also flies trails to various part of the world in support of combat aircraft on exercises or operational deployments.

This tasking has continued to put a great strain on 101 Sqn crews and its VC.10s. The FSTA programme is currently being finalised and it is planned to see the VC.10 replaced from 2008. In June 2005 it was announced that three of the VC.10 fleet would be withdrawn to assist in the provision of spares for the remaining aircraft. This will see the total number operated from 19 to 16. From 14 October 10 and 101 Sqn amalgamated and 10 Sqn disband as its history is around 18 months shorter of the two. To alleviate some of the load on the VC.10, 2,000 hours of their tanker tasking was transferred to 216 Sqn who operate the more fuel-efficient Tristars but

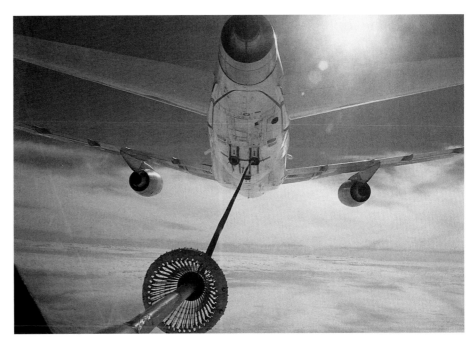

216Sqn provides a strategic-transport capability with its Tristars, some of which are also equipped for the aerial-refuelling role.

they can only operate with a single refuelling hose compared to the VC.10's three, which could cause difficulties in refuelling on multi-aircraft operations or trails.

101 Sqn operate the VC.10, C.1K, K.3 and K.4 from their base as Brize Norton plus the C.1K from October 2005.

No. 216 Squadron

RAF Brize Norton
Lockheed Tristar K.1, KC.1 & C.2
2 Group
Strike Command
Role: Air Transport/Tanker
Motto: *CCXVI Dona Ferens* – 216 bearing gifts

The origins of 216Sqn can be traced back to when it was formed at Villesneux on 1 April 1918, from elements of 16Sqn of the RNAS – hence its traditionally being referred to as 'two sixteen'. Prior to then it had been 'A' Squadron, RNAS – a detachment of 7Sqn RNAS which became 207Sqn. It was initially equipped with the 0/400, which was flown nearly all of the war in the strategic-bomber role. In July 1919, 216Sqn moved to Egypt.

Beginning in 1920, the 0/400s were replaced by the DH.10 bomber, which was used mainly for carrying freight and mail.

These were later replaced by the Vimy, Victoria, Valentia and, eventually, the Bombay in October 1939.

For the early part of the war, 216Sqn had a mixed role, with the Valentias continuing to be operated for transport and the Bombays in the bomber role. The squadron's main role was to assist other squadrons deploying to Greece and the Middle East, as well as maintaining the supply route down into Africa and the Gold Coast. It assisted in evacuations from Greece and resupply of the besieged forces in Habbaniya and Tobruk.

Hudsons arrived in July 1942 and, the following March, the first Dakota was delivered, enabling the Bombays to be withdrawn a few months later. The squadron continued in-role, but was now capable of dropping airborne forces, which it did on the Aegean Islands. It also extended its area of operation east to Burma, from where it could re-supply the 14th Army.

After the war ended and the Valetta replaced the Dakota in November 1949, 216Sqn continued in its transport role.

In November 1955, 216Sqn was brought home and, the following June, was re-equipped with the Comet C.2, becoming the first military jet-squadron in the world. In February 1962, these were supplanted by and eventually replaced with the larger

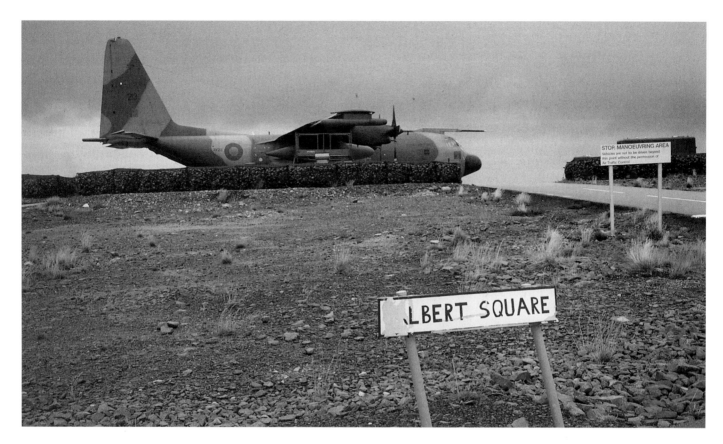

1312 Flight operates the Hercules to provide a maritime patrol capability around the territorial waters of the Falkland Islands and an aerial support to South Georgia. A VC.10 is also borrowed from Brize Norton to provide an air-to-air refuelling capability, primarily for the Tornados.

Comet 4. In addition to the normal transport role, these were also tasked with VIP and Royal flights, up to their disbanding in June 1975.

In July 1979, 216 re-formed with Buccaneers at Honington in the maritime strike/attack role. In 1980 it moved to Lossiemouth, but disbanded shortly afterwards.

As a result of a post-Falklands revue, which highlighted a shortage of aerial tankers, six surplus Tristar 500s were bought from British Airways and four converted for their new role. The other two were used to re-form 216Sqn in August 1983 and train the crews under the supervision of BA crew. In 1985, a further three ex-Pan-Am Tristars were added to the fleet. By the time all had become operational, 216Sqn operated two K.1, four KC.1, two C.2 and one C.2A.

Once they became fully operational, 216Sqn were tasked with flying special trips for widows and ex-prisoners of war to visit war graves in the Far East, as well as participating in numerous exercises and

trails, including the *Golden Eagle* round-the-world Tornado F.3 deployment by 29Sqn.

During the Gulf War, 216Sqn tankers were operationally deployed, the huge, white fuselages of two of their aircraft being painted in a pink ARTF camouflage. Five were deployed to operate in the tanker role during operations and the policing of the former Yugoslavia and Kosovo, during which a Serb MiG-29 unsuccessfully fired an air-to-air missile at one of their Tristars. Here they dispensed over 6 million kg of fuel to 1,580 aircraft. They have also been deployed as part of *Southern Watch*, enforcing the no-fly zone over southern Iraq. More recently, they were also deployed for operations in Afghanistan, as well as the operation to depose the oppressive regime in Iraq. During the latter, squadron tankers dispensed over 900,000kg of fuel to coalition aircraft and squadron transports airlifted some 16,000 personnel and 700 tonnes of freight.

While these operational tasks were

going on, the squadron was also providing tanking for exercises and trails, as well as fulfilling their air transport role, much of which was in support of these operations.

No. 216Sqn currently operates the Tristar K.1, KC.1, C.2 and C.2A from their base at Brize Norton.

No. 1312 Flight

RAF Mount Pleasant, Falkland Islands
BAC VC.10 K.3 & K.4, Lockheed Hercules C.1
2 Group
Strike Command
Role: Tanker/Air Transport
Motto: Desire the right

On 19 April 1944, 1312 Flight was formed with the Dakota at Llandaw, but disbanded after only three months, when the personnel, aircraft and equipment were transferred to 2nd Allied Tactical Air Force (2 ATAF).

In September 1954, 1312 (Transport Support) Flight was re-formed at Abingdon from the Transport Support Flight with Hastings, then disbanded again in April 1957.

On 1 September 1983, 1312 Flight was re-formed again at Stanley on the Falkland

Islands with the Hercules C.1K tanker aircraft, which had been operating as the Hercules Detachment since 15 October 1982. In 1985, the Flight moved to its new home at Mount Pleasant. The Hercules tankers were withdrawn in April 1996, to be replaced by a VC.10 K.3 or K.4 on loan from 101Sqn, providing a refuelling capability for the Tornado F.3s of 1435 Flight, significantly increasing endurance and range and, therefore, its capability. The VC.10 tends to be a K.3, as there is no local passenger-carrying requirement. As both 10 and 101Sqn operate the tankers, the crew on detachment to 1312 can be from either squadron.

No. 1312 Flight also operates a Hercules C.1 on loan from Lyneham. Crews were provided by 24 and 30Sqn until April 1999, when this was taken over by 47 and 70Sqn. The Hercules is used to provide a maritime radar-reconnaissance, as well as a 'top cover' rescue capability for the Falklands territorial waters and also transport to South Georgia for air-dropped supplies. All vessels within the designated areas are reported and visually identified where possible. Some may be photographed as well. Most of these vessels are fishing ships from Japan, Poland, Russia and Thailand.

The Hercules is also used to provide an air drop – of mail and small stores, using a harness pack – for the garrison at Grytviken on South Georgia. This is conducted approximately every six weeks and includes a reconnaissance around South Georgia plus the islands in South Sandwich chain, as well as the waters.

The VC.10 and Hercules are also both capable of medevac. Although rarely used, this can provide an emergency capability of transferring a patient to the South American mainland.

No. 1312 Flight operate one VC.10 tanker plus one Hercules C.1 from Mount Pleasant on the Falkland Islands in the South Atlantic.

No. 1 Air Control Centre

RAF Kirton-in-Lindsey
2 Group
Strike Command
Role: Deployable radar and Air Command and Control
Motto: Ever Alert

On 27 August 1965, 1 Air Control Centre (1 ACC) was established at Rattlesden. Almost immediately it was deployed to Lusaka, Zambia, where it was used to assist in monitoring the borders of neighbouring Rhodesia and to control the 29Sqn Javelins, which had also deployed. It returned to the UK at Wattisham and, in 1968, was deployed to Akrotiri on exercise. Because of the nature of the equipment in use at that time, twenty-three Hercules sorties were used for the deployment. As a result, 1 ACC was not deployed overseas operationally again. In July 1979, it moved to Portreath, where it provided cover of the South West Approaches, until the station was upgraded and 1 ACC was disbanded in September 1980.

When the Falklands conflict broke out, in 1982, the RAF lacked a established mobile radar-unit. A suitable radar was found in storage and deployed, along with a hastily assembled crew. It eventually arrived and was set up towards the end of the conflict. Afterwards, when a list of participating units was being compiled, a member of the unit, presumably ex-1 ACC, gave that as the identity of the anonymous unit, resulting in a battle honour being allocated to a unit disbanded four years previously.

On 1 April 1995, 1 ACC was re-formed at Boulmer, in response to the ending of the Cold War and the consideration that future operations would be Out Of Area (OOA). It was initially equipped with ex-Argentinian Type 99 radar, brought back from the Falklands. In 1997, it acquired the Type 101 radar and, in 2002, took delivery of the Thales Tactical Air

Since taking delivery of their Type 101 Radar and the Thales Tactical Air Control Centre system, 1 ACC have deployed operationally to Cyprus and Iraq in support of operations.

Control Centre system. This enabled the formation of the RAF's first deployed Air Surveillance and Control System Counterpart (UKDAC), which was initially deployed to Cyprus in January 2003, to provide coverage not only for Akrotiri but also the US Navy's 6th Fleet. They returned to Boulmer at the end of April and then deployed again a couple of weeks later to Iraq.

In April 2004, it was announced that, following a review, all communications-based units would be co-located at Scampton. As a result, 1 ACC re-located temporarily to Kirton-in-Lindsey in early 2005, before it eventually moves to Scampton by 2009.

No. 1 ACC is currently based at Kirton-in-Lindsey.

No. 5131 (Bomb Disposal) Squadron

RAF Wittering
2 Group
Strike Command
Role: EoD
Motto: *E Nocentibus Innocentia* – To make the harmful harmless

In April 1943, 5131 (Bomb Disposal) Squadron was formed at Snaith as the first of six RAF bomb-disposal teams. Kept very busy during the war, once it ended they were employed by the Allied Disarmament Organization to dispose of large stocks of weapons, including 161,008 tons of ordnance, 28,088 tons of chemical weapons and 4,370 'V'-weapons. Once the task was completed, all but 5131 (BD) Sqn were disbanded. In June 1965, the squadron was reduced to two Flights. In 1975, they became part of the RAF Armament Support Unit, as 1 EOD and 2 EOD. In 1984, 1 EOD became EOD Operations Flight and 2 EOD became the Airfield EOD Training Flight. In 1987, the Airfield EOD Development Team was added – their role being to get airfields back to safe operations following an air attack.

On 1 June 1995, 5131 (Bomb Disposal) Squadron was re-formed. Since then the squadron has been busy in peacetime, clearing weapons in storage sites, such as Chilmark and Bicester, old ranges at Cowden, Braid Fell, Goswick Sands and Theddlethorpe, and old chemical filling-sites – many dating back to the Second World War and earlier. Estimates of some sixty years' work remaining will see the squadron busy well into the future. They also provide teams for emergency EOD calls. However, recent operations have also seen them deployed on Operations *Corporate* in the Falklands, *Granby* in Iraq, *Fingal* in Afghanistan and *Telic* in Iraq again. Operationally, 5131Sqn's role is to clear airfields sufficiently to ensure safe operation by Allied aircraft.

No. 5131 (BD) Sqn is a sub-unit of the Armament Support Unit based at Marham.

No. 5131 (Bomb Disposal) Squadron is based at Wittering.

Station Flight

RAF Northolt
Britten Norman BN-2T Islander CC.2 & CC.2A
2 Group
Strike Command
Role: Communications

The Station Flight was formed at Northolt in August 1991 and, in December, the first of two BN-2T Islanders arrived. Designated CC.2, the second, subsequently, was delivered as a CC.2A. The exact purpose of the flight is not revealed – officially it is light communications with a photographic mapping role.

Northolt's Station Flight operates the Islander CC.2 and CC.2A from its base at Northolt.

Tactical Communications Wing

RAF Brize Norton
2 Group
Strike Command
Role: Communications
Motto: *Ubique Loquimur* – We speak everywhere

The Tactical Communications Wing (TCW) was originally established as 50 Tactical Signals Unit in 1962 at Odiham, to provide deployable support for air operations where little or none already exist.

In 1967, the Unit was renamed Tactical Signals Wing and changed again in 1969 to its current title, following its move to Benson. In 1976, the TCW moved to Brize Norton.

The current role of TCW is to install and operate a transportable tactical communications and information system, which is used to support squadrons and other units. While this will be in support of national interests, it may be to support NATO or UN operations.

In addition to frequent training exercises, TCW have been deployed to

5131(BD)Sqn are continually working to clear bombs and other toxic materials from various locations in the UK. Operationally, they have also been extremely busy to ensure airfields are safe for RAF and other aircraft. Here they are recorded working at Kabul Airport, Afghanistan.

ABOVE: Northolt's Station Flight operate the RAF's only Islanders for various roles, which include light communications and a photographic-mapping role.

BELOW: Communications equipment of the Brize Norton-based Tactical Communications Wing (TCW). By 2006 it should have re-located to Scampton.

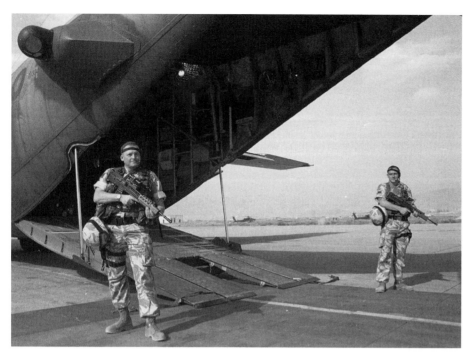

Members of the TPW providing Air Transport Security (ATSy) for a Hercules C.3a on the ramp at Kabul Airport, Afghanistan.

fitness. TPW can also provide security personnel to NARO (Nuclear Accident Response Organization).

Amongst the numerous countries around the world where the TPW has been deployed are, most recently, Afghanistan and Iraq. Besides a HQ staff, TPW comprises two operational squadrons, which are boosted by a third, provided by the Auxiliary Provost Squadron when required. To enable them to meet these varied and demanding roles, the operational TPW conduct a ten-week operations-and-training cycle, ensuring that teams are available when required and at short notice.

The Tactical Provost Wing is located at Henlow.

UK Mobile Air Movements Squadron

RAF Lyneham
2 Group
Strike Command
Role: Air Movements
Motto: Swift to move

The United Kingdom Mobile Air Movements Squadron (UKMAMS) was formed at Abingdon on 1 May 1966. Its role was to provide a mobile movements capability, as required, for stations not needing a permanent movements establishment. As the draw-down of RAF presence in the Far and Middle East progressed in the early 1970s, so UKMAMS's remit was expanded to overseas locations without movements personnel.

On 1 February 1974, UKMAMS moved to Lyneham, where it absorbed the stations movements personnel and operated a dual role. Since then the role has changed very little, although the tasking has increased dramatically.

UKMAMS comprises three flights. The Base Air Movements Flight handles all movements tasking at Lyneham and provides a detachment to the Joint Air Mounting Centre at nearby South Cerney. The Mobile Air Movements Flight maintains a team on ninety-minutes standby. While this has, in the past, predominately required UKMAMS teams to support forward airheads on exercises, more recently this has meant that a UKMAMS team has been amongst the first personnel into operational theatres. These opera-

Angola, Bosnia, Italy, Nepal, Rwanda, Saudi Arabia and Turkey for operational and humanitarian tasking, in addition to Afghanistan and Iraq. While some sites can be operating to provide expanded capability alongside existing similar facilities, it can also be at a bare field with no facilities, as could be operated by the Harrier. TCW has the capability to support up to thirteen deployed sites concurrently, in addition to its deployed HQ.

It was announced in 2003, that the TCW would move out from Brize Norton by 2006. In April 2004, a further announcement gave the new location to be Scampton.

Tactical Communications Wing (TCW) is currently based at Brize Norton.

Tactical Provost Wing

RAF Henlow
2 Group
Strike Command

The Tactical Provost Wing (TPW) was formed on 1 April 2000 at Henlow. Prior to that it was part of the HQ P&SS as the UK Support Squadron, which was formed at Debden on 1 October 1968. It moved to

Northolt in July 1974 and on to Rudloe Manor in 1977 and, in November 1966, was re-named the Tactical Police and Security Squadron.

TPW is tasked with providing a provost and security support within the Force Rear Support Area on deployed operations, until the arrival of RAFP. They also provide security to the Air Transport (AT) fleet during operations and non-operational deployments, such as relief operations. If required, they can also provide this support for any operations or exercises, as well as ceremonial events in the UK and around the world through to air shows.

As a result of their commitments, which can often be at short notice, the members of TPW are highly trained in policing, which includes law, procedures and defensive tactics, as well as some minor investigation. They are frequently tasked with close protection of senior officers, government officials and VIPs and provide the RAF's only dedicated Service Police Specialist Search Teams, who conduct searches wherever a terrorist threat is perceived, at home and abroad. To this are added tactical skills, such as fighting in built-up areas and field skills for when they are required to operate in austere locations, as well as a high degree of personal

tional tasks have included the former republic of Yugoslavia, Sierra Leone, Afghanistan and Iraq. Not only are UKMAMS amongst the first in, by their very nature they are the last to return home. The third flight is the Support, Standards and Training Flight (SSTF), whose task is to ensure that all the personnel are trained to the highest level. It also includes an engineering team, to repair squadron equipment.

UKMAMS is based at RAF Lyneham.

MoD Fire Services Central Training Establishment

Manston
2 Group
Strike Command
Role: Fire services training

The first RAF School of Fire Fighting and Rescue was established at Sutton-on-Hull on 18 August 1943 and remained there until October 1959 to provide specialist training for fire crews. It then moved to Catterick until the RAF Fire Fighting and Rescue Squadron moved to Manston to join the Air Force Department Fire Service Central Training Establishment in January 1989. The combined unit became the RAF Fire Services CTE. In 1995 it became the MoD FS CTE, tasked to train the MoD/Defence Fire Service, as well as RAF fire crews, in various aspects of aircraft crash and structural fire-fighting, for which a variety of qualifications are awarded. Nearly half of the instructors are RAF and the school has a number of obsolete airframes, as well as simulators, which are used during training.

Manston ceased to be an RAF airfield on 31 March 1999 and is now operated as a civil airport – London Manston. MoD FS CTE continues to be located at the airfield, though discussions are underway for a possible merger with other similar training establishments.

ABOVE RIGHT: **Movers of the UKMAMS loading freight into the cavernous hold of a C-17 Globemaster.**

RIGHT: **The MoD FS CTE uses Manston to train MoD and RAF fire crews to be able to quickly control and extinguish large fires and to be able to provide the initial rescue from a crashed aircraft. Crown Copyright**

The Royal Auxiliary Air Force

RAF High Wycombe

2 Group

Strike Command

Role: Reserves

Motto: *Comitamur ad Astra* – We go with them to the stars

The origins of the Royal Auxiliary Air Force (R Aux AF) date back to 9 October 1924, when it was formed as the Auxiliary Air Force (AAF) – the world's first ever reserve air-arm. The majority of the squadron would be part-time and would be administered by the County Territorial Association. The first of six Auxiliaries was 502 (Ulster) Sqn, formed at Aldergrove on 15 May 1925, followed, in September, by 602 (County of Glasgow) Sqn at Renfrew.

By September 1939, twenty AAF squadrons were operational, utilizing a variety of types. The first Luftwaffe aircraft was shot down over the UK by 603 (City of Edinburgh) Sqn on 16 October 1939, followed by another by 602 a few moments later. These squadrons had become an integral and vital part of the UK's defence. During the Battle of Britain, the AAF provided fourteen of the sixty-six squadrons in the Fighter Command Order of Battle. Post-war analysis showed that AAF squadrons accounted for a third of all kills during the Battle of Britain. They continued to operate in various roles throughout the war and, in July 1944, 606 (South Yorkshire) Sqn became the first Allied squadron to operate a jet fighter – the Meteor.

At the end of the war the AAF was disbanded, but was reconstituted within the Reserve Command on 1 May 1946. Twenty-one flying squadrons were re-activated with Spitfires and Mosquitos – later to operate Vampires and Meteors. In addition, a number of ground units, including AOP, AA and fighter-control units, were also established. In 1947, King George VI conferred the Royal prefix, due to the wartime bravery of the AAF and their *esprit de corps*.

The 1957 defence review was famous for a variety of reasons, especially the perceived end of the manned fighter, which was to be replaced by missiles. As a result, all R Aux AF flying squadrons were disbanded in March 1957, along with the regiment's light anti-aircraft squadrons and the auxiliary fighter-control units. They had been manned by some 11,000 personnel. Following these swingeing cuts, three Maritime Headquarter Units (MHU) were formed during 1959–60. These units provided additional personnel that could be called on to provide reinforcement in operations rooms, as well as intelligence and communications centres at Command and Group HQ levels. During 1960 to 1965, a similar unit was established at Aldergrove. During this period, AAF manning levels remained at around 500, until the late 1970s.

Following an increase in tension that had been triggered by the Russian invasion of Afghanistan, three R Aux AF Regiment Field Squadrons were formed in June 1979. Established on a trial basis, they were to

Gunners from 501 (County of Gloucester) Sqn firing a 51mm mortar. Crown Copyright

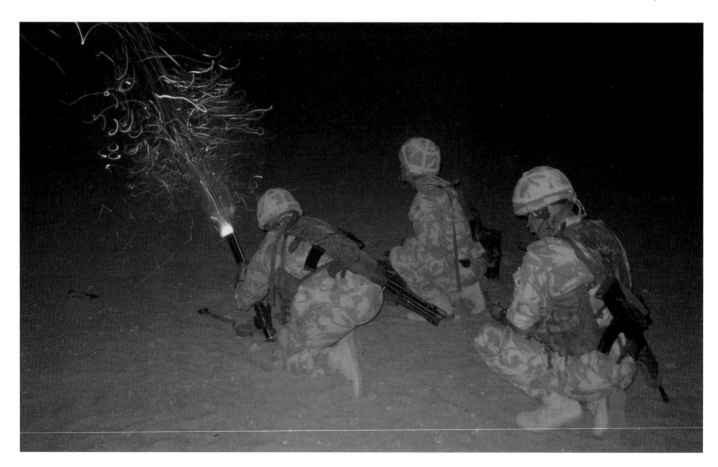

provide local defence at the front-line UK airfields of Honington, Lossiemouth and Scampton. Deemed to be successful, two more squadrons were formed in 1982 and another the following year. At the same time, consideration was being given to providing reservists for a number of other specialized roles.

The Falklands campaign in 1982 brought home the need for additional capacity in a number of areas and, as a result, a Movements and an Aeromedical Evacuation Squadron were formed. In addition, captured Argentinian Oerlikon guns provided radar-controlled equipment for a further two light anti-aircraft squadrons. Four airfield-defence flights were also formed, to provide point defence and guards at specific locations. In 1989, a further air-defence squadron was formed at Waddington, to introduce Rapier on a cadre basis.

In 1994, the re-introduction of reserve aircrew saw the establishment of 1359 Flight at Lyneham, following a period of trials, providing additional Hercules aircrew to augment the regular squadrons.

In April 1997, the RAF Volunteer Reserve was merged into the R Aux AF, which resulted in four new squadrons being incorporated into the single RAF reserve force.

The Reserve Forces Act 1996, which was implemented in April 1997, enabled the RAF to call upon a flexible, well trained and highly motivated reserve force, which it could call out for operations worldwide. This could include peacekeeping, humanitarian and disaster relief. The Act also introduced new categories of reserves and enables reservists to undertake full-time service.

Since then, personnel from the R Aux AF have been mobilized to serve in virtually all of the operations which have involved British Forces. The busiest has been 4624Sqn, which provides an air-movements support role, with air transport always being at the forefront of most operations. However, most squadrons have provided personnel when required and some reservists remain on active service.

The Squadrons of the R Aux AF are:

No 501 (County of Gloucester) Sqn – Brize Norton
No 504 (County of Nottingham) Sqn – Cottesmore
No 600 (City of London) Sqn – Northolt

No 603 (City of Edinburgh) Sqn – Edinburgh (det at Kinloss)
No 606 (Chiltern) Sqn – Benson
No 609 (West Riding) Sqn – Leeming
No 612 (County of Aberdeen) Sqn – Leuchars
No 2503 (County of Lincoln) Sqn – Waddington
No 2620 (County of Norfolk) Sqn – Marham
No 2622 (Highland) Sqn – Lossiemouth
No 2623 (East Anglian) Sqn – Honington
No 2625 (County of Cornwall) Sqn – St Mawgan
No 4624 (County of Oxford) Movements Sqn – Brize Norton
No 4626 (County of Wiltshire) Aeromedical Evacuation Sqn – Lyneham
No 7006 (VR) Intelligence Sqn – Waddington
No 7010 (VR) Photographic Interpretation Sqn – Waddington
No 7630 (VR) Sqn – Chicksands
No 7644 (VR) Sqn – High Wycombe
No 1359 Flight – Lyneham
Provost Sqn – Henlow

No. 501 (County of Gloucester) Squadron, R Aux AF

RAF Brize Norton
2 Group
Strike Command
Role: Operations Support
Motto: *Nil Time* – Fear Nothing

The origins of 501 (County of Gloucester) Squadron can be traced back to 501 (City of Bristol) Squadron. It was originally formed on 14 June 1929, with regular and reserve personnel, as a special reserve squadron and flew the DH.9A as a day-bomber unit. In 1930, it changed its name to 501 (County of Gloucester) Sqn and converted to the Wapiti. These were replaced by the Wallace in 1933 and, in May 1936, it was transferred to the Auxiliary Air Force. Harts were delivered in July and then Hinds in March 1938. From December, it changed to Hurricanes for the fighter role. It deployed to France, before returning to take its part in the Battle of Britain.

In July 1940, 501Sqn moved briefly to Middle Wallop with its Hurricanes and, having been located at Gravesend, Kenley and Filton, re-equipped with Spitfires at

Colerne in May 1941. In October 1942, it moved to Northern Ireland, returning to southern England in April 1943 and operating from a number of bases, including Hawkinge and Manston, from where it operated Tempests from August 1944. It disbanded at Hunsdon in April 1945.

In May 1946, 501Sqn was re-formed at Filton, with its Spitfires arriving a few months later. These were replaced by the Vampire in November 1948, which it operated until it disbanded again in March 1957.

In 1982, 501 (County of Gloucester) Sqn, R (Aux) AF was re-formed as 2624 (County of Oxford) Sqn, to provide ground defence for Brize Norton as a regiment unit and, later, assigned to RAF Germany for Harrier support.

On 1 April 1998, the squadron was re-roled to support the Air Transport and Air-to-Air Refuelling (AT&AAR) force. During this time they included a Flight comprising Hercules C.1K aircrew.

In October 1999, the squadron re-roled again to operations support at Brize Norton. On 1 May 1999, the squadron was re-numbered 501Sqn.

The current role of 501Sqn is to assist station operations, enabling it to continue operating in all situations. It also can provide specialist support, as required, for contingency force, peacekeeping, humanitarian or disaster relief operations. In February 2003, the squadron was mobilized for Operation *Telic*, seeing personnel deployed to a number of locations initially and then assisting in the security at Basra Airport. In April 2004, the squadron came under the command of 4 FP Wing HQ.

No. 501 (County of Gloucester) Squadron, R Aux AF, operates from its base at Brize Norton.

No. 504 (County of Nottingham) Squadron, R Aux AF

RAF Cottesmore
2 Group
Strike Command
Role: Operations Support
Motto: *Vindicat in Ventis* – It avenges in the wind

On 26 March 1928, 504 (County of Nottingham) Special Reserve Squadron, was formed at Hucknall with the Horsley. These were operated as day bombers, until

A gunner of 603(City of Edinburgh)Sqn checks the NBC sensors to ensure that no toxic traces have been detected. Crown Copyright

replaced by the Wallace in February 1935, followed by the Hind from May 1937.

In May 1936, 504Sqn became a part of the Auxiliary AF and in August 1936 became the first Auxiliary unit to become an active fighter squadron within the RAF. It was designated a fighter unit in October 1938, although it took until March for Hurricanes to arrive. It operated from Digby and Debden, prior to a short deployment to France in May 1940. The following month, it guarded Scapa Flow from Wick, before joining the Battle of Britain from Hendon in September. Having re-equipped with Spitfires, it later undertook offensive sweeps, before moving to Northern Ireland in August 1941, Middle Wallop in October 1942 and returning to Scotland in September 1943. It moved south again during preparations for Operation *Overlord*. By March 1945, it had moved to Colerne and was converting to the Meteor but, in August, it was disbanded, when it was re-numbered 245Sqn.

In May 1946, 504Sqn was re-formed at Syerston with trainers but, in April, it converted to Mosquitos and re-equipped with Spitfires in May 1948. In October 1948, it received Meteors again, but was disbanded in March 1957.

The Offensive Support Role Support Squadron (OSRSS) was formed at Cottesmore on 1 January 1998 and renamed 504 (County of Nottingham) Squadron on 1 October 1999, although wasn't officially reformed until a year later.

The role of 501Sqn is to provide a survive-to-operate capability for the RAF and multi-trade support to Joint Force Harrier operations, during contingency force, peacekeeping, humanitarian or disaster relief operations. From April 2004, it comes under the command of 1 FP Wing HQ.

No. 504 (County of Nottingham) Squadron is based at Cottesmore.

No. 600 (City of London) Squadron, R Aux AF

RAF Northolt
2 Group
Strike Command
Role: HQ Augmentation
Motto: *Praeter sescentos* – More than six hundred

On 14 October 1925, 600 (City of London) Sqn was formed at Northolt as a bomber squadron, with the DH.9 and Avro 504K. These were replaced by

Wapitis in August 1929 and then Harts in January 1935, before Demons were operate in the fighter role from February 1937. In January 1939, it re-equipped with the Blenheim and, with these, flew its first mission in May 1940. Unfortunately, the squadron lost five of its six aircraft to Bf.110s, with seven aircrew killed. Shortly after, the squadron converted to night-fighters with Beaufighters and became one of the first to operate Airborne Intercept (AI) radar.

It was deployed to North Africa in November 1942, then Malta in June 1943 and Italy in September. It converted to Mosquitos in January 1945 and was disbanded in August, having shot down more aircraft than any other Allied night-fighter squadron.

It was re-formed in May 1946 at Biggin Hill with Spitfires, then received Meteors in March 1950, but disbanded again in 1957.

On 1 October 1999, 600Sqn was re-formed at Northolt by the re-naming of 1 and 3 Maritime Headquarters Unit, which had formed in 1959 to support maritime aircraft and whose duties were expanding.

The current role of 600Sqn is to provide trained personnel for RAF and Joint Headquarters worldwide. These include intelligence, flight operations, fighter control, communications, supply, MT and admin.

No. 600 (City of London) Squadron, R Aux AF, is based at Northolt.

No. 603 (City of Edinburgh) Squadron, R Aux AF

Edinburgh
2 Group
Strike Command
Role: Operations Support
Motto: *Gin Ye Daur* – If you dare

Formed at Turnhouse on 14 October 1925, 603 (City of Edinburgh) Sqn was equipped as a light-bomber squadron, initially with DH.9As and then Wapitis in 1930 and Harts in 1934. In 1938, its role was changed to fighter while still flying the Hind and it re-equipped with the Gladiator from March 1939, prior to taking delivery of the Spitfire in September 1939. In October, 603Sqn intercepted the first German raid, during which it became the first squadron to shoot down a Luftwaffe aircraft – an He.111 – over British soil.

While operating from Hornchurch in September 1940, Pilot Officer Caister had been involved in close aerial-combat and, although probably exhausted, managed a perfect landing. The bad news was that this was a Luftwaffe airfield in Northern France. Unfortunately, the disorientated pilot had presented the Germans with their first airworthy Spitfire. Caister was not the only pilot to make this mistake, with a number of Luftwaffe and RAF aircraft being captured in similar circumstances. An encounter was also made with Italian AF CR.42s, during which a number were shot down, resulting in their not appearing over the UK again.

In December 1940, it returned to Scotland and then came back several times, until April 1942, when 603Sqn was deployed to defend Malta along with 601Sqn, having forty-seven Spitfires

between them. In August, the surviving aircraft were absorbed into 229Sqn. The groundcrew had already moved to Cyprus, where they operated as a servicing unit. In February 1943, 603 was re-activated in Egypt with Beaufighters and operated around Italy and along the North African coast. In January 1945, 603 re-appeared in the UK with the re-numbering of 229Sqn with Spitfires at Coltishall. One of the tasks flown included divebombing V-2 launch sites. It then returned to Turnhouse in April and disbanded again in August 1945.

The squadron re-formed at Turnhouse in May 1946 with Spitfires, converting to Vampires in May 1951, which it temporarily operated from Leuchars while the runway was lengthened at Turnhouse. The demise of the auxiliary fighter squadrons resulted in 605Sqn disbanding in March 1957.

On 1 October 1999, 603Sqn was re-formed from 2 MHU, which had

previously been formed from 3602 (City of Edinburgh) Fighter Control Unit in 1959.

The current role of 603Sqn is survive to operate by providing force protection. The squadron also has a detachment to provide mission support, primarily for maritime forces. It comes under the control of 3 Force Protection Wing HQ.

No. 603 (City of Edinburgh) Squadron are based in Edinburgh and have a detachment at Kinloss.

No. 606 (Chiltern) Squadron, R Aux AF

RAF Benson
Joint Helicopter Command
Role: Helicopter Support
Motto: Steadfast in Support

On 1 October 1996, 606 (Chiltern) Sqn, R Aux AF was formed as the Helicopter Support Squadron (HSS) at Benson. Initially, this was formed to trial the concept of multi-traded Role Support

Gunners of 606(Chiltern)Sqn climb aboard a Puma to be airlifted to enable them to rapidly move to their objective. Crown Copyright

Squadrons (RSS). Having established its value, the HSS was re-named 606Sqn on 1 October 1999 and control transferred to the newly formed Joint Helicopter Command – a part of the army's HQ Land at Wilton.

The current role of 606Sqn is to provide trained personnel to augment and reinforce the Support Helicopter Force (SHF). This includes operations, transport, catering, general ground-engineering, helicopter handling and marshalling, as well as regiment trades.

No. 606 (Chiltern) Squadron is based at Benson.

No. 609 (West Riding) Squadron, R Aux AF

RAF Leeming
2 Group
Strike Command
Role: Operations Support
Motto: Tally Ho

On 10 February 1936, 609Sqn was formed at Yeadon with Harts. It re-equipped with Hinds in December 1937 and, although re-designated a fighter squadron in December 1938, did not begin to convert to Spitfires at Catterick until August 1939. It moved to Drem, where the first kill was a He.111. In 1940, it moved to Northolt, covering the evacuation of Dunkirk and then taking part in the Battle of Britain. From July 1940 until November, it was based at Middle Wallop. On 21 October 1940, it shot down a Ju.88 and became the first Spitfire squadron to shoot down 100 aircraft. The squadron moved to Biggin Hill in 1941 and, in April 1942, received Typhoons, enabling a steady increase in its close air-support operations against German targets. From mid-1944, this further increased with the use of rockets. It moved to Manston and then onto the continent, eventually reaching Wunstorf in Germany. The squadron disbanded in September 1945.

In May 1946, 609Sqn R Aux AF was re-formed at Yeadon with the Mosquito and began converting to Spitfires in April 1947. These were replaced by the Meteor F.8 in January 1951 at Church Fenton, before being disbanded in March 1957.

On 1 July 1998, 609 (West Riding) Sqn,

R Aux AF was originally re-formed as the Air Defence Support Squadron. It was re-named 609Sqn on 1 October 1999, although the actual reforming parade didn't take place until November the following year.

The current role of 609Sqn is survive to operate, with personnel trained in a number of trade specializations to provide support on exercises or operations at home or abroad. It comes under the control of 2 Force Protection Wing HQ.

No. 609 (West Riding) Squadron, R Aux AF, is based at Leeming.

No. 612 (County of Aberdeen) Squadron, R Aux AF

RAF Leuchars
2 Group
Strike Command
Role: Surgical support
Motto: *Vigilando custodimus* – We stand guard by vigilance

On 16 June 1937, 612 (County of Aberdeen) Sqn, Auxiliary Air Force was formed as an army co-operation unit at Dyce with Tutors. These were replaced with Hectors by the end of the year and then Ansons, in November 1938.

The squadron spent much of the war flying anti-submarine patrols with Whitleys and then Wellingtons, before disbanding at Langham in July 1945.

It re-formed in May 1946 with Spitfires at Dyce and converted to Vampires, before being disbanded again in March 1957.

The Air Transportable Surgical Squadron (Designate) was formed on 1 January 1997, becoming independent at Leuchars in April, and was re-numbered 612Sqn on 1 October 1999. The squadron comprises two Air Transportable Surgical Teams, each of which can accommodate twenty-five beds, and are capable of holding patients, including two intensive treatment, for up to forty-eight hours until stabilized, before being medevaced out of theatre.

The current role of 612Sqn is to provide surgical and medical support to any Aeromedical Evacuation units or

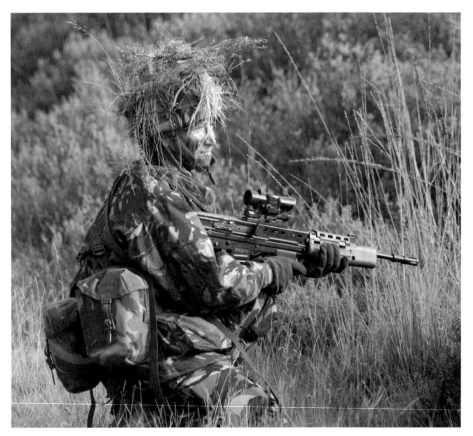

A female Gunner of 609(West Riding)Sqn armed with an SA80 rifle crouches to check for any movement during a patrol. Crown Copyright

Deployed Operating Base Medical Centres, at air-heads where secondary care support is required. It was deployed to Oman for *Saif Sareea II* and, during this exercise, treated over 100 patients. It has also provided volunteers for operations in Kosovo and Iraq.

No. 612 (County of Aberdeen) Squadron is based at Leuchars.

No. 2503 (County of Lincoln) Squadron, R Aux AF Regiment

RAF Waddington
2 Group
Strike Command
Role: Ground support
Motto: *Libertas Coelorum et Agrorum* – Freedom of the
ground for control of the air

In 1979, 2503 (County of Lincoln) Sqn, R. Aux AF was formed at Scampton to assist with the ground defence of the Vulcans based at there. As the fleet was retired, 2503Sqn moved to Waddington, in preparation for the arrival of the Nimrod AEW. When this was cancelled, 2503Sqn moved temporarily to Coningsby, to assist in protecting the Tornado until the arrival of the Sentry AEW.1.

In view of the ending of the Cold War and the reduction of threat to UK bases, 2503Sqn have seen their role expanded to support the RAF Regiment deployed overseas.

The current role of 2503Sqn is to provide a sustainment capability to the regular RAF Regt Field Squadrons. It comes under the control of 2 Force Protection Wing HQ.

No. 2503 (County of Lincoln) Squadron, R Aux AF is based at Waddington.

No, 2620 (County of Norfolk) Squadron, R Aux AF Regiment

RAF Marham
2 Group
Strike Command
Role: Ground support
Motto: *Cum Patria Mea Vocat* – When my country calls

On 1 March 1983, 2620 (County of Norfolk) Sqn, R Aux AF was formed at

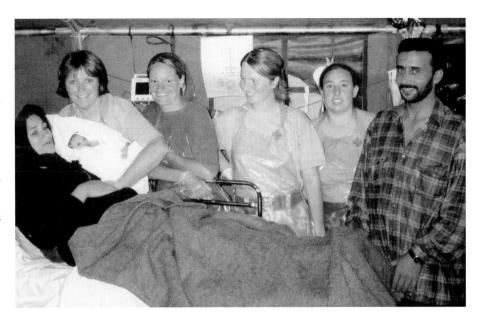

ABOVE: Medical staff from 612(County of Aberdeen)Sqn assist an Iraqi mother in the birth of her baby. Crown Copyright

BELOW: A section commander of 2503(County of Lincoln)Sqn directing one of his gunners. Crown Copyright

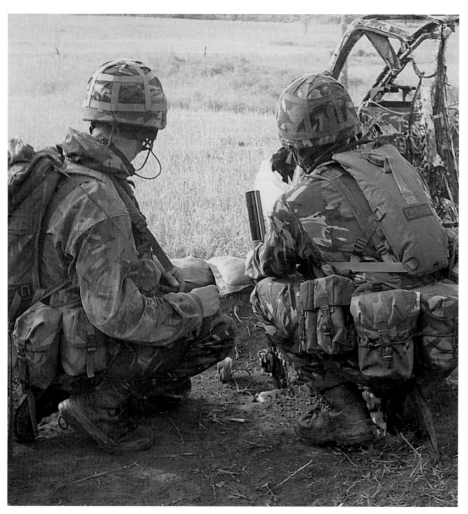

Gunners from 2620(County of Norfolk)Sqn take part in a US Army training exercise at Fort Drum near New York. Crown Copyright

Marham to provide ground-force defence of the station.

In January 1999, the squadron re-roled to become an operations support squadron and has trained personnel to augment regular force-protection resources. Personnel are also trained in a branch or trade, to enable them to provide an additional secondary peacetime or crisis role.

During Operation *Telic* 2620Sqn was mobilized and personnel fulfilled both their primary and secondary roles. On returning home they reverted to the field squadron role. From April 2004, they came under the control of 1 FP Wing HQ.

The current role of 2620Sqn is sustainment for the RAF Regiment Field Squadrons and it comes under the control of 1 Force Protection Wing HQ.

No. 2620 (County of Norfolk) Squadron, R Aux AF is based at Marham.

No. 2622 (Highland) Squadron, R Aux AF Regiment

RAF Lossiemouth
2 Group
Strike Command
Role: Ground support
Motto: *Seasaidh Sinn Ar Tis* – We stand our ground

In 1979, 2622 (Highland) Sqn, R Aux AF Regiment was formed at Lossiemouth to assist in providing the ground defence for the airfield.

In February 2003, 2622 (H) Sqn were mobilized for the first time and were deployed on Operation *Telic*, where they provided additional manpower for 15, 26, 34 and 51Sqn of the RAF Regt, as well as the STOs.

The current role of 2622Sqn is to provide a sustainment capability to the regular RAF Regt Field Squadrons and it comes under the control of 3 Force Protection Wing HQ.

No. 2622 (Highland) Squadron, R Aux AF, is based at Lossiemouth.

No. 2623 (East Anglian) Squadron, R Aux AF Regiment

RAF Honington
2 Group
Strike Command
Role: NBC Support
Motto: *Gebeorgan Ond Werian* – Protect and defend

In 1979, 2623 (East Anglian) Sqn, R Aux AF Regiment was formed to provide ground defence for Honington in time of war.

In 1994, the squadron was disbanded, but re-formed again the following year with a new training role. As such, it became the central training unit for all the Auxiliary Regiment squadrons until 1997, when this was undertaken by the Training Wing at the RAF Regiment Depot. As a result, 2623Sqn was suspended.

The Strategic Defence Review (SDR) highlighted a need to provide sustainment personnel who were trained to operate the Rapier Field Standard 'C' (FSC). As a consequence, 2623Sqn was re-roled in 1998, undertook recruiting and training and became operational on 1 April 2002. On 1 April 2004, the squadron re-roled again and is now a Biological Detection unit, primarily to augment the JNBC Regiment.

No. 2623 (East Anglian) Squadron is based at Honington.

No. 2625 (County of Cornwall) Squadron, R Aux AF Regiment

RAF St Mawgan
2 Group
Strike Command
Role: Ground support
Motto: *Onen Hag Ol* – One and all

On 1 November 1982, 2625 (County of Cornwall) Sqn, R Aux AF Regiment was formed to assist in the ground defence of St Mawgan, which then was operating Nimrod MR.1s.

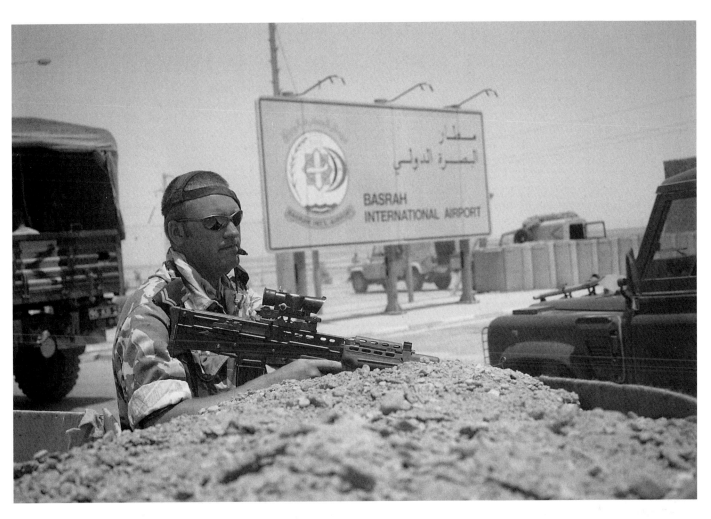

ABOVE: **A 2622 (Highland) Sqn gunner on security duty at the entrance to Basrah Airport.**

RIGHT: **Dressed in Ghille suits, enabling them to blend into the natural surroundings, these gunners from 2625(County of Cornwall)Sqn are equipped with sniper rifles and sensors. Crown Copyright**

With operational tasking for the regular services over the last few years steadily increasing, opportunities for reservists to assist are increasing. During 2001, personnel from 2625Sqn were deployed to Sierra Leone, Kuwait, the Falkland Islands and Kosovo.

The current role of 2625Sqn is to provide a sustainment capability to the regular RAF Regt Field Squadrons. It comes under the control of 4 Force Protection Wing HQ.

No. 2625 (County of Cornwall) Sqn is based at St Mawgan.

No. 4624 (County of Oxford) Movements Squadron, R Aux AF

RAF Brize Norton
2 Group
Strike Command
Role: Air Movements
Motto: Ready to move

In 1982, 4624 (County of Oxford) Movements Squadron, R Aux AF was formed at Brize Norton to provide support to the RAF's movements organization in the UK or overseas in time of emergency.

When it was allocated the number 4624, the squadron adopted the 624Sqn Association. The origins of 624Sqn can be traced back to 1575 Flight, which was formed on 28 May 1943 at Tempsford for Special Operations Executive duties. It was equipped with Halifax and Venturas and, in June, moved to Maison Blanche in North Africa. Later that month, it commenced operations over Corsica, Sardinia and Italy. It was disbanded when the Flight became 624Sqn in September 1943, while based at Blida in North Africa, and continued in its special-duties role. Stirlings were added in July 1944, before being disbanded in September 1944. It was re-formed in December 1944 with Walrus at Grottaglie and a couple of Hurricanes and Ansons were added in spring 1945, but then finally disbanded in November 1945.

Within a year of forming, three flights of 4624 (County of Oxford) Movements Squadron had been established, trained and were already being deployed. Besides assisting the movements personnel at Brize Norton and nearby Lyneham, because of the importance of air transport for exercises and operations, personnel from the squadron have been and still are increasingly required for tasks all over the world. In 1987, it was declared fully operational with six flights.

In January 1991, the squadron was mobilized for Operation *Granby* (Gulf War) and personnel were deployed to a number of locations in the UK, as well as Wildenrath, Akrotiri and others with UKMAMS. Many remained mobilized for a lengthy period after the war ended, to assist in the recovery of troops and equipment back to their bases.

As a result of the increased tasking, the squadron was increased in size by 40 per cent in 1999. Once again, the squadron was mobilized, due to the Balkan crisis, resulting in a third of the operational Flights serving for six months, and again during operations in Afghanistan, plus Operation *Telic*, when 128 members were called up.

The current role of 4624Sqn remains to provide movements support to allied operations worldwide.

No. 4624Sqn, R Aux AF is based at Brize Norton.

No. 4626 (County of Wiltshire) Aeromedical Evacuation Squadron, R Aux AF

RAF Lyneham
2 Group
Strike Command
Role: Aeromedical Evacuation
Motto: *Tute Domum* – Safely home

On 9 September 1983, 4626 (County of Wiltshire) Sqn, R Aux AF was originally formed at Princess Alexandra Hospital, Wroughton. It moved to Hullavington in 1986, before arriving at Lyneham in May 1993.

The squadron has been involved in bringing thousands of personnel home from locations all over the world, during which they have travelled millions of miles. They were the first reserve unit to be mobilized since 1945, when they were called for active service in the Gulf in January 1991. During that time, they operated aero-

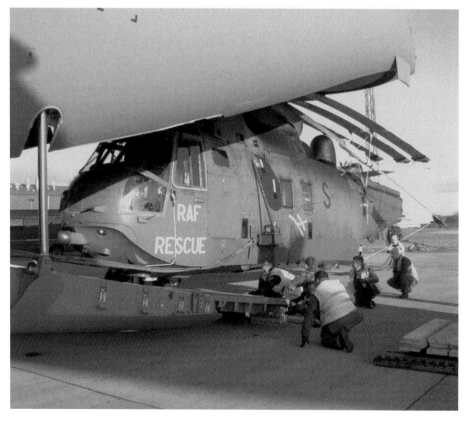

Members of 4624 (County of Oxford) Movements Squadron unloading a 78Sqn Sea King brought back from the Falklands in a C-17. Crown Copyright

medical facilities at Riyadh, Al Jubail, Dhahran and Muharraq. During *Saif Sareea* in Oman in 2001, some 700 casualties were flown home in a thirteen-week period, including one flight with forty-two patients – the largest peacetime airlift.

The current role is to operate in support of the RAF's Tactical and Strategic aeromedical evacuation of casualties across the spectrum of military operations. No. 4626 (County of Wiltshire) Squadron is based at Lyneham.

No. 7006 (VR) Intelligence Squadron, R Aux AF

RAF Waddington
2 Group
Strike Command
Role: Intelligence support
Motto: *Florebo Quocumque Ferar* – Flourish wherever we are planted

No. 7006 Flight had existed during the 1940s and early 1950s, but records appear to be missing and their details cannot be included.

On 1 April 1986, 7006 (VR) Intelligence Squadron, R. Aux. AF was reformed at High Wycombe as 7006 (VR) Flight. This was as the result of awareness by the RAF Board that there were insufficient trained intelligence personnel. As a consequence, regular and VR personnel from other trades were being used to fill the posts. It was formed to try to create an improved structure for the intelligence branch and, as a consequence, it was decided to form a new RAF VR flight for this role. Initial 7006Sqn personnel were drawn from 7010 (Photograph Interpretation) Flight at Wyton and 7630 (Interrogation) Flight at Ashford.

In April 1997, 7006 Flight changed to its current title as a result of the merger of the two reserve forces. Squadron personnel operated in support of various units during 1999, partly as a consequence of events in Kosovo.

In 2000, following a reorganization of the intelligence reserves, 7006 Flight reported to the HQ Intelligence Reserves, located within the AWC at Waddington in conjunction with 7010 and 7630Sqn. In October 2000, it moved from High Wycombe to Waddington.

The current role of 7006Sqn is to provide trained intelligence personnel to support the RAF intelligence organization in times of national crisis or war.

No. 7006 (VR) Intelligence Squadron, R Aux AF is based at Waddington.

No. 7010 (VR) Photographic Interpretation Squadron, R Aux AF

RAF Waddington
2 Group
Strike Command
Role: Reconnaissance support
Motto: *Vocati Veniemus* – When summoned we shall be there

No. 7010 (VR) Photographic Interpretation Squadron, R Aux AF was originally formed as 7010 RAFVR in April 1953. It had over 500 officers and its role was to exploit strategic imagery at the Joint Air Reconnaissance Intelligence Centre (JARIC), then located at Nuneham Park.

In 1965, the Flight became the first reserve unit to augment RAF Germany and it was also the first time that it had been used for tactical Imagery Analysis (IA).

In 1992, 7101 Flight received its first operational call-out, which was in support of Operation *Warden*. It became a squadron in April 1997.

Although it still provides support for JARIC, the role of the squadron has moved towards supporting tactical reconnaissance with the Jaguars and Tornados. It reports to the HQ Intelligence Reserves, which are located within the AWC at Waddington.

The current role of 7010Sqn is to provide operational Imagery Analysis (IA) support to the RAF.

No. 7010 (VR) Photographic Interpretation Squadron, R Aux AF, is based at Waddington.

No. 7630 (VR) Squadron, R Aux AF

DISC Chicksands
2 Group
Strike Command
Role: Intelligence support
Motto: Persevere

No. 7630 (VR) Sqn, R Aux AF was originally formed around 1956. Its role was

to provide a pool of linguists for intelligence duties. At that time, all the members were Russian speakers. Later that year, the Flight moved to the Intelligence Corps HQ at Maresfield and, later, to Ashford.

From 1972, the unit utilised non-linguists to provide officers with intelligence analysis and briefings. These were subsequently transferred, to join the newly formed 7006 Flight.

Deployment opportunities reduced as British Forces withdrew from various Middle East and Far East locations, so officers' work with other members of NATO increased.

During the Gulf War, officers formed part of the Defence Debriefing Team that interviewed evacuees from Kuwait. Subsequently, some officers deployed to the former Yugoslavia and operated in Bosnia and Kosovo.

No. 7630Sqn also provide training for other units by helping to simulate unfriendly forces for 'captured' personnel.

Having amalgamated into the R Aux AF in April 1997, the unit moved to Chicksands, where it operates within the Defence Intelligence and Security Centre (DISC), which formed in October 1996. It reports to the HQ Intelligence Reserves, which are located within the AWC at Waddington.

The current role of 7630Sqn is to gather information of intelligence value by debriefing subjects in their own language.

No. 7630 (VR) Sqn, R Aux AF, is based at Waddington.

No. 7644 (VR) Squadron, R Aux AF

RAF High Wycombe
2 Group
Strike Command
Role: Communications support
Motto: *Verité à jamais* – The truth always

No. 7644 (VR) Sqn, R Aux AF was formed in 1981. However, its origins date back to just before the Second World War, when it was decided that it was going to be vital to be able to collect news about the RAF. Journalists seemed the best personnel and so a number were recruited into the RAF VR to help allay service fears. By 1940, this had expanded to include servicemen and women who would tell

LEFT: An officer from 7630(VR)Sqn continues with his task, despite having donned his NBC respirator following an alert alarm. Crown Copyright

BELOW: Members of 7644(VR)Sqn interview a Tornado pilot to provide TV footage for use by national broadcast media. Crown Copyright

their own story, thus helping to keep the public informed.

The value of these Public Relations (PR) specialists had been proven and so a small number were maintained as a PR element of 7802 Flight, RAFVR. They later transferred to 7630 Flight, before being established as 7644 Flight in 1981, becoming part of the R Aux AF in 1997.

Members of the PR reserve have deployed on most RAF and allied operations all over the world. During the Gulf War, the whole of the unit volunteered and were deployed in theatre.

In 2000, the unit became an asset of the Directorate of Corporate Communications (DCC) at Strike Command. Due to new, varied tasking, a substantial recruiting drive resulted in their being brought up to full strength. The unit moved from Waddington to Halton later that year, although the adjutant remained within the DCC at Strike.

The role of 7644 (VR) Sqn is to provide PR support to RAF and NATO forces worldwide in peace and war.

No. 7644 (VR) Sqn is based at Halton.

Mobile Meteorological Unit (RAF Reserve)

RAF Benson
2 Group
Strike Command
Role: Meteorological support
Motto: Tomorrow's weather today

The history of the Mobile Meteorological Unit (MMU) can be traced back to the First World War, when Meteorological Office personnel served in uniform to provide squadron with weather forecasts. During the 1960s, these forecasts were provided from fixed sites, which were not always near to squadrons, especially when on exercise or on deployment. With weather playing a more important part in flight planning, the RAF tasked the Met Office with providing on-site advice for commanders in the field.

In September 1962, a Met Office forecaster from Odiham was commissioned into the RAF Volunteer Reserve for fourteen days to accompany an exercise in Greece. This proved to be successful and resulted in the MMU being formed.

The withdrawal from the Far and Middle East and the majority of operations

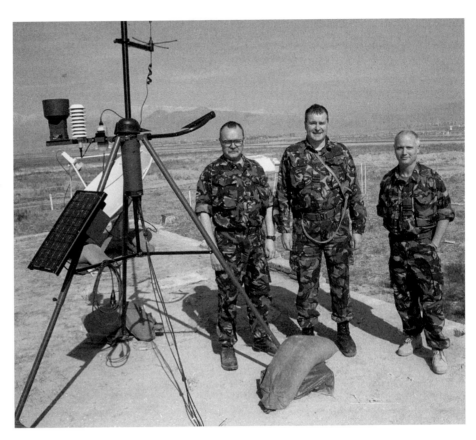

A Mobile Meteorological Unit team at Kabul provide aircrews with full weather-briefings. Their role is to deploy to austere locations and assist aircrew with good met-forecasting to incorporate in their flight plans.

within the NATO boundaries meant that the MMU was only occasionally required. This all changed when the Argentinians invaded the Falklands. An MMU team was deployed on Operation *Corporate* and provided a valuable tool to commanders, enabling them to make maximum use of their limited resources. More recently, the MMU has been deployed to the Middle East and Balkans, with teams in Afghanistan, Bosnia and Iraq.

The Mobile Meteorological Unit is based at Benson.

Provost Squadron, R Aux AF

RAF Henlow
2 Group
Strike Command
Role: Tactical Provost Wing
Motto: Without fear or favour

The Provost Sqn, R Aux AF was formed on 1 April 2000 as 3Sqn within the Tactical Provost Wing, to provide support

for the regular units on deployed operations.

As a new unit, the squadron is still recruiting and training personnel and anticipates being declared operational in April 2005.

The role of the squadron includes the policing of the lines of communication (LOC-P), air transport security (ATSy) and specialist security search, and the policing of deployed military populations.

The Provost Squadron, R Aux AF, is based at Henlow.

No. 1359 Flight, R Aux AF

RAF Lyneham
2 Group
Strike Command
Role: Hercules aircrew

On 1 December 1945, 1359 Flight was formed at Lyneham. It was equipped with Lancastrians and Yorks to replace the Northolt-based VIP Flight, which had

A Corporal of the Provost Squadron on a range practising firing her 9mm Browning pistol. Crown Copyright

A Hercules reserve aircrew of 1359 Flight at work in his office. Crown Copyright

been disbanded several months previously. It is believed to have operated C-54 Skymasters for a short while, prior to their being returned to the USA at the end of the Lend Lease arrangement. It moved to Bassingbourn in February 1946 and, the following month, broke the flight record to New Zealand with two Lancastrians. In July, it was absorbed into 24Sqn, along with its five Yorks, five Lancastrians and twelve Dakotas.

Following the disbanding of 57 (R) Sqn in November 2001, the Hercules Reservist Aircrew (HRA) Flight was re-named 1359 Flight. It then became embedded within 70Sqn, sharing its building and facilities.

The role of 1359 Flight is to provide the RAF with a number of volunteer Hercules aircrew, which it achieves by recruiting retired Hercules crews. Ideally, they will have just retired and will, therefore, hold current qualifications. Most members are also currently employed by airlines, requiring reduced continuation training on the Hercules.

The initial plan for the Flight was to provide a number of crews sufficiently trained to enable them to be called up in times of crisis and war. This was subsequently broadened to include a 'peacetime utility'. As a result, the Flight are able to provide the squadrons with a number of Limited Combat Ready (LCR) and Combat Ready (CR) crews. The LCR crews requiring minimal burst-training before squadron tasking and the CR maintaining all their qualifications to enable availability at short notice. Such has been the tasking for the 1359 Flight over the last few years, that all crews are CR and it is anticipated that some further recruiting will be made before long for the 'J' model. Recently, members of the Flight have been called out on Operations in Afghanistan and Iraq, as well as other operations in the Middle East and Africa.

No. 1359 Flight is based at Lyneham and have no aircraft of their own, but are tasked in support of Lyneham flight operations.

RAF Regiment

2 Group
Strike Command
Role: Ground defence
Motto: *Per Ardua* – Through adversity

A recommendation in November 1941, by the Committee on Airfield Defence, that the RAF should have its own airfield defence force resulted in the formation of the RAF Regiment on 1 February 1942 at Belton Park near Grantham, where training immediately commenced. Until then the RAF had substantially relied on assistance from the army. Now it was to have a protection force under its own control, in much the same way as the Royal Navy have the Royal Marines. In theory, the services should be able to protect each other but, during the Second World War, the army was unable to provide sufficient manpower to adequately protect RAF installations. That this was necessary was exemplified by the losses suffered in Crete. Prior to this, the RAF had armoured-car companies that were formed during the 1920s for the very same role, but they were insufficient in numbers during the Second World War. They were incorporated into the RAF Regiment in 1946.

As the Second World War progressed, the RAF Regiment expanded its role and even took part in some operations, such as Monte Casino in 1943. They were at Juno beach on D-Day+1 and took control of captured airfields, removing mines and preparing them for use by Allied aircraft.

In 1944, the RAF Regiment was active in the Far East, where they were parachuted into battle. As in Europe, they undertook the capture and restoration of airfields for the Allies. By the end of the war, the RAF Regiment strength was over 55,000.

With the war over, the RAF Regiment's role continued, with substantial forces in Malaya, Iraq and Aden and, to a lesser extent, in Palestine and Suez, plus all the other 'exposed' airfields operated from by the RAF. More recently, these have included Northern Ireland, Cyprus, the Falklands and, very recently, the former Yugoslavia, Kuwait, Afghanistan and Kuwait again, in 2003.

Today, the RAF Regiment provide a specialist ground-warfare capability for the RAF, providing defence for its airfields and aircraft and maintaining a Survive-To-Operate/Force Protection capability. While the Field Squadrons included armoured vehicles during the 1980s, these have been dispensed with and they now rely on fast manoeuvrability with Land Rovers. This force protection includes an NBC detection capability, SAMs with the Rapier (FSC), as well as field squadrons equipped with a range of weapons and surveillance equipment. One squadron (2Sqn) retains a parachute capability and, in October 2003, achieved its jungle qualification.

During Operation *Telic*, a new composite RAF Regiment was formed that, apart from three officers, was made up with auxiliaries. No. 1 Composite Resident Field Squadron (1 CRFS) was formed to provide security of the British area of responsibility at Ali Al Salem, when all other field force units were deployed elsewhere. Personnel were taken from nine regiments and a section was later moved up to Basra.

The regiment also have their own band – the Band of the RAF Regiment. It was formed in 1942 from the Coastal Command Band at Belton Park and moved to Catterick in 1946. It then spent a short period at Uxbridge from 1994, before spending three years at Northolt, then returning to Uxbridge. It is now based at Cranwell. Besides their musical role, which has taken them around the world, the musicians have a medical-support role and were deployed for this during Operation *Granby*.

Recruit training is undertaken by Training Wing at Honington. Officers undergo the initial officer training at Cranwell before starting their regiment training at Honington. This lasts for six months and covers a broad range of foundation skills, including tactics and weapon handling, before they join a squadron. For regiment gunners, the course lasts eighteen weeks, during which a substantial amount of fitness training is conducted. It also includes training on fieldcraft, map reading, radio procedure, tactics and weapons.

The RAF Regiment currently comprises:

1 Squadron – Field squadron – St Mawgan
2 Squadron – Field squadron (parachute trained) – Honington
3 Squadron – Field squadron – Aldergrove
15 Squadron – Rapier FSC squadron – Honington
16 Squadron – Rapier FSC squadron – Honington
26 Squadron – Rapier FSC squadron – Waddington

The basic role of the RAF Regt gunners is to provide airfield defence to prevent enemy troops or terrorists getting anywhere near a potential target. Crown Copyright

27 Squadron – RAF element of Joint NBC Regiment – Honington

34 Squadron – Field squadron – Leeming

37 Squadron – Rapier FSC squadron – Wittering

51 Squadron – Field squadron – Lossiemouth

Queens Colour Squadron/63 Squadron – Ceremonial/Field squadron – Uxbridge

Ground Based Air Defence Force HQ – Honington

Force Protection Centre – STO training – Honington

1 RAF Force Protection Wing HQ – Wittering

2 RAF Force Protection Wing HQ – Leeming

3 RAF Force Protection Wing HQ – Marham

4 RAF Force Protection Wing HQ – Lyneham

Joint Rapier Training Unit – Honington

No 2503Sqn, R Aux AF – Waddington

No 2620 (County of Norfolk) Sqn R Aux AF Regt – Marham

No 2622 (Highland) Sqn, R Aux AF Regt – Lossiemouth

No 2623 (East Anglian) Sqn, R Aux AF Regt – Honington

No 2625 (County of Cornwall) Sqn, R Aux AF Regt – St Mawgan

In 2004 it was announced that the armed forces would undergo a restructuring. Due to their not having fired a missile in anger and the perceived reduction of an enemy air-threat, RAF Rapier SAMs would be withdrawn, commencing in 2005 and completed by 2008. As a result, the four GBAD units would be disbanded. Of the current total of forty-eight fire units, twenty-four will remain, but these would be operated by the army under a new Joint HQ within the RAF Command Structure.

No. 1 Squadron, RAF Regiment

RAF St Mawgan

2 Group

Strike Command

Role: Ground defence

Motto: *Ar-His Sur-Ris* – Swiftly suddenly

The origins of 1Sqn RAF Regiment can be directly traced back to 1 Armoured Car Company (1 ACC), which was formed at Heliopolis, Egypt on 19 December 1921.

This company was formed to assist the air elements in the enforcing of law and order in the British-mandated territories of Mesopotamia, Palestine, Transjordan and Egypt, after the collapse of the Ottoman/Turkish Empire. They were equipped with Rolls Royce Type A armoured cars, which were nicknamed 'tin trams'.

No. 1 ACC quickly grew, to the extent that the sections became companies in their own right. Unfortunately, a result of its success was that these five other companies, which were given operational taskings, were undermanned and under-equipped. The solution was to disband 1 ACC in December 1923 and distribute its assets across these other companies.

A nucleus of 1 ACC was retained to form 1 Armoured Car Wing HQ. During the rest of the 1920s, the Wing struggled to separate the various feuding tribes across the region. By February 1930, they had managed to achieve the surrender of all the hostile elements, in co-operation with the flying units.

With their task achieved, the Wing was reduced in size and re-named 1 ACC in April 1930. It continued its role in Iraq and achieved a peace treaty with rebels in the north-east in 1931. In 1936, troubles were brewing in Palestine with the settlement of Jews and, in May, two sections deployed to assist British Army forces trying to quell rioting. In October, they were recalled to Iraq, where they continued patrolling.

Following the outbreak of war, Germany attempted to gain control of Iraq with its oil fields and sever the British route to India and the Far East. The airfield at Habbaniya was surrounded in April 1941. The surrounding Iraqi force, of some 9,000 men, was fought off by 1 ACC (106 men) plus aircraft from 4 SFTS, 1,000 RAF personnel and six companies of levies (1,000 local men). Assisted by the Kings Own Royal Regiment, 1 ACC and one company of levies followed the retreating Iraqi Army to Sin El Dibban, where they captured 500, as well as substantial amounts of equipment. A Section of 2 ACC were despatched from Egypt and, en route, Luftwaffe He 111s began to attack Habbaniya from Fellujah. Subsequently, a successful attack was made on Fellujah and an unsuccessful German counter-attack resulted in some 300 more prisoners taken by the ACCs and levies. This resulted in an armistice being agreed, in May 1931, that halted the Nazi forces entering the

region, which could otherwise have had disastrous consequences.

In October 1941, 1 ACC detachments were deployed to Helwan, Egypt and the Western Desert and advanced across to Tunisia, protecting advanced landing-grounds. Once Rommel's forces had surrendered, 1 ACC returned to Egypt.

On 3 October 1946, 1 ACC became part of the RAF Regiment and was merged into 2701Sqn at Quastina, Palestine. In April 1941, 2701Sqn had been formed as 701Sqn, then re-numbered 2701 in February 1942. It provided LAA defence in London, before advancing through Europe. It was re-numbered as 1 (Armoured Car) Squadron, RAF Regiment in February 1947, served in Palestine and was disbanded in December 1947.

In March 1948, 1 (AC) Sqn re-formed in Germany by the re-numbering of 4 (AC) Sqn at Sunden. It moved to Lübeck in February, where it assisted in loading during the Berlin Airlift. In August 1949, it moved on to Luneberg.

October 1951 saw it at Wunstorf, re-equipped with the Humber armoured car, but then it lost these in December 1953, when it changed role and became 1 (Field) Sqn. In December 1955, it was re-named 1 (Light Anti-Aircraft) Squadron and operated L40/70 Bofors Guns, until disbanded in September 1957.

In June 1958, 62 (F) Sqn was re-numbered 1 (F) Sqn while serving at El Adem, Libya. In addition to airfield defence, it was also involved in minefield clearance, as well as assisting in SAR operations and running desert survival and navigation courses. In July 1961, it was deployed to RAAF Butterworth, Malaysia. Again, it provided SAR support and one flight was parachute trained for this task. It also operated security detachments at Gan.

In November 1963, the role was changed to low-level air-defence and saw it based the UK for the first time, at Bicester. However, detachments were deployed to Aden, Muharraq and Hong Kong. It also assisted in the foot and mouth epidemic of 1967. In August 1970, the squadron moved to Laarbruch, Germany, where it reverted to a Field Squadron in 1974 and undertook a tour in Northern Ireland in 1979. In 1978, it changed to its original armoured-role with Ferrets, Saladins and Saracens. In February 1982, these were replaced with CVR (T) Scimitars, as well as Spartans, a

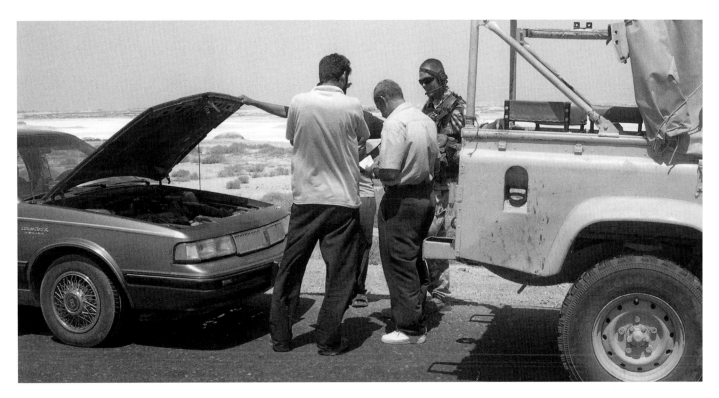

**A Gunner from 1Sqn, RAF Regt checking an Iraqi driver's car and papers at a VCP (Vehicle Check Point).
Crown Copyright**

Sultan and Samson, for a primary role of protecting the Harrier force.

In January 1991, 1Sqn was deployed to the Gulf, to provide protection for the SHF operating in Saudi Arabia and Bahrain, before advancing into Iraq to support the helicopters. It then returned to Laarbruch in March and, in November 1993, re-roled as a field squadron. It operated a detachment to Cyprus in December for internal security tasking and, in 1994, to Northern Ireland.

In January 1994, 1Sqn responded to a Dutch emergency request when nearby towns were in danger of flooding. Within hours, the squadron was deployed and, over eight days, laid 612,000 sandbags to provide a 6km protective perimeter around Arcen. Despite higher water than that which had previously flooded the town, the homes of 9,000 were protected, as a result a section of the wall was incorporated in the new flood defences and named 'The RAF Regiment Dyke'.

From June 1995 until November, 1Sqn were deployed to Ploč, Croatia to provide protection for SHF and 24 AMB. It then returned to the region in July 1997, as part of the SFOR peacekeeping force, providing internal security.

In January 1999, 1Sqn moved to St Mawgan and, in March, it deployed its first *roulement* to Ali Al Salem, Kuwait, where they provided protection for the British sector and subsequently the Kuwaiti sector. December 2000 saw the squadron return to Kuwait. Benefiting from the previous deployment, many personnel had learnt Arabic, which proved valuable in local relations and the gathering of intelligence. Having returned from Kuwait after a short break, they were then deployed to Macedonia at short notice. March 2002 saw part of the squadron deployed to Kabul for four months and then Ali Al Salem in December during the build up for Operation *Telic*. In April, it moved into Iraq – where it was originally formed. After securing the oilfields, US and local oilworkers were able to restore oil production, enabling valuable revenue to be earned. In May, the squadron returned home for a short break, before being tasked with providing security at the RIAT airshow.

As has been described, being declared to NATO as a Reaction Forces (Air) unit means that 1Sqn, RAF Regt can be deployed at short notice to secure a base, prior to deployment of NATO aircraft. In

April 2004, they came under the control of 4 FR Wing HQ.

No. 1Sqn, RAF Regiment is a Field Squadron based at St Mawgan.

No. 2 Squadron, RAF Regiment

RAF Honington
2 Group
Strike Command
Role: Ground defence
Motto: *Nunquam Non Paratus* – Always prepared

Originally formed as 2 Armoured Car Company (2 ACC) at Heliopolis, Egypt on 7 April 1922 with Rolls Royce armoured cars, this company was formed to assist in the enforcing of law and order, mainly in Transjordan, along with 1 ACC.

It initially had a reconnaissance role in North Africa at the start of the Second World War and, later, took part in the *Crusader* Offensive and the battle for El Alamein, where its role was to protect the forward landing-strips. During the advances on the German fortified Mareth Line, in April 1943, 2 ACC made use of their radios to direct Allied aircraft onto enemy targets, prior to their surrendering the following month. The company then

2Sqn, RAF Regt display just some of the weaponry that they have gathered while on patrol in Iraq. Crown Copyright

returned to Transjordan and, later, Palestine.

On 3 October 1946, 2 ACC became part of the RAF Regiment when it was re-numbered 2702Sqn, before being re-numbered as 2 Armoured Car Squadron (2 (AC) Sqn) in February 1947. In December, it absorbed the assets of 1 (AC) Sqn when it was disbanded. In May 1948, it moved to Iraq and then Sharjah in January 1953, where it was re-named 2 (Field) Sqn. In March 1955, it moved to Cyprus and then on to Malta in 1959.

In 1962, 2 (F) Sqn was selected as the Regiment's parachute unit and moved to Colerne for training. Once complete it was deployed on numerous operational deployments, including against the EOKA in Cyprus, as well as to Aden, Zambia and Ulster. The title changed again, on 1 January 1970, to 2Sqn, RAF Regt and the deployments continued, including Hong Kong and Oman, where it was successful in repelling rebel attacks on Salalah airfield.

After a tour in Northern Ireland, 2Sqn moved to Catterick in June 1976, under 3 Wing, prior to a move to Hullavington in August 1980. A year later, it was designated an armoured unit and moved to Germany, under 5 Wing, to support the Harrier Force.

In 1990, 2Sqn was deployed to Akrotiri for security purposes, during the build up of the Gulf War. In 1992, it returned to Catterick, where it became a field squadron under 3 Wing. It moved to Honington in May 1994 and, in October 2003, became jungle warfare specialists. In January 2004, 2Sqn were deployed to Iraq to assist in the on-going security operation and, in April, 2Sqn came under the command of 1 FP Wing HQ.

No. 2Sqn RAF Regiment are based at Honington.

No. 3 Squadron, RAF Regiment

RAF Aldergrove
2 Group
Strike Command
Role: Ground defence
Motto: *In Arduis Audax* – Bold in adversity

Originally formed as 3 Armoured Car Company (3 ACC) at Basra, Iraq, on 3 November 1922 with armoured cars to assist the flying units in the security operations, in April 1925 it was disbanded, with personnel and equipment distributed amongst other armoured car companies.

In 1940, 757 Defence Squadron was formed at Nutts Corner and re-numbered 2757Sqn in December 1941. When the RAF Regt was formed in February 1942, 2757Sqn was incorporated and, in 1943, it changed role from defence to field, before changing again, in August 1944, to an armoured car squadron and deploying to Europe.

During the latter stages of the war, 2757Sqn's main role was to provide protection for Air Technical Intelligence Staff as they undertook reconnaissance missions on radar and other sites. Once the war ended, it remained in Germany as part of the 2nd Tactical Air Force. In August 1947, 2757Sqn was re-numbered 3 (AC) Sqn and continued to remain in Germany, until disbanded at Güsloh in October 1957.

On 27 July 1987, 3Sqn was reformed at Hullavington, moving to Aldergrove in February 1988 as the resident RAF Regt Sqn. It operated a detachment at Bishops Court until its closure in 1990 and has frequently operated other deployments in the region, in support of the army and the RUC/police service of Northern Ireland (PSNI).

No. 3Sqn, RAF Regiment is a Field Squadron and is based at Aldergrove.

No. 27 Squadron, RAF Regiment

RAF Honington
2 Group
Strike Command
Role: NBC Detection
Motto: *Defensores Defendo* – I defend the defenders

On 3 September 1951, 27Sqn, RAF Regiment was formed at Yatesbury as a Low-Level Air Defence Unit (LLAD), equipped with the L40/60 Bofors gun. It was deployed to Abu Sueir in the Canal Zone and, shortly after, saw its first action while undertaking a patrol.

From 1956, the squadron spent much its time on security duties in Cyprus, until 1975, when it returned home to equip with the Rapier. It then spent twenty years based at Leuchars (Scotland), with deployments to Belize and the Falklands. In 1995, 27Sqn moved to Waddington (Lincolnshire) and was disbanded in 1998.

On 1 April 1999, 27Sqn was re-formed at Honington, where it formed 25 per cent of the Joint NBC Regiment.

No. 27Sqn, RAF Regiment is currently based at Honington, where it forms part of the Joint Nuclear, Biological and Chemical Regiment.

No. 34 Squadron, RAF Regiment

RAF Leeming
2 Group
Strike Command
Role: Ground defence
Motto: *Feu de Fer* – Fire from iron

On 19 November 1951, 34Sqn, RAF Regiment was formed at Yatesbury as a Light Anti-Aircraft (LAA) unit, equipped with the L40/60 Bofors gun. It was deployed to El Hamra in Egypt and mounted a number of detachments in the Canal Zone. In September 1953, it was absorbed into 8 Wing as 8/34Sqn.

In February 1956, it was re-named 34Sqn again and moved to Nicosia in Cyprus a few months later, where it took over from Royal Artillery units. It was involved in the peacekeeping and internal security (IS) role, due to EOKA terrorist activity. It also converted to LLAD with the Bofors gun.

In January 1975, 34Sqn was re-rolled as a field squadron and, in 1982–3, designated as a light-armour squadron with the CVR (T) Scorpion. However, the majority of its vehicles were held by the Regiment Depot for use by the Light Armour Training Squadron. The squadron had been given a war role of defending one of the RAF bases in Germany.

The squadron continued to be based at Akrotiri and was subjected to a number of alerts, due to events, primarily, in the Middle East. In 1990, it was put on a war footing as a result of the Iraqi invasion of Kuwait. As it was already considered acclimatized, 34Sqn was deployed to protect RAF forces, initially to Muharraq in Bahrain and then Dhahran in Saudi Arabia. It was later replaced by units from the UK and returned to Cyprus.

As the last light-armoured unit, 34Sqn was re-roled as a field squadron in 1993.

Members of a 3Sqn, RAF Regiment Force Protection team brief Royal Engineers at Camp Souter in Kabul, Afghanistan, prior to a drive through the city.

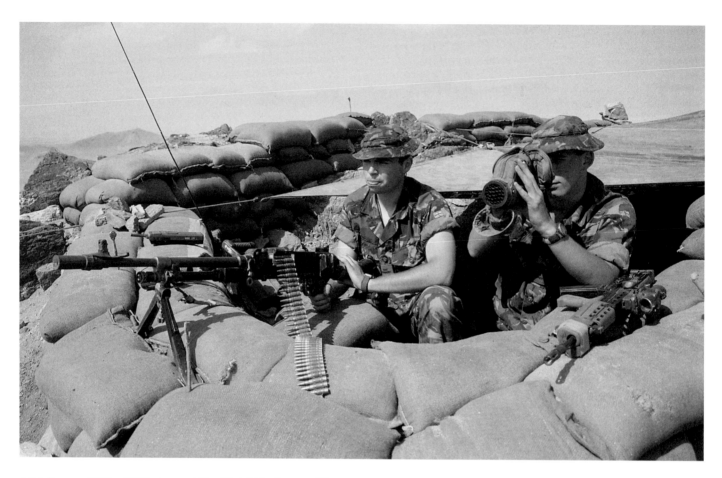

ABOVE: Gunners of 34Sqn, RAF Regt man a hilltop OP in Afghanistan, enabling them to monitor movement over a wide area, thereby contributing to ISAF's role in helping the Afghans maintain a secure and peaceful environment.

BELOW: Having arrived at a new desert location, gunners of 51Sqn, RAF Regt quickly dig-in to provide themselves with some protection from potential enemy fire once the dust storm has ended. Crown Copyright

This included equipping with Land Rovers and mortars. In 1995, members of the squadron were deployed as special constables in the Military Aid to Civil Powers role, in support of the Sovereign Base Area Police during trouble in the area.

In 1996, 34 returned home and was based at Leeming, where it trained for a new role in the Rapid Reaction Force and in support of the Harriers and the Joint Helicopter Force.

More recently, it has been deployed to the former republic of Yugoslavia, Saudi Arabia, Macedonia and Afghanistan and took part in Operation *Peninsula*, assisting MAFF in controlling the foot and mouth epidemic.

No. 34Sqn, RAF Regiment is currently based at Leeming as a field squadron.

No. 51 Squadron, RAF Regiment

RAF Lossiemouth
2 Group
Strike Command
Role: Ground defence
Motto: *Celeriter Defendere* – Swift to defend

In April 1940, 51Sqn, RAF Regt was originally formed as 713 Defence Squadron Bentley Priory – the HQ of Fighter Command – as a Light Anti-Aircraft (LAA) unit during the Battle of Britain, equipped with just Lewis machine-guns and small arms.

When the RAF Regiment was formed in February 1942, the Squadron became 2713 (Rifle) Sqn and, in 1943, formed the nucleus of the Fighter Command Battle School at Hazelmere. In October 1943, it changed role to a field squadron, assisting with airfield defence, plus security escort for many VVIPs.

In April 1944, 2713 (Rifle) Squadron deployed to France as part of 83 Group, 2nd Tactical AF. In July, it became a rifle squadron and was tasked with the protection of airfields, as well as isolated radar and special signals units, moving through France and Belgium and into Germany. It remained at Celle in Germany after the surrender and, on 21 August 1947, was re-numbered 51 (Rifle) Sqn. In 1955, it reverted to the LAA role and re-equipped with the Bofors 40/60 gun, eventually disbanding, in September 1957, at Celle.

On 13 July 1964, 51Sqn was re-formed as a field squadron at the regiment depot, located at Catterick. It deployed detachments to Cyprus and Aden during the first half of 1965 and then, in November, it deployed to Zambia when Rhodesia declared UDI. There it spent six months protecting 29Sqn Javelins, before returning to Catterick. In January 1967, it was deployed to Aden and, the following year, spent four months in Oman.

In March 1969, 51Sqn arrived at Wittering to operate in support of the Harrier Force. In August, it deployed three flights to Northern Ireland and these continued on a four month *roulement* until January 1987. It also undertook *roulements* to Salalah, from 1969, and Hong Kong, from 1972 until 1975.

The squadron returned to Catterick once more in October 1982, where it was re-roled as a light-armoured unit and equipped with the CVR (T). It was also allocated the wartime role of protecting the Harrier Force in Germany.

In November 1990, 51Sqn was deployed to the Saudi airfield of Dhahran, as part of Operation *Granby*. It also operated detachments at Tabuk and Muharraq. Once the Gulf War ended, 51Sqn returned home to Catterick and was disbanded in March 1993.

On 8 May 2001, 51Sqn, RAF Regt was reformed at Lossiemouth. During 2003, 51Sqn was deployed to Iraq to assist in security operations, at sites including Basra Airport and its near surroundings.

No. 51Sqn, RAF Regiment is based at Lossiemouth as a field squadron.

Queen's Colour Squadron (No. 63 Squadron, RAF Regiment)

RAF Uxbridge
2 Group
Strike Command
Role: Ceremonial and Ground defence
QCS motto: Escort
63Sqn motto: *Vigilo et Arceo* – Watch and ward

On 1 June 1943, 63Sqn, RAF Regt was originally formed as 2865 (Light Anti-Aircraft) Sqn at Bone in Algeria. The following year, it moved forward to Italy, before being rested in Scotland in November. Three months later, the squadron took part in the Allied advance into Germany.

In September 1946, 2865Sqn was deployed to Gatow to provide the security

A 63Sqn gunner mans a pintle-mounted gun on a Land Rover to provide cover while the rest of the patrol try to resolve a security problem for local Iraqis. When not on operational service, the unit performs ceremonial duties as the Queen's Colour Squadron.

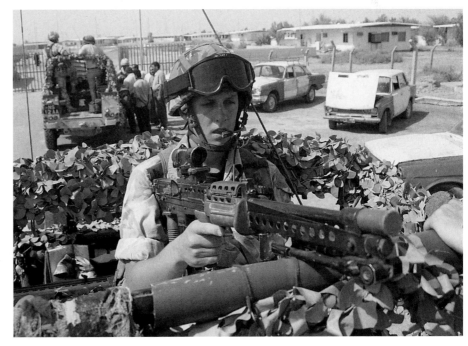

force for the airfield. On 21 August 1947, it was re-numbered 63Sqn and, in December, it moved to the UK as a field squadron. In 1956, it was deployed to Malta during the Suez Campaign and then returned to Felixstowe in February 1957.

In December 1957, 63Sqn moved to Ayios Nikolaos in Cyprus and stayed until December 1960, when it moved to Tengah in Singapore. While there, it converted to the LLAD role and equipped with the Bofors gun. During its stay, security detachments were deployed to Kai Tak in Hong Kong and Gan. In 1971, the squadron moved home to North Luffenham.

In January 1972, it was announced that 63Sqn would become the first regiment to equip with the Rapier but, prior to the deployment in Germany, they were tasked with a duty in Northern Ireland, where they provided close defence for Aldergrove. In May, they moved to Güsloh, Germany, to provide the SHORAD.

Following the Argentinian invasion of the Falklands, in May 1982, 63Sqn formed part the South Atlantic Task Force and headed south on the *QE II* during Operation *Corporate*. The squadron was deployed at San Carlos to protect the Harrier forward-operation base, prior to moving by sea to Stanley after the Argentine surrender. In September 1982, it returned to Güsloh. Since then it has participated in the *roulement* providing Falklands cover by the Germany-based Rapier units.

In May 1992, 63Sqn was disbanded and was absorbed into the Queen's Colour Squadron.

The Queen's Colour Squadron was formed on 1 November 1960, from a ceremonial unit that was originally established in the 1920s. Following the entrusting of 63Sqn's number plate and Standard to the QCS, it was declared operational in February 1994 as Queen's Colour Squadron (No. 63Sqn RAF Regiment). As a result, the squadron have a unique role within the RAF, in that they are dual-roled. Predominately during the summer months, they perform their ceremonial role, which can range from performing continuity drill at a Tattoo through to guard duties at Buckingham Palace. When not conducting ceremonial duties, the QCS become an RAF Regt Field Squadron and undertake operational training and exercises.

In December 2002, the QCS stopped ceremonial duties to prepare for deployment on Operation *Telic*. Having secured a forward-operating base for the Joint Helicopter Force, they were also tasked with custody of Iraqi prisoners and distribution of humanitarian aid, while maintaining the airfield security. Within a few months of returning home, they resumed their share of ceremonial duties by providing the guard at Buckingham Palace.

Queen's Colour Squadron (No 63Sqn RAF Regiment) is based at Uxbridge.

Ground Based Air Defence Wing HQ

RAF Honington
2 Group
Strike Command
Role: GBAD HQ
Motto: Air to defend

The RAF Ground Based Air Defence Wing (RAF GBAD) was formed in October 1998 at Honington. However, its history can be traced back to 1304 Wing, which was formed on 1 April 1944. It was part of the assault force for Operation *Overlord*, landing on Juno Beach in the early hours of D-Day+1. As the Allies progressed through Belgium and Holland, then Germany, the Wing's primary role was to secure and defend the forward airfields. They were also required to hold sectors of the front line, as part of the 1st Canadian/2nd British Armies. Units of 4 Wing contributed to the capture of fifteen airfields and 50,000 German PoWs by the Regiment.

During the early post-war years, 4 Wing were deployed to Utersen, commanding 5 LL and 1 Rifle Squadron, to provide airfield defence, VP guards, patrols and escort duties. It moved to Lübeck in March 1946, then on to Celle, where it was tasked in defending Fassberg, Wunstorf and Celle.

In August 1947, 1304 Wing were re-numbered 4 Wing and commanded two armoured-car squadrons and two rifle squadrons. It moved to Luneberg in 1949, followed by Jever in 1952, Laarbruch 1955, then Oldenburg in 1956, where it disbanded in September 1957.

In December 1973, 4 Wing was re-formed at Catterick, then deployed to

Bruggen in January to command 16, 58, 63 and 66Sqn with Rapier SAMs. In June 1978, it moved to Wildenrath.

Following the Argentinian invasion of the Falklands in April, 63Sqn was ordered to prepare to deploy in May 1982, together with reinforcements from 4 Wing. Personnel travelled down on the *QE II* and equipment on the *Atlantic Causeway*, then air defences were established at San Carlos. Despite initial problems getting systems operational, of the twenty-four missiles fired, the Rapier SAMs were responsible for the destruction of fourteen Argentinian aircraft plus six probables.

During the 1980s, 4 Wing commanded 16, 26, 37 and 63Sqn but, following the disintegration of the Warsaw Pact and the subsequent Options for Change, 4 Wing was disbanded in 1991.

In October 1998, the RAF GBAD was formed at Honington to command all of the RAF GBAD squadrons. As the RAF's sole GBAD force HQ, it naturally continues the function and role of 4 Wing and continues the command of three of its squadrons – 15, 26 and 37Sqn plus 16Sqn. In March 2008 it will be disbanded.

The Ground Based Air Defence Wing HQ is located at Honington.

No. 15 Squadron, RAF Regiment

RAF Honington
MBDA Rapier FSC
2 Group
Strike Command
Role: Ground-based air defence
Motto: *Yang pertama di-mana mana* – To be reckoned with anywhere

On 1 June 1946, 15Sqn RAF Regiment was originally formed as 2700 Light Anti-Aircraft (LAA) Squadron at Nethertown. As such, it was equipped with the L40/60 Bofors gun. In 1947, it was re-numbered 15 LAA and moved to Watchet, where it played the role of demonstration squadron for the RAF School of Gunnery.

In October 1958, 15 LAA was re-named 15 (Field) Squadron. In November 1959, it deployed two flights to Gan for three months, while the rest of the unit deployed to Changi for internal security.

Reloading a Rapier launcher during an NBC exercise – in normal circumstances all eight missiles can be replaced in a matter of minutes. MBDA

In 1962, the squadron deployed to the Far East during the Indonesian Conflict, operating from various locations, including Brunei, Gan and Malaysia. In September 1964, it moved to Seletar, where it stayed, until returning to UK at the end of December 1969.

January 1970 saw 15 (Field) Sqn move into Wittering. From here it operated a number of deployments, including the Middle and Far East, Cyprus and Malta, as well as Northern Ireland.

In March 1982, 15Sqn was equipped with the Scorpion CVR (T) reconnaissance vehicle. During the conversion, 'C' Flight were deployed to Ascension to assist in protecting the island during Operation *Corporate*. By September, the squadron was fully operational and deployed to Northern Ireland the following January, staying until May. It then moved into Hullavington in June and provided a detachment the following month to Greenham Common for Operation *Roust*, protecting the USAF

cruise missiles from the anti-nuclear campaigners. This task kept it occupied until 1985, although it also undertook another NI tour. Further NI tours and deployments to Germany for Harrier defence exercises continued until July 1990, when the squadron disbanded.

The 15Sqn identity was not lost because, on 1 August 1990, 54Sqn at Leeming assumed 15's identity and equipped with Rapier surface-to-air missiles. In March 1996, the event was to be repeated, when 15Sqn disbanded and 20Sqn at Honington assumed the 15Sqn title the following month, after completing its task as a USAF-funded Rapier unit.

On 1 April 1996, 15Sqn was restored to its air defence role with the Rapier SAM and was declared operational to NATO by June. Since then it has participated in various exercises from Norway to Malaysia. In January 2001, 15Sqn was dropped into Sierra Leone by Hercules, as part of a reinforcement demonstration. In

September, it was deployed operationally to Kuwait.

In 2005, it was announced that 15 Sqn will be disbanded by March 2008.

No. 15Sqn, RAF Regt is based at Honington with Rapier FSC.

No. 16 Squadron, RAF Regiment

RAF Honington
MBDA Rapier FSC
2 Group
Strike Command
Role: Ground-based air defence
Motto: All points we defend

On 12 January 1948, 16Sqn, RAF Regiment was formed at Watchet as a Low-Level Air Defence Unit (LLAD) and equipped with the L40/60 Bofors gun. It spent the next eight years providing protection for various bases in East Anglia.

In 1956, it converted to a field squadron and, in November, deployed to Akrotiri to protect the RAF base from the EOKA terrorist threat. The following year, it

A Rapier surface-to-air missile is launched at an airborne target. It can be controlled automatically using radar or manually using the passive optical-tracker. MBDA

returned to the UK and was deployed to Northern Ireland. In 1958, it moved to Felixstowe, followed by Upwood in 1962 and Aden the following year. In July, it returned to Upwood, before returning to Cyprus, where it assisted in maintaining the 'Greenline'.

In March 1964, 16Sqn moved to Catterick, during which stay it undertook short operational deployments to Aden, Hong Kong, British Honduras, Antigua, Zambia and Northern Ireland.

The squadron returned to the LLAD role in 1970 with the Bofors and, in 1975, underwent training on the Rapier at North Luffenham. The following year, it moved to Wildenrath, where it provided the SHOrt Range Air Defence (SHORAD). Following the Falklands War, 16Sqn was one of the four Germany-based squadrons to provide SHORAD cover at Stanley and, later, Mount Pleasant.

On 31 March 1992, following the Options for Change, 16Sqn was disbanded. However, the name was transferred to the Rapier Training Unit at West Raynham.

In March 1993, 16Sqn moved to Honington and, in April 1995, absorbed elements from the disbanding 66Sqn. In July, it was declared to SACEUR as a fully operational SHORAD unit. In 1996, it deployed to the Falklands, converting to the Rapier FSC when it returned to Honington.

In 2005 it was announced that 16 Sqn would be disbanded by March 2007.

No. 16Sqn, RAF Regiment is currently based at Honington as a Rapier FSC squadron.

No. 26 Squadron, RAF Regiment

RAF Waddington
MBDA Rapier FSC
2 Group
Strike Command
Role: Ground-based air defence
Motto: Action – Reaction

On 27 August 1951, 26Sqn, RAF Regiment was formed at Yatesbury as a Low-Level Air Defence Unit (LLAD) unit with the Bofors L40/60 gun. Two months later, it moved to Abu Sueir in Egypt and took part in many Canal Zone air-defence exercises.

In 1954, it moved to Habbaniya in Iraq and then Mafraq in Jordan in 1956. While there, the squadron came to the rescue by preventing a fire from destroying a complete year's harvest in the town of Ramtha. In December 1956, the squadron moved to Cyprus, on security duties during the EOKA threat. In 1964, it was deployed to Changi in Singapore during the Indonesian confrontation. The year of 1966 saw it in Oman and, later, Anguila.

From June 1970, 26Sqn provided LLAD to Güsloh, followed by a Northern Ireland tour in 1973. In 1974, it converted to the field role and was assigned to the Harrier Force, but this was interrupted by a deployment to Akrotiri, following the Turkish invasion of the island in 1976.

In 1976, 26Sqn was deployed to Belize to provide air defence for the airport. However, while it was there, a reorganization of the regiment came to the decision that 26Sqn should be a Germany-based unit. As a result, 26 exchanged identities with the Laarbruch-based 58Sqn on 1 April 1976.

While based at Laarbruch, 26Sqn became the first in Germany to equip with

ABOVE: The Nimrod MR.2 provides maritime-patrol capability and a surveillance role, which will be further enhanced when modified to become the MRA.4.

ABOVE: Afghanistan is just one of the many locations ranging from Northern Ireland to Iraq in which this Puma HC.1 has seen operational service.

BELOW: The Sentry AEW.1 was a tremendous leap in technology when it replaced the Shackleton. Since then they have been deployed operationally in the Balkans, Middle East and even the USA for a period post-9/11.

ABOVE: The Sea King HAR.3 provides a valuable rescue service, not only to servicemen and women, but also to thousands of holiday-makers and sailors around our coast.

ABOVE: The Spitfire is a further memorial to the fighter pilots of the Second World War. This Mk.II flew during the Battle of Britain and is the only RAF aircraft currently in service to have shot down another aircraft in anger.

BELOW: A DHFS Squirrel HT.1 landing in a confined area during student training near its base at Shawbury.

BELOW: Besides the colour-scheme, the RAF's Twin Squirrel features an enlarged upper fuselage to house the second engine.

ABOVE: Launching a Brimstone missile, this Tornado GR.1 is one of the few remaining GR.1s – the operational survivors having been converted to GR.4/4A. MBDA

BELOW: With wings fully swept to 67 degrees, the Tornado F.3 is capable of flying up to Mach 2.2.

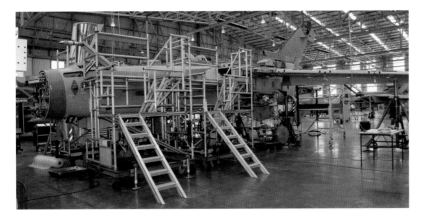

ABOVE: Like the GR.1, the Tornado F.2 no longer flies operationally with the RAF. This last remaining airworthy example, shown undergoing maintenance, continues to be operated for trials by QinetiQ at Boscombe Down and has been modified for the TIARA (Tornado Integrated Avionics Research Aircraft) role. QinetiQ

BELOW: Attack Tornados currently in service have been upgraded to GR.4 or GR.4a standard. Although modified for reconnaissance, the GR.4a retains the attack capability and this aircraft has been busy dropping a range of bombs in Operation *Telic*, as can be seen from the mission markings.

ABOVE: Two of the Tristar K.1 tankers that participated in Operation *Granby* over Iraq were painted pink for camouflage over the desert. Recorded on their return home to Brize Norton, the paint was a temporary ART finish that could be washed off after the application of an alkali solution.

BELOW: ZD948 at Mount Pleasant Airport (MPA) is one of the ex-Pan Am Tristar C.2s that have been modified to carry freight as well as passengers.

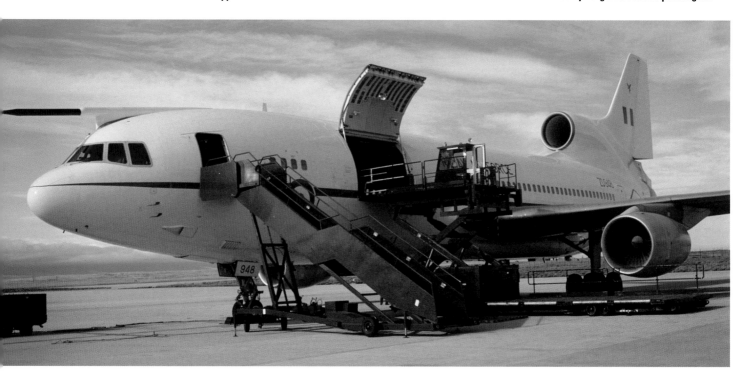

BELOW: The Tucano T.1 is the RAF's basic-flying trainer – all of which are operated by 1 FTS at Linton-on-Ouse.

BELOW: The Tutor replaced the Bulldog as the RAF's Elementary Flying Trainer. It is operated by the UASs for pilot training and the AEFs for cadet air-experience.

A pair of Typhoon T.1s from 29(R)Sqn breaking over the runway at Akrotiri during their first overseas deployment, which took them to Singapore in 2004.
Crown Copyright

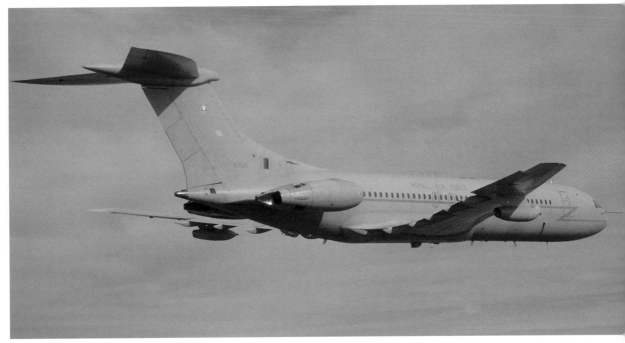

The RAF are the last operators of the impressive VC.10. The C.1s were delivered new to 10Sqn in the mid-1960s and during the early 1990s were modified to C.1K, which enabled refuelling pods to be fitted for air-to-air refuelling.

BELOW: The VC.10 K.3, illustrated refuelling a Typhoon, is one of the ex-East African Airlines Super VC.10s that were converted for use as tanker aircraft, becoming force-extenders for combat aircraft.

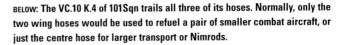

BELOW: The VC.10 K.4 of 101Sqn trails all three of its hoses. Normally, only the two wing hoses would be used to refuel a pair of smaller combat aircraft, or just the centre hose for larger transport or Nimrods.

ABOVE: The all-glassfibre Vigilant is used by the Air Cadets to provide air experience and flying training to members of the ATC and the CCF. Crown Copyright

BELOW: The Viking T.1 is also glassfibre and provides a greatly improved performance over its predecessors. It equips a network of VGSs across the country to fly cadets. Crown Copyright

The A330 proposal for the RAF's new tanker aircraft by AirTanker is the preferred option to replace the current VC.10 and Tristar, but remains subject to contract. AirTanker

The Airbus A400M has been ordered to provide further tactical- and strategic-airlift capacity from around 2009. Airbus Military

ABOVE: The Nimrod MRA.4 took to the air for the first time on 26 August 2004 and is currently undergoing development prior to it entering service. BAE Systems

LEFT: The Joint Strike Fighter is to be the next-generation combat aircraft that will replace the Harrier.

BELOW: The Sentinel R.1 will provide the RAF with an impressive battlefield intelligence, target-imaging and tracking-radar capability once it is operational with 5Sqn. Raytheon

the DN181 Blindfire Radar, giving it a highly accurate all-weather capability. It subsequently became the first unit to receive the Rapier B1, FSB1 (M) and, most recently, the Rapier Field Standard 'C' (FSC).

From 1979, 26Sqn has provided detachments for Belize and, from 1983, the Falklands. In 1991, it was deployed to Tabuk in Saudi Arabia, to provide protection for the Tornado GR.1s.

On 1 April 1996, 26Sqn converted to and was declared operational on the Rapier FSC.

In 2005 it was announced that 26 Sqn would be disbanded by March 2008.

No. 26Sqn, RAF Regiment is based at Waddington as a Rapier FSC squadron.

Although it has been operationally deployed several times, Rapier has not been used in anger since the Falklands War in the early 1980s. MBDA

No. 37 Squadron, RAF Regiment

RAF Wittering
MBDA Rapier FSC
2 Group
Strike Command
Role: Rapier FSC squadron
Motto: *Versatilis* – Versatility

On 12 December 1951, 37Sqn, RAF Regiment was formed at Yatesbury as a Light Anti-Aircraft (LAA) unit, equipped with the L40/60 Bofors gun. In 1952, it was deployed to Abu Sueir in the Canal Zone, where it was also tasked with Internal Security (IS) and desert rescue.

In 1955, 37 moved to Cyprus to provide defence for Akrotiri, but was also tasked with providing anti-sabotage detachments at Limassol, Nicosia and Kevides.

The year 1961 saw 37Sqn return to the UK, to be based at Sealand and then Upwood, in 1962, where it converted to a field squadron. The following year it was deployed to Khormaksar, Aden for twelve months. It then came home to Catterick and, during its ten-year stay, saw detachments to Kenya, Tanganyika, Cyprus, Northern Ireland and Antigua. It also had a war role to support Bruggen.

In 1975, 37Sqn moved to Bruggen, where it was renumbered as 66Sqn and became a SHORAD unit with the Rapier. As a result of the 1976 review of the regiment, 66Sqn reverted to 37Sqn, but retained its new SHORAD role. In 1982, the squadron provided the first post-war SHORAD detachment for Stanley, a role it continued to share with others of the Germany-based units.

In October 2001, 37Sqn moved to Wittering to provide protection for the Harrier force.

In August 2005, it was announced that 37 Sqn would be the first of the GBAD Sqns to disband. This will have been completed by March 2006.

No. 37Sqn, RAF Regiment is currently based at Wittering as a Rapier FSC squadron.

RAF Force Protection Centre

RAF Honington
2 Group
Strike Command
Role: Ground Defence Training

The RAF Force Protection Centre (RAF FP Centre) was originally formed as the RAF Survive to Operate Centre (RAF STO Centre) on 1 January 1994. Prior to that, it was known as the Support Command Ground Defence School (RAF SCGDS) and based at St Athan.

The RAF STO Centre was established to run ground-defence courses for Ground Defence Command and Control personnel, provide the 'core' of the Health Control and Monitoring Force (HCMF) in support of the RAF Nuclear Accident Response Organization (NARO), run special safety-team courses for RAF NARO personnel and shooting-range authorization courses for Air Training Corps staff. Courses run for RAF Regiment training personnel covered Common Core Skills (CCS), active and passive defence-measures, post-attack recovery, ground-defence areas, home-defence radio comms, plus planning and conducting ground-defence exercises. A Small Arms Trainer Custodian course was added in September 1997 for SNCOs.

The RAF STO Centre moved to Honington in September 1994 and, in November 1996, it was spit into two divisions – the Operations and Training (Ops & Trg Div) and the STO Div. In June 1996, a mobile training team was formed to train overseas stations.

From February 1999, the STO Centre commenced a surge in tri-service Individual Reinforcement Training (IRT) specific for personnel deploying on Operation *Agricola* to Kosovo, in addition to that already being conducted for Operation *Palatine* – Bosnia and Croatia. This was conducted under the auspices of the UN Training Advisory Team (UNTAT). Initially, these were run at Honington and by mobile training teams but, from June, all were run on camps in the Stanford Training Area (STANTA).

OPPOSITE: The Rapier is a portable GBAD system and can be easily transported by Chinook. MBDA

Within the first six months, some 1,500 personnel had completed the two-day course, which ranged from mine awareness to using Bosnian refugees for training personnel in how to use interpreters. From October 1999, two-day Individual Deployment Training (IDT) courses were added for RAF personnel deploying on expeditionary operations. These ranged from tent erection to basic-navigation skills.

Commencing April 1999, when the Joint NBC Regt was formed, the STO Centre ran a series of Collective Protection (COLPRO) courses for the NCO instructors and offered advice and assistance in all areas of NBC defence. Biological Warfare COLPRO drills for those deploying on Operation *Bolton* were also added to the repertoire of courses.

On 1 April, the RAF STO Centre was renamed RAF Force Protection Centre. It provides an HQ function for 3Sqn and QCS/63Sqn, RAF Regt, plus 2623Sqn R Aux AF.

The RAF Force Protection Centre is based at Honington.

No. 1 RAF Force Protection Wing HQ

RAF Wittering
2 Group
Strike Command
Role: Force Protection
Motto: *Ersten zum Letzen* – From first to last

On 1 April 1998, 1 RAF Force Protection Wing HQ was formed at Laarbruch as 1 Tactical Survive to Operate HQ (1 Tac STO HQ), although its history can be traced back to 33 Wing, which was formed at Innsworth in 1952.

In 1960, 33 Wing, RAF Regt moved to Felixstowe, where it took command of the RAF Regiment Strategic Reserve Squadrons. In 1964, it was deployed to Cyprus, followed by Northern Ireland in 1969–70. It was then moved to Wildenrath for Harrier force protection and also spent periods at Güsloh and Laarbruch, as well as Ascension during Operation *Corporate* in 1982. The year 1990 saw 33 Wing in Bahrain on Operation *Granby*. Soon after returning home, the Regt Wing HQ were considered unnecessary but, since the Harrier force still required a Survive to Operate

Command and Control capability, 33 Wing continued in this more specialized role and, in 1994, the unit was renamed Tactical Survive to Operate HQ (Tac STO HQ).

Since its formation, the role of 1 FP Wg HQ has widened to provide a high-readiness unit capable of providing command and control for any RAF unit anywhere in the world – not just the Harrier GR.7 units. This takes the form of planning, advice and protection for these units when deployed. This will include making a reconnaissance of the location and establishing command and control. For this role, it forms a small team of officers and RAF Regiment gunners.

Since forming, the 1 FP Wg HQ has had many operational deployments, including Ploč, Croatia in 1998 to support the JHF, Kuwait for the Tornados on Operation *Bolton* and Pristina, Kosovo in 1999 on Operation *Agricola*. It was while deployed to Kuwait that the unit was re-named 1 Tactical Survive to Operate HQ (1 Tac STO HQ). When Laarbruch closed in 1999, it moved to Wittering and has since seen operations in Kuwait, Kosovo, Sierra Leone, Kenya and, in 2003, Iraq.

In April 2004, all the STO HQ underwent a significant organizational change, which resulted in the change to their current title. They now provide the HQ element for 2Sqn, RAF Regiment (at Honington), 504 (County of Nottingham) Squadron, R Aux AF (at Cottesmore) and 2620 Squadron, R Aux AF (at Marham).

No. 1 RAF Force Protection Wing HQ is based at Wittering.

No. 2 RAF Force Protection Wing HQ

RAF Leeming
2 Group
Strike Command
Role: Ground-defence HQ
Motto: *Facta non verba* – Deeds not words

On 1 April 1998, 2 RAF Force Protection Wing HQ (2 FP Wg HQ) was originally formed as 2 Tactical Survive to Operate HQ (2 Tac STO HQ) at Leeming, to provide support for the Tornado F.3 units in the form of planning, advice and protection for these units when deployed. This includes making a reconnaissance of the location and establishing command and control. For this it forms a small team of officers and RAF Regiment gunners.

Within a month of forming, the HQ was tasked with the preparation and completion of the first Tornado F.3 Force NATO Operational Evaluation. This was conducted at St Mawgan and was successfully performed. It provided valuable experience for when the HQ was deployed to Ali Al Salem in June 1998, for six months, on Operation *Bolton*, commanding all Force Protection units at the base. Having returned home they participated in exercises and assisted in an advisory capacity for the Harrier Det at Gioia del Colle, Italy.

September 1999 saw the HQ return for another operational tour at Ali Al Salem. Having returned in January, they were placed on standby to deploy to Sierra Leone on Operation *Palliser*. They completed their preparations in just seven hours, following the capture of 300 UN personnel (including a British officer) by the RUF (Revolutionary United Front). However, the situation was resolved with the deployment of the Paras of the Spearhead Battalion and they subsequently stood down.

In November, the HQ supported 15 Brigade during Operation *Waterfowl* – assisting the emergency services during the severe flooding in North Yorkshire. This was followed in January by another six-month operational tour at Ali Al Salem. A month after returning, they were tasked with protecting facilities at Menwith Hill from peace protesters, who had previously entered the site. With the aid of 15Sqn, RAF Regt, plus a section of Gurkha Engineers, a 9km fence was erected in under three days. During autumn, elements of the HQ were deployed to Oman for Exercise *Saif Sareea II*. In December, confirmation of the HQ's imminent deployment to Afghanistan was received. In January, they deployed, together with a Flight from 34Sqn RAF Regt, to establish and maintain the security of the airport at Kabul. July 2003 saw the HQ deployed to Basra International Airport for six months, where they provided a FP command-and-control function.

Following a significant re-organization, the HQ was renamed 2 RAF Force Protection Wing HQ in April 2004. As a result of the re-organization, the Wing provides the HQ function for 34Sqn, RAF

Regt (Leeming), 609Sqn, R Aux AF (Leeming) and 2503Sqn, R Aux AF (Waddington).

No. 2 RAF Force Protection Wing HQ is based at Leeming.

No. 3 RAF Force Protection Wing HQ

RAF Marham

2 Group

Strike Command

Role: Force Protection

Motto: *Parare et Protegrere* – Prepare and protect

Although it was formed on 1 March 1999, the origins of 3 RAF Force Protection Wing HQ (3 FP Wg HQ) can be traced back to 3 Wing, RAF Regt, which was formed in 1951.

In October 1951, 3 Wing was formed at El Hamra, Egypt to provide anti-aircraft defence and was equipped with Bofors guns. It consisted of 26, 27 and 37Sqn, RAF Regt and was tasked with also providing internal security within the Suez Canal zone. In December 1955, it was deployed to Nicosia with 27 and 37Sqn, during the EOKA uprising, moving to Akrotiri the following year. In December 1960, 37Sqn replaced 34 and 3 Wing remained until 1975, having provided internal security and peacekeeping, in addition to its Low-Level Air Defence (LLAD) role, especially during the Turkish invasion of Cyprus in 1974.

Having moved to Catterick in January 1975, 3 Wing now commanded 16, 37 and 48 Regiment Squadron and, by 1976, changes resulted in these becoming 2, 48, 58 and 66Sqn plus a Tigercat flight. In July 1978, 66Sqn disbanded, 48Sqn converted from Tigercats to Rapier in December 1978 and 2Sqn moved to Hullavington in August 1980, remaining under 3 Wing.

In May 1982, 3 Wing deployed to Ascension Island for Operation *Corporate* and took with it 15Sqn's 'C' Flight. Later, all of 15Sqn arrived, to assist with the island's defence and the handling of Argentinian PoWs, before returning home in July 1982.

In October 1982, 58Sqn, RAF Regt converted to armoured reconnaissance CVR (T) vehicles and 2Sqn was replaced by 51Sqn. Elements of 51 and 58Sqn conducted operations in Cyprus, Greenham Common and Northern

Ireland over the following few years and also assisted in the Lockerbie disaster.

In September 1990, 3 Wing were deployed to Tabuk, Saudi Arabia, where they co-ordinated the build up of the airfield's defences – their control centre using twenty-one ISO containers welded together. Organizing of exercises and rehearsals took place, so that, when the Iraqi started firing Scud missiles at the base, a full action plan was in place. Its job done, 3 Wing returned home to be replaced by 6 Wing.

In March 1992, 58Sqn was disbanded and 2Sqn moved back to Catterick but, in October 1992, 3 Wing was disbanded.

On 1 March 1999, 3 Tac STO HQ formed at Honington, deploying to Ali Al Salem in Kuwait on 10 March as part of Operation Bolton. Once there, the Tac STO HQ provided support for the Tornado GR.4 units, in the form of planning, advice and protection for these units while deployed. Under their control were RAF Police, 1 and 63 Field Squadrons of the RAF Regiment, plus a Prototype Biological Detection System detachment.

Their role is to swiftly make a reconnaissance of the location, establishing a command and control plus effective security for aircraft arriving or departing from the airfield. For this it forms a small team of officers and RAF Regiment gunners. Having returned from Kuwait in September 1999, they were re-deployed in August 2000 – again in support of Operation *Bolton*. During that deployment there was a perceived, increased terrorist threat and additional regiment gunners were deployed.

In January 2002, 3 Tac STO HQ returned to Ali Al Salem for Operation *Resonate South* (formerly Operation *Bolton*) where it controlled 16, 26, 51 and 34Sqn, RAF Regt. It returned home in July 2002. February 2003 saw it return to the Middle East to provide protection for the helicopters of the Joint Helicopter Command (JHC). This included the move forward into Iraq and the formation of a coalition Forward Arming and Replenishment Point (FARP). This additionally included elements of the Tactical Supply Wing, 5131 (BD) Sqn, plus communications and medical personnel.

Having been amongst the first British servicemen to enter Iraq, they secured an airstrip at Safwan and operated it until required to move even further forward. Reconnaissance selected Shaibah and

Basrah International as new bases, with the latter being established as a JHC base and becoming the main entry point for British troops. As such, the areas were secured and, as a result, a large proportion of the troubles being caused by regime loyalists subsided before they returned home.

Following the re-organization, 3 Tac STO HQ was re-named 3 RAF Force Protection Wing HQ in April 2004 and provides the HQ function for 51Sqn, RAF Regt (Lossiemouth) plus 603Sqn, R Aux AF (Edinburgh) and 2622Sqn, R Aux AF (Lossiemouth).

No. 3 RAF Force Protection Wing HQ is based at Marham.

No. 4 RAF Force Protection Wing HQ

RAF Lyneham
2 Group
Strike Command
Role: Ground-defence HQ

On 1 May 2002, 4 RAF Force Protection Wing HQ (4 FP Wg HQ) was originally formed at Honington as 4 Tactical Survive to Operate HQ (4 Tac STO HQ). Their role, then and now, is to provide a compact command-and-control unit that maintains a very high state of readiness. As a highly mobile self-contained unit, it is capable of being deployed worldwide, by air, land or sea, to take control of all Force Protection elements that are dedicated to the defence and security of RAF airheads on deployed operations.

Once deployed, their tasks range from organizing rapid reconnaissance and deployment planning, to the organization and control of force protection in hostile environments. Because of its role, the HQ is a flexible and agile organization that provides specialist advice and co-ordination to any air commander.

Consisting of a wing commander and eleven staff – of which elements of the RAF Regiment staff include specialists in active and passive defence, battlefield communications and force-protection training – 4 FP Wg HQ are based at Lyneham. Their role is aligned with air transport plus air-to-air refuelling, which also closely links them with Brize Norton.

Within two months of forming, 4 Tac STO HQ were deployed to Ali Al Salem,

Kuwait in July 2002, to assume responsibility for the force protection of RAF assets deployed there. While there, their role expanded as the base prepared for conflict. Active and passive defences were established and recuperation measures developed, to ensure the highest level of operational readiness when Operation *Telic* commenced in 2003. In keeping with their highly mobile capability, in the short time that they have existed, they have also been deployed on operations in Afghanistan and the Democratic Republic of Congo.

In April 2004, all the STO HQs underwent a significant organizational change, which resulted in the change to their current title. The most significant result of these changes is that 4 FP Wing is now the HQ for three Force Protection Units. These are 1Sqn, RAF Regt and 2625Sqn, R Aux AF (both based at St Mawgan) and 501 Operations Support Squadron, R Aux AF (at Brize Norton), which have been re-brigaded to become a 'fighting wing' under the command of 4 FP Wing HQ. This will not only forge greater links between Regular and Aux AF Protection Squadrons but will also deliver a potent total-force package to support future expeditionary air operations.

No. 4 RAF Force Protection Wing HQ is based at Lyneham.

Joint Rapier Training Unit

RAF Honington
MBDA Rapier FSC
2 Group
Strike Command
Role: Rapier OCU

The Joint Rapier Training Unit (JRTU) was formed on 1 April 1999 at Honington. It was formed to establish a common training programme between RAF and Army Rapier SAM units.

Its origins date back to 1992, when the Rapier FSC Operational Conversion Unit was formed to convert army and RAF units using the original Rapier system to the Rapier Field Standard 'C' (FSC). The exercise was deemed successful but, when all the units had been converted, the OCU was disbanded. With future training to be undertaken by the individual services, the Directorate of Operational Capability voiced concern. As a consequence, the Strategic Defence Review

(SDR) resulted in the forming of the JRTU.

A small implementation team began preparatory course-development from 5 January and most of the army personnel arrived in March, enabling the official formation on 1 April – the first course commencing on 12 April. JRTU provides all-syllabus-based operator training on the Rapier for both services, plus GBAD training for RAF personnel. With a complement of fifty, the unit comprises two elements – Instruction and Support. This is further broken down into 'A' Flight, which conducts all executive courses and trains experienced Rapier operators for the instructor role within the units, and 'B' Flight, which provides basic operator, tactical controller and junior commander courses. Training and Development Section (TDS) designs and provides computer-based training facilities, as well as course support and documentation, and monitors the courses to maintain quality. The Support Element provides the admin, equipment engineering, manpower, planning and training support for the Instruction Element.

JRTU personnel may be required to support operational Rapier units on deployment, as they were recently in the Middle East, and also on unit-level training, as required, including their annual collective assessment. They may also be required to support equipment trials and demonstrations.

In 2004, a decision was made to restructure the Armed Forces. One of the consequences was the decision to withdraw the RAF Rapier SAMs. As the JRTU trains personnel from both services, it will be transferred to the Royal Artillery, prior to its withdrawal in 2008.

JRTU is equipped with Rapier FSC and based at Honington.

Joint Nuclear, Biological and Chemical Regiment

RAF Honington
2 Group
Strike Command
Role: NBC Detection

The Joint Nuclear, Biological and Chemical Regiment (JNBC Regt) was formed on 1 April 1999, as a result of the Strategic Defence Review. It provides a

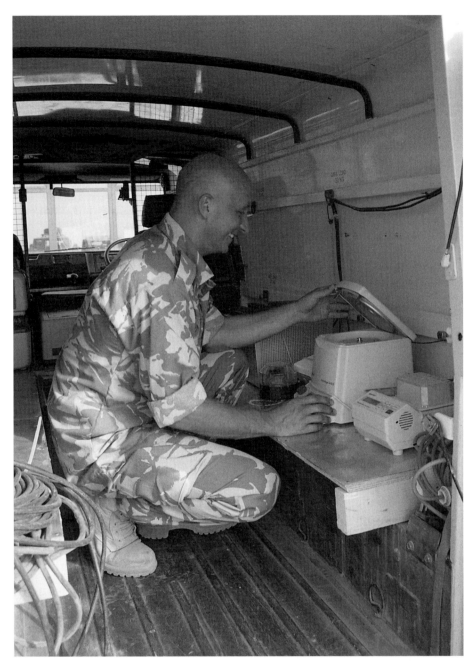

A member of the Light Role Specialist Monitoring Team (SMT) of the Joint NBC Regt checks their equipment before going out on patrol.

No. 3 Group

High Wycombe
Strike Command
Role: Air Battle Management
Motto: *Niet zonder arbyt* – Nothing without labour

On 10 May 1919, 3 Group was formed at Cambridge within South-Eastern Area. It became 3 (Training) Group in August 1918 and, later, moved to Mousehold Heath. It was transferred to Northern Area in October 1919 and, while at Spittlegate, the 'Training' was dropped. Having transferred to Inland Area in August 1921, it was disbanded.

In April 1923, 11 Wing was re-numbered 3 (Training) Group but, in April 1926, it was re-numbered, becoming 23 (Training) Group.

It was re-formed at Andover in May 1936 as 3 (Bomber) Group at Abingdon from Western Area ADGB. It moved to Mildenhall the following January. From October 1938, its squadrons at Feltwell, Warwell, Honington, Marham and Mildenhall began to be modernized with the arrival of the Wellington. These were joined by Stirlings from August 1940, by which time it was at Exning. The Halifax and Lancaster arrived later on. A substantial portion of 3 Group's operations took their aircraft over Holland, where a number were lost. The Group's Dutch motto is a refection of this and the help given to downed crews.

With the war over, 3 Group moved back to Mildenhall in October 1946 and Lincolns were replacing the Group's Lancasters. In 1950, Washingtons were obtained as a stop-gap, prior to the arrival of the Canberra in 1953. With over sixty squadrons operating the Canberra, it was the UK's most successful jet-bomber and all but one came under the control of 3 Group. The southern sector of the Thor Force was controlled by the Group, from the arrival of the first missiles in September 1958, until the last of the twenty squadrons was disbanded in August 1963. It also controlled the V-bomber force, from the introduction of the Valiant from June 1954, until it was absorbed into 1 (Bomber) Group in November 1967.

In April 2000, 2 Group was reformed at High Wycombe as one of the three Groups of the restructured Strike Command. It was responsible for the newly formed Joint Force Harrier, which consisted of the

specialist force, able to provide support to all three services and civil authorities following an NBC attack or accident. It comprises 25 per cent of 27Sqn RAF Regiment and 75 per cent 1st Royal Tank Regiment and is based at Honington.

They are equipped with various highly specialized vehicles, including the Fuchs survey-and-detection vehicles, plus MPDS decontamination vehicles, as well as Pinzgauers. These vehicles can be deployed to potential areas of threat and, having located and identified hazardous areas, they are able to mark the area contaminated. Because of their role, they were deployed to Afghanistan in 2001 and Iraq in 2003. They were also used to provide support during the foot and mouth outbreak in 2001.

The Joint Nuclear, Biological and Chemical Regiment is based at Honington.

Harrier GR.7s plus the Royal Navy Sea Harrier FA.2s. It also included the Nimrod MR.2s, the Search and Rescue helicopters,plus the mountain-rescue teams.

For the first time in the RAF, 3 Group was responsible for squadrons from another service and, uniquely, its AOC was not RAF but Rear Admiral Henderson, who was followed by Rear Admiral Scott Lidbetter – both of the Royal Navy.

In 2003–4, 3 Group was reorganized and became responsible for Air Battle Management. As such, it lost the JFH but now manages Intelligence, Surveillance, Target Acquisition and Reconnaissance (ISTAR), plus Battlefield Management assets. This includes all the Nimrods (R.1 and MR.2s), the Sentry, and Canberras. It will also operate the Sentinel and Nimrod MRA.4 when they enter service. In addition, 3 Group controls the Aerospace Surveillance and Control Systems (ASCAS) and Air Traffic Control (ATC) staff.

No. 3 Group is based at High Wycombe.

No. 5 (Army Co-operation) Squadron

RAF Waddington
Bombardier Sentinel R.1
3 Group
Strike Command
Role: Air Defence
Motto: *Frangas non Flectas* – Thou mayst break but shall not bend me

On 26 July 1913, 5Sqn was formed at Farnborough from a nucleus from 3Sqn. It moved to France in August 1914 with Avro 504s and Henry Farmans. There, it operated in the reconnaissance role until the end of the war, by which time it was operating RE.8s. It then formed part of the army of occupation, until it returned to the UK in September 1919 and was disbanded in January 1920.

A few months later, on 1 April, 5Sqn was re-formed in India by the re-numbering of 48Sqn, flying the F.2b Fighter and later re-equipping with the Wapiti in 1931. These were replaced by the Hart light-bombers from June 1940. The arrival of the Audax in 1941 and Mohawk 1942 resulted in a role change to fighter as well as ground attack.

In June 1943, Hurricanes were delivered, followed by Thunderbolts in September 1944 and Tempests in 1946. On 1 August 1947, 5Sqn disbanded.

It was re-formed on 11 February 1949 at Pembrey, when 595Sqn was re-numbered, and took on the role of anti-aircraft co-operation with various aircraft, until it took its Vampires to Wunstorf in September 1951. Here it operated in the fighter-bomber role, changing to Venoms the following year. In October 1957, it was disbanded yet again.

In January 1959, 68Sqn was re-numbered 5Sqn at Laarbruch with

The Sentinel R.1 will re-equip 5Sqn at Waddington as deliveries commence in 2005. Raytheon

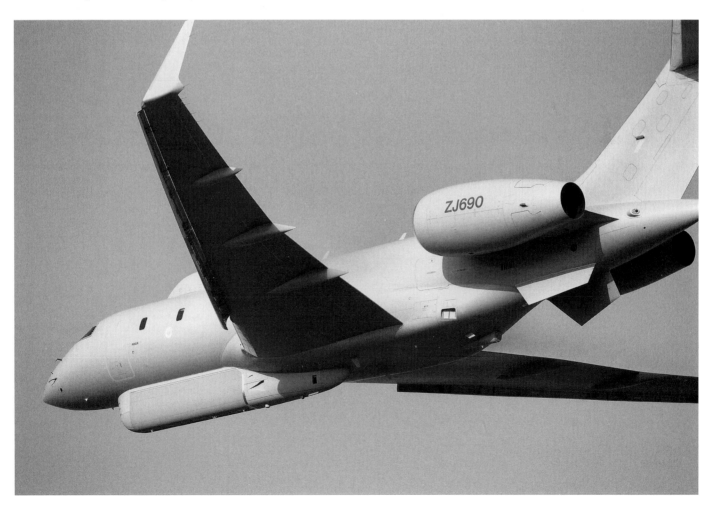

Meteors, which were exchanged for Javelins a year later. In October 1962, it moved to Geilenkirchen and, in October 1965, the squadron disbanded.

A new 5Sqn was formed at Binbrook the following day to fly the Lightning, although it was the middle of November before the first one was received. These were operated until April 1988. Meanwhile, a cadre had been formed at Coningsby in December 1987 to train up on the Tornado F.3 and was officially re-formed in May 1988.

In August 1990, 5Sqn were completing their APC in Akrotiri and were about to hand over to 29Sqn for their camp. They were instructed to cancel the training and then deployed to Dhahran, where they were flying CAP within a couple of hours of arriving. The squadron continued to fly the Tornado until 28 September 2002, when it was disbanded – two years earlier than originally announced.

In February 2002 – when it was announced that 5Sqn would disband – it was also announced that it would be re-formed on 1 April 2004 to operate the Sentinel R.1 at Waddington. Accordingly, the first personnel for the new 5Sqn arrived at Waddington and formed a cadre in September 2003; 5Sqn officially re-formed on 1 April 2004, although the first Sentinel R.1 will not be delivered until 2006.

No. 5Sqn is based at Waddington and will operate the Sentinel R.1.

No. 8 Squadron

RAF Waddington
Boeing Sentry AEW.1
3 Group
Strike Command
Role: Airborne Early Warning
Motto: *Uspiam et Passim* – Everywhere unbounded

On 1 January 1915, 8Sqn was formed at Brooklands and moved to Gosport, to become the first RFC unit to equip with a single type – the BE.2c. In April it moved to France, flying bombing and recce missions. Later, designated a recce unit, 8Sqn converted to FK.8s in August 1917 and specialized in anti-tank-gun spotting for the Tank Corps the following year. Captain F M F West was awarded a Victoria Cross during one such mission, when he spotted a huge troop and transport concentration. Having been attacked by enemy aircraft and severely injured, he managed to fly back to base, where he insisted that he gave his report before being taken to hospital, despite falling in and out of consciousness. Re-equipping with the F.2b Fighter, 8Sqn formed part of the Army of Occupation until July 1919, when it returned home and disbanded the following January at Duxford.

In October 1920, 8Sqn re-formed with the DH.9A in Egypt, moving to Iraq the following February and then to Aden from 1927. It received the Fairey IIIF in 1928, followed by Vincents in 1935 and Blenheims in April 1939, although some Vincents were still being operated until March 1942. In May, 8Sqn was designated a general reconnaissance unit and re-equipped with the Blenheim IV, to which some Mk.Vs were added in September. There followed a lengthy period of monotonous patrols to locate submarines. None were seen until July 1943, when one was attacked with a Hudson, which had been operated for the previous six months. The following January they were replaced by the Wellington, which were operated until 1 May 1945, when the squadron disbanded.

On 10 May 1945, 8Sqn was re-formed at Jessore in India, as a result of the re-numbering of 200Sqn with Liberators. It moved to Ceylon shortly after, from where it dropped supplies to guerrilla forces in Malaya in the battle against the Japanese. On 15 November 1945, the squadron disbanded again.

In September 1946, 8Sqn was re-formed with Mosquitos at Aden from the re-numbered 114Sqn. The following April, Tempests VIs arrived for the fighter/ground-attack role. A detachment were sent to Somaliland to assist 6Sqn quell

The five Sentry AEW.1s are operated by two squadrons. 8Sqn markings are applied to the left side. Jeremy Flack

local unrest in early 1948. In July 1949, the Tempests were replaced by Brigands, following which the squadron entered the jet age with Vampires in December 1952. During April and May, they were deployed to Kenya for operations against the Mau Mau. The Vampires were swapped for Venoms in 1955, which were operated from Cyprus for a while during the Suez Crisis and Operation *Musketeer*. A few photo-reconnaissance Meteors were added a little later.

The Venoms were replaced by Hunter FGA.9s in January 1960 and the Meteors by the Hunter FR.10 in April 1961. They were deployed to Bahrain in June when Iraq threatened Kuwait. As this trouble died down, further hostilities arose requiring its return to Aden, along with 43Sqn and Shackletons of 37Sqn, to form the Aden Strike Wing. For a while, the FR.10s formed 1417 Flight, before the whole squadron withdrew to Bahrain in September 1967 and, later, to Sharjah, before disbanding on 15 December 1971.

On 8 January 1972, 8Sqn was re-formed with the Shackleton AEW.2 at Kinloss. In August, they moved to their new home at Lossiemouth. Although their Shackleton and the AEW radar were considered obsolete before their planned retirement date in 1984, they were require to continue soldiering on, due to the delays in building the Nimrod AEW.3. This was eventually cancelled in December 1986, requiring the Shackleton to continue flying, awaiting the arrival of its replacement. Eventually, on 30 June 1991, 8Sqn was disbanded with the Shackleton and re-formed the following day at Waddington with the Sentry AEW.1. In the space of a day, 8Sqn had progressed from operating the oldest aircraft in the RAF to the newest.

The leap forward in technology was tremendous and 8Sqn were soon declared operational, regularly taking place in exercises as part of the NATO Airborne Early Warning Force Command (NAEWFC). Missions are flown from a number of Forward Operating Bases (FOBs) around Europe as well as others further afield.

Operations have been flown on UN and NATO operations and 8Sqn has flown missions in the former Yugoslavia, Afghanistan and Iraq .

No. 8Sqn operate the Sentry AEW.1 from their base at Waddington. The aircraft are pooled with 23Sqn and have both squadron markings applied, with 8Sqn's appearing on the port side.

No. 22 Squadron – Headquarters

RMB Chivenor
3 Group
Strike Command
Role: Search & Rescue
Motto: *Preux et Audacieux* – Valiant and brave

On 1 September 1915, 22Sqn was formed at Gosport, initially with Blériots and BE.2cs. It then re-equipped with the FE.2b, prior to deploying to France in April 1916. It was deployed as a reconnaissance unit, flew missions along the Hindenburg Line and saw action on the Somme. However, following re-equipping with the F.2b Fighter in July 1917, this role took secondary place to that of a fighter. In just one month, 22Sqn destroyed eighty-four enemy aircraft. In September 1919, it returned to the UK at Ford and disbanded at Croydon at the end of the year.

The squadron re-formed in July 1923 at Martlesham Heath, to undertake trials with the A&AEE. A number of long-distance trials were also conducted, including a non-stop flight from Cranwell to Karachi in a Fairey Long Range Monoplane in April 1929 – 4,130 miles (6,645km) in 50hr 48min. It was later re-titled the Performance Testing Squadron in March 1934.

In May 1934, 22Sqn was re-established at Donibristle with Vildebeests. It deployed to Hal Far, Malta, in October 1935, in the torpedo-bomber role during the Abyssinian Crisis and returned the following August, moving to Thorney Island in March 1938. During November 1939, it began to convert to the Beaufort, with which it began operations in April. In 1940, while at North Coates, some Marylands were delivered and it became the first RAF unit to operate the type.

As a result of his actions with 22Sqn in April 1941, Flying Officer Kenneth Campbell was posthumously awarded a VC – the only one awarded to an RAF torpedo-bomber crew. He was tasked with attacking the *Scharnhorst* and *Gneisenau* in Brest harbour. Flying his Beaufort, of the three tasked, he was the only aircraft to reach the target and he successfully torpedoed the *Gneisenau* before crashing.

In January 1942, the squadron ground-crew embarked for Ceylon, followed by the aircrew in March. They had been deployed to Ceylon to fly escort and anti-submarine

patrols, but were diverted to operate from Malta for a short period before continuing. By July 1944, the squadron had re-equipped with Beaufighters and it moved to Burma in December. Once the Japanese surrendered it moved back to Gannavaram, India and was disbanded in September 1945.

It was reformed at Seletar, Singapore with Mosquitos, in May 1946, from the re-numbered 89Sqn. This was short-lived, as it was disbanded again in August.

On 15 February 1955, 22Sqn was re-formed as a Search and Rescue (SAR) squadron with borrowed Sycamore helicopters at Thorney Island. In June these were replaced by the much-delayed Whirlwind HAR.2 and 22Sqn moved to St Mawgan in June 1956. By this time, Flights had been formed at Felixstowe, Martlesham Heath (and closed), St Mawgan, Thorney Island and Valley. An additional Flight was formed at St Mawgan in October 1956, for deployment to Christmas Island. In January 1957, two Whirlwinds were flown onto HMS *Warrior* and sailed for the Pacific, where they provided an SAR and communications role during Operation *Grapple* – the detonation of British hydrogen bombs in the Christmas Islands. It gradually built up to eight Whirlwinds, before they were handed over to 217Sqn.

In March 1969, 'D' Flight at Manston was closed, following a short-notice governmental decision. As when it moved out from Thorney Island in 1959, this loss of cover caused a strong public reaction, which eventually resulted in Bristow Helicopters being contracted to provide SAR cover for the Coastguards in 1971.

In April 1974, the squadron HQ moved back to Thorney Island, where it remained until January 1976. By now, Flights were based at Brawdy, Chivenor, Coltishall, Leuchars and Valley. In January 1976, it moved to Finningley, where the HQ SAR Wing was established along with 202Sqn. From May 1976, the Wessex began to replace the Whirlwind.

During December 1992, the HQ SAR Force moved to St Mawgan and 22Sqn HQ moved with it. By then, the squadron operated Flights at Chivenor, Coltishall, Leuchars and Valley

In June 1994, 22Sqn received its first Sea King HAR.3 and, in May 1997, it received its first Sea King HAR.3A, replacement being completed by July 1997. On 22 September 1997, 22Sqn HQ

'A' Flight of 22Sqn at Chivenor is especially busy during the summer months, rescuing holidaymakers in trouble around the Devon and Cornish coast.

moved to Chivenor, where it is co-located with 'A' Flight.

Standard practice is for each Flight to maintain two aircraft on standby, with one crew ready to scramble 24-hours a day, 365-days a year. A second crew is held at one hour's notice to scramble. The primary role of the SAR Flight is to rescue military aircrew but, in practice, the bulk of their work involves civilian rescues.

No. 22Sqn has its HQ at RMB Chivenor, where 'A' Flight is co-located, 'B' Flight is based at Wattisham and 'C' Flight at Valley. 'A' and 'B' Flights are equipped with the Sea King HAR.3A, while 'C' has the HAR.3.

No. 22 Squadron – 'A' Flight

Westland Sea King HAR.3A
RMB Chivenor
3 Group
Strike Command
Role: Search & Rescue
Motto: *Preux et Audacieux* – Valiant and brave

'A' Flight of 22Sqn was originally formed on 15 February 1955 at Thorney Island, with Sycamores borrowed from St Mawgan. The first Whirlwind HAR.2s arrived in June 1955. In June 1956, it moved to St Mawgan and, in November 1958, moved to Chivenor, replacing 'E' Flight of 275Sqn, which had been operating Sycamores.

In August 1962, the Whirlwind HAR.2s were replaced by the more capable HAR.10s. In November 1981, 'A' Flight converted to the Wessex and flew the last RAF operational sortie of a Whirlwind HAR.10 in December. 'A' Flight then took over the Sea King HAR.3s of 'B' Flight, 202Sqn from Brawdy in June 1994. These were replaced by the improved HAR.3A in May 1997.

In March 2004, 'A' Flight received the first two Forward-Looking Infra-Red (FLIR)-equipped HAR.3As, which has greatly enhanced their capability.

'A' Flight, 22Sqn operates the Sea King HAR.3A from its base at Chivenor.

No. 22 Squadron – 'B' Flight

Westland Sea King HAR.3A
Wattisham
3 Group
Strike Command
Role: Search & Rescue
Motto: *Preux et Audacieux* – Valiant and brave

'B' Flight, 22Sqn was formed on 25 June 1955 at Martlesham Heath with Whirlwind HAR.2s. It moved to Felixstowe in April 1956 and disbanded in May 1961.

In June 1961, 'B' Flight reformed at Tangmere with the Whirlwind HAR.2. These were replaced with the HAR.10 in August 1962. The Flight moved to Thorney Island in May 1964, but was disbanded in February 1973 – all men and helicopters were transferred to Lossiestowe, to form 'D' Flight of 202Sqn.

A new 'B' Flight was formed at Coltishall in April 1973, replacing 'D' Flight of 202Sqn. In April 1976, an exchange of locations occurred with 'B' Flight and the Leuchars-based 'C' Flight of 202Sqn. In July, it re-equipped with the Wessex. 'B' Flight continued to provide its SAR service from Leuchars, until it was disbanded in March 1993.

In July 1994, 'B' Flight was re-formed at Wattisham with the Sea King HAR.3, by the re-numbering of 202Sqn's 'C' Flight, which had moved from Manston. With its superior capability, it also took over the cover that had previously been provided by 'E' Flight at Coltishall. It converted to the Sea King HAR.3A in July 1997.

'B' Flight, 22Sqn operates the Sea King HAR.3A from its base at Wattisham.

No. 22 Squadron – 'C' Flight

Westland Sea King HAR.3
RAF Valley
3 Group
Strike Command
Role: Search & Rescue
Motto: *Preux et Audacieux* – Valiant and brave

'C' Flight, 22Sqn was formed on 27 September 1955 at Valley with the Whirlwind HAR.2 and converted to the HAR.10 in October 1962.

It converted to the Wessex in October 1976 and, on 30 May 1976, completed its 5,000th Wessex SAR mission. It became the last and longest-serving UK operator of the SAR Wessex when it finally retired its last example on 30 June 1997, by which time the Flight had converted to the Sea King.

'C' Flight, 22Sqn operates the Sea King HAR.3 from its base at Valley.

No. 23 Squadron

Boeing Sentry AEW.1
RAF Waddington
3 Group
Strike Command
Role: Airborne Early Warning
Motto: *Semper Aggressus* – Always having attacked

On 1 September 1915, 23Sqn was formed with an Avro 504 and a Blériot at Fort Grange, Gosport, from a small nucleus provided from 14Sqn. The squadron was working up, prior to deploying to France in March 1916, and a detachment was flown to Sutton's Farm (near Hornchurch), which was being opened as a fighter station to protect London. While there,

ABOVE: Because of the nature of their work, the rescue Sea Kings can often find themselves using impromptu landing grounds. However, despite the helicopter's noise, these cows are more interested in the photographer.

BELOW: Constant training by aircrew on different scenarios enables difficult and frequently dangerous rescues to be regularly achieved.

Second Lieutenant J C Slessor attempted to intercept Zeppelin L15 on the night of 13 October 1915 – this was the first night-intercept attempt over England.

In March 1916, 23Sqn deployed to the Western front with FE.2bs, undertaking mainly offensive patrols. The SPAD S.VII was received the following January, followed by Dolphins in March 1918. A year later, the squadron returned home to Waddington and was disbanded at the end of the year.

In July 1925, 23Sqn re-formed at Henlow with Snipes, which were replaced with Gamecocks the following spring. A move to Kenley was made in February 1927 and it converted to the Bulldog in 1931. The following year, the squadron moved to Biggin Hill and took delivery of Hart fighters for evaluation.

In September 1935, 23Sqn was briefly deployed to Malta during the Abyssinian crisis, before transferring to Northolt for a training role. The Hart fighters were re-named Demon and, in 1937, the squadron was issued with the new model, which was fitted with the first Frazer-Nash hydraulically operated gun-turret. These were replaced by the Blenheim IF, following the squadron's move to Wittering in December 1938. When war broke out, the squadron initially undertook convoy patrols off the east coast, before becoming a night-fighter unit from September 1940, when they were based at Middle Wallop. Beaufighters and Bostons joined the squadron during the autumn of 1940 and,

later, Havocs, when the role changed to night-intruder for attacks on German-held airfields in France. Deliveries of Mosquitos began in July 1942 while at Ford, before a move was made to Manston.

In December 1942, 23Sqn moved to Luqa, Malta to undertake long-range intruder-missions over Sicily and Italy. As the number of major targets reduced or became out of range, the role changed to interdictor. In May 1944, the squadron returned to the UK, to be based at Little Snoring with Mosquitos, providing night escorts for bombers, until disbanding in September 1945.

It was re-formed in September 1946 with Mosquitos again at Wittering, as a night-fighter unit once more. In January 1947, it moved to Coltishall, from where the Mosquitos continued to be operated until December 1951 and the delivery of its first jet fighter – the Vampire in October. On these, it resumed displaying its squadron colours, as previously sported during the 1930s. The Vampires gave way to the Venom in June 1954 and the Gloster Javelin in March 1957, by which time the squadron had moved to Horsham St Faith. The squadron then became involved in the development of in-flight refuelling and became the first Fighter Command squadron to deploy non-stop to Singapore, using air-to-air refuelling, in January 1963.

Having moved to Leuchars in March 1963, 23Sqn received its first Lightning in August 1964. Besides the impressive, supe-

rior performance, this was also the first single-seat fighter that the squadron had operated since the Bulldog. The Lightning F.3s gave way to F.6s in May 1967, which they continued to fly until disbanding in October 1975.

Although it didn't officially form until December, 23 (Designate) Squadron had already formed at Coningsby the previous month with the Phantom FGR.2. It moved to Wattisham in February 1976, where it continued to provide air defence with the Phantom until March 1983.

In April, 1983, 23Sqn was reformed at Stanley, Falkland Islands, where it took over the role of air defence for the Islands from 29Sqn. In April 1986, the squadron re-located to Mount Pleasant, but was disbanded in October 1988, when the unit was re-numbered 1435 Flight.

The following day, the squadron re-formed at Leeming with the Tornado F.3. It took part in Operation *Granby*, but disbanded again in February 1994.

On 1 April 1996, 23Sqn re-formed with the Sentry AEW.1 at Waddington, where it initially operated as the Sentry Training Squadron. The RAF's seven Sentries are pooled, being operated jointly with 8Sqn and flown with both squadron markings.

The Sentry Training Squadron now operates within 23Sqn and runs a variety of courses. These range from the long course for new pilots to the Sentry, which lasts six months, to the short course for retraining previously qualified Sentry pilots, which depends on their experience but would last a minimum of three weeks.

Because of the role of the Sentry, members of 8/23Sqn have seen extended periods of

With 23Sqn markings on the right side, three Sentry AEW.1s can be seen at Aviano AB, Italy during operations over the Baltic Region.

operation and deployment to provide their valuable service. This is required not only for the RAF combat aircraft, but also other NATO and coalition forces during the seemingly continual periods of conflict and endless peacekeeping patrols in parts of Europe and the Middle East.

No. 23Sqn operates the Sentry AEW.1 from its base at Waddington. Aircraft are pooled with 8Sqn and have both squadron markings applied, with 23Sqn's appearing on the starboard side.

No. 39 (No. 1 Photo Reconnaissance Unit) Squadron

RAF Marham
English Electric Canberra PR.9
3 Group
Strike Command
Role: Reconnaissance
Motto: *Die Noctuque* – By day and night

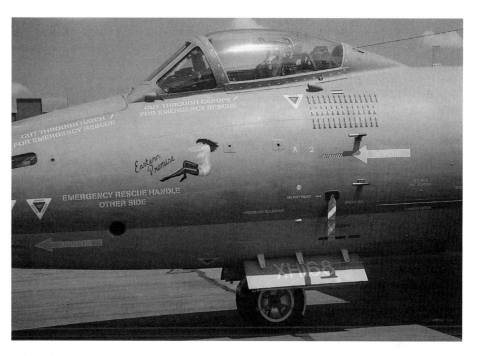

39 (1 PRU)Sqn continues to be heavily in demand, as can be seen from their Operation *Telic* mission markings.

On 1 July 1992, 39 (1 PRU) Squadron was formed when No 1 Photographic Reconnaissance Unit (1 PRU) and 39Sqn were merged and renumbered.

The origins of 39Sqn commence on 29 January 1916 with BE.2cs at Hounslow as 19 (Reserve) Sqn. On 15 April, it was re-numbered as 39Sqn and designated as the first Home Defence squadron. Two detachments were formed to guard London's eastern approaches. These were located at Hainault Farm (Chadwell Heath) and Sutton's Farm (Hornchurch), plus the HQ at Hounslow. During September 1916, one of its pilots – Lieutenant W Leefe Robinson – was responsible for shooting down the first German airship over the UK. For this he was awarded the VC. Another was shot down in October, but this pilot was only awarded a DSO. In mid-1917 the flights all moved to North Weald and, from September, converted to the F.2b Fighter. The squadron was preparing to deploy to France when the war ended. Instead, it disbanded less than a week after the signing of the Armistice in November 1916.

In July 1919, at Biggin Hill, 39Sqn was re-formed. Initially it was a cadre unit, until equipping with the DH.9a in February 1923. It moved to Kenley and then Spitalgate, where it became a fully operational bomber-squadron. In 1928, it moved to Birch Newton, prior to leaving the DH.9s to 101Sqn and deploying to Risalpur, India and the North West Frontier to operate the Wapiti bomber. In November 1931, it re-equipped with the Hart, prior to the arrival of the Blenheim in June 1939. In August it deployed to Tengah, Singapore.

In April 1940, 39Sqn pulled back to India, then moved to Aden, from where it patrolled and attacked targets in Italian East Africa. In November, it moved to Helwan, Egypt and, shortly, received Marylands for strategic reconnaissance. Beauforts began to be operated alongside these from August, for maritime attack. A detachment was sent to Malta in August 1942, while the remainder operated from forward bases in Egypt and Libya. In Malta, it absorbed detachments from 86 and 217Sqn to form a new 39Sqn, while the rest were absorbed into 47Sqn. In June 1943, it moved to Tunis and converted to Beaufighters, which were operated throughout the western Mediterranean. In November 1943, it moved to Algeria and deployed a detachment to southern Italy. By February, it had moved to Sardinia, before operating in Italy in July 1944. In December, it converted to the Marauder. At the same time, a detachment of Beaufighters were deployed to Greece to stem attacks from communist forces.

After the end of the war, 39Sqn continued to operate the Marauder in Italy. In October 1945, it moved to Khartoum, Sudan, where Mosquitos augmented the fleet from February 1946, but suffered from the humidity. In September 1946, it was disbanded.

The squadron was reformed at Manston in April 1947 with Tempests. It disposed of them in March 1949 and moved to Fayid, Egypt to protect the Suez Canal, but had to wait until the following month for a delivery of Mosquitos. In March 1953, 39Sqn entered the jet age with the Meteor, which it took to Luqa, Malta in June 1955. It flew several security deployments to Cyprus during operations in Suez, against EOKA terrorists and in the course of the Lebanon crisis. Then, in June 1958, the squadron disbanded again.

The following day – 1 July 39Sqn – it took over the role of the re-numbered 69Sqn with Canberra PR.3s. These were operated in the survey photography role until November 1962, by which time deliveries of the PR.9 were being made. On 1 October 1970, the squadron moved from Malta to Wyton and continued to operate until 29 May 1982, when it was disbanded due to its reduced size. The following day it was formed as 1 Photo Reconnaissance Unit (PRU). As a result of increased requirement the unit needed to enlarge and, on 1 July 1992, it was re-named once more – this time to its

42(R)Sqn provide the training at Kinloss, but all of the Nimrod MR.2s operate on a pooled basis as the Kinloss Wing.

current title of 39 (1 PRU) Squadron. In September 1993, it was relocated to Marham.

No. 1 PRU was formed in July 1940. Its origins can be traced back to 2 Camouflage Unit, which was formed in November 1939 and became the Photographic Development Unit in January the next year. Its name was to disguise its reconnaissance role. From Heston, 1 PRU operated Spitfires and Hudsons, moving to Benson in December 1940. Mosquitos were added and the unit continued until, in October, it was used to form five new squadrons and disbanded.

On 1 June 1982, 1 PRU was re-formed at Wyton with a flight of Canberra PR.9s from 39Sqn. Its role – to continue aerial survey and other photographic tasks in the UK and overseas.

As 1 PRU grew, it established its own engineering facilities, as well as photo processing, until 1992, when the name changed to the current title.

Despite the age of its aircraft, 39 (1 PRU) Sqn has remained busy, operating in the tactical, medium and high-level vertical and oblique photographic role. Amongst tasks undertaken are photographic surveys of Denmark, Germany, Kenya, Norway, Oman, St Helen and Zimbabwe.

During operations in Afghanistan, the Canberra PR.9s of 39 (1 PRU) Sqn were in great demand, assisting in the tracking down of members of Al Qaeda and contin-uing with operations in Sudan. Most recently, they flew 150 missions in support of coalition forces over Iraq. In 2003, a Canberra was deployed to the Falklands to undertake a survey of the islands.

It is anticipated that the Canberra will continue to be operated by 39Sqn until it is withdrawn in August 2006, with the loss of its unique capability.

No. 39 (No 1 PRU) Sqn currently operates four Canberra PR.9s from their base at Marham.

No. 42 (Reserve) Squadron

RAF Kinloss

Nimrod MR.2

3 Group

Strike Command

Role: Nimrod OCU

Motto: *Fortiter in re* – Bravely in action

Originally, 42Sqn was formed at Filton on 1 April 1916 with the BE.2c and deployed to France in August with the BE.2d, which it flew in the reconnaissance role. In April, it converted to the RE.8 and then deployed to northern Italy in November, returning to France in March 1918. It returned to the UK in February 1919 and was disbanded at Netheravon on June.

On 14 April 1936, 42Sqn was re-formed at Donibristle from 'B' Flight of 22Sqn. It was equipped with Vildebeest IIIs as one of only three torpedo strike-units in the UK.

It moved location a number of times, before arriving at Bircham Newton in August 1939, exchanging its aircraft for Beauforts the following April. These were used in the anti-shipping and mine-laying role along the northern European coast.

In June 1942, it was deployed to Ceylon, but was diverted for operations in the Middle East with 47Sqn. In December, it eventually arrived, then moved to India and converted to Blenheims by March, followed by a further re-equipping with the Hurricane in October. It disbanded in June 1945, but was re-formed the following day from 146Sqn with the Thunderbolt, but was disbanded again in Burma at the end of December 1945.

In October 1946, 42Sqn was re-formed from 254Sqn at Thorney Island with the Beaufighter, only to be disbanded in October 1947.

In June 1952, 42Sqn was formed at St Eval with the Shackleton. These were superseded by the MR.2 in April 1954 and, in October 1958, the squadron moved to nearby St Mawgan. In December 1965, the Shackleton MR.3s were introduced and continued to be operated until 1971.

In April 1971, 42Sqn converted to the Nimrod MR.1. These were upgraded to MR.2 and deliveries began in 1983. The squadron was deployed during Operation *Corporate* in 1982 as well as Operation *Granby* in 1992 but on 1 October 1992, 42 (Torpedo Bomber) Sqn was finally disbanded as a front-line unit.

Its identity was revived the same day, when 38 (R) Sqn, which had operated as the Nimrod OCU (previously 236 OCU), was re-numbered 42 (Reserve) Squadron with the role of training of aircrew onto the Nimrod.

No. 42 (R) Sqn operates the Nimrod MR.2 from its base at Kinloss, using aircraft from the fleet, pooled with all of the other Nimrod squadrons. Other than for special occasions, the Nimrods do not carry and squadron identification.

No. 51 Squadron

RAF Waddington
Hawker Siddeley Nimrod R.1
3 Group
Strike Command
Role: Reconnaissance
Motto: Swift and Sure

On 15 May 1916 at Thetford, 51Sqn was formed as a Home Defence Squadron with BE.2c, BE.2d and BE.12 reconnaissance aircraft. Later, these were replaced by the FE.2b for a night-fighter role to combat Zeppelins. It also operated the Avro 504K, modified as a single-seat fighter. In addition, a number of DH.4s were used on the night-fighter training role. The squadron disbanded in June 1919 at Sutton's Farm (later Hornchurch).

The squadron re-formed at Driffield in March 1937 with the Anson and the Virginia biplane-bomber. These were

replaced by the Whitley in February 1938 at Linton-on-Ouse. On the day war was declared, 51Sqn took part in a leaflet raid over the Hamburg and Bremen area. Having moved to Dishforth, in March 1940, it participated in the first Bomber Command attack on Germany, targeting the seaplane base at Hornum. It also took part in the first attack on the marshalling yards at Turin, Italy on 11 June – the day after Italy entered the war.

In February 1941, 51Sqn crew flew 78Sqn aircraft from Malta in the first airborne assault on Italy. The squadron also flew paratroops and RAF specialists to the Normandy coast to attack the Bruneval radar station and capture vital equipment. In May 1942, 51Sqn was attached to Coastal Command, attacking German submarines and sinking six. From October, it returned to Bomber Command and resumed attacks on German targets with the Halifax from Snaith. In April 1945, it had moved to Leconfield and, when the war ended, 51Sqn converted to Stirlings and then Yorks, in April 1946, before moving to Waterbeach. These it used to repatriate PoWs from the Far East, before taking part in the Berlin Airlift and moving to Bassingbourn, where it disbanded in October 1950.

In August 1958, 192Sqn was renum-

bered 51Sqn. Based at Watton, it operated the Comet 2R and various Canberras on electronic-reconnaissance duties, which were to become referred to as ELINT (ELectronic INTelligence), and other specialized reconnaissance roles with Signals Command. In March 1963, it moved to Wyton and became part of the Strategic Reconnaissance Wing, then Brampton's Central Reconnaissance Establishment. A number of their sorties took them around the Baltic and, although they didn't infringe enemy air space, they were frequently intercepted by Soviet and Warsaw Pact fighters and even some from neutral Sweden.

In 1974, the Canberras and Comets were replaced by Nimrod R.1s, to continue tasks around the Baltic and other areas, although a few Canberras continued until 1976. On 1 April 1995, 51Sqn moved to Waddington. During May, one of their Nimrods was undergoing a post-maintenance air-test when a major fire broke out. The captain managed a classic ditching in the Moray Firth, with the aircraft remaining afloat, and all the crew were rescued by a 202Sqn Sea King. For his action, Flight Lieutenant Stacey was awarded the Air Force Cross.

The squadron continues its role of ELINT and has seen its aircraft frequently deployed operationally into areas of trouble. It was involved in Operation *Corporate* to recover the Falkland Islands, the Gulf War, former republic of Yugoslavia (FYR), monitoring Iraq,

The Nimrod R.1s of 51Sqn are readily identified by the lack of MAD boom on the tail. They also sport a substantial number of additional aerials, which are used in the gathering of electronic intelligence.

Afghanistan and the Iraqi War. Due to the role of 51Sqn, in recent operations has usually been deployed at an early stage, as trouble is building up, and has not returned for some time after hostilities have ceased.

No. 51Sqn operates the Nimrod R.1 from their base at Waddington.

No. 78 Squadron

RAF Mount Peasant, Falkland Islands
Boeing Chinook HC.2, Westland Sea King HAR.3
3 Group
Strike Command
Role: Support Helicopter
Motto: *Nemo non Paratus* – Nobody unprepared

On 1 November 1916, 78 Squadron was formed with the BE.2 at Harrietsham, Kent, as an RFC Home Defence unit protecting London from attack by German Gotha bombers and Zeppelins. The following year it was equipped with Camels, F.2b Fighters and Dolphins. Shortly after the Armistice it began to re-equip with the Sopwith 1½ Strutter, but was disbanded in December 1919 before they were all delivered.

In November 1936, 78Sqn was re-formed with Heyfords from 'B' Flight of 10Sqn at Boscombe Down. It moved to Dishforth in the following February and slowly converted to the Whitley. It had temporary moves to Ternhill, Linton-on-Ouse and Middleton St George, ending at Croft in October 1941. In March 1942, it began re-equipping with the Halifax. It moved on to Middleton St George in June and Linton-on-Ouse in September, from where it operated until June 1943, when it moved on to Breighton. By May 1945, having completed over 6,000 sorties, 78Sqn transferred from Bomber to Transport Command, re-equipped with the Dakota and then moved to Egypt. It conducted route flying to various locations around the Mediterranean, Middle East and North Africa. It received Valettas in 1950 and continued the role until September 1954, when the squadron disbanded at Fayid.

In April 1956, 78Sqn was re-formed at Aden with Pioneers, adding Twin Pioneers later. Due to the hostilities in that region, these aircraft were considered vulnerable, so guns were fitted in the rear door of the

Twin Pioneer and rockets under the wings, which were later fired in its army-support role. The squadron converted to the Wessex in 1965, at Sharjah, from where it operated until December 1971, when it was disbanded once again.

Following the war in the Falklands, in August 1983, 1310 Flight was formed at Kelly's Garden with Chinooks and 1564 Flight with Sea Kings HAR.3s at Navy Point. When the newly built Mount Pleasant airfield was completed, these two Flights were amalgamated and re-numbered 78Sqn on 22 May 1986.

Currently, 78Sqn operate the Chinook HC.2 as a transport in support of the army, while the Sea King is primarily tasked with search and rescue for both military and civilians. When not on task, the Sea Kings can also be used in the support helicopter role. Unlike the other RAF SAR helicopters, 78Sqn's Sea Kings are painted dark-grey for operational reasons.

No. 78Sqn operate the Chinook HC.2 and Sea King HAR.3 from their base at Mount Pleasant on the Falkland Islands.

The Falkland Islands is the only location where the Sea King HAR.3 operates in a toned-down colour scheme. There, 78Sqn also provide additional army support when capability is available.

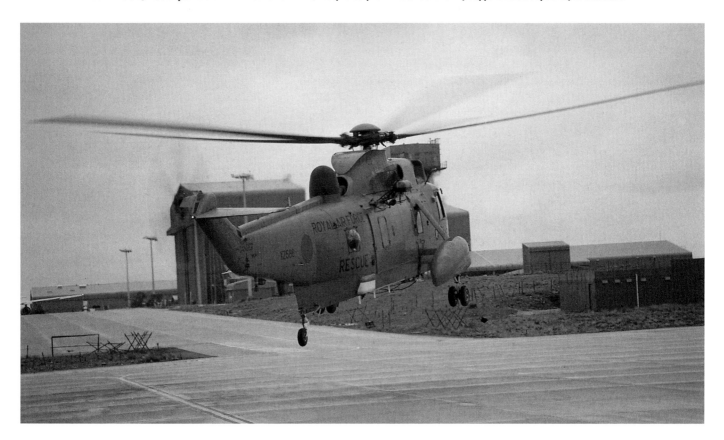

No. 84 Squadron

RAF Akrotiri. Cyprus
Bell Griffin HAR.2
3 Group
Strike Command
Role: Support Helicopter/Search & Rescue
Motto: *Scorpiones Pungunt* – Scorpions sting

On 7 January 1917, 84 Squadron was formed at Beaulieu, equipping with the SE.5a from August and deploying to France in September. Captain Beauchamp-Proctor was awarded a VC for his actions in 1918, during which he took part in twenty-six air combats and brought his total aircraft destroyed to twenty-two, plus sixteen balloons. During operations, the squadron destroyed 129 enemy aircraft and fifty observation balloons. After a year with the Army of Occupation in Germany, it returned to the UK as a cadre to Tangmere and was disbanded in January 1920.

In August 1920, 84Sqn was re-formed in Baghdad, Iraq with the DH.9a and moved to Shaibah in September. It re-equipped with the Wapiti in October 1928 and became the first unit to operate Vincents, from December 1934, followed by conversion to Blenheim in February 1939. It moved to the Western Desert in October and, later, took part in the campaigns in Greece, Iraq, Persia and Syria, before deploying to Sumatra in the Far East in January 1942. There, it attacked Japanese positions in Batvia, Java and Sumatra, before being overrun. Most of the squadron were captured, apart from the CO and some aircrew. The squadron was re-established in India, where it received more Blenheims. Vengeance dive-bombers eventually arrived in December 1942, replaced by Mosquitos in July 1944. but glue-softening in the high humidity soon brought this to a halt. The Vengeances soldiered on until October, but it was February before new Mosquitos arrived. The Japanese surrendered before they became operational.

With the war over, 84Sqn moved to Singapore, with detachments to Java and then Malaya in May 1946, before returning to Singapore in September, where it converted to Beaufighters the following month. In November 1948, it was moved to Iraq and converted to Brigands in February. In April 1950, it returned to Singapore, where it flew missions against communist terrorists in

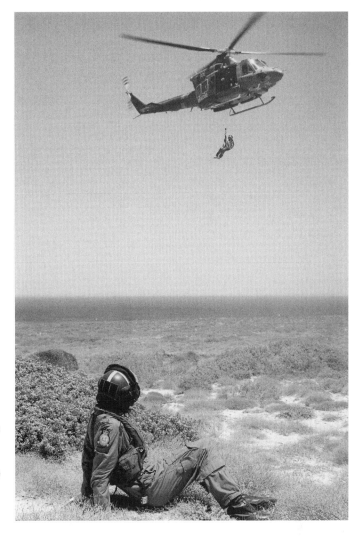

An airman simulates an injured aircrew for a training exercise. 84Sqn at Akrotiri is the only RAF SAR squadron that is not equipped with the Sea King but operates the Griffin HAR.2. Crown Copyright

Operation *Firedog*, before disbanding in February 1953, after having dropped 1,883 tons of bombs.

The same day, 204Sqn was re-numbered to form a new 84Sqn at Fayid, Egypt with the Valetta, to operate in the Canal Zone and, then, Aden in 1957. The Beverley arrived the following year. In September 1960, the Valetta Flight became 233Sqn. With Aden closing, 84Sqn re-equipped with the Andover in August 1967 and moved to Sharjah the following month. In October 1971, the squadron was disbanded.

In July 1972, 84Sqn was re-formed from 1563 Flight and a 230Sqn detachment with the Whirlwind at Akrotiri, commencing its role to support UN forces and an SAR squadron. In March 1982, they converted to the Wessex HC.2. In March 1985, these were replaced with ex-RN Wessex HU.5s, although the HC.2s returned in 1995. In 2002, Flight

Lieutenant Nicky Smith was appointed as CO of 84Sqn, becoming the RAF's first female to hold this position in an operational squadron. In early 2003, the Wessex was retired, being temporarily replaced with the Sea King from 203 (R) Sqn while 84Sqn prepared to take delivery of the their new Griffin HAR.2s.

The primary task of 84Sqn is providing SAR cover for resident and visiting British Forces. It can also be called upon to assist UN forces on the island – hence the blue band. In addition, it can be used for support helicopters, as well as assisting the local authorities. In a classic example, two Griffins assisted a pair of Russian-built 'Helix' helicopters of the Republic of Cyprus in extinguishing a fierce fire that threatened a village. They brought water from a source several miles away in under-slung buckets.

No. 84Sqn operates four Griffin HAR.2s from its base at Akrotiri in Cyprus.

A Nimrod MR.2 of the Kinloss Wing climbs away using its powerful Spey engines on another sortie. 120Sqn is one of the three MR.2 squadrons based at Kinloss.

No. 120 Squadron

RAF Kinloss
Hawker Siddeley Nimrod MR.2
3 Group
Strike Command
Role: Maritime Patrol
Motto: Endurance

On 1 January 1918, 120 Squadron was formed at Cramlington with DH.9s. It was preparing to deploy to the continent to join the Independent Bombing Force, attacking targets in Germany. Before it became operational, the Armistice was signed and the role changed to flying mail between Hawkinge and France. In May 1919, it converted to the DH.10, with which it managed to deliver mail between Hawking and Cologne in three hours. In late-summer 1919, the squadron was disbanded.

In June 1941, 120Sqn was re-formed with Liberators at Nutts Corner in Northern Ireland, on anti-submarine patrols to protect the transatlantic convoys. It moved to Ballykelly the following month and, having operated detachments at Reykjavik and Aldergrove, in April 1943, it moved to Reykjavik, Iceland but returned to Londonderry the following March. A further detachment was operated at Cain from April. By the end of the war, it had become the RAF's highest scoring anti-submarine squadron, with fourteen U-boats destroyed plus three shared and eight damaged. It was disbanded in June 1945.

In October 1946, 120Sqn was re-formed with Liberators at Leuchars by the renumbering of 160Sqn and re-equipped with Lancasters shortly after. In November 1947, it deployed to Palestine, where its role was searching for illegal immigrants. It returned to the UK in 1950, where it converted to the Shackleton during 1951. It then moved to Aldergrove in 1952, returning to Kinloss in 1959, during which time it operated the Shackleton MR.1, MR.2 and MR.3 and saw wide service throughout the world.

From December 1970, 120Sqn converted to the Nimrod at Kinloss, with which it continued in the anti-submarine and surface-surveillance roles plus SAR. It flew numerous surveillance missions during the 'Cod War' with Iceland in 1973. From January 1977, it was on Operation *Tapestry*, tasked with patrolling the UK's oil rigs and 200-mile fishery limits.

In 1981, it began to receive the improved Nimrod MR.2 and was soon taken into action for the first time. The squadron's Nimrods were the first to be operated in the South Atlantic in 1982 from Ascension Is, after they were hastily fitted with refuelling probes and armed with Sidewinder missiles for self defence. They were also the first to be deployed on Operation Granby and flew numerous surveillance missions in 1991.

It is anticipated that 120Sqn will be the first to be equipped with the Nimrod MRA.4 when it enters service in 2009.

No. 120Sqn operates the Nimrod MR.2 from their base at Kinloss. The aircraft are drawn from the Maritime Wing and are shared with 42 (R) and 201Sqn.

No. 201 Squadron

RAF Kinloss
Hawker Siddeley Nimrod MR.2
3 Group
Strike Command
Role: Maritime Patrol
Motto: *Hic et Ubique* – Here and everywhere

On 16 October 1914, 201Sqn was originally formed as 1Sqn, RNAS at Fort Grange. In June 1915, Flight Sub-Lieutenant Warneford was awarded a VC for destroying the Zeppelin LZ-37 over Bruges. He achieved this by throwing bombs at the airship. The award was the first for any aerial combat. The navy had further success, when two submarines were sunk in August 1915. In 1917, the squadron was awarded the Croix de Guerre for assisting the French during the Third Battle of Ypres.

When the RAF was formed in April 1918, the squadron was re-numbered 201Sqn. Coastal patrols were flown from Dover, followed by fighter missions. Aircraft operated included Farmans, Caudrons and Moranes plus Sopwith Camels and Triplanes.

As a result of his action in October 1918, Major W G Barker was awarded a VC. He had attacked a two-seat enemy aircraft, which broke up in the air, and was then attacked by formations of Fokker fighters. During this he was injured in both legs, had an elbow shattered and lost consciousness twice. Despite this, when he came to, he returned to the combat and shot down a further three enemy Fokkers. He finally flew his damaged aircraft back to base and crashed on landing.

At the end of 1919, 201Sqn was disbanded, having been credited with over 280 aircraft destroyed during First World War operations.

In 1929, 201Sqn was re-formed as a flying boat unit at Calshot with the Southampton and operated anti-submarine and warship-reporting patrols. The Southampton was replaced by the London in 1936 and, when war broke out, the squadron was based at Sullom Voe in the Shetlands, where it operated from the depot ship *Manella*. During that initial part of the war, the squadron flew search and rescue (SAR) missions to aircraft searching for submarines in the North Atlantic and managed to locate and recover a number of crews. The Londons were replaced by Sunderlands in November 1939, during a few months at Invergordon. Having returned to Sullom Voe, the squadron moved on to Castle Archdale in Northern Ireland in September 1941, followed by Pembroke Dock in March 1944. During these moves, various detachments were also operated, including Reykjavik in 1941.

Although a number of attacks on submarines had already been recorded by 201Sqn, the first confirmed sinking was of U-384 in March 1943. A further three were sunk in the South West Approaches during Operation *Overlord*. By the end of the war, it had clocked up some 20,000 hours flown and was credited with seven German U-Boats confirmed sunk.

During 1948, 201Sqn Sunderlands were tasked as part of the Berlin Airlift. Because of the nature of their design, they were particularly useful in transporting salt, as this was corrosive for other aircraft, which had not been proofed.

In 1956, the squadron flew a detachment out to the Far East, prior to disbanding briefly in 1958. It then re-formed with the Shackleton, which was operated far and wide.

In autumn 1963, 201Sqn was deployed to Nassau in the Bahamas, where their primary role was to provide protection against Cuban infiltration. Interestingly, when the region was hit by a severe hurricane, the squadron flew emergency aid into Havana. The squadron were also deployed to Singapore in 1965, during the Malaysian Emergency, and to Sharjah, to patrol the Arabian Gulf during the withdrawal of British Forces from the Middle East during the late 1960s.

Having returned to the UK, in November 1970, 201Sqn became the first to re-equip with the Nimrod at Kinloss. These were used to monitor Soviet submarine movements, not only in the North Atlantic but also, through detachments in the Far East, the Malacca Straits.

During early 1982, 201Sqn started to convert to the Nimrod MR.1 and, in May, some were deployed to Ascension for operations in the South Atlantic, off the Argentine coast.

In August 1990, the first 201Sqn Nimrod arrived at Seeb in Oman, following the Iraqi invasion of Kuwait. In October 1992, Nimrods were deployed to Sigonella, Italy for Operation *Sharp Guard*, to enforce UN sanctions during the civil war in the former republic of Yugoslavia (FRY).

No. 201Sqn operate the Nimrod MR.2 from their base at Kinloss. The aircraft are drawn from the Maritime Wing pool.

No. 202 Squadron – Headquarters

RAF Boulmer
3 Group
Strike Command
Role: Search & Rescue
Motto: *Semper Vigilate* – Be always vigilant

No. 202Sqn originated as 2Sqn RNAS, which was formed on 17 October 1914 at

201Sqn have operated the Nimrod since 1982 and flew some of their early missions on Operation *Corporate* in the South Atlantic. Today it continues to operate the Nimrod MR.2 as part of the Kinloss Wing. Crown Copyright

Eastchurch. It was equipped with various aircraft and tasked with flying missions against Belgian ports and anti-Zeppelin patrols. In June 1915, it became part of 2 Wing. On 5 November 1916, it was re-formed from 'B' Squadron of 1 Wing, RNAS at St Pol, France and equipped with Farman F40s, with which it was tasked to fly reconnaissance missions over Belgium. During March 1917, it converted to the DH.4. On 1 April 1918, at Bergues, France, the squadron became 202Sqn of the RAF, still operating the DH.4 –plus the DH.9 which was operated for just four months from May. It continued in the reconnaissance role and, in November 1918, moved to Varssenaere in Belgium, before setting foot in the UK for the first time in March 1919. It arrived at Eastburn Airfield (later to be re-named Driffield) and was disbanded in January 1920.

The squadron was re-formed in April 1920 at Alexandria, Egypt with the Short 184 to fly fleet co-operation. However, with cut backs and the Royal Navy's preference to operate its own aircraft, 202Sqn was disbanded again in May 1921.

In January 1929, 481 Flight at Marsaxlokk Bay, Malta was re-numbered 202Sqn, Equipped with Fairey IIIDs, these were replaced with IIIFs from June 1930. In February 1922, the squadron was involved in the location of a Dornier Wal flying boat, which had come down some

fifty miles from Malta. It was soon located and a Royal Navy ship directed to the spot. The squadron's first SAR task and a taste of things to come!

During the 1930s, 202Sqn made several flag-waving tours of the Mediterranean and, in 1935, converted to the Scapa flying boat. Following the Italian invasion of Ethiopia, the squadron undertook anti-submarine patrols around Malta. Once over, it resumed the flag waving and included surveys of some potential temporary bases – an exercise which would prove useful a few years later!

The squadron commenced conversion to the London in 1937, by which time the Spanish Civil War was causing problems, with several unarmed merchant ships being sunk. The squadron provided part of an international 'police force', during which 111 patrols were flown. When Germany annexed part of Czechoslovakia, 202Sqn were deployed to Alexandria and, despite Neville Chamberlain's assurance that he had obtained a peace agreement with Hitler, 202Sqn spent a while photographing Libyan and Sicilian airfields and ports, just in case!

September 1939 saw 202Sqn at Gibraltar, where they continued their patrols around the progressively more hostile Spanish coast and into the Bay of Biscay. Following the defeat of the French and the establishment of Vichy France,

the Allies requested they surrender the French Fleet to them, rather than let it get into German hands. When they refused, a 202Sqn London was tasked with a reconnaissance mission over Oran, in July 1940, and photographed the fleet, enabling British warships to accurately bombard and destroy them.

With operational tasking significantly increasing, 202Sqn were joined by two Sunderlands of 228Sqn. Over the next few months, four Londons were lost, although one Italian submarine was attacked and forced to the surface, where a destroyer was able the effect its capture. In October 1940, 3 AACU with Swordfish was absorbed into the squadron, for local patrols. In April 1941, it began conversion to the Catalina and some Sunderlands were added towards the end of the year. The invasion of North Africa and Operation *Torch* in 1942 saw increased patrols, during which U-620 was sunk by one 202Sqn Catalina in February 1943 and another contributed to the sinking of U-761 a year later. In September 1944, 202Sqn returned to the UK, where it continued to operate in the anti-submarine role from Castle Archdale until disbanded in 1946.

In October 1946, 202Sqn was reformed with the Halifax at Aldergrove by the re-numbering of 518Sqn. Its new role was meteorological reconnaissance, flying

A 202Sqn Sea King heads a line of SAR types. Although the Sycamore was used in the SAR role it is incorrectly marked, as it was never operated by 202Sqn. The Squadron commenced SAR duties with the Whirlwind and converted straight to the Sea King. It therefore never operated the Wessex, which appears in the background, either.

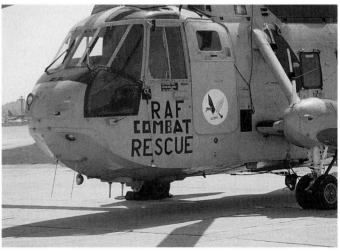

This 202Sqn Sea King HAR.3 has been unofficially marked as 'Combat' Rescue. The RAF have no dedicated Combat Rescue helicopters but could potentially use the Sea King if so required. There is little reason why the SAR helicopters could not be used with a toned-down colour-scheme, as in the Falklands. It has a reasonable range and could be armed with a pintle-mounted machine gun for self defence.

lengthy patterns out into the Atlantic. In 1950, it converted to the Hastings, which it operated until disbanded again in July 1964.

In September 1964, 228Sqn at Leconfield was re-numbered 202Sqn and continued to perform the search and rescue (SAR) role with the Whirlwind. Flights were operated at Acklington, Coltishall, Leconfield and Leuchars.

In January 1976, 202Sqn HQ moved to Finningley, forming the SAR Wing with 22Sqn, by which time Flights were operating from Boulmer, Coltishall, Leconfield, Leuchars and Lossiemouth. From August 1978, the Whirlwinds were replaced by the Sea King, with 202Sqn being the first to convert. A central maintenance facility, along with the HQ SAR Wing, was also established at Finningley, jointly with 22Sqn. 'C' Flight at Coltishall was deployed to the Falklands in August 1982 and was re-numbered 1564 Flight the following August. In December 1992, the HQ moved to Boulmer.

No. 202Sqn's HQ is based at Boulmer. They operate the Sea King HAR.3 with 'A' Flight at Boulmer, 'D' Flight at Lossiemouth and 'E' Flight at Leconfield.

The RAF Sea Kings have proved invaluable in saving lives, not only of British servicemen but also casualties at sea and ashore. By far the biggest customers for the squadrons are holiday-makers, who frequently seem to leave their common sense at home and manage to get themselves into life-threatening situations.

No. 202 Squadron – 'A' Flight

Westland Sea King HAR.3
RAF Boulmer
3 Group
Strike Command
Role: Search & Rescue
Motto: *Semper Vigilate* – Be always vigilant

In September 1964, 202Sqn's 'A' Flight was established at Acklington with Whirlwinds It moved to Boulmer on 21 October 1975 and converted to the Sea King 1 January 1979.

No. 202Sqn's 'A' Flight operated the Sea King HAR.3 from Boulmer.

No. 202 Squadron – 'D' Flight

Westland Sea King HAR.3
Lossiemouth
3 Group
Strike Command
Role: Search & Rescue
Motto: *Semper Vigilate* – Be always vigilant

'D' Flight of 202Sqn was originally formed in August 1964 with Whirlwinds at

Coltishall and continued to operate them until April 1973, when replaced by 'B' Flight of 22Sqn.

'D' Flight was re-formed in September 1973 at Coltishall with the Whirlwind. Later that year it was re-named 'C' Flight and, in 1982, it moved to Port Stanley, where it became 1564 Flight.

On 18 February 1973 'B' Flight from 22Sqn at Thorney Is was re-numbered 202Sqn 'D' Flight and moved to Lossiemouth with the Whirlwind.

'D' Flight re-equipped with the Sea King in September 1978 and currently carries out an average of 250 emergency call-outs each year – in 2001 it carried out its 5,000th rescue. It is planned to move 'D' Flight to Kinloss in May 2005.

No. 202Sqn's 'D' Flight operates the Sea King HAR.3 from Lossiemouth.

No. 202 Squadron – 'E' Flight

Westland Sea King HAR.3
Leconfield
3 Group
Strike Command
Role: Search & Rescue
Motto: *Semper Vigilate* – Be always vigilant

In November 1988, 202Sqn's 'E' Flight was established with Sea Kings at Leconfield from 'D' Flight of 22Sqn.

No. 202Sqn's 'E' Flight operates the Sea King HAR.3 from Leconfield.

No. 203 (Reserve) Squadron

RAF St Mawgan
Westland Sea King HAR.3
3 Group
Strike Command
Role: Sea King OCU
Motto: *Occidens oriensque* – East and West

On 1 September 1914, 203Sqn was originally formed as 3Sqn, RNAS at Eastchurch with Nieuports and Farmans. It was deployed to the Dardanelles, where it performed spotting duties for the guns of RN warships.

In November 1915, the squadron commander – Richard Bell-Davies – was leading a bombing mission on Ferrijik Junction, Bulgaria. During the attack one of the aircraft was hit, but the pilot managed a safe landing and then set light to his aircraft. Despite intense fire from troops on the ground, Bell-Davies swooped down and managed to rescue him, just as Bulgarian troops were coming into rifle range. For this, Bell-Davies was awarded the VC. By the end of the year, 3Sqn had returned to the UK and been disbanded.

Six months later, 'C' Squadron, RNAS,

203(R)Sqn provides the type-training for Sea King HAR.3 crews prior to joining the operational squadrons.

with Bristol and Nieuport Scouts, was re-numbered 3Sqn. It flew patrols over Belgium and saw action over the Somme, supporting RFC units. The role continued when it was transferred to the RAF and re-numbered 203Sqn, remaining in Belgium until March 1919, when it returned home and disbanded at Scopwick (later re-named Digby) in January 1920.

In March 1920, 203Sqn was reformed with Avro 504s and Camels and main-tained its early connections by operating as a naval co-operation unit. These links continued when it converted to the Nightjar and flew carrier-borne fighter duties. It deployed to Turkey during the Chanak crisis in 1922 with Nightjars, then disbanded in April 1923.

The Mount Batten-based 482 Flight was re-numbered 203Sqn in January 1929 and took its Southamptons to Basra, Iraq, tasked in the anti-piracy and policing role. In 1931, it received Rangoons, followed by Singapores and then, in May 1940, the Blenheim in Aden. When Italy entered the war in June 1940, 203Sqn was heavily tasked in the East African campaign, before deploying to Crete to provide cover

for the evacuation from advancing Axis forces.

Operations in the Middle and Far East continued, with 203Sqn flying Baltimores from August 1942, Wellingtons at Santa Cruz from November 1943 and, finally, Liberators, which it operated from November 1943 at Madura, Ceylon until May 1946. It then returned to the UK, operating from Leuchars before deploying to St Eval, where it converted to the Lancaster.

In 1952, 203Sqn moved to Topcliffe, where it converted to the Neptune maritime patrol aircraft, which it flew until September 1956, when it disbanded.

In November 1958, the Ballykelly-based 240Sqn was re-numbered 203Sqn. Equipped with the early Shackletons, these were subsequently exchanged for later marks, before it moved to Luqa, Malta in January 1969. It converted to the Nimrod in October 1971 and continued to maintained patrols in the Mediterranean until the end of 1977, when it was disbanded once again.

On 1 November 1996, 203Sqn was re-formed as a reserve squadron by the

re-numbering of the Sea King Operation Conversion Unit (SK OCU) at St Mawgan. Originally formed as the RAF Sea King Training Unit (RAFSKTU) – officially on 17 February 1978 at Culdrose, although it came into existence on 1 November 1977– it became the Sea King Training Flight in October 1979, before being re-named SK OCU on 1 April 1996.

No. 203 (R) Sqn take aircrew from the SARTU at Valley and train them to operate the Sea King, prior to posting to 22 or 202Sqn.

In 2003, three 203 (R) Sqn Sea Kings were temporarily deployed to Akrotiri, Cyprus, to provide a stop gap between the disbanding of the Wessex and the intro-duction of the Griffin with 84Sqn.

Of the various courses run by 203 (R) Sqn, the long course for *ab initio* pilots lasts twenty-three weeks and includes seventy hours flying plus a further fifty in the simu-lator, while the short refresher-course lasts just three weeks with fifteen hours flying and five in the simulator.

In 2004, it was announced that 203 (R) Sqn would be relocated to Valley by June 2006.

No. 203 (R) Sqn currently operates the Sea King HAR.3 from St Mawgan.

No. 1115 Flight

RQ-1A Predator UAV (USAF owned)
Indian Springs Auxiliary Field, USA
3 Group
Strike Command

No. 1115 Flight is a recently established unit and has no previous history. It is currently located at Indian Springs Auxiliary Field, which is near to Nellis AFB and the extensive Nellis ranges. It is a small unit, consisting of some forty-four personnel, which operates alongside the USAF's 11th and 15th Reconnaissance Squadron, which are equipped with the General Atomics RQ-1A Predator.

The personnel of 1115 Flight are being trained up and gaining experience in the

1115 Flight has been formed to work with USAF forces to gain experience in the role and operation of UAVs such as RQ-1 Predator.

operation of the Predator UAV. With this rapidly advancing technology, the RAF are using this opportunity to evaluate the role of Predators, which are currently being flown by the RAF, but are owned by the USAF.

It is thought that the RAF is very interested in obtaining its own UAVs. These would probably be for use in the high-altitude long-endurance role and even as an armed CUAV able to launch weapons – both of which roles Predator is capable.

No. 1115 Flight is based at Indian Springs in the USA.

Ballistic Missile Early Warning Squadron

RAF Fylingdales
3 Group
Strike Command
Role: Air Surveillance & Control

The Ballistic Missile Early Warning Squadron (BMEWS) began operations in 1963 to counter the perceived threat from the Soviet Union of a possible missile attack being launched across the North Pole. Three BMEWS sites were selected to provide the early warning for the UK and USA. The other two sites are located at Thule in Greenland and Clear in Alaska. Because of the benefit to the US Defences,

The Ops Room of the BMEWS, where operators monitor signals that may indicate a hostile threat by ballistic missile or from satellites in space. Crown Copyright

the USA paid around £36m of the £45m that it cost to build the site at Fylingdales – the three large 'golf ball'-like structures being a major feature.

In 1986, it was decided that a significant upgrade of the site was required. Not only was the equipment getting more costly to maintain but there were potential new threats from additional countries with ballistic missiles. This upgrade cost £160m of which £112m was paid by the USA. The new system saw the end of the 'golf balls', with their 112-ton scanners mounted inside, and their replacement by a single pyramid-like structure, on the three surfaces of which a Solid State Phased Array Radar (SSPAR) is mounted. Each face has 2,560 transmitters, which use electrical phase to steer the beam. Not only does this enable the system to operate effectively with some transmitters down (either failed or on maintenance) but also the static arrays can provide a full 360-degree cover and, thus, are unique.

Although now capable of 'seeing' beyond that range, the effort at Fylingdales is concentrated on a 3,000-mile radius. The system is now also capable of tracking some 800 objects in space simultaneously.

In December 2002, the US Government formally requested to incorporate some of the missile early warning facilities at Fylingdales in its 'Son of Star Wars'

National Missile Defence system (NMD). The new computer will result in a more accurate detection and analysis of threats. The current system was only required to determine where an incoming missile was going to land, the proposed US-upgrade requires more accurate information, to enable actual interception of the attacking missile.

Fylingdales is purely a BMEWS and plays a vital role in the British and NATO defences and deterrence. There is no airfield at Fylingdales and, therefore, no aircraft are based there.

RAF Mountain Rescue Service

RAF Stafford (HQ)
3 Group
Strike Command
Role: Mountain Rescue
Motto: Whensoever

The Mountain Rescue Service was established on 6 July 1943 at Llandwrog. It evolved from the uncoordinated and untrained attempts to locate crashed aircrews dating back to the 1930s. As a result of the increasing number of callouts, the station medical officer and keen mountaineer at Llandwrog – Flying Officer Graham – began training airmen in the skills of mountaineering and rescue techniques. After thirty-three crewmembers had been rescued from twenty-two crashes, he realized that formalized training and better equipment was required. He presented his finding to the Air Ministry, was given the support that he requested and, so, the organisation was officially formed.

Initially, Mountain Rescue Teams (MRT) were formed at Harpur Hill, Llandwrog, Millom and Montrose. These gradually expanded and, by 1947, included teams located in the Middle and Far East. Their role had also expanded and included searching for civilian aircrew and passengers.

During the mid-1970s, the Mountain and Desert Rescue Teams were withdrawn. This left only the UK MRTs at Kinloss, Leeming, Leuchars, St Athan, Stafford and Valley. Valley was closed in October 1996 and its equipment and area of responsibility transferred to Stafford.

Although the equipment and clothing used by the MRTs has improved greatly over the years, the task remains largely a physical one of searching in often difficult terrain and poor weather. Their role remains the same – primarily to locate and recover crashed military aircrew. By regular training they maintain a high level of fitness, enabling a specialized ability to be able search all types of terrain in all types of weather. They are also trained to provide first aid to survivors and co-ordinate their safe delivery to hospital.

Although the numbers of crashes has dramatically reduced, the MRTs still provide a valuable role for the occasional crash. They provided a major contribution to the efforts that were put into the Lockerbie and East Midlands accidents. However, the majority of their call-outs are now for civilian walkers and climbers who get into difficulties. MRTs are available on a one-hour standby, 365 days per year. The MRTs are also called out under the Military Aid to the Civil Community (MACC) scheme during periods of flooding and other extreme weather conditions.

Each team comprises seven full-time staff and up to twenty-nine volunteers. Unpaid, these volunteers are required to train on at least two weeks per month and one evening per week. They take part in regular exercises with civilian and military

A stretcher being lowered by a member of the Mountain Rescue Service using a 'guiding line' technique to keep it away from the cliff. The Mountain Rescue Service can rapidly deploy teams, primarily to locate and assist injured aircrew and passengers, in any terrain. In peace time this frequently includes lost or fallen climbers. Crown Copyright

The Chinook HC.3 has enlarged fairings either side of the fuselage containing additional fuel to provide extra range, and will be operated by 7Sqn. Crown Copyright

rescue organisations to maintain maximum effectiveness. Training of a raw recruit takes approximately three years before they become an MRT expert.

The RAF Mountain Rescue Service HQ is based at Stafford. Teams are based at Kinloss, Leuchars, Leeming, St Athan and Stafford.

Joint Helicopter Command

Wilton
HQ Land (Army)
Role: Support Helicopter
Motto: Across all boundaries

Joint Helicopter Command (JHC) was formed on 1 October 1999 and based at the Army's Land HQ at Wilton. It became operational on 1 April 2000.

It was formed as a result of the 1998 Strategic Defence Review. Its role is to train, plan, prepare, sustain and resource battlefield helicopters and air-assault assets. As a result, the unified force is able to operate with a more effective capability.

While the SAR Sea Kings and Griffins of 78 and 84Sqn are not included, the Support Helicopter Force Chinook, Merlin and Puma all are. Their bases at Aldergrove, Benson and Odiham also provide helicopter support for army and other units, to enable tasks to be successfully completed.

To enable the helicopters to be operated effectively, it was decided to establish the Joint Helicopter Support Unit, which became operational in July 1982. Consisting of 30 per cent RAF and 70 per cent Army personnel from a range of corps, they assisted in the preparation of under-slung loads and landing sites. Members of the embryo unit were aboard the *Atlantic Conveyor* when she was hit and sunk by an Argentinian Exocet missile – fortunately, they survived. The Unit has been involved in many other operations – humanitarian relief as well, providing aid to civil authorities.

Since being formed, JHC has been extremely active, with operations in Afghanistan, Bosnia, Kosovo, Mozambique, Sierra Leone and, most recently, Iraq.

Joint Helicopter Command (JHC) is based at Wilton.

No. 7 Squadron

RAF Odiham
Boeing Chinook HC.2, Westland Gazelle AH.1
Joint Helicopter Command
Role: Support Helicopter
Motto: *Per Diem Per Noctum* – By day and by night

On 1 May 1914, 7Sqn formed at Farnborough, but was dispersed within three months to reinforce other squadrons, prior to their being deployed to France. On 28 September, 7Sqn re-formed and was itself deployed to France the following April with the FB.5 in the reconnaissance and bombing role. In August 1915, both having been hit by enemy ground-fire, Captain Liddell was posthumously awarded the VC for saving his badly wounded observer's life, despite his own severe injuries. The squadron later operated BE.2cs and then RE.8s, before returning home and being disbanded at the end of 1919.

On 1 June 1923, 7Sqn re-formed at Bircham Newton as a heavy-bomber unit, initially with Vimys and then Virginias, and moved to Worthy Down in 1927. In October 1935, 'B' Flight were re-numbered 102Sqn. It re-equipped with Wellesleys in 1937, then Ansons and Hampdens in spring 1939. The squadron moved to Finningley in September 1939, prior to being re-named 16 OTU at Upper Heyford and disbanded in May 1940.

At Leeming, 7Sqn re-formed as the RAF's first Stirling bomber unit on 1 August 1940. It then moved to Oakington and commenced bombing missions in February 1941. In October 1942, it was designated and remained a Pathfinder unit for the rest of the war, re-equipping with the Lancaster the following May. In July 1945, it moved to Mepal. During this period it flew over 5,000 sorties and lost 157 aircraft. Some 800 aircrew lost their lives and 546 were awarded decorations and medals.

Following VE day, 7Sqn flew food drops to the starving Dutch civilians, as well as

bringing PoWs home. In July 1946, it moved to Upwood, where it converted to the Lincoln in August 1949. It continued operating from Upwood until December 1955, apart from when it was deployed to Malaya in 1949 and the Middle East. It subsequently returned home and was disbanded at Oakington in January 1956, but not before it had won the Lawrence Minot Trophy – a prestigious American Bombing Competition – eight times.

On 1 November 1956, 7Sqn re-formed as a member of the V-Force, flying Valiants from Honington. It moved to Wittering in 1960 and was disbanded in September 1962.

In May 1970, 7Sqn was re-formed at St Mawgan to provide target facilities with the Canberra. This it continued to do until it disbanded in January 1982.

It was re-established on 1 September 1982 at Odiham with the Chinook HC.1, later upgraded to HC.2 – 7Sqn has also operated a few Gazelle HT.3 and HCC.4s, primarily to check low-flying routes prior to their being flown by the Chinooks at night. As the last operators of the RAF's Gazelle, 7Sqn retired their last examples in October 2001 and now has two AAC AH.1s attached, enabling a rationalization of the JHC Gazelle fleet.

Since re-equipping with the Chinook, 7Sqn has been involved in various operations, including the Falklands, Northern Ireland, Beirut, Gulf War, the former

18Sqn Chinooks have seen wide service, having been based in Germany before moving to Odiham. Here one is landing in Oman during Exercise *Saif Sareea II*, creating a dust cloud.

republic of Yugoslavia (FRY), Afghanistan and Iraq, in addition to numerous exercises. During the squadron's return from the Gulf War, 7Sqn was tasked to assist in humanitarian relief operations for the Kurdish refugees. This resulted in their flying food and supplies from Turkey into Northern Iraq.

No. 7Sqn is earmarked to operate the Chinook HC.3 when it enters service.

No. 7Sqn currently operates the Chinook HC.2 and two Army Gazelle AH.1s from their base at Odiham.

No. 18 (Bomber) Squadron

RAF Odiham
Boeing Chinook HC.2
Joint Helicopter Command
Role: Support Helicopter
Motto: *Animo et Fide* – With courage and faith

On 11 May 1915, 18 Squadron was formed at Northolt from a nucleus provided by 4 Reserve Squadron and equipped with Longhorns. It equipped with the FB.5 Gunbus, DH.2s and a Bristol Scout at Norwich and deployed to France in November. It operated the FE.2b bomber from April 1916, followed by the DH.4 in

May 1917 and DH.9A in October 1918, until disbanded at the end of December 1919, by which time it had scored 200 victories.

The squadron was re-formed with the Hart light-bomber at Upper Heyford in October 1931 and, later, re-equipped with the Hind. It entered the Second World War with Blenheims and a deployment to France, where it suffered heavy losses. In October 1941, part of the squadron was deployed to Malta from East Anglia with Blenheim IVs to attack Axis shipping, until disbanded in Egypt in March 1942. However, in the UK, the rest of the squadron was being built-up to strength at Waddington with Blenheims and flying operations. During this period, an artificial leg was dropped for Douglas Bader after he lost his when shot down over France by a Bf.109. The whole squadron moved to North Africa in November 1942. It was all but wiped out in December during an attack near Chouigui, on which the CO – Wing Commander Malcolm – was awarded a posthumous VC for his skill and daring, which were of the highest order. In January, their surviving aircraft were passed to 614Sqn and they re-equipped with the Boston. Gradually, the squadron moved through Sicily, Italy and into

Greece, where it was disbanded in March 1946.

For just two weeks in September 1946, 621Sqn with Lancasters at Ein Shemer, Palestine was re-numbered 18 (B) Sqn, before becoming 'B' Flight of 38Sqn. The squadron then re-formed again in March 1947 with Mosquitos at Kabrit, Egypt, moving on to Burma and Changi, Singapore, where it disbanded in November 1947 when re-numbered 1300 (Meteorological) Flight.

In December 1947, 18 (B) Sqn re-formed with Dakotas at Netheravon and took part in the Berlin Airlift from Gütersloh and Wunstorf, before disbanding in February 1950 at Oakington.

In August 1953, 18 (B) Sqn re-formed with the Canberra at Scampton, moving to Upwood in May 1955. It disbanded in January 1957. It re-formed again in December 1958, by the re-numbering of 199Sqn, equipped with the Valiant bomber, which it used in the ECM role. In 1958, it moved to Finningley, where it continued to operate until disbanded in March 1963.

It re-formed again in January 1964 at Odiham, as the first Wessex HC.2 squadron, following the re-numbering of the Wessex trials unit. It subsequently moved to Acklington and deployed to Cyprus to operate as part of the UN forces, then on to Gütersloh, in August 1970, to support the British Army, until the squadron disbanded in November 1980.

On 4 August 1981, 18 (B) Sqn was re-formed once more at Odiham as the RAF's first Chinook squadron. It was deployed to the Falklands in April 1982 as part of the Task Force. It lost three of its Chinooks when the MV *Atlantic Conveyor* was sunk by an Argentinian Exocet missile, leaving just one operational aircraft. This single Chinook made a substantial contribution to the British forces in reclaiming the Islands.

In May 1983, 18 (B) Sqn was moved back to Gütersloh in support of 1 (BR) Corps. In January 1991, they were deployed to Saudi Arabia in support of coalition forces and, although the squadron returned to Gütersloh afterwards, many of the air and groundcrew were rapidly re-deployed to Turkey to help provide humanitarian aid to the Kurds in northern Iraq.

While based in Germany, 18 (B) Sqn was heavily tasked with providing support, not only for the Harrier force, but also the Army's 1 (BR) Corps. As a result of the

Options for Change, the squadron lost some of its Chinooks but gained a flight of Puma HC.1s. In December 1992, it moved to Laarbruch and continued to fulfil its commitments in Belize, the Falkland Islands and Northern Ireland.

In 1996, a pair of Chinooks was deployed to Split in Croatia as part of IFOR, to help bring peace and stability to Bosnia, and, in July 1997, the squadron moved back to Odiham, becoming a Chinook-only unit.

In support of operations, 18 (B) Sqn was deployed to Sierra Leone and, in 2003, the squadron was deployed to Iraq, where it played its part in freeing the Iraqi people from Saddam's oppressive regime.

In addition to their operational role, 18 (B) Sqn also conduct the aircrew training on the Chinook. Established as a Flight within the squadron, the Operational Conversion Flight trains *ab initio* helicopter pilots on their first operational tour with a 24-week course, during which they will fly ninety-one hours plus spend a further sixty hours in the simulator. Other courses are shorter, with a refresher lasting approximately eight weeks and hours flown tailored to meet the individual's needs.

No. 18 (B) Sqn is based at Odiham and operates the Chinook HC.2.

No. 27 Squadron

RAF Odiham
Boeing Chinook HC.2
Joint Helicopter Command
Role: Support Helicopter
Motto: *Quam Celerrime Ad Astra* – With all speed to the stars

On 5 November 1915, 27Sqn was formed at Hounslow and deployed to France with the Martinsyde G.102 in March 1916. Nicknamed the 'Elephant', this resulted in the squadron badge featuring the elephant. The squadron conducted numerous bombing raids in the Somme, Ypres and Amiens areas, as well as on Zeppelin Sheds. At the same time it was pivotal in the development of high-altitude reconnaissance and all-weather flying. From September 1917, it began to convert to the DH.4 which was replaced by the DH.9 in July 1918. It remained in Germany as part of the Army of Occupation, returning to the UK in March 1919, and disbanded in January 1920.

Re-formed during April 1920 at Mianwali, India from the re-numbered 99Sqn, it policed the North West Frontier with the DH.9a, assisting in the evacuation of 586 people from Kabul in 1928. It re-equipped with Wapitis and, in October

Royal Marines deploy from a 27Sqn Chinook HC.2 during operations in Afghanistan. The use of the Chinooks enabled patrols to quickly move location and maintain an element of surprise during their patrols for suspect terrorists.

1939, it became a training unit at Risalpur.

In 1940, 27Sqn returned to operations with the Blenheim and, in February 1941, it moved to Singapore, then Malaya, but was wiped out when the Japanese overran the region, resulting in it being disbanded in February 1942. Fortunately, many personnel managed to escape back to India and the squadron was eventually re-formed in September 1942 with the Beaufighter, to resume attacks on the Japanese. In April, it received its first Mosquito and began converting towards the end of the year. However, problems with the glue softening in the wooden wings resulted in their being handed back and ops continuing with the Beaufighter, which was now being capable of firing rockets. During one raid, two aircraft managed to destroy half a million gallons of fuel. Once the war ended, the squadron was disbanded in February 1946.

Re-formed in November 1947 at Oakington as a Dakota squadron, 27Sqn assisted in the development of snatch-towing of gliders. It also participated in the Berlin Airlift, only to be disbanded again in November 1950.

In June 1953, 27Sqn was re-formed at Scampton with the Canberra. It moved to Cyprus to take part in Operation *Musketeer* – the Suez Crisis – in 1956, attacking Egyptian targets. In January 1957, it returned home, where it was disbanded.

In April 1961, it was re-formed at Scampton with the Vulcan B.2 bomber. It was disbanded in March 1972, before it re-formed in November 1973 with the Vulcan again, but this time in the Maritime Radar Reconnaissance (MRR) role – monitoring Soviet shipping movements. This role ended in March 1982, when it was disbanded again.

In May 1983, 27Sqn was re-formed at Marham with the Tornado GR.1 and crews took part in the Gulf War, where they used laser-guided bombs (LGBs) operationally for the first time. The squadron disbanded on 24 September 1993, when its Tornados were transferred to 12Sqn at Lossiemouth.

On 1 October 1993, 240 OCU, which operated the Chinook and Puma HC.1s at Odiham, was re-numbered 27 (R) Sqn. Its Chinooks were gradually upgraded to HC.2 standard over the next couple of years. When the SHF was reorganized, the Puma Flight was transferred to the squadrons at Benson and, on 1 January 1998, it was re-classified to full operational status, although it retained a training flight for training all Chinook crews.

During September and October 1999, two Chinooks from 27Sqn deployed on HMS *Ocean* for Exercise *Bright Star* in Egypt, along with seventeen other countries. This was the first time that the RAF Chinooks had operated as an integral part of an Amphibious Task Group for an extended period aboard ship. Pre-exercise training was undertaken to acclimatize air and groundcrews to navy procedures and evolve safe flying techniques on a relatively small deck – not only was there a potential of crew getting blown overboard by the powerful down draughts, but also other helicopters. Even the difficulty of getting a Chinook below deck was tested by the removal of the rotor blades. Once the exercise was underway, the capabilities of the Chinook came into their own, especially when it came to the carrying of freight. By the time the exercise ended, the marines, ship and squadron were much better aware of each other's needs and capabilities, which was a valuable lesson for future operations.

In 2002, 27Sqn Chinooks joined those of 7Sqn at Bagram, Afghanistan to take part in operations against the Taliban and Al Qaeda forces still operating in that country. In 2003, they deployed again, as part of the coalition forces, to fly joint operations with US aircraft and troops from Royal Marines, US and Australian armed forces again – this time in Iraq.

No. 27Sqn operates the Chinook HC.2 from its base at RAF Odiham.

No. 28 (Army Co-operation) Squadron

RAF Benson
Westland Merlin HC.3
Joint Helicopter Command
Role: Support Helicopter
Motto: *Quicquid Agas Age* – Whatsoever you may do, do

On 7 November 1915, 28Sqn was formed at Gosport as a training squadron and operated a number of different types,

A 28Sqn Merlin HC.3 flies low-level over Bosnia on peacekeeping duties in support of NATO's SFOR.

33Sqn operates the Puma HC.1 from its base at Benson in support of the Army, transporting troops and cargo around the battlefield.

including FE.2bs. In September 1917, it moved to Yatesbury, where it became part of the Home Defence as a fighter squadron with Camels, before its planned deployment to France, briefly from October 1917. Instead, it was deployed to Italy, where it operated until it returned to the UK in February 1919. It was disbanded in January 1920 at Eastleigh.

It was re-formed at Ambala, India from the re-numbered 114Sqn with their F.2b Fighters in April 1920. These were replaced by Wapitis in September 1931 and then the Audax in 1936, before converting to Lysanders in September 1941. These were used for bombing and army co-operation against the Japanese in Burma. The squadron lost most of the Lysanders, withdrew to Lahore, India and re-equipped. Hurricanes arrived in December 1942 and these flew in the tactical reconnaissance role, until replaced by Spitfires from July 1945. In November, it moved to Malaya and then to Kai Tak, to reinforce units in Hong Kong in May 1949, during the Chinese Civil War.

In February 1951, the Vampire replaced the Spitfire FR.18s and were operated until replaced, in turn, by the Venom in February 1956. It re-equipped with Hunters in May 1962 but was disbanded at Kai Tak in January 1967.

A detachment of 103Sqn at Kai Tak was re-numbered 28Sqn in April 1968 with the Whirlwind, converting to Wessex in January 1972. It moved to Sek Kong in March 1978 and then returned to Kai Tak in November 1996. It remained the RAF's last remaining squadron in the Far East

until Hong Kong was handed back to the Chinese, resulting in 28Sqn disbanding on 3 June 1997.

Deliveries of the Merlin HC.3 commenced in March 2001 for training. However, 28Sqn officially reformed on 17 July at Benson. This was the first time that the squadron had operated in the UK since 1920.

The introduction of the Merlin was initially a little turbulent, especially when the Royal Navy lost one of theirs. However, 28Sqn quietly progressed with their training and exercises and were declared fully operational in 2005.

Having undertaken an earlier training exercise in Norway, a pair of Merlin HC.3s were deployed to Banja Luka in April 2003 for twelve months, to relieve 33Sqn Pumas in the humanitarian role, where they proved highly successful.

No. 28Sqn operate the Merlin HC.3 from its base at Benson.

No. 33 Squadron

RAF Benson
Westland Puma HC.1
Joint Helicopter Command
Role: Support Helicopter
Motto: Loyalty

On 12 January 1916, 33Sqn was formed at Filton from a nucleus provided by 12Sqn. It had a two-fold role – defence duties in

Yorkshire at night and training by day. In April, the training role was taken over by 57Sqn and 33Sqn continued its night defence with the BE.2 and FE.2 from November 1916. In 1918, it was re-equipped with F.2b Fighters and Avro 504s. Having made no successful interceptions, the squadron disbanded in June 1919.

In March 1929, 33Sqn was re-formed with the Horsley bomber at Netheravon. Having moved to Eastleigh in September, it became the first Hart squadron the following February. Moving to Bicester in 1930 and Upper Heyford in 1934, it was then deployed to Egypt in October 1935, to assist in the Abyssinian Crisis. While there, it converted to the Gladiator in March 1938. In October, it moved on to Palestine, but returned to Egypt with Gauntlets the following March.

From June 1940, 33Sqn flew a series of successful combat missions against Italian units. In September, it began to convert to the Hurricane and moved to Greece in early 1941. With the fall of Greece, it was forced to withdrew to Crete as the Luftwaffe rapidly advanced and it lost all of its aircraft. After a fierce ground battle, many of the squadron were evacuated to Egypt and re-equipped. The squadron then began to fly its Hurricanes on patrols over the Western Desert from June 1941. A few Tomahawks arrived in February, but further deliveries were halted and so more Hurricanes were

The role of 230Sqn in supporting the security forces in Northern Ireland has significantly reduced in recent years due to the decrease in terrorist activity.

added instead. Deliveries of Spitfires started in early 1943, but the desert patrols continued and it wasn't until April 1944 that 33Sqn eventually left North Africa for the UK.

The squadron then transferred to Fighter Command at North Weald, from where it flew fighter sweeps with the Wing, as well as escort missions. As the Germans retreated, 33Sqn moved forward from August, returning briefly to Predannack to re-equip with the Tempest. It stayed in Germany as part of the Occupation Forces at Fassberg from October 1945. Spitfires were briefly flown before the Tempests returned and, in November 1947, it moved to Güsloh. In July 1949, it flew to Renfrew, where the aircraft were crated and shipped to Hong Kong. After a short period at Kai Tak, it was deployed to Malaya to help combat the communist terrorists. There, it re-equipped with the Hornet in April 1951 but, in March 1955, it was disbanded after having flown 5,000 sorties in Malaya and the aircraft were transferred to 45Sqn.

In October 1955, it was re-established again with Venom night-fighters at Driffield, but disbanded in June 1957.

At Leeming in September 1957, 264Sqn with Meteors was re-numbered 33. These were flown until it moved to Middleton St George and converted to Javelins in July 1958. It deployed to Luqu, Malta in February 1959 but, in November 1962, it was disbanded.

It was re-formed again in March 1965 with the Bloodhound SAM in Malaya, where it remained until disbanded in June 1970.

On 14 June 1971, 33Sqn became the first RAF squadron to fly the Puma HC.1 and was officially re-formed at Odiham on 29 September. Since then, the squadron has been involved in numerous exercises where it operated in support of land forces. It also has been deployed operationally to many parts of the world, including Ascension Island, Belize, Venzuela and Zimbabwe. It was deployed to the Gulf for Operation *Granby*, where it carried over 4,000 troops and 68,000kg of freight. It has provided Pumas for Northern Ireland and provided disaster relief in Jamaica. On 13 June 1997 it moved to Benson and also took over the role of the Puma OCU the same day.

More recently, Pumas from 33Sqn were deployed during the operations in Afghanistan and were re-deployed to Iraq in December 2003 during the peace-keeping operations..

No. 33Sqn is equipped with the Puma HC.1 and operate from their base at Benson.

No. 230 Squadron

RAF Aldergrove
Westland Puma HC.1
Joint Helicopter Command
Role: Support Helicopter
Motto: *Kita Chari Jauh* – We seek far

The origins of 230Sqn can be traced back to 1913 at Felixstowe, when the Naval Air Station was established. A number of experiments were conducted with various seaplanes and a Flight was established. This were used for coastal patrols when

war broke out and, in April 1917, it became known as the War Flight. Over 600 patrols were flown over the following twelve months, during which the Flight attacked twenty-five submarines and destroyed the L.43 Zeppelin. Following the incorporation of RNAS units into the new RAF, Felixstowe's War Flight became part of 230Sqn in August 1918 at Felixstowe, along with 327 and 328 Flights with F.2As/F.5s and 328 Flight with Camels. It survived the wholesale disbanding of squadrons at the end of the war and moved to Calshot in May 1922. In April 1923, it was reduced to a flight status and re-numbered 480 Flight.

In December 1934, 230Sqn was re-formed at Pembroke Dock and was equipped with the Singapore III flying-boat in April. The following October, it was deployed to Egypt, returning home for a few months in August 1936, before deploying to Seletar, Singapore. It re-equipped with Sunderlands from June 1938. Tasked with patrolling the Indian Ocean, a detachment was operated out of Ceylon but, gradually, the whole squadron moved across. By February 1940, the squadron was officially based in Ceylon and those still at Seletar transferred to 205Sqn.

In May 1940, 230Sqn returned to Alexandria, Egypt to operate on anti-submarine patrols and reconnaissance operations, which it continued to fly until January 1943. During this period, in April 1941, 230 flew reconnaissance around Crete and at night was landing by the beaches to evacuate troops from the advancing German Army. It then moved to Dar-es-Salaam in Tanganyika (now Tanzania), to resume patrols over the Indian Ocean, and operated detachments at Madagascar, as well as Greece.

In February 1944, it returned to Ceylon, deploying a detachment to Calcutta the following year to transport casualties and freight to and from Burma. In April, it moved on to Burma to attack Japanese shipping and, by December, was back at Singapore. It eventually left to return to the UK in March 1946 – spending some time at Calshot. It took part in the Berlin Airlift, operating from Lake Havel prior to returning home to Pembroke Dock in February 1949. The squadron was eventually disbanded in February 1957.

In September 1958, 230Sqn was re-formed by the re-numbering of 215Sqn. It was based at Dishforth and equipped with the Pioneer CC.1. It deployed to Cyprus a few months later for policing duties. A few Twin Pioneer CC.2s were added in 1960, while at Upavon, and a Flight was established in the Cameroons in September 1960 to support peacekeeping troops, then returned home the following year.

In June 1961, 230Sqn began to convert to the Whirlwind HAR.10 and moved to Germany in January 1965 for two years. Just two months later, 230Sqn was deployed to Borneo for a further two years. It moved into Odiham on its return home, where it stayed until November 1969. It then moved to Wittering in October 1971 and, while a detachment was operated at Nicosia, Cyprus, another detachment began converting to the Puma. In December 1971, 230Sqn disbanded,

On 1 January 1972, the Puma detachment was officially re-formed as 230Sqn. In October 1980, the squadron was transferred to Gütersloh, Germany. It continued to operate from the station until April 1992, when its Pumas were transferred to 18Sqn and 230Sqn disbanded.

On 4 May 1992, 230Sqn was re-formed at Aldergrove to continue operating the Puma HC.1 and working alongside the Wessex of 72Sqn. The role of 230Sqn is to support the security forces, enabling them

to undertake their role. This can involve moving troops quickly, to provide highly mobile vehicle check-points to frustrate action by terrorists. It also is a quicker and more secure mode of transport, especially near the border.

In March 2002, it absorbed the Pumas from the disbanding 72Sqn, to become one of the RAF's larger units, with fifteen aircraft on strength. With the progressive improvement in the security situation in the region, it was announced, in June 2004, that the number of Pumas operated would be reduced by six.

No. 230Sqn operates the Puma HC.1 from its base at Aldergrove.

No. 1310 Flight

Basra International Airport, Iraq
Chinook HC.2
Joint Helicopter Command
Role: Support Helicopter

No. 1310 Flight was originally formed on 10 April 1944 at Llandow with Ansons,

tasked with transport. Following a move to Bognor in June 1944, it flew in the aeromed role to France, for casualties following the D-Day landings. It was disbanded in May 1946.

In March 1953, 1310 Flight was re-formed at Upavon, but operated their four Yorks from Mellala, Australia in support of nuclear weapons trials, from May 1953 until the end of the year.

In July 1964, 1310 Flight was re-formed at Odiham with Whirlwinds, three of which were transported to Atkinson Field, British Guyana to assist with internal security, leading to the country's independence in May 1966. The Flight disbanded in October and were flown back to the UK on one of the new Belfasts of 53Sqn shortly after.

Following the surrender of the invading Argentine forces of the Falkland Islands in May 1982, 1310 Flight was re-formed at Kelly's Garden, in August 1983, in the support-helicopter role. It continued to operate as such until May 1986, when it was merged with 1564 Flight of Sea Kings, located at Naval Point, Stanley, to form

1310 Flight have provided a heavy-lift capability for British and NATO IFOR peacekeeping forces in Bosnia. More recently, they were reformed to provide a similar role for coalition forces in Iraq.

78Sqn at the newly built Mount Pleasant airfield.

In December 1995, 1310 Flight was re-formed at Divulje Barracks near Split in Croatia, to support the NATO peacekeeping operations in Bosnia. The Flight was disbanded in December 2000.

On 1 August 2003, 1310 Flight was re-formed at Basra International Airport with Chinooks, to provide support-helicopter capability for the deployed Allied forces.

No. 1419 Flight

Basrah, Iraq
Westland Merlin HC.3
Joint Helicopter Command
Role: Support Helicopter

1419 Flight was formed 1 March 1941 as a Special Duties unit. It formed by the re-numbering of 419 Flight which had formed in August 1940 at North Weald with Lysanders moving to Stapleford Tawney, Tangmere and Stradishall. Around the time of the re-numbering the Flight added a few Whitleys and a Marylands and commenced operating from Newmarket. However, as their tasking to drop agents and supplies into occupied France grew, 1419 Flight was re-designated 138 (Special Duties) Sqn in August 1941.

On 1 March 2005, 1419 Flight was re-formed at Basrah, Iraq, to operate Merlin HC.3s on detachment from 28 Sqn. They replaced the Chinooks of 1310 Flight and it is probable that the two units will operate alternately in support of the security forces in Iraq until they are withdrawn.

Proving their capability, the Merlins were self deployed to Iraq during which they flew some 3,500 miles. Once in theatre they quickly adopted their role which includes assisting in the rapid positioning of vehicle check-points, surveillance and troop movements including casualty evacuation.

1419 Flight operates the Merlin HC.3 from Basra, Iraq.

No. 1563 Flight

Basra International Airport, Iraq
Westland Puma HC.1
Joint Helicopter Command
Role: Support Helicopter

On 22 December 1942, 1563 Meteorological Flight was originally formed at Helwan, Egypt with Gladiators. The following month it moved to Benina, Libya and, in June, re-equipped with Hurricanes. These were replaced by Spitfires in June 1945 and the Flight disbanded in May 1946.

In July 1963, 1563 was re-formed when 103 Sqn with Sycamores at Nicosia, Cyprus was split into 1563 Flight, which remained at Nicosia, and 1564 Flight, which moved to Al Adem. In November 1963, 1563 Flight re-equipped with Whirlwinds, which it took to Akrotiri in November 1967. In January 1972 a Detachment of 230 Sqn was joined with 1563 Flight to re-form 84 Sqn at Akrotiri, within which it became 'A' Flight with a SAR role.

On 1 November 1983, 1563 Flight was re-formed in Belize with Pumas. These had arrived in October 1975 to provide support for the Army units that had deployed to Belize as a result of hostile posturing and mobilization by neighbouring Guatemala. It disbanded again in July 1994.

On 12 December 2003, 1563 Flight was re-formed at Basra International Airport in Iraq with the Puma HC.1 and it is anticipated that it will remain in theatre for twelve months.

No. 1563 Flight operates the Puma HC.1 from its base at Basra in Iraq.

Rotary Wing Operational Evaluation and Training Unit

RAF Benson
Joint Helicopter Command
Role: Helicopter OEU

The Rotary Wing Operational Evaluation and Training Unit (RWOETU) was formed in October 1997 at Benson.

It was formed from the Support Helicopter Tactics and Trials Flight at Odiham and the Sea King OEU at St Mawgan, to conduct operational evaluation and standardization and develop synthetic training to maintain the effective capabilities of the RAF's helicopter forces. Unlike the other OEUs, the Rotary Wing incorporates training within its remit. While this is a relatively small portion of its workload, the larger portion is associated with the Merlin HC.3 and Chinook HC.3.

The primary role of RWOETU is the co-ordination and conduct of trials for all RAF helicopters and the continued development of in-service and new equipment. As a result, personnel within the unit include Chinook, Merlin, Puma and Sea King crews.

A Merlin HC.3 of 1419 Flight 'somewhere' in Iraq. Crown Copyright

1563 Flight operated for eleven years in Belize to support army units and re-formed in 2003 for a similar role in Iraq.

Although a JHC unit, functional control of RWOETU comes from Waddington's Air Warfare Centre, as with other OEUs.

The RWOETU is based at Benson and borrows helicopters as required.

Chief of Staff Operations

Air Warfare Centre

RAF Waddington
CoS Ops
Strike Command
Role: Tactics support
Motto: *Arma Iudicare Consilium Dare* – To judge and access arms and to give advice

The Air Warfare Centre (AWC) was formed in October 1993 by the amalgamation of various units, including the Central Trials and Tactics Organization (CTTO), Department of Air Warfare (DAW) and the OEUs.

The AWC was formed to provide the expertise to contribute to the fully integrated support provided by Strike Command. This is achieved by the permutation of and development of operational doctrine and comprises five main areas of responsibility. Support is provided by the Operational Division at HQ level and instruction provided on Air Warfare courses. The Defence Electronic Warfare Centre provides support at tactical level for all three services. The Intelligence Division provides air-intelligence support to Strike Command and its units. The Development Division operates through the various OEUs to evaluate new aircraft, weapons and directly associated equipment. Finally, the Operational Analysis Division is integrated with all of the other divisions, to provide scientific support to all AWC activities.

The AWC is located at eleven locations. The other main location to Waddington is Cranwell, which houses the Operational Doctrine and Training element. The OEUs form the flying elements of the AWC, with the SAOEU and the Tornado F.3 OEU being the only ones with their own aircraft. Others borrow aircraft from operational squadrons as required. In March 2003, the Tornado F.3 OEU temporarily deployed to Waddington, while work was carried out on the runway. Following its return, it is due to be merged with the SAOEU at Boscombe Down and the Air Guided Weapons OEU at Valley, to form a Fast Jet and Weapons OEU to be based at Coningsby.

The Air Warfare Centre (AWC) HQ is at Waddington.

Fast Jet OEU

RAF Coningsby
Panavia Tornado F.3
CoS Ops
Strike Command
Role: Tornado OEU

The Fast Jet Operational Evaluation Unit (OEU) was formed on 1 April 2004 at Coningsby by the amalgamation of the resident Tornado F.3 OEU with the Strike Attack Operational Evaluation Unit (SAOEU) from Boscombe Down and the Air Guided Weapons OEU from Valley.

The Tornado F.3 Operational Evaluation Unit was formed at Coningsby on 1 April 1987. Although parented by the station, it was part of the Air Warfare Centre (AWC) at Waddington. Equipped with Tornado F.3s, their role was to evaluate new equipment and develop techniques for its use, including trials. Their Tornados were adapted for this role and the unit was able to maintain an interface between manufacturers and DPA, along with MoD and DLO, and the operational Tornado F.3 squadrons. As such, the OEU was instrumental in the successful introduction of numerous pieces of equipment – some of great urgency during Operations such as *Granby*, *Deny Flight* and, most recently, *Telic*.

The origins of the Strike Attack Operational Evaluation Unit (SAOEU) date back to January 1983 and the formation of the Tornado OEU – this unit was

A formation of Tornado GR.4s and Harrier GR.7s of the Fast Jet OEU returning from a series of live trials in the USA. Kevin Wills

equipped with a pair of Tornado GR.1s and based at Boscombe Down.

Like the F.3 OEU, the original brief for the Tornado OEU was for specific service trials, although its planned life was just two years. The unit proved so successful that it continued to operate and, in July 1988, Harriers were added and the unit renamed the Strike Attack OEU (SAOEU). Amongst the Harrier work carried out were the tactics to be used for the GR.7. In 1996, the tasking of the SAOEU was further expanded by the adding of the Jaguar, to trial the new avionics of the GR.3.

The SAOEU trial equipment, weapons and flying techniques, following contractor trials, prior to their entry into operational service. As a result, SAOEU undertake a number of interesting trials. A recent example was digital data-transfer, in which an aircraft needs to pass information to another. Simple enough, until a mountain or even a hill blocks the transmission. The SAOEU investigated solutions, including the use of a UAV as relay. As a result, they enhance the capability and survivability of strike aircraft.

The oldest component of the Fast Jet OEU is the Air Guided Weapons Operational Evaluation Unit (AGWOEU), which can trace its history back to June 1957, when it was formed as the Guided

Weapons Development Squadron with Swifts. It subsequently became the Guided Weapons Training Squadron, then disbanded, to be replaced by Fighter Command Missile Practice Camp in June 1962. This was renamed Strike Command Missile Practice Camp (STCAAME) in April 1968. The unit's role was to provide a facility for squadrons to fire live air-to-air missiles at targets over Cardigan Bay. These targets have usually been the radio-controlled Jindivik drones launched from the Qinetiq facility at Llanbedr, or the supersonic Stiletto missile launched from a Canberra. In 1996, this became the Air Guided Weapons Operational Evaluation Unit (AGWOEU) and it currently provides the planning, briefing and facilities for the Missile Practice Camps. On 1 April 2004, the AGWOEU amalgamated with the SAOEU and the Tornado F.3 OEU to form the Fast Jet and Weapons OEU at Coningsby.

While the runway was closed at Coningsby, in March 2003, the Tornado F3 OEU temporarily moved to Waddington. Having returned, on 1 April 2004, it amalgamated with the SAOEU from Boscombe Down and the Air Guided Weapons OEU at Valley to form the Fast Jet and Weapons OEU at Coningsby.

The Fast Jet OEU is based at Coningsby and operate the Harrier GR.7, Jaguar GR.3 plus Tornado F.3 and GR.4.

RAF Provost & Security Services

RAF Henlow
CoS Ops
Strike Command
Motto: *Fiat Justitia* – Let justice be done.

Policing within the RAF was administered by the army until 1 April 1918, when the RAF Police were established. It wasn't until 1931 that an RAF Provost Marshal was appointed and that element of the service began to develop. An RAF Police HQ was eventually established at Uxbridge in 1937.

During 1940, an RAF Security School was established at Halton to train security officers and NCOs in roles that, by then, included general security, special investigations, passes and VIP security, as well as discipline of air and ground personnel. RAF Police were also a vital element in maintaining a security black-out on a number of highly secret operations. In addition, some of the personnel were trained to become dog-handlers. In 1941 the RAF Police HQ moved to Burnham, near Maidenhead.

When the D-Day invasion commenced, RAF Police were at the forefront, to assist in the directing of troops and equipment away from the beaches and in maintaining security for some of the vital stores and positions. Besides operating in all the theatres of the fighting, RAF Police had also served in Canada.

As the war ended, RAF Police were issued with white caps and webbing to assist in their easy identification, which resulted in their being referred to as 'snowdrops'.

During 1947, the RAF Police became responsible for security within the RAF and the Provost Marshal for the regional policing. In February 1951, the latter organization was titled the RAF Provost & Security Service (RAF P&SS).

The RAF Police School moved to Netheravon in 1952 and, in doing so, became the RAF Police Depot. The Depot moved on to Debden by September 1960 and courses expanded to incorporate new subjects, such as nuclear security. Later, drug detection became an important new role for the dogs.

In 1975 the RAF Police School moved to Newton, while the HQ P&SS moved to Rudloe Manor and, in November 1998, to its current base at Henlow.

Units of the RAF Police are located at every RAF station, while the HQ RAF P&SS provides the centralized assets to enable specialist teams to conduct criminal investigations, security and counter intelligence, as and where required. They also include specialists in computer forensics and flying complaints. A Tactical Provost Wing (TPW) was formed in April 2002 to provide a high-readiness capability, enabling security personnel to be operationally deployed to provide protection of transport aircraft and personnel, as well as a counter-terrorist search capability. The TPW are assisted in their role by the R Aux AF Tactical Provost Squadron.

HQ P&SS is based at Henlow.

Chief of Staff Support

RAF Firefighting and Rescue Service

CoS Support

Strike Command

Role: Firefighting and rescue

Motto: *E Flammis atque ruinis salus* – Out of fire and catastrophe, salvation

The trade of fireman within the RAF was not formally introduced until 1943. Prior to that it was an ad hoc arrangement, with personnel being detailed to provide cover from a variety of other trades.

The RAF School of Firefighting and Rescue was established at Sutton-on-Hull in August 1943 and began formal training of personnel. During the late 1950s, the RAF Fire Service was briefly amalgamated with the RAF Regiment.

During the early 1960s, the service was unable to attract sufficient service recruits, which resulted in the formation of the Air Force Dept Fire Service. This civilian-manned body merged with a similar army organization in the 1990s and became the Defence Fire Service. The current result is that some stations are served by the Defence Fire Service, while the RAF Firefighting and Rescue Service provides the cover for the rest.

The RAF Firefighting and Rescue Service operates at various stations in the UK and overseas.

The RAF Firefighting and Rescue Service provide emergency cover, not only in the event of a crash but also for all buildings on a station, and assist in non-military emergencies when requested. They are also deployed with flying units when flying to locations where insufficient or no cover is available, such as here at Basra in Iraq.

RAF Police dog-handler with his Alsatian patrolling an airfield's perimeter.

Personnel and Training Command

RAF Innsworth
Role: Command
Motto: *Ut Aquilae Surgant* – That eagles might soar

Personnel and Training Command (P&TC) was created on 1 April 1994 as a result of a major restructuring of the RAF, effectively taking over from Support Command.

P&TC is responsible for all aspects of recruiting, training, career management, welfare, conditions of service, resettlement and pensions for RAF regular and reserve forces worldwide.

P&TC employs some 17,000 people, which includes 4,000 civilians, and is spread over some thirty locations. It is responsible for over 500 training aircraft, of which 150 are ATC gliders. Headquarters staff are based at Innsworth and number some 1,500, of whom half are civilian.

The two major components of P&TC are the Training Group Defence Agency (TGDA), which is responsible for administering the training role of the command, plus administration of the Red Arrows, and the Personnel Management Agency (PMA).

The function of the PMA has existed since pre-RAF days, when it was conducted by the RNAS and then the RFC, and has continued in various guises since. RAF personnel records were computerized by 1973, by which time the organization was named Personnel Management Centre and located at Barnwood. Currently named the Personnel Management Agency (PMA), it was formed in 1997. Its role is to manage the careers of RAF and reserve personnel, to encourage their full development and their retention and to ensure that the RAF has the right manpower to meet all of its tasks. It also looks after their pay.

The TGDA was formed in April 1994 and is responsible for the recruiting of all RAF personnel and their training up to the OCUs. It is also responsible for the flying training of army and Royal Navy personnel to a similar standard.

A further component is the Armed Forces Personnel Administration Agency (AFPAA). It was formed in 1997 and is a Joint-Service organization, which administers servicemen's pay and pensions. It was also tasked with reducing overall costs, standardizing the service throughout the armed forces.

As part of the continued need to reduce costs, in 2004, it was announced that P&TC would be co-located with Strike Command. This would enable a new structure and result in a reduced manning level to around 2,000. Once determined, this enabled selection of a suitable site. High Wycombe was chosen and co-location will be completed by 2008.

Personnel and Training Command (P&TC) HQ is based at Innsworth.

No. 19 (Reserve) Squadron

RAF Valley
Hawk T.1, T.1A & T.1W
Personnel and Training Command
Role: Advanced Flying Training
Motto: *Possunt Quia Posse Videntur* – They can because they think they can

On 1 September 1915, 19Sqn was formed at Castle Bromwich from a nucleus provided by 5 Reserve Squadron. It flew various aircraft, until it converted to the RE.7 in December. It deployed to France as a fighter squadron in July 1916 with BE.12s and operated SPAD S.VII from December and, later, S.XIIIs. It then re-equipped with the Dolphin in January 1918, which was flown until it returned to the UK in February 1919 and disbanded at the end of that year. The association with the Dolphin is reflected in its badge.

The squadron was re-formed in April 1923 at Duxford as a training flight within 2 FTS. It remained at Duxford as a full squadron when 2 FTS moved out that December. A variety of aircraft were operated by the squadron, including the Grebe, Siskin, Bulldog and, then, the Gauntlet by June 1935. Still at Duxford, in August 1938, 19Sqn became the first Spitfire squadron.

Operating as a fighter squadron, it also used the satellite airfield at Fowlmere. It moved to Matlaske then Ludham in 1941, prior to a series of further moves, including

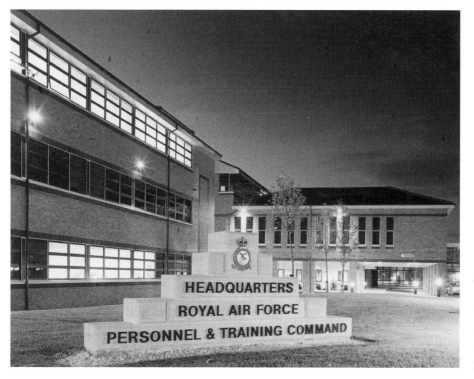

The HQ of Personnel and Training Command (P&TC) is based at Innsworth. It is planned to be co-located with Strike Command by 2008 at High Wycombe. Crown Copyright

Yorkshire and the West Country. In February 1944, 19Sqn converted to Mustangs and began daylight escort-duties. In February 1945, it moved to Peterhead, Scotland and returned south to Andrews Field then Molesworth after a few months rest.

In March 1946, it re-equipped with the Spitfire, prior to receiving the Hornet in October at Church Fenton. These gave way to the Meteor in 1951 and then the Hunter in 1956. In 1959, it moved to Leconfield, where it re-equipped with the Lightning in 1962. In September 1965, the squadron moved to Güsloh, Germany. The demise of the Lightning saw the beginnings of the new squadron form at Wildenrath with Phantoms in September 1976. When 19Sqn's Lightnings were retired, the squadron disbanded at the end of 1976 and 19 (Designate) Squadron became operational on New Year's Day. The Phantoms continued to be operated by 19Sqn until January 1992, when it was disbanded.

On 23 September 1992, the squadron was re-formed by the re-numbering of 63 (R) Sqn, to become 19 (R) Sqn within 7 FTS. When 7 FTS was disbanded in September 1994, 19 (R) Sqn became part of 4 FTS and provides students who have completed the AFT course with 208 (R) Sqn the tactics and weapon training elements of the course. This course lasts about twenty weeks, during which the student flies sixty-three hours, including fifteen solo. Once successfully completed, the student progresses to a type OCU, prior to joining an operational squadron. No. 19 (R) Sqn also hosts the CFS Hawk element, which trains and checks the QFIs. In addition, 19 (R) Sqn maintains a Tactical Armament Flight at St Athan. Manned mainly by armourers from contractor Babcock, the Hawks, operated from Valley, use the range at Pembrey then re-arm at St Athan to reduce flying time. Once the exercise is over, the Hawks return to Valley. On successful completion of the course, the students will effectively be pooled with those that completed the NFTC course in Canada and will be posted to the OCU to the aircraft type that it has been determined they are best suited for.

It is anticipated that 19 (R) Sqn will start to receive the Hawk 128, which first flew on 27 July 2005, from 2008.

No. 19 (R) Sqn operates the Hawk T.1, T.1A and T.1W from its base at Valley.

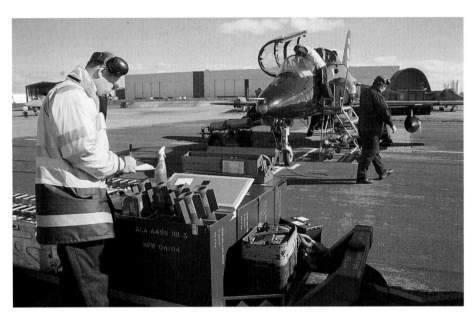

Valley-based 19(R)Sqn provide the weapon training for fast-jet pilots. Groundcrew of St Athan's TAF Det re-arm the Hawk T.1A ready for a return to the nearby ranges at Pembrey Sands.

No. 45 (Reserve) Squadron

RAF Cranwell
King Air B200
Personnel and Training Command
Role: Multi-engine training
Motto: *Per Ardua Surgo* – Through difficulties I arise

On 1 March 1916, 45Sqn was formed at Gosport and deployed to France that October with the Sopwith 1½ Strutter and Nieuport 12. In November 1917, it was deployed to Italy with Camels, where it destroyed 114 enemy aircraft for a loss of only six of its own. In September 1918, they returned to France and then to the UK in February, where they were disbanded at the end of 1919.

The squadron was re-formed in April 1921 with DH.9s in Egypt. These were soon replaced with Vimys in November, then Vernons in March 1922, prior to moving to Iraq to provide a Baghdad–Cairo air-mail service. In 1923, Squadron Leader Arthur Harris – later to become CinC Bomber Command during the Second World War – took command of 45Sqn. The squadron were also tasked in policing the Middle East from the air. For this, Harris had bomb racks added to the Vernon troop carriers, converting them to 'heavy bombers'.

In January 1927, 45Sqn was absorbed into 47Sqn, but was quickly re-formed at Heliopolis, Egypt with the DH.9a once more. These were replaced by the Fairey IIIF in September 1929, Vincents in November 1935 and the Wellesley in December 1937. During this period, 'B' Flight had been deployed to Nairobi, Kenya in September 1935, where it became 223Sqn in December 1936. By the time war broke out, 45Sqn were at Fuka in North Africa with Blenheims.

January 1942 saw preparation for deployment to Calcutta the following month. Unfortunately, the Japanese led a successful attack on the advance base, in which most of their aircraft were destroyed. This resulted in a major setback for 45Sqn and it wasn't until June 1943 that they were able to launch a successful return attack. Now equipped with the Vengeance, the squadron used the dive-bombers until they were replaced by Mosquitos in February 1944. Their attacks continued until Rangoon was recaptured and 45Sqn then withdrew to India to prepare for Operation *Zipper* – to invade Malaysia – but the dropping of the atom bombs finally halted the war.

In May 1946, 45Sqn moved to Ceylon and began converting to Beaufighters in November. August 1948 saw the uprising of terrorists in Malaya and the squadron moved to Kuala Lumpur soon after. Brigands were introduced in November 1949 while at Tengah, and the Hornet in January 1951. Jet aircraft were operated by 45Sqn from May 1955, initially with the

Overflying the college buildings at Cranwell is a formation of King Air B200s of 45 (R) Sqn, which are used for training students to fly multi-engine aircraft. Crown Copyright

Vampire, then Venoms from December 1955. It disbanded in March 1957, reforming a short while later at Coningsby, before returning to Tengah in December 1957, where it remained until it disbanded in January 1970.

In August 1972, 45Sqn was re-formed with Hunters at West Raynham, moving to Wittering later in the year. The new role of 45Sqn was to provide holding graduate pilots with some advanced flying, before joining the Buccaneer or Jaguar OCU, to resolve a temporary problem in the training sequence. As a result, 45Sqn was disbanded in July 1976.

On 1 January 1984, the Tornado Weapons Conversion Unit (TWCU) at Honington was given the shadow identity of 45 (Reserve) Squadron in a policy designed preserve some of the more important squadrons. Their role was to train aircrew in RAF weapons and their delivery techniques, prior to joining the TTTE. However, when more squadrons were disbanded as part of the Options For Change in the early 1990s, 45 (R) Sqn was disbanded on 31 March 1992 and the former TWCU took on the identity of 15 (Reserve) Squadron.

On 1 July 1992, the Jetstream equipped Multi-Engine Training Squadron within the 6 FTS and based at Finningley was re-named 45 (R) Sqn. In October 1995, 45 (R) Sqn moved to Cranwell when Finningley closed down and became part of No 3 FTS.

On 1 April 2004 the aircraft operation for multi-engined training became privatised and Serco introduced the King Air B200 to replace the Jetstream T.1. As a result Serco are required to provide a specified number of aircraft to meet 45 (R) Sqn's daily flying programme.

45 (R) Sqn provides training for pilots who have been selected at the elementary training stage to fly multi-engined aircraft such as the Hercules or Sentry. They commence training with a short MELIN (Multi-Engine Lead IN) course on the Firefly. After an 8 week course which includes 30 hours flying, the students progress to the King Air. Students take a 29 week course during which 70 hours will be flown before departing to the appropriate OCU / training squadron. For students who do not complete the Advanced course at Valley there is an opportunity to retrain for multi-engined aircraft. Courses range from 30 to 45 hours depending on previous experience.

No. 45 (R) Sqn operates the King Air B200 from Cranwell.

No. 55 (Reserve) Squadron

RAF Cranwell
Hawker Siddeley Dominie T.1
Personnel and Training Command
Role: Multi-crew training
Motto: *Nil Nos Tremefacit* – Nothing shakes us

55 Sqn was formed on 27 April 1916 at Castle Bromwich as a training unit and was equipped with FK.8 and Avro 504. It re-equipped with DH.4s in January 1917 and was deployed to France in March in the bombing, photographic and reconnaissance role and later strategic bombing against targets in Germany. After the war the Squadron undertook mail carrying duties. It returned home in January 1919 and disbanded in 1920.

In February 1920, Suez based 124 Sqn with DH.9s was re-numbered 55 Sqn. It was moved to Turkey on HMS *Ark Royal* and assisted in the defence of Constantinople and the Dardanelles. In August it was moved again – this time to Iraq for policing duties staying there until 1939. It re-equipped with the Wapiti in 1930 followed by the Vincent from 1937 and Blenheim in March 1939.

During the first ten months of the war, 55 Sqn was deployed to patrol the Suez followed by bombing missions over Libya. In March 1942, it converted to the Baltimore which were operated in the desert campaigns, including El Alamein, and then into Italy. While there they re-equipped with the Boston in October 1944 before moving on to Hassani in Greece in September 1945 where it performed mail carrying duties once more. Having converted to Mosquitos, 55 Sqn was disbanded in November 1946.

55 Sqn was re-formed in September 1960 with the Victor bomber at Honington and commenced in the refuelling role with the tanker variant in May 1965 at Marham. These were flown intensively during Operation Corporate refuelling Hercules, Nimrods plus the Vulcans taking part in the recovery of the Falkland Is. Eight Victors were deployed to Bahrain during Operation Granby to support the Jaguars and Tornados. With the Gulf War over, 55 Sqn returned to Marham and were disbanded at the end of 1993.

55 Sqn re-formed by the re-numbering of the VC10 OCU at Brize Norton in October 1993. It borrowed aircraft from the regular squadrons as required. However, this incarnation was short lived and it disbanded on March 31st, 1996. The role of the unit being absorbed into 10 and 101 Sqns.

The Squadron identity survived when it was transferred to the Dominie element of 3 FTS on November 1st, 1996. Based at Cranwell, 55 (R) Sqn provides air and ground training for aircrew Officers and NCOs (excluding pilots). In April 2003 these aircrew were reclassified as – Commissioned – Weapon Systems Officers (WSO) and – NCO who are now referred to as NCA (Non Commissioned Aircrew) – Weapon Systems Operators (WSOp). The close relationship between WSOs and WSOps has resulted in them being united under a single flying badge, the Common Rear Crew Brevet. Further rationalisation has resulted in reduction of the number of the specialisations. With improved technology, especially GPS, the role of pure navigator has changed. The new title reflects this more modern role whether that be Fast Jet or Multi-Engined (Maritime or Transport/Air Refuelling/ ISTAR (AAI)). NCOs are no longer recruited as Air Electronics Operators, Loadmasters or Air Engineers. They are recruited as WSOps who will be streamed either Crewman, EW or Acoustics at a juncture which is approximately half way through their professional training. Linguists are still recruited as Linguists, however, they are remain within the WSOp cadre throughout their career.

NCA cadets destined for 3 FTS will have completed their initial recruit training at Halton and now join serving servicemen / women who are re-rolling on a 10 week Non-Commissioned Aircrew Initial Training Course (NCAITC) conducted by the Officer and Aircrew Cadet Training Unit at Cranwell. On successful completion of this course the cadets are promoted to acting Sergeant (unpaid) before commencing their WSOp training. A WSOp Generic Training Course follows during which the foundations of the aircrew skills and knowledge are built over a 24 week period. Subjects include basic survival training and aviation medicine as well as some maths and science. This then leads on to electrical theory and aircraft systems plus communications systems and flight planning. This is followed by 20 hours training in the Dominie. All the way through the course SNCO development and operational skills are being developed and cadets are encouraged to plan and participate in adventurous training.

The Linguists – WSOp (L) – will have already been streamed and now departs for the Defence Special Signal School at Chicksands for a course which may last up to 19 months. The rest of the cadets that have successfully completed the course will now be streamed as Crewman, Electronic Warfare or Acoustics WSOps.

The Crewman – WSOp (Cmn) – are further split into Fixed or Rotary Wing with the Rotary moving on to the DHFS at Shawbury for their course which includes 105 hours on the Squirrel and Griffin. The Fixed Wing WSOp (Cmn) undertakes a 15 week course which covers training in basic aircraft systems, weight and balance, loading and restraint as well as cargo handling and first aid. The course provides a mixture of class and practical training as well as some flying. On successful completion the student moves either to Lyneham for a 14 week conversion course onto the Hercules or a 16 week course at Brize Norton. On successful completion the students are awarded their Brevets and become an acting Sergeant (paid).

The Electronic Warfare (28 weeks) – WSOp (EW) – training concentrates on radar, EW and communications systems which includes synthetic, practical as well as additional Dominie training. On successful completion students are awarded their Brevets and become an acting Sergeant (paid) before being posted to Nimrod R.1, MR.2 or Sentry AEW.1 for conversion training with 42 or 54 (R) Sqns.

The Acoustic (27 Weeks) – WSOp (Aco) – undergoes training in oceanography plus submarine and surface vessel propulsion systems. Further training is given on the analysis of acoustic noise, how to locate and identify vessels.

55(R)Sqn fly their Dominie T.1s to provide navigation training to weapon system officers/operators plus air engineers and air loadmasters.

Additional Dominie flying is given and once successfully completed students are awarded their Brevets and become an acting Sergeant (paid) before they are posted to 42 (R) Sqn, the Nimrod MR2 OCU.

Junior officers will have completed their 24 week Initial Officer Training at the OATCU at Cranwell before they commence their flying training with 55 (R) Sqn. WSOs commence their basic navigation course with a 14 week course comprising of 5 weeks of ground school followed by 14 flights with the CFS Tutor Squadron. They then progress to the Tucano Air Navigation School (TANS) at Linton-on-Ouse where a further 28 hours are flown during their 12 week course. They then return to 55 (R) Sqn for a 9 week simulator and Dominie flying course. On successful completion, the students are selected for Fast Jet or Multi-Engine.

The Fast Jet students fly 30 hours over 11 weeks in the Dominie on increasingly arduous sorties with waypoint timing accuracy of +/– 15 seconds being expected. Meanwhile, the Multi-Engine are split into Maritime or AAI elements continue with their appropriate 14 week course on the Dominie during which 41 hours will be flown.

Having successfully completed the courses so far, the fast jet students depart to join the Navigator Training Unit within 100 Sqn at RAF Leeming, where they commence a 21 week course during which they fly 35 hours in Hawks. The Multi-Engine students will depart to join the appropriate OCU / Training Flight for final training before being posted onto an operational squadron.

Having completed their Initial Training Course, WSOp students hold the acting rank of sergeant. Students are then split into four They then progress onto the specialist training courses 28-week WSOp Basic course. Students are then split into four courses. Air Engineer, which is 46-weeks long and includes 13 Dominie sorties. Air Loadmasters (ALM) commence on an 8-week course followed by further training on survival, first aid and leadership as well as visits to squadrons. On completion they are split into fixed and rotary wing prior to a 3-week course. Fixed-wing students continue with a further 5-week airmanship phase on the Dominie course before departing to Brize Norton or Lyneham while the rotary-wing depart for the DHFS at Shawbury.

From joining 55 (R) Sqn, until they depart all students remain part of 3 FTS despite flying with other units as part of their course. The appropriate Brevets are presented to all WSOs and WSOps prior to departing to the OCU / Training units. In addition to new entry students the squadron also runs courses for refresher training and to re-role.

55 (R) Sqn operates the Dominie T.1 from their base at Cranwell.

No. 60 (Reserve) Squadron

RAF Shawbury

Griffin HT.1

Personnel and Training Command

Role: Multi-engine helicopter training

Motto: *Per Ardua Ad Aethera Tendo* – To strive through difficulties to the sky

On 1 May 1916, 60Sqn was formed at Gosport. It deployed to France in June 1916, initially with the Morane Bullet, followed by Nieuport Scout and, later, the SE.5a. The squadron evolved into a fighter unit; assisted by the skills of top scoring aces – Major Albert Ball and Captain W A Bishop – the squadron amassed a total of 274 'kills', as well as numerous decorations, including Bishop's VC. He was awarded this for his actions in June 1917 when, alone, he overflew a German airfield near Cambrai. Several aircraft already had their engines running and one took off. He fired at it and then attacked a second: the first crashed and the second collided with a tree. A pair then took off and he shot down the first and caused the second to dive away before he returned to base. Ball was awarded a DSO and Bar while with 60Sqn. Having returned to the UK in February 1919, 60Sqn was disbanded the following January at Bircham Newton.

The squadron was re-formed by the re-numbering of 97Sqn in April 1920 at Risalpur, India, where it patrolled the North West Frontier and then Afghanistan with DH.10 Amiens. Later types included the DH.9A in 1923 and Wapiti from 1930. During this period, Aircraftsman Shaw served for a while with the squadron and later became better known as 'Lawrence of Arabia'.

In June 1939, 60Sqn converted to the Blenheim, with which it undertook patrols of the Indian coast. In February 1941, the squadron moved to Burma, where it operated out of Rangoon. While there it also had a Flight of Buffalos, which were used

60(R)Sqn provide advanced rotary-wing training for aircrew on the Griffin HT.1 from their base at Shawbury.

72(R)Sqn provide basic flying-training for student pilots on the Tucano T.1 at Linton on Ouse as part of 1 FTS. Kevin Wills

to re-form 67Sqn. It lost most of its aircraft to the rapidly advancing Japanese and combined with 34Sqn before withdrawing to India. Operational again from May 1943 with fresh Blenheims, it continued to attack Japanese targets. In May 1943, it re-equipped in the ground-attack and fighter role with Hurricanes and, later, Thunderbolts. After the war, it became part of the policing force in Indonesia, prior to moving to Tengah, Singapore and re-equipping with the Spitfire. The squadron flew the first combat missions of Operation Firedog, bombing and firing rockets over Malaya at communist terrorists who were infiltrating. It also flew the RAF's last operational Spitfire mission, on 1 June 1951.

At Tengah, the Spitfires were replaced by the Vampire from December 1950. These gave way to the Venom from January 1955 and the combat missions continued. It re-equipped with the Meteor in the UK in 1959 and returned to Tengah. Again, it became the last squadron to fly the type operationally when they gave way to the Javelin in July 1961. More operational flying resulted from the Malysia/Indonesia confrontation and it continued to fly the Javelin until April 1968, when it was disbanded at Tengah.

In February 1969, 60Sqn's title was transferred to the RAF Germany Communications Squadron at Wildenrath. From here it operated the

Basset, Devon, Pembroke and the RAF's last Heron, carrying VIPs and freight around Germany, and to and from the UK. In 1987, the Andover arrived and, in 1990, it had completely replaced the remaining Pembrokes. In March 1992, it disbanded, with aircraft and crew transferring to 32Sqn.

In May 1992, 60Sqn was re-formed, with the establishment of a new Wessex HC.2 squadron at Benson. The squadron was to fulfil two roles: one-third provided a Wessex OCU function for itself, as well as 72 and 84Sqn, and the other two-thirds undertook the operational Support Helicopter (SH) role, providing support for the army, as well as a VIP and a Northern Ireland function. On 26 March 1997, it was disbanded once again.

Shortly after, 60Sqn was reformed on 1 April 1997 as 60 (Reserve) Sqn. The squadron's current role is as a Wing within the DHFS flying school, to provide multi-engined advanced rotary-training for pilots, navigators and crewmen of the RAF.

No. 60 (R) Sqn provides RAF pilot, navigator and crewman students multi-engined helicopter training on a 36-week course, prior to progressing on to the SARTU or tactical helicopter squadrons.

No. 60 (R) Sqn is part of the DHFS and operates the Griffin HT.1 from its base at Shawbury.

No. 72 (Reserve) Squadron

RAF Linton-on-Ouse
Tucano T.1
Personnel and Training Command
Role: Basic Flying Training
Motto: Swift

On 10 July 1917, 72Sqn was formed at Upavon from a CFS training flight with Avro 504s. It deployed to Mesopotamia in the Middle East shortly after, with G.102 Elephants and Bristol M.1 Scouts, flying missions against the Turks. It later converted to DH.4, SE.5a and SPAD S.VII, before it was disbanded in September 1919 at Baghdad, Iraq.

Re-formed as first the first Gladiator unit at Tangmere, in February 1937, 72Sqn converted to Spitfires in April 1939 at Leconfield. It took a significant part in the evacuation of Dunkirk, flying cover from Gravesend, as well as in the Battle of Britain, spending some time at Acklington, Biggin Hill and Croydon. In 1942, it was deployed to the Middle East, taking part in Operation *Torch* in North Africa, followed by action in Malta, Sicily and Italy, as well as the invasion of southern France. It formed part of the occupation of Austria, prior to disbanding at Tissano, Italy in December 1946.

In February 1947, 72Sqn re-formed at Odiham to became the first squadron to re-equip with the Vampire. This was subsequently replaced by the Meteor from July 1952 and, in April 1959, by the Javelin, which it flew from Odiham, North Weald, Church Fenton and Leconfield, where it disbanded in June 1961.

In November 1961, 72Sqn re-formed at

207(R)Sqn operates the Tucano T.1 to provide student pilots with basic training. It is part of 1 FTS, based at Linton on Ouse.

Odiham to convert to the Belvedere HC.1, which it flew until the arrival of the Wessex HC.2 in August 1964. With this versatile helicopter, it saw detachments throughout the world, including Cyprus, Libya, Far East and even the USA. Although it had previously participated in exercises in the Province, a detachment was sent to Northern Ireland in July 1969, becoming the first RAF support helicopters to be deployed to the troubled region. The continuing troubles eventually saw the whole squadron move, in November 1981. Besides assisting the army, it was also responsible for Search and Rescue (SAR) for that region.

In December 1967, 72Sqn were tasked with providing SAR cover when the Whirlwind fleet were grounded. But, later, a yellow Wessex was delivered in July 1974 and, the following month, 'D' Flight was formed and undertook SAR training, before becoming operational at the end of September at Manston. It continued to operate until June 1976, when it was replaced by 22Sqn.

In January 1997, 72Sqn received five Puma HC.1s to operate alongside the Wessex HC.2s. In March 2002, the Wessex was removed from UK operation and the squadron retired. The Pumas were transferred to 230Sqn.

In July 2002, it was announced that the squadron would assume a reserve status and it was allocated to 1Sqn of 1 FTS, with whom Tucano T.1s are operated at Linton-on-Ouse.

Students who have successfully completed the UAS course undergo a ten-month course with 72 (R) Sqn, which will include 120 hours flying the Tucano. This is the identical course to that run by 207 (R) Sqn.

No. 72 (R) Sqn operates Tucano T.1s at Linton-on-Ouse as part of 1 FTS.

No. 207 (Reserve) Squadron

RAF Linton-on-Ouse
Short Tucano T.1
Personnel and Training Command
Role: Training
Motto: *Semper paratus* – Always prepared

On 1 April 1918, 207Sqn was formed from 7Sqn, RNAS, whose history can be traced back to August 1915 with the forming of 4Sqn at Eastchurch. No. 4Sqn became 4 Wing at Petit Synthe, which expanded and ,by the following June, was split into 1 and 2Sqn. These were renamed 'A' and 'B' Squadron the following month, flying the Nieuport, BE.2c and Caudron – each were capable of bombing and fighting. In November, the roles were configured so that 'A' Squadron operated fighters and was re-named 6Sqn. 'B' Squadron was equipped with bombers and became 7Sqn, converting to the Short Bomber soon after. It became the first squadron to fly them operationally.

'A' Flight, formed from 7Sqn in July 1917, was used to form RNAS 14 and

16Sqn the following year. When the RAF was formed, 7Sqn was transferred from the RNAS, re-numbered 207Sqn and operated the Handley Page 0/400 bomber. When the war ended, 207Sqn returned to the UK and was disbanded in January 1920 at Uxbridge.

It was re-formed in February 1920 at Bircham Newton, from a nucleus from 274Sqn. Initially, it was equipped with the DH.9A, with which it was deployed to San Stefano, Turkey during the Chanak Crisis. In 1927, it converted onto Fairey IIIFs and then Gordons in 1932. It was re-equipped with the Vincent in 1936, while at Gebit in Sudan, before converting to Wellesleys at Worthy Down in 1937, then moving to Cottesmore and converting to the Battle in April 1938. In April 1940, it was merged into 12 OTU at Benson.

In November 1940, 207 was re-formed at Waddington and became the first squadron to be equipped with the Manchester. During February 1941, the squadron provided a nucleus from which 97Sqn was re-formed. The Manchester suffered problems and some Hampdens were operated, until the arrival of Lancasters in January 1942 following a move to Bottesford. These were flown on raids all over Europe, including Italy and Poland, while operating from Langar and Spilsby. From April 1943, it operated as part of the Pathfinder Force for a year. By the end of the war, 540 operations had been flown, but at a cost of 154 crew lost. In July 1949, it converted to the Lincoln, then disbanded in March 1950.

In June 1951, 207 was re-formed at Marham with Washingtons and continued to operate with Canberras from March 1954, until disbanded again in March 1956.

It re-formed in April 1956 as a V-bomber unit with the Valiant, which it flew operationally from Malta on Operation *Musketeer* against Egyptian targets in October 1956. It was disbanded in May 1965, following the grounding of the Valiant force the previous year.

In February 1969, 207 was re-formed by the re-naming of the Southern Communications Squadron. It was equipped with the Basset, Devon and Pembroke at Northolt to fly VIPs and senior officers around the UK. In April 1974, the squadron was advised that their Basset CC.1s would be retired the following day. The Pembrokes were retired in 1977 and it continued to operate the Devon until being disbanded in June 1984.

On 12 July 2002, 207 Squadron was reformed as a Reserve squadron, which was allocated to 2Sqn of 1 FTS, which operated the Tucano at Linton-on-Ouse.

Students who have successfully completed the UAS course undergo a ten-month course with 72 or 207 (R) Sqn This includes 120 hours flying the Tucano. The courses run by both squadrons are identical.

No. 207 (R) Sqn operates Tucano T.1s at Linton-on-Ouse as part of 1 FTS.

No. 208 (Reserve) Squadron

RAF Valley
BAe Hawk T.1 and T.1A
Personnel and Training Command
Role: Advanced Flying Training
Motto: Vigilant

On 26 October 1916, 208Sqn was originally formed as 8Sqn, RNAS, at le Vert Galant, France. It came into existence as a result of an RFC request for reinforcements for operations in the Somme; each of the existing RNAS squadrons provided one flight to enable the new unit to be formed. This resulted in Naval 8Sqn initially operating three different types – the Nieuport Scout, Sopwith Pup and 1½ Strutter. In February, it moved to St Pol, where it re-equipped with the Sopwith Triplane. It then moved to Furness, followed by Auchel and Mont St Eloi. Here, they re-equipped with the Camel. In early 1918, Naval 8Sqn came home to Walmer for a rest, but was rushed back to

France at the end of March to help halt the advancing Germans.

When the RFC and RNAS squadrons merged to form the RAF in April 1918, 'Naval 8' became 208Sqn. They operated from Teteghem, then La Gorgue. Unfortunately, while there, the Germans overran the Portuguese lines that the squadron was supporting and, due to thick fog precluding take-off, had to burn all sixteen of its aircraft before abandoning the airfield. Two days later, it was re-equipped at Serny and, over the following five months, destroyed eighty-six enemy aircraft for the loss of only six. In July 1918, it moved to Tramecourt for a couple of months, where one of its duties was protection for King George V, who was staying in a nearby chateau. It then moved to Foucacourt on the Somme, followed by Estrée-en-Chaussée and Moritz, where it re-equipped with the Snipe just as the war ended. It operated from various locations in Belgium and Germany as part of the Army of Occupation, before returning to the UK, where it was disbanded at Netheravon in November 1919.

In February 1920, 208Sqn was re-formed at Ismailia, Egypt from 113Sqn, which was still flying RE.8s. These were replaced by the F.2b Fighter, which it operated in the army co-operation role. It was deployed to San Stefano in September 1922, during the Chanak Crisis in Turkey, where it undertook photo-reconnaissance missions before returning to Ismailia in September 1923. In 1927, it moved to Heliopolis and

then on to Ramleh, Palestine to police Arab-Jewish troubles. It re-equipped with the Atlas, which was flown to many parts of the Middle East. In 1935, it converted to the Audax, plus 'D' Flight with the Demon. However, 'D' Flight was absorbed into 64Sqn the following January. With trouble brewing, the squadron deployed to Mersa Matruh, to stem Mussolini's expansion in North Africa. Before long, the troubles in Palestine required it to return, initially to Ramleh and then to operate detached flights from Jerusalem and Haifa. In December, the whole squadron returned to Heliopolis.

In January 1939, 208Sqn re-equipped with the Lysander and, when war broke out, it was located at Qasaba. Initial tasking was to patrol the Libyan/Egyptian border, but the Lysander was too slow and vulnerable, resulting in several being shot down. In November 1940, Hurricanes arrived and they were tasked with photo reconnaissance of Bardia, Tobruk and el Adem. After several moves, 208Sqn was deployed to Greece to help stem the Axis invasion, but was heavily outnumbered. The last two remaining Hurricanes were taken by 80Sqn and 208Sqn finally ran out of aircraft when the last Lysanders were destroyed at Argos. Having marched to a beach-head, they were evacuated to Crete and on to Palestine, where they were re-established in May 1941 at Gaza. From there, detachments were operated from Habbaniya, Amman, Haifa and Aqir and attacked enemy positions from Damascus.

A 208(R)Sqn Hawk T.1a flies through the mountains of North Wales, providing RAF student pilots with excellent low-level training. Philip Stevens – TargetA

In December 1943, 208Sqn converted to recce Spitfires, as part of the preparations to move into Italy. There it took part in many operations, including the battle for Monte Casino. In September 1944, it moved to Florence.

Despite the war ending, operations continued, with 208Sqn returning to Petah Tiqvah, Palestine, this time to counter Jewish terrorists, during which seven aircraft were blown up. In March 1948, it re-located to Nicosia, Cyprus, although a detachment continued at Ramat David. In May 1948, Egyptian AF aircraft destroyed another seven aircraft 'accidentally'. When another wave arrived, two Spitfires managed to shoot down five.

In November 1948, 208Sqn moved on to Fayid, Egypt. While there, a further four unarmed Spitfires were shot down by the Israelis, just hours before an international ceasefire. In 1950, the Spitfires were replaced with Meteors at Abu Suier. The squadron finally left the Middle East and arrived at Hal Far, Malta in January 1956. In March, it moved to Akrotiri, Cyprus, returning to Malta in August, during the Suez Campaign, to protect forces operating from there. Detachments were also later operated in Bahrain and Aden and 208Sqn eventually disbanded in 1958.

In the meantime, 34Sqn at Tangmere was re-numbered 208Sqn in January 1958 and moved back to Nicosia, Cyprus in March, where one was damaged by terrorists. While there, a detachment was sent to Amman, Jordan to help stabilize the government when King Feisal of Iraq was assassinated in July 1958. It was disbanded in March 1959.

The following day at Eastleigh, Kenya, 208Sqn was re-formed from the re-numbered 142Sqn with Venoms, although a detachment was maintained in the Persian Gulf. In March 1960, 208Sqn flew back to Stradishall and re-equipped with the Hunter, before returning to Kenya while still maintaining the Middle East detachments at Aden and Bahrain. The Kuwaitis requested help to stem threats from Iraq and, in July, 208Sqn deployed into Kuwait for three months. From there it moved to Khormaksar, Aden then Muharraq, Bahrain in June 1964, where it was later disbanded in September 1971.

The squadron was re-formed at Honington in July 1974 with Buccaneers. In 1977, it became the first non-USAF participant in the *Red Flag* series of exer-

cises. In July 1983, 208Sqn moved to Lossiemouth, where it operated in the Maritime Strike Attack role with Sea Eagle missiles, in addition to its land-strike role. In September 1983, 208Sqn deployed six Buccaneers to Cyprus, from where they flew a number of missions over Beirut in support of the multinational peacekeeping forces in Operation *Pulsator*.

In January 1991, they formed part of the Buccaneer Wing that was deployed during the Gulf War, flying their pink Buccaneers to provide laser designation for the Tornados using the Pavespike system. The Buccaneers also dropped a number of LGBs themselves. A total of 107 missions were flown. Until they were disbanded on 31 March 1994, 208Sqn continued to operate their Buccaneers, plus Hunters for training, from Lossiemouth.

On 1 April 1994, 208Sqn was re-formed as a reserve unit by the re-numbering of 234Sqn, to operate as one of the two squadrons of 4 FTS, along with 19Sqn. The Advanced Flying Training for students from Tucano courses and refreshers for existing pilots is provided by 208Sqn. The AFT course lasts about twenty weeks, during which students fly sixty-three hours, of which fifteen are solo. Those that successfully complete this stage then progress on to 19 (R) Sqn for the Tactics and Weapon Training elements of the course. Not all Tucano students will have come to 208Sqn. On successfully completing the course, some students will be selected go to Canada, where they join the NFTC (NATO Flying Training in Canada) course and receive similar training, flying the more modern Hawk 115. The rest will progress to 19 (R) Sqn or be creamed off to become instructors with 208.

It is anticipated that 208 (R) Sqn will start to receive the Hawk 128 from 2008.

No. 208 (R) Sqn operates the Hawk T.1A/T.1W from their base at Valley.

No. 1 Flying Training School

RAF Linton-on-Ouse

Tucano T.1

Personnel and Training Command

Role: Basic flying training

Motto: *Terra Marique Ad Gaelum* – By land and sea to the sky

The RAF's first Flying Training School (FTS) was formed at Netheravon on 29

July 1919, initially as the Netheravon Flying School. It was equipped with Avro 504s, F.2b Fighters and DH.9As.

Royal Navy and Marine students arrived in June 1924, but their training was moved to Leuchars in 1929. By 1930, the pilot's course took 150 flying hours, initially flying the Tutor then progressing to the Atlas. However, the reduction in the RAF's size during the early 1930s resulted in the closing of the school in February 1931.

On 1 April 1935, the training school at Leuchars was re-named 1 FTS. It was transferred from Coastal Command to Training Command's 23 Group in July. Training of naval and army pilots continued and the first references to instrument flying are recorded, as well as a one-day catapult course. No. 1 FTS also had a different approach to training. The 1938 syllabus used civilian Elementary Flying Training Schools to provide the fifty-hour *ab initio* course, but 1 FTS conducted this itself – the first of the 'all through' training that was to become standard after the war. However, the navy and army preferred the old system and it reverted back to using the civilian schools. In August 1938, 1 FTS returned to Netheravon.

The Harvard arrived for intermediate training in 1939, while Harts and Hinds were used for the advanced course, with Blenheims being added shortly after. In September, the school was re-named 1 Service FTS. Having been training predominately naval pilots, from June 1940, 1 SFTS began to supply pilots to RAF operational units. The relief landing-ground at Shrewton was being used for night flying, but as Luftwaffe attacks increased, so many of the training schools were moved to the Commonwealth. As a result, 1 SFTS closed in March 1942 and relocated to Ambala, India, where it became 1 SFTS (India) in June. Although the school was manned by RAF instructors, it was used to train Indian Air Force pilots only and, in December 1946, it became Advanced Flying Training School (India).

In June 1947, 1 FTS was re-formed at Spitalgate by the re-numbering of 17 FTS. It was equipped with Tiger Moths and Harvards and trained Royal Netherlands Air Force pilots as well as RAF. However, its life was limited and, in February 1948, it was disbanded.

December 1950 saw 1 FTS re-form at Oakington with Harvards, as part of the

This impressive line-up of Tucano T.1s from 1 FTS is used to provide basic flying-training for hopeful RAF aircrew at their base at Linton-on-Ouse.

post-war expansion. Training was provided for re-entrants, as well as National Service pilots. The following year, VR pilots were added and, in October, it moved to Moreton-in-Marsh. At its peak, 1 FTS had sixty aircraft and was flying 3,500 hours per month. In April 1955, the school was disbanded again.

Just ten days later, 22 FTS, equipped with Provosts at Syerston, was re-named 1 FTS. Here it returned to its earlier role of providing initial training for naval pilots. In September 1957, it moved to Linton-on-Ouse, where it commenced the 'new' style of all-through training, taking naval pilots from *ab initio* through to 'Wings' (a touch of déjà vu) using Provosts and Vampires. Jet Provosts replaced the piston Provosts in June 1960, although a few Chipmunks were added in March 1961 for the naval pilots destined for helicopters. In July 1969, the Royal Navy commitment ended when it was transferred to 2 FTS at Church Fenton.

No. 1 FTS then concentrated on training RAF pilots at Linton-on-Ouse, with Topcliffe used as a RLG from 1974 and Dishforth from 1983. On 1 April 1992, 1 FTS's first Tucano arrived, enabling the Jet Provost to be retired in July 1993. By this time over 630,000 hours had been clocked up by 1 FTS on the JP, training RAF and many Commonwealth pilots.

The 1998 Strategic Defence Review detailed a need for an increase in the numbers of 'fast jet' pilots, resulting in an increase in 1 FTS's work-load. With a fleet of nearly eighty Tucanos, nearby Church Fenton was added to the list of RLGs used by the school.

In July 2002, it was announced that 1 and 2Sqn of 1 FTS would assume reserve squadron status and they were allocated the identities of 72 (R) and 207 (R) Sqn. No. 1 FTS also operate the Tucano Air Navigation Squadron (TANS) and CFS (Tucano).

No. 1 FTS operates the Tucano T.1 from its base at Linton-on-Ouse, with 72 and 207 operated as Reserve Squadrons.

No. 3 Flying Training School

RAF Cranwell
Personnel and Training Command
Motto: Basic flying training
Motto: Achieve

On 26 April 1920, 3 Flying Training School (3 FTS) was formed at Scopwick, but disbanded in April 1922, having used aircraft such as the Avro 504, Snipe and F.2b Fighter.

In April 1928, 3 FTS was re-formed at Grantham, operating a variety of aircraft, including the Siskin, followed by Bulldog, Fury and, in the 1930s, the Tomtit. These were followed by the Bulldog in 1934 and the Fury II, prior to moving to South Cerney in August 1937 with the Hart and Oxford. In September 1939, it was renamed 3 Service Flying Training School

By June 1940, the Harts had been passed on, when the school concentrated on twin engine training. In 1942, it became known as 3 Pilots Advanced Flying Unit, providing refresher training for experienced pilots, and made use of various landing grounds in the area.

With the war over, in April 1946, the school, which had reverted back to 3 SFTS, moved from South Cerney to Feltwell with its Tiger Moths, Harvards and Ansons. In 1947, the Prentice arrived, replacing the Tiger Moth, and it became 3 FTS again. By 1954, all types had been replaced by the Provost. It was disbanded in June 1958.

In September 1961, 3 FTS was reformed at Leeming with the Jet Provost. It absorbed the Vampire Advanced Training Unit from 7 FTS in 1966, the School of Refresher Training from Manby in 1973 and the RN EFTS with Bulldogs in 1974. In April 1984, it was disbanded,

On 1 February 1989, the Flying Training School at Cranwell was re-named 3 FTS, flying Jet Provosts. In 1991, these were replaced by the Tucano. During 1995, 3 FTS absorbed the CFS Bulldog Squadron, followed by 6 FTS Bulldogs, Dominies and Jetstreams, of which the latter two were allocated reserve squadron status. However, it lost the basic-flying role on the Tucano, which was moved to Linton-on-Ouse to be operated by 1 FTS.

No. 3 FTS comprises Flying Wing plus 55 (R) Sqn, with which it provides the

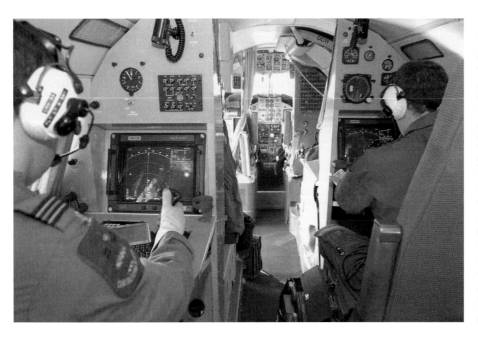

A CFS QFI checks a navigation instructor from 55 (R) Sqn inside a Dominie T.1. Crown Copyright

front-line conversion units with qualified multi-engine pilots, Weapon Systems Officers (WSO), who are all commissioned officers, and non-commissioned aircrew (NCA), including Weapons Systems Operators (WSOp), Air Engineers and Loadmasters.

Flying Wing comprises 45 (R) Sqn, which is now equipped with the King Air (replacing the Jetstream T.1s in April 2004), Ops Sqn, Air Traffic Control Sqn, General Service Training Sqn and Groundschool. No. 55 (R) Sqn is equipped with the Dominie and conducts all the RAF's non-pilot aircrew training.

No. 3 FTS is based at Cranwell and comprises 55 (R) Sqn with the Dominie T.1 and 45 (R) Sqn with the King Air T.1.

No. 4 Flying Training School

RAF Valley
Personnel and Training Command
Role: Advanced flying training
Motto: *E Sabulo ad Sidera* – From the sand to the stars

On 1 April 1921, 4 Flying Training School (4 FTS) was formed at Abu Sueir in the Canal Zone, Egypt. It was equipped with two Avro 504Ks at the time and was the only overseas RAF training unit. Its role was to teach pilots for the Middle East squadrons.

During the mid-1930s, 4 FTS was able to concentrate on advanced training, due to the use of civilian flying schools for ab initio training. For this and an army co-operation role, they were equipped with a variety of aircraft, including the 504N, Audax, Atlas, DH.9A, F.2b Fighter, Hart, Tutor and Vimy and, in October 1938, the Anson was added.

In January 1930, during a flight to Cairo in a DH.9A, the engine came off its mounting, causing control to be lost. Although parachutes had been available for some time, this crew became the first RAF personnel to successfully jump from an aircraft.

On 1 September 1939, 4 FTS moved to Habbaniya, Iraq. When war broke out a few days later, the Audax were allocated for air defence with pilots kept at readiness. As student pilots became short in supply from the UK, 4 FTS took recruits from the Commonwealth and even from other countries, such as Egypt and France.

In February 1940, the name was changed to 4 Service Flying Training School and, in July, Gladiators were added to the fleet. With an increased demand for observers and air gunners for Middle East Command, the school's role changed, with only half of its capacity used for training pilots on Harts. The air gunners trained on Gordons and observers on Oxfords, but this halted in early 1941.

The Empire Training Scheme schools in Rhodesia and South Africa were soon training sufficient pilots for the Middle East and, as a result, it was decided to disband 4 SFTS. However, in April, while the last course was being trained, Rashid Ali, who was a Iraqi rebel and sympathizer with the Germans, seized power in Baghdad, assisted by four Generals and a revolutionary army. This caused the Regent to flee to Habbaniya. Britain quickly sent reinforcements, to which Rashid Ali reacted by sending 9,000 troops and twenty-eight artillery guns. On 1 May, 4 SFTS was transformed to the 'Habbaniya Air Striking Force', adapting its various aircraft to carry bombs and arming them with machine guns. Having had an ultimatum to withdraw ignored by the Iraqis, the 'Striking Force' commenced their attack, flying 193 sorties on the first day. However, this cost them five of their seventy aircraft.

Although their aircraft losses mounted, the bombing attacks continued. After five days the Iraqis withdrew, having been subjected to 584 sorties with a total of 45 tonnes of bombs dropped. While this battle had been won, rumours of Luftwaffe aircraft were confirmed when a pair of He.111s attacked the airfield on 16 May. More aircraft were discovered at Mosul and attacks against each other continued virtually daily. The Germans were reinforced with Italian CR.42s, but these were quickly destroyed. Sensing defeat, Rashid Ali and his conspirators fled to Persia, enabling the Regent to return to Baghdad.

During the hectic activity, the 'Habbaniya Air Striking Force' had flown 1,605 operational sorties, the majority of which were flown by students. A small force of Hurricanes and Gladiators was established to provide protection but, on 1 July 1941, 4 SFTS was disbanded.

On 3 February 1947, 4 FTS was reformed at Heany, Southern Rhodesia with Tiger Moths, Harvards and Ansons. The Ansons were transferred to 3 Air Navigation School (3 ANS), along with the role of navigator training, but kept its strength up with the additional Harvards and Tiger Moths of the disbanded 5 FTS. In 1951, the Tiger Moths were replaced by Chipmunks. The school was disbanded once again in January 1954.

As a consequence of the re-organization of RAF flying training, 4 FTS was re-established by re-numbering 204 Advanced Flying School (204 AFS) on 1 June 1954. It operated the Meteor F.4 and T.7 from Middleton St George, until the arrival of the Vampire FB.5 and T.11 in October 1954. From January, RAF training comprised 130 hours basic training on the Provost, followed by 110 hours of advanced training on the Vampire – the latter being with 4 FTS.

In June 1956, 4 FTS moved to Worksop, absorbing 211 FTS, which still operated the Meteor T.7 and F.8. These continued to be flown until December 1957, when it became all-Vampire again, but disbanded in June 1958, when the role was taken over by 7 FTS at Valley.

On 15 August 1960, 7 FTS was re-numbered 4 FTS. The Varsity T.1 was added to the fleet for Coastal and Training Command crew training, but they were transferred to 5 FTS in March 1962. In November, the first Gnat T.1 was delivered and, by August 1963, had completely replaced the Vampire.

In 1964, the 4 FTS Gnat display team – the Yellow Jacks – were formed. Following winter maintenance at Kemble, they emerged the following year as the CFS Red Arrows.

The Hunter F.6 and T.7 joined 4 FTS in 1967 and were operated along with the Gnats, proving especially useful, not only better for the longer-legged students, who had problems with the small Gnat, but also preferred by many of the Commonwealth and Foreign students. On successfully completing the seventy-hour course, students then progressed to 229 OCU at Chivenor.

During 1971, both the Gnats and Hunters operated from Fairford while the runway at Valley was being resurfaced.

On 4 November 1976, the first Hawks were delivered to 4 FTS, which led to the retirement of the Gnat and Hunter in November 1979. Training of QFIs commenced in April 1977, followed by the first student course in July. In September 1992, 234Sqn became part of 4 FTS when the school took over the role of the disbanded Tactical Weapons Units (TWU). It was joined by 74 (R) Sqn in October 1992. In April 1994, 234Sqn was re-numbered 208 (R) Sqn and, in October, it was joined by 19 (R) Sqn. In September 2000, 74 (R) Sqn was disbanded and the instructors joined an enlarged 19 (R) Sqn.

No. 4 FTS is the UK's last advanced flying-training unit and is responsible for the training of fast-jet pilots for the RN as well as the RAF. In addition to training its own instructors, 4 FTS trains Qualified Tactics and Weapons Instructors plus Exchange Officers and Foreign and Commonwealth Officers.

No. 4 FTS comprises 19Sqn, which undertakes tactics and weapons training, and 208Sqn, which provides the advanced flying-training. In addition, it incorporates the BAe Systems Hawk Synthetic Training Facility, with procedure and simulator trainers for ground training.

Central Flying School

RAF Cranwell
Personnel and Training Command
Role: Training
Motto: *Imprimis Praecepta* – Our teaching is everlasting

The Central Flying School (CFS) was formed at Upavon on 12 May 1912 and is the oldest military flying school in the world – No. 1 Course commenced in August 1912 and was completed in December 1912. It had trained a total of ninety-four RFC pilots by the outbreak of the First World War. It also rapidly became one of the main centres for experimental flying. When the RAF was formed in 1918, the CFS became responsible for the training of flying instructors, however, it continued to provide this service for the army and navy on request.

It was briefly re-named the Flying Instructors School in December 1919, but reverted to CFS in April. It moved to Wittering in October 1926 and a Refresher Flight was formed the following year. During the late 1920s, Flight Lietenant D'Arcy Greig led the first CFS aerobatic display team, flying de Havilland Genet Moths, and so commenced the tradition of display aerobatics that was a feature of the Hendon Air Displays during the following decade.

In 1935, rotary-wing aircraft entered service following the purchase of six Cievra C.30 Autogyros for the RAF School of Army Co-operation. However, the first true helicopter to enter service was the Sikorsky R-4 Hoverfly in 1944.

In 1942, the CFS was split into the Empire Central Flying School at Hullavington and 7 Flying Instructors School (7 FIS).

In 1946, the CFS was re-established at Little Rissington with Tiger Moth, Harvard, Mosquito, Lancaster and Spitfire, plus jet-powered Vampire. South Cerney was opened for basic flying and the EFTS disbanded in 1949. In 1953, training consolidated on the Provost T.1 and Vampire.

Such was the value of the helicopter during the Malaysian emergency that the CFS Helicopter Development Unit (HDU) was formed at Middle Wallop, in March 1954, with three Westland Dragonfly helicopters. A substantial portion of the HDU's initial tasking was to provide VIP transport, including the Royal Family. It moved to South Cerney in June 1957, where it quickly established its real role. The Sycamore and Whirlwind were added to its fleet and, by 1957, it was training pilots for all three services. The CFS (H) moved to Tern Hill in August 1961. A reorganization resulted in it being formed as a wing with two squadrons. The larger one was responsible for pilot and QHI training and the other for establishing and maintaining standards. At this point the CFS (H) was equipped with the Dragonfly, Whirlwind, Sycamore and Skeeter. Later they were replaced by the Whirlwind and Sioux, then the Wessex and Gazelle.

Concurrently, the Jet Provost was introduced in 1959, the Varsity in 1960, followed by the Gnat in 1962 and, later, by the Bulldog, Gazelle and Jetstream in 1973, and Hawk in 1977. In the meantime, January 1967 saw the Primary Flying Squadron (PFS) at South Cerney moved to Church Fenton.

Little Rissington flying ended in April 1976, with the Bulldogs moving to Leeming and the detached Gnats at Kemble to Valley – they were being replaced by Hawks from the end of the year. The Jet Provosts and HQ moved to Leeming in November 1977, while the CFS (H) moved from Ternhill to Shawbury in 1976. The Red Arrows moved from Kemble to Scampton in 1984, the Tucano replaced the Jet Provost in 1989, the CFS Hawk unit was re-named 19 (R) Sqn in September 1994 and the HQ moved back to Cranwell in 1995. In 1997, the CFS (H) role of training instructors on the Gazelle and Wessex ceased when they were withdrawn and is now carried out on the Squirrel and Griffin at Shawbury, using helicopters borrowed from DHFS.

Today, the CFS continues to fulfil its role of training flying-instructors and providing examiners to ensure that the necessary high standards of pilots are maintained at squadron level.

Consequently, every UK military flying unit has a CFS representation.

The CFS Tutor Squadron, formed in 1994, has an additional role of providing elementary navigator instruction on behalf of 55 (R) Sqn, in addition to conducting flying instructor courses for experienced pilots for all three services.

The CFS HQ is located at Cranwell, together with the CFS Tutor Squadron. Neither have any aircraft of their own, borrowing them as required. The Hawk-equipped Red Arrows at Scampton are part of the CFS.

The CFS HQ is located at Cranwell and operates elements at all of the flying training establishments. However, aircraft are borrowed as required. The only CFS aircraft are the Hawk T.1/T.1As of the Red Arrows.

Central Flying School Tutor Squadron

RAF Cranwell
Grob Tutor
Personnel and Training Command
Role: Elementary Training

The origins of the CFS Tutor Squadron can be traced back to 1952 at South Cerney, where RAF pilots were taught how to give basic instruction on the Piston Provost. This unit was amalgamated with the advanced instructor-training at Little Rissington in November 1954 and formed the Chipmunk flight of CFS's 4Sqn. It became a unit in its own right and was named CFS Bulldog Squadron, when the Bulldog aircraft entered service in 1974. It moved from Little Rissington to RAF Leeming in 1977, where it stayed until September 1984, when it relocated to Scampton. Finally, on 3 September 1995, the squadron moved to its present location at Cranwell, where it was absorbed into 3 FTS as part of the Defence Costs Studies 'rustication' of the CFS flying squadrons. At the same time, it also adopted the task of providing airborne training to basic navigator courses for the Navigator and Airman Aircrew School. During the gradual replacement of the Bulldog in RAF service by the Tutor, the squadron was renamed CFS Tutor Squadron on 2 October 2000, when the balance of its task shifted to the new aircraft. The squadron became part of No. 1 Elementary Flying Training School (1 EFTS) in March 2003.

The CFS Tutor Squadron provides training for flying instructors for all three services. The main course lasts six months and includes eighty hours on the Tutors, while a refresher course takes two months with forty hours. The Tutor element of the navigator training lasts two months and includes just under twenty flying hours.

The CFS Tutor Squadron is based at Cranwell, but has no aircraft. It uses the Tutor from a combined Cranwell-based fleet shared with East Midlands UAS, 7 Air Experience Flight and the No 1 EFTS UAS Standards Flight.

Defence Elementary Flying Training School

RAF Barkston Heath
Slingsby Firefly 260
Personnel and Training Command
Role: Elementary Training

The Defence Elementary Flying Training School (DEFTS) originally evolved from the RNEFTS and commenced life as the Joint Elementary Flying Training School (JEFTS). It is a civilian flying school, which was established by Hunting Contract Services and was taken over by Babcock in 2001.

JEFTS was initially set up to provide elementary flying training for all three services. The RAF joined it in 1994 and it moved to Barkston Heath from Topcliffe in 1995. In 1996, the army joined in and, the following year, it took on army grading. It was planned to include navy grading, but it was decided that the skies of Lincolnshire were getting too crowded and it remained at Roborough. With some 17,000 hours per year being flown, one element moved to Church Fenton to ease congestion. The contract was fixed by student numbers and a price fixed for getting those students through.

The company provided 80 per cent of the instructors and management running the school. Of the instructors, 20 per cent of the unit were military, but 80 per cent of the civilian tutors were highly qualified ex-military.

In July 2003, the Tri-service contract ended and the RAF switched its elementary training to be incorporated within the UAS system. At the same time, control of the school passed back into military hands, with the establishment of a RAF Chief Flying Instructor and RN and Army Squadron Commanders in charge of 703 Naval Air Squadron and 674Sqn AAC. Manning reflects this increased military presence with 40 per cent military instructors.

Consequently, the name changed to Defence Elementary Flying Training School (DEFTS) and it now only provides

The CFS Tutor Squadron operates the Grob Tutor for continuation training for existing QFIs, as well as for teaching new ones. Crown Copyright

initial training to army and navy aircrew. It does, however, provide some lead-in training for the multi-engine course at Cranwell, which lasts for eight weeks and includes thirty hours flying. DEFTS also provides army flying grading at Middle Wallop with the Firefly 160.

DEFTS operate the Firefly 260 at Cranwell and Barkston Heath plus the 160 at Middle Wallop.

Defence Helicopter Flying School

RAF Shawbury
Eurocopter Squirrel HT.1, Bell Griffin HT.1.
Personnel and Training Command
Role: Basic and advanced helicopter-training

The Defence Helicopter Flying School (DHFS) was formed on 1 April 1997, to provide basic and advanced single-engine helicopter training for pilots of all three services, plus advanced twin-engine helicopter training for RAF pilots, aircrew and navigators. For this role, the DHFS is equipped with the single-engine Squirrel HT.1 and twin-engined Griffin HT.1.

Having successfully completed their *ab initio* training with the UASs, student heli-

The RAF has cut the majority of training on the Defence Elementary Flying Training School (DEFTS) Fireflys and transferred it to the UAS Tutor. It is currently only used for students on the Multi-Engine Lead-IN (MELIN) course prior to joining 45(R)Sqn and the King Air.

copter pilots from all three services arrive at the DHFS where they initially join 660 Sqn for the Single Engine Basic Rotary Wing Squadron – 660 Sqn. This unit is commanded by an Army Major and equipped with the Squirrel. The course lasts 12 weeks comprising of ground and simulator training and 35 hours are flying. From there successful student progress to the Single Engine Advance Rotary Wing Squadron with 705 Sqn. This commanded by a Royal Navy Lt Commander and also equipped with the Squirrel. The number of hours flown during the eight week course depends on the service and is tailored for their specific requirements. For RAF students the course includes 37 hours flying. Once successfully completed, the Army students depart for Middle Wallop and Navy students to Yeovilton or Culdrose. RAF students remain at Shawbury and join the Multi Engine Advance Rotary Wing Squadron – 60 Sqn. This unit is commanded by a Sqn Ldr and equipped with the Griffin HT.1. Here pilots, navigators and WSOp (Cmn) are taught to work together and undertake a variety of training including the carrying of underslung loads during the 39 week course which includes 63.5 hours flying.

The Defence Helicopter Flying School is equipped with the small Squirrel HT.2 for basic helicopter-pilot training for all three services and the Griffin HT.1 for RAF twin-engined and advanced aircrew training.

For part of the course they are detached to the DHFS SARTU at Valley for three weeks for advanced SAR technique training during which a further 13.5 hours will be flown. Additional DHFS courses are run for refresher as well as hover conversion for student Harrier pilots undertaking their fast jet training at Valley.

DHFS comprises 660Sqn AAC and 705 NAS, which both operate the Squirrel HT.1, plus 60Sqn with the Griffin HT.1 – all based at Shawbury. In addition, the SARTU is operated as a detachment at Valley.

No. 1 Elementary Flying Training School

RAF Cranwell
Personnel and Training Command
Role: Elementary Training
Motto: *Ab Initio* – From the beginning

On 3 September 1939, 1 Elementary Flying Training School (1 EFTS) was originally formed at Hatfield with Tiger Moths. It was operated by de Havilland initially, on behalf of the RAF, before being taken over by them in January 1940. Its origins can be traced further back, to the establishment of a reserve school at Stag Lane in May 1923 that moved to Hatfield in May 1930. In August 1935, it was re-named 1 Elementary & Reserve Flying Training School, before becoming 1 EFTS in September 1939. It moved to Holywell Hyde (re-named Panshangar in September 1943) in September 1942, equipped with Tiger Moths and Proctors. In May 1947, it was re-named 1 Reserve Flying School.

On 1 May 2003, 1 EFTS was re-formed at Cranwell by the re-naming of HQ Elementary Flying Training (HQ EFT). It is responsible for the elementary flying-training of students for all three services, plus a small number from foreign and Commonwealth air forces. These students either have been selected by the OASC and have completed their initial officer training with the Officer and Aircrew Cadet Training Unit (OACTU), or have joined a University Air Squadron (UAS) and will complete the OASC/OACTU process on completion of their university course.

From 1993 until 2003, most RAF Direct Entry (DE) student pilots were put through an elementary flying-training course with JEFTS at Church Fenton. Latterly, this was supplemented by Direct Entry Flights at Yorkshire and London UAS. However, following the ending of the JEFTS ten-year contract on 7 July 2003, 1 EFTS re-organized the future elementary flying-training of RAF students. As a result, all RAF student aircrew now enter either as university students through the UAS or as DE students, who will undergo basic initial officer training with OACTU at Cranwell before joining a UAS. Both sets of students will undergo ground training, plus sixty-two hours of flying training, with DE students achieving this in around four months. University students, meanwhile, take three to four years to intersperse this training with that of their undergraduate syllabus.

No. 1 EFTS is also responsible for the elementary flying-training of army and navy students. This was undertaken by JEFTS, which has been re-named Defence Elementary Flying Training School (DEFTS) since July 2003.

Through its area of responsibility, 1 EFTS accounts for some 62,500 flying hours per year.

No. 1 EFTS is responsible for the fourteen UAS, including the AEFs at various locations around the country with the Tutor, DEFTS at Barkston Heath with the Firefly and UAS Standards Flt at Cranwell, plus the CFS Tutor Squadron, which operate the Tutor, pooled with East Midlands UAS.

RAF Aerobatic Team/ The Red Arrows

RAF Scampton
BAe Hawk T.1/T.1A
Personnel and Training Command
Role: Aerobatic Team
Motto: *Éclat* – Brilliance

The Red Arrows are the RAF's display team and were formed as part of the Central Flying School (CFS) on 1 March 1965. Officially, they were based at Little Rissington and equipped with seven Gnats, however, they were actually based at Fairford before settling at nearby Kemble for the next sixteen years.

When the CFS moved to Cranwell in 1976, the Red Arrows remained at Kemble and were parented by Brize Norton. In November 1979, they received their first Hawk and, in spring 1983, they moved to Scampton. With plans for Scampton's closure in 1995, the Red Arrows were earmarked to move to Marham but, for operational reasons, this was could not happen until 1999. As a result, they temporarily moved to Cranwell in 1995, but continued to practice over Scampton. When Marham was earmarked for the Tornado, plans to re-open Scampton were announced in August 1998, enabling the return of the Red Arrows and also its use as a RLG for Cranwell. In December 2000, they returned to Scampton.

The Red Arrows gave their first performance to the media at Little Rissington on 6 May 1965, but this was marred by bad weather and they were forced to fly a straight-and-level display. Their first public display was at Biggin Hill nine days later. By the end of their first season, they had flown sixty-five displays, not only in the UK but also in Belgium, France, Germany, Holland and Italy.

Two spare pilots were incorporated in the team, but this required a huge amount of additional work to get them qualified to fly in any position and they were rarely needed. As a result, in 1968, it was decided to enlarge the team to nine display aircraft, which led to them flying the Diamond Nine that has become their trademark.

For the 1980 season, the Gnats were exchanged for the BAe Hawk T.1, reflecting the RAF's change in advanced trainer. Since then, the Red Arrows have displayed before crowds in Africa, Australia, Eastern and Western Europe, Middle and Far East, as well as the USA.

Each year, normally, two new pilots are selected to join the team with whom they will stay for three years. Each pilot will have volunteered and undergone a tough selection process. These new pilots will join the team shortly before the end of the season, to get used to the schedules. At the end of each season, the Hawks will be given a complete overhaul, in order that the aircraft are ready for the start of the new season. In the meantime, training is conducted with aircraft on loan.

It is normal for ten aircraft to be flown to airshows. This extra aircraft is flown by the team manager, who also acts as the commentator during the team's performance. This will also enable him to get from one show to another independently,

should, for instance, the team not be land-ing at the venue. It also acts as a spare aircraft, should it be needed. The other nine aircraft will also normally each carry a member of the groundcrew. This enables the aircraft to be quickly turned round, as the Red Arrows usually perform several airshows on each day over the season's weekends.

The Red Arrows fly the Hawk T.1 and T.1A and are based at Scampton.

Search and Rescue Training Unit

Griffin HT.1
RAF Valley
Personnel and Training Command
Role: SAR aircrew training
Motto: That lives may be saved

The origins of the Search and Rescue Training Unit (SARTU) can be traced back to early April 1962 and 3Sqn, CFS (H), which commenced training specialist SAR aircrew at Valley. Equipped with the Whirlwind, the unit was part of the CFS (H) establishment, which was based at Ternhill. In September 1976, it was re-

ABOVE: The Red Arrows aerobatic team provides a visual spectacle for thousands of people at airshows all over the country. They also undertake occasional overseas tours.

BELOW: The role of the Search and Rescue Training Unit is exactly as its title states – providing SAR training at Valley using the Griffin HT.1. Kevin Wills

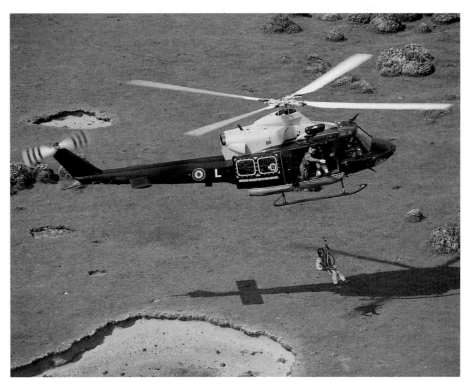

named the Search and Rescue Training Squadron and, in December 1979, it was changed again to Search and Rescue Training Unit (SARTU).

The Whirlwind was replaced by the Wessex in February 1981.

On 1 April 1997, the SARTU became a detached unit of the Shawbury-based DHFS, which superseded 2 FTS for helicopter training. The Wessex was replaced by the Griffin HT.1, which differs from the Shawbury-based model with the fitting of rescue hoists and flotation gear. However, these kits can be moved from one airframe to another relatively easily.

The role of the SARTU is to provide SAR training to all RAF helicopter aircrews. The location at Valley enables an ideal source of training environments, with locally based vessels, sea cliffs around Anglesey and the nearby mountains of Snowdonia. The course for pilots lasts fifteen days and includes fifteen hours flying. Crewmen undergo a ten-day selection course, during which they fly 8 hours. Those selected then join the SAR Crewman Course, which lasts eight weeks, during which they fly a further 61 hours.

The SARTU is a lodger unit at Valley and operates the Griffin HT.1.

RAF Centre of Aviation Medicine

RAF Henlow
BAe Hawk T.1A
Personnel and Training Command
Role: Aviation medicine training
Motto: *Ut Secure Volent* – To fly safely

The origins of the Centre of Aviation Medicine date back to the First World War and the establishment of a number of medical and physiological establishments. Amongst these were the RAF Physiological Laboratory, formed in 1918, and the RAF Institute of Health, formed in 1919 at Halton. From this was evolved the Medical Training Establishment and the Institute of Health.

The Physiological Laboratory moved from Hendon to Farnborough in 1939 and was re-named RAF Institute of Aviation Medicine (IAM) in 1945. Its role was to undertake research and approve various systems and equipment for aircrew. Initial test equipment included decompression and low-temperature chambers. A large climatic facility was commissioned in 1952 and a man-carrying centrifuge in 1955. A high-performance hypobaric

chamber, a 46m-long decelerator track and an advanced helmet-impact test facility were subsequently added.

In addition to ground-based equipment, the IAM also operated various aircraft, starting with the Meteor, followed by the Canberra and Hunter. In 1994 the IAM was re-named School of Aviation Medicine (SAM)

In the meantime, the Aeromedical Training Centre was formed in 1960, to issue, fit and provide centralized standard training for aircrew with their personal equipment. Initially, it was located at Upwood, before moving to North Luffenham in 1964, where it was later re-named Aviation Medicine Training Centre (AMTC). Part of the training sequence was a session in the hypobaric chamber, to experience hypoxia, and on the Spatial Disorientation Familiarization Device, to help crews experience and be more aware of these significant contributors to accidents.

In December 1998, the School of Aviation Medicine (SAM) and the Aviation Medicine Training Centre (AMTC) were amalgamated to form the Centre of Aviation Medicine (CAM) at Henlow. In April 1999, it was transferred from Strike Command to Personnel and Training Command as a directly administered unit. Since then, it has been expanded to incorporate the Central Medical Board in April 2000, Institute of

The pair of Hawks of the Aviation Med Flight provide various functions for the Centre of Aviation Medicine, including desensitising aircrew prone to air sickness. Crown Copyright

A Canberra T.4 is gradually stripped for spares at the Aircraft Maintenance & Storage Unit, Shawbury.

Health from Halton in June 2000 and the Communicable Diseases Control Wing in June 2003.

The CAM currently provides courses for new and experienced doctors in all aspects of aviation medicine. It also provides aviation-medicine training for aircrew in hypoxia, disorientation, NVG and NBC, as well as personal flying clothing. It also undertakes a variety of other functions, which can range from investigating the human factor in air accidents to curing motion sickness for aircrew.

The RAF CAM is a lodger unit at Henlow and the detached Aviation Med Flight operates two of the Hawk T.1As, which are based at and operated from Boscombe Down.

Central Air Traffic Control School

RAF Shawbury

Personnel and Training Command

Role: Air Traffic Controller training

Motto: *Securi Transeant* – Let them go safely

The Central Air Traffic Control School (CATCS) was formed on 11 February1963 at Shawbury, but its origins date back to the beginning of the Second World War.

The exact origins of the CATCS are a little vague, however, Bomber Command was probably the first to establish an organized ATC system, in 1937, using a system called 'ZZ', which used Direction Finding (DF) to guide aircraft through cloud. At the beginning of the Second World War there were only eight 'qualified' flying controllers in the RAF. During the war years these number significantly increased, along with improvements in technology from the early use of DF equipment to the developments in radar.

The Regional Control School probably ran the first ATC courses. Formed at Mildenhall in September 1940, it moved to Reading in May 1941, was re-named School of Flying Control in December and re-located to Watchfield. This was re-named School of Air Traffic Control in November 1946 and operated Ansons. Together with the Central Navigation School, it was absorbed into the Central Navigation and Control School (CN&CS), which was formed at Shawbury in February 1920. It operated a range of aircraft, from Chipmunks and Provosts to Lancasters and Lincolns. It subsequently absorbed the Ground Controlled Approach (GCA) School from Wyton, in March 1953. CN&CS re-equipped with Vampires in 1954 and Provosts in 1958, which were flown by pilots from Marshalls of Cambridge. In 1963, navigation training was split off and moved to Manby and the school was then re-named the Central Air Traffic Control School (CATCS). In 1972, all of the RAF's ATC training was located at Shawbury, with the arrival of the Area Radar Training Squadron.

The CATCS re-equipped with the Jet Provost in 1970. These were retired in July 1989 after 122,480 hours had been flown since 1954 by Marshalls without an accident. By this time, all training was being conducted on simulators.

The CATCS currently trains air traffic controllers and assistants for the RAF and RN, as well as some overseas countries. It also trains selected qualified controllers in advanced radar-control techniques, instructors and personnel for station operations-centres. In 2002, AMS delivered six advanced Terminal Radar Simulators to the CATCS. Such is the capability of these simulators that the school were able to map Bagram airfield and its surrounds, to provide controllers with some training before being deployed to Afghanistan.

CATCS is based at Shawbury.

Aircraft Maintenance & Storage Unit

RAF Shawbury

Personnel and Training Command

Role: Aircraft maintenance and storage

The Aircraft Maintenance & Storage Unit (AM&SU) was formed at Shawbury during 1981–82, following the closure of 5 MU at Kemble. It was originally operated by FRA Services but has more recently changed to FB Heliservices.

The role of the AM&SU is to prepare

and store aircraft at various states of readiness, as part of the fatigue-life management strategy of the RAF's front-line and training fleet. Since it was opened, it has handled approaching 700 aircraft. These have included aircraft such as the Meteor, Hunter, Lightning, Whirlwind and Phantom, which are no longer in service, through to the Tucano, Viking T.1 and Harrier GR.7, which are currently operated. By careful management, the individual fleets are able to maintain a balanced number of flying hours.

The AM&SU provides a service for all three services – both fixed wing and rotary. Most recently it has received army Apaches from Westlands. They also provide temporary storage of aircraft prior to disposal. The Bulldogs were an example of this function. AM&SU does not operate any aircraft of its own, but will usually have over a hundred aircraft under its control.

No. 1 School of Technical Training

RAF Cosford
Personnel and Training Command
Role: Trade training
Motto: *Crescen les discimus* – Growing we learn

In March 1920, 1 School of Technical Training (1 SoTT) was formed at Halton from the School of Technical Training (SoTT) that had evolved during the First World War.

Currently, 1 SoTT provides airframe, avionics, electrical, propulsion and weapon training for new and existing personnel. Courses are ranged from basic, through further, to advanced, to provide the high standard of tradesmen and women required by the RAF. Students are taught in various environments that include classroom, computer simulation and on aircraft, for which some ninety time-expired airframes are utilized.

The variety of courses is run by different specialist squadrons: the Principles and Advanced Training Squadron, Engineering Skills Training Squadron, Airframe Training Squadron, Avionics Systems & Electrical Training Squadron, Propulsion & Weapon Training Squadron, Line Training Flight and Airfield Flight. These provide the whole cross-section of engineering and supervisory tradesmen and women and include the opportunity

for suitable NCO candidates to progress for commissioning as an officer.

For students who successfully complete the courses, a range of qualifications are awarded that are civilian-recognized. These include NVQ, City and Guilds certificates, BTEC at National Certificate (ONC) level and BTEC Higher National Certificates (HNC).

Tucano Air Navigation Squadron

RAF Linton-on-Ouse
Short Tucano T.1
Personnel and Training Command
Role: Navigation training

The Tucano Air Navigation Squadron (TANS) was formed in April 1995 at Topcliffe with the Tucano T.1. Its origins date back to 1992, with the formation of the Bulldog and Tucano Squadro (BATS) at Finningley, to provide initial training for navigator students and replacing the Jet Provost within 6 FTS.

Prior to Finningley closing, the BATS was disbanded and TANS formed at Topcliffe in April 1995, within 1 FTS, located at Linton-on-Ouse. TANS initially shared aircraft and accommodation with the CFS Tucano Squadron until the CFS unit moved to Cranwell in 1997. In June 2003, TANS moved to Linton-on-Ouse, where it continues to operate as a unit within 1 FTS, using the school's pooled aircraft.

Initially training navigators, following their new title, TANS provides the navigation training for Weapon System Officers (WSO) on the Tucano, teaching them basic fast-jet visual-navigation techniques. The TANS course lasts thirteen weeks, during which students receive a range of air and ground training, to enable them to complete the course on navigation using ground classes, then simulators. During the latter stage of the course, students have to prepare, brief, fly and debrief sorties in the Tucano. Twenty-eight and a half hours are allocated to practical, during which navigational exercises are flown in the Tucano. Once successfully completed, students progress to 55 (R) Sqn and the Dominie.

The TANS operates the Tucano T.1 from its base at Linton-on-Ouse.

University Air Squadrons

The concept of the University Air Squadrons was formed by Lord Trenchard in 1919, with the object of encouraging an interest in flying, as well as maintaining an association with universities and aviation-related studies. Cambridge and Oxford were his original suggestions, but it took until 1925 for this to happen.

The squadrons were initially commanded by ex-regular officers but, in 1928, they became serving wing commanders. They were akin to a civil flying club with members paying a subscription. They didn't wear a uniform and were not subject to military regulations.

The squadrons subsequently standardized on the Avro 504N and Tutor. So successful was the scheme that London UAS was formed. In 1937, approval was given for suitable third-year members to be commissioned as pilot officers. As such, they could fly current front-line aircraft.

As war broke out, the UAS were disbanded, but the quality of their students was quickly realized and they were re-established the following year, plus an additional twenty squadrons. They provided pre-service training for potential officers, but flying was limited to just occasional air experience, usually with Tiger Moths and Harvards. The UAS re-equipped with the Chipmunk T.10 in 1950.

By 1947, only fourteen squadrons remained. Now part of the RAF Volunteer Reserve (VR), their role was to provide flying training to graduates who wished to become officers in the RAF or Royal Navy. Following the introduction of the Graduate Entry Scheme in 1969, some 50 per cent of pilots entering the RAF were university graduates.

A 1968 cost-cutting exercise saw a reduction in student numbers of 15 per cent, although the number of universities covered increased.

From 1973, the Bulldog began to replace the Chipmunk, enabling the pilot to watch his student in the side-by-side seat arrangement.

Students who were selected as pilot members flew an RAF training syllabus of up to ninety hours spread over three years. They were expected to attend ground training and fly once a week and during summer, Easter and Christmas camps, which had periods of continuous flying-training available with RAF full-time Qualified Flying Instructors (QFIs).

Since 1996, the Air Cadets Air Experience Flights (AEF) have become subordinated to the UAS and their Chipmunk fleet sold off. Most UAS were allocated an AEF and received additional Bulldogs, which were pooled and used as a joint fleet. This arrangement continued with the conversion to the Tutor in 1999. The Tutors are civilian-owned and military-operated aircraft. The contractor, who owns the aircraft, is paid per flying hour – this charge includes not only all of the flying costs but also any other services, such as ATC, catering and security.

Today most UAS are commanded by a squadron leader and consist of three flights: a military flight, which has full-time RAF instructors teaching the soon-to-be-military students; an AEF, with a reservist flight commander and volunteer-reserve pilots flying air cadets; and a civilian support staff.

In July 2003, the RAF elementary flying training programme changed, with all RAF pilots receiving elementary training on the UAS. The role of training Direct Entry students changed from the previous system, using the tri-service JEFTS at Barkston Heath, to all undertaking their elementary flying training with the University Air Squadrons. Students have ground-school training and then all continue with a 62-hour flying course. For the Direct Entry students this will be completed in eighteen to twenty-four weeks. For the UAS students this will take three to four years, depending on the length of the academic course, and includes up to 90 hours flying on the Tutor.

At any one time, there are in the region of 1,000 students who have joined the UAS from the universities, of which some 650 will be student pilots. A number drop-out for various reasons and those that 1 EFTS see as potential RAF pilots will be offered sponsorship. Of the students that complete the EFT course, about 60 per cent will have come through this route; direct entry accounts for the other 40 per cent. Following a tie-up with the CAA, completion of the EFT course qualifies the student for a PPL, although they are responsible for paying the appropriate fee.

The UAS also provide university students with navigator training, as well as Ground Branch.

There are currently fourteen UAS at various locations around the UK and they are all equipped with the Tutor. Most are co-located with an Air Experience Flight and share the aircraft on a pooled basis.

The University Air Squadrons are:

Birmingham University Air Squadron – Cosford
Bristol University Air Squadron – Colerne
Cambridge University Air Squadron – Wyton
East Midlands University Air Squadron – Cranwell
East of Scotland University Air Squadron – Leuchars
Universities of Glasgow & Strathclyde Air Squadron – Glasgow Airport
Liverpool University Air Squadron – Woodvale
London University Air Squadron – Wyton
Manchester & Salford Universities Air Squadron – Woodvale
Northumbrian Universities Air Squadron – Leeming
Oxford University Air Squadron – Benson
Southampton University Air Squadron – Boscombe Down
Yorkshire University Air Squadron – Church Fenton
University of Wales Air Squadron – St Athan

Birmingham University Air Squadron

RAF Cosford
Grob Tutor
Personnel and Training Command
Role: Elementary flying training
Motto: *Scientia dabit alas* – Knowledge gives wings

The Birmingham UAS was formed in May 1941 and commenced formal training in October 1942, for pre-entry graduates prior to joining the RAF.

In October 1946, the UAS began flying training on the Tiger Moth from Castle Bromwich. In July 1950, it converted to the Chipmunk and, in October 1951, was re-named University of Birmingham Air Squadron (UBAS). With the closing of the airfield at Castle Bromwich, the squadron moved to Shawbury in March 1958. In June 1975, the Chipmunks were replaced with the Bulldog. A 'temporary' move was made to Cosford in March 1978, but there are no plans for their return! UBAS took over the responsibility of 8 AEF in 1996 and it converted to the Tutor in April 2001.

Besides Birmingham University, UBAS takes students from Aston, Central England, Coventry, Keele, Staffordshire, Warwick and Wolverhampton Universities.

Birmingham UAS operates the Tutor from its base at Cosford and pools its aircraft with 8 AEF.

Bristol University Air Squadron

Colerne
Grob Tutor
Personnel and Training Command
Role: Elementary flying training
Motto: *Audentitor Ito* – Forward more valiantly

Bristol UAS was formed on 25 February 1941 and performed the role of an Initial Training Wing for a Officer Cadets Training Unit throughout the Second World War. It was disbanded in July 1946.

Bristol UAS was re-formed during November 1950 at Filton with four Tiger Moths, where it continued to operate until March 1992. During this time, it had converted to the Chipmunk then Bulldog in 1975. It then briefly relocated to Hullavington, before settling in at Colerne in 1993. From 1996, it incorporated 3 AEF, to provide air experience for air cadets, and their aircraft were pooled. In October 2000, the Bulldogs were replaced by the Tutor.

In addition to Bristol University, the UAS takes students from the Universities of Bath, Exeter and Plymouth, as well as the West of England.

The Bristol University UAS operate the Tutor and have their HQ on the airfield at Azimghur Barracks, Colerne, pooling their aircraft with 3 AEF.

Cambridge University Air Squadron

RAF Wyton
Grob Tutor
Personnel and Training Command
Role: Elementary flying training
Motto: *Doctrinam Accingimus Alis* – We equip learning with wings

Cambridge University Air Squadron became the first UAS when it was formed on 1 October 1925 and was equipped with the F.2 Fighter at Duxford. All the initial members were undergraduates. The old F.2b Fighters were soon replaced with the Avro 504N and Tutor, which became standard for later UAS squadrons.

The UAS established a Research Flight, which undertook a number of experiments – a wind tunnel, built as a joint project, was used by Sir Frank Whittle to assist in his experiments while he was at the university in 1939.

As a result of the deepening crisis during the late-1930s and the urgent need for more pilots, the UAS programme was expanded and new squadrons formed. Just prior to the war, Cambridge UAS HQ moved to Cambridge Airport. Tiger Moths were flown during the early war years and later replaced with the Harvard. The Chipmunks arrived in 1950, to be replaced by the Bulldog in 1973. Shortly after, 5 AEF came under the control of the UAS. It moved to Wyton and re-equipped with the Tutor T.1 in 1999.

As well as taking from Cambridge University, the UAS also draws from the Universities of Essex, East Anglia and the Anglia Polytechnic University.

The Cambridge UAS HQ is located in Cambridge and they operate the Tutor from Wyton, which are pooled with 5 AEF.

East Midlands University Air Squadron

RAF Cranwell
Grob Tutor
Personnel and Training Command
Role: Elementary flying training
Motto: Strength in Reserve

East Midlands UAS was originally formed on 26 February 1941, as Nottingham UAS at Newton, for the initial training of students for the RAF. Its first aircraft was a single Tiger Moth for air experience, although a pair of Oxfords were operated during the late-1940s. By the end of the war, 216 Nottingham UAS members had entered the RAF as aircrew, a further nineteen going to the FAA.

In 1947, the number of Tiger Moths was increased to five. These were subsequently exchanged for the Chipmunk in June 1951. A Harvard was also operated from October 1952 to April 1957.

In November 1967, Nottingham UAS was officially named East Midlands UAS

in recognition of the additional universities that provided recruits. In 1974, the Chipmunks were replaced by the Bulldog. At the same time, 7 AEF came under its control. In November 2000, the airfield at Newton was closed and EMUAS moved to Cranwell, where it exchanged the Bulldogs for the new Tutor T.1.

East Midlands UAS takes students from De Montfort, Leicester, Loughborough, Nottingham, and Nottingham and Trent Universities, plus the University of Lincolnshire and Humberside.

East Midlands UAS HQ is located in Nottingham and they operate the Tutor, based at Cranwell and pooled together with 7 AEF.

East of Scotland University Air Squadron

RAF Leuchars
Grob Tutor
Personnel and Training Command
Role: Elementary flying training
Motto: Trust nobody

The East of Scotland University Air Squadron is the newest of all the UAS. It was formed on 1 September 2003 at Leuchars, by merging the Aberdeen, Dundee and St Andrew UAS and the East Lowlands UAS. Both of these units have seen significant changes over the years – perhaps this latest one will enable them to settle down for a while.

The East of Scotland UAS can be traced back to the 1940s, with the Aberdeen UAS and the St Andrews UAS. Aberdeen UAS was formed in 1941 at Marischal College, Aberdeen, with flying undertaken at Dyce. Having been equipped with Chipmunks in the early 1950s, this arrangement continued until 1980, when the flying was transferred to Leuchars due to the increasing traffic being generated by the North Sea oil industry. The following year, the squadron merged with St Andrews UAS. In May 1993, the squadron's HQ, located in Aberdeen, was closed and moved to Leuchars. In 1996, it took responsibility for 12 AEF and the Bulldogs from both units were pooled.

St Andrews UAS was formed in 1942 and took students from both the University of St Andrews and Queen's College Dundee. Queen's College became Dundee University in 1967. On 1 January

1969, the squadron became part of the newly formed East Lowlands UAS, which was based at Turnhouse. On 3 October 1981, the squadron was separated from East Lowlands UAS and amalgamated with Aberdeen UAS, resulting in Aberdeen, Dundee and St Andrew UAS. In 2000, it re-equipped with Tutors.

In the meantime, the East Lowlands Universities Air Squadron (ELUAS) had been formed on 1 January 1969, by the amalgamation of St Andrews UAS and Edinburgh UAS. These had been formed in 1942 at Leuchars and 1941 at Turnhouse, respectively, with Tiger Moths and then converted to Chipmunks during the early 1950s.

When it formed, the ELUAS continued to be linked with the Edinburgh Universities. Later in 1969, the Heriott-Watt University was added, as was Stirling University in 1974 and Napier College of Commerce and Technology (now Napier University) in 1977.

The Chipmunk T.10 was replaced by the Bulldog T.1 in 1975 and, in 1981, St Andrews University was transferred to the newly formed Aberdeen, Dundee and St. Andrews Universities Air Squadron. With Turnhouse closing in April 1995 as an RAF airfield, ELUAS moved to Leuchars. In May 2000, the Bulldogs were replaced with the Tutor.

East of Scotland UAS takes students from each of the Aberdeen, Dundee, Edinburgh, Robert Gordon, Herriot-Watt, Napier, St Andrews and the Stirling Universities Queen Margaret College, plus the University of Abertay.

The East of Scotland UAS operates the Tutor and their HQ from Leuchars, pooling their aircraft with 5 AEF.

Universities of Glasgow & Strathclyde Air Squadron

Glasgow Airport
Grob Tutor
Personnel and Training Command
Role: Elementary flying training
Motto: *In Utrumque Paratus* – Either peace or war

The Universities of Glasgow and Strathclyde Air Squadron (UGSAS) was originally formed on 13 January 1941 as the Glasgow UAS.

It wasn't until the reorganization of the RAFVR in 1946 that Glasgow UAS received its first aircraft, in the form of the Tiger Moth and Magister, which were operated from the RNAS base – HMS *Sanderling* – at Abbotsinch airfield. They continued to operate from there until 1950, when, in September, they converted to the Chipmunk. The construction of runways required the UAS to move in December and it took up temporary residence at Scone – a temporary move which lasted until 1969! The Chipmunk continued to be flown until 1974 and the introduction of the Bulldog. In 1996, it took over the administration of 4 AEF and March 2000 saw the Bulldog replaced with the Tutor.

In addition to the Universities at Glasgow and Strathclyde, the UGSAS takes students from the Universities of Paisley and Stirling, plus Glasgow Caledonian University and the Glasgow School of Art.

The HQ of the Universities of Glasgow and Strathclyde AS is located in Glasgow, they fly the Tutor from Glasgow Airport and their aircraft are pooled with 4 AEF.

Liverpool University Air Squadron

RAF Woodvale
Grob Tutor
Personnel and Training Command
Role: Elementary flying training
Motto: *Studiis divisi, volando sociati* – In studies we are divided, in flying we are united.

Liverpool UAS was formed on 13 January 1941 in premises at No. 10 Abercromby Square. Initial equipment were two aircraft engines and cadets were given air experience flights in a Tiger Moth at Speke or Sealand. Having provided much valuable training during the war, the UAS was closed in June 1946.

In December 1950, the UAS was reformed with an HQ in Liverpool and began providing flying training, initially from Hooton Park then from Woodvale from July 1951. Initially Tiger Moths were flown and these had begun to be replaced by the Chipmunk in June. At various times, Harvards, Prentices and Provost were also operated on loan.

In 1974, the Chipmunks were replaced by the Bulldog and then the Tutor in 2000.

Liverpool UAS draws students from the University of Liverpool, John Moores University, University of Lancaster and the Central University of Lancaster, as well as universities and colleges whose students take examinations accredited to these universities.

The Liverpool UAS HQ is located in the city and the Tutor is operated from their base at Woodvale.

London University Air Squadron

RAF Wyton
Grob Tutor
Personnel and Training Command
Role: Elementary flying training
Motto: Learn by Degrees

University of London Air Squadron (ULAS) was formed in September 1935, with its Town HQ at Imperial College and Flying HQ at Northolt. Although there was no uniform for students, they normally wore blue blazers and grey flannels. Initially, they operated the Avro 504N but, the following year, ULAS re-equipped with the Tutor and later the Hart.

When war broke out, the squadron was initially disbanded, but re-formed in April 1941 as a training unit for volunteer aircrew. To cope with the numbers, ULAS consisted of three squadrons – 1Sqn at Kensington, 2Sqn at Holloway and 3Sqn at Twickenham.

When the war ended, ULAS reverted to its original role, with the flying element re-forming at Biggin Hill with Tiger Moths on 28 February 1946. The ULAS Flying HQ moved fairly regularly, arriving at Fairoaks in 1947, Booker in 1950, Kenley in 1954, Biggin Hill in 1957, White Waltham in 1959, Abingdon in August 1973 and then Benson in June 1992, before moving to its current base of Wyton in 1999. During this period, the Tiger Moths were replaced by Chipmunks in 1950, Bulldogs in 1973 and the Tutor in November 1999.

ULAS is the biggest of all the UAS and, besides the University of London, it also takes students from the Universities of Brunel, City, Greenwich, Hertfordshire, Kent plus Canterbury Christ Church College.

The ULAS HQ is located in London and operates the Tutor from Wyton.

Manchester & Salford Universities Air Squadron

RAF Woodvale
Grob Tutor
Personnel and Training Command
Role: Elementary flying training
Motto: *Scientia in Alto* – Knowledge in the sky

Manchester University Air Squadron was formed in March 1941 in Manchester using the Tiger Moth from Ringway. Their initial flying consisted mainly of air experience in regular RAF aircraft. In 1945, more Tiger Moths arrived and they moved to Barton, where the aircraft were replaced by Chipmunks in 1950.

In March 1953, Manchester UAS moved its aircraft to Woodvale, where it continued to operate with the Chipmunks until 1973, when they were replaced with the Bulldog. In April 1975s recruiting at the Salford University was brought under the jurisdiction of the squadron and the name, appropriately, changed to Manchester & Salford Universities Air Squadron (MSUAS). In 1996, the UAS took over administration of 10 AEF and, in April 2001, the Bulldogs were replaced with the Tutor.

In addition to taking students from Manchester University, the UAS draws from Manchester Metropole and the University of Manchester Institute of Technology.

Manchester & Salford Universities Air Squadron operate the Tutor from their base at Woodvale and these are pooled with 10 AEF.

Northumbrian Universities Air Squadron

RAF Leeming
Grob Tutor
Personnel and Training Command
Role: Elementary flying training
Motto: *Dat scientia alas* – Knowledge gives wings

Northumbrian UAS was originally formed as Durham UAS in February 1941 at Woolsington (now Newcastle Airport) with five Tiger Moths. It later moved to Usworth in May 1949 and then Ouston, where, in 1957, it re-equipped with the Chipmunk T.10.

In 1963, the University of Newcastle-

A Tutor of the Oxford UAS based at Benson is also used to provide cadets with air experience with 6 AEF.

upon-Tyne was established from King's College and, as a result, Durham UAS was re-named Northumbrian Universities AS, to reflect the greater catchment area.

When Ouston closed, the squadron moved to Leeming in December 1974, where it later re-equipped with the Bulldog in November 1995. In 1996, it took over the administration of 11 AEF and the aircraft were pooled. The Bulldogs were replaced with the Tutor T.1 in February 2001.

Northumbrian UAS draws students from the Universities of Durham, Newcastle upon Tyne, Northumbria, Sunderland and Teeside.

Northumbrian UAS operates Tutors from its base at Leeming and these are pooled with 11 AEF.

Oxford University Air Squadron

RAF Benson
Grob Tutor
Personnel and Training Command
Role: Elementary flying training
Motto: I walk the skies and keep my thoughts on the sun

Oxford University Air Squadron (OUAS) was formed on 11 October 1925 but, with

no allocated aircraft, the UAS air-experience flying was restricted to summer camps at Manston, on Avro 504s and F.2B Fighters. By 1927, they were operating a 504K from Upper Heyford.

In 1932, OUAS moved to Abingdon and, by 1939, Tutors had been added to the squadron. In addition, advanced flying was being undertaken on Harts at the RAFVR Flying School at Kidlington. The UAS was closed at the outbreak of the war, but re-opened in October 1940 as an Initial Training Wing for the undergraduates – many of whom were attending short university courses under Air Ministry auspices, with flying in Tiger Moths carried out at Abingdon.

Many famous names were members of OUAS during the Second World War. Military names include Group Captain Leonard Cheshire and Captain the Lord Lyell (both whom were to be awarded VCs), Sir Christopher Foxley-Norris and Richard Hillary. Civilian names include Richard Burton, Robert Hardy and Warren Mitchell.

With the war over, OUAS reverted to training RAFVR students with Tiger Moths. It moved from Abingdon to Kidlington in April 1949, where it converted to the Chipmunk the following year and continued to fly until 1958, when it moved to Bicester.

In February 1975, conversion was made to the Bulldog and, in September, a return to Abingdon. In June 1992, it moved on to Benson and, in January 2000, converted to the Tutor.

In 1996, the UAS absorbed 6 AEF, which still retains its own identity and provides air experience for the Air Cadets using pooled aircraft.

Besides Oxford University, Oxford UAS takes students from Oxford Brookes and Reading Universities, plus the RMCS Shrivenham.

Oxford UAS HQ is in Oxford and they operate the Tutor from Benson, pooled with 6 AEF.

Southampton University Air Squadron

Boscombe Down
Grob Tutor
Personnel and Training Command
Role: Elementary flying training
Motto: *Forbitus Ardua Cedunt* – Difficulties lead to gallant men

Southampton UAS was formed in February 1941 at Worthy Down. Early air-experience flying was carried out with the Tiger Moth and, later, the Anson.

Subsequent moves have seen the UAS move to Eastleigh (now Southampton) Airport in October 1946, followed by Hamble in March 1947. During the early

1950s it converted to the Chipmunk. In June 1978, it moved to Hurn (now Bournemouth International) Airport, where it converted to the Bulldog in 1974. It moved on to HMS *Daedalus* at Lee-on-Solent in 1987, before becoming a lodger unit at Boscombe Down in April 1993. In 1996, it took over administration of 2 AEF and their aircraft were pooled. It converted to the Tutor in 2000.

Besides Southampton University, the UAS also takes students from the universities at Bournemouth and at Portsmouth, plus the Southampton Institute and King Alfred College.

The Southampton UAS HQ is located in Southampton and they operate the Tutor from Boscombe Down, pooled with 2 AEF.

Yorkshire University Air Squadron

RAF Church Fenton
Grob Tutor
Personnel and Training Command
Role: Elementary flying training
Motto: *Universtate sublimis* – Aloft in the world

The origins of the Yorkshire UAS can be traced back to the forming of Hull UAS at Driffield, on18 February 1941, and Leeds UAS at Yeadon, on 31 January 1941 – both operating Tiger Moths. They were formed to provide pre-service ground and flying training for potential officers. Later in the war they were disbanded, but re-formed straight after the war as part of the Volunteer Reserve.

On 15 March 1969, Hull and Leeds UAS were amalgamated to form Yorkshire UAS at Church Fenton. The Chipmunks were replaced with the Bulldog T.1s in 1974 and, in August 1975, it moved to Finningley, returning to Church Fenton in October 1995. The Bulldogs gave way to the Tutor in August 2000. The UAS also incorporates 9 AEF, to provide air experience for air cadets.

Yorkshire UAS take students from the Universities of Bradford, Huddersfield, Hull, Leeds, Leeds Metropolitan, Sheffield, Sheffield Hallam and York.

The Yorkshire UAS HQ is at Church Fenton, from where they operate the Tutor, pooled with 9 AEF.

University of Wales Air Squadron

RAF
Grob Tutor
Personnel and Training Command
Role: Elementary flying training
Motto: *Ar Esgyll Dyfg* – On wings of learning

The origins of the University of Wales Air Squadron (UWAS) can be traced back to 1941 and the formation of three UAS in Wales.

Aberystwyth UAS was formed on 15 January 1941 in the town. A Flight was formed at Trinity College, Camarthen in October 1941, but transferred to Swansea UAS once established. A further Flight was established at Bangor University in November 1941, but was disbanded in October 1944. Use was made of a Moth Minor from May 1942 at Aberporth, to provide air experience for the students. The UAS was disbanded in 1945.

Cardiff UAS was formed on 19 February 1941, initially located within the University, but it was disbanded in June 1943.

Swansea UAS was formed on 7 February 1941 in Swansea and, in October, was established as 'A' Flight, with 'B' Flight having been formed at Trinity College. No aircraft were operated, but visits and annual camps provided some air experience for the students. The UAS disbanded in June 1946.

UWAS was re-formed on 10 September 1963 at St Athan with Chipmunks. These were replaced by the Bulldog in September 1974 and the squadron converted to the Grob in June 2000.

In June 2003, UWAS was one of the squadrons selected to take on the task of training RAF Direct Entry student pilots. The first course commenced in June, followed by graduation in October. This new tasking was additional to their existing role of recruiting and training undergraduates. As a result, the number of instructors was increased.

UWAS takes students from the various University of Wales locations at Aberystwyth, Bangor and Cardiff, Lampeter, Newport and Swansea, plus the University of Glamorgan.

The University of Wales AS HQ is located at St Athan, from where they operate the Tutor.

Air Cadet Organization/ HQ Air Cadets

RAF Cranwell
Personnel and Training Command
Role: Cadet training
Motto: Venture Adventure

The Air Cadet Organization (ACO) is a national voluntary youth organization for young people aged 13–20. It comprises the Air Training Corps (ATC) and the RAF section of the Combined Cadet Force (CCF).

Its origins lie in the formation of the Air Defence Cadet Corps (ADCC) in 1938. This organization was run by local people in many towns and cities to train young men in aviation skills.

In those days, with war looming, every effort was being made to prepare for the defence of the UK. The ADCC was playing its part in preparing the youths with the right instruction and skills should they be required to join the RAF or Fleet Air Arm (FAA). In 1939, basic gliding instruction began at Dunstable Downs.

As the war approached and ADCC staff were called up, the organization was limited in its capabilities. However, the keen cadets managed to assist in a variety of roles, ranging from helping to push aircraft around to loading belts of ammunition. They even assisted in guarding the airfield at Cambridge.

The quality of the ADCC cadets soon became apparent and the Government asked the organization to provide pre-service training to those waiting to join up. During 1940, the Government took control of the ADCC and, on 5 February 1941, the Air Training Corps (ATC) was established.

The training continued with visits to RAF and FAA airfields. Air-experience flying was given as often as possible, but opportunities were limited. The value of this introduction to flying was considered important and so a scheme to develop a series of gliding schools was introduced. By 1943, a gliding programme was operating and an ATC Flight was established with ten Oxfords and Dominies to provide air-experience flying. By December 1945, eighty-four gliding schools were in existence.

In May 1946, the ATC came under Reserve Command and the number of gliding schools reached eighty-seven. A variety of gliders were operated, including Primary, Grunau Baby, Tutor, Gull, Kite and Falcon, in various numbers. The Cadet Mk.I was the first glider to be ordered in quantity for the ATC, but this was single seat. More single-seat Cadet Mk.IIs followed, before the two-seat Cadet Mk.3 and the Sedbergh were ordered and single-seat Prefects replaced most of the old gliders.

The RAFVR flying schools closed in 1958 and the opportunities for cadet to fly in the more advanced aircraft of the time were considered limited. As a consequence, fifty surplus Chipmunks were used to establish a number of Air Experience Flights (AEF) during August/September 1958. They were located throughout the country, with ATC squadrons and CCF (RAF) sections affiliated to provide balanced numbers of cadets.

A Husky was donated to the fleet in January 1969 and, in 1978, 13 AEF converted to the Bulldog,

The year 1977 saw the delivery of an initial batch of fifteen Venture motor gliders and, following training, their distribution to some of the schools. A further twenty-five were accepted from 1980. In 1983 came the arrival of three new gliders in the form of the ASK.21, ASW.19 and Janus C. The first two types were renamed Vanguard and Valiant in Air Cadet service. In 1984 came delivery of the first of 100 Grob 103 gliders, which were named Viking. Initial deliveries enabled the Vanguard to be phased out. During this period of change, the title of the gliding schools was changed to Volunteer Gliding Schools (VGS) in 1979.

In 1996, the AEFs were reduced from thirteen to eleven, following the withdrawal of the Chipmunk, and then amalgamated with the UAS, flying the Bulldog. These were subsequently replaced by the Tutor.

The ATC is made up of some 1,000 squadrons, spread throughout the country, with around 35,000 cadets. These are grouped into Wings. The Wings are administered in Regions and the HQ is located at Cranwell. CCF (RAF) sections are located at 191 public schools throughout the country.

The RAF sponsors the ACO organization but does not actively use the organization for recruiting. The role of the ACO is to:

- promote and encourage a practical interest in aviation and the Royal Air Force among young people.
- provide training which will be useful both in Service and in civilian life.
- foster the spirit of adventure and to develop the qualities of leadership and good citizenship.

In addition, there is the opportunity to gain BTEC qualifications in Public Service and Aviation Studies that may benefit a young person in whatever walk of life they choose. Both of these are also valued by employers.

For those cadets who wish to join the RAF, the ACO provides a good insight into RAF life, with the opportunities and personal development provided perceived as a positive benefit by the RAF in their recruiting. A substantial proportion of RAF recruits are ex-cadets. Air Cadets also join the other arms of the regular services in some numbers.

There are currently twenty-seven VGS, which provide up to 1,900 Gliding Scholarships per year, plus 13,000 Gliding Induction Courses on either the Viking T.1 glider or the Vigilant T.1 motor-glider. Powered flying is provided by eleven Air Experience Flights (AEF), which provide 45,000 twenty-minute flights per year, in which the cadets are allowed to take control under supervision from qualified instructors. The Air Cadet Pilot Scheme provides opportunities for selected cadets to receive further flying training to solo standard.

Challenging activities include hang-gliding, microlighting and parachuting, while non-flying opportunities include sailing, skiing, shooting and swimming, plus seven other major sports. The ACO participate in the International Air Cadet Exchange, enabling cadets to take part in reciprocal visits to a variety of countries. Cadets may also travel abroad on approved RAF flights or outward-bound expeditions. Every year, a substantial number of cadets takes part in the Nijmegen March and in overseas expeditions, often to help underprivileged communities.

While the ACO has encouraged cadets to participate in the Duke of Edinburgh Award Scheme and, more recently, the Millennium Volunteers programme, cadets can qualify for the BTEC Award in Aviation Studies. This is considered equivalent to a GCSE at grade 'A' to 'C' for employers. The RAF will accept it in lieu

of a science subject for the non-commissioned entry.

Cadets and staff are now given the opportunity to undertake First Aid qualifications. Cadets learn in the classroom but also on courses, such as those who help in the National Air Cadet Adventure Training Centres in Wales and in the Lake District.

The organization is very dependent on its 15,000 adult staff and is always looking to recruit more uniformed and non-uniformed volunteers. The experience that adults gain as staff is often very useful to them in civilian life, as they also gain leadership, management and organizational skills and qualifications.

The Air Cadet Organization has its HQ at Cranwell and operates the Viking T.1 glider and Vigilant T.1 motor-glider from various VGS sites throughout the country. They also operate the Tutor, which are pooled with the UAS and flown as required by the AEF.

Air Training Corps

RAF Cranwell
Personnel and Training Command
Role: Cadet training
Motto: Venture Adventure

The origins of the Air Training Corps (ATC) date back to the Air Defence Cadet Corps, which was founded in October 1938 under the auspices of the Air League. In 1941, it became the Air Defence Cadet Corps, which was a pre-entry training organization. After the end of the Second World War, the ADCC became the ATC as a voluntary youth organization, which was tasked not only to encourage an interest in aviation and the RAF but also to provide some training of benefit to service and civil life. In addition, they were to foster and develop a spirit of adventure and leadership, as well as good citizenship. These tasks remain the objectives of the ATC today.

The ATC is a voluntary youth organization, which is supported by the RAF. This organization is broken down into regions and then individual squadrons based in towns all over the country. Regular evening meeting are provided for male and female youths between 13 and 21 to encourage an interest in aviation and the RAF training in various subjects and to foster a sense of adventure, as well as developing qualities of leadership and good citizenship. It is hoped that cadets will find this of value in their future life be it in the RAF or other job.

A range of opportunities are available to the cadets, including flying in RAF aircraft. In addition, the ATC organization operate aircraft with Air Experience Flights (AEF) and Volunteer Gliding Schools (VGS), to provide experience flying in gliders and small powered-aircraft, as well as cadet flying training at various locations around the country.

For those interested in joining the RAF, the ATC provides a good insight into RAF life, including annual camps at RAF stations and opportunities to fly in RAF aircraft. ATC cadets can experience a wide range of adventurous opportunities and, for those that wish to join the RAF, the ATC is considered to have provided a good background – as a result the majority of recruits have previously been members of the ATC.

The ATC operates the Tutor with the Air Experience Flights plus the Viking glider and Vigilant T.1 motor glider with the Volunteer Gliding Schools.

No. 2 Air Experience Flight

MoD Boscombe Down
Grob Tutor
HQ Air Cadets
Personnel and Training Command
Role: Cadet experience flying

In June 1958, 2 AEF was formed at Hamble with the Chipmunk and commenced flying cadets in September.

During 1960, the Chipmunks were deployed daily to Sandown, Tangmere and Thorney Island to enable the cadets to fly in their local areas. The following year Bembridge, Odiham, Old Sarum and Shoreham were used.

In June 1978, the AEF moved to Hurn and departed in April 1996 for Boscombe Down, where it became administered by Southampton UAS and the aircraft were pooled

No. 2 AEF provides air experience flying for air cadets from the Hants and IoW Wing and part of each of the Dorset and Wilts, Norfolk and Suffolk, Surrey and Sussex Wings, plus the Channel Islands, as well as some CCF (RAF) units.

No. 2 AEF is based at Boscombe Down and operates Tutors, which are pooled with the Southampton UAS.

No. 3 Air Experience Flight

Colerne
Grob Tutor
HQ Air Cadets
Personnel and Training Command
Role: Cadet experience flying

In September 1958, 3 AEF was formed at Filton with the Chipmunk.

The AEF operated from Staverton during the summer of 1972 and from Swansea and St Athan for the Welsh cadets, prior to the opening of the Severn Bridge. It moved to Hullavington in June 1989, before settling at Colerne in 1993, where it was amalgamated with Bristol UAS.

No. 3 AEF provides air experience flying for air cadets from 1 Welsh, Bristol and Gloucester, Devon and Somerset, plus Plymouth and Cornwall Wings, and parts of 3 Welsh, Dorset and Wilts, plus some CCF (RAF) units.

No. 3 AEF is based at the airfield at Azimghur Barracks, Colerne and operates the Tutor, pooled with the Bristol UAS.

No. 4 Air Experience Flight

Glasgow International Airport
Grob Tutor
HQ Air Cadets
Personnel and Training Command
Role: Cadet experience flying

In September 1958, 4 AEF was formed at Exeter Airport with the Chipmunk.

No. 4 AEF is somewhat unique, in that it has never been based at an RAF station. However, it operated camps at Brawdy, Chivenor, St Athan and St Mawgan. In 1995, when all of the AEFs were absorbed into the UAS with which they were co-located, 4 AEF was unable to do so and was disbanded.

In 1996, 4 AEF was re-formed in name within 12 AEF. As a result, as required, 12 AEF staff transit to Glasgow, where they operate as 4 AEF and are administered by Universities of Glasgow and Strathclyde AS.

No. 4 AEF provides air experience flying for air cadets from Glasgow and West of Scotland, plus part of the Edinburgh and South Scotland Wings, and two CCF (RAF) units.

No. 4 AEF is based at Glasgow Airport and operates the Tutor, pooled

with the Universities of Glasgow and Strathclyde AS.

No. 5 Air Experience Flight

RAF Wyton
Grob Tutor
HQ Air Cadets
Personnel and Training Command
Role: Cadet experience flying

Formed at Marshall's Airfield at Cambridge in July 1958 equipped with Chipmunks, 5 AEF commenced flying cadets in October.

In 1968, a Husky was donated to the ATC by Hughie Green and Billy Butlin and was operated by 5 AEF until October 1987. In 1996, 5 AEF came under the control of Cambridge UAS and converted to the Bulldog. In 1999, the AEF moved to Wyton, where it became the first Air Cadet unit to convert to the Tutor.

No. 5 AEF provides air experience flying for air cadets from the Essex Wing, plus parts of each of Beds and Cambs, Herts and Bucks, Kent, London, Norfolk and Suffolk, Sussex, plus the South and East Midlands Wings, as well as a number of CCF (RAF) units.

No. 5 AEF is based at Wyton and operates the Tutor pooled with the Cambridge UAS.

No. 6 Air Experience Flight

RAF Benson
Grob Tutor
HQ Air Cadets
Personnel and Training Command
Role: Cadet experience flying
Motto: *Exemplo Excitamus* – By example we inspire

In July 1958, 6 AEF was formed at White Waltham with the Chipmunk.

Annual summer camps were held at Colerne until September 1973, when the AEF moved to Abingdon. In July 1992, it moved to Benson.

The AEF was initially selected to train all cadets on the Pilot Navigation Training Scheme. The two-week course consists of eight one-hour flights, during which the cadets are required plan and brief the instructor pilot on a route. The cadet provides him with the courses and heights before they actually fly the route. On completion of the course, the cadet is awarded the Cadet Navigators Wings.

In 1996, the 6 AEF was absorbed into Oxford UAS, but still retains its own identity and provides air experience for the Air Cadets using pooled aircraft,

No. 6 AEF provides air experience flying for air cadets from Middlesex, plus the Thames Valley Wings, as well as parts of each of Herts and Bucks, Kent, London, Surrey, Sussex Wings, plus some thirty CCF units .

No. 6 AEF is based at Benson and operate the Tutor, pooled with the Oxford UAS.

No. 7 Air Experience Flight

RAF Cranwell
Grob Tutor
HQ Air Cadets
Personnel and Training Command
Role: Cadet experience flying

In September 1958, 7 AEF was formed at Newton with Chipmunks, staying there until it was required to move, due to the imminent close of the station.

Having been absorbed into East Midlands UAS in 1996 and converted to Bulldogs, both units moved to Cranwell in September 2000, where they converted to the Tutor.

No. 7 AEF provides air experience flying for air cadets from Trent Wing and parts of Beds and Cambridge, plus South and East Midlands Wings, plus some CCF (RAF) units. Recently, it has commenced AEF Flying Courses, on which cadets are taught the core elements of elementary flying training, apart from formation flying. This replaces the old Flying Scholarship Course.

No. 7 AEF is based at Cranwell and operate the Tutor, pooled with the East Midlands UAS.

No. 8 Air Experience Flight

RAF Cosford
Grob Tutor
HQ Air Cadets
Personnel and Training Command
Role: Cadet experience flying

In October 1958, 8 AEF were formed at Cosford with the Chipmunk.

In February 1960, the AEF moved to Shawbury. In 1978, it moved back to Cosford, returning to Shawbury the following year. In 1996, 8 AEF came under the control of Birmingham UAS and converted to the Bulldog by March, before moving back to Cosford in April, along with the UAS. In May 2001, 8 AEF began converting to the Tutor.

Like 6 AEF, 8 AEF is one of the few AEF selected to operate the Cadet Pilot Navigation Training Scheme, on successful completion of which the cadet is awarded the Cadet Navigators Wings.

No. 8 AEF provides air experience flying for air cadets from Staffordshire, Warwick and Birmingham, and West Mercian Wings, plus part of both 2 and 3 Welsh Wings, as well as the CCF (RAF).

No. 8 AEF is based at Cosford and operates the Tutor, pooled with the University of Birmingham AS.

No. 9 Air Experience Flight

RAF Church Fenton
Grob Tutor
HQ Air Cadets
Personnel and Training Command
Role: Cadet experience flying

In September 1958, 9 AEF was formed at Yeadon with the Chipmunk.

The AEF moved to Church Fenton in November 1959, then on to Dishforth in March 1932, before returning to Church Fenton in 1968. In August 1975, it moved

Cranwell-based 7 AEF utilizes the Tutors of East Midlands UAS to provide cadets with air-experience flights.

to Finningley but, when it closed in 1995, 9 AEF returned to Church Fenton once again. In 1996, 8 AEF was amalgamated into Yorkshire UAS and converted to the Bulldog. In August 2000, the Yorkshire UAS and 9 AEF converted to the Tutor.

No. 9 AEF provides air experience flying for air cadets from South and West Yorkshire Wings, plus part of Central and East Yorkshire Wings, as well as CCF (RAF) units.

No. 9 AEF is based at Church Fenton and operates the Tutor, pooled with the Yorkshire UAS.

No. 10 Air Experience Flight

RAF Woodvale
Grob Tutor
HQ Air Cadets
Personnel and Training Command
Role: Cadet experience flying

In August 1958, 10 AEF was formed at Woodvale with many pilots drawn from 610 (County of Chester) and 611 (West Lancashire) Auxiliary AF Squadron, which had disbanded at Hooton Park just previously, in March 1957. Cadet flying commenced in October.

In its early days, 10 AEF used to deploy to Jurby, Squires Gate and Valley, as well as Ronaldsway on the Isle of Man, to provide the widely dispersed cadets with local flights. For the benefit of Welsh cadets, briefings were given in Welsh as well as English. In 1996, 10 AEF was amalgamated into Manchester and Salford UAS.

No. 10 AEF currently provides air experience flying for air cadets from East Lancs, East Cheshire and South Manchester, Merseyside, plus Northern Ireland Wings and part of the Cumbria and North Lancs, and 2 Welsh Wings, as well as the Isle of Man and CCF (RAF) units.

No. 10 AEF is based at Woodvale and operates the Tutor, pooled with the Manchester and Salford UAS.

No. 11 Air Experience Flight

RAF Leeming
Grob Tutor
HQ Air Cadets
Personnel and Training Command
Role: Cadet experience flying

In September 1958, 11 AEF was formed at Ouston with Chipmunks.

In September 1974, 11 AEF moved to Leeming. In December 1985, it moved to Middleton St George, before returning to Leeming in January 1988. In November 1995, the Chipmunks were retired and, the following year, the AEF was absorbed into Northumbrian UAS, with whom the Bulldogs became pooled.

No. 11 AEF provides air experience flying for air cadets from the Durham and Northumberland Wing, plus parts of Cumbria and North Lancashire, plus the Central and East Yorkshire Wings, as well as some CCF (RAF) units .

No. 11 AEF is based at Leeming and operates the Tutor, pooled with the Northumbrian UAS.

No. 12 Air Experience Flight

RAF Leuchars
Grob Tutor
HQ Air Cadets
Personnel and Training Command
Role: Cadet experience flying

In September 1958, 12 AEF was formed at Turnhouse with Chipmunks. The first cadet flying commenced in November. Due to the large cadet catchment area of 12 AEF, detachments have been operated at various times from Carlisle, Dyce, Kinloss, Leuchars, Lossiemouth, Machrihanish, Prestwick, Wick and even Stornoway.

In 1962, the AEF operated for several months from East Fortune and Kinloss, while the runways at Turnhouse were worked upon.

The East Lowlands UAS, along with 12 AEF, moved to Leuchars prior to Turnhouse closing in April 1995. In 1996, East Lowlands UAS became responsible for its administration. About the same time, 4 AEF was re-established within 12 AEF to fly cadets at Glasgow. As a result, when required, staff from 12 AEF operate from Glasgow as 4 AEF.

No. 12 AEF provides air experience flying for air cadets from Aberdeen and NE Scotland, Dundee and Central Scotland, plus the Highland Wings and part of the Edinburgh and South Scotland Wing, as well as a number of CCF (RAF) units in the region.

No. 12 AEF is based at Leuchars and operates the Tutor, pooled with the Aberdeen, Dundee and St Andrews UAS.

Air Cadets Central Gliding School

RAF Syerston
Grob Vigilant T.1, Grob Viking T.1 and Robin 400
HQ Air Cadets
Personnel and Training Command
Role: Cadet Gliding School

The Air Cadets Central Gliding School (ACCGS) was formed in January 1972, but its origin can be traced back to the forming of the Home Command Gliding Instructors School (HCGIS) on 1 July 1949 at Detling. When the station closed, the HCGIS moved to Hawkinge.

In March 1959, the Home Command was disbanded and the air cadets organization came under the responsibility of Flying Training Command. A re-organization resulted, with HCGIS being split into two – 1 Gliding Centre (1 GC) remained at Hawkinge to cover the southern region and 2 Gliding Centre (2 GC), for the north, was based at Newton. In 1960, 2 GC moved to Kirton-in-Lindsey, followed by Spitalgate in October 1965. Meanwhile, 1 GC moved to Swanton Morley in December 1961.

The Cadet Mk.3 and Sedbergh had been the workhorses of the Air Cadets, augmented with a few Prefects, plus five Swallows donated by the McRoberts Trust. In the late-1960s, 1 and 2 GCs were required to trial a new all-metal T.53, but found it unsuitable. This was followed by the Falke T.61, a motor-glider that was subsequently ordered as the Venture.

In January 1972, the Central Gliding School (CGS) was formed at Spitalgate from 1 and 2 GCs and was renamed Air Cadets Central Gliding School (ACCGS) in 1974. When Spitalgate closed as an airfield in March 1975, the detachment (previously 2 GC) at Swanton Morley remained and, in August 1977, moved to Syerston.

The delivery of an initial batch of fifteen Venture motor-gliders came in 1977 and, following training, their distribution to some of the schools. A further twenty-five were accepted from 1980. The year 1983 saw the arrival of three new gliders in the form of the ASK.21, ASW.19 and Janus C. The first two types were renamed Vanguard and Valiant in Air Cadet service. The year 1984 saw delivery of the first of 100 Grob 103 gliders, which were named Viking. Initial deliveries enabled the Vanguard to be phased out.

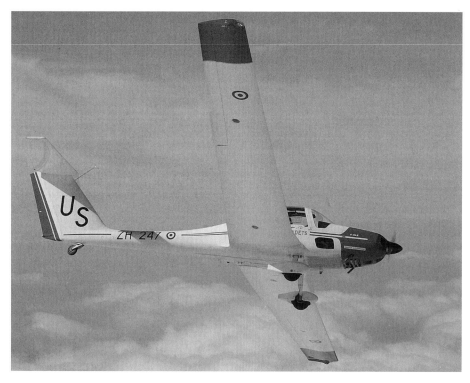

The Air Cadets Central Gliding School (ACCGS) at Syerston operates the motorized Vigilant T.1 and the Viking T.1 gliders. They provide training for the volunteer instructors and develop flying techniques for new gliders. Crown Copyright

A Chipmunk from 7 AEF was frequently borrowed to provide aero-tows for instructor courses, but this became increasingly difficult. As a result, a Robin 400 was hired from 1987. This has since been replaced by another civilian-registered Robin operated under contract.

The co-location of the Police Dog Training School at Syerston from 1988 resulted in the Venture operations being partially conducted from nearby Newton.

In March 1990, the arrival of the Grob 109b, as the Vigilant motor-glider, resulted in the replacement of the Valiant from June 1991 and, by June 2000, the Valiant and Janus C had also been withdrawn.

ACCGS operated the Vigilant T.1 and the Viking T.1, plus a Robin 400, from their base at Syerston.

No. 611 Volunteer Gliding School

Watton
Viking T.1
HQ Air Cadets
Personnel and Training Command
Role: Cadet Gliding School

In 1943, 611 VGS was originally formed as 102 Gliding School at the Hethersett Racecourse near Norwich and operated the Dagling Primary glider. It moved to Horsham St Faith in 1945 and re-equipped with the Cadet Mk.1.

The Cadet Mk.2 was added in 1948, followed by the Grunau Baby IIb sailplane. In 1950 came the introduction of the Sedbergh and the Cadet Mk.3 followed in February 1953. In June, 102 GS moved to Swanton Morley and, in October 1955, it was re-numbered 611 Gliding School.

In 1962, 1 Gliding Centre at Hawkinge moved to Swanton Morley and their gliders were used by the school at weekends. These included the Prefect and Swallow. This enabled a role change from purely teaching cadets proficiency in gliding and enabling them to fly solo, to widening the horizon to offer Air Experience Gliding. In 1977, 1 GC moved out to Syerston.

The arrival of the Venture T.2 motor-glider in 1978 saw the end of the conventional glider operations. In 1987, they reverted, with the conversion to the Viking glider. In June 1991, the school managed to achieve 611 launches over a single weekend.

When it was announced in 1995 that

Swanton Morley was to close as part of the Options for Change, it was decided that 611 VGS would relocate to Watton but, due to lack of accommodation, it would operate from Marham while this was being built. One Viking was also detached to Wethersfield and operated with 614 VGS for some staff currency.

In September 1996, the new hangar and accommodation was completed and 611 VGS moved across, with four of the Vikings being aerotowed.

No. 611 VGS provide glider training, including scholarship and advanced level, as well as air experience flying, for Air Cadets from part of Beds and Cambs, plus the Norfolk and Suffolk Wings.

No. 611 VGS operate the Viking T.1 from the STANTA airfield at Watton.

No. 612 Volunteer Gliding School

Abingdon
Vigilant T.1
HQ Air Cadets
Personnel and Training Command
Role: Cadet Gliding School
Motto: Venture

In June 1945, 612 VGS was originally formed at Ipswich Airport as 104 Gliding School with Primary and Cadet Mk.1 gliders. In 1947, it moved to Martlesham Heath, where it was joined by 145 GS from Colchester and the schools merged. Around the same time the Grunau Baby IIb was introduced.

The early 1950s saw standardization on the Cadet Mk.3 and the Sedbergh two-seat gliders and, in October 1955, 104 GS was re-numbered 612 GS. Due to the closure of Martlesham Heath, the school was disbanded in May 1963.

On 1 December 1978, 612 VGS was re-formed from the 613 VGS detached flight at White Waltham. Their stay was short lived, as the airfield was sold the following year and the school moved to Benson. During July 1980, the school hosted HRH Prince Edward and presented him with his solo gliding wings, after he successfully completed his course on the Sedbergh.

In September 1980, 612 VGS converted to the Venture T.2. These fabric-covered motor-gliders gave way to the glass-fibre Vigilant in September 1990. The increase in operational flying at Benson required

612 VGS to move out in 1992 and a temporary home was found at Halton, alongside 613 VGS. On 8 June 1995, 612 VGS moved to Abingdon, which had recently been transferred from the RAF to the army as Dalton Barracks.

No. 612 VGS provide glider training to Air Cadets from Thames Valley Wing, as well as part of each of the Hants and the IOW, London and Middlesex Wings.

No. 612 VGS operate the Vigilant T.1 from their base at Dalton Barracks, Abingdon.

No. 613 Volunteer Gliding School

RAF Halton
Vigilant T.1
HQ Air Cadets
Personnel and Training Command
Role: Cadet Gliding School
Motto: *Docemus Volatum* – We teach flying

The origins of 613 VGS date back to October 1942 with the forming of C122 Elementary Gliding School at Northwick Park, Harrow. It was equipped with Grunau Baby IIb, Primary and Falcon III gliders.

In April 1946, the school moved to Leavesden, but became homeless in September 1947, when it was forced to move out. The gliders and equipment were stored at Hornchurch and all training suspended.

In February 1948, a new site was occupied at Halton and, soon after, the school was re-equipping with the Cadet Mk.3 and the Sedbergh.

In 1955, C122 EGS was re-numbered 613 Gliding School. In 1968, a detached flight was formed from the old HQ Air Cadets Glider Flight at White Waltham and continued to operate their gliders. In 1978, the detached flight was re-numbered 612 VGS. During this period, the school operated various Prefect and Swallow gliders on loan.

By the end of May 1980, the venerable Cadet Mk.3 and Sedbergh gliders had been retired and were replaced by the Venture T.2 motor-glider. Over the next eleven years, 613 VGS achieved some 750 Proficiency awards, as well as many thousands of air-experience flights for cadets.

In June 1991, 613 VGS converted to the Vigilant T.1 motor-glider.

No. 613 VGS provide glider training, including scholarship and advanced level, as well as air experience flying, for Air Cadets from part of each of the Herts and Bucks, London and Middlesex Wings.

No. 613 VGS operate the Vigilant T.1 from their base at Halton.

No. 614 Volunteer Gliding School

MDP Wethersfield
Viking T.1
HQ Air Cadets
Personnel and Training Command
Role: Cadet Gliding School
Motto: *Aere sust enta* – The air sustains us

No. 614 VGS was formed in September 1955, but its origins can be traced back to the Second World War,

In October 1943, 142 GS was formed in at Stapleford Tawney. It moved to North Weald in August 1946, followed by Hendon in August 1950, arriving at Hornchurch in 1953.

In May 1944, 146 GS formed at Shenfield then moved to Fairlop in 1944 and then Hornchurch in 1946.

612 VGS execute a pairs take-off from Fairford. They had participated in the Royal International Air Tattoo at Fairford and were departing for their base at Abingdon.

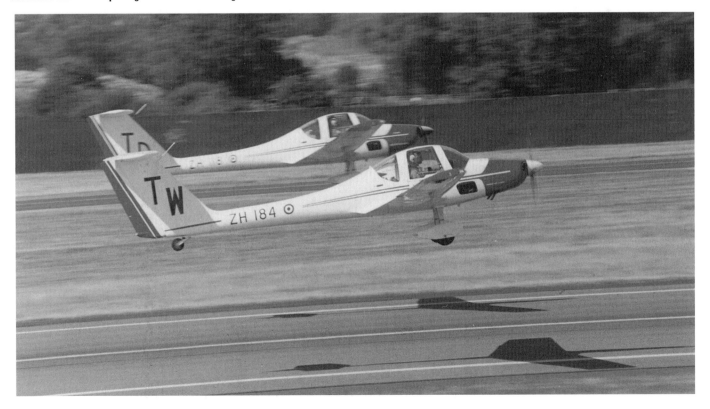

In 1945, 147 GS was formed in Laindon and moved to Fairlop. It then merged into 146 GS.

In September 1955, 142 and 146 GS merged to become 614 GS at Hornchurch. For many years, the school led in the number of Proficiency , Advanced and Soaring certificates awarded. Its instructors gained a number of Silver Cs and a Gold during this period and often displayed at Biggin Hill airshow. It moved to North Weald in June 1962, Debden in 1965 and Wethersfield in June 1982.

No. 614 VGS provide glider training for Air Cadets from Essex Wing, as well as part of each of the Beds and Cambs, Norfolk and Suffolk and the London Wings.

No. 614 VGS operate the Viking T.1 from their base at Wethersfield.

No. 615 Volunteer Gliding School

RAF Kenley
Viking T.1
HQ Air Cadets
Personnel and Training Command
Role: Cadet Gliding School
Motto: *Qui docet discit* – Who teaches learns

No. 615 VGS was formed in September 1955, but its origins can be traced back to the Second World War.

In 1943, 126 GS was formed at Booker.

In 1942, 141 GS was formed at Kidbrooke, then moved to Gravesend in 1945, West Malling in 1969, then Detling in 1951.

In 1945, 168 GS was formed at Rochester, then moved to Detling in 1949.

In 1942, 143 GS was formed at Hamsey Green near Kenley and moved to Croydon in 1945. During this period it had operated the Cadet Mk.1 and Mk.2, Falcon III, Grunau Baby IIb and Primary. In 1948 it moved to Kenley and gliding continued.

Following the re-organizing of the Gliding Schools, all four schools were merged and re-established as 615 CG at Kenley, operating along with 661Sqn, London UAS and 61 Group Communications Flight. At that time, the airfield became rather congested with Austers, Chipmunks, Provosts and Harvards. However, by 1961, 615 GS was the sole flying unit.

In October 1978, the school suffered a major disaster when the Bellman hangar that it occupied was destroyed, along with all of its gliders and equipment. By February 1980, a new Bessoneau hangar had been built and replacement Cadet Mk.3 and Sedbergh gliders delivered, enabling it to recommence glider operations.

Following its suggestion, 615 VGS was tasked with evaluating a scheme to introduce air-experience gliding to all ATC cadets. After a year's trial, the scheme was adopted. In June 1983, the school achieved a total of 615 launches in a single day.

In April 1986, 615 VGS ceased using its old wooden and canvas Cadet Mk.3 and Sedbergh gliders and converted to the fibre-glass Viking T.1. Disaster struck the school once again, when half of the portable Bessoneau hangar collapsed the following January, under the weight of snow that had accumulated on it. All of the gliders in the hangar were damaged. A Viking was loaned from the ACCGS but, without a hangar, it had to be stored in a trailer and required rigging and de-rigging every day that it was flown. A new hangar was built the following month.

In 1993 a new hangar and HQ was opened and, in 1995, it was joined by 618 VGS from West Malling, followed by 617 VGS from Manston in 1999. In 2000, 618 VGS moved on to Odiham, while 617 has been disbanded, although a new site is being sought.

No. 615 VGS provide glider training for Air Cadets from parts of each of the London, Kent, Surrey and the Sussex Wings.

No. 615 VGS operates the Viking T.1 from its base at Kenley.

No. 616 Volunteer Gliding School

RAF Henlow
Vigilant T.1
HQ Air Cadets
Personnel and Training Command
Role: Cadet Gliding School

In June 1958, 616 VGS was formed at Henlow with Sedbergh gliders. These were soon joined by Cadet Mk.3s. At later dates, a Prefects and a Swallow were also operated on loan.

In June 1978, 616 VGS was re-equipped with the Venture T.2, then the Vigilant in 1991.

No. 616 VGS provide glider training for Air Cadets from part of each of the Beds and Cambs, Herts and Bucks, South and East Midlands, and the Middlesex Wings.

No. 616 VGS operate the Vigilant T.1 from its base at Henlow.

No. 618 Volunteer Gliding School

RAF Odiham
Vigilant T.1
HQ Air Cadets
Personnel and Training Command
Role: Cadet Gliding School
Motto: *Volamus Acriter* – We fly harder

In March 1963, 618 VGS was formed at Manston. It had been established with Cadet Mk.3 and Sedbergh gliders, plus equipment from 671 GS that had been disbanded at Bishops Court in Northern Ireland the previous year, due to security considerations.

In March 1965, 618 VGS moved to West Malling, where it increased in size and operated seven Cadet Mk.3s and three Sedberghs. A number of annual detachments were made to Halesland near Cheddar for staff training.

The school was selected to be the first to re-equip with the Vanguard T.1 glider and, in June 1983, initial deliveries commenced. By September, the last Cadet Mk.3 had been retired. In the end, 618 became the only VGS to operate the Vanguards but, in February 1988, they were retired and replaced by Vikings. As the airfield was developed into a business park, flying activities became more difficult and 618 were given notice to leave by September 1994.

Despite an on-going search, only the small site at Challock, near Ashford, could be found. Shared with Kent Gliding Club, room for only two Vikings and poor winter conditions resulted in gliding ceasing in March 1996.

The school managed to provide some courses by temporarily using other airfields – Syerston in 1996 and 1997, Kenley and Portmoak 1998. However, the additional closure of 617 VGS at Manston resulted in a dire shortage of gliding facilities in the region.

On 1 July 1999, 618 VGS was re-formed at Odiham with the Vigilant T.1 motor-glider. Instructors initially trained at Abingdon with 612 VGS and, in September, they commenced cadet training.

No. 618 VGS provide glider training for Air Cadets from parts of each of the Kent, Surrey and the Sussex Wings.

No. 618 VGS operate the Vigilant T.1 from their base at Odiham.

No. 621 Volunteer Gliding School

Hullavington
Viking T.1
HQ Air Cadets
Personnel and Training Command
Role: Cadet Gliding School

No. 621 VGS was formed in September 1955, but its origin can be traced back to 87 GS, which was formed in the spring of 1943 at Weston-super-Mare airfield with the Primary glider and the Cadet Mk.I.

In 1947, 87 GS re-equipped with the Cadet Mk.II, followed by the Mk.3 in 1951, adding the Sedbergh in 1952. In September 1955, 87 GS was re-numbered 621 GS. Draycott in the Mendips north of Bath was used for advanced and instructor courses. This airfield became known as Halesland, but ceased to be used for air cadet gliding in 1985.

In 1985, the old wooden and canvas gliders were replaced by the modern GRP Viking T.1. Plans to develop the airfield led to a search for new site. Merryfield looked ideal and a short deployment was undertaken. At the end of it, a public meeting was held and the Royal Navy gave in to local opposition, who claimed it would be intrusive and noisy!

Following Weston's owners going into receivership, 621 VGS moved to Hullavington in 1993, having spent fifty years at Weston. There they were joined by 625 VGS.

No. 621 VGS provide glider training for Air Cadets from part of each of the Bristol and Gloucester, Devon and Somerset, and the Hants and IoW Wings.

No. 621 VGS operate the Viking T.1 from their base at Hullavington.

Once they have passed a basic qualification, all teenage cadets in the Air Training Corps are allocated air-experience flying time in the Tutor aircraft and the Vigilant or Viking gliders. They can later apply for an instruction course, on which they are taught to fly. Crown Copyright

No. 622 Volunteer Gliding School

Upavon
Viking T.1
HQ Air Cadets
Personnel and Training Command
Role: Cadet Gliding School

In September 1955, 622 VGS was formed, although its history dates back to the forming of 89 GS in March 1944 at Christchurch with the Primary glider. Subsequent additions were the Cadet Mk.I and Grunau Baby, followed by the Mk.II.

The last Cadet Mk.IIs had been retired by 1950 and replaced by the Sedbergh, then augmented by the Cadet Mk III and a Prefect. During the 1953 National Gliding Championships at Great Hucklow, one of the 89 GS Sedberghs, flown by the school's CO, managed to get to Leicester aerodrome – a distance of sixty miles! Flushed with their success they participated in the championship the following year and achieved seventy-three miles.

In 1955, 89 GS was re-numbered 622 GS and, in 1963, the school moved to Old Sarum, following the closure of the airfield at Christchurch. When the RAF disposed of Old Sarum in 1978, 622 GS moved on

to its present site at Upavon. It was converted to the Viking T.1 in January 1985. Despite the handing over of the station to the army in 1993, the school continues to operate from the airfield.

No. 622 VGS provides air experience and advanced flying courses to air cadets from each of the Dorset and Wilts, Hants and IoW, and the Middlesex Wings.

No. 622 VGS operate the Viking T.1 from their base at Upavon.

No. 624 Volunteer Gliding School

RMB Chivenor
Vigilant T.1
HQ Air Cadets
Personnel and Training Command
Role: Cadet Gliding School

No. 624 VGS was formed in September 1995, but its history dates back to August 1944 and the formation of 84 GS at the Halden Moor airfield near Teignmouth. It operated the Primary, and the Cadet Mk.I. The Cadet Mk.III and Sedbergh were added later.

In 1946, 84 GS moved to Exeter Airport and were re-numbered 624 GS in 1955, but the number of flights that the school

The Viking T.1 glider allows student and instructor an excellent view from the cockpit and the light but strong glass-fibre construction enables good performance. Crown Copyright

could operate was limited by the increased traffic for the civil airport and the operation of the CAACU. However, a bonus was that many cadets were able to fly in the Mosquitos and Oxfords of the CAACU.

In October 1965, 624 GS moved to Chivenor, where circuits over the estuary required cadets and instructors to wear life jackets. With a reduced number of cadets in their catchment area, the school was reduced down to a single glider by 1968. In 1974, the Hunters had moved out and Chivenor was placed on care and maintenance. In 1979, preparations for the return of jet training resulted in the school being grounded completely.

In January 1981, the school re-opened with the Cadet Mk.III and Sedbergh, but had to train new staff. In May 1983, it re-equipped with the Venture T.2 motor-glider, requiring more staff training. In 1991, these were replaced by the Vigilant T.1. In 1995, the RAF finally vacated Chivenor and the station was handed over to the Royal Marines, although 22Sqn's 'A' Flight also remained.

No. 624 VGS provide cadets with air experience, with the Gliding Induction Course and further training with the Gliding Scholarship, through to Advanced Gliding Training courses.

No. 624 VGS provide glider training for Air Cadets from part of the Devon and Somerset, plus the Plymouth and Cornwall Wings.

No. 624 VGS operate the Vigilant T.1 from their base at RMB Chivenor.

No. 625 Volunteer Gliding School

Hullavington
Viking T.1
HQ Air Cadets
Personnel and Training Command
Role: Cadet Gliding School

Formed at South Cerney in August 1958, 625 VGS was equipped with the Sedbergh and the Cadet Mk.3 gliders.

During the summer of 1966, the school temporarily moved to nearby Kemble while the World Gliding Championships were held at South Cerney.

In 1972, the army took over the site, but the school continued operating. In September 1978, 625 GS converted to the Venture T.2 motorized glider. By 1985, they reverted back to gliders, when they converted to the Viking T.1. Instructor conversion training was carried out at

Catterick with 645 VGS. The World Aerobatic Championships required a deployment to Upavon for the duration and, in 1988, a short deployment was made to Swanton Morley.

With Hullavington due to close in 1993, a shuffle began. A new home was needed by 3 AEF and its Chipmunks, so they were moved to Colerne. This caused the army's Silver Stars parachute display team to move to South Cerney. As a result, 625 VGS were required to move out. They temporarily moved to nearby Kemble in July 1992 but, with it also due to close, the school moved on to Hullavington in December 1992 and, in April 1993, the airfield became army controlled. In July 1993, they were joined by 621 VGS.

No. 625 VGS provides air experience and Gliding Induction Courses, with further training on Scholarship and Advanced Glider Training Courses, for cadets from parts of each of the Bristol and Gloucester, Dorset and Wilts, West Mercian and 1 Welsh Wings.

No. 625 VGS operate the Viking T.1 from their base at South Cerney.

No. 626 Volunteer Gliding School

RNAS Predannack
Vigilant T.1
HQ Air Cadets
Personnel and Training Command
Role: Cadet Gliding School

Although formed in 1955, the history of 626 VGS dates back to 1945 as 82 GS at Roborough (Plymouth) airfield. In 1948, it moved to Harrowbeer near Exeter and a Detached Flight was operated at RNAS St Merryn until 1954. This Flight was then disbanded, but was re-formed shortly after as 626 GS at Trebelsue, which is now part of St Mawgan. It was equipped with the Cadet Mk.3, Prefect and Sedbergh gliders and, later, the Swallow.

In 1961, 626 GS moved to St Eval and then on to RNAS Culdrose in May 1964. The replacing of the runway lighting at Culdrose resulted in the cessation of gliding for nearly a year from August 1965, so limited flying was conducted at nearby RNAS Predannack. With an unsecured, damaged hangar, this required the towing of the gliders from Culdrose for each day's flying. By October 1968, proper facilities were built at Predannack, enabling 626 VGS to move across.

In September 1985, 626 VGS converted from its old gliders to the higher performance Viking, although it has also operated the Valiant and Janus C in the past.

During a storm, their wooden-framed Bessonneau hangar collapsed, severely damaging the Vikings. As a result, gliding was suspended for several months before re-commencing, with the replacement gliders kept in trailers requiring re-rigging for each day's flying. In November 1990, 626 VGS moved back to St Mawgan and operated out of one of the HAS. However, this was only a temporary move, due to limited facilities, and, in July 1991, it moved back to Predannack, but had to wait until 1995 before proper facilities were completed.

No. 626 VGS provide air experience, basic and advanced flying courses to air cadets from parts of the Plymouth and Cornwall Wing.

No. 626 VGS operate the Viking T.1 from their base at RNAS Predannack.

No. 631 Volunteer Gliding School

RAF Sealand
Viking T.1
HQ Air Cadets
Personnel and Training Command
Role: Cadet Gliding School

Although 631 VGS was formed in September 1955, their origins date back to 186 Gliding School, which was formed in April 1944 at Speke. It was then equipped with a Primary and two Cadet Mk.I gliders.

In 1946, 186 GS moved to Hooton Park, followed by a move to Woodvale in December 1947. Shortly after this, the Sedbergh and Cadet Mk.II were added to the fleet, enabling circuits to be achieved. The school moved on to Hawarden in November 1952 and delivery of the Cadet Mk.3 commenced. Here it operated alongside 192 GS, which it absorbed in May 1953.

In July 1944, 192 GS was formed at Little Sutton, moving to Sealand. Over the following few years, it moved around – Woodvale, Hooton Park, returning to Sealand several times, arriving at Hawarden, then being absorbed into 186 GS.

In November 1955, 186 GS was re-named 631 GS.

In 1959, 631 GS provided the nucleus for the forming of 635 GS and, in June 1963, moved to its current site at Sealand. By this time, the school was operating eight Sedberghs and a single Cadet Mk.3, with a single Swallow and a Prefect occasionally being operated for staff training. The Cadet was lost in 1973 and, in 1984, the school converted to the Viking.

No. 631 VGS provide glider training for Air Cadets from part of each of the East Cheshire and South Manchester, Merseyside and 2 Welsh Wings.

No. 631 VGS operate the Viking T.1 from their base at Sealand.

No. 632 Volunteer Gliding School

RAF Ternhill
Vigilant T.1
HQ Air Cadets
Personnel and Training Command
Role: Cadet Gliding School
Motto: *Excelle Contende* – Strive to excel

Although it was formed in September 1955, the origins of 632 VGS can be traced back to August 1942 with the forming of 45 GS at Meir, near Stoke-on-Trent. It was then equipped with an acquired, civilian Primary glider. Another was subsequently built and then augmented, in 1945, by the Cadet Mk.I.

Delivery of the Sedbergh two-seat glider began in 1949, followed by the Cadet Mk.3 in 1951. During the following period, 45 GS ran various courses at Castle Bromwich and Fradley, near Litchfield, due to the lack of accommodation at Meir.

In September 1955, 45 GS was re-named 632 GS. During 1963, the school moved to Tern Hill and, in May 1978, converted to the Venture T.2 motor-glider, which eliminated the winch launch. Unfortunately, this resulted in a reduction in staff. In March 1984, the school was tasked with training instructors of 635 VGS. In 1990, the school returned to conventional gliding once more, when they were re-equipped with the Vigilant glider.

Following the establishment of the DHFS at Shawbury, the airfield at Tern Hill has seen increased usage, resulting in 632 VGS being unable to operate its summer camp training courses. As a result, these have been undertaken at other locations, such as Salmesbury and Halton.

No. 632 VGS provide glider training for Air Cadets from part of each of the Staffordshire, West Mercian, East Cheshire and the South Manchester and 2 Welsh Wings.

No. 632 VGS operate the Vigilant T.1 from their base at Tern Hill.

No. 633 Volunteer Gliding School

RAF Cosford
Vigilant T.1
HQ Air Cadets
Personnel and Training Command
Role: Cadet Gliding School

Although 633 VGS was formed in September 1955, its origins can be traced back to 1943 and 42 GS, which was formed at Loughborough with the Grunau Baby and Kite. It moved to Bruntingthorpe in 1946, followed by Bramcote in 1947. In November 1949, 42 GS moved to Cosford, where it operated the Cadet Mk.II and Mk.3.

In 1952, the school standardized with the two-seat Cadet Mk.3 and Sedbergh gliders, which it continued to operate until 1978 and the introduction of the Venture T.2. In September 1955, 42 GS was re-named 633 GS. In 1991, it converted to the Vigilant.

No. 633 VGS provide glider training for Air Cadets from part of each of the Staffordshire, Warwick and Birmingham, and the West Mercian Wings.

No. 633 VGS operate the Vigilant T.1 and is located at Cosford.

No. 634 Volunteer Gliding School

RAF St Athan
Viking T.1
HQ Air Cadets
Personnel and Training Command
Role: Cadet Gliding School

Although 634 VGS was formed in September 1955, its origins date back to

December 1944 and the formation of 68 GS at Bridgend with a mixed fleet, including the Falcon, Cadet Mk, II, Kite and Tutor.

In 1945, the school moved to Stormy Down and then on to St Athan in 1947. The Sedbergh was added to the fleet in 1950 and operated alongside the surviving Cadet Mk.IIs.

In September 1955, the school was re-numbered 634 GS and continued to operate until 1963, when OC Flying at St Athan suspended flying, following a cable-launch incident that pulled the radar scanner out of the ground. A move to Swansea Airport, on the old airfield of Fairwood Common, saw flying recommence but, in 1964, the school returned to St Athan. Part of the school remained at Fairwood Common and became 636 GS.

During the 1980s, 634 VGS became a Sedbergh-only school, until it re-equipped with the Viking in July 1986. In spring 1999, the school operated a Valiant single-seat glider for staff conversion.

No. 634 VGS provide glider training for Air Cadets from part of both the 1 and 2 Welsh Wings.

No. 634 VGS operate the Viking T.1 from their base at St Athan.

No. 635 Volunteer Gliding School

BAe Systems Salmesbury
Vigilant T.1
HQ Air Cadets
Personnel and Training Command
Role: Cadet Gliding School
Motto: *Sapientia Provenienti* – Training for tomorrow

In October 1959, 635 VGS originated at Hawarden from a cadre of staff from 631 GS. It was officially formed on 1 November 1959 at Burtonwood with the Cadet Mk.3 and Sedbergh gliders.

Over the following twenty years, the Grasshopper, Prefect and Swallow gliders were also operated for various periods, until 1983, when a series of setbacks resulted in flying ending at Burtonwood. Opening of a public road across the middle of the airfield, use of a substantial part of the airfield and its hardstanding for the M62 motorway, plus new power lines and, finally, the re-stocking of the US/NATO stockpile, including fuel and ammunition, made flying progressively more restricted, until gliding ended on the site in September.

A search and then negotiations had been underway for some time and 635 were able to commence their move to the BAe airfield at Salmesbury in early 1984. With only limited unobstructed-grass available for winch launches, it was decided to convert the school to the Venture T.2 motor-glider, staff instruction being provided by 632 VGS at Tern Hill and their aircraft coming from 625 VGS at South Cerney.

In 1991, 635 VGS converted to the Vigilant T.1.

No. 635 VGS provide glider training for Air Cadets from Cumbria and North Lancs plus East Lancs Wings and part of the Merseyside Wing.

No. 635 VGS operates the Vigilant T.1 from its base at Salmesbury Aerodrome.

No. 636 Volunteer Gliding School

Swansea
Viking T.1
HQ Air Cadets
Personnel and Training Command
Role: Cadet Gliding School

On 1 October 1964, 636 VGS were formed at Swansea Airport from a cadre unit formed from 634 GS and was

The motorized Vigilant T.1 combines the easy self-launch of a powered aircraft with a gliding capability. Crown Copyright

equipped with two Cadet Mk.3s and a Sedbergh.

In 1986, the old gliders were exchanged for the modern Viking, improving performance and maintenance. In October 1996, the school moved to the DERA airfield at Aberporth, enabling increased flying to take place without the restrictions of a civil airport. However, the nature of work undertaken at Aberporth in trialling weapons and equipment did cause some difficulties – a classic example being during the testing of a remote-controlled Land Rover, which crashed into the hangar when control was lost. Fortunately nobody was injured, but three gliders suffered considerable damage.

Planned development of the airfield at Aberporth resulted in the return of 636 VGS to Swansea Airport in April 2001.

No. 636 VGS provides air experience and courses for air cadets from part of the 3 Welsh Wing.

No. 636 VGS operates the Viking T.1 from its base at Swansea Airport.

No. 637 Volunteer Gliding School

Little Rissington
Vigilant T.1
HQ Air Cadets
Personnel and Training Command
Role: Cadet Gliding School

In March 1966, 637 VGS was originally formed at Gaydon with the Cadet Mk.3 and Sedbergh gliders.

Within three months, the school was fully operational, flying cadets either on air experience or Glider Proficiency training. Staff continuity training included annual opportunities to fly in the Prefect and Swallow.

Following the vacating of Gaydon by 1 ANS, RAF flying ceased and various other activities began to creep in, including parascending, which began to restrict glider flying. Parts of the airfield were leased to farmers and, in 1997, the airfield was sold for vehicle testing and the school was required to move out.

In November 1977, 637Sqn moved to the ex-CFS airfield at Little Rissington, where it occupied one of the main hangars. However, when the USAF adapted part of

the site into a Contingency Hospital, they were required to move across the airfield into one of the old 8 MU hangars, while the main hangars were converted into hospital wards and operating theatres.

Little Rissington is the highest airfield in the UK, at 740ft (226m) above sea level, and often experiences different weather from other parts of the country – not always better. While some additional lift generated by the hills is useful, the hill fog can be a disadvantage.

In June 1981, 637 VGS converted to the Venture T.2 motor-glider. Supported by the USAF, who occupied the buildings and left the school complete freedom of the airfield, Little Rissington proved to be a good site – so much so that they had a number of visitors. While the runways at Benson were re-surfaced, 612 VGS operated alongside and even 663 VGS from Kinloss came down for their summer detachment in July 1990.

In October 1990, 637 VGS converted to the Vigilant motor-glider but, in January 1991, the hospital was activated during preparations for the Gulf War. In February, the school was required to move out and sought reciprocal hospitality with 612 VGS at Benson. Fortunately, the hospital was not required and 637 returned home in May.

The change of USAF base commanders saw a change in the school's fortunes and, in 1993, their hangar was condemned and they were required to move to the next hangar. In actual fact, this was even worse. When the USAF estates gave them a week to move out, the Vigilants and Venture still on site were returned to the ACCGS and the school closed down.

Fortunately the station commander at Cosford offered some facilities and 637 was able to commence flying again in August 1993, alongside 633 VGS. Within a few months, a US Presidential change saw the closing of the USAF hospital facilities and the school was able to return in the summer of 1994. Still, all was not well, as the accommodation allocated was the initial reception area for the casualties and the offices were theatres without windows. Security fencing also required the Vigilant wings to be folded and re-rigged every time they were moved. Operations continued through perseverance and another accommodation building was allocated – only marginally better. In the meantime, a new location at the DRA site at Pershore was being negotiated but, eventually, this was

cancelled on security grounds. Basic amenities were added to the accommodation block but ,when the technical site was sold, the new owner required the school's removal.

Temporary accommodation was found at Brize Norton, while a Rubb hangar was built at Little Rissington. With Bicester airfield about to be sold, the RAF Gliding Centre was also looking for a new home and consideration to them moving to Little Rissington made retention of the airfield more viable. Sadly, a vociferous local community complained about the noise of the gliders, so that the operation of 637 VGS at Little Rissington cannot be assured.

No. 637 VGS provide glider training for Air Cadets from part of each of the Warwick and Birmingham, Bristol and Gloucestershire and the West Mercian Wings.

No. 637 VGS operate the Vigilant T.1 from its base at Little Rissington.

No. 642 Volunteer Gliding School

RAF Linton-on-Ouse
Vigilant T.1
HQ Air Cadets
Personnel and Training Command
Role: Cadet Gliding School

Although 642 VGS was formed in September 1955, its origins can be traced back to 1945 when 23 GS was established at Hedon near Hull, initially equipped with Cadet Mk.I and Mk.II gliders.

A Grunau Baby was added during the late-1940s and the school moved to Rufforth, near York, in 1948. June 1949 saw the first of the Sedberghs arrive, followed by Cadet Mk.3s in 1951. Following the reorganization of the gliding schools in September 1955, 23 GS was re-numbered 642 GS.

In July 1959, 642 GS moved to Linton-on-Ouse, where it has remained – apart from short periods at Driffield in 1970 and Church Fenton in 1985, when Linton's runway was resurfaced.

In August 1978, 642 VGS re-equipped with the Venture T.2 motor-glider. In August 1990, these were replaced by the Vigilant.

No. 642 VGS provide glider training for Air Cadets from part of each of the

Central and East Yorkshire and the South West Yorks Wings.

No. 642 VGS operate the Vigilant T.1 from their base at Linton-on-Ouse.

No. 643 Volunteer Gliding School

RAF Syerston
Vigilant T.1
HQ Air Cadets
Personnel and Training Command
Role: Cadet Gliding School

Formed on 29 December 1955, 643 VGS can trace its history back to September 1942, when 107 GS was formed at West Common, Lincoln. It was established primarily by 204 and 1237 ATC Squadrons and equipped with Dagling Primary and Grunau Baby gliders, plus a privately owned BA Swallow light-aircraft.

In June 1945, E107 GS moved to Coleby Grange near Lincoln, from where it operated the Primary and Cadet Mk.I. The following year, the school moved to Digby and was re-numbered 22 GS, where Cadet Mk.IIs were added to the fleet. In 1949, the school was designated 22 Detached Flight (22 DF) and moved to Waltham, near Grimsby. In 1950, it moved to Kirton-in-Lindsey, where it re-equipped with the Cadet Mk.3, adding the Sedbergh in October 1951. The following March, a pair of single-seat Prefects were added.

In December 1955, 22 DF was re-numbered 643 GS. In October 1965, it moved to Hemswell and then, in April 1974, on to Lindholme. In March 1982, it was moved again – this time to Scampton. It was soon in good company, with the Red Arrows arriving the following year and the CFS in 1984.

October 1985 saw 643 VGS re-equip with the Vikings and a further change saw the school convert to the Vigilant motor-glider, just prior to Scampton being mothballed in 1991. As a result, the school was moved again, temporarily to Binbrook. A further temporary move saw the school move to Syerston a year later, where it joined the ACCGS (Air Cadets Central Gliding School), 644 VGS and the Four Counties Gliding Club. It has since converted to the Viking.

No. 643 VGS provide glider training for Air Cadets from part of each of the South and East Midlands, South and West Yorks,

Warwick and Birmingham and the Trent Wings.

No. 643 VGS operate the Viking T.1 from their base at Syerston.

No. 644 Volunteer Gliding School

RAF Syerston
Vigilant T.1
HQ Air Cadets
Personnel and Training Command
Role: Cadet Gliding School

The formation of 644 VGS was on 29 December 1955, although its origins date back to December 1943 and the formation of 29 GS, which operated from a field at Sheffield. The early gliders operated were the Kite, Gull 2 and Cadet Mk.I.

In February 1944, 29 GS moved to Askern, followed by Doncaster Aerodrome in May 1946 and, later, Spitalgate in 1955.

During this period, 44 GS had originally formed in 1943 at Rearsby, moved to Bruntingthorpe and then, by 1949, Desford, where it was disbanded. It was re-formed at Cottesmore in July 1951, then moved to Spitalgate in 1955.

Both 29 and 44 GS had converted to the Cadet Mk.3 and Sedbergh, plus an occasional Prefect on loan. They both disbanded in September 1955 and became 644 VGS.

The school operated alongside the ACCGS, which provided some additional tasking in the preliminary trials for the all-metal Slingsby T.53 glider and the Venture T.1 motor-glider. The ownership of the airfield at Spitalgate passed over to the army in 1975, resulting in 644 GS and the ACCGS moving out to Syerston.

In 1977, 644 GS became the first school to convert to the Venture motor-glider and it subsequently assisted the ACCGS convert other schools.

The school became the first again to convert to the Vigilant motor-glider in 1990 and converted to the Viking in March 2004.

No. 644 VGS provide glider training for Air Cadets from part of each of the Beds and Cambs, South and East Midlands and the Trent Wings.

No. 644 VGS operate the Viking T.1 from their base at Syerston.

No. 645 Volunteer Gliding School

Allanbrook Barracks, Topcliffe
Viking T.1
HQ Air Cadets
Personnel and Training Command
Role: Cadet Gliding School

Although was formed on 8 September 1958, the origins of 645 VGS date back to 1943.

In 1943, 26 GS was formed at Greatham near Hartlepool and operated the Baby, Cadet Mk.I, Falcon 3 and Kite. It moved to Middleton St George in 1946 and disbanded in September 1955.

Meanwhile, 31 GS had been formed at Usworth in 1944 and the resources of both schools subsequently merged, to form 645 GS in September 1958.

On 8 September 1958, 645 GS was formed at Middleton St George and equipped with the Cadet Mk.3 and Sedbergh. In May 1960, the airfield was designated a Master Diversion Airfield, which required the school to move out.

The school re-located to Catterick, which was home for the RAF Regiment Depot. When 641 GS disbanded at Ouston in 1973, 645 took over its tasking, resulting in a doubling of the workload.

In 1982, 645 VGS, along with 618, became the first schools to operate the Vanguard. A Valiant was also operated, most of the time, for staff continuation training, replacing the Prefect and Swallow that were previously operated.

In November 1984, the Vanguard was replaced by the Viking. During the mid-1980s, 645 VGS was used by the ACCGS to provide advanced-soaring courses, prior to their using the facilities at Portmoak. Occasionally the airfield became unavailable mid-week and so some courses were conducted at Hemswell, Swanton Morley and Acklington.

In July 1994, Catterick ceased to be an RAF airfield and was taken over by the army. On agreement, 645 VGS continued to operate from the airfield with its Viking until 2003, when it moved to the former RAF airfield at Topcliffe, which is also now occupied by the army as Allanbrook Barracks.

No. 645 VGS provide glider training for Air Cadets from part of each of the

The wings of the Viking are liberally covered with high-visibility red panels to try to ensure that they are easily seen in the air by other aircraft. Crown Copyright

Central and East Yorks and the Durham and Northumberland Wings.

No. 645 VGS operate the Viking T.1 from their base at Allanbrook Barracks, Topcliffe.

No. 661 Volunteer Gliding School

Kirknewton
Viking T.1
HQ Air Cadets
Personnel and Training Command
Role: Cadet Gliding School

Although formed on 24 November 1955, the origins of 661 VGS lay with the formation of 1 Elementary Gliding School in 1942 at Stathaven, Lanark.

In December 1942, this became 1 GS and moved to Dungavel in March 1944. In April 1950, it relocated to Dumfries and was re-numbered 661 VGS in September 1955.

Turnhouse was transferred to civilian ownership for development into Edinburgh airport. The increase in aircraft movements, including operation of airliners, resulted in 661 GS being suspended in January 1964.

This was considered to be a temporary

measure until a new location was found. The staff were retained, enabling them to retain the categories and attend ACCGS courses. They were also able to fly with 662 and 663 GS, to enable them to maintain the continuation training.

Eventually, the site at Kirknewton became available, following the withdrawal of the occupying USAF communications unit. On 2 April 1967, 661 GS officially re-commenced operations with the Cadet Mk.3 and Sedbergh gliders. Initial operations were hampered by the remains of the communications aerials and problems were exacerbated by a bad winter. As a result, flying was suspended while parts of the runway were resurfaced. A Swallow was later added to the fleet and operated until 1976.

In July 1985, 661 VGS converted to the Viking. A government initiative saw Defence Estates becoming more active in trying to get revenue to cover airfield running costs. This has resulted in the addition of various other activities, including some private flying.

No. 661 VGS provide glider training for Air Cadets from part of each of the Durham and Northumberland, Edinburgh and South Scotland, and the Glasgow and West Scotland Wings.

No. 661 VGS operates the Viking T.1 from their base at Kirknewton.

No. 662 Volunteer Gliding School

RMB Arbroath
Viking T.1
HQ Air Cadets
Personnel and Training Command
Role: Cadet Gliding School

In September 1955, 662 VGS was formed at Edzell, but its origins lie with the formation of 2, 5 and 6 GS, which eventually came together to form the new school.

In October 1942, 2 GS was formed at East Fortune and moved to Grangemouth in November 1947.

On 20 October 1944, 5 GS was formed at Fordoun, moved to Dyce in May 1946 and, subsequently, to Edzell.

On 25 October 1942, 6 GS was formed at East Fortune, but disbanded in 1945–6. It re-formed on 1 November 1947 at Grangemouth.

In 1951, 6 GS was disbanded and was absorbed into 2 GS. In September 1955, 2 GS was disbanded, along with 5 GS, and the merged resources used to form 662 GS.

Initially Baby, Falcon and Kite gliders were flown, to which the Cadet Mk.I, Grasshopper and Kite were added, followed by the Cadet Mk.II. The schools then standardized on the Cadet Mk.3 and Sedbergh from the early 1950s. The Prefect was occasionally operated for staff training.

In 1955, at Edzell, 6 GS was re-numbered 662 GS and absorbed 5 GS, which continued to operated from Dyce as a Detached Flight. In 1963, the Prefect was replaced with a Swallow. This was one of four Swallows presented to the Air Cadets by the MacRoberts Trust. In 1958, 662 GS moved to HMS *Condor*, Arbroath and, in July 1967, the Detached Flight was re-established as an independent unit and numbered 663 VGS.

No. 662 VGS provide glider training for Air Cadets from the Dundee and Central Scotland Wing and part of each of the Edinburgh and South Scotland, and the Glasgow and West Scotland Wings.

No. 662 VGS operates the Vigilant T.1 from their base at HMS *Condor*.

No. 663 Volunteer Gliding School

RAF Kinloss
Vigilant T.1
HQ Air Cadets
Personnel and Training Command
Role: Cadet Gliding School

663 VGS was originally formed on 16 November 1959 at Abbotsinch Airport Glasgow with the Cadet Mk 3, but was disbanded only three years later in 1962.

On 7 July 1967, 663 VGS was re-formed at Dyce/Aberdeen Airport from a Detached Flight of 662 VGS. It initially operated one each of the Cadet Mk.3 and Sedbergh gliders with a second cadet Mk.3 arriving in 1969.

In May 1968, the school moved to Dalcros/Inverness Airport, but moved back to Aberdeen Airport in November. However, the number of movements soon proved to be too restrictive and a new location was sought.

On 8 July 1973, 633 GS moved to Milltown, a satellite of Lossiemouth, where it operated alongside Fulmar RAF GSA. When it became a transmitter site for 81 SU in March 1977, the aerials made gliding hazardous and so 633 GS, together with the Fulmar RAF GSA, moved to Kinloss.

In August 1986, the school converted to the Venture motor-glider and operated detachments to Lossiemouth and one to Little Rissington in 1990. In 1991, another equipment change saw the conversion to the Vigilant.

No. 663 VGS provide glider training for Air Cadets from Aberdeen and North East Scotland, and the Highland Wings.

No. 663 VGS operate the Vigilant T.1 from their base at Kinloss.

No. 664 Volunteer Gliding School

Newtownards
Vigilant T.1
HQ Air Cadets
Personnel and Training Command
Role: Cadet Gliding School

In August 1986, 664 VGS was established at Bishopscourt with a single Venture motor-glider.

Northern Ireland was somewhat sensitive and one of their trailers was reported as a cruise-missile launcher in a Greenham Common report. One unusual flight resulted from a request to photograph a Russian Auxiliary General Intelligence vessel, which was anchored offshore.

When Bishops Court was closed in 1990, 664 VGS was left without a home and so was suspended in October. An ongoing search led to a trial at Newtownards that, despite various problems (apart from the political difficulties), resulted in a positive result and the school re-opened in February 1996 with two Vigilants.

No. 664 VGS provide glider training for Air Cadets from Northern Ireland Wing. They operate the Vigilant T.1 from their base at Newtownards.

Miscellaneous Units

Combined Air Ops Centre Nine

RAF High Wycombe
NATO's Allied Air Forces North
Role: Air surveillance & Control

Combined Air Ops Centre Nine (CAOC9) was formed on 1 September 1999 at High Wycombe. It came into being following a re-organization of the NATO Alliance Allied Command Europe, which resulted in a new structure. HQ Allied Forces North Western Europe (HQ AFNW) and HQ Allied Air Forces North Western Europe (HQ AIRNW) were both closed and their tasks subsumed into Allied Air Forces North.

CAOC9 is a detached element of AIR NORTH, part of NATO's Allied Air Forces North (AIRNORTH), and thus responsible to the Commander Air North (COMAIRNORTH) for the command and control for all NATO and Air, Ground and Maritime units of the RAF assigned to CAOC9. It is responsible for policing the air, as well as training and preparing forces to support crisis management actions and the transition to war. It plans and directs Air Operations and produces the Air Tasking Order. It also provides protection to vital assets and areas during crises, which may be co-ordinated with land and naval forces.

CAOC9 provides a continuous monitoring service. The Duty Controller monitors warnings from the Control and Reporting Centres (CRC), fed from the Reporting Heads (RH), and can order an appropriate response – usually in the form of a launch of QRA aircraft to investigate.

Plans to close the NATO element of the CAOC were announced in June 2003, as part of a larger programme to create a more efficient NATO command structure.

Combined Air Ops Centre Nine is based at High Wycombe.

Empire Test Pilots School

MoD Boscombe Down
QinetiQ
Role: Test Pilots School
Motto: Learn to Test: Test to Learn

The Empire Test Pilots School (ETPS) was formed in 1944, but its origins date back to 1914, when an Experimental Flight was formed as part of the CFS at Upavon. Its aircrew were some of the few experienced pilots left, following the deployment of four squadrons to France. They were tasked with assessing aircraft and equipment before it entered service.

In 1943, it was decided to form a test-pilots' school at Boscombe Down, to train and develop the specialist skills for the selected pilots. In recognition of the number of Commonwealth students being trained, the prefix 'Empire' was added to the school's name in 1944.

In 1974, a rotary-wing course was added, followed by a flight-test engineers course in 1974. More recently, a major civil flight test course was added in 2000, enabling the ETPS to train test pilots for the commercial market and, more recently, modular courses. Although manned by service personnel, ETPS is part of QinetiQ, which is a PFI, established in July 2001 to take over much of what was DERA.

ETPS operates a varied fleet, which includes the Hawk – including the specially modified example that has a Variable Stability System (VSS) and is used as a Advanced Stability Training and Research Aircraft (ASTRA).

ETPS is based at Boscombe Down and operates the Alpha Jet, Andover, Bassett, Gazelle, Harvard, Hawk, Jaguar, Lynx, Sea King, Tornado, Tucano and Squirrel.

Forward Support (Fixed Wing)

RAF St Athan
Defence Logistics Organization
Role: Recovery and repair

The Forward Support (Air) was formed in April 2000 at St Athan, as part of the DLO, but its origins lie back in the 1940s and the establishment of around 100 Repair and Salvage Units (RSU). While it is difficult to trace precisely which one links to the current Forward Support (Air), it is generally accepted that it is most closely aligned with 5 Salvage Centre, which was actually formed at St Athan in September 1939. It moved almost immediately to Shipton, where it was re-named 60 MU in October 1940. Its role was to recover crashed aircraft and either repair them or break them for spares, hence they became known as 'Crash and Smash'.

In November 1945, 60 MU moved to Rufford. In 1957, the surviving RSUs were merged into three MUs – 49 (Colerne), 60 (Rufford) and 71 (Bicester). All three moved to Church Fenton in 1959 and 49 MU was absorbed into 60 MU in 1962, prior to them moving to Dishforth in March. The country was split into two

regions, with 71 MU responsible for the area south of Cottesmore/Shawbury and 60 MU for the area to the north. In 1966, 60 MU relocated to Leconfield and 71 MU to Bicester.

In September 1970, the Repair and Salvage Squadron from 60 MU was merged with 71 MU and, in November 1976, 60 MU closed, its tasking being absorbed by 71 MU, which moved to Abingdon. In 1992, Abingdon closed, along with 71 MU. The MU's tasking was transferred to St Athan Engineering Wing, where it was split into three sections – Aircraft Salvage and Transportation Flight (AS&TF), Repair & Support Squadron (RSS) and the RAF Repair & Design Authority (RAFRDA). The latter was a merger of Abingdon's aircraft repair design and the St Athan mechanical design functions. AS&TF were subsequently re-named Aircraft Recovery & Transportation Flight.

Following the formation of DARA in April 1999, the three sections were merged back together to form the Forward Support (Fixed Wing) and are a part of the DLO's Forward Support (Air). The other component of FS (Air) being the Royal Navy-orientated Forward Support (Mobile Aircraft Support Unit) at Fleetlands, which also supports RAF helicopters.

At present staffed with 250 personnel, the current role of the FS (FW) remains basically similar to the RSU of the Second World War – to provide structural

The Empire Test Pilots School operates a small fleet of highly colourful varied types of military aircraft, including this Jaguar T.2. Although commanded by an RAF wing commander and staffed by service personnel, ETPS actually comes under the control of QinetiQ.

The Forward Support (Fixed Wing) operate a recovery-and-repair service from their base at St Athan. They effect repairs to damaged aircraft that require specialized rebuilding techniques. Here a Hawk is being repaired after it collided in mid-air with a gull while flying low-level over the nearby ranges.

repair-and-recover support to fixed-wing aircraft deployed on operations. As such, they are deployed as an Air Combat Service Support Unit. When not deployed operationally, the unit trains for its primary role and provides a similar repair-and-recovery support service. It provides specialist engineering support to the Nuclear Accident Recovery Group, aircraft repair design and technical-information support to fixed-wing aircraft. It provides a design support on aircraft ground-equipment and aircraft modifications. It also operates a tri-service aircraft-weighing service.

The Forward Support (Fixed Wing) is based at St Athan.

Joint Arms Control Implementation Group

RAF Henlow
Ministry of Defence
Role: Conflict Prevention and Arms Control
Motto: *Per Fidem Mutuam Securitas* – Security through mutual trust

An 'Open Skies' initiative was originally proposed by President Eisenhower in 1955 as an inspection process to reduce fears of potential build-up of opposing forces. This was immediately rejected by the Russians, who distrusted the scheme.

In 1989, the proposal was re-introduced as a multinational scheme and, in 1992, a treaty was signed with twenty-seven countries in east and west Europe, plus USA and Canada, to promote confidence and security through openness and transparency between the signatory states. The treaty was ratified, came into force at the beginning of 2002 and a number of other countries has since joined.

'Open Skies' is the trust-building programme in which treaty signatories are able to operate observation aircraft equipped with cameras and sensors, plus send ground inspectors, at short notice to check routes or specific locations for military activity.

The British component of 'Open Skies' is operated through the Joint Arms Control Implementation Group (JACIG), which was formed in 1990 at Scampton and moved to Henlow in May 1996. JACIG is a tri-service unit that comes under the Conflict Prevention and Arms Control (CPAC) at MoD and whose primary role is to implement the UK's Arms Control commitments, as agreed in various treaties. This includes providing access for other signatories' forces, in order to dispel hostility and build a level of trust to ensure future peace.

An Andover was originally operated on contract from DERA (now QinetiQ), which was primarily equipped with a 12in focal-length camera, but could also carry additional film or video cameras. Fitted with a GPS receiver, it was able to accurately fly specified routes. The aircraft was normally operated by a crew of four, plus two sensor operators/technicians. An additional ten monitors could be carried from either the observed or observer countries. In April 2003, the contract to maintain the Andover ended and brought about a temporary halt in British-operated 'Open Skies' flights. The Andover remains part of the QinetiQ fleet.

In January 2004, an agreement was signed with the Swedish Government, which resulted in joint operations with the R Sw AF. This will result in future JACIG 'Open Skies' missions being flown in the SAAB 340.

JACIG is based at Henlow.

RAF Flying Club Association

An RAF Flying Club Association (RAF FCA) was initially formed in April 1933 at Hatfield, to provide reasonably priced flying for Reserve Officers pilots who had to cease active training at age thirty-eight. In January 1934, its activities were extended to all members of the flying services – past as well as present. A branch was also established at Heliopolis, Egypt. It was closed at the outbreak of the Second World War and the aircraft requisitioned, along with all other flying clubs. After the war, there was an effort to revive the FCA at Panshanger but, in 1950, it closed,

In September 1980, the RAF Powered Flying Association (RAFPFA) was established to support four flying clubs that had operated as independent organizations at Brize Norton, Cranwell, Halton and Laarbruch. Besides promoting light aircraft flying to members of the Armed Forces, it had also been formed to provide a body to co-ordinate and resolve the civil and military regulations, which were resulting in making it difficult for civil aircraft to operate at military airfields. Although it did not formally close, the RAFPFA appears to have faded away.

The current RAF Flying Club Association (RAF FCA) was officially inaugurated at Halton on 7 July 2001, without knowledge of the previous associations, but still formed to try to resolve the same issues. The aims were defined to facilitate the Air Force Board's objective of enabling servicemen and women, regardless of rank or trade, to have the opportunity of learning to fly at the lowest practical cost. This is achieved by advising and assisting in the formation of new clubs and encouraging the communication between all FCA clubs, in addition to promoting general aviation within the RAF. Although it isn't currently fully recognized by the Tri-Service Sports Board, the association also encourages members to participate in competitive sport-flying competitions.

RAF FCA clubs are based at Akrotiri, Benson, Brize Norton, Coltishall, Cosford, Cranwell, Halton, Leuchars, Lyneham, Kinloss, Marham, Waddington and Wyton.

RAF Gliding and Soaring Association

RAF Halton

The RAF Gliding and Soaring Association (RAFGSA) was formed in 1949, to enable all members of the RAF to have the opportunity to enjoy the sport of gliding and soaring in their spare time.

The RAFGSA operate around seventy single- and two-seat gliders, ranging from basic trainers through to high-performance aircraft. Volunteer qualified instructors ensure that all members, from novice upwards, are given the opportunity to build up their experience according to a syllabus. Those already with intermediate and advanced experience, and novices as they progress, are able to participate in cross countries and competitions at local, national and international levels. Even adventurous training expeditions are organized outside the UK.

Glider launches are by winch or aerotow and, because it is subsidized, it can prove to be enjoyable sport for personnel of all ranks, as well as their families, without the high costs that are incurred in civilian clubs.

The RAFGSA Centre was located at Bicester but moved to Halton in June 2004. Gliding sites are located at Bicester, Cosford, Cranwell, Dishforth, Halton, Keevil, Kinloss, Marham, Syerston and Wattisham. A further site is located at Dhekeila Garrison, Cyprus.

ABOVE: **The Lyneham Aviation Centre is affiliated to the RAFFCA and also looks after microlight interests on the station, as well as the club's Cherokee 180.**

BELOW: **The RAF Gliding and Soaring Association provide servicemen and women with the opportunity to fly a range of standard- and high-performance gliders in their spare time, irrespective of their service rank or role.**

CHAPTER FOUR

RAF Equipment and Weapons

Combat aircraft are impotent without equipment and weapons. This section describes those operated by the RAF on a range of aircraft. While the old-fashioned iron bombs fall from aircraft much as they did in the early days of the First World War, their destructive power is clearly greater. However, they still rely on the skill of the pilot to ensure the accuracy of their delivery. This has been greatly enhanced with modern navigation and avionics, but they can still miss the target.

During the 1992 Gulf War, the use of laser- and TV-guided bombs reached a level not seen before. As video footage was released, we were able to see bombs being dropped through windows and down chimneys – an effect that would have taken a squadron of Second World War bombers to match now achieved by a single aircraft. The result is fewer crew subjected to threat from AAA or SAMs and less collateral damage to civilian property. The next generation of bombs that are on order – the Paveway IV – incorpo-

rates GPS, which will further improve this capability.

While bombs have been the bread and butter of attack aircraft since the early days, missiles saw their introduction in the Second World War and have experienced a steady improvement in their capabilities ever since. Today, the RAF inventory includes a range of missiles to meet varied requirements. These can range from the basic CRV rockets through to the Storm Shadow long-range stand-off missile. In between are a range of air-to-air and air-to-ground missiles capable of destroying aircraft or tanks. Virtually all of these weapons are new or have seen recent upgrades to ensure that they are of a high capability and details of weapons currently on order are also described.

While integral guns are not included in this section, machine guns used in helicopters, such as the Chinook and Puma, on recent operations to provide self protection, are included.

Equipment provided to add a capability

to an aircraft has been incorporated. These include reconnaissance pods, which can be fitted to enable a far larger number of aircraft to be used in the intelligence gathering role than the few specialist aircraft available. The current generation of JRP, and especially the RAPTOR pods, provide a reconnaissance capability that the RAF only dreamed of a couple of decades ago. With an electro-optical sensor, it can recognize a man at sixteen miles and a car at sixty. In addition to storing these images for downloading on landing, they can be transmitted immediately back to a ground facility by data-link for immediate analysis. Another piece of equipment is the TIALD pod, which can provide automatic tracking and laser designation of targets for the laser-guided bombs.

While none of these items of weaponry or equipment will result in the elimination of pilots in the RAF, they will enable them to gather intelligence and deliver weapons more accurately and safely than ever before.

An inert 1,000lb GP bomb fitted onto a Harrier GR.7.

BAe Systems 500lb and 1,000lb General Purpose Bomb

Role: Bomb
Length: 2.0m (6ft 6.75in); 2.29m (7ft 6in)
Span: 0.46m (1ft 6in); 0.58m (1ft 11in)
Weight: 260kg (573lb); 439kg (968lb)

The General Purpose Bomb is a standard 'iron bomb' that differs little from those of the Second World War, although it has seen some developments that enable it to be carried by modern fast-jets.

One of the most significant changes is that to the tail. One of the modern fast-jet tactics is low-level operation. The problem with this is the potential of the bomb to bounce or ricochet, resulting in potential damage to the aircraft. To avoid this, a retarding system can be fitted that deploys on bomb-release and acts as a brake, allowing the aircraft to depart before the bomb explodes.

The accuracy of the General Purpose Bomb, which is available in 500lb and 1,000lb sizes, is totally reliant on the skill of the aircrew. Modern weaponry, with its laser- or GPS-guidance enabling pinpoint accuracy and minimal collateral damage, has dramatically reduced the requirement for this type of bomb.

The 1,000lb bomb can be adapted to a Paveway II LGB with a kit produced by Portsmouth Aviation.

The 500lb and 1,000lb bombs can be carried by the Jaguar GR.3/3A, Harrier GR.7/GR.9, Hawk T.1 and Tornado GR.4.

An AGM-65G-2 Maverick air-to-ground missile fitted onto a Harrier GR.7.

Raytheon AGM-65 Maverick

Role: Short/medium-range air-to-surface missile
Engine: Solid propellant motor
Length: 2.49m (8ft 2in)
Span: 0.72m (2ft 4.25in)
Speed: Mach 1.0+
Weight: 220kg (485lb)
Range: 25km (16 miles; 13nm)

In the mid-1960s, Hughes commenced design of the AGM-65 Maverick as a TV-guided missile for use against tanks and other valuable ground-targets. It entered USAF service in 1972. Since then, Maverick has undergone various improvements over the years, with different warheads and seekers.

The RAF has taken delivery of the AGM-65G2 variant of the Maverick in an initial £42m contract. A further order was placed and includes the AGM-65K.

The AGM-65G Maverick has an Infra-Red (IR) guidance system and is designed to operate against a range of targets. An image of the target, as seen by the missile, is displayed in the cockpit and the pilot simply selects the aim point and fires. The missile is locked onto the target, enabling the aircraft to break off. The AGM-65G contains a 300lb penetrator.

The AGM-65K Maverick is fitted with a TV seeker, which enables the pilot to see the target displayed in his cockpit. Once locked on, the guidance will maintain the target, making it a good system to tackle moving targets, but it is limited to daylight operation.

The Maverick has been acquired by the RAF and was first used operationally by them in Iraq in 2003.

Maverick is carried by the Harrier GR.7/GR.9.

Raytheon AIM-9 Sidewinder

Role: Air-to-air missile
Engine: Solid-propellant motor
Length: 2.87m (9ft 5in)
Span: 0.63m (2ft 1in)
Speed: Mach 2+
Weight: 86kg (190lb)
Range: 16km+ (10 miles+; 9nm+)

The design of the AIM-9 Sidewinder began with the US Naval Weapons Centre at China Lake during the late-1940s. It was first fired in 1953

The AIM-9 Sidewinder air-to-air missile fitted onto a Hawk T.1A.

and entered service in 1956 as a short-range, infra-red-guided air-to-air missile.

Early Sidewinder AAMs were limited in their capabilities, but they were basically simple in construction and cheap to build. Gradually their technology improved, resulting in a very capable missile. By the time of the AIM-9L – or 'Lima' as it was known – it had become an all-aspect missile, with a sensor capable of sensing the heat generated by friction on the wing leading-edge. Although Sidewinders were being built in substantial numbers and exports were being made, various European armed forces were interested in acquiring the new 'Lima' missile and a European licence production-facility was established during the early 1980s.

Amongst these European armed forces were the RAF and RN. In 1982, the conflict in the Falklands erupted, but the European 'Lima' was yet to enter service. As a result, the US supplied around 100 from their own stocks. These were used by RN Sea Harriers to shoot down eighteen Argentinian aircraft.

The Sidewinder missile is being replaced by the ASRAAM.

The Sidewinder is carried by the Harrier GR.7, Hawk T.1A, Jaguar GR.3/3A, Nimrod MR.2, Tornado F.3 and GR.4, and will be carried by the Typhoon F.2.

Raytheon AIM-120 AMRAAM

Role: Medium-range air-to-air missile
Engine: Solid-propellant motor
Length: 3.65m (12ft 0in)
Span: 447mm (1ft 5.6in)
Speed: Mach 4
Weight: 157kg (345lb)
Range: 50km (31 miles; 27nm)

The AMRAAM (Advanced Medium-Range Air-to-Air Missile) was developed in the late-1970s by Hughes, under joint sponsorship with the USAF and US Navy, to replace the AIM-7 Sparrow. Designated AIM-120, it has an active radar and is a look-down, shoot-down, fire-and-forget air-to-air missile with a multiple-launch capability. It entered service with the USAF in 1991.

The RAF ordered AMRAAM to replace the Sky Flash missile carried by the RAF Tornado F.3s and it will be carried by the Typhoon. It is also carried by Royal Navy Sea Harrier FA.2s.

AMRAAM is an all-weather, all-aspect, active radar-guided missile. The missile is normally launched using target-position information provided by the carrier aircraft. Further information is provided mid-course, to update the missile's naviga-

tion system, and then the missile automatically activates its own radar-seeker to home onto the target. A 22kg (48.5lb) charge is initiated by a proximity fuse. For a close attack, the missile would simply use its own radar.

A further order for AMRAAM missiles was announced in August 2004. This is for the improved AIM-120C-5 model, which will replace those already in service from 2007.

The AMRAAM is carried by the Tornado F.3 and will be carried by the Typhoon F.2.

MBDA AIM-132 ASRAAM

Role: Shortrange air-to-air missile
Engine: Solid propellant motor
Length: 2.90m (9ft 6in)
Diameter: 0.166m (6.5in)
Speed: Mach 3.0+
Weight: 87kg (192lb)
Range: 15km (9 miles; 8nm)

The ASRAAM (Advanced Short-Range Air-to-Air Missile) was designed as a result of a failed European agreement for a new missile specification. The MoD issued its own specification for this new air-to-air

The AIM-120 AMRAAM air-to-air missile on a Sea Harrier FA.2.

The ASRAAM air-to-air missile fitted to a Tornado F.3.

missile in April 1992. It entered service with the RAF in January 2002 and features a significant improvement over the AIM-9 Sidewinder, which it will eventually replace. It can be fitted on existing Sidewinder rails.

ASRAAM features a highly advanced homing-head with an IR-imaging seeker and an in-flight agility that will make it almost impossible to evade. It can operate passively using the advanced IR-imaging seeker or use radar. It can engage targets from gun range to almost beyond-visual range.

The wingless missile has three operating modes. It can be fired normally against a target in the forward hemisphere in lock-on before mode. For targets beyond the seeker acquisition range, a lock-on after launch mode can be selected. In this case, the target data is fed from other sensors on the aircraft or even from another source. During close-in combat, the pilot can use the aircraft sensors or his helmet-mounted display to provide data for a variation of the lock-on after launch. This gives the capability to fire outside the normal +/– 90 degrees off-bore sight, enabling targets to be attacked 'over-the-shoulder'.

Initial deliveries of ASRAAM commenced in September 2002 and have been made to the RAF's Tornado F.3 squadrons, with whom it was used operationally during patrols over Iraq in 2003. Although capable of taking cueing data from a Helmet Mounted Sight (HMS), enabling over the shoulder aiming, it is not anticipated that this capability will be realized for several years to come.

ASRAAM is carried by the Tornado F.3 and will eventually be carried by the Harrier GR.7/GR.9, Typhoon F.2 and Joint Strike Fighter.

BAe ALARM

Role: Anti-radar missile
Engine: Solid propellant motor
Length: 4.3m (14ft 2in)
Span: 720mm (1ft 4.25in)
Speed: n/a
Weight: 265kg (584lb)
Range: 93km (58 miles; 50nm)

The ALARM (Air-Launched Anti-Radar Missile) is a missile that BAe began developing during the 1980s for the RAF, to replace the existing US Shrike missiles.

ALARM is a fire-and-forget missile, which has various modes of operation. A Tornado GR.4 can carry up to nine missiles, depending on its role. As it approaches an area suspected of operating SAM radars, it can fire an ALARM. The missile can be pre-programmed with a database of threat transmissions, which can be reprogrammed in flight if necessary. As the missile reaches the threat area, it climbs to its operational altitude of around 12,000m. A parachute opens and it searches for emissions. Should no threat be detected it remains on the parachute while the attacking formation flies through. Should a radar be switched on, the parachute would be jettisoned and the ALARM would make its attack at supersonic speed. Incidentally, it is probable that one of these parachutes was what an Iraqi saw falling into the Tigris in Baghdad, which resulting in the horrific scenes of weapons being fired from the river banks at a suspected aircrew.

As an alternative mode of operation for area suppression, a ripple of missiles can be launched and it is possible to create a safe corridor or area. Onboard processors ensure that no more than one missile gets targeted to a single target. The universal mode provides an even greater stand-off range.

During Operation *Granby* 123 Alarm

ALARM anti-radiation missiles under a Tornado GR.4.

rounds were fired. As with most technology, advances in radar have required a upgrade to the Alarm missile, which is being implemented, resulting in the Mk.2 variant. During Operation Telic a further forty-seven rounds were fired.

The ALARM is carried by the Tornado F.3 and GR.4. It will also be cleared for use with the Typhoon F.2.

Hunting BL755

Role: Cluster bomb
Length: 2.45m (8ft 0.5in)
Weight: 277kg (610lb)

The Hunting BL755 cluster bomb was developed in the late-1960s to meet an RAF requirement for a cluster-bomb unit (CBU) for use against soft and hard targets.

BL755 contains 147 shaped-charge bomblets and uses a gas-generating cartridge to release the outer casing and eject the bomblets. Two type of bomblet can be fitted into these CBUs. The BL755 No. 1 is armed with a general-purpose munition, which has a petal-like tail, is designed primarily for use against soft targets, such as aircraft, SAMs and un-armoured vehicles, using a fragmentation warhead and has a limited capability against armour. The CBU No. 2 (or IBL-755) is specifically for use against

armoured vehicles. These bomblets are fitted with a parachute to give a higher impact angle and have a high-velocity jet that is triggered on impact and can burn a hole through armour. These BL755s are designed for release at low level, the bomblets being distributed over an area 150m long and 60m wide.

Development of the BL755 system have led to the RBL755 and BL755PS. RBL755 is similar to the standard BL755, but is designed for medium-level launch and is fitted with a ground-detecting sensor to ensure separation of the bomblets at the optimum height over the target. The BL755PS is fitted with a Doppler radar and can be used at high or medium level or tossed from low level. A kit has been produced to enable the Mk.3 ground sensing capability to be retro-fitted to the earlier models.

The BL755 is a free-fall weapon and, so, can be carried by virtually any aircraft with the standard NATO fitting-lugs.

In May 2004, it was announced by the Armed Forces Minister that stocks of the BL-755 and RBL-755 were to be withdrawn. The IBL-755s would be withdrawn by the end of 2004, as Brimstone will replace that capability. It is anticipated that all the final stocks will have been withdrawn by the end of the decade.

BL755 and the variants can be carried by the Harrier GR.7/GR.9, Hawk T.1, Jaguar GR.3 and Tornado GR.4.

MBDA Brimstone

Role: Anti-armour missile
Engine: Solid-propellant motor
Length: 1.80m (5ft 11in)
Span: 0.3m (1ft 0in)
Speed: Mach 1.0+
Weight: 49kg (108lb)
Range: 8km (5 miles; 4nm)

Brimstone is an air-to-ground missile that has been developed for use against armour and other important battlefield targets. It has been designed with a millimetre-wave radar (mmR), enabling it to operate without external guidance to locate and attack armoured vehicles. It is intended to replace the BL755.

The Brimstone was originally conceived back in the late-1980s when, under the Cold War scenario, it was anticipated that there was a need for such an anti-armour weapon, to counter a potential massed advance of Soviet tanks in central Europe.

Early development was stalled by the Options for Change spending review that followed the Gulf War. However, the continued requirement for such a weapon resulted in its continued funding. The initial development of Brimstone took the existing AGM-114 Hellfire missile, which is only capable of being operated from static, vehicle or helicopter platforms. The Brimstone design fitted a new mmR seeker-head – replacing the laser – and redesigned the structure to make it capable of withstanding the stresses encountered on a fixed-wing aircraft. As a result, the missile has more than a passing resemblance to the Hellfire missile but the similarity ends there.

The Brimstone seeker is fitted with a number of target algorithms that enable it to detect various specific targets. This enables it to prioritize them, rather than to attack the first encountered. It can also be fed with an area of attack, enabling it to be launched over friendly forces and not commence an attack until it reaches the enemy. Alternatively, it can be configured with friendly forces, or perhaps a town in the background, and will self-destruct when it passes through a specified line.

In 1994, the Staff Requirement (Air) 1238 was issued for an Advanced Anti-Armour Weapon (AAAW). This requirement was for an autonomous fire-and-forget weapon with a multi-kill/single-pass capability in all-weather, 24-hours a day. It had to have a stand-off

ABOVE: **A pair of RBL-755 cluster bombs on a Harrier GR.7. The RBL-755 variant can be identified from the BL-755 by the additional bumps just forward of the tail fins. This Harrier was operating out of Gioia del Colle, Italy against Serb targets in Kosovo. It has obviously flown a number of missions, according to the markings by the cockpit.**

BELOW: Mock-ups of the Brimstone air-to-ground missiles on a Harrier GR.7.

capability, operate at medium- and low-level and have the capability to destroy current and potential/future targets.

Brimstone can be fired singly or in a fast ripple (0.5 second intervals) at a target area. The range of potential attack profiles is varied. They may give the missile a free hand over a suspected area; the pilot may indicate an area through his helmet-mounted sight or the FLIR for visual targets; Beyond Visual Range (BVR) targets can be programmed for a specific area of attack or targeted from a second aircraft, such as an Apache, J-STARS, ASTOR or even a datalink signal from a Forward Air Controller (FAC).

The first airborne-launch of Brimstone was from a Tornado GR.1, operated by DERA, on 17 December 1998, and flight trials commenced the following August at the Yuma Proving Ground in Arizona. Sixteen inert missiles were fired during the first phase, of which nine were fitted the active seeker-head. Of these nine, seven successfully located and hit their targets. The first fully guided firing of Brimstone was made on 19 December 2001, from a Tornado GR.1.

Brimstone is subject of a £820m order, but it is suffering from delay. It missed its original September 2001 entry into service date, but deliveries commenced in 2005.

It has suffered from a moving of the goal posts, where the original Cold War scenario has not been born out by recent engagements. As a result, the automated fire-and-forget capability could now result in collateral or even 'friendly fire' damage. As a result, a later development will include a dual-mode seeker, which incorporates a laser guidance and enables some control when required.

Brimstone has been designed to be carried by Tornado GR.4, Harrier GR.7/GR.9 and, eventually, the Typhoon F.2.

Bristol CRV-7

Role: Air-to-ground rocket
Engine: Solid-propellant motor
Length: 1.04m (3ft 5in)
Span: 186mm (7.25in)
Weight: 6.6kg (14.5lb) + warhead

The Canadian-designed CRV-7 (Canadian Rocket Vehicle) is an unguided rocket, for which design commenced in the 1970s by the Canadian Department of National Defence and Bristol Aerospace and which entered service in 1975. A number were purchased to replace the Matra SNEB rockets and some of these were fired from Jaguars during the Gulf War.

The 70mm (2.75in) body can be fitted with a range of warheads, depending on the anticipated targets. They are fitted

A CRV-7 rocket pod with an example of one of the rockets.

into the six-tube LAU-5002 or nineteen-tube LAU-5003 pods.

Further quantities were purchased during the late-1990s for use with the Harrier GR.7 and were used operationally during Operation *Telic* in Iraq.

The CRV-7 is used by the Harrier GR.7/GR.9 and Jaguar GR.3/3A.

Boeing Harpoon

Role: Air-to-surface missile
Engine: Teledyne turbojet
Length: 3.85m (12ft 6in)
Span: 0.91m (3ft 0in)
Speed: Mach 0.85
Weight: 556kg (1,226lb)
Range: 120km (75 miles; 65nm)

The Harpoon was selected as an anti-ship missile in 1971 by the US Navy, entering service with them in 1977 as the AGM-84.

This sea-skimming anti-ship missile has an inertial-guided navigation system that was originally designed to be carried by aircraft, but variants have since been built to operate from land, ship and even submarine.

The Harpoon is launched either with the position of the target known or just the bearing. Depending on this information, the missile automatically switches on its acquisition radar at an appropriate time – the more accurate the target position, the less search-time needed for this radar. Once the target has been located, it homes in and the warhead is designed to enter the ship before exploding to cause maximum damage.

The Harpoon was introduced into RAF service in 1982 during the Falklands campaign, to provide additional armament for the Nimrod MR.2.

Harpoon is carried by the Nimrod MR.2.

Thales Optronics Joint Reconnaissance Pod

Role: Reconnaissance Pod
Length: 2.81m (9ft 3in)
Diameter: 1.4m (4ft 6in)
Weight: 254kg (559lb)

The Joint Reconnaissance Pod (JRP) was initially referred to as the Jaguar Reconnaissance Pod or, more technically,

ABOVE: **The Nimrods can be armed with the AGM-84D Harpoon missile, which looks similar to this US Navy example. It is, in fact, an inert training-round mounted on a P-3 Orion – their equivalent of the Nimrod.**

RIGHT: **The Joint Reconnaissance pod fitted under a Jaguar GR.3.**

the GP1 Electro-Optical (EO) pod. It is a reconnaissance pod carried by the Jaguar GR.3A. It contains electronically scanned sensors and an Infra-Red Line Scanner (IRLS). The data is then recorded onto tape and can be interpreted by software to produce high-quality images. A variety of cameras can be fitted into the pod, although they are normally configured for medium- or low-level operation.

The IRLS is normally fitted to provide horizon-to-horizon images. In the nose, one camera is fitted for the medium level, which can be rotated through 180 degrees. For the low-level mode, which is the speciality of 41Sqn, two fixed-cameras are fitted – one either side of the pod at a set angle.

The pod has been designed to operate in a fully automated role with targets having been pre-planned in the Jaguar Mission Planner (JMP). A further mode enables the pilot to manually control the system, using the helmet-mounted sight, enabling the recording of targets of opportunity.

The JRP has undergone several stages of development, with a number of models in service with the RAF. The JRP has also

changed name to Joint Reconnaissance pod following clearance for it to be operated by the Harrier GR.7 and Tornado GR.4A, as well as the Jaguar, enabling non-recce-designated aircraft to be used when required.

The Joint Reconnaissance Pod can be fitted to the Harrier GR.7/GR.9, Jaguar GR.3/3A and Tornado GR.4.

SACO Defence 7.62mm M60D gun

Role: Automatic machine-gun
Length: 1.077m (3ft 6.6in)
Weight: 8.51kg (18.75lb)

The M60 is a US-built 7.62mm automatic machine-gun that dates back to 1957. It is capable of firing at up to 550 rounds per

minute. It is normally mounted on the rear ramp of a Chinook, although it can also be fitted in the crew door or escape hatch.

General Electric M134 machine-gun

Role: Gatling machine-gun
Length: 0.8m (2ft 7.5in)
Weight: 15.75kg (35lb)

The M134 is a US-built 7.62mm mini Gatling-type machine-gun designed for use from helicopters and fixed-wing aircraft. It is an electrically driven, six-barrelled gun capable of firing up to 4,000 rounds of 7.62mm ammunition per minute. One can be fitted in the forward-cabin door or the escape hatch of a Chinook.

An M60D machine-gun mounted on the tail ramp of a Chinook HC.2 during a mission in Afghanistan.

A M134 minigun mounted in the doorway of a Chinook. This weapon is capable of firing up to 4000rpm.

Portsmouth Aviation/ Raytheon Paveway II (UK) LGB

Role: Laser-guided bomb
Length: 3.55m (11ft 7.75in)
Span: 420mm (1ft 5.5in) diameter; 1.68m (5ft 6in) tail extended
Weight: 450kg (992lb)

Paveway was originally a code name for a programme to provide smart bombs for use in the Vietnam War. The joint USAF/ Texas Instruments development resulted in their first LGB being dropped in 1965. By 1971, a range of eight Paveway I LGBs had entered production including 500lb Mk.82, 1,000lb Mk.83 and 2,000lb Mk.84 bombs.

The Paveway kit comprises a nose and tail, with adapters to enable it to fit various bombs. A gimballed detector is fitted onto the front of the bomb; once it detects the appropriate, coded, laser-reflection it is ready to be released and provides guidance signals to the tail section, guiding the bomb onto the target. The source of the laser can be from somebody on the ground or from another aircraft.

In the mid-1970s, the RAF investigated the possibility of adapting Paveway to fit their 1,000lb GP bombs. This led to the Paveway II (UK) kits being produced by Portsmouth Aviation. When stocks began to run low, following operations in Iraq and the former republic of Yugoslavia, a

quantity of the Enhanced Paveway IIs were acquired.

During Operation *Telic*, 265 Paveway II LGBs were dropped by RAF aircraft

Paveway II can be carried by the Harrier GR.7/GR.9, Jaguar GR.3/3A and Tornado GR.4.

Raytheon Enhanced Paveway II

Role: Laser-guided bomb
Length: 3.45m (11ft 4in)
Span: 1.7m (5ft 7in) wings deployed
Weight: 558kg (1,228lb)

Recent operations have seen RAF Paveway II and III stocks substantially depleted. As a result, the RAF has taken delivery of a quantity of the Enhanced Paveway II kits, which have a dual-mode Laser/GPS delivery system, as well as being capable of a greater range. Should the sensor on the bomb be unable to locate the laser designation, due to weather, smoke or any other obstruction, then the GPS system takes over the guidance.

During the operation in Iraq, USAF and RAF forces used more Paveway weapons than any other guided munitions, which included the Enhanced Paveway as well as the standard models. A total of 394 Enhanced Paveway II weapons were dropped by the RAF during Operation *Telic*.

Enhanced Paveway II can be carried by the Harrier GR.7/GR.9, Jaguar GR.3/3A and Tornado GR.4.

Portsmouth Aviation/ Raytheon Paveway III (UK) LGB

Role: Laser-guided bomb
Length: 3.49m (11ft 5.25in)
Span: 1.68m (5ft 5.5in) wings extended
Weight: 1,065kg (2,348lb)

The Paveway III is a continued development of the Paveway II that originated in the 1980s. It is instantly recognisable, with a longer solid-state nose and larger tail that extends from 0.94m to 2m once dropped. This gives a greater flexibility of operation, increased accuracy and also extends its range, lack of which was one of the short-comings of the earlier model.

A new warhead has been developed by BAe Systems and can be fitted onto standard bombs. The BROACH (Bomb Royal Ordnance Augmented CHarge) enables attacks on hardened targets at low level. These attacks would otherwise require a munition, such as the BLU-109, which has to be dropped at altitude to obtain the necessary kinetic energy to achieve the same penetrative power. This new warhead fires a jet of molten copper at the target, which causes considerable damage and weakens the structure, immediately prior to the impact of the main warhead. The BROACH warhead can be fitted to a number of existing bombs, including the Paveway II and III LGBs.

The RAF has also taken delivery of the dual-mode Enhanced Paveway III kits, which also have a GPS delivery system. During Operation *Telic*, ten of these were dropped.

Paveway III can be carried by the Harrier GR.7/GR.9, Jaguar GR.3/3A and Tornado GR.4.

Raytheon Enhanced Paveway III

Role: Laser-guided bomb
Length: 4.39m (14ft 5in)
Span: 2.06m (6ft 9in) fins extended
Weight: 1051kg (2,315lb)

As with the Paveway II, recent operations have seen RAF Paveway III stocks depleted and a quantity of the Enhanced Paveway III kits ordered. These also have a dual-mode Laser/GPS delivery system, as well as being capable of a greater range. Should the sensor on the bomb be unable to locate the laser designation, due to weather, smoke or any other obstruction, then the GPS system takes over the guidance.

While only ten Enhanced Paveway III weapons were dropped by the RAF during Operation *Telic*, during the trials, it was considered that the weapon was so accurate that a number of inert bombs were dropped on Iraqi tanks located in built-up areas. The kinetic energy was sufficient to knock out the tanks without the collateral damage that would have resulted from the bomb's explosion.

Enhanced Paveway II can be carried by the Harrier GR.7/GR.9, Jaguar GR.3/3A and Tornado GR.4.

TOP RIGHT: **A 1,000lb Paveway II bomb mounted under a Jaguar GR.3.**

CENTRE RIGHT: **The Enhanced Paveway II LGB can be identified by the round bulges at the top and bottom of the nose, just forward of the fins.**

BOTTOM RIGHT: **A Paveway III mounted on a Harrier GR.7**

MBDA Rapier FSC

Role: Surface-to-air missile
Engine: Solid fuel
Length: 2.24m (7ft 4in)
Span: 0.17m (6.75in)
Speed: Mach 2.5+
Weight: 43kg (95lb)
Range: 10km (6 miles; 5nm)

The Rapier FSC (Field Standard C) is a surface-to-air missile (SAM) designed to counter enemy UAVs and cruise missiles, as well as aircraft and helicopters. In April 1967, during its first live trials, the Rapier destroyed the Meteor target.

The first Rapiers entered service with the RAF Regiment in 1971. It has since become the primary weapon for the Low Level Air Defence (LLAD) squadrons. Rapier was first used operationally during the Falklands campaign and although found to be sensitive to being moved. This and the fact while a number of the launchers were placed on high ground for maximum surveillance, they were then unable to fire down on the low flying attacking aircraft. As a result Rapier only achieved one verified kill although there were also several unconfirmed.

Rapier is normally operated by a two-man team, consisting of an NCO, who controls the engagement procedures, and an airman, who tracks the target through an optical sight. The equipment is a launcher armed with eight ready-to-fire missiles. The launcher also incorporates its own passive electro-optical surveillance and tracking system. This detects, tracks and can destroy enemy targets, including those flying fast-and-low, even at night. A 3D Surveillance Radar can track over seventy-five targets simultaneously and automatically prioritize them for engagement. A tracker radar can be used for night or low-visibility conditions – with its ultra-narrow beam-width, it can acquire and track the targets and provide a unique dual-engagement capability. Rapier is considered to be a 'hittile', in that it is designed to actually hit the target and explode, to cause maximum damage, rather than explode near the target with a proximity fuse. An alternative fragmentation-head can be used against smaller cruise missiles and UAVs.

In 1998, it was announced that the earlier models of the Rapier B1 and B1X were to be withdrawn and, in 1999, the MoD signed a £1.3bn contract for the improved Rapier Mk.2. As a result, it is considered that the Rapier will remain effective until at least 2020. However, plans are currently underway to provide a new integrated air-defence command-and-control system that will include all of the UK's air-defence assets, to improve their ability to protect against new threats, which include cruise missiles and UAVs. In 2004, it was announced that the RAF's Rapier GBAD systems would be withdrawn and the units disbanded. The first Rapier Squadron will disband in 2005, followed by the next in 2007 and final withdrawal in 2008. The RAF will then depend on the army and other coalition forces for its GBAD.

Rapier is currently operated by 15, 16 and 37 RAF Regiment Squadrons at Honington and 26Sqn at Waddington, plus the Joint Rapier Training Unit at Honington.

Goodrich RAPTOR pod

Role: Reconnaissance pod
Length: 5.8m (19ft 2in)
Width: 0.8m (2ft 7in)
Height: 0.75m (2ft 6in)
Weight: 1,000kg (2,200lb)

The RAPTOR (Reconnaissance Airborne Pod for TORnado) is a new reconnaissance pod that entered service with II (AC) and 13Sqn just prior to Operation *Telic* and was used operationally in Iraq.

The RAPTOR was originally ordered for development by Raytheon in 1997 and used DB-110 technology, developed by Hughes prior to their take-over by Raytheon in 1997. It has been designed to be able to recognize targets at a range of 72km in the electro-optical mode or 36km in infra-red. According to a post-war briefing, it was stated that the imagery was capable of recognizing a man at 16 miles and a car at 60 miles. The navigator is able to use a video display to view the digital image, enabling him to conduct a battle-damage assessment in real time. The pod can also transmit imagery live to a Data-Link Ground Station.

RAPTOR can be fitted to the Tornado GR.4A and may later be fitted to the Typhoon F.2.

A Rapier FSC launches a missile. Unfortunately, it has been decided that the RAF Rapier units will all be disbanded by 2009. MBDA

BAe Sky Flash

Role: Medium-range air-to-air missile
Engine: Solid-propellant motor
Length: 3.66m (12ft)
Diameter: 203mm (8in)
Speed: Mach 2.0+
Weight: 195kg (430lb)
Range: 40km (25 miles; 22nm)

The Sky Flash is a medium-range air-to-air missile, on which development commenced in 1973. It was based on the US-designed AIM-7 Sparrow missile, for which it was to be fully interchangeable. It incorporated a British-designed, Marconi-built, advanced semi-active radar-seeker and EMI proximity fuse, which replaced the existing components, in addition to the auto-pilot and power supply.

Sky Flash entered service with the RAF in 1978 and it became the RAF's primary air-defence weapon. Sky Flash was initially fitted to Phantoms when they took over the air-defence role of the Lightning and was subsequently fitted to the Tornado F.3. The missile is carried in a semi-recessed position under the fuselage and is forced out into the slipstream by a Frazer-Nash launcher as part of the firing sequence. Four Sky Flash missiles can be carried by the Tornado F.3.

Sky Flash is currently being replaced by AMRAAM.

Sky Flash missiles are carried by the Tornado F.3.

A Sky Flash supersonic air-to-air missile being fitted under the belly of a Tornado F.3.

The Raptor pod has proved to be a very useful piece of kit, capable of recording high-resolution images at long range. Crown Copyright

MBDA Sting Ray

Role: Light torpedo
Length: 2.6m (8ft 6.24in)
Diameter: 0.35m (1ft 2in)
Speed: 75km/h (47mph; 40kt)
Weight: 265kg (584lb)
Range: n/a

Development of the Sting Ray advanced light-torpedo was begun in the mid-1970s by Marconi, to produce an air-launched weapon capable of homing-in on a submarine, either in shallow or deep water.

Sting Ray entered service with the British armed forces in 1985. It features a 29kg (64lb) shaped-charge warhead, which is similar to that used against tanks. This shaped charge produces a directional jet of molten copper to penetrate the pressure hull. It was the first torpedo to use this technology. An improved variant entered service in the mid-1990s.

Dropped from a Nimrod, a parachute deploys to reduce its speed before it enters the water. Being autonomous, Sting Ray then measures the sea depth to determine the search profile. It searches a pattern for a submarine, which it then classifies, before instigating the appropriate attack

Sting Ray is a lightweight electrically driven torpedo that can be carried by the Nimrod MR.2 and later by the MRA.4. BAE Systems

profile. Should the torpedo miss, it has the capability of re-attacking. Up to eight Sting Ray torpedoes can be carried in the Nimrod MR.2's bomb bay.

Sting Ray is currently undergoing an upgrade to increase its effectiveness, which should enable its life to be extended to 2025.

The Sting Ray torpedoes are carried by the Nimrod MR.2 and it will be carried in the MRA.4.

MBDA Storm Shadow

Role: Stand-off weapon
Engine: 1 × Microturbo TRI 60-30 turbojet
Length: 5.1m (16ft 9in)
Span: 3.0m (9ft 11in)
Speed: Mach 0.8
Weight: 1,300kg (2,866lb)
Range: 250km+ (155 miles+; 135nm+)

The Storm Shadow commenced as the Franco/German Apache SOW in 1983 and was developed with BAe into the SCALP when the Germans withdrew.

SCALP and Storm Shadow were developed in parallel, with minor differences incorporated – mainly tailored to French and British mission-preparation systems. After a competition, Storm Shadow was selected in 1997 to meet the RAF requirement for such a weapon to be carried by the Harrier GR.7, Tornado GR.4 and Typhoon. The Harrier requirement has since been dropped.

Storm Shadow is a Conventionally Armed Stand-Off Cruise Missile (CASOM)

that can be operated in all weather, by day or night, as a precision-guided weapon. It is designed to attack high-value targets that would be expected to have a heavy defence and therefore provide the aircrew with protection by enabling launch at a distance outside this defence. It has been designed with stealthy characteristics to reduce detection during its attack mode.

The Storm Shadow navigation system uses a combination of TERrain PROfile Matching (TERPROM), together with GPS. It is also fitted with a terminal seeker. The warhead features a double BROACH (Bomb Royal Ordnance Augmented CHarge) penetrator, which has been designed to be able to successfully attack command-and-control bunkers. It can also be used against other forms of hardened buildings or bunkers and bridges. It can also be used to attack docked naval ships.

The first fully guided firing of SCALP was by a Mirage 2000N at the end of December 2000. Storm Shadow was first fired from a Tornado GR.4 on 25 May 2001. By the middle of 2002, it had completed virtually all of its system tests and was ready to enter service trials. Once these were completed, Storm Shadow was ready to enter service

Storm Shadow was first used operationally by Tornado GR.4s of 617Sqn during operations against the Saddam Hussain regime in Iraq in 2003, although it had not been declared fully operational. A total of twenty-seven were launched.

Storm Shadow is carried by the Tornado GR.4 and will be carried by the Typhoon F.2.

BAe TIALD pod

Role: Designator pod
Length: 2.9m (9ft 6in)
Diameter: 0.3m (12in)
Weight: 230kg (507lb)

The Thermal Imaging Airborne Laser Designator (TIALD) programme, commenced in 1987, is the response to an RAF requirement for a replacement for the Pavespike pod. Initially designed by Ferranti (which became part of GEC Marconi and was subsequently taken over by BAe), it was close to completing its development when the Gulf War commenced. As a result, it was rapidly brought into service to enable to enable some of the Tornado GR.1s to provide a designation to the Laser Guided Bombs (LGBs). Only two demonstrator TIALD pods were available and, after modification of both the pod and Tornado to be compatible, they were flown to the Gulf, where they flew the first operational mission on 10 February 1991. During their use during the Gulf War, the TIALD was flown on ninety-one missions over eighteen days. During these missions they were credited with scoring 229 direct hits – a rate that was only bettered by the USAF F-117s.

TIALD is a unique unit, in that it not only provides the laser designation, but that this is combined with a TV image.

Since the Gulf War, modifications to the TIALD systems have enabled the system to self-designate – as opposed to mutual designation, with one aircraft

designating for another. Another useful modification introduced enabled the Navigational Attack System (NAS) to be updated through the TIALD.

ABOVE: **Storm Shadow is the RAF's new cruise missile, first used operationally against Iraqi targets in 2003.**

BELOW: **A TIALD pod fitted to a Harrier GR.7 to enable the pilot to 'illuminate' the target with a laser beam, so directing LGB bombs from itself or another aircraft.**

Post-Gulf War, the improved TIALD was being used by Tornados being flown on Operation *Jural/Southern Watch* during monitoring of Iraqi positions south of the 32nd parallel. During these missions, TIALD was used in the surveillance role and occasionally used, as originally designed, to hit targets such as SAM positions being set up south the 32nd parallel.

Further modifications to TIALD have been included as part of the Tornado Mid-life Update Programme. As a result, TIALD 500 has been developed into a highly effective system – far in advance of the original concept.

The TIALD pod can be fitted to Harrier GR.7/9, Jaguar GR.3/3A and Tornado GR.4.

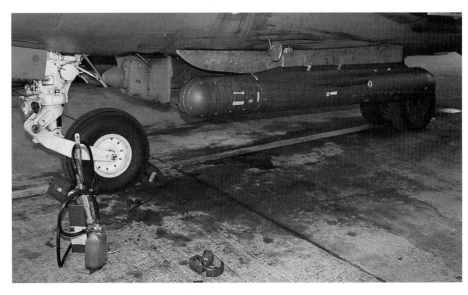

Forthcoming Weapons

MBDA Meteor

Role: Long-range air-to-air missile
Engine: Ramjet
Length: 3.67m (12ft 2in)
Speed: Mach 4.0+
Range: 100km+ (62 miles+; 54nm+)

The Meteor has been selected to become the primary BVRAAM (Beyond Visual Range Air-to-Air Missile) to arm the Typhoon for the RAF, with entry into service in 2012. A £1.2bn contract was signed in December 2002 to develop and produce Meteor for the British, French, German, Italian, Spanish and Swedish Governments, for their armed forces to arm their Typhoons, Gripens and Rafales. The scheduled first air-launched live-firing of Meteor is in 2005.

Meteor is an autonomous missile with an all-weather, shoot-up/shoot-down capability. Its design combines advanced air-breathing ramjet technology for endurance, along with state of the art sensors and processors. It will have a range in excess of 100km and cruise speed of over Mach 4. This missile is being designed to be effective against not only aircraft but also cruise missiles, even in an intense electronic-warfare environment. It will also be an agile missile, capable of tracking and destroying a manoeuvring target. It will also have a multi-target engagement capability.

For detection, the Meteor will be equipped with an active radar-seeker and

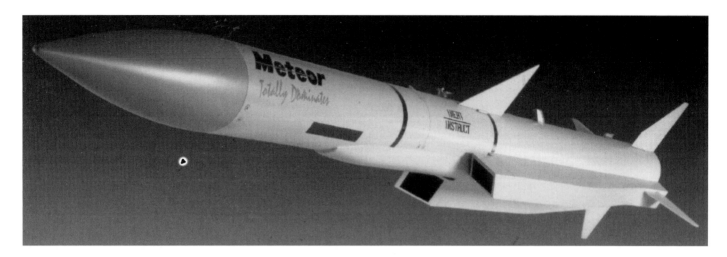

The Meteor is to be the RAF's BVRAAM (Beyond Visual Range Air-to-Air Missile), which will arm the Typhoon from 2012. MBDA

armed with proximity, impact fuses and fragmentation warheads for maximum effectiveness.

The Meteor is scheduled for delivery in 2012 and will be carried by the Typhoon F.2.

Raytheon Paveway IV

Role: Laser-guided bomb
Length: 3.04m (9ft 11.7in)
Span: 1.32m (4ft 4in) folded
Weight: 227kg (500lb)

In June 2003, MoD announced that Raytheon had been selected to supply their Paveway IV to meet the RAF's Precision Guided Bomb (PGB) requirement.

Paveway IV is the latest generation of this extensive range of PGBs. It provides a highly accurate all-weather delivery system, which uses GPS and inertial navigation, as well as anti-spoofing and anti-jamming technology. It also includes a late-arming device that confirms with the guidance system that it is on target during the drop before completing the arming – reducing collateral damage. This is a development from the Enhanced Paveway and will be used primarily by the RAF on 500lb bombs. Because of the improved accuracy of this new generation PGB, less destructive force is required

and the collateral damage is reduced. However, the guidance kits can easily be fitted to any size of bomb.

Although not part of the initial order, a laser-designated variant is available. It has an alternative head, which increases the overall length to 3.33 (10ft 11in).

Prior to it entering service, Paveway IV will be subjected to a variety of trials by QinetiQ, including fire, rough handling and dropping, as well as bullet- and fragmentation-attack testing. It is anticipated that Paveway IV will enter RAF service in 2007 and replace most of the existing range of dumb and laser-guided bombs.

Paveway IV will be carried by Harrier GR.7/GR.9, Jaguar GR.3/3A, Tornado GR.4 and Typhoon F.2.

The Paveway IV is to be the RAF's next generation of Precision Guided Bomb (PGM) and will enter service in 2007. Raytheon

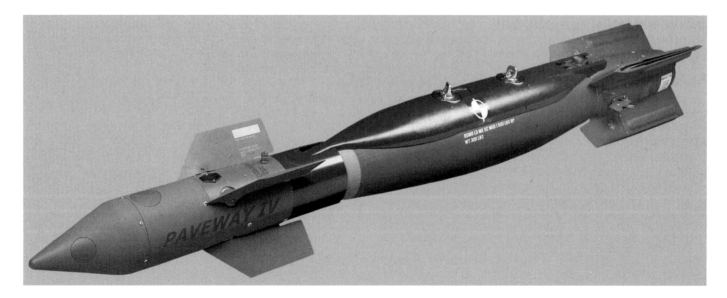

Index